STALIN AND GERMAN COMMUNISM

STALIN and
German Communism

A Study in the Origins of
the State Party

By RUTH FISCHER

WITH A PREFACE
By SIDNEY B. FAY

HARVARD UNIVERSITY PRESS · CAMBRIDGE 1948

CONTENTS

4. THE PERIOD OF TRANSFORMATION

5. THE STATE PARTY IS INSTALLED

6. SUMMARY AND CONCLUSION

MAPS

PREFACE

It was a tragic misfortune for Germany—and for the world—that at the end of World War I the German working classes were not united in a single coherent working-class party. Such a party might have been able to make the "revolution" of 1918 a really democratic revolution and might have given effective support to the newly established Weimar Republic. It would have counteracted the forces of militarist reaction, of extreme Left radicalism, and of social chaos resulting from the defeat and the rapid demobilization of millions of officers and men. These military elements, with habits developed in wartime, were cast adrift on society and were unable to find jobs or to adjust themselves to postwar conditions. They banded together in Free Corps that at first contained some good and idealistic elements but gradually degenerated into disorderly and defiant military organizations which sought to overthrow the Weimar Republic, murdered its ministers, and formed a large element in the Nazi Storm Troop formations which finally did wreck the Republic in 1933.

Instead of forming a single political party, the German workingmen were divided into at least three rival groups, each seeking to capture the support of the German masses. This contributed to the develop-

ment of that multiplicity of political parties—there were soon more than
a score of them—which caused the extreme instability of all coalition
cabinets and was one of the fatal weaknesses of the Weimar Republic.
It also led to an unhealthy internecine strife among the three parties
representing primarily the German working classes.

The first, oldest, and strongest of these three proletarian parties in
1918 was the SPD (*Sozialdemokratische Partei Deutschlands*) or Social
Democratic Party, led by Ebert and Scheidemann. It arose in 1875 from
a merger of Marxists and Lassalleans. The former, led by Bebel and
Wilhelm Liebknecht, had been affiliated with the First International and
believed ideologically in the inevitable class struggle and the ultimate
triumph of the revolutionary proletariat. The Lassalleans, more nationalist, had a socialist program of practical reforms which seemed very
radical in those days but which has been mostly won today by workingmen in all industrially advanced countries. They believed in achiev-
ing their program, not by violent revolution, but by gradual legal means
—by getting and using the secret ballot and parliamentary power to secure improved social and legal conditions for the workingmen. The
two wings, Marxist and Lassallean, each continued to keep something
of their ideological origins, and at congresses of the Social Democratic
Party adopted platforms which reflected the two somewhat contradictory plans of action. Gradually, however, as German industry and
commerce made tremendous strides at the end of the nineteenth and
beginning of the twentieth centuries, the German working class became far better off in the matter of wages, working conditions, legal
rights, and political power. In the Reichstag election of 1912, Social
Democratic candidates won more than a third of the total popular vote
and formed the strongest party numerically in the Reichstag. But with
increased well-being and political power the Social Democratic Party
leadership became more conservative, less international and more national, and even somewhat bourgeois in its outlook and action.

The second workingman's party was the USPD (*Unabhängige
Sozialdemokratische Partei Deutschlands*) or Independent Socialists.
With Marxian antimilitarist and international traditions, they developed as a split-off in 1916 from the Social Democratic Party who represented the more conservative, nationalist and bourgeois tendencies of
the original Lassallean group before the merger of 1875. They believed

that "the main enemy is in our own country"—the monarchists, militarists and big industrialists who were criminally prolonging the war. They advocated peace at once on the basis of "no annexations and no indemnities," and promoted strikes to bring it about. The party ceased to exist soon after the end of the war. At a party convention at Halle in October, 1920, two thirds of the delegates voted to secede and join the recently formed Communist Party. Fifteen months later the remainder decided to reunite with the Social Democratic Party from which they had split off in 1916.

The third party, KPD (*Kommunistische Partei Deutschlands*) or Communist Party, did not have a separate existence until the end of December, 1918. Most of its members had formed the left wing of the Independent Socialists within which they existed as the Spartacus League. They were more violently antimilitarist and more fanatically in favor of social revolution than the rest of the Independent Socialists. They drew their intellectual guidance and emotional inspiration from Rosa Luxemburg and Karl Liebknecht. The former was a brilliant young Polish intellectual—"an eagle," Lenin called her, though he differed sharply from many of her views—who had escaped from Tsarist oppression. She settled down in Germany in 1897, and by marriage with a German workman acquired German citizenship. Karl Liebknecht was the son of Wilhelm Liebknecht, one of the militant founders of the German Social Democratic Party in Bismarck's day. Karl published in 1911 an influential book against imperialism and the German army, *Militarismus und Antimilitarismus*. Early in the war he was the first Reichstag member of the Social Democratic Party to refuse to vote credits for carrying on the conflict, and was active in the movement which led the Independent Socialists to split off from the Social Democrats in 1916. Because of their opposition and incitement to mutiny, both Liebknecht and Luxemburg were imprisoned by the Kaiser's government and not released until October and November, 1918, at the time of its downfall.

The influence of Luxemburg and Liebknecht increased rapidly during the last weeks of 1918 as a result of the German military defeat, the growing strikes in the factories, the mutiny of sailors in Kiel followed by uprisings all over Germany, and the indignation felt by workingmen in uniform against the Kaiser's old officers. It was also increased by the success of the Bolshevist revolution in Russia, and by hopes of Russian assistance in utterly destroying militarism in Germany and in preparing a radical socialist revolution there also. Workers' and Soldiers' Councils, similar to the Russian soviets, sprang up all over Germany. Among the metal workers of Berlin and in the industrial centers of Hamburg, Bremen, the Ruhr, and elsewhere, there also appeared a new radical type of organization—factory councils which chose their own shop stewards.

After Ebert replaced Prince Max von Baden as Chancellor on November 9, there was a confused struggle for power between the Social Democrats, the Independent Socialists, and the leaders of the Spartacus League. In order to avoid anarchy, protect the fluid frontiers, and prevent too hasty and violent a revolution, Ebert, with the approval of many Independent Socialists, called for support from the army. To the Spartacus League this was treason to the sacred cause. On December 30, 1918, its members broke away from the Independent Socialist Party and formed their own separate organization, the Communist Party (KPD). Hardly had it been born when its two most brilliant guiding spirits were arrested by monarchist troops and a few hours later, on January 15, 1919, murdered "while attempting to escape." It was shortly after this that Ruth Fischer came to Berlin and quickly assumed a leading position in the new party.

The German Communist Party, strongly based on the teachings of Marx, was more genuinely international in its character and outlook than the other two socialist parties. It was also, in view of Germany's great industrial population, the most important Communist party in Europe outside Russia. It exercised consequently a magnetic attraction upon Communists outside Germany, both upon the Bolsheviks who wanted to use it for their own nationalist purposes and upon other individuals who hoped that it would establish international socialism. It is perhaps significant that Ruth Fischer, like several of its other leaders—Rosa Luxemburg, Leo Jogiches, Arkadi Maslow—were not born in Germany but were attracted to it.

Ruth Fischer was born in Austria and brought up in Vienna, where her father, Rudolf Eisler, was a noted professor and the author of several works on philosophy and sociology. During World War I, as a young student at the University of Vienna, she joined the Social Demo-

cratic Party of Austria. But since this party in the multi-national em-
pire stood for the preservation of the framework of the Austro-
Hungarian state, and conceded only cultural autonomy for the various
nationalities, she was driven to the extreme left of the party. The "Left
Radicals" fought for the right of all nationalities to break away from
Hapsburg rule and work out their own destinies.

This right of self-determination, upheld by Lenin and put forward
in the Brest-Litovsk negotiations, made a tremendous impression upon
the young students in Vienna. It gave Ruth Fischer an active interest
in Bolshevism. She had some minor clashes with the Austrian police
and published some "underground" socialist pamphlets. She was encouraged by messages from the Bolsheviks, first from Switzerland and
later from Moscow. At the collapse of Austria-Hungary, a Bolshevik
delegation from Moscow, disguised as a Red Cross Mission, suggested
that she and her radical group of students and young workers found a
Communist Party in Austria, which would affiliate with the Communist Third International then in process of formation. On November 4, 1918, she became charter member No. 1 of the Communist Party
of Austria, one of the first Communist parties in Europe. In this way
she came into direct contact with the Soviet regimes in Hungary and
Bavaria, and met leading figures like Béla Kun, Eugen Varga, Max
Levin, and others.

The Austrian Communist Party, however, was a rather inefficient,
artificial, and weak creation, especially after the dissolution of the Hapsburg Empire and the breaking away of its parts. Furthermore, the
bulk of the Vienna workers did not wish to leave their old party. In
1919, therefore, Ruth Fischer moved to Berlin, which she believed had
become the real center of the revolutionary struggle in Europe. She
became active for the Communist Party as an organizer and writer. In
November 1921, to her surprise, she was elected chairman of the Berlin
branch of the party. It was an unusual step to put a young woman in
her early twenties, and not even a German citizen, in command of the
largest Communist Party organization in the Reich. It was taken partly
because of the ability she had shown, and partly just because of her
youth; many of the rank and file of the party distrusted the old leaders,
and wanted to avoid having the organization become an instrument in
the hands of a small clique or a tool to be used by Russian agents. Al-

though Karl Radek had long been active in Germany in Russian interests, the German Communists had not yet fallen so completely under Soviet influence as they did later.

Ruth Fischer represented the Left Opposition in the Communist Party. This group believed the party should have a democratic organization and an autonomous policy in Germany. It wanted the Comintern to preserve its original international and revolutionary character, instead of being transformed into an agency for Soviet State dictatorship and aggressive nationalist and military aims.

In 1922 Ruth Fischer was elected delegate to the Fourth World Congress of the Comintern, and from 1924 to 1926 she was a member of the Comintern Presidium. Here she fought, but ultimately without success, for the views of the Left Opposition. She was also elected a Communist deputy to the German Reichstag, and was a member of its Foreign Affairs Committee, 1924–1928.

As holder of these various important positions she traveled a dozen times to Russia between 1922 and 1926. She came to know the Russian Bolsheviks much more intimately than was possible from a distance. She became acquainted with Lenin, Zinoviev, Bukharin, Kamenev, Radek, Trotsky, and many other old Bolsheviks whom Stalin gradually eliminated in order to establish his own dictatorship. Zinoviev and Bukharin were her best friends and supporters. She also observed at first hand and learned to know Manuilsky, Dimitrov, Vyshinsky, Thorez, Togliatti, Foster, and many other Stalinists who are still playing leading roles in various countries today.

As a consultant on German Communism she gained an insight into the workings of the Comintern, where "the German question" was the dominant one in the Third International during these years. She perceived how Comintern questions were dangerously intertwined with the internal Bolshevik conflicts which were taking place just before and after Lenin's death in the struggle as to who was to be his successor. Among the men intriguing to inherit his mantle, as is well known, Stalin proved the shrewdest and most ruthless. Observing these conflicts at close range, she realized how Stalin was transforming Lenin's organization into a highly centralized and totalitarian machine of a new type—a State Party dictatorship through the instrumentality of the Red Army, the secret police, terror, and eventually economic domination. She saw also how the same totalitarian methods were transforming the Comintern into an agency of the Russian State Party and introducing the same tendencies into the Communist parties which composed it.

Seeing this dangerous transformation through the "Stalinist revolution" which followed the Leninist revolution, Ruth Fischer became an active member of the oppositionist bloc led by Zinoviev and Trotsky in Russia, and by Maslow in Germany. She thereby incurred the hatred of Stalin. She describes the private interviews in which Stalin tried, in vain, to win her over. During her last visit to Moscow, called as a member of the Comintern's Executive Committee to attend its Fifth World Congress, she was detained for ten months, at Stalin's instigation, under the surveillance of his secret police in the Lux Hotel. She managed, however, to maintain contacts with her friends, Zinoviev, Kamenev, and Bukharin. At a wink from them and with their assistance, she took advantage of Stalin's absence from Moscow on a brief trip to the Caucasus and made her escape back to Germany in June, 1926.

Meanwhile she had been elected in 1924 a member of the German Reichstag. She continued to head the minority Left Opposition within the German Communist Party, but after her escape from Moscow she was expelled from the Party by the Party machine which had fallen into the hands of Stalinists. They also demanded that she resign her seat in the Reichstag, but she refused. The Stalinists who henceforth controlled the Party were men like Thälmann and Torgler who were put in concentration camps by the Nazis, or Pieck and Ulbricht who fled to Moscow after 1933 and then returned to Berlin in 1945 to serve as Stalin's main tools in the administration of the Russian Zone in Germany.

During the years from 1926 to 1933 Ruth Fischer remained in continuous and close contact with her oppositionist friends in Russia. She also observed how the rising Nazis adopted many of Stalin's totalitarian and terroristic ideas and methods. When Hitler seized power in 1933, his Storm Troopers sacked her house and took her young son as hostage. She herself fled to Paris, where she lived until 1940, still keeping up secret relations with her friends in Germany and Russia. Because of her continued opposition to Stalinism, she and her comrade,

Maslow, were included in the great Moscow purge trials of 1936 and condemned *in absentia*. They were charged by Vyshinsky with having sent an agent to Moscow in 1933, at the order of Trotsky, to murder Stalin!

After the occupation of Paris by the German armies in 1940, Ruth Fischer fled via the Spanish border to Lisbon. The next year she came to the United States, and eventually became an American citizen. Here she has collected a mass of valuable material on the ups and downs of the German Communist Party, on the transformation of the Bolshevist party into a totalitarian dictatorship, and on the degeneration of the Comintern. On the basis of this material, as well as on her own vivid recollections and experiences, she has told the story for the years 1918 to 1929. In a later volume she plans to show how the Stalinist State Party and terrorist totalitarianism were further tightened and strengthened during the critical years of the 5-Year Plans and the Moscow mass purges, while at the same time Hitler was building up his war machine and totalitarian dictatorship.

There are three strong threads which run through Ruth Fischer's present volume and bind its diverse details and complicated ideological expositions firmly and closely together.

The first thread is the history of the German Communist Party, 1918–1929. Others have given an account of this: Paul Merker (*Deutschland: Sein oder nicht Sein?*, Mexico, 1944) from the Stalinist propagandist point of view, and Friedrich Stampfer (*Die Vierzehn Jahre der Ersten Deutschen Republik*, Karlsbad, 1936) from the Social Democratic historical angle. But no one, so far as we know, has given it in such detail and with such detached and authentic inside information as Ruth Fischer.

The second thread is the story of the internal Soviet struggle for political power during Lenin's last years and immediately after his death up to the point where Trotsky was eliminated by exile. It is the confused, shifting, and complicated struggle between Stalin, Trotsky, Zinoviev, Bukharin and many others. It involved varying concepts of economic, organizational, and foreign policy which the author disentangles with real insight. She writes with inside information because of the many official positions which she held and because she was personally acquainted with the protagonists in Moscow and with the many

Russian agents like Radek who were active in Germany. She has read, and frequently cites, a great many pamphlets by Russians and official Soviet records. It may be that in attributing motives she occasionally depends more upon her own intuition than upon clear historical proof. Attributing motives is always a delicate and uncertain matter. But she has clearly tried conscientiously to follow strict historical evidence. In any case, her interpretations are valuable as a corrective to the legends and myths which Soviet official writers and historians have built up around Stalin and the formative years of the Soviet totalitarian regime.

The third thread is the connecting tie-up between the other two threads—the interrelation between German Communist policy and the internal conflicts in the Soviet Politburo and the Moscow Comintern; or, to put it more bluntly, Russian efforts to manipulate German Communist policy, not for Germany's own good, but in the interests of Russian internal factions or of Soviet foreign policy. It was this, together with Stalin's use of terror and secret police, and his ruthless elimination of those who stood in his way, which led Ruth Fischer to break with Moscow and with the pro-Soviet German Communists, including her own brother, Gerhart Eisler. It is her exposition of the beginnings of this aspect of Stalinism which is so significant for the world today, when, as Léon Blum has so often pointed out, Communist parties in France and elsewhere work solely and servilely in the interests of their Moscow masters, rather than as honest patriots for the good of their native land. All the features of terrorist totalitarianism were tested out and matured in the wide scope of Russian society during these years 1918–1929, and then transferred to the Comintern branches. All later forms of totalitarian rule are only offshoots from the model Ruth Fischer saw being formed, integrating in each country its specific national characteristics, but based fundamentally on the example that Stalin had set.

Having known Ruth Fischer a number of years and having read her book, I am impressed with her amazingly vivid recollection of events and wide information about Communist leaders everywhere, not only in Germany and Russia. The numerous footnotes in which she records their liquidation or promotion by Stalin reads like a "Who's Who" of Communism of the past thirty years. Her detailed reconstruction of the interrelation between the internal conflicts within the Rus-

sian Politburo and Comintern on the one hand, and the confused conflicts and vacillations within the German Communist Party on the
other hand, is made clear as never before. Her searching analysis of
the fine-spun ideological debates and theories is highly enlightening,
and a valuable corrective to a common tendency, especially in America,
toward oversimplification. Her book is important both for the historian
of the past thirty years and for everyone who wants to understand how
the present aggressive and terrorist Soviet dictatorship came into being.
It is thus an essential contribution to a good understanding of Communism in the world today.

SIDNEY B. FAY

Cambridge, Mass.

ACKNOWLEDGMENTS

In presenting this study to the American public, I am deeply indebted to Sidney B. Fay, Professor Emeritus of History at Harvard University, and K. D. Metcalf, Director of the Harvard University Library, who by their sympathy and assistance have made this detailed and non-conformist history of the Russian State Party possible. During the years when a critical approach to Russian Communism had everywhere a feeble response, they not only encouraged me to work on this study but enabled me to finish and publish it.

Among the many friends who have read portions of the manuscript and offered valuable suggestions, I want to mention in particular Dr. Karl Korsch, Dr. Heinz Langerhans, Dr. Karl Menges, and Dr. Karl August Wittfogel. Albert Gates and Maurice Buchs checked the chapters on the Zinoviev-Trotsky opposition during the twenties, and Adolf and Carola Weingarten have helped in collecting source material and in overcoming various technical difficulties.

I was enabled to present this book in English by the substantial assistance of William Petersen, who edited the manuscript for language and saw the book through the proofs. In this respect, I want also to express my appreciation to the editorial staff of the Harvard University Press.

The maps were drawn by Robert Winslow.

RUTH FISCHER

April 28, 1948

THE ORIGINS
OF GERMAN COMMUNISM

1.

MAXIMUM CENTRAL POWERS
EXPANSION AFTER THE
TREATY OF BREST-LITOVSK

■ CENTRAL POWERS

UNDER CENTRAL POWERS
OCCUPATION IN MARCH 1918

HIGHPOINT (AUG.1918) OF
CENTRAL POWER EXPANSION

RUSSIAN BOUNDARIES AFTER
BREST-LITOVSK TREATY-MAR.
1918-AND THE SUPPLEMENT-
ARY TREATY OF AUG.1918

NOTE: German-controlled Rumania
annexes Bessarabia-March 27 1918

ALLIED INTERVENTION

On the eve of the outbreak of the war in 1914, Germany, of all the belligerents, had in the Left wing of its Social Democratic Party one of the strongest and most conscious anti-war movements. In 1914 the party comprised one million members, the trade-unions some two and a half millions. The Italian Socialist Party, second in size to the German, had about half its membership.

In the fifty years before the war during which the party had grown, it had nurtured a steadfast anti-militarist tradition. The strongest labor organization of Europe was expected to be a decisive factor in breaking Germany's war potential; the German Social Democrats, it was believed, would resist mobilization—they would not fight the Kaiser's war. When instead the Social Democratic deputies in the Reichstag voted for war credits and the workers submitted to the draft without protest, there was a cry from the socialist and liberal world against this betrayal of its expectations. But these critics had failed to note both the power of the Bismarckian Reich and the fundamental change, behind the continuing façade of revolutionary rhetoric, that had taken place in the imposing Social Democratic Party.

The latent rebellion against the war in the ranks of the party and among some of its second-file leaders was not able to find an appropriate channel immediately, but it did make itself felt by a kind of inner rust on the party structure. Later, when events moved faster, it could be seen what had happened to the authority of the party in the interim. The German worker, conditioned to believe that his organizational strength of itself made war impossible, suffered a rude shock at the outbreak of the conflict; and during its progress, with the ever gloomier prospect of defeat before him, he continued to learn.

By the turn of the century the German party had become the heart of the Socialist International, the model throughout the world of Social Democrats. It was not only its membership figure that was impressive; it was the unparalleled strength of organizational discipline, the creation of a unique combination of political with trade-union loyalties into one amalgam—the first modern mass organization. Oswald Spengler, a philosophical forerunner of Nazism, admired the great mass organizer, the great mass leader, in August Bebel, the party's founder; he compared him with a general of a modern army. Lenin wrote that in the struggle to organize more effectively the weak, dispersed groups of Russian Social Democrats, Russian Bebels would emerge to mold their cadres into a powerful socialist army.

The Social Democratic Party participated, however, in neither the central government nor the administration of the various states. The Kaiser's Reich was a bastard form between Russian autocracy and English parliamentarianism. Bismarck had created a German parliament on the Western model, but governmental power was vested in the Bundesrat, the council of princes, who continued to rule Germany with semifeudal prerogatives. He fought the Social Democrats with violence, and his successors admitted them to full citizenship only slowly and under pressure.

This isolation from national politics that Bismarck imposed was in part self-defeating, for it served to increase the devotion of the worker to his party. The German Social Democrats were able to realize a type of organization that was more than a loosely knit association of individuals coming together temporarily for temporary aims, more than a party for the defense of labor interests. The German Social Democratic Party became a way of life. It was much more than a political machine; it gave the German worker dignity and status in a world of his own. The individual worker lived in his party, the party penetrated into the worker's everyday habits. His idea, his reactions, his attitudes, were formed out of this integration of his person with his collective.

In Marxist social science—"scientific socialism"—its adherents believed that they possessed a coherent and complete theory of history, independent of the institutional science of the bourgeois world. Socialist ritual began to be substituted for religious ceremonies in the most important personal relations—in baptisms, weddings, funerals. Organized recreation, travel and sport helped create the new type of worker. For the Social Democrat the unorganized worker became a lower species of human; nowhere else in the world could the epithet "indifferent" be applied with the specific contemptuous flavor it had among German socialists. A man was stigmatized who would not raise himself into the elite of his class, to join there the millions ardently certain that the future was theirs.

Social Democracy and War

It is difficult today to understand the naïveté of our grandfather's generation toward war. Germans and British alike, the French and the Americans, had lived for the fifty years before 1914 through a period of relative stability, of expanding industrialism. Society was being pushed forward by technological change, accompanied by the opening of new trade routes, the development of the natural and the social sciences, the flourishing of art and literature. In one way or another, every member of Western civilization shared the pride in its industrial achievement. The growing cities, all felt, would stand forever, with ever more and better libraries and museums, schools and churches, hospitals. Humanity was climbing up the ladder of progress.

At the turn of the century a vast number of studies was produced on the flaws of society: on slums and on juvenile delinquency, on the care of mother and child, on city planning, on education, on an international language, on—a favorite topic—sex and prostitution. Progressive ideas were assimilated by the socialist parties of Europe and integrated, according to the needs of the working class, the fourth estate rising to a new status in society, into a single pattern of social reform. When the Social Democratic theorist, Eduard Bernstein, attacked Marx's laws of societal motion, he was only one example of this adaptation of socialist thought to the general optimistic temper. The conflict between Bismarck and the rising workers' organizations had given the Social Democratic Party prestige as a rebel against the social order, but the revolutionary prospect, the motive power of the early years, had faded into mere propaganda. The revolutionary tactics of 1789 and 1848 were felt to have become obsolete.

Karl Kautsky, before 1914 the party's leading theorist, had been in his early phase not only a loyal disciple of Marx and Engels but a stimulating teacher of the young Lenin. Later, together with Rudolf Hilferding in Vienna, he turned towards a new interpretation of the development of capitalist society. Step by step, they held, the anarchy of the free market would disappear, to be replaced by monopolist control. Parallel with this growth of organized capitalism, mass organizations of the workers would grow irresistibly. In a not too far distant future, the trade-unions and the Social Democratic parties would comprise the majority of the people. More and more, the intelligentsia would get to have the same status in society as the manual workers, and finally would join with them in their organizations. Ultimately machinery would transform agriculture into a type of production increasingly similar to manufacture; the peasant would emerge into the new era as a farmer. The fusion between capitalist monopolies and the state apparatus would become so nearly complete that the borderline would soon be almost invisible. The change to socialism would then be possible by a shift of ruling cadres; labor organizers would replace capitalists. On a world scale, such an organized capitalism would promote peaceful progress. The colonies, industrialized by capitalism, would achieve their independence; their severance from the mother countries would follow once they had acquired a comparable technological base.

This was in substance the credo of the German Social Democrats and their associates in Europe. By this analysis, a system of super-imperialism was in the making in which rational coöperation for the peaceful delineation of world spheres, for bigger and better industrialization, would replace the irrational costly methods of war and civil war.

During the last weeks of diplomatic maneuvers following the assassination of Archduke Franz Ferdinand of Austria, the party maintained its pacifist protest to the very day of the war's outbreak, without believing, however, in the imminence of the conflict. After war was declared, the party found itself at a fork in the road. Organized labor in Germany had only two possibilities: an immediate audacious decision to resist the war policy, which would have led to an underground fight and the temporary loss of all party and union property, or qualified coöperation with the Imperial government.

The problems of a revolutionary policy, including the strategy of a general strike, had been discussed; for decades the possibilities and the dangers of a mass uprising had been scrutinized by party and trade-union organizers. At the party conventions in Jena and Mannheim in 1905 and 1906, Carl Legien, the leader of the trade-unions, had opposed the idea of a general strike stubbornly. At these conventions and immediately after them, Rosa Luxemburg, inspired by the mass strikes in Russia, Belgium, and France, had vigorously attacked Legien's formulations.

It was absurd to expect German Social Democracy to change its character from August 2 to August 3, to abandon in twenty-four hours a decades-old policy restricted to the legal limits set by the Imperial Constitution. The leaders had learned political horse sense, to cross bridges when they were come to, to discard adventurism. In August the Social Democratic Party, loyal to its reformist past, bound the destiny of German labor to that of the German Reich. The socialists of Great Britain and France did the same; on July 31, the outstanding opponent of the war in France, Jean Jaurès, had been assassinated. The thirteen Social Democratic deputies to the Russian Duma, of whom six were Bolsheviks, split into Defensists and Defeatists; the Bolsheviks were arrested and sent to Siberia. Only a year later, after the first international opposition to the war began to be felt, did an important legal mass party, the Italian Socialists, oppose the entry of its country into the war.

In Germany, as in the other countries, the most demonstrative gesture of opposition was a vote in the parliament against war credits. On the 3rd of August, the Social Democratic Reichstag deputies met separately and deliberated on whether to support war credits. Of the 111 deputies, 14 fought for a vote of Nay, among them Karl Liebknecht, Georg Ledebour, Otto Rühle, and Hugo Haase. The formal request of this minority to be released from party discipline on the issue was denied, and the vote in the Reichstag the next day was unanimous. It was only in December that Liebknecht broke discipline and voted in the Reichstag against further war credits. The average Social Democrat found it even more difficult to liberate himself immediately from the discipline of his own party and feel his way alone through the entanglement of Germany's war policy.

Anti-war leaflets were already being distributed in the fall of 1914. Karl Liebknecht, Rosa Luxemburg, Franz Mehring, and Clara Zetkin signed a letter attacking the party's war policy, and this initiative stimulated the protest movement in the party, which gained weight and began to disquiet its National Executive Committee, the *Parteivorstand*. Opposition to the war policy was strong among the metal workers of Berlin, who struck on several occasions. These strikes were in fact strikes against the war, despite their formal restriction to union demands. There was unrest in all industrial centers—in Hamburg, in the Ruhr, in Bremen, in Stuttgart. In 1915 the kernel of the industrial proletariat in Germany, of the organized Social Democratic units, of the trade-unions, was already in incipient rebellion.

This mood crystallized around the figures of Karl Liebknecht and Rosa Luxemburg, who together worked to make it articulate and mature.

Liebknecht and Luxemburg

Karl Liebknecht, the bearer of an illustrious socialist name, was the son of one of the party's founders. Old Wilhelm Liebknecht had participated in the revolution of 1848. He had lived in London with Marx, and with August Bebel he had laid the groundwork for the new Social Democratic Party in Germany. For the older generation of German socialists, "Bebel and Liebknecht" had the same ring as, in 1917 Russia, "Lenin and Trotsky." In 1871 he protested the annexation of Alsace-Lorraine; he called the stand of the intellectuals, journalists, professors, and other literati who did not oppose the war "high treason to civilization and humanity." For a few months in 1872 he was imprisoned for his anti-war propaganda, which he continued even from his Prussian fortress, maintaining his intimate connection with Marx in London and carrying on his attack on the government.

A year before Liebknecht's imprisonment, on August 13, 1871, Karl was born in Leipzig. As editor of the *Vorwärts* ("Forward"), the Berlin party daily, his father had so small an income that Karl and his brother Theodor were able to study law at the university only with the party's help. Karl, thus born and bred in the Social Democratic Party, carried his heritage with enthusiasm. In 1905, with the German party rocked by the Russian revolution, he became more active in the fight against imperial militarism, propagandizing particularly among the young men about to be drafted. In 1907, after a trial at which the book he had just published, *Militarismus und Antimilitarismus,* was an exhibit, he was sentenced to eighteen months in prison. During his imprisonment he was elected to the Prussian Diet, and in 1912 he became a Reichstag deputy. But despite his great party name and his personal courage, nothing before 1914 foretold the unique role he later played.

Liebknecht's co-leader in the fight against the imperialist war, Rosa Luxemburg, was one of the socialists who, fleeing from Tsarist persecution, had joined the German movement.[1] She was born in 1870 in a small town of Russian Poland, the youngest of five children of a wealthy cultivated Jewish family. Early in life she was afflicted with an ailment of the hip, which kept her in bed for a year and left her somewhat handicapped. Her parents sent her to a Warsaw Gymnasium, an unusual thing for a Jewish girl of that period, and here she became involved in revolutionary youth circles. In 1889, threatened with imprisonment, she escaped hidden in the hay of a peasant's wagon "over the green border" into Germany and went to Zurich, whose university was the rallying point of Russian socialists forced into exile. After a short excursion into zoology and botany, she studied economics, which for her meant Marxism.

From her exile, Rosa participated actively and passionately in the life and struggles of the Polish underground. She fought against the

---

[1] This group of Easterners in the German party—which included several of Luxemburg's close friends, among others Leo Tyszko-Jogiches, Julian Marchlewski-Karski, and Adolf Warszawski-Warski—played an important part in the formation of German Social Democratic ideology. In the main they were of the extreme Left; they brought with them an underground experience, an uncompromising militancy, a hatred of German imperialism stronger than usual among German socialist circles.

Among these refugees, A. L. Parvus-Helphand was notable in many respects. Entering the German party in the 1890's, he contributed to all the Social Democratic theoretical organs and built up a solid reputation. In 1905 he returned to Russia and after the defeat was exiled to Siberia. He escaped and lived for a while in Constantinople, where during the Balkan wars he acquired a fortune. In 1914 he was one of the leaders of the pro-war wing of German Social Democracy and at the same time a war profiteer. In 1917, he tried, in vain, to reconcile the German party with the Bolsheviks, and later the Independent Socialists with the Ebert-Noske leadership.

Polish nationalism flourishing among Polish Social Democrats and in 1893, together with Jogiches and others, helped to organize a split and to found a new party, the Social Democratic Party of the Kingdom of Poland and Lithuania. She led a double political life: while her importance in the legal German party was growing, she was also still involved in the continual feuds and calumnies that are the inevitable accompaniment of major political differences between illegal parties. Rosa, who defended her point of view with vigor, went the full gamut of *ad hominem* attack. She was accused of being an agent of the Okhrana, the Tsarist secret police; it was rumored that she had been able to escape from Poland only with the help of Colonel Markgrafski of the Warsaw gendarmerie. At the 1896 London conference of the Polish socialists, Daszynski, a deputy to the Austrian parliament, shouted, "It is intolerable that our movement is encumbered with such scoundrels as Rosa Luxemburg, Urbach, etc. . . . If our international army is not freed of this band of journalistic brigands, they will destroy our liberation movement."

Despite her lifelong activity in the Polish party, Rosa could not be satisfied with the vicarious activity from abroad in an underground movement; she did not want to live in perpetual exile. She longed for a Western socialist movement to absorb her energy; and when she decided to settle down, she chose Germany, irresistibly drawn to the mass organization of the Social Democratic Party. The first period was filled with difficulties. She acquired German citizenship through a formal marriage to a comrade, Gustav Lübeck, and began to travel about the country, speaking at party meetings and writing for various party papers. She was attacked as a fanatic intruder from the East, as one unable to understand the particular features of the German labor movement; even old Wilhelm Liebknecht wrote a rather disagreeable article attacking her personally. For long years her German articles were corrected by her intimate friend, the wife of Karl Kautsky, but later Luise could write her, "You write better and more beautiful German than anyone else, and my corrections have become completely superfluous."

When the revolution broke out in St. Petersburg in 1905, Luxemburg went to Warsaw and took part in the struggle there. After a short imprisonment, she returned to Germany and participated in the prolonged discussion that absorbed the German party on the strategy of the general strike. Invigorated by her latest Polish experience, she attacked the reformist attitude of the party leadership as opportunism; in 1909 her stand led to a break with Karl Kautsky, who had been her devoted friend and perhaps her principal teacher. It was during these years that her fame spread outside the party and she became a national figure. Luxemburg attracted to her person the hatred of the German authorities, for she was a dangerous propagandist against the Reich and its policies, a virulent exposer of German militarism, a principled opponent of those Social Democratic politicians whom, in spite of their pacifist phraseology, she regarded as potential supporters of a future war. Under the spell of her personality and attracted by the experiences she had brought with her from the East, a group formed around her. It was the nucleus of the future Spartakusbund—among others, Franz Mehring, later the author of a biography of Marx and a party history, and Clara Zetkin, an organizer of women.

With the outbreak of war, Luxemburg's activity increased. Indefatigably she called for mass action to enforce a peace with no annexations or indemnities. In February 1915 she was taken into custody to serve an old two-month sentence; with an interruption of several months at the beginning of 1916, she was held in prison at Wronke, near Breslau, until November 1918.

The most concise statement of Luxemburg's anti-war view is her so-called Junius pamphlet. Reading it today, one is impressed by her cry of despair at the collapse of the Socialist International, of socialist solidarity. If, she said, the workers of all countries do not now, by their concerted action, stop the slaughter of their proletarian brothers, socialism is doomed and Europe's decay is certain. "The present massacre, one whose like has never been seen, is reducing the adult working population to women, the aged, and cripples. It is a bloodletting that threatens to drain the last drop from the European labor movement. Another such world war and the prospects for socialism will be buried under the rubble heaped up by imperialist barbarism. . . ."[2]

---

[2] [Rosa Luxemburg], *Die Krise der Sozialdemokratie,* published illegally (Berlin, 1916), p. 91. Its popular title, the Junius pamphlet, derives from English history. From 1769 to 1772, a man signing himself Junius (probably from Lucius Junius Brutus, the Roman patriot) addressed a series of letters to the London *Public Advertiser* attacking the ministry of the Duke of Grafton with sharp invective. In

Luxemburg opposed the illusion that the belligerent statesmen would come to terms without the intervention of the Social Democratic mass parties. In substance, however, her concept of the post-war world was a qualified *status quo ante;* she did not grasp the scope of the irreversible breakdown of European society. Her vision encompassed the transformation of Germany into a republic, with no immediate structural changes; Social Democracy would take up again its long fight in close solidarity with brother parties in other European countries. In contrast to Lenin, she did not look upon the war as a prelude to a civil war that would usher in European socialism.

Until the war broke out, relations between Rosa Luxemburg and Karl Liebknecht had been sporadic, but now their efforts to fight against it brought them together. The resistance movement gathered momentum during 1915; Social Democratic locals and particularly the youth were restive under the patriotic policy of the party leadership. In April there appeared the first and only issue of an anti-war magazine, *Die Internationale,* edited by Luxemburg and Franz Mehring and with an article by Liebknecht; it was immediately confiscated.

The anti-war wings of European socialism met twice in Switzerland, in 1915 and 1916, at the conferences of Zimmerwald and Kienthal. Luxemburg and Liebknecht were unable to attend, but their followers, who called themselves now *Die Gruppe Internationale,* were represented.[3] These faint manifestations of anti-militarist internationalism gave the German opposition new impetus and strengthened it in its fight against

---

their day, they achieved a certain fame; as late as 1927, a book was published attempting once again to solve the mystery of Junius' identity. For this wartime pamphlet, Luxemburg used the same pseudonym.

[3] The Russian delegates to the Zimmerwald conference were Lenin, Zinoviev, Axelrod, Martov, Martynov, Natanson, Chernov, Bersin, Trotsky; the German delegates were Georg Ledebour, Adolf Hoffmann, Josef Herzfeld, Ernst Meyer, Bertha Thalheimer, Julian Borchardt; the Polish delegates were Karl Radek, Warski, Lapinski. The following countries were also represented: Italy, Holland, Scandinavia, Rumania, Bulgaria, Switzerland. The Independent Labour Party of Great Britain intended to participate but its delegates were not granted passports.

About forty delegates from essentially the same countries participated in the Kienthal conference. The third and last conference of the Zimmerwald Union took place in Stockholm in September 1917; after the Communist International was formed in 1919, it was dissolved.

The dominant position of the Zimmerwaldists was to end the war by the concerted action of the socialist parties. Within this minority, the group around Lenin was a smaller minority, the so-called Zimmerwald Left, which called for a sharp break with Social Democracy and revolutionary opposition to the war.

the party leadership. Dissatisfaction was growing, and the elements of a new party were forming.

Only a few small groups, mainly intellectuals in Bremen and Leipzig who before the war had worked with Karl Radek, editor of Social Democratic newspapers in both these cities, had become vaguely familiar with Lenin's ideas. The weeklies *Arbeiterpolitik* ("Workers' Policy"), edited in Bremen by the teacher Johann Knief, and *Lichtstrahlen* ("Light Rays"), edited in Berlin by a personal friend of Radek, Julian Borchardt, were closest to Lenin. Radek himself, writing articles for German papers from Switzerland, began to have an important influence in the anti-war wing. But in general Lenin was still almost unknown and certainly without important influence in Germany— a situation that did not change until after the Bolsheviks seized power in Russia.

On New Year's Day 1916 a secret conference of *Die Gruppe Internationale* in Liebknecht's Berlin apartment adopted Luxemburg's thesis, *The Crisis of Social Democracy,* as its statement of policy. The formulation of this policy associated with Liebknecht, the title of one of the manifestos he published, was "The main enemy is in our own country."

On January 12, Liebknecht was expelled by the party faction of the Reichstag. Two days later Otto Rühle made a statement defending him and was also expelled.

The tendency toward a new party was increasing. To split the party, however, was against the tradition of forty years of unity. In 1875, at the Gotha unity convention, the Bebel wing, the "Eisenacher" (so called after the town of Eisenach, Thuringia, the site of the party's founding convention), had joined with the Rhineland socialists, organized under Lassalle in the General German Workers' Association (*Allgemeiner Deutscher Arbeiterverein*). Ever since then, Social Democrats had looked on any policy that might lead to a split not merely as a political error but as ultimate infamy—with the same moralistic abhorrence associated, say, with murder. For them no issue was important enough to divide the party: the concept of class unity was, as it is today, dogma for all labor organizations in Germany.

None the less, on March 24, 1916, the Social Democratic Party split. The minority wing, the USPD (*Unabhängige Sozialdemokratische*

Partei Deutschlands, Independent Social Democratic Party of Germany), whose founding convention was at Gotha, April 6–7, rapidly became a second Social Democratic mass party.

The opposition to the war developed to such a point that on May Day Liebknecht decided to act, expecting a mass response to his protest. He had meanwhile been drafted into the army and put in a punishment company. In this uniform he went to a point in Berlin near the large railroad stations, which were filled to capacity with troops awaiting transport to the two fronts. He shouted repeatedly, "Down with the imperialist war! Get out of the army! Long live socialism!" He was arrested, but his protest was not at all the isolated gesture of a crank; Liebknecht, standing alone on the Potsdamer Platz, was supported by hundreds of thousands of German Social Democrats. The Imperial government was very well aware of the prestige that Liebknecht had won by his direct action. During his trial and imprisonment in Luckau, Silesia, there were demonstrations and strikes which failed of their principal aim, Karl's liberation, but brought to the attention of the government and the party bureaucracy the growing warweariness.

On September 20, there appeared the first of a series of political letters signed Spartakus (after the leader of a slave revolt against Rome in 73 B.C.), which were soon eagerly read in party circles. Their main political direction came from Luxemburg, who wrote her articles in her prison cell, but others of the group contributed. *Die Gruppe Internationale,* which became known from these letters as the Spartakusbund, formed the Left wing of the USPD.

Several USPD organizers were imprisoned. All the leading Spartakists were taken into protective custody—not only Luxemburg and Liebknecht but later Franz Mehring, Clara Zetkin, Wilhelm Pieck, and Hugo Eberlein. Berlin organizers of the metal workers' union, among them Richard Müller, the chronicler of the German revolution,[4] were sent to the front. The increasing resistance of the German workers to the war had to be considered by all forces involved in the conflict. The Entente watched it carefully, hoping to coöperate with the pacifists of

---

[4] Richard Müller, *Vom Kaiserreich zur Republik: Ein Beitrag zur Geschichte der revolutionären Arbeiterbewegung während des Weltkrieges,* 2 vols. (Berlin: Malik-Verlag, 1924).

the Center Party and the USPD. Ludendorff and the General Staff watched it no less carefully; this undercurrent of workers' resistance was impairing the morale of the German army just on the eve of America's declaration of war. The party bureaucracy was also much concerned with the growing rebellion against its authority; now, after two years of war, the power of the party machine was bound to the success of its alliance with the Imperial government.

Peace propaganda found an especially ready ear among sailors. They greeted each other with "Long live Liebknecht!" and founded small clandestine committees. In March 1917 the diffuse unrest crystallized into a mutiny; the two leaders, Reichpietsch and Köbes, were executed as an example—the first political execution of the war—but unrest in the navy continued none the less, and even grew. Hundreds of sailors were sentenced to terms ranging from one to fifteen years.[5]

Following Liebknecht's protest, there sprang up groups of revolutionaries: underground sailors' committees, underground committees in the Berlin factories. The trade-unions and the party were represented in the factories by their "men of confidence"—*Betriebsvertrauensleute*. These men, mainly trade-union functionaries, exerted a decisive influence inside the party. From among them an underground organization developed known as the *Betriebsobleute*—the Shop Stewards.

The Shop Stewards, bound to their specific plants, were distinctly different from the Workers' and Soldiers' Councils, which were formed in 1918 and represented loose units of various local organizations. The Shop Stewards were a new form of political organization, beyond the traditional party and trade-union bodies. The resistance movement did not take the same form as in Berlin throughout the Reich, but its content was similar in all industrial regions. The workers' representatives gathered regularly and plotted against the party machine, to organize a movement to end the war. Measured by the standards of the time, these workers took considerable risks. Many of the middle-aged men, engaged in war production, had been exempted from military service; a quick transfer from the factory to the trenches was the price paid for militant activity.

---

[5] Cf. Icarus, *The Wilhelmshaven Revolt* (London: Freedom Press, 1944).

The general mood against the war was not limited to socialist workers. In 1917 the Catholic workers of the Ruhr, the Rhineland, and Upper Silesia, who formed the mass base of the Center Party, were also advocating an immediate peace settlement—another expression of the effort of German workers to transcend Wilhelmian society.

Liebknecht and Luxemburg in prison, a sailors' rebellion going on, the indestructible Social Democratic Party split and its anti-war wing growing, the mood spreading among wide sectors of the population, strikes in all industrial areas, unrest everywhere—that was the political scene of 1917 Germany. The resistance movement grew, independent in its forms and in its content of Russian Bolshevism, and contributed finally in large part to the downfall of the Reich. It revitalized the dream of the Social Democratic worker in the transformation of Germany into a people's republic. "You will all see the socialist state, all you delegates who are sitting here," August Bebel had declaimed to the 1891 Erfurt convention. In the mind of the German worker, internationalism, reborn of mobilization and war, regained its religious character.[6]

Luxemburg versus Lenin

Lenin, who came to Western Europe in 1900, a few years later than Luxemburg, after one year in prison and three years in East Siberia, was virtually unknown among Western socialists.[7] He settled down in turn at the libraries of Munich, London, Geneva, Zurich, with notebook and pencil and began producing a prodigious quantity of pamphlets, but except among a few socialist experts with special contacts to Russia, they were not read in the West.

Superficially his background was identical with Luxemburg's: they

---

[6] For a contemporary account of the German resistance movement see Emil Barth, *Aus der Werkstatt der deutschen Revolution*, Berlin [1919?]. This confused report has been severely criticized by contemporary writers, but it is a valuable source book. See also Heinrich Ströbel, *Die deutsche Revolution, ihr Unglück und ihre Rettung*, Berlin [1920]; Eugen Prager, *Geschichte der U.S.P.D.: Entstehung und Entwicklung der Unabhängigen Sozialdemokratischen Partei Deutschlands* (Berlin, 1922).

[7] In 1911, when Michels wrote his survey of socialist parties (Robert Michels, *Zur Soziologie des Parteiwesens in der modernen Demokratie*, Leipzig, 1911), he did not so much as mention either Lenin or Trotsky, and this in spite of the fact that his prime concern was with party organization. Luxemburg, on the other hand, is listed ten times in the index.

were both socialist refugees from the Tsarist police. Lenin was much more mature, however (Rosa was still in her teens when she came to Zurich); he had been more active in the underground for a longer period, and the main ideas of his later life were already in gestation. He had no hint of Luxemburg's desire to be part of a legal mass party in the West. He lived in Switzerland as in an asylum; it was a working place, an organizational outpost. Wherever he stayed, Lenin lived in Russia. His personal life, his travels, were arranged according to the needs of the party. During the fifteen formative years of Bolshevism, wherever he went the party center went with him. He studied the West eagerly, but it was in order to bring the latest word of European socialism to his native country; to the end of his life he never lost his respect for "the highly civilized European worker."

During the first years of the new century, Lenin worked out his theory of party organization, and by gathering around him a large portion of the Russian socialist exiles began to put it into practice. This concept, a central doctrine of Bolshevism, aroused considerable excitement in all of the Eastern parties; not only the Russian Social Democrats themselves but the Poles, the Jewish Bund, the Letts, the Caucasians, spent years in debating the pros and cons. At the Second Russian Social Democratic Congress, in London in 1903, there was a split over the question of party structure into Bolsheviks and Mensheviks—majority and minority. This schism, and the innumerable articles and debates around its central issue, aroused little interest among European socialists, but Luxemburg, as an active member of the Polish party, was involved in the polemics from the beginning. Through the Polish delegates to the conference, Hanecki and Warski (elected by the party's Central Committee, of which she was a member), Luxemburg was informed in detail of the complicated debates; and in Germany she published an article attacking Lenin's view. Both concepts of party structure played a part in the formation of German Communism and its subsequent relation to Russian Bolshevism.

For Lenin, the labor movement is a product of the antagonism in capitalist society, which creates what he terms trade-union consciousness, the awareness of the working class that its interests run counter to those of the capitalist class. Spontaneously, the workers can develop only this trade-union consciousness; spontaneously, they can never reach the higher form of political consciousness. The class struggle does not develop automatically into political forms, into the revolution. Socialist concepts can result only from deep scientific insight, and, as Kautsky had written, "the vehicles of science are not the proletariat but the bourgeois intelligentsia." Lenin quoted Engels: "Socialism, having become a science, demands the same treatment as every other science—it must be studied." Hence, the working class needs bourgeois intellectuals; and those who come over to the revolutionary movement, bringing with them the knowledge of scientific method, shall be taken into the proletarian party.

A proletarian ideology cannot develop spontaneously, he held. To limit the labor movement to its economic phase, to trade-unions; to renounce political struggle through the party, is not to destroy capitalist society but to adjust the workers' movement to it. The worker must take a stand on all political interests of the other classes, must assimilate and understand their intellectual, moral, and political implications. The Social Democrat must appeal to all classes of the people, not only to the workers; the typical Social Democrat must be not a trade-union leader but a people's tribune.

A strictly disciplined party structure, he maintained, is imperative in the highly developed class struggle of our time. The party is a factor in the historical process; it intervenes in it, and is not merely its product. The Russian party is intended to be first of all an effective instrument for the destruction of the Tsarism of the moment. Its fundament, a guiding elite, bases its political acts on a scientific analysis of the historical process and is kept free of adulteration by a constant fight for correct interpretation and application of its principles. The continued functioning of a central body, able to develop its political theory undisturbed, is a necessity—the reason for the revolutionary headquarters in exile. The branches submit to the center because they recognize the superior worth of its political theory and vision, and thus the center is able to bring the local experiences to a higher level of integration. The center transfers its directives to the branches through professional revolutionaries, men who submit their entire being to the necessity of carrying out the orders of the center. This revolutionary fraternity is a close conspiratorial group, to enter which is not to indicate a transitory political preference but to bind oneself to a cause. Lenin's organizational ideas derived from both the Jacobins and his revolutionary predecessors in Russia, but they were linked to an analysis of the revolutionary role of the proletariat. For Lenin, the party is the catalyst that will bring the labor movement, in the widest meaning of the term, into action; the party is the vanguard of the proletariat. And the central figure of the party is the professional revolutionary, bound to the party center and carrying its ideas, program, and decisions to the party locals; he is the pivot around which the entire organization revolves.[8]

In her reply to Lenin, Luxemburg recognized that this question of party organization was one that concerned "the entire younger socialist generation" of Russia, where Tsarist absolutism set especially difficult conditions. None the less, she rejected Lenin's concept that a centrally organized elite must be built up and isolated by strict discipline; she rejected rules permitting the interference of the Central Committee in the life of the locals, their dissolution and re-formation by the Central Committee, which could thus influence the convention that elects it. Such rules would permit the Central Committee to become the only active kernel, with all other sections of the party only the instruments of its executive will, in contradiction to the natural unfolding of the class struggle.

Apart from general principles of struggle, she held, there is no one set of tactics that can be set in advance, by which the Social Democratic membership can be drilled by the Central Committee. There is constant fluctuation; there is no rigid boundary between party leadership, membership, and mass. Social Democracy is not only the organization

---

[8] The ideas here summarized were first developed by Lenin in an article published in May 1901 called "Where To Begin" (*Collected Works,* New York, 1929, vol. IV, Book I, p. 109 ff.). This was expanded the following year into the famous pamphlet, *What Is To Be Done?* (*ibid.,* Book II, p. 91 ff.). Both were written as a polemic against the Economists, the school of socialist thought in Russia that sought to guide the nascent labor movement principally into trade-unionist channels.

In recent discussions, Lenin's concept of the professional revolutionary has been a main object of attack because of the extreme power it gave to the Central Committee; the Stalinist GPU agent has been identified in the popular mind with Lenin's professional revolutionary. That Stalin's State Party does indeed stand on the foundation of Lenin's Bolshevik Party is, however, only one aspect of a complicated historical process and does not take into account the diverse elements of the metamorphosis of a revolutionary underground organization seeking power when once that power has been attained—which is precisely the subject of this book.

of the working class, but the movement inherent in the working class. Lenin's concept of the revolutionary party results from a mechanical transfer of Blanqui's conspiratorial groups to the Social Democratic movement.[9]

Russia, Luxemburg argued, is on the threshold not of the proletarian but of the bourgeois revolution. In Germany, on the contrary, we already have strong proletarian cadres, of which the Social Democrats are the leading strata. There can be no constitutional rule against the growth of opportunism and *embourgeoisement;* only the spontaneous development of the class struggle can finally overcome all obstacles and direct the class struggle into the correct path. "Historically, errors committed by a real revolutionary labor movement are immensely more fertile and valuable than the infallibility of the most perfect Central Committee." [10]

Luxemburg's vision of the extrapolation of the dictatorship of the Central Committee beyond the taking of power has, in the light of later developments, attained enormous weight. She spoke as the representative of a Western mass movement at the time of its full vigor, before any signs of decadence had developed. Lenin spoke as the representative of underground conspiratorial groups in a feudal country, which three years later was shaken by a revolution.[11]

---

[9] Louis Auguste Blanqui, the French revolutionary, attempted a coup in 1839 and was released from prison just in time to participate in the revolution of 1848. He was in prison during the Commune of 1871, about half of whose leaders were Blanquists. He organized underground "clubs" and taught that "the war between the rich and the poor" must be won by "the revolutionary dictatorship."

[10] Rosa Luxemburg, "Organisationsfragen der russischen Sozialdemokratie," *Die Neue Zeit* (Stuttgart, 1904), vol. 22, Book I, pp. 484–492 and 529–535. When Lenin submitted a reply, the editors of the *Neue Zeit* ("New Times"), the principal theoretical organ of the German party, rejected it because of its unclear presentation; printed afterward in Russian, it was entitled "You Can Feed Nightingales on Fables." Even later, Lenin was never published in the periodical; the only time his name appears in the index is for the 1921 volume, when his *Zur Frage der Diktatur* was reviewed.

[11] Lenin defended his concept of organization not only against the Economists, and later Luxemburg, but also against many adversaries in the Russian movement, of whom we mention here only Trotsky. But it would be an over-simplification to set the democrat Trotsky against the autocrat Lenin, even in this early period of Bolshevism. Lenin attacked the undemocratic character of Trotsky's concept of the permanent revolution and counterposed his own theory of the democratic dictatorship of the workers and peasants. Trotsky, who criticized the centralization of the party, set a narrower boundary to the revolutionary task and limited its immediate realization in the main to the proletariat.

The tenor of this debate indicates the divergent evolution between the new Leninist party and the Luxemburgist tendency. There was one moment of rapprochement, in the wake of the defeat of the Russian revolutionaries. At the International Socialist Congress in Stuttgart in 1907, Lenin and Luxemburg joined forces to oppose the general optimistic temper of European socialists and to move a resolution demanding a renewal of the revolutionary struggle to overthrow capitalism during a war.[12]

After this one instance of coöperation, relations between the Leninists and Luxemburgists again became cold, if not hostile. The status of the Bolsheviks in the Socialist International was never quite certain; Lenin and his group lived on its fringe. He was regarded by the leaders of the Western mass parties as an unimportant but potentially dangerous fanatic, and Luxemburg, though on certain fundamental issues she was closer to Lenin, tended to agree.

In the years immediately preceding the outbreak of the war, the struggle among the various parties and factions of Russian Social Democracy reached an apex; Lenin was opposed not only by the Mensheviks but, to one degree or another, by almost every one of the other groupings. In May 1914, following an appeal by the Menshevik Party to the Socialist International to inhibit the Bolsheviks' splitting tactics, the Belgian Emile Vandervelde went to St. Petersburg as its representative to investigate the possibility of uniting the two wings. In spite of the now ominous war danger, the International planned to meet in the usual way in August 1914 in Vienna, and a preparatory conference sat on July 16–17 in Brussels, where a special committee was constituted to hear Vandervelde's report on the Russian party.

The delegates represented on this committee illustrate the bizarre

---

[12] *VIIe Congrès Socialiste International, tenu à Stuttgart du 16 au 24 août 1907* (Brussels, 1908), p. 152 ff. The central paragraph of the resolution that *was* adopted ran as follows:

"If war threatens, the working classes and their parliamentary representatives in the countries involved, supported and coördinated by the International Bureau, are duty-bound to mobilize all their forces to hinder its outbreak by the measures that appear most effective to them, which will change with the sharpening of the class struggle and of the general political situation. If war breaks out none the less, they are duty-bound to stand for its rapid close, and with all forces to utilize the economic and political crisis the war has created to awaken the people, and thus to accelerate the end of capitalist class rule" (*ibid.*, pp. 421–424).

state of disintegration that Russian Social Democracy was in; the following factions were represented: the Mensheviks, represented by Martov, who in 1912 together with Trotsky and Axelrod and the Jewish Bund had formed the "August Bloc," an anti-Leninist combination; one faction of Polish Social Democrats, represented by Luxemburg; Plekhanov, representing his own group; the *Vperyod* ("Forward") group, a Left grouping represented by Lunacharsky; another Polish faction, the Warsaw group, represented by Unschlicht and Hanecki (who sided with Lenin); and the Lettish Social Democrats (who supported the Bolsheviks). The Bolsheviks delegated Ines Armand to represent them; the fact that neither Lenin nor Zinoviev left Zurich is a sufficient indication of their feeling toward the purpose of the conference. With the Bolsheviks and their supporters abstaining, the conference decided to unite all the groups on the basis of a program to be proposed by the International Bureau; to implement this decision a general party congress was to be convoked. Axelrod and Luxemburg "were charged with drawing up a manifesto on the necessity of unity, directed against the splitting politics of the Bolsheviks. Lenin's faction was thus completely isolated. . . . However, the World War, breaking out after a few weeks, brought the unity effort thus begun to an end." [13] This unification would have meant, in effect, the expulsion of the Bolsheviks from the International, for Lenin would never have accepted submitting his organization to the discipline of a hostile majority —a fact of which Luxemburg and Axelrod were certainly aware when they accepted the assignment of writing the manifesto.

The sharpness of this organizational conflict reflected the sharpness of the ideological dispute between Lenin and Luxemburg. They were united in their general analysis of the epoch in which they lived: socialist parties, they agreed, could not win a victory by gradualist change of the capitalistic system but had to face a period in which war would follow inevitably from the imperialist competition. But this agreement on the fact of imperialism did not imply any unity concerning its main features or the methods by which socialism might best supplant it. Though Luxemburg did not live long enough to

[13] J. A. Martov, *Geschichte der russischen Sozialdemokratie,* mit einem Nachtrag von Th. Dan, *Die Sozialdemokratie Russlands nach dem Jahre 1908* (Berlin, 1926), p. 268.

develop her ideas to their full maturity, they have none the less had an important influence not only on German Communism but on Left socialist thought generally in its give-and-take with Bolshevik theory.

Deeply affected by the aggressive spirit of the German Reich and its drive for colonies, Luxemburg interpreted the main trend of the twentieth century as a ruthless search of all capitalist states for foreign markets and new investment areas. With the British colonization of Egypt and India as a model, she analyzed the creation of new industries based on cheap, native labor in a milieu favoring capital accumulation. As long as the world offered such possibilities of exploitation to capitalists, the competitors could postpone their collapse for a certain period; but after all the non-capitalist peoples had been absorbed into the world's capitalist systems, capitalist accumulation would reach a dead end, and capitalist society would collapse into a world war, which could not be avoided but could be combated through the mobilization of the entire working class in a series of mass strikes. Luxemburg did not, however, tie this theory concerning an indefinite future to the political reality of the Europe of her day.[14]

Lenin disagreed with Luxemburg's analysis of imperialism; basing himself on Hobson and Hilferding, he developed their ideas on the expansionist drive of capitalist states and asserted that the fight for the *re*-division of the world had begun. The peaceful period of 1872–1914 had passed; Europe, Lenin wrote in 1913, was "a barrel of gunpowder." Monopoly capitalism, he argued, strives to control all factors of production and all markets, and only possession guarantees complete control. Only the conscious intervention of the proletariat, the seizure of power in a series of revolutions accompanying the series of world wars, could bring to an end this era of decay. The world war, which for Lenin was an immediately imminent prospect, was the basic premise of reality, to which all policies had to be adjusted.[15]

In particular, Lenin adapted his concept of the Russian revolution and the program of his party to the expansionist drive of Imperial Russia—her will to subject the peoples on her Caucasian border, her

---

[14] Rosa Luxemburg, *Die Akkumulation des Kapitals: Ein Beitrag zur ökonomischen Erklärung des Imperialismus* (Berlin, 1913).

[15] Lenin, *Imperialism, the Highest Stage of Capitalism* (Petrograd, 1917). See also *New Data for V. I. Lenin's Imperialism,* ed. E. Varga and L. Mendelsohn (New York, 1940).

plans to expand into China, her Pan-Slav smokescreen for the domination of the Balkans. The more acute the internal antagonisms in
Tsarist Russia became, the more necessary were new adventures, further conquests, additional territories; for only war could offer a hope
that a domestic change might be once again postponed. From this
vision of the impending imperialist conflict, Lenin derived his doctrine
of the right of national self-determination, for him an important
weapon in the anti-imperialist struggle.

Around this question of self-determination, especially around the
particular aspect of Polish independence, there was for many years a
feud between Lenin and Luxemburg, who rejected self-determination
as unrealizable under capitalism. Luxemburg's concept of a far-distant
socialist society, based on a fully developed planned economy, determined her current political attitudes on many questions. In such a
perfect socialist society of the future, national animosities would be
reduced to cultural variations, national differences would no longer
be factors in social structures, which would be conceived along the
contours of economic regions alone. In this vision, Luxemburg was
influenced not only by the force and vitality of the great utopians and
Marx's critique of the artificiality of national division under capitalism,
but by her opposition to the Polish nationalists, whose narrow vista
she fought as a Polish internationalist. This difference on such a key
question as the right of nations to political equality illustrates how
dangerous it is to follow the common juxtaposition of the autocratic
socialist Lenin against the democratic socialist Luxemburg.

Her position can be best illustrated by an overstatement of it, a resolution adopted by the Polish party two years after the outbreak of the
war; [16] on many occasions, and most explicitly during the war, Luxemburg herself expressed the same policy in more general terms. It
was the premise of the Polish socialists that the tendency of finance-
capitalism to expand into greater state combinations, even if without
regard to the nationality of the people involved, is in the end "economically progressive," for these brutal forms of imperialist oppres-

---

[16] "Thesen über Imperialismus und nationale Unterdrückung," adopted by the
Central Committee of the Social Democratic Party of Russian Poland and printed
in their central organ, *Gazeta Robotnicza* ("Workers' Journal"), No. 2, April 1916;
cited from Lenin, *Sämtliche Werke* (Vienna, 1930), XIX, 528 ff.

sion prepare for socialism by political and economic concentration within the capitalist world. Thus, in fully developed capitalist countries, Social Democrats cannot demand a return to dated forms, cannot fight for either the reëstablishment of old national states or the establishment of new ones. Their slogan must be, "Down with frontiers!" The fight against national oppression can now be made only as a part of the general fight against imperialism and for socialism, and in a socialist world national aspirations will no longer be an issue.

> We have no reason to assume [the resolution stated] that in the socialist society the Nation will have the character of an economic-political unit. According to every preconception, the Nation will be merely a cultural and language community, since territorial division of the socialist cultural entity—to the extent that such a thing will exist—will be on the basis of production requirements. Thus it will not only be individual nations, in the full development of their own power, that decide on this division (as they would under the principle of "national self-determination"); all interested citizens will have the right to participate in the decision. To transfer the formula, "the right of self-determination," to the socialist society indicates a complete misinterpretation of the nature of the socialist commonwealth.

With this ironclad vision of the world commonwealth, governed by the world economic board, the authors of the thesis went on to characterize national self-determination as a heritage from the Second International, whose ambiguity might lead to the defense of the capitalist fatherland. How obsolete the issue of nationalism had become they illustrate by the example of their native Poland:

> The World War has proved that the period of formation of national states in Europe has come to an end. . . . The attitude of the Polish bourgeoisie in all parts of divided Poland has strikingly demonstrated that the ideal of the National State is an anachronism in the imperialist era, and confirms the correctness of the position of the Social Democratic Party of Russian Poland towards such independence currents. The Polish proletariat has never made national independence its goal. . . . Today, in the light of the World War experiences, to put forward the slogan of national independence as an instrument in the fight against national oppression would be not only a dangerous utopia but also the negation of the most basic principles of socialism.

When Lenin polemized against this point of view, he was most careful to take into account Luxemburg's internationalism, the difficulties she had in opposing Polish nationalists. But on the main issue he was forthright; the defense of national minorities was an integral part of his revolutionary doctrine. In his struggle against feudal Russia, he took over the traditions of nineteenth-century revolutionary democracy and made them his own.

In an article summing up twenty years of polemics on the question, Lenin begins, it would be a betrayal of socialism to renounce the right of national self-determination. The economic analysis of the Polish socialists completely disregards the question of the state and state power; organized economy is only one aspect of the future socialist society. Quoting Engel's pamphlet, *Po and Rhine,* Lenin states that there are natural borders in Europe, created over a period of centuries by language and national affinity. In the process of history, the great viable states have sucked in smaller and weaker ones, so that the natural borders of the earlier period have now been obliterated.

> Reactionary imperialist capitalism will leave as a heritage to the socialism that succeeds it a series of annexations in Europe and other continents. Shall victorious socialism, which will reëstablish perfect democracy and carry it to completion, renounce the democratic determination of national borders? Will it not take into account the "sympathies" of the peoples? It is enough to put these questions to see how our Polish colleagues are driving from Marxism toward "imperialist Economism." [17]

Lenin's prime example was his native country.

> In Russia—where no less than 57 per cent, i.e., over 100,000,000 of the population, belong to oppressed nations, where those nations mainly inhabit the border provinces, where some of those nations are more cultured than the Great Russians, where the political system is distinguished by its particularly barbarous and medieval character, where the bourgeois-democratic revolution has not yet been completed—the recognition of the right of nations oppressed by Tsarism to free secession from Russia is absolutely obligatory for Social Democracy in the interests of its democratic and socialist tasks. . . . Russian socialists who fail to demand freedom of seces-

---

[17] Lenin, "Die Ergebnisse der Diskussion über die Selbstbestimmung," *Sämtliche Werke,* XIX, 295 ff.

sion for Finland, Poland, the Ukraine, etc., etc., are behaving like chauvinists, like lackeys of the blood- and mud-stained imperialist monarchies and the imperialist bourgeoisie.[18]

Their differences on the national question point up the essential contrast between these two great revolutionary figures—Lenin with his eye always to the immediate problem, to the actual possibilities, to what is to be done; Luxemburg looking over these to her vision of the socialist future, and then returning from this to the present.[19]

---

[18] Lenin, "The Attitude of the Russian and Polish Social Democracy and of the Second International on Self-Determination," *Selected Works* (Moscow, 1935), V, 278–279.

[19] Later Lenin summed up his lifelong differences with Luxemburg as follows: "Rosa Luxemburg was mistaken on the question of the independence of Poland; she was mistaken in 1903 in her appraisal of Menshevism; she was mistaken on the theory of the accumulation of capital; she was mistaken in July 1914, when side by side with Plekhanov, Vandervelde, Kautsky and others, she advocated unity between the Bolsheviks and the Mensheviks; she was mistaken in the works she wrote while in prison in 1918 (she corrected most of these mistakes at the end of 1918 and the beginning of 1919 after she was released). But in spite of her mistakes, she was—and remains for us—an eagle." ("Fox-Hunting, Levi and Serrati," *ibid.*, X, 312).

When the centuries-old Romanov dynasty came to its end in February 1917, the first of the houses that had governed Europe to topple, its death was the result of a combination of variegated ailments, some of which had been gnawing at its inner body for many decades. Of the multitudinous factors that led to the overthrow, one was dissatisfaction with the conduct of the war, combined with a growing realization that the Tsar, partly because he feared the probable effect of a too complete defeat of Germany on Imperial Russia, could not wage an efficient war.

Russia's contribution to the war had been a disappointment to the Entente. Between 1912 and 1914, Allied diplomats had written back to their capitals of a "steamroller" Russian army, but this judgment had been based too much on the impressively garbed Cossack troops that paraded each fortnight in St. Petersburg. The enormous resources of manpower were ineffective, for they took with them into the army the dying social order of civilian life; despite the courage of the privates and the brilliance of many generals, the army failed to sweep away the Germans. It became restive.

In February 1917, two months before the entrance of the United States was to make Germany's defeat certain, the most Western-minded among Russian politicians took steps to bring their country fully into the war. It was feared that if the Tsar was not removed, he might, following the advice of Rasputin, arrange a separate peace with

Germany, just as the decisive turn of the war was at hand. Russia had suffered, and now she would be deprived of her just share of the peace settlement unless a thoroughgoing change was effected. The revolutionaries who engineered the coup against the "pro-German" Tsarist government were encouraged by their French and British advisers.

Thus, the men who succeeded Nicholas II were united in their ardent desire to continue the war, and they were supported in this by substantial socialist groups. This was the Russia to which the political refugees streamed back from all over the world. By the boldest of bargains, Lenin was enabled to return in a train that passed through German territory under the protection of Ludendorff himself. In the heavy anti-German atmosphere of Petrograd politics, this arrangement hung like a dark shadow over the first months of Lenin's participation in Russian politics, the first since 1905 that was not from exile. The story has often been told how he brusquely attacked the Bolshevik Party's indeterminate stand and pushed it forward. Emerging from long years of underground activity, the weakened Bolshevik cadres that appeared above the surface were confused, with no clear alternative to Lenin's forthright program. He met stiff resistance from other socialist groups, but the tiny Bolshevik group was embedded in a strong if diffused peace current. The Soviets of Workers', Soldiers', and Peasants' Deputies, elected on March 10, 1917, convened in Petrograd and on March 27 appealed for an immediate end to the war: "The Russian democracy calls upon the peoples of Europe for concerted decisive action in favor of peace."

Lenin prepared the Bolshevik coup d'état impelled by a certainty that in Europe—and particularly in Germany—the revolution was moving yet faster; at every crucial point his decisive argument was the latest scant news of the German anti-war movement. "I think it better," Lenin said, referring to the vote in the Reichstag on war credits, "to remain alone like Liebknecht, one against a hundred and ten" than to follow the Mensheviks and Populists. Five months later, when Lenin was fighting against a substantial opposition in his own party, he referred again to the resistance movement in Germany. During the discussion in the Central Committee immediately preceding the events of November 7, he stated that "the international situation of the Russian revolution places the armed uprising on the order of the day." "If in a country like Germany there is a mutiny in the navy," he stated on October 29, "this proves that things have gone very far."

The Bolshevik coup created panic in London and Paris, less because of the social change in Russia, about which there was little concrete knowledge at the time, than because Lenin might push for an immediate peace with Germany. The strength of the German army was still overrated in Allied headquarters, which had plans for mobilization and future campaigns through 1920.

On November 8, when Lenin appeared at the Congress of Soviets to report on the coup (whose success was by no means yet assured), he proclaimed the Bolsheviks' peace policy without ambiguity. "The first thing is the adoption of practical measures to realize peace. We shall offer peace to the people of all belligerent countries on the basis of the Soviet terms—no annexations, no indemnities, and the right of self-determination of peoples." The Bolsheviks lived in the illusion that the withdrawal of Russia would stop the war immediately. They hoped that their proposal for a three-month armistice would have to be accepted by all governments, under pressure from the weary soldiers, and that in these three months all fundamental questions could be settled.

Only the Central Powers reacted to this call for peace; on November 26, 1917, the Reich expressed its willingness to come to terms.[1] An arrangement in the East was vital, so that all German forces could be concentrated in the West. During the preliminaries, the Bolsheviks intensified their peace propaganda. Copies of the peace proclamation, together with a special manifesto to the German army, were dropped from airplanes far behind the lines. Newspapers in German written for soldiers were printed in editions fantastically large for this period—that of *Die Fackel* ("The Torch"), for instance, was half a million a day—and sent by special trains to Minsk, Kiev, and other points on the front, where the soldiers of Germany were approached in the name of Karl Liebknecht. In the first days of the revolution

---

[1] "General Hoffmann's staff was publishing a paper called *Russky Vyestnik* (The Russian Messenger) for the benefit of the Russian prisoners" (Trotsky, *My Life*, New York: Charles Scribner's Sons, 1930, p. 363). Trotsky reports that in the first period the German General Staff spoke in this propaganda literature of him and the Bolsheviks "with admiring affection."

Trotsky set up in the Foreign Office a press bureau headed by Karl Radek, who because of his long stay in the German Social Democratic Party was regarded as an expert for German affairs, and a bureau of international revolutionary propaganda, comprising among others the American, John Reed. Zinoviev, sent to the frontier with the assignment to proceed to Central Europe, was turned back by the Germans.

Separate Peace

On December 2, 1917, less than a month after they had taken power, Soviet delegates met with German representatives at Brest-Litovsk in their first conference and arranged a provisional truce, which became a formal armistice on December 15. This first step toward peace startled war-torn Europe; the eyes of every diplomat, of every general, and of every common soldier followed the zigzag of the negotiations as they wandered through December and into the new year. After three and a half years of war, with empires at stake, and lives, here was the prospect—or the danger—of a negotiated peace, which would set the vast ambitions on both sides at naught.

The Bolsheviks did not expect leniency from the German army, but they reasoned that under the pressure of the mood for peace, which was general in Europe but particularly strong among the peoples of the Central Powers, the German General Staff would be forced to accept a compromise. If so, then a treaty ending the war without indemnities or annexations would topple the whole war edifice, and the Entente diplomats also would be forced to come to the conference room. In the name of the Soviet government, Trotsky issued a proclamation throwing the responsibility of the separate peace on those who continued the war. The Bolsheviks, he said, did not feel themselves bound by the secret treaties that had taken Russia into the war, the treaties whose text the Soviet government had published as one of its first acts.

"Socialists of all countries," the Petrograd Telegraph Agency broadcast, "especially the socialists of Germany, must understand that between the program of the Russian workers and peasants and the program of the German capitalists, landowners, and generals there is an irreconcilable contradiction. . . . The workers of Germany, Austria-Hungary, Bulgaria, and Turkey must substitute for the imperialist program of their ruling classes their own revolutionary program of solidarity and collaboration between the workers of all countries."

During the week of December 22–28, 1917, at the first conference in Brest-Litovsk to discuss peace terms, the Bolsheviks offered a simple but radiant hope to a Europe torn by marching armies: withdrawal of all troops, guaranteed return of refugees, a plebiscite in all disputed areas, no annexations or indemnities. Richard von Kühlmann, the German delegate at Brest, said he would have to withdraw to consider the offer, but intimated that it would not be rejected out of hand. In the middle of the conference, in an attack on Entente public opinion, the Central Powers issued their famous Christmas Day declaration: they were for a peace without indemnities or annexations, provided only that the war end immediately and all belligerents take part in the negotiations. The Allies ignored the appeal, as indeed Germany intended.

Meanwhile Russia was slipping into civil war. Tsarist generals—Kaledin, Kornilov, Alexeyev—were gathering troops. In the Ukraine, the Rada, the legislative assembly that had been instituted after the February revolution, combined a program of Ukrainian nationalism with strong opposition to a Bolshevik-sponsored peasants' uprising. On November 20, it declared a Ukrainian People's Republic; at the Brest conference the Ukrainian delegate, M. Holubovich, declaimed that after 250 years the Ukrainian Republic had regained its national existence and did his best to use the German plans against the Soviet government to the advantage of his own infant state. The increasing tension in the Ukraine gradually developed into an intertwined war and civil war. On December 17, the Soviet government issued an ultimatum to the Rada, demanding a satisfactory reply within twenty-four hours. The right of the Ukraine, as of any part of the Russian empire, to secede was "once more confirmed," but the Bolsheviks insisted that it cease assisting "the counter-revolutionary forces of the Cadets and of Kaledin."

On January 8, 1918, President Wilson proclaimed his Fourteen Points, centering around national self-determination. The USPD faction in the Reichstag issued a manifesto attacking the German war aim as they had been "openly laid down at Brest-Litovsk."

We were assured over and over again in the past that the German government wanted only to protect the frontiers of the Empire and that it did not intend to make annexations. No thinking person can believe this assertion any longer.

Germany wants the annexation of Russian territory. . . . If Germany succeeds in making a peace of conquest against the Russian people, it will be a misfortune for Russia, the Poles, the Lithuanians and Latvians. But it would be an even greater misfortune for ourselves. The result would be a postponement of general peace, new threats and a desire for revenge, increased armaments and intensified reaction in our land. . . . Only a peace without annexations and indemnities and on the basis of the self-determination of peoples can save us.[2]

In mid-January mass strikes broke out in Vienna and Berlin. The desire for peace was particularly strong in Austria-Hungary. Workers of the Görtz factory and the Arsenal, two of the largest plants of Vienna, stopped work in the middle of a shift because bread had not been distributed for several days. They marched from one factory to another, closing the entire war industry in a few hours. This Bread Strike rapidly became a demonstration of solidarity with the Bolsheviks, who felt bitter disappointment when an adjustment in the bread ration brought it to an end.

In the second phase of the negotiations, Trotsky replaced Adolf Joffe as the head of the Russian delegation at Brest. Under the guise of giving the Russian program of national self-determination full support, von Kühlmann and General Max Hoffmann pushed for independent governments in the Baltic states, in Poland, in the Ukraine—all under the protection of the German army. "The significance of the Brest-Litovsk pourparlers," the Soviet government wirelessed "To ALL" on January 22, "is that they have stripped from German imperialism its false cloak, temporarily borrowed from the democratic wardrobe, and exposed the cruel reality of annexationism of owners and capitalists."

Against the actuality of Russian dismemberment, the majority of the Bolshevik Party revolted. Bukharin and Radek proposed that a revolutionary war be waged against Germany, thus inspiring the Ger-

---

[2] Quoted in Judah L. Magnes, *Russia and Germany at Brest-Litovsk* (New York, 1919), pp. 63–64.

man workers to join their Russian comrades and rise against their government. This position was supported by the Left Social Revolutionaries,[3] who were at this time in the government; and it was welcomed by many anti-Bolshevik groups in the country who, reflecting the resurgence of Russian nationalism induced by the German peace terms, wished to continue the war at the side of the Entente.

Lenin, who none the less advocated accepting the German terms immediately, for a time was in a hopeless minority in the party. He based his argument first of all on the impossibility of continuing the war with the Russian army, which had been melting away from the front—partly under the pressure of Bolshevik propaganda. These peasants in uniform were interested in only one thing: getting home in time to get their share of the landed estates that were being divided. The officers, who certainly felt no loyalty to the Soviet government, were wavering between a nationalist will to resist the Germans and a wish to exploit to the full this good opportunity to weaken the new Russian regime. "Our army is destroyed and is demobilized," Lenin declared, "and refuses to fight at all. But in Dünaburg Russian officers are again promenading with epaulets."

When Trotsky returned from Brest, after having used the rostrum of the conference table to call Europe to revolt, he also recognized that no war could be waged with the old Russian army. His compromise formula, "No war, no peace," met halfway the nationalist outrage and frustration that the German terms had generated in the country and

---

[3] The Social Revolutionary Party, founded by M. Gotz and V. Chernov in 1901, was heir to the Narodnik (Populist) revolutionary peasant groups and followed their tradition of individual terrorism in the fight against Tsarism. During the war a Left faction developed, and after the February revolution this wing, led by Maria Spiridonova, Boris Kamkov, and Mark Natanson, repudiated any collaboration with bourgeois parties. At the Second Congress of Soviets, in November 1917, the Left wing had 169 of 193 Social Revolutionary delegates, and for a few weeks it attempted to bring the Right minority into collaboration with the Soviet government, but without success. Only after this policy failed did the Lefts SRs themselves enter the government; by an agreement entered into on November 30, a Left SR was to be included in every commissariat. Immediately afterward, on December 2, the group constituted itself a separate party.

During the Brest crisis, on March 16, the Left SRs left the government and four months later attempted a coup against it. They were driven into illegality and the illegal party gradually disintegrated. Small groups were formed, the Revolutionary Communists and the Narodnik Communists, which sponsored collaboration with the Soviet government and were later fused into the Bolshevik Party.

left the way open to another revolutionary policy. "The supporters of revolutionary war," Trotsky writes in his memoirs, "obtained 32 votes, Lenin 15, and I 16" at the meeting of active party workers on January 21.

> But these figures [he continues] are not really indicative of the mood of the party. In the upper stratum, if not in the masses, the "left wing" was even stronger than at this particular meeting. It was this fact that insured the temporary victory of my formula. . . .
>
> In all the directing institutions of the party and the state, Lenin was in a minority. Over two hundred local Soviets . . . stated their views on war and peace. Of them all, only two large Soviets . . . went on record as being in favor of peace. . . . Lenin's point could have been carried out by means of a split in the party and a coup d'état, but not otherwise.[4]

On February 9, the Central Powers signed a separate peace with the Rada, and the next day Russia broke off negotiations on the basis of Trotsky's formula. "In refusing to sign a peace of annexation, Russia declares, on its side, the state of war with Germany as ended."

On February 15, three days before the end of the armistice, the German army advanced along the Eastern front. This brought the dispute in the party to a climax; the Bukharin wing began to behave like an independent party. On February 18, after Trotsky changed his view during the day to support Lenin and tendered his resignation as Commissar of Foreign Affairs, the Central Committee voted to accept the German terms.

> I was very sceptical about the possibility of securing peace even at the price of complete capitulation. But Lenin decided to try the capitulation idea to the utmost. Since he had no majority in the Central Committee, and the decision depended on my vote, I abstained from voting to insure for him the majority of one vote. I stated this explicitly when I explained my reasons for not voting. If the surrender should fail to obtain peace for us, I reasoned, we would straighten out our party front in armed defense of the revolution thrust on us by the enemy. . . .
>
> On the twenty-second of February, at the meeting of the Central Committee, I reported that the French military mission had conveyed the French and English offers to help us in a war with

---

[4] Trotsky, *My Life*, pp. 382–383.

Germany. I expressed myself as in favor of accepting the offer, on condition, of course, that we be completely independent in matters of foreign policy. Bukharin insisted that it was inadmissible for us to enter into any arrangements with the imperialists. Lenin came vigorously to my aid, and the Central Committee adopted my resolution by six votes against five. As far as I can remember now, Lenin dictated the resolution in these words: "That Comrade Trotsky be authorized to accept the assistance of the brigands of the French imperialism against the German brigands." He always preferred formulas that left no room for doubt.

After I left the meeting, Bukharin overtook me in the long corridor of the Smolny, threw his arms about me, and began to weep. "What are we doing?" he exclaimed. "We are turning the party into a dung heap." Bukharin is generally ready with his tears, and likes realistic expressions. But at this time the situation was becoming really tragic. The revolution was between the hammer and the anvil.[5]

The German army continued to advance. The Bolshevik government declared a revolutionary war against "the bourgeoisie and imperialists of Germany" and ordered complete destruction of property in case of retreat.

On February 23, new German peace terms were received in Petrograd. They called for the virtual cession of Dvinsk, Livonia, and Estonia to Germany and of Anatolia to Turkey; the recognition of the Ukrainian government; the evacuation of Finland and the Ukraine; the immediate demobilization of the Russian army. They specified that "the above conditions must be accepted within forty-eight hours."

On that same day the Central Committee voted to form a Red Army. February 23rd has since been celebrated as Red Army Day.

Lenin was convinced that the only way to maintain the young Soviet government in power was to accept the German terms immediately. They were accepted in form, and at the session of February 24, the day after the new German terms were received, the Central Committee discussed who should represent Russia at Brest to sign the treaty. George V. Chicherin and Leo M. Karakhan had been nominated and, in order, he said, to maintain continuity with the previous delegation, Lenin proposed that Adolf A. Joffe, Trotsky's intimate friend, opponent of the peace treaty, go as well. Joffe declined categorically, and Lenin

---

[5] Trotsky, *My Life*, pp. 389–390.

withdrew his nomination and proposed instead that Joffe be sent to Brest as a consultant. Joffe would not be needed there, Trotsky pointed out, for there would be nothing to do but sign the peace. G. Y. Sokolnikov then nominated Zinoviev as delegate, and Zinoviev nominated Sokolnikov. Lenin proposed that they both go. With that, Sokolnikov declared that he could not go, and if he was ordered to go he would resign from the Central Committee. Lenin asked the comrades not to get nervous.

Trotsky's resignation as Commissar for Foreign Affairs was discussed. Lenin's motion, "that the Central Committee ask Comrade Trotsky to postpone his decision until its next session on Tuesday" (amended to read "until the return of the delegates from Brest-Litovsk"), was passed with three abstentions. After the vote, Trotsky declared that he had made his proposal, that it had not been accepted, and that he felt himself compelled not to participate in the sessions of the leading bodies. Lenin proposed that Trotsky abstain from the sessions of the Council of People's Commissars for Foreign Affairs, but attend all other meetings; this motion was adopted.

G. I. Lomov, M. S. Uritsky, V. M. Smirnov, G. L. Pyatakov, among others—all "Left Communists," members of the Bukharin wing—had resigned from their various posts in the party and the soviets. Lenin moved "that the Central Committee ask the comrades who have made these declarations to postpone their decision until the return of the delegation from Brest-Litovsk and to reconsider this resolution of the Central Committee in their group." A party convention was imminent, Lenin pointed out, at which they could win their position. By an amendment to his motion, Lenin offered the group a guarantee by the Central Committee that their statement would be published in *Pravda*. These proposals of Lenin were adopted.[6]

---

[6] Aeusserungen Lenins in der Sitzung des Zentralkomitees der SDAPR(B)," *Sämtliche Werke* (Zurich, 1934), XXII, 306 ff.

This report, taken from the stenographic record of the committee's session, can be compared with the impression of outsiders, for example, one of the best informed at the time, Bruce Lockhart: "I remember Chicherin giving me an account of a Soviet Cabinet meeting. Trotsky would bring forward a proposal. It would be violently opposed by another Commissar. Endless discussion would follow, and all the time Lenin would be writing notes on his knee, his attention concentrated on some work of his own. At last some one would say: 'Let Vladimir Ilyitch decide.' Lenin would look up from his work, give his decision in one sentence, and all would be peace." (R. H. Bruce Lockhart, *British Agent*, New York, 1933, p. 236.)

On March 3, 1918, Chicherin, as chief of the Russian delegation, signed the Treaty of Brest-Litovsk.[7] But, under the pretext of protecting the local population from brigands, the German army continued to advance, and the dispute in the Bolshevik Party rose to a climax. On March 5, two days after the signing of the treaty, the Bolsheviks shifted the capital from the vulnerable Petrograd, which they were afraid the Germans would seize as a guarantee for the treaty, to Moscow. By March 20, the Austro-German advance in the Ukraine had encompassed Kiev and Odessa, and the Turks had recovered Trebizond and Erzerum; the Central Powers were in full control of the Black Sea. If the Bolsheviks broke again with the Germans, the Entente was considering a realignment with Russia. No one regarded the settlement at Brest as final, and both Germany and the Entente accused the Soviet government of double dealing.[8]

At the Seventh Party Congress, which met in Moscow March 6–8, the struggle between the two factions was continued at an increased tempo. In a sharp statement, Lenin developed his principal point: that the question of advisability of a war against Germany was irrelevant, since the condition of the Russian army made it impossible. The signing of the peace, he pointed out, though it had not stopped the German advance, had saved Petrograd from seizure. "We do not know how long the breathing spell will last, but we will try to make use of this moment. Perhaps the breathing spell will be of longer duration, but perhaps it will last only a few days. Everything is possible. . . ."

The Russian revolution, from February on, had proceeded from one triumph to the next, but now it must look forward, Lenin said, to "a

---

[7] Estonia and Livonia were ceded to Germany, and the Anatolian provinces and the districts of Erivan, Kars, and Batum to Turkey. Russia agreed to evacuate her troops from the Ukraine and to recognize the Ukrainian People's Republic; to evacuate Finland and the Åland Islands, and to raze the fortifications on the latter. "The contracting parties mutually renounce indemnification of their war costs . . . as well as indemnification for war damages," said the treaty, but Russia had to pay "compensation" of three hundred million gold rubles. Various subsidiary clauses regulated the economic relations between Russia and each of the powers of the Quadruple Alliance.

[8] It was reported in Allied circles that there was a German Control Commission in Petrograd, which from behind the scenes controlled the Bolshevik Foreign Office. When General Berthelot arrived in Moscow at the head of a French military mission, his services in training Russian troops were offered to Trotsky, since the alternative was assumed to be German officers. On the other side, the Germans accused the Soviet government of welcoming the British troops when they landed at Murmansk. Cf. Lockhart, *British Agent*.

series of torturous defeats." The central task of the moment was the preservation of the Soviet state, even if considerably weakened, as a starting point for a new advance at a more propitious moment. The shattered and dispersed forces of Soviet power had to be tightened and centralized. The decision to build a Red Army had to be implemented, for this would be the only ultimate guarantee of the victory of the European revolution. Time was in favor of Soviet Russia, for Europe was heading toward a revolutionary cataclysm, and it was necessary only to endure, to hold out, till it came. "No one knows—no one can know—what will happen, for every one of the big powers is under pressure, compelled to fight on several fronts. The attitude of General Hoffmann is defined by three factors—that he must destroy Soviet power, that he must fight on several fronts, and that the revolution in Germany is growing." But Hoffmann might take Petrograd and Moscow "tomorrow."

Doggedly, Lenin held to this view and maintained it not only against the opposing stand of the Left Communists under Bukharin but against weakening amendments offered by Zinoviev and Trotsky, among others. From the party congress Lenin carried his view to the Fourth Congress of the Soviets, meeting a few days later, March 15–17, where he had opposing him not only the Bukharinists, rankling under party discipline, but the very active Left Social Revolutionaries, who so fought the ratification of the treaty that they left the coalition government. For them, sitting and waiting for the German advance, which would mean not only the end of Soviet power but the annihilation of all revolutionary organizations, was the height of folly.

The Left Communists

From the same basic premise as Lenin, that Europe was on the brink of a revolutionary crisis and time was with the Soviets, the Left Communists drew an opposite conclusion. The principal difference in the analysis was a different appreciation of the actual force of the Central Powers. Even if Hoffmann did take Moscow, they argued, it would be a short-lived victory, for Germany was in the last phase before an Entente victory, which was now assured by the arrival of the fresh and well-equipped American troops. The Reich was facing collapse, and Austria-Hungary was facing dismemberment. These historical facts, which could be predicted with certainty, would create a revolutionary opportunity in Central Europe of unprecedented magnitude, and the task in Russia was to foster this opportunity, to prepare to collaborate with the revolutionaries who would spring from the fires of dying Europe. The mighty German army, whose possible advance on Moscow put the very discussion under a strain, was a mighty façade only, which tomorrow would fall before the Allied attack.

The Lefts proposed a new type of war—the formation in the rear of the enemy army of partisan groups composed of workers and poor peasants, who would fight with a combination of machine gun and *Communist Manifesto*. Let the Germans advance; the farther into Russia they came, the more certain would be their annihilation. The guerrilla bands that surrounded and harried them would grow in the process of fighting, assimilating new recruits from the countryside. The Bolsheviks might lose Petrograd and Moscow but they would emerge immensely strengthened, not only by the creation of mobile units of Communist forces but by the dissemination of a passionate faith in the ultimate victory of Communism that the imminent bourgeois catastrophe made inevitable.[9]

This inevitable crisis, the Left Communists insisted, would mature fastest with this strategy. If the German General Staff was deprived of the temporary stabilization that a separate peace with Russia would give it, the illusion among the German masses that the war might be ended by orderly and relatively advantageous negotiations would be dispelled. The weak cadres of the German revolutionaries would be encouraged and inspired to fight harder and strike sooner. Most important of all, the German generals would be deprived of their last decisive drop of self-confidence, which they needed in a defeat much more than

---

[9] Under other circumstances, these military tactics of the Left have been realized successfully in various places—in Yugoslavia during the Second World War, in Greece since then, in China since 1931. Mao Tse-tung has told how, by an adaptation of Marxist principles to the Chinese scene, he created a new type of mobile peasant army. "We have lived for twenty years in what might be called military communism. . . . It is a system by which the personnel of army and government is not paid in money but draws part of its food from taxation and part from joint productive work. 'By this method,' said Liu, 'we can support an army and government staff of two or three million without too seriously burdening the people's livelihood. With this system we have been able to carry on war for twenty years and can carry it on till final victory.'" (Anna Louise Strong, "The Thought of Mao Tse-tung," *Amerasia*. New York, June 1947, vol. XI, No. 6, pp. 161–174.

in a victory if they were to maintain the dominant position they had established during the war.

Like all the Bolshevik leaders, the Left wing looked forward to a widespread fraternization among the troops of all nations. "Workers of all countries, unite!" was reinforced by "Soldiers of all armies, unite!" That despite many isolated incidents a general intermingling never materialized on a mass scale was at least in part the result of the Brest-Litovsk Treaty. Widespread fraternization between the soldiers of the Russian armies and those of the disintegrating German armies on the Eastern front would have resulted, in the concept of Bukharin and his supporters, in international brigades composed of Russians and Germans, of Austrians and Hungarians and Czechs, who would together have carried the revolution to their various homelands. According to this grandiose concept, Europe would emerge from international civil war as a federation, organized from local councils up and not vice versa.

It has become a commonplace that, among others, Karl Kautsky and Rudolf Hilferding and Rosa Luxemburg foresaw some of the implications of the Bolsheviks' experiment, but that a similar anxiety was expressed from the Left is less well known. The effect of the Brest-Litovsk Treaty on the new state was such, the Bukharinists feared, that the revolution would develop in the opposite direction.

> Once we renounce an active proletarian policy, the achievements of the workers' and peasants' revolution will be petrified into a system of state capitalism with petty bourgeois economic relations. "The defense of the socialist fatherland" will then in fact be the defense of a petty bourgeois fatherland that is subject to the influence of international capital. . . .
>
> Instead of a transition from the partial nationalization to the general socialization of big industry, this will in the main be formed into immense trusts directed by industrial captains, which from the outside will appear to be state enterprises. Production so organized creates the social basis for an evolution toward state capitalism and is in fact a transitory stage to it. With the factories administered on the principles of broad capitalist participation and semi-bureaucratic centralization, the labor policy bound to them would naturally be the introduction of work discipline (as proposed by the Right Bolsheviks), piece work, longer working days, etc.
>
> With this beginning, the form of the state administration can-

not but develop in the direction of bureaucratic centralization, the rule of the commissars, the quashing of the independence of local soviets, the renunciation in fact of the type of commune state governed from below.[10]

Although Lenin had won another victory at the Congress of Soviets, nothing was definitely settled. With the continuing advance of the Germans, the proponents of a revolutionary war, in and outside the party, grew ever more frantic. War and civil war were raging in the Ukraine, where the Germans had disbanded the Rada and installed Hetman Skoropadsky. That food from the Ukraine granary was going to feed the German troops enraged the nationalists and made them even more bitterly opposed to the Brest-Litovsk policy. In this complex situation, where the Social Revolutionaries represented both the disgruntled peasantry and the nationalist furor, the Communist Party (the new name had been adopted at its Seventh Congress) fumbled its way to a one-party dictatorship.

In accordance with their long tradition, the Left Social Revolutionaries began to fight the Soviet government by a series of terrorist plots, which were intended to bring to power a government that would reopen the war against Germany. Lenin's government, they said, is not the dictatorship of the proletariat but the dictatorship of Mirbach (the German ambassador). On June 20, as the climax of a month of heightening tension, People's Commissar for Propaganda V. Volodarsky was killed by a Social Revolutionary.

The kernel of Soviet power shriveled further, surrounded by hostile camps in the Ukraine, on the Don, in the North Caucasus, in Siberia, on the Volga. Moscow was swarming with refugees, from the Ukraine in particular, who related everywhere their tales of cruelty under the German occupation.

On June 24, the Central Committee of the Left Social Revolutionaries met in Moscow under the leadership of one of the great revolutionaries of Tsarist Russia, Maria Spiridonova. The minutes read:

> The Central Committee of the Left Social Revolutionary Party, having examined the present political situation of the Republic,

---

[10] "Thesen der 'Linken Kommunisten' über die gegenwärtige Lage," quoted in Lenin, *Sämtliche Werke*, XXII, 627 ff.

resolves that in the interests of the Russian as well as of the international Revolution, an immediate end must be put to the so-
called "breathing-space" created by the Treaty of Brest-Litovsk.

The Central Committee believes it to be both practical and
possible to organize a series of terrorist acts against the leading
representatives of German imperialism. In view of the fact that
this, contrary to the wishes of the party, may involve a collision
with the Bolsheviks, the Central Committee makes the following
declaration:

"We regard our policy as an attack on the present policy of
the Soviet Government, not as an attack on the Bolsheviks themselves. As it is possible that the Bolsheviks may take aggressive
counteraction against our party, we are determined, if necessary,
to defend the position we have taken up with force of arms. In
order to prevent the party from being exploited by counter-revolutionary elements, it is resolved that our new policy be stated clearly
and openly, so that an international social revolutionary policy
may subsequently be inaugurated in Soviet Russia." [11]

On July 4, some nine hundred to one thousand delegates assembled
at the Great Theater in Moscow for the Fifth Congress of Soviets.
Count von Mirbach, together with Entente observers, listened to the
bitter debates between Left Social Revolutionaries and Bolsheviks on
the Brest-Litovsk Treaty, which was here finally ratified. At the same
time the plan to build a Red Army was sanctioned.

From the first the atmosphere is charged with electricity. The
opening day is devoted to speeches by minor delegates. The
speeches are on strictly party lines. The three great crimes are
the Brest-Litovsk peace, the Poverty Committees and the death
sentence. The Left Social-Revolutionaries denounce all three. They
support their denunciation of the Peace Treaty with blood-

---

[11] Quoted in I. Steinberg, *Spiridonova, Revolutionary Terrorist* (London, 1935),
pp. 208–209. Born of a middle class family of Tambov, Maria Spiridonova entered
the Social Revolutionary Party in her teens. She became a leading revolutionary figure on January 16, 1906, when, at the age of twenty-one, she carried out the death
sentence the Social Revolutionary Central Committee had pronounced on General
Luzhenovsky. Clad as a school girl, she carried a revolver in her muff and shot the
general at the Borissoglebsk railroad station. She was arrested immediately and raped
and tortured by two Cossack officers, but she became the heroine of all anti-Tsarist
groupings so rapidly that the police did not risk sentencing her to death. In 1917, she
returned to Moscow from Siberian exile and exerted an enormous influence during
the first period of the revolution. After the July Days of 1918, she was arrested; the
last word of her, in 1935, was that she was in exile in the Urals.

curdling accounts of the German atrocities in the Ukraine. The Bolsheviks are on the defensive.[12]

On July 6, the Social Revolutionaries carried out the death sentence they had pronounced on Count Wilhelm von Mirbach. Jacob Blumkin, Social Revolutionary and member of the Cheka (later a Bolshevik and secretary of Trotsky), was enabled by his credentials to gain admittance to Mirbach by saying that he wished to warn him personally of a plot against his life. When Mirbach asked how the assassins proposed to kill him, Blumkin replied, "Like this!" and emptied a pistol into his body. As he escaped through the window, he threw a bomb back into the room.[13]

This was the signal for a Social Revolutionary coup; the party captured the telegraph office and sent out messages over the country announcing the imminent downfall of the Bolsheviks. When Dzerzhinsky went to the party headquarters to remonstrate over the Mirbach assassination, he was arrested for a few hours. It was planned to arrest all the Bolshevik leaders the next day at the Congress, but the Bolshevik delegates did not appear, and the theater was surrounded instead by Lettish troops.[14] This broke the force of the coup, but it reappeared sporadically for some weeks in isolated incidents. During the Bolshevik counteraction, on July 17, the Tsar and his family were executed at Ekaterinburg. On July 30, Field Marshal Hermann von Eichhorn, the German commander in the Ukraine, was assassinated by a Social Revolutionary.

The abortive Social Revolutionary coup had an effect opposite to what was intended: it strengthened the authority of Lenin within the

---

[12] Lockhart, *British Agent,* p. 294.

[13] "As the trial of the Rightist-Trotskyist bloc proved, Bukharin, Trotsky, and the other conspirators intended by this assault on Mirbach to break the Brest-Litovsk Treaty, to overwhelm the Soviet government, to arrest and kill Lenin, Stalin, and Sverdlov, and to restore capitalism in the land of the soviets" (*Bolshaya Sovetskaya Entsiklopediya,* Moscow, 1938, XXXIX, 486).

[14] A fear has since pervaded the politburo that the Soviet power could be destroyed by arresting the whole of a party congress. In the 1938 trial, H. G. Yagoda, who for sixteen years was head of the GPU, was convicted of having worked during those sixteen years for the overthrow of Stalin. He had known, he confessed, of a coup being prepared by the anti-Stalinist Bloc, which intended to arrest the Seventeenth Party Congress in January 1934. (Cf. *Report of Court Proceedings in the Case of the Anti-Soviet "Bloc of Rights and Trotskyites,"* Moscow, 1938, p. 570).

party and the authority of the party in the country. With the Allied offensive on the Western front and the ever more imminent defeat of the German army, the political opposition of the Left Communists was weakening. During the first phase of the Brest negotiations, from January to March 1918, while the Left Social Revolutionaries were in the government, the majority of the Bolshevik Party under Bukharin had coördinated their actions with the Social Revolutionaries on the basis of a joint opposition to the treaty. In July the ill-conceived coup of the Social Revolutionaries closed the Bolshevik ranks and widened the rift between the Social Revolutionaries and the Bukharinists that had begun when the coalition was broken.

The Social Revolutionaries continued their terrorist acts. On August 30, they killed Mikhail Uritsky, chairman of the Petrograd Cheka, and on the same day, as Lenin was leaving the Michelson factory in Moscow, he was wounded by Dora Kaplan, a Left Social Revolutionary who once had been in prison with Spiridonova. With this attempt on Lenin's life, measures of reprisal were enormously increased; the period of Red Terror dates from this day.

The Bolsheviks had traveled far from the utopian group that had broadcast messages "to the workers of the world." They had signed a treaty with the German General Staff; they had lost the collaboration of the Mensheviks and the Left Social Revolutionaries and were building a one-party regime; they had founded the Red Army and the Cheka. Moving into a period of two and a half years of civil war, with troops of half a dozen foreign nations on Russian soil attempting to overthrow Soviet power, the Bolsheviks were pushed ever farther in the direction of repressive measures and centralization. But the vision of Year One still remained; it was still thought possible to return to the original concepts when their German revolutionary associates joined them.

Spartakus and Brest-Litovsk

The Bolshevik evaluation of the German revolution, as it developed in this major crisis of the party, is of the greatest interest today, for in it we see a basic difference between Leninism and Stalinism, one that regained primary importance during World War II. First of all,

Lenin rejected mechanical dependence on the timing of the German uprising. He emphasized that the German revolution was ripening but that it was impossible to expect it to follow a fixed schedule:

> We know that Karl Liebknecht will be victorious; we know that he will come to our assistance, and that Liebknecht's revolution in Germany will liberate us from all international difficulties and from the necessity of revolutionary war. Liebknecht's victory will annul the consequences of our stupidities. But it would be the peak of folly to expect that Liebknecht will be victorious at just one moment and to count on speedy deliverance in such a mechanical way. The German revolution needs time. It needs preparation, propaganda, fraternization in the trenches, a period of development.[15]

Against Trotsky's argument that his "no war, no peace" policy would intensify the rebellion in the German army and make it impossible for the General Staff to send reliable troops against revolutionary Petrograd, Lenin replied:

> One could want nothing better if it turns out that Hoffmann is not strong enough to send troops against us. But there is little hope of that. He will find specially selected regiments of rich Bavarian farmers for it. And then, how many of them does he need? You say yourself that the trenches are empty. What if the Germans resume fighting? [16]

Against both the Bukharin-Radek faction and Trotsky, Lenin insisted that the overthrow of the German imperial government was much more difficult than the elimination of Tsarism in February 1917. Russia had been predominantly a peasant country, with an economy exhausted by the war and a deteriorating and corrupt upper class that was unable to resist even an inexperienced and weak workers' movement. In Germany, on the other hand, the revolution had to combat an "organized state capitalism technically splendidly equipped," directed by a self-assured and well-organized upper class, which would defend its interests with extreme brutality.

"This wild beast will let nothing escape it," he declared when General Hoffmann reopened the war by sending German troops back into

---

[15] Lenin, *Sämtliche Werke*, XXII, 283.
[16] Quoted in Trotsky, *My Life*, p. 381.

the Ukraine. During the following weeks, as the German army penetrated deeper into the Ukraine and the Caucasus, sacked villages and
cities, summarily executed all Bolsheviks and other revolutionaries,
neither Lenin nor Bukharin nor any other Bolshevik leader wavered
for a single moment in his solidarity with the German worker. When
the oppositionists pointed to the danger of an estrangement between
German and Russian workers as a result of the Brest-Litovsk Treaty,
Lenin replied that the German worker would understand the Bolshevik
position because "he is an intelligent, an educated worker, because he
is used to living in an advanced culture."

The German revolution, in the Bolshevik concept, would not merely
bring "assistance"; it would not merely lighten the unbearably heavy
load that the Russian revolutionaries were carrying. In the general
concept of European socialism, revolution in Germany was imperative
for the structural change that still had to be made in Russian society;
and the fact that the socialists in Russia took power first did not change
this relationship. The Russian soviets are raw, Lenin declared at the
Seventh Congress, "but as we create Soviet power, we can see what we
are doing, for we stand on the shoulders of the Paris Commune
and the development over many years of German Social Democracy."

The base of the social revolution was in Germany, but the tempo
at which the German revolution developed was slower than even the
most pessimistic in Russia had anticipated. The stabilization of the
army afforded by Brest-Litovsk had indeed been a setback, and the
peace that the Bolsheviks had signed with the German General Staff
led to widespread misunderstanding and criticism among German
socialists.

The most famous expression of this criticism is that by Rosa Luxemburg—another example of the wide divergence between her and Lenin.
Luxemburg never expected the Bolshevik experiment to last. The
Soviet government would not be able to hold out alone, she wrote to
Luise Kautsky on November 24, 1917, not only because the backward
economy made a socialist government an anomaly, but because the
Western Social Democrats were lamentable cowards, who would
quietly watch the Russians bleed to death. It would be better to perish
in such a fight, she added, than to live for the defense of the imperialist

fatherland; even a defeat would have salutary effects on the future of socialism.

The Brest-Litovsk negotiations, however, changed her friendly pessimism into bitter criticism of every aspect of Lenin's policies: she was in a mood of depression concerning the future of Russian and German socialism.

Since the end of 1915 or earlier, Luxemburg had expected Germany's military defeat. She called for a defeat of world imperialism by the proletariat, but saw as the most favorable alternative an Allied victory. For a victory of German imperialism would enslave all Europe and perhaps reach into other continents, demoralizing and disintegrating the international labor movement. With the breathing spell that Brest-Litovsk had given the German army, such an imperialist victory was now again possible. During the summer of 1918, she even speculated in the *Spartakusbriefe* on the possibility of a Soviet-German war alliance against the West.

> Above all, Rosa feared that the Bolsheviks might join in the game of German diplomacy and thus, by designating a peace based on violence as "a democratic peace, a peace without annexations or indemnities," slink into the good graces of the German General Staff. The revolutionaries would then be degraded into politicians, and the disintegrating element of distrust would have been carried into the movement.[17]

This view was not shared by even such intimate friends as Paul Levi and Leo Jogiches, and during the summer months in prison, in order to clarify these differences in her inner circle, Luxemburg wrote a general evaluation of the fundamentals of Bolshevik policy. She was in basic disagreement with Lenin on every major question, and that she coöperated with him after her release from prison in 1918 was undoubtedly the result of the pressure of her own organization.

In a mixture of visionary criticism of the shortcomings of the proletarian dictatorship with an organic inability to grasp the realities of the moment, Luxemburg summed up in this pamphlet, published after

---

[17] Paul Frölich, *Rosa Luxemburg, Gedanke und Tat* (Paris, 1939), pp. 236–237. Paul Frölich's study suffers from his wish to blur the controversy between Lenin and Luxemburg and to present their positions as fundamentally the same. Compare Rosa Luxemburg's article, "Die russische Tragödie," in *Spartakusbriefe* (Berlin: Kommunistische Partei Deutschlands [Spartakusbund], 1920), pp. 181–186.

her death, her old disagreement with Lenin on every principled issue: land policy, suffrage, the constituent assembly, dictatorship and democracy.[18] Once again, the differences come out most sharply in her attack on the Bolshevik's "so-called right of self-determination of peoples, or —something which was really implicit in this slogan—the disintegration of Russia."

> The mere fact that the question of national aspirations and tendencies towards separation were injected at all into the midst of the revolutionary struggle, and were even pushed into the foreground and made into the shibboleth of socialist and revolutionary policy as a result of the Brest peace, has served to bring the greatest confusion into socialist ranks and has actually destroyed the position of the proletariat in the border countries.[19]

As a prime example of this nationalist urge that the Bolsheviks have injected into the class struggle, Luxemburg cites the Ukraine, whose national aspirations she ironically compares to those of the Wasserkante, a region in Germany where the Plattdeutsch dialect is spoken.

> Ukrainian nationalism in Russia was something quite different from, let us say, Czechish, Polish, or Finnish nationalism in that the former was a mere whim, a folly of a few dozen petty bourgeois intellectuals without the slightest roots in the economic, political, or psychological relationships of the country; it was without any historical tradition, since the Ukraine never formed a nation or government, was without any national culture, except for the reactionary-romantic poems of Shevchenko. It is exactly as if, one fine day, the people living in the Wasserkante should want to found a new Low German nation and government! And this ridiculous pose of a few university professors and students was inflated into a political force by Lenin and his comrades

---

[18] Rosa Luxemburg, *The Russian Revolution*, translated by Bertram D. Wolfe (New York: Workers Age Publishers, 1940). The pamphlet was first published in full at Berlin in 1922 with an introduction by Paul Levi. In the middle thirties, the *Spartacus* group in Paris issued a French translation by Marcel Ollivier. In general, the pamphlet has been important in the Left Socialist attack on Bolshevism. It was answered by Clara Zetkin, *Um Rosa Luxemburgs Stellung zur russischen Revolution* (Hamburg, 1923), and Adolf Warski, *Rosa Luxemburgs Stellung zu den taktischen Problemen der Revolution* (Hamburg, 1922). Both Zetkin and Warski were close friends of Luxemburg, and their reply to the pamphlet was intended to confuse the differences between her and Lenin and to accuse Levi of bad faith in publishing a hasty manuscript that she would have wished to revise fundamentally.

[19] *The Russian Revolution*, pp. 27–28.

through their doctrinaire agitation concerning the "right of self-determination, including, etc." To what was at first a mere farce they lent such importance that the farce became a matter of the most deadly seriousness—not as a serious national movement for which, afterward as before, there are no roots at all, but as a shingle and rallying flag of counter-revolution! At Brest, out of this addled egg crept the German bayonets.[20]

The almost quaint naïveté of this passage cannot be matched, but the same rigidity of analysis characterizes her criticism, for example, of the Bolshevik land policy. Socialist land reform, she said, consisted not in the division of land among the peasants but in the nationalization of the large landed estates.

But the weakness of her political analysis became her strength when, with great hostility, she looked at the new form of dictatorial state emerging from the revolution. Conditioned to think as a revolutionary democrat, having fought all her life against autocracy and bureaucracy, she sensed intuitively the deformation inherent in Lenin's creation. The concluding paragraphs of the same pamphlet constitute one of the most penetrating prophecies of degeneration that had yet been formulated by any of the Social Democratic critics of the Bolshevik experiment.

> When all this is eliminated, what really remains? In place of the representative bodies created by general, popular elections, Lenin and Trotsky have laid down the soviets as the only true representation of the laboring masses. But with the repression of political life in the land as a whole, life in the soviets must also become more and more crippled. Without general elections, without unrestricted freedom of press and assembly, without a free struggle of opinion, life dies out in every public institution, becomes a mere semblance of life, in which only the bureaucracy remains as the active element. Public life gradually falls asleep, a few dozen party leaders of inexhaustible energy and boundless experience direct and rule. Among them, in reality only a dozen outstanding heads do the leading and an elite of the working class is invited from time to time to meetings where they are to applaud the speeches of the leaders, and to approve proposed resolutions unanimously—at bottom, then, a clique affair—a dictatorship, to be sure; not the dictatorship of the proletariat, however, but only the dictatorship of a handful of politicians, that is a dic-

---

[20] *The Russian Revolution*, pp. 30–31.

tatorship in the bourgeois sense, in the sense of the rule of the Jacobins (the postponement of the Soviet Congress from three-month periods to a six-month period!). Yes, we can go even further: such conditions must inevitably cause a brutalization of public life: attempted assassinations, shooting of hostages, etc. (Lenin's speech on discipline and corruption.) [21]

---

[21] *The Russian Revolution,* pp. 47–48.

Though the open rebellion that the Bolsheviks expected in Germany did not develop immediately, in the months following the Brest-Litovsk Treaty there was a growing restiveness in all strata of German society. The German government began a policy of double dealing: on the one hand, they strove to derive the maximum possible benefit on the Western front from the separate peace in the East, and, on the other, they looked forward to a possible future collaboration with their present foes in stamping out Bolshevism. But with the fresh American troops on the Western front and the growing weariness in Germany, the General Staff had not sufficient power at its disposal for its ambitious scheme. In overreaching itself, it failed everywhere: it antagonized the new peoples in its orbit in the East; it aggravated the Bolsheviks' resistance; it failed to get even a stalemate in the West.

The German General Staff, however, did gain first-hand experience with a revolutionary government. It saw Bolshevism eye to eye, first across the conference table at Brest-Litovsk and then in the towns and villages as the German troops marched into Bolshevik territory. At Brest-Litovsk the German officers had met a type of socialist quite different from the moderate Social Democrat with whom they were used to dealing. In these early months of 1918, before the Red Army became a force, the Bolsheviks had only one weapon at their disposal—peace propaganda. It was assumed that their regime in Russia would be short-lived, but the possibility that the revolution might spread to Germany was a nightmare that grew more terrifying with the passing weeks. The possibility of the general fraternization and breakdown of the armies that the Bolsheviks hoped for made war in the East a perilous affair. Kaiser Wilhelm, deeply impressed by the fate of his cousin, the Tsar, was unnerved by the possibility that his own regime might go tumbling after the Romanovs. In the discussions of both the General Staff and the Cabinet, it was recognized that if the armies of the Central Powers on the Eastern front were dissolved into the red ocean that already was lapping on Germany's border, it would rise in a tide that no dam could hold back.

The Kaiser wrote: "Generals von Gallwitz and von Mudra reported to me on the front. They described the internal situation in the army —the great number of desertions behind the front, the cases of insubordination, the appearance of the red flag on leave trains returning to the front. . . ."[1]

In February 1918, the Petrograd soviet had elected as honorary members Karl Liebknecht, the symbol of German resistance, and Fritz Adler, the Austrian Social Democratic leader who in 1916 had assassinated Count von Stürgkh, the Foreign Minister, and was in prison at the time of his election. The first German-language pamphlets of Lenin, Trotsky, and Zinoviev began to appear, and the Bolsheviks immediately adopted the radio to broadcast their peace slogans. The Bolsheviks spoke in a language "such as had never been heard in German socialist circles. It gave the sleepy burghers the jitters."[2] The politically trained and active officers of the German General Staff studied the Bolshevik leaflets and pamphlets and were bewildered by the new language, the aggressive approach to all problems, the well-conceived proposals for direct action. The military commander of Berlin-Brandenburg, General von Linsingen, was especially troubled.

Through regular diplomatic channels based on the Brest-Litovsk Treaty, Joffe and Bukharin had been sent to the Russian embassy in Berlin. The leaders of the USPD—Hugo Haase, Rudolf Breitscheid, Oscar Cohn—attended a May Day celebration at the embassy, and

---

[1] Kaiser Wilhelm II, *Ereignisse und Gestalten aus den Jahren 1878–1918* (Berlin, 1922), p. 235. Cf. Erich Ludendorff, *Ludendorff's Own Story* (New York, 1918), II, 326 ff.

[2] Helmut Tiedemann, *Sowjetrussland und die Revolutionierung Deutschlands, 1917–1919*, Historische Studien, Heft 296 (Berlin, 1936).

Haase toasted the Soviet government. The Reich used an incident at the Friedrichsstrasse railroad station to break the coöperation between the embassy and German socialists. Luggage of the Russian embassy was opened, ostensibly by accident, and subversive leaflets printed in Russia were found.[3] With this as a pretext, the Russian emissaries were expelled. Certain concessions had to be made, however, to the resistance movement. Liebknecht was released from prison and was permitted to return to Berlin.

At Kiel

In its spring offensive on the Western front, the General Staff fought with restive troops against a new combination of forces and a new weapon, the tank, while the German hinterland lived in the hope that peace was near and regarded each continuing week of war with increasing weariness. Facing the 191 German divisions were 220 Entente divisions, including 40 of fresh American troops, but the decisive factor was the flow of matériel supporting them.

At the beginning of August, the German General Staff lost its hope for a military victory. The entire power of the Central Powers began to crumble: Austria-Hungary pushed for an immediate negotiated peace; Bulgaria was no longer reliable; Turkey was engaged in the pursuit of its own interests in the Caucasus. The General Staff discussed repeatedly the twelve divisions in the Ukraine; they were needed badly in the West, but if they were withdrawn would the Bolsheviks follow? The Ukrainian wheat that had been expected could not be delivered through a country in civil war; the breadbasket intended to bolster home morale was empty.

At the end of September, the situation became untenable. Ludendorff conferred with Hindenburg, and together they met with the leading Cabinet members.

> Revolution was standing at our door, and we had the choice of meeting it with dictatorship or concessions. A parliamentary government seemed to be the best weapon of defense . . . As a result of our conference, we placed our proposals for a peace step before His Majesty. It was my duty to describe the military situ-

---

[3] Cf. Oberst W. Nicolai, *Geheime Mächte: Internationale Spionage und ihre Bekämpfung im Weltkrieg und Heute* (Leipzig, 1924), p. 161.

ation, the seriousness of which was realized by the Emperor to provide a foundation for the necessary political action.[4]

On September 29, Hertling was replaced as Chancellor by Prince Max von Baden, whose reputation as a Southerner, less militaristic than the Prussian government, would make it easier, it was thought, to deal with the Entente.

On October 2, General Ludendorff stated flatly in a memorandum to the civilian authorities that the army could not hold the Western line much longer. Between October 5 and 21, Germany sent three offers of peace to Wilson, who, it was felt, would accept less harsh terms than the French. When this last hope proved illusory, the catastrophe set in.

Ludendorff proposed that the war be continued on a completely different basis: that the original war aims be renounced and that the German people be inspired to a mass uprising for the defense of the soil of the Fatherland. Though the revolutionary forces were still amorphous, the Cabinet recognized that they were too strong to combat, and rejected Ludendorff's plan as unrealizable. He was forced to resign, in order to clear the way to further negotiations, and was replaced by General von Gröner, an intimate of Hindenburg.[5] Three days later, on October 29, the government ordered a large draft, principally to increase its bargaining power with the Entente; this created great excitement and only stiffened the resistance in the industrial centers.

Ludendorff's stand inspired the admiralty to an action of its own, which it hoped might turn the situation to Germany's advantage at this eleventh hour. The German navy lay undamaged in the harbor at Kiel, and under Admiral von Hipper the top navy men hatched a plan to fight a last-ditch battle against the British fleet. On October 29, the day before this "death cruise" was scheduled, sailors on two or three of the ships made it clear that they were not eager to share the honorable death their officers were seeking. Order was restored, but

---

[4] Field Marshal Paul von Hindenburg, *Out of My Life* (London, 1920), II, 261–262.

[5] Gröner posted signs all over Berlin reading, "When Hindenburg calls for guns, only a bastard would strike" (Ein Hundsfott, wer streikt, wenn Hindenburg ruft). From then on he was known in the factories of Berlin as Hundsfott Gröner.

the men had to be put in irons. By midnight of the 29th, even the *Baden,* Admiral Hipper's flagship, was affected, and he ordered that special maneuvers be substituted for the proposed operation. The next day the men refused to sail; they barricaded themselves in the forward hatches and sang socialist songs. On the 31st the worst mutineers, on the *Thüringen* and the *Helgoland,* surrendered and were taken away. The Third Squadron was sent to its home base at Kiel in the belief that the heightened morale resulting from a stay in port would give the officers a chance to regain control.

This move was fatal. Kiel was in a revolutionary mood; there had been a serious strike in January. From the meeting halls where the sailors and the workers met that evening, the German revolution started, and it spread during the next days along the whole Northern coast, and then to the Central and Southern provinces.[6] A mass uprising broke out, of a scope unparalleled in any modern industrial country, transcending all manipulations and manipulators. When the seamen demonstrated in Kiel, Hamburg, and Bremen on the 3rd and 4th of November, they were joined by tens of thousands of workers, singing the socialist songs of their fathers and proclaiming the republic. Several seamen were arrested in Kiel; soldiers in full field equipment gathered from various regiments quartered near by and under red flags marched to the jail to liberate them. Red flags were raised on the battleships.

On November 6, the government sent to Kiel Gustav Noske, member of the party's National Executive Committee, who restored a certain measure of control by assuring the sailors that the armistice was already under negotiation. Nevertheless, the sailors and the soldiers seized trains and proceeded to Hamburg. Here the officer corps decided to fight. With a general at their head, they marched towards the railroad station, intending at all costs to halt the march of the Kiel sailors to the center of Hamburg. The general was so sure of his authority, so used to having his orders obeyed, that he thought it would be enough to confront the first groups of seamen with a pointed revolver and an energetic command. When, however, one of the seamen merely knocked the revolver out of the general's hand, the demoralized officers retreated without a fight.

---

[6] Cf. Harry R. Rudin, *Armistice, 1918* (New Haven, 1944), p. 244 ff.

Twenty-four hours later the uprising was general in Hamburg, Lübeck, Neumünster, Bremen, Wilhelmshaven, Bremerhaven, Rendsburg, Schleswig, Cuxhaven, Brunsbüttel, Schwerin, Lüneburg, Hanover. The moderate Social Democrats were eliminated in such centers of their traditional dominance as Hamburg, Bremen, Brunswick.

The rebellion reached Berlin last. When Liebknecht had arrived at the end of October, he had become the center of attention and authority in the Shop Stewards' Committee, to which he and two other members of the Spartakusbund, Wilhelm Pieck and Ernst Meyer, had been coöpted.

The USPD was very hesitant and rejected a demonstration proposed by Liebknecht and Pieck for November 3 as "revolutionary gymnastics." Demonstrations were senseless, the political leaders said. "Total revolution" was the order of the day, and nothing else. On November 2, the Shop Stewards' Committee discussed a plan for the uprising and rejected it by 22 votes to 19. Liebknecht and Pieck got only five votes for their slogans: "Peace now! Lift the state of siege! Germany a socialist republic!"

When news about the Kiel uprising reached Berlin, Liebknecht called another meeting of the committee and proposed the uprising for November 8 or 9. "The organizers refused to accept this timetable because these days were paydays, on which the workers would not be disposed to leave the factories." [7]

At the beginning of the month, one Oberleutnant Walz had put himself and his regiment at the disposal of the Shop Stewards. He was arrested on November 8, and this news caused the committee to transfer its session to the Reichstag building, which was inviolable to the police. On the way to the Reichstag, one of the leaders of the planned uprising, Ernst Däumig, was arrested. In his brief case the police found detailed plans for the uprising and a list of the conspirators. Däumig, former editor of the *Vorwärts,* had been elected head of military operations because with his long service in the French Foreign Legion

---

[7] Wilhelm Pieck, "Um den 9. November 1918 in Berlin," *Inprekorr* (Berlin, November 9, 1928) vol. VIII, No. 125, p. 2475 ff. Pieck had returned to Berlin from Holland on October 27, 1918.

The International Press Correspondence, the most important serial publication of the Comintern, was published in English, German, and French. The title of the English edition is abbreviated to *Inprecor,* the German to *Inprekorr.*

he was regarded as an expert in military strategy. Luise Zietz, another Independent Socialist deputy, was with Däumig but managed to escape. Her arrival at the Reichstag brought the nervous tension to a climax; the conspirators realized that the government possessed all the details of the plot and might arrest them at any moment. That was decisive for setting the date of the uprising for November 9.

November 9th in Berlin

On the same day the Reich Chancellor, Prince Max von Baden, ordered some reliable regiments to Berlin for the protection of government buildings. The most rustic groups were singled out for this assignment, for instance, regiments from the Spreewald, the Lübben Hussars. The next morning, on the 9th of November, these soldiers deserted their assigned quarters. At ten the same morning, the Fourth Jäger Battalion arrived, freshly supplied with hand grenades and ammunition. These soldiers refused to obey the order to patrol the streets and began to discuss whether to join the revolution.[8] The bewildered officers joined in the discussion and were able to dissuade the soldiers from demonstrating with the workers only by announcing the abdication of the Kaiser, which had not yet taken place. The soldiers assembled in the barracks, stripped off all insignia of rank, tore off their medals and crosses, elected a soldiers' council.

The Schloss, the residence of the Imperial family, was a lodestone to Berlin. Twice at the beginning of the war, Kaiser Wilhelm had spoken from its balcony, to exhort his people to fight the war with a united front. From the big windows of the ground floor, Prussian kings had been wont to watch their troops march in the Lustgarten; the castle was a shrine to Hohenzollern prerogative.

The Imperial family had left the castle on August 16, 1914, leaving only the personnel of the Imperial household, but Berlin expected the monarchists to center the fight for survival around the Schloss. The castle commander, General Freiherr von Richthofen, decided to put it in a state of defense. Military police were posted on the bridges over

---

[8] Kaiser Wilhelm reports: "On the 9th of November the Minister of War reported insecurity of parts of the troops in Berlin—the 4th Jägers, the 2nd Company of the Alexander Regiment, the 2nd Battery Jüterbog, have gone over to the rebels. No street fighting." (*Ereignisse und Gestalten*, p. 243.)

the Spree, and during the night of November 8–9 several armed cars were added to the castle detachment. The garrison was given the order to shoot to kill.

At nine in the morning of November 9, the commander asked for reinforcements. At ten, in the confusion, Richthofen gave the order to clear the surrounding area of troops. An hour later the police troops got another reversal, and were ordered to resist the demonstrators. At noon civilian authorities reported the Emperor's abdication and flight. The castle garrison did not believe it until 2:30, when the news was confirmed from military sources. The *Oberkommando in den Marken,* the military head of the Berlin-Brandenburg area, gave Richthofen the order, "Don't shoot at the people under any circumstances. Withdraw all troops from the neighborhood of the castle." At three o'clock the people were streaming toward the Schloss. "The castle guard lay down their arms immediately. One detachment, jubilantly greeted by the mass, marched away across the Lustgarten under a red flag." [9]

At 3:30, an hour before Liebknecht arrived, a storekeeper drafted for auxiliary service in the neighborhood, one Schlesinger, climbed to the Imperial balcony and implored the populace not to touch the Imperial property, now national property. He hoisted a red blanket taken from a servant's room (or, according to other versions, a red slipcover or even a red handkerchief), and for weeks this symbol flew from the Kaiser's balcony. The masses, though delighted that the Schloss had been taken so easily, believed that the Imperial troops had retired through an underground passageway to the nearby Marstall, the former Imperial stables, which they would attempt to hold.

By noon people were streaming from the suburbs toward the center of the city. The civilian crowd was spotted with uniforms; women participated in an amazing proportion. The demonstrators occupied power plants for a few hours. Several trolley and bus drivers wanted to continue and were forced to drive their cars back into the barns. But incidents were on a small scale. From the center the demonstration moved back towards the Imperial barracks dispersed through

---

[9] Rudolf Rotheit, *Das Berliner Schloss im Zeichen der Novemberrevolution* (Berlin, 1922), p. 9. Cf. also the report of the castle librarian, Dr. Bogdan Krieger, *Das Berliner Schloss in den Revolutionstagen 1918* (Leipzig, 1922).

Berlin suburbs, to appeal to the soldiers and disarm the officers. At the Maikäfer Barracks, one of the few shootings took place and several people were killed. In the afternoon Berlin resembled a giant army camp, the camp of the revolution. Automobiles went around, with propagandists—Karl Liebknecht at their head—haranguing the masses. Wherever an officer appeared, his epaulets were torn off. "The joy over the defeat of the old regime was indescribably great," writes a chronicler of the revolution, Heinrich Ströbel.

At about four Liebknecht arrived at the castle with a small group of sailors and workers and spoke from the Imperial balcony:

> The day of liberty has dawned. A Hohenzollern will never again stand at this place. Seventy years ago Friedrich Wilhelm IV stood here and doffed his cap to the procession honoring the fifty blood-soaked victims to the cause of freedom, fallen on Berlin's barricades. Today there is another procession passing by . . . Today a numberless crowd stands on the same spot to cheer the new liberty . . .
>
> I proclaim the free socialist republic of Germany, which shall comprise all Germans . . . We want to build the new order of the proletariat, an order of peace and happiness, with liberty for all our German brothers and for our brothers throughout the world. We extend our hands to them and call on them to complete the world revolution. Those among you who want a free socialist German republic and the world revolution, raise your hands to an oath.[10]

Cheers. Raised hands. The palace guard threw away their rifles. Soldiers armed with machine guns poured in from all sides and joined in.

Meanwhile Prince Max von Baden was negotiating with Friedrich Ebert to arrange a Social Democratic caretaker government, possibly under the Crown Prince, as successor to the Kaiser. Despite this wish to conserve the monarchy, the Republic was proclaimed some hours later. How this happened is best described in the eyewitness report of Philipp Scheidemann, the veteran Social Democratic leader, who had been in Prince Max's cabinet and was one of the six People's Commissars who constituted the first republican government:

---

[10] This speech was not taken down, but the versions of various observers, Müller, Ströbel, *et al.*, are essentially identical.

On the morning of the 9th of November, 1918, the Reichstag was like an armed camp. Working men and soldiers were going in and out. Many bore arms. With Ebert, who had come from the Chancery to the Reichstag, and other friends, I sat hungry in the dining hall. . . . Then a crowd of workers and soldiers rushed into the hall and made straight for our table.

Fifty of them yelled out at the same time, "Scheidemann, come along with us at once. Philipp, you must come out and speak."

I refused; how many times had I not already spoken!

"You must, you must, if trouble is to be avoided. There are thousands upon thousands shouting for you to speak. Come along quick, Scheidemann. Liebknecht is already speaking from the balcony of the Schloss!"

"Well, if I must."

"Come along now. You must.". . .

"Liebknecht intends to proclaim the Soviet republic."

Now I clearly saw what was afoot. I knew his slogan—supreme authority for the Workers' and Soldiers' Councils. Germany to be therefore a Russian province, a branch of the Soviet. No, no, a thousand times no!

There was no doubt at all. The man who could bring along the "Bolshies" from the Schloss to the Reichstag, or the Social Democrats from the Reichstag to the Schloss, had won the day.

I saw the Russian folly staring me in the face—the Bolshevist tyranny, the substitute for the tyranny of the Tsars. No, no, Germany should not have that on the top of all her other miseries . . .

I only said a few words, which were received with tremendous cheering.

"Workers and soldiers, . . . the cursed war is at an end . . . The Emperor has abdicated and he and his friends have decamped. The people have triumphed over them all along the line. Prince Max von Baden has handed over his office as Chancellor to Ebert. Our friend will form a labor government, to which all socialist parties will belong . . .

"Stand united and loyal. The old and the rotten—the monarchy—has broken down. Long live the new! Long live the German republic!"

Endless cheering broke out, and then the crowds began to move towards the Schloss. The Bolshevist wave that threatened to engulf Germany had spent its force. The German Republic had become a thing of life in the plans and the heart of the masses.

Directly after my speech, I went back to the dining hall of

the Reichstag to rescue my "skilly". . . . A few working men and soldiers who had come with me into the hall . . . were all agog to speak with Prince Max . . . "Scheidemann has proclaimed the republic.". . .

Ebert's face turned livid with wrath when he heard what I had done. He banged his fist on the table and yelled at me. "Is it true?" On my replying that it was not only true but a matter of course, he made a scene which passes my understanding. "You have no right to proclaim the republic. What becomes of Germany—whether she becomes a republic or something else—a constituent assembly must decide.". . .

Now, many years after this critical day, I understand Ebert's conduct better, for now we have various books and reports from which it can be gathered that these private conversations about monarchy, republic, a substitute for the Kaiser, about which I knew nothing, actually took place. Ebert to a certain extent was not a free agent . . .[11]

The story of how the last Berlin chief of police of Imperial Germany, von Oppel, ceded his place to the revolutionaries is as indicative as the taking of the Schloss of the debility of the old regime. Von Oppel, nervous at his desk in the police presidium on Alexanderplatz, had only one thought, how to get out safely. Alexanderplatz, situated in the midst of proletarian precincts, was surrounded by streets and squares full of demonstrating workers and soldiers, parading and shouting and waving their little red flags. The police were apprehensive. As it was obvious that the USPD represented the majority of the Berlin workers, Oppel telephoned to the party headquarters on Dircksenstrasse to send someone who could take over as police chief. Emil Eichhorn, a Social Democratic veteran, a metal worker, a USPD deputy, had been designated for this post. He was regarded almost as a Bolshevik because he had been on friendly terms with Joffe and Bukharin at the Soviet Embassy and in August 1918 had even joined the staff of the first Russian press agency in Berlin, the Rosta. When he got von Oppel's message, he walked to the police presidium, accompanied by only one member of the socialist youth. He found a big demonstration going on before its closed doors, which were guarded by soldiers in lively discussion with the beleaguerers. He said simply, "I am the new police

[11] Philipp Scheidemann, *The Making of New Germany* (New York: D. Appleton and Company, 1929), II, 261 ff.

president, Eichhorn, who was called by telephone, and I have come to take over." The soldiers saluted the new chief and opened the gates. The senior executives had already deserted their desks; the men greeted him with enthusiasm.[12]

The men of the regiment quartered in this precinct stood around and discussed with the senior lieutenant the problem, Shall we join the revolutionary movement, or shall we stand at attention? The men, peasants from Mecklenburg and Pomerania, felt apart from the people of the big city and preferred to be restricted to their barracks; they asked the USPD to guarantee their food and supplies, and this was done. In the following days they left one after the other and returned to their homes.

With Eichhorn a group of demonstrators streamed into the police building and freed 650 prisoners, who had been brought in during the past few days. In the back yard of the building a mound was rapidly growing, composed of the rifles, sabers, and revolvers of the Berlin policemen, who were most eager to disarm themselves voluntarily and get out of it all.

In the evening of the 9th of November, shooting in various quarters of Berlin became more intense. But it developed nowhere into actual street fighting. There were particularly violent clashes around the University and the Royal State Library on Unter den Linden, which had been occupied by students. Groups of soldiers temporarily seized the *Vorwärts* and *Lokalanzeiger* buildings, Wolff's telegraph agency, and various other newspaper buildings. The personnel of the *Lokalanzeiger* resisted stubbornly, and the first issue of the *Rote Fahne* ("The Red Flag") did not appear till November 21. Government officials became panicky. They quit in the midst of their routine and escaped by side doors. "In the press division of the Foreign Office, all the documents remained scattered on the tables. The state of the offices indicated clearly that the executives of the press division had left their jobs in hurried flight."[13]

The next day Berlin was in the hands of the newly formed Workers' and Soldiers' Councils. All over Germany, dynasties and state govern-

---

[12] Emil Eichhorn, *Die Januar-Ereignisse* (Berlin, 1919).

[13] *Berliner Tageblatt*, November 11, 1918, quoted in Richard Müller, *Vom Kaiserreich zur Republik*, II, 15–16.

ments were abdicating in favor of cabinets led by Social Democrats. The parallel councils, which in this period had more power than the legal successor cabinets, issued uncountable proclamations for a German socialist republic.

As a token of this wish to establish socialist power, and as a counter measure to the garrison troops, the local councils occupied the public buildings. The caretaker governments took them back, and the councils back again; the instability of power was reflected in the continual shift.

The temporary seizure of public buildings, newspaper plants, tele-graph agencies, was characteristic of the upheaval in Central European countries during the November weeks.[14] This spontaneous occupation

---

[14] In Vienna, where I lived at this moment, there was no organization compa-rable to the Spartakusbund within the well-organized Austrian Social Democratic Party. A group of socialist students and young workers contacted the armament plants in Vienna and Lower Austria and propagandized for the Bolsheviks. After the Bread Strike, this group called themselves the Left Radicals (to be distinguished from the Lefts, led by Otto Bauer and Robert Danneberg, author of the 1926 Linz program of the Austrian Social Democratic Party; Danneberg died in Buchenwald in 1945).

Messages from the Bolsheviks, first from Switzerland and later from Moscow, reached our small group. Encouraged by them, we proudly called ourselves the Communist Party of Austria, founded on November 4, 1918, one of the first Com-munist parties in Europe. I was charter member No. 1. We produced a lot of propaganda literature, but our influence among organized labor was small.

Independently of this organization, a group composed of remnants of all Austrian regiments seized the barracks in western Vienna. They called themselves the Red Guard; their commander was Egon Erwin Kisch, the well known Czech writer, who had returned from service with the Austrian army with the rank of Ober-leutnant. (Kisch, after many adventures, lived in exile in Mexico City during 1941–1945. He has returned to his native Czechoslovakia, where he is now one of the best-known state journalists of the new Russophile republic.)

When the Austrian republic was proclaimed on November 12, groups from the large plants in Floridsdorf appeared with over-sized posters: "Long live the Socialist Republic of Austria!" That was literally all, for no organization whatever stood behind these posters. A group of socialist students proceeded to the balustrade of the Austrian parliament to submit to the newly established republican government "the demands of the Vienna workers." The general nervousness of the times was such that the guards were ordered to defend the building against the demonstrators —or perhaps the guards shot without orders. Anyway, a panic broke out. One of the newly baptized Communists, Franz Koritschoner, got a bullet in his belly. (He died in disgrace in Russia in the late thirties.) I was trampled down by the panicky crowd and lost consciousness. I awoke at the desk of the managing editor of Vienna's largest daily, the *Neue Freie Presse*. Soldiers of the Red Guard had found me lying on the pavement and had brought me to the building, seized the news-paper, and proclaimed me chief editor. The entire personnel appeared in the room and assured me of their loyalty. I was about twenty years old and rather bewildered with the idea that we had seized power. For two or three days we put out special

of the seats of power was partially due to the war experiences of the returning soldiers. After its entrance into a conquered city, an army always seizes the main buildings. In part it followed the Russian example: the victory by the Bolshevik minority had been most strikingly demonstrated by the workers' seizure of main governmental centers in Moscow and Petrograd. Millions who hardly knew the names Lenin and Trotsky, and had certainly never read a line of Marx or Lenin, accepted instinctively their method of seizing power by taking its strong places.

As the news flowed in from all over Germany, Fritz Ebert realized that his party was not able to stem the tide alone. It was itself torn by conflicting currents. The rank and file coöperated with the Workers' and Soldiers' Councils and were not at all disposed to disconnect themselves from the revolutionary minority. The pressure on Ebert was so strong that he offered a cabinet post to Liebknecht, who replied to this gesture with the expected refusal.

The evening of the 9th of November, Ebert telephoned to General Gröner, key man at Hindenburg's headquarters at Wilhelmshöhe, near Kassel, and asked his support for the new cabinet. As a Social Democratic leader, Ebert had coöperated with the army on a friendly basis during the war, and it was natural for him to seek help from at least a part of the army against the threatening revolution.[15]

---

editions, which stated that the occupation of the press buildings had been for demonstrative purposes. Then we all left peacefully and the *Neue Freie Presse* reappeared, unhindered until the Nazi days. A few days later I was arrested by the new government and accused of high treason against the Austrian state, but got an amnesty after six weeks.

[15] A report on this much discussed telephone conversation is given in E. O. Volkmann (Archivrat im Reichsarchiv), *Revolution über Deutschland* (Oldenburg, 1930), p. 68. Cf. also General Gröner's testimony as cited in Beckmann, *Der Dolchstossprozess in München* (Munich, 1925), pp. 110–111, quoted by Arthur Rosenberg, who had access to the court proceedings, in *A History of the German Republic* (London, 1936), p. 324.

The coöperation between Ebert and Gröner has been the subject of interminable polemics, lasting until today. The fact of coöperation is not denied by Ebert's apologists; the area of discussion is rather his motives and the effects of the combination. The reliability of Gröner's affidavit in particular has been questioned. Rosenberg, who has given the best material on the matter, himself defends Ebert's loyalty to the Republic. "There is no proof that Ebert actually entered into a plot with the officers against the revolutionary working classes. Ebert never failed in his duty of loyalty towards his fellow-members [i.e., his comrades] of the USPD. But he was oppressed with a sense of the immense difficulties confronting the German Gov-

The Workers' Councils

In Russia, the motive force of the worker and peasant had been the desire to end the war and to partition the land. In Germany, the war had already come to an end, and the peasants were not involved in the revolutionary process; in spite of many residual feudal features, they were incomparably better off than those in Russia. In November 1918 the dynamic question was whether or not to conserve the army, that is, whether or not to maintain the force by which the Reich could regain its lost status in Europe. For the average soldier, capitalism was an impersonal force. In the difficult period preceding the defeat, his natural enemy, the representative of the ruling class to which he was daily directly opposed, was the officer. From this deeply rooted experience, the worker in uniform brought home the conviction that the army skeleton had to be destroyed if, within a historically short period, the Kaiser were not to return and Germany were not to go back into the war.

The army had grown up in a rapidly industrialized nation, with vulnerable frontiers on all sides, constricted between two big powers, Russia and France-England. Without protective forces, Germany's industrial expansion into Europe would have been impossible. As Kaiser Wilhelm put it, the well-being of a country can be assured only if real power protects its industry and commerce.

From the beginning of the Reich, the German army had built up its tradition of being a political army. The General Staff, the incarna-

ernment. To economic troubles and the anxieties of foreign policy were added a threat of separatist movements not only in the Rhineland, but also in various other parts of the country. In these circumstances Ebert wished to reduce to a minimum the possibilities of friction and to act as mediator between all parties. If the High Command made professions of loyalty to him, Ebert saw no reason to administer a rebuff. Nevertheless it was a tactical error for Ebert to have admitted the High Command too far into his confidence." (Rosenberg, p. 50.)

In my opinion, this discussion is dated and irrelevant. Ebert's motives, his sincere belief that by this understanding with the military he was saving Germany, cannot be doubted. His actions must be judged on the basis of a general political evaluation of the whole civil war period; the fact that discussion has narrowed to the actions and character of Ebert, only one of many complex factors involved, has been due largely to Communist propaganda. From any point of view, however, it cannot be denied that the temporary alliance between the Right leadership of the Social Democratic Party and the army was of decisive importance in shaping the young Republic.

tion of an ambitious and not yet vanquished social stratum, was shattered but morally unbroken by the defeat of November 1918. These men saw clearly that, with all pending settlements decisively disturbed by the unknown factor in the balance, revolutionary Russia, Germany's post-war come-back was possible. The temporary alliance with the Social Democratic Party, emanating from the bitter needs of the defeat and loaded from the beginning with mutual distrust and hatred, was entered by the General Staff only to save the officer corps and the technical skeleton of the army from the onslaught of the revolution. The big landowners of the East, the big industrialists of the West, a large portion of the middle class, could not conceive of a Germany without the army.[16]

The internal enemy was an excellent argument for opposing the military limitations set by Versailles, for fighting for the maintenance of a skeletal army organization. The frontiers of the Reich were in flux from the palpable pressure of the newly founded small states surrounding it, and the defense of these fluid border regions was another factor giving weight to the arguments of the army's spokesmen.

> The internal breakdown uprooted state authority, gave the upper hand at first to elements hostile to the state. This meant the victory of all those forces that had for decades been in opposition to the Reich—the internationalists, the pacifists, the advocates of class struggle, the individualists. The Reichswehr was created in the fight against all of these. At first it fought them in alliance with the majority of the bourgeoisie and the moderate wing of labor, under the political leadership of the Social Democrats . . . Out of this coöperation the new state was born.[17]

---

[16] General Hans von Seeckt, the creator of the Republican army, the Reichswehr, was later military delegate to the Versailles peace conference. On May 26, 1919, he submitted a memorandum to the leader of the German delegation, Graf Brockdorff-Rantzau, protesting the military clauses of the treaty and explicitly rejecting joint responsibility. "I want to state clearly," he wrote, "that according to all competent military opinion an army of 100,000 men, with a limited officer corps, is not sufficient to fulfill the foreign tasks still remaining to Germany, even presuming a League of Nations, or to give the necessary backbone to its domestic policy. . . . If Germany accepts these conditions, she becomes helpless in both the domestic and the foreign fields." (Erich Otto Volkmann, "Der Organisator der Reichswehr," *Generaloberst von Seeckt: Ein Erinnerungsbuch*, Deutsche Gesellschaft für Wehrpolitik und Wehrwissenschaften, Berlin, 1937, p. 35.)

[17] Major Marks, "Reich, Volk und Reichswehr," *Wissen und Wehr*, 12. Jahrg. Heft 1, 1931. Marks was a member of the General Staff; he collaborated with Noske

Politically conscious workers, that is, the majority of German workers at this time, understood the crux of the question, but their organizations lost their time in entangled discussions. Even the best leaders were caught in irreconcilable controversies over the question of what to do and what not to do. The worker in the street, the soldier returned to his industrial home town, the sailor discharged from his ship, lying idle in one of the dead harbors of Germany—these were loyal to their parties. But across the borderlines of the respective organizations, socialist and Catholic workers alike were united in one simple obsession: to disarm the General Staff, to deprive them of troops and facilities, to dispossess the officer corps. In this aim the workers were united with broad strata of the German middle class, especially those who after the defeat had turned pacifist and democratic. These groups sought an alternate policy to imperialist expansion. The parliamentary alliance between Ebert and the Left wing of the Center Party expressed this tendency.

On November 9 the Social Democratic caretaker authorities gave the General Staff the responsibility of returning the troops to their homes. This reinforced the authority of the officer corps, whose status was being challenged by soldiers' councils. The German army, dispersed over the continent, was in part unaware of the events at home. In good part, however, especially on the Eastern front, the soldiers reflected the events both in Russia and in Berlin. The officers' response was flexible; when the pressure was too strong they abdicated voluntarily and submitted to the authority of the soldiers' councils. Sometimes they commanded the election of councils and incorporated them in the commanding group. Wherever it was possible, and to the extent possible, the old discipline was kept intact.

In 1918, the danger of plunder or banditry by German soldiers was relatively small. These men were entirely able to organize the return to their home barracks themselves. Ebert's insistence that the officer corps was irreplaceable flowed from politics rather than logistics; he, and the officers, understood that their main role was to combat possible contagion from revolutionary sore spots. The General Staff took full advantage of this opportunity to reorganize; Ebert's appeal

during the January days as member of the Berlin Kommandatur. He later became one of the principal experts of the Reichswehr Ministerium.

to Gröner for his assistance on the evening of November 9 increased its advantage.

In contrast to the amorphous and enormous mass movement of the workers, the General Staff established small select cadres, made up out of the disbanded army divisions, under Imperial officers. The Garde Kavallerie Schützen Division, whose very name emphasized its continuity with Imperial tradition, became the best known of these counter-revolutionary cadres, which were assembled mainly in small towns around Berlin.

Between the army and the revolutionaries the fight for authority continued. The officers insisted that their men, intimidated by the upheaval in the streets, should face it and parade there in closed ranks, both to restore their own morale and to impress the populace with their discipline.

The first parade of the Berlin garrison took place as early as November 23. A few days later, General von Mudra, commanding the 17th Army, forbade his soldiers to wear revolutionary emblems and insisted that demobilized soldiers still in uniform continue to salute officers. General Gröner publicly praised Hindenburg, the supreme commander in chief, as the savior of the Fatherland, who had led the army back in good order. His statement was intended to restore confidence in the officer cadres dispersed throughout the Reich and panic-stricken before the growing mass rebellion.

On December 5, groups of the Garde Kavallerie Schützen Division, composed mainly of two thousand sergeants, marched through the main streets of Berlin. The following day, in the northern part of the city, there was a bloody clash when these newly formed "Freikorps" (independent corps) troops tried to arrest several deputies of the Workers' and Soldiers' Councils. On December 6, the Freikorps marched to the palace of the Reich Chancellor, where they called on Ebert to assume dictatorial power. Ebert had just been warned by Gröner that he must take more energetic measures. The next day Berlin was showered with leaflets demanding the assassination of Liebknecht and the extermination of the revolutionaries. This propaganda was tainted with anti-Semitic tones: "Kill Liebknecht! Kill the Jews!" Giant placards were carried in the streets, with such slogans as the following:

Arbeiter, Bürger!
Das Vaterland ist dem Untergang nahe.
Rettet es!
Es wird nicht bedroht von aussen, sondern von innen:
Von der Spartakusgruppe.
Schlagt ihre Führer tot!
Tötet Liebknecht!
Dann werdet ihr Frieden, Arbeit und Brot haben!

Die Frontsoldaten [18]

(Workers, citizens: Our fatherland is close to ruin; save it. It is menaced not from the outside but from within, by the Spartakus group. Kill its leaders; kill Liebknecht! Then you will have peace, work, and bread. The Front Soldiers.)

In this atmosphere, on December 16, 1918, the first national conference of the Workers' and Soldiers' Councils took place.[19] Its delegates had been elected in a miasma of confusion, without either a clear procedure or a definite program. There was one delegate to 200,000, based on the 1910 census; between the delegates and so large a constituency there could be no intimate relation.[20] Thus the strongest political machine controlled the election; of the 490 delegates, 298 were Social Democrats. There were 195 paid party or trade-union functionaries, 71 intellectuals, 13 army officers, 179 workers. The conference refused to seat Luxemburg and Liebknecht.

The convention debates were even more confused and involved than the parallel discussions in the various party organizations. Socialism was proclaimed necessary on the one hand, and on the other declared impossible because of the economic chaos. Maneuvers, intrigues, personal quarrels, jealousies, gave the upper hand to Ebert, who was then opposed even by a large portion of his own party. But this picture of

---

[18] Quoted in Paul Frölich, *Rosa Luxemburg: Gedanke und Tat* (Paris, 1939), p. 266.

[19] The second conference convened on April 15, 1919, also in Berlin. It was without importance, for in the interval the Shop Stewards' movement had been exhausted in the battles of the civil war. On August 23, Noske dispossessed the office of the Greater Berlin Council. For a contemporary report on both conferences, see Stenographic Record, Die Reichskonferenz der Arbeiter- und Soldatenräte, *Deutscher Geschichtskalender,* Dr. Friedrich Purlitz, ed., *Die deutsche Revolution* (Leipzig, n.d.), I, 201–259; II, 186–201; and Heinrich Schäfer, *Tagebuchblätter eines Rheinischen Sozialisten* (Bonn, 1919).

[20] Richard Müller, *Vom Kaiserreich zur Republik,* II, 203.

impotence cannot obscure the major trend of the convention, the unanimity against the old Imperial army.

The debates were interrupted several times by delegates from the quarter of a million workers demonstrating outside, marching endlessly up and down, demanding the proclamation of a German socialist republic and the transfer of all power to the Workers' and Soldiers' Councils. At one time thirty soldiers, carrying the banner of their regiment, entered the meeting hall and surrounded the dais. Soldier Felchner, in the name of the Soldiers' Councils of Berlin, took the floor and demanded that: "(1) the Supreme Soldiers' Council, composed of elected delegates from all Soldiers' Councils, assume command of all army troops and of the navy; (2) all insignia of rank be prohibited; (3) all officers be disarmed." "This rule," he added, "is to go into effect immediately, after all returning troops have laid down their arms in the barracks. The Soldiers' Councils will be responsible for the reliability and discipline of the troops."

These items are typical of the trend in all soldiers' organizations throughout the Reich. For example, the very moderate Hamburg Soldiers' Council, composed mainly of Social Democrats, formulated substantially the same program, with such additional touches as prohibiting the wearing of medals and decorations. Trained in loyalty to their elected party chiefs, the delegates hoped to enforce the realization of their demands by mass pressure and precision in formula. They were really and truly democrats; they believed under all circumstances in the efficiency and value of democratic procedure.[21]

Ebert fought energetically for the maintenance of the army, emphasizing that it was necessary to keep enough divisions to protect the German frontiers. "In the border land between Germany and Poland, irregular troops, deserters, and vagabonds create a state of emergency. A protective frontier cover is necessary. The proposal of Emil Barth, identical with the points of the Soldiers' Councils, makes the organization of the army impossible. If Barth continues in this way, then I

---

[21] Later Hindenburg proclaimed: "I do not recognize the resolution adopted by the Central Council of Workers' and Soldiers' Deputies concerning military matters and specifically concerning the status of officers and non-commissioned officers. . . . Now as before, the army supports the Ebert government, and expects the government to carry out its promise to preserve the army." (Müller, II, 222.)

doubt whether we can continue to coöperate." [22] At this point of Ebert's speech another delegation of soldiers appeared with flags and posters, and supported Barth.

The convention adjourned in confusion and disagreement. The directives it adopted did not tie the hands of Ebert and permitted him to continue collaborating with the army. Immediately after the convention, the plans of the General Staff for liquidating the revolutionaries began to materialize. On December 23, 1918, Ebert ordered General Lequis, the commander of the Brandenburg garrison, to march into Berlin. His first assignment was to disband the Volksmarine Division (People's Naval Division).

The Volksmarine Division was a peculiar and significant product of the time. It consisted originally of about six hundred sailors, natives of Berlin, who were later joined by several thousand other sailors and soldiers. To be a sailor had a revolutionary glamor, the result of the Kiel revolt. During the first days of the revolution, the sailors had occupied as temporary quarters the former Imperial Schloss and its annex, the Marstall. Not affiliated with any party, they put themselves at the disposal of the new Republican government. Ebert feared these unwanted associates and wished to be rid of them as soon as possible.

This ambiguous situation led to constant quarrels. The sailors felt themselves entitled to regular pay by the new administration, both as sailors not yet formally demobilized and as members of the new Volksmarine Division. For a few hours on December 23 the men occupied the Reich Chancellery and the telegraph office, to protest the intentional delay in paying them. They withdrew after the intervention of Emil Barth, who promised to negotiate with the cabinet. Here General Lequis stepped in. His troops, under the command of one Major von Harbou, surrounded the Schloss and the Marstall. After a ten-minute ultimatum, they opened artillery fire. The sailors evacuated the Schloss, which was difficult to defend, and barricaded themselves successfully in the Marstall; after one day von Harbou was compelled to retreat. Then the government granted the sailors the right to remain in the Marstall, but imposed the condition that there be no further recruitment to their division. This unexpected result accelerated the show-

---

[22] Stenographic Record (cited above, note 19), pp. 220–221.

down between the army command and the Berlin revolutionaries. The officers had estimated the military value of the revolutionaries as negligible; this unorganized and poorly armed populace should have disbanded at the first approach of organized troops. "When the report of Major von Harbou on the Marstall affair reached the chief command in Kassel, for the first time a deep depression and lack of courage were visible." [23]

The officers wanted to sharpen the conflict and bring about a complete break between Ebert and the Berlin revolutionaries. They tried to get Ebert to transfer the seat of the government to Kassel. "On December 24, I spoke again with Ebert," General Gröner reported.[24] "He asked me what we ought to do. I told him we had only about 150 men left in Berlin and that therefore the General Staff would remain near Kassel."

That was a clear threat, and Ebert understood it. He reacted accordingly. "I will go home, too," he said. "I will go home to sleep for three days. I need it. I will just vanish from the Chancellery and will take good care that all the other gentlemen of my cabinet will also desert the Reich Chancellery. We will leave only the doorman. If the Liebknecht group takes power now, there will be just no one to resist. Maybe we will reconstitute our government after a few days, perhaps in Potsdam."

Ebert wanted to remain in Berlin because he realized that if his alliance with Gröner should be made public, his authority among the workers would be destroyed, and in this case the revolutionaries might succeed. While the force of the revolution thus almost cracked the caretaker government, the brain of the revolution, the Spartakusbund, floundered in indecision and uncoördinated gestures.

The Communist Party of Germany Is Founded

Rosa Luxemburg had returned from prison on November 10. She was greeted in the *Lokalanzeiger* building by Leo Jogiches, the Polish socialist, her closest collaborator and friend. They were much concerned with the attitude of Liebknecht, who had identified himself unambiguously with the Shop Stewards' movement. Luxemburg con-

---

[23] E. O. Volkmann, *Revolution über Deutschland*, p. 163.
[24] According to his testimony at the Munich trial in 1925. Cf. Rosenberg, p. 325.

sidered it premature to establish council power at that time; for her the principal task of the Spartakusbund was to arouse a socialist spirit and consciousness in the workers. Of the two wings of the Social Democratic movement, the USPD seemed at the moment to comprise the overwhelming majority of German workers, and Luxemburg and Jogiches were therefore in favor of maintaining the Spartakusbund within the USPD.

The conflict between Luxemburg and Liebknecht was intensified during November and December. Luxemburg presented her position without ambiguity at the conference that founded the Communist Party of Germany. Her report on the political tasks of the new party represents most concisely her concept of the course of the German revolution. It was a mixture of a passionate appeal to the masses for direct action with a program of political abstentionism.

> It would be a criminal error [she said] to seize power now. The German working class is not ready for such an act. Of course, the government of Ebert and Scheidemann cannot be accepted as a workers' government, since these traitors collaborate with the remnants of the Imperial Army and the General Staff. No compromise with such a government is possible. The workers should fight, fight within the factories and on the streets, against Ebert and Scheidemann, but they should not aim at the overthrow of the Ebert government. It is useless, it is childish, to overthrow it and replace it by another if the masses are not ready and able to organize Germany. Our battlefield is within the factories.[25]

Luxemburg envisioned a chain of strikes that would gain momentum and gradually embrace the large majority of the workers. These strikes would organize them, educate them, fill them with the fervor of the class struggle. With this class consciousness, they would unite against the bourgeoisie and its allies in the Social Democratic bureaucracy, which would find itself completely isolated from the common man. This period of mass strikes was for Luxemburg the indispensable prerequisite for the organization of a revolutionary party, and the necessary preliminary phase to all further action. Based on this premise,

---

[25] *Bericht über Gründungsparteitag der Kommunistischen Partei Deutschlands (Spartakusbund) vom 30. Dezember 1918 bis 1. Januar 1919*, printed illegally (Berlin, 1919).

the Spartakist program consisted in an involved but definite rejection of Lenin's policy for Germany.

> The Spartakusbund rejects the sharing of governmental power with Scheidemann and Ebert, the tools of the bourgeoisie . . . The Spartakusbund will also reject gaining power through the collapse of the Scheidemann-Ebert government or because the USPD has reached an impasse in its collaboration with them.
>
> The Spartakusbund will never assume governmental power unless it is supported by the clear, unambiguous will of the great majority of the proletariat in Germany, and in no other way except with their conscious acceptance of the ideas, aims, and fighting methods of the Spartakusbund . . .
>
> The victory of the Spartakusbund stands not at the beginning but at the end of the revolution. It is identical with the victory of the millions of masses of the socialist proletariat.[26]

In substance this decision meant that the Spartakusbund would not participate in any kind of workers' or democratic party alliance. If the present government reached an impasse, the Spartakusbund would neither attempt to support it nor attempt to overthrow it; it would neither share in a caretaker successor government, nor take power alone. In effect, the Spartakist program was equivalent to a critical toleration of the Ebert government, combined with militant propaganda against the army and for socialist aims.

Another passage of the program formulated the rejection of revolutionary terror, again a conscious and strong rejection of Bolshevik practice. The Spartakusbund emphatically denied punitive measures against their enemies; "the socialist revolution hates and despises violence and murder."

Thus Rosa Luxemburg formulated a program of non-interference in the policy of the new Republic—of abstentionism concerning the formation of the new state; that is, participation in elections to the national assembly but as a mere propaganda instrument. According to her interpretation, Germany was entering a long period of sharp class struggle, during which the Spartakusbund would mature. The forces of the revolution, still weak and ineffectual, would grow organically by the combination of strikes and political education. After a long

---

[26] *Was will der Spartakusbund?* (Berlin, December 1918).

period of such preparation, the movement would take over almost without bloodshed and rule almost without compulsory measures. In the speeches and writings of Luxemburg during the few weeks when she could present her point of view, she did not dwell on the changed status of Germany, the chasm between the old Germany and the new. She fought with all her force against the regrouping counter revolution, but gave nowhere an analysis of the new balance of power in Europe, with Germany between revolutionary Russia and the West.

At the first Spartakusbund convention, this hidden conflict between Luxemburg and Lenin, well known to her intimates, influenced the decisions in an involved manner. Radek was there as official Bolshevik delegate to the German Communists; Luxemburg refused even to see him and had to be persuaded by Levi that this was an impossible procedure. Their meeting, when it took place, was cold and formal. The split in the Polish "organization in 1912 [had] naturally caused an estrangement between Rosa Luxemburg and me," Radek wrote later.[27] These basic differences on all major issues gave the Spartakist convention an atmosphere of confusion, of disintegration. Since open criticism of the Russian revolution and the tactics of the Bolsheviks was taboo—for the first workers' victory rated officially only praise— these conflicting policies had to seek other, and more devious, channels of expression.

Liebknecht was much closer to Lenin in his ideas, but he could not develop them. He had no intention of building a caucus to support his policy; he was unable even to present it clearly. The basic political differences were drowned in a sea of resolutions welcoming the Soviets and Lenin and Trotsky with ambiguous enthusiasm. Through this atmosphere of confusion, Liebknecht and his friends opposed Luxemburg's concept as a dangerously unrealistic interpretation of the pivotal situation in Germany after the Kaiser's downfall. They attacked her premise that conditions for the revolutionary camp would constantly improve. Against this criticism, in tragic tones, Rosa asked for a firm stand against adventurist policy, against putschism. "Comrades," she said, "you are falling into the trap of comfortable radicalism."

The debates illustrate strikingly the confusion of the German revo-

---

[27] *Entsiklopedischeski Slovar*, Russian Bibliographical Institute Granat, Moscow [191?–1934], Vol. 41, Part II (appendix), p. 155.

lutionaries. No general analysis of the crucial dangers of the hour was attempted; instead the convention considered the following topics: The crisis in the USPD, Karl Liebknecht; The national convention, Paul Levi; Our program and the political situation, Rosa Luxemburg; Our organization, Hugo Eberlein; Economic conflicts, Paul Lange; The international conference, Hermann Duncker. The chairmen were Wilhelm Pieck and Jakob Walcher; the secretaries Fritz Heckert and Rosi Wolfstein. There were delegates representing forty-six districts.

Liebknecht was chosen to defend the split from the Independent Socialists because he had the greatest influence among the USPD workers. Referring to the entrance of the USPD into the Ebert cabinet on November 9, he proposed instead a united front of the Spartakusbund and the USPD against the Social Democrats.

Karl Radek made a welcoming speech in the name of the Bolshevik Party and Soviet Russia. The convention sent a carefully worded telegram of greeting to the Russian Soviet Republic, avoiding any direct contact with the Bolshevik Party.

Paul Levi reported on the question of participation in the Constituent Assembly. He defended Luxemburg's point of view that the Spartakists should participate, and fought against the idea of overthrowing the government by violence. "That would be possible only if we, the Spartakusbund, supported by the power of the working class, could take over. But now we have first to win over [the majority of] the proletariat."

Otto Rühle,[28] delegate from Pirna, Saxony, opposed this view. "Our participation would be equivalent to a political endorsement of the Constituent Assembly, . . . would be a suicidal policy . . . Our only task is to build up the Workers' and Soldiers' Councils. If in fear of the masses the Constituent Assembly moves to Schilda,[29] then we will build a new government in Berlin."

Rosa Luxemburg defended participation in the elections. Fritz Heckert told the saga of "the fifty-year struggle" of the Social Democratic Party to get the electoral franchise, but got no response; Rosi

---

[28] Author of a biography of Marx. He died in Mexico City in 1943.

[29] A town famous for its merry pranks, here used as the symbol of complacent middle-class stupidity.

Wolfstein, of Duisburg, recommended political mass strikes against the Constituent Assembly.

The convention rejected participation in the Constituent Assembly by a vote of 62 to 23. "Liebknecht confessed he went to bed believing in participation in the elections and awoke opposed to it." [30]

> PAUL LANGE: The war has ruined small factories, and industry is ripe for socialization. Production is concentrated. As a consequence of the lack of coal and of raw materials, the state has had to intervene in private enterprise in varying degrees. Socialization should be carried out by the factory councils. Trade-unions are in theory for socialization, but in fact against it.

The discussion of Lange's report was combined with one on the trade-union question. "The fight for socialization," Luxemburg said, "cannot be waged without posing the question whether or not the trade-unions should be liquidated." Fritz Heckert looked forward to a transformation of the trade-unions with the progress of the revolution; he was absolutely opposed to leaving them. In summing up, Lange expressed a doubt that the trade-unions would change.

> ROSA LUXEMBURG: The 9th of November was rather a breakdown of the old than the victory of a new idea. What followed can be described as chaos, a movement without a plan, without consciousness, in which the only unifying principle was the formation of Workers' and Soldiers' Councils. That was the birth-cry of the revolution, the slogan around which all forces were rallied . . . There was an illusion of unity under the banner of so-called socialism . . . Ebert was elected as a socialist . . . The first period of illusions in Ebert-Scheidemann is passed . . . They are the counter revolution, and now the revolution marches forward. We need not a change of the government but an undermining of it. The revolution was political only and not economic . . .

Motions were passed against the troops in the Baltic region, who were committing "high treason against the German working class"; against the international conference proposed by the British Labour Party; for the formation of Workers' and Soldiers' Councils as the "strategic points" of class organization of the proletariat.

---

[30] Paul Frölich, *Rosa Luxemburg*, p. 274.

After these abstruse discussions on policy, the conference came to its decisive point, how to integrate with other revolutionary groups. It would have been wise to remain in the USPD, whose loose organization permitted wide differences; once this connection was rejected, the minimum should have been a program of unity with the Shop Stewards' Committee, but Liebknecht's efforts to effect a unification were in vain. The Shop Stewards set five conditions: (1) participation in the elections, (2) a joint program commission on a parity basis, (3) precise instructions concerning the tactics of street demonstrations, (4) joint editing of propaganda literature, (5) giving up the name "Spartakusbund." Luxemburg and Jogiches found these conditions unacceptable. The convention decided to sever its connection with the USPD and to found an independent party, the "Communist Party of Germany (Spartakusbund)." [31]

The major issue of the involved and confused debates at this convention was a different appreciation of the November upheaval. The delegates, most of them still in uniform, had just returned from the trenches. They had learned direct action by participating in the direct action of the army in occupied countries. They knew their enemy, and they knew that the dispossessed groups would not wait, would not lose any opportunity to restore the old Hohenzollern regime.

Gustav Noske

At the end of 1918, the situation in Berlin turned to the disadvantage of Ebert. Following the Marstall incident, the three USPD Peoples' Commissars—Hugo Haase, Emil Barth, and Wilhelm Dittmann—resigned from the cabinet. At this moment, when the precarious power of the caretaker government was teetering, Ebert turned to Noske, the man who had saved the day at Kiel, and made him responsible for liaison with the old army in common action against the revolutionaries.

Gustav Noske was one of the most interesting personalities of the

---

[31] A participant in the first Spartakus congress, Mr. G. F., has told me that during the session Jogiches asked him whether he should not blow up the whole affair. The attitude of Jogiches is indicated also in another incident. Clara Zetkin, who had been elected to the Wurttemberg Landtag as a USPD deputy, had difficulty with the rank and file in retaining her seat after the Spartakusbund left the USPD. Jogiches wrote her a letter advising her to remain as a USPD deputy, since he doubted whether it was opportune to found a new party at that moment.

German Social Democratic Party. Born in 1868 in a small town near Berlin, Brandenburg an der Havel, of proletarian stock, he has told in his posthumous autobiography [32] how this social status was felt to be a stigma. He wanted to be a forester, but his family's poverty made this impossible. He became apprentice to a basket weaver attached to a baby-carriage factory, and hated the work; but he emphasizes that it was chosen for him so that he could acquire a skill—Bebel, after all, had been a master carpenter. Drawn into the trade-union movement and into the Social Democratic Party, he quickly gained local authority and became a Social Democratic editor, first in Brandenburg, then in Königsberg, and later in Chemnitz. In these years, "no one ever talked of Marx or Marxism"; Noske read Marx's elementary pamphlets for the first time during a short prison term in 1903, after having been editor of Social Democratic newspapers for six years.

Noske went up with the party, representative of the stratum who identified its rise to national status with their own ambitions. In party discussions, he was always at the Right, condemning all criticism of its nationalist policies as folly. He had little patience with the *Ostleute,* the Russian and Polish socialists who had escaped from Tsarist persecution to Germany, and particularly with Rosa Luxemburg. After the International Socialist Conference at Stuttgart in 1907, he reported back to his Chemnitz organization about her, sarcastically commenting on "the ambiguous credentials characteristic of *Ostleute."* Bebel sent him an abusive letter attacking his stand and warmly defending Luxemburg. "There was a time," Bebel wrote, "when I hoped that you would develop. Now I must say that this hope was in vain."

In the years before the war, as one of his party's military experts in the Reichstag, Noske excited the approval of certain nationalist circles and the opposition of the party rank and file. As early as 1907, his jingoism was satirized in the German press in the following doggerel:

---

[32] Gustav Noske, *Aufstieg und Niedergang der deutschen Sozialdemokratie* (Zurich, 1947). The manuscript was finished in 1933, and Noske writes in the foreword that until 1936 he maintained the illusion that the book could be published under the Nazis.

During the Second World War, he was arrested twice, first for a few days at its outbreak and then on July 22, 1944, in connection with the generals' revolt. He escaped from the Moabit prison in Berlin in April 1945, when the Russians were already in the suburbs. He died on November 30, 1946, at the age of seventy-eight.

Geht es mal in ferner Frist,
Ans Kanonenfuttern,
Denkt so mancher Reservist:
"Nee—ich bleib' bei Muttern."
Doch das soll uns Kampf und Schlacht
Nimmermehr vergällen,
Denn es ist heut' ausgemacht:
Noske wird sich stellen! . . .

Noske schnallt den Säbel um,
Noske geht aufs Ganze,
Noske feuert, bum, bum, bum,
Noske stürmt die Schanze,
Noske schreit Hurra, Hurra!
Noske hält die Wachen,
Noske schiesst Viktoria,
Noske wird's schon machen.

(When in the distant future, we have to feed our guns, many a reservist will think, "Nix, I'll stay home with Mom." But that won't lose us the war and battles, for one thing is certain: Noske will be there . . .
(Noske belts his saber on, Noske goes all out, Noske fires boom, boom, boom, Noske storms the bulwarks, Noske cries Hurrah, Hurrah! Noske walks his post, Noske shoots the final shot, Noske will do it.)

But neither this public abuse nor Bebel's grumbling nor the enormous opposition from the pacifist-minded party membership deflected Noske from his nationalist credo, from his conviction in particular that the Reich must acquire colonies in Africa. In defense of his stand he wrote a book, *Social Democracy and Colonial Policy,* which appeared just at the outbreak of the war and was submerged by it.

During the war Noske was among the staunchest "social patriots," and his past made him the most obvious choice among plebeian figures to quell the revolutionary upsurge with which it ended. Noske was the party organizer par excellence; his life was in the party, and even after he acquired considerable power as a bureaucrat, he never lost evidences in his speech and behavior of his proletarian origin. He had an understanding for military affairs (he boasts in one place, referring to his intention to reorganize the German army under Social

Democratic auspices, that he might have been the Trotsky of Germany!); he had a skill in organizing, but his principal advantage over his confrères in the party's National Executive Committee was a greater audacity, a more vigorous personality. The Social Democratic worker could find a better life only in a better Reich, and it was the function of the Social Democratic Party to work toward a richer and more powerful Germany. The party, synchronized with the army, should become one of the two foundation pillars of an expanding empire. That he was not able to carry out this grandiose plan, he repeats again and again in his memoirs, was because of the rubber-spined vacillations of the other Social Democratic leaders, particularly Scheidemann, who were always content with half-measures against the bothersome Left wing. But at the end of 1918 Noske was at the peak of his enthusiasm, convinced that a few well-organized skirmishes would dispel the revolutionary follies.

Bloody January

On December 25, five hundred men again occupied the *Vorwärts* building, which act had to be countered immediately if Ebert was not to suffer an irreparable loss to his prestige and authority within the party. The Social Democratic newspaper had been built through the efforts of the Berlin organization, which through decades of common work had collected the necessary money. Legally it was the property of the organization. When the majority of the Berlin Social Democrats left the Ebert party to help form the USPD, they regarded the *Vorwärts* building, printing plant, and other installations as rightfully theirs. Thus, broad circles of Berlin workers looked on the occupation of the building as an act designed to get the property back to the organization from which it had been stolen.

When Noske accepted the cabinet post for military affairs, the situation seemed hopeless for the government, which had no reliable troops at its disposal. The decisive conflict crystallized around the figure of the pacifist police president, Emil Eichhorn, the man who had got his office so easily and who did not understand how to use it. Eichhorn had organized a security guard of about 3500 men, which, enlarged by several thousand demobilized soldiers, could have relieved the *Vorwärts* partisans. But Eichhorn was far from such belligerent plans. On the contrary, he tried to clear the *Vorwärts* build-ing of its occupants, at the instigation of Dittmann and Haase, his party associates; and even the Shop Stewards' Committee was dis-posed to join him in this arbitration of the conflict. This peaceful settlement could have been arranged if the military had not been seeking an opportunity for a decisive punitive action. They got it.

In the first days of January 1919, the newly elected Central Commit-tee of the Communist Party of Germany (Spartakusbund) convened and considered the critical situation. Karl Liebknecht proposed uni-fication of the various revolutionary movements in Berlin—the Volks-marine Division, the Shop Stewards' Committee, the USPD, the Spartakusbund. Luxemburg, supported by Leo Jogiches, opposed Liebknecht. Jogiches proposed that the *Rote Fahne* publish a sharp statement, to be signed by Luxemburg in the name of the Spartakist Central Committee, to the effect that Liebknecht no longer repre-sented the Spartakusbund at the Shop Stewards' Committee.[33]

All eyes were on Berlin. The Berlin Shop Stewards were the best incarnation of "the internal enemy," the nucleus of a militant organ-ization. They had more elements of power in their hands than the vague assembly of Workers' and Soldiers' Councils. Deliberately to provoke the Shop Stewards, on January 4 Ebert ordered Eichhorn to leave the police presidium and appointed as his successor Social Demo-crat Eugen Ernst. On January 5, Noske ordered the attack on the police presidium and on the newspaper building. The Executive Com-mittee of the Shop Stewards, recognizing the importance of this test, decided to fight to retain Eichhorn. The Spartakist Central Commit-tee, meeting on the same day, passed a motion denying support to Eichhorn because this might lead to the fall of the Ebert government. When they later reversed their position, they stated explicitly that they were still opposed to overthrowing the cabinet.

Thus, the first and most important group of German resistance to the restoration of *Kaiserlich* imperialism, the Shop Stewards, had to act alone, estranged from all party leadership and organization. They

---

[33] Two documents exist concerning this conflict between the two leading Spar-takists: Paul Levi's statement in the Central Committee of the German Communist Party, on May 4, 1921, published in his pamphlet *Was ist das Verbrechen?* (Berlin, 1921), cf. Rosenberg, pp. 330–333; and a letter of Karl Radek, published in *Illustrierte Geschichte der deutschen Revolution* (Berlin, 1926).

gave the Ebert cabinet an ultimatum, demanding that Eichhorn be maintained and the army be disarmed and disbanded immediately (together with the usual host of social demands). The Shop Stewards, however, did not call for the resignation of the Ebert cabinet; in spite of verbal polemics, they did not realize until the last moment (and of course they did not know of the agreement between Ebert and the army) that Comrade Ebert was really their enemy. They expected him to yield to their pressure ultimately and accept a compromise.

On January 6, there was a pro-Eichhorn demonstration, larger than anyone had expected. In Berlin hundreds of thousands marched through the Siegesallee. Contemporary observers were impressed with the mass mood, which had developed considerably in the last few months. It was a gigantic army, lacking only leadership and organization to be irresistible.

Liebknecht, accompanied by Wilhelm Pieck, went to the Shop Stewards' Committee and declared that the Eichhorn incident was the starting point for a decisive blow against the counter revolution. The occupation of the *Vorwärts* building should continue, the committee decided, and it issued a proclamation for a general strike. Fifty-three members were designated as the Action Committee, which elected three co-presidents—Liebknecht, Georg Ledebour, and Paul Scholze. This committee, the first tentative organized direction of the German revolutionaries, was composed of shop stewards representing not parties but their factories, and included only those few political leaders who, against the outspoken will of their organizations, had joined them. Neither Ledebour nor Liebknecht was authorized to participate.

The situation was confused and complex. The Shop Stewards did not feel themselves secure in their political function. Their relations with the Volksmarine Division were strained; the sailors were difficult to handle. These congenital weaknesses notwithstanding, the Shop Stewards' Committee was becoming most dangerous for the army and the Ebert cabinet. Gustav Noske correctly analyzed the situation as serious for the government.

> Since there might be tumult in Wilhelmstrasse [seat of the government], the members of the government had arranged to

meet somewhere else [that is, go underground]. I met Ebert and Baake there, as I had my belly full of Down with Noske! . . . Somewhat later a message came that the Spartakists had occupied the *Vorwärts* building and, a little later, other newspaper buildings. We sat together in a depressed mood. The continued threats made it inadvisable to return home. To go out to a restaurant for dinner was not possible, for the waiters were on strike. I telephoned to an acquaintance, who gave us some food. In his apartment, later in the evening, I met Scheidemann and the same Baake. We spoke a lot, but arrived at no decision. It was not possible even to guess how Berlin would look to us the next morning.[34]

The military needed time to prepare their march into Berlin. "Many more troops were required for the salvation of Berlin than the, at most, few hundred that the Colonel had at his disposal on January 6."[35]

The rapid overthrow of the Ebert cabinet, the establishment of a workers' government in Berlin, would have acted like a bellows to the smoldering fires in Germany. Once the industrial centers were set in motion, the demoralized military would have been unable to regroup enough cadres. They would have lost their chance to march on Berlin. Just this was their *cauchemar*. In 1919, in spite of all their shortcomings, the Shop Stewards could have crushed the counter revolution with a minimum of effort and sacrifice. In the continuing duel between the Berlin workers and the General Staff, the officer corps was at its most disadvantageous point since the foundation of the Reich.

The Shop Stewards did not realize how strong in fact they were. Blinded by their internal tension and uneasy because of the desertion of the politicians, after losing precious hours in deliberations they still could not agree on such concrete measures as a call to arms to all Berlin workers, immediate action against the few army strongholds in the Berlin area, a march on Potsdam. It was crucial to prevent the regrouped army forces from entrenching themselves in strategic points in Berlin.

---

[34] Gustav Noske, *Von Kiel bis Kapp: Zur Geschichte der deutschen Revolution* (Berlin, 1920), p. 67. This incident took place the evening of Sunday, January 5.
[35] *Von Kiel bis Kapp*, p. 70.

The masses in the Siegesallee, Noske wrote, waited, waited endless hours, for instructions, for an appeal, for a concrete plan. In silence and discipline they waited, and finally they went home.

On January 7 the students of the Berlin University issued a manifesto calling for the defense of "the holy order in Germany." The conservatives, still unfriendly toward the Red Ebert cabinet, were called on by the students to forget their grievances and fight shoulder to shoulder with the Social Democratic Party.

For two precious days, the troops of General von Lüttwitz were able to gather in the environs of Berlin. Under the immediate command of Lequis, they were awaiting the order to invade the city. On January 8 Ebert, Scheidemann, Noske, Landsberg, and Wissell declared in a manifesto against the Spartakists that they would meet violence with violence. Everyone in Berlin understood that this was the signal to the army to march. The Spartakusbund, no longer able to abstain, issued a manifesto declaring its solidarity with the fighting workers. A few hours later, the Potsdam regiment marched in. It was a motley combination of residua of the old army—officers, staff sergeants, soldiers of the First Garde Regiment, the Garde Jäger Battalion, a Sergeants' School, the Garde Kavallerie Schützen Division, and two artillery groups.

The military marched into the center of the city without opposition. The proletarian suburbs watched them take this strategic position full of passionate hatred but already demoralized by their lack of organization, leadership, and program.

Their first objective, to take the *Vorwärts* building, was delayed a few hours, pending negotiations with the revolutionaries. Meanwhile mortars and cannon were placed all around the building, in the Belle Alliance Square and the surrounding streets. On the morning of January 9 the troops opened fire. In this crowded quarter, with its narrow streets, the effect was deadly. With the first shot fired in the center of Berlin, the revolutionaries had lost the day. The small group in the *Vorwärts* building, considering their position hopeless, sent seven emissaries to the troop commander under a flag of truce to negotiate their surrender. Berlin saw its first Nazi atrocity. The men were taken to a military post in Dragonerstrasse, beaten with whips and clubs, and shot.

Street fighting in Berlin flared up sporadically. One of the most popular leaders of the Berlin workers, the Independent Socialist Georg Ledebour, was arrested. This arrest broke the last psychological bond to the Ebert cabinet; the Shop Stewards' Committee proclaimed a Liebknecht-Scholze-Ledebour government—a futile gesture after the invasion of the Potsdam regiment.

On January 10 the Spartakusbund tried again to end its connection with the Shop Stewards. Again it forbade the participation of Liebknecht, but without effect.

The revolutionaries were seized by a growing demoralization. By January 12, the Potsdam regiment had occupied all important points and buildings. The Shop Stewards' Committee, hunted by the troops, went underground. Berlin streets were barred with barbed wire. There were military posts everywhere, and everywhere the inscription, *Wer weiter geht, wird erschossen* (If you go farther, you will be shot).

On January 15, Luxemburg and Liebknecht were arrested. Instead of leaving immediately and going to any one of the hundred places where they could have found safety (as Lenin had been forced to go to Finland in July 1917), they had hid at the home of a sympathizer in West Berlin, without even an adequate bodyguard. The precious game were easily caught. They were taken to the Hotel Eden, a temporary military headquarters, which did not bother to report the arrest to Ebert, who had given no instructions what to do in case of their arrest. In my opinion and in that of many other contemporaries, General Lüttwitz' headquarters had been determined from the beginning to kill them.

There was no trial, no investigation. They were killed the same night.

The hand-picked soldiers conducting them through the Tiergarten brutally manhandled them and shot them. The frail body of Rosa Luxemburg was thrown into the Landwehr canal and not found until much later. "The cowardly and brutal assassination of Karl Liebknecht and Rosa Luxemburg . . . is among the most dastardly outgrowths of these insecure times . . . The murderers came before a military tribunal and were given mild prison sentences. Their excuse was accepted: 'shot while trying to escape.' This phrase, invented at this time, had a terrible resurrection fifteen years later." [36]

---

[36] Otto Braun, *Von Weimar zu Hitler* (New York, 1940), p. 84. Braun was Social Democratic premier of the Prussian cabinet.

The defeat of the Shop Stewards and the assassination of Liebknecht and Luxemburg marked the end of the first phase of German Communism. From their German premises, both the Spartakusbund and the Shop Stewards had tried to develop a socialist policy designed to prevent the regrouping of the Imperial forces. Both had failed. The humanitarian Rosa Luxemburg, who had solemnly rejected terror as a weapon, was killed by terrorists.

The semi-official assassination of socialist leaders, one of them a frail and crippled woman, in the middle of a civilized city was a feature new in German society. The incident had tremendous after-effects. The workers wanted to avenge the murder of the Spartakist leaders. They developed a new grimness; they shed the first layer of their naïveté. It was the simplest, the most easily understandable, example of what might happen to all those who opposed the forces of restoration. After the 15th of January, a good part of the original good-mindedness of the German revolutionaries was a thing of the past. The disappearance of Liebknecht and Luxemburg as the leaders of young German Communism was tragic indeed. Their death symbolized the end of all attempts to develop to maturity the best traditions of the German Social Democratic movement and to adapt them to the new phase of Germany's history.

The position of Ebert, Luxemburg's obverse, must also be put against the background of the shaking balance of power in 1918 Europe. The German Social Democrats, men with little imagination but in their own way liberals and democrats, fought to regain Germany's status in post-Versailles Europe. They preferred any arrangement with France and England to coöperation with Russia. The stubborn resistance of Ebert to the Spartakists reflects this stand, as does his persistent will to conserve the old pattern of German society.

In allying himself with the German army, he was, among the ideologues and phraseologues of his party, the realistic politician. Concerted action with the USPD and the Spartakists would have opened wide the gates to the torrent of the German socialist revolution. This torrent, he thought, would have destroyed every vestige of the Imperial Reich and every possibility of its restoration, in however moderate a form. Such a transformation into a socialist economy would have linked Germany with revolutionary Russia. Germany would have dropped out of the sphere of the Western powers and would have become one end of the axis Russia–Germany, which would have been laid along the line Moscow–Königsberg–Berlin and would have comprised Warsaw, Prague, Vienna, Budapest.

Thus, at all costs and by any means, Ebert and Noske wanted to save the Reich. In saving the Reich, Ebert looked forward to a long-range program of gradual social reform, which would give labor a rising status and a strengthened influence. His policy was nothing new; it was the adaptation of the pre-war Social Democratic ideas to changed circumstances. In Paris and London alike, he was acclaimed for his insight into the implications for Germany of the new Europe; Ebert was the savior of Germany. "Indeed, the Social Democratic workers may be said to be the one politically educated class in Germany and its leaders, who are now everywhere in power, the only experienced administrators among German political parties." [1]

But the peculiar and ambiguous situation of Germany between Russia and the West could not be resolved so easily—by the extermination of the visible portion of the revolutionary movement, the Spartakists and the Shop Stewards' Committee. The Reich was in disintegration. Its economic and political status in Europe was shattered. The effects of the defeat were felt by all strata of German so-

---

[1] *The Economist*, London, November 16, 1918, vol. 87, p. 682.

ciety and could not be blurred by pretending that nothing had happened, that no substantial change had taken place.

The Freikorps and National Bolshevism

The Freikorps, the illegal regrouping cadres of the Imperial army,[2] were led by officers whose dominant and continuing impulse was to exterminate the labor movement in whatever form it was found, including their temporary allies, the Social Democrats; for in disintegrating Germany the entire labor class was potentially Bolshevist. The disintegration of the old German regime was reflected also in the groups that wanted most to conserve it. The nationalist youth, uprooted by the war, was restless and dissatisfied with the older generation. The generals, the monarchists, the intimates of the former high bureaucracy, intrigued and maneuvered. They protested, or they did not protest, against the Versailles treaty; in any case their fulminations were an alibi and not a call to action. The younger men wanted active resistance against the victorious powers, terroristic plots against the occupation, elimination of the collaborating Republicans, demonstrative assassinations. In their conspiratorial fraternities, these young men sought in an endless stream of debate a master plan to liberate Germany quickly.

The Freikorps added to the impetus of the nationalist youth the experienced skill of the army cadres. The gulf between the revolutionaries and the Freikorps is illustrated by an anecdote of Ernst Friedrich Karl von Salomon, the talented chronicler of the Freikorps and the Fehme,[3] who sums up the feeling of his generation in his autobiography, *The Outlawed*. A student of the Military Academy in Berlin-Lichterfelde, a boy in his teens, he wandered about Berlin during the November days, sick at heart at the fate of his Fatherland. Everywhere he saw "the yelling mob" tearing the epaulets from the shoulders of the officers who dared to appear on the streets wearing them, trampling on these symbols of German honor. As a reaction to this experience, Salomon joined a Freikorps, and served with it in the Baltic campaign.

---

[2] Cf. F. W. von Oertzen, *Die deutschen Freikorps, 1918–1923* (Munich, 1939).

[3] In medieval Germany, the Fehme was a secret self-appointed tribunal for the extermination of criminals who managed to evade official prosecution. The assassination of political opponents, as carried out by the Freikorps and later by the Nazis, was organized by a group that designated itself the Fehme.

On his return to Germany, his Freikorps was ordered to Harburg, a gray workers' town near Hamburg where all life centered around the rubber factory. The next morning Hoffmann, a comrade of Salomon's, spoke to him:

> HOFFMANN: Come with me. There are a lot of things I don't like. [He dragged Salomon to the big corner window of the school room.] Look, machine guns are posted in the schoolyard against us. And for half an hour I have been watching them pile up ammunition. Not only men, but women and children. The streets are full of armed workers. But that isn't all. Look here, at the open lot behind the school. Regular trenches. We are encircled, simply surrounded.
>
> SALOMON: But do our officers know all this?
>
> HOFFMANN: Of course. But what are they doing? They have been negotiating for hours with deputies and committees of the Workers' Guard and of the Burghers' Guard and with the army command.
>
> SALOMON: What? The regular army is here? That's good.
>
> HOFFMANN: On the contrary. The 9th Regiment is here, but this morning these pigs arrested their officers. They opened the storerooms and distributed the rifles to the workers.
>
> [Salomon's narrative continues:] We looked out of the window in silence, feeling very lonely. A wave of hatred arose from the mass around the school. The hatred of two races: the physical revulsion of one for the other. The painful abhorrence of one by the other. They could not stand the smell of each other.
>
> We stared round-eyed at the mass, not at the armed individuals, who were more dangerous. But it was this eyeless mass that impressed us more.[4]

Among the same young nationalists—and in the same von Salomon —a counter current sprang up: a confused and vague reaching toward a possible German-Russian alliance against the West. The chains of Versailles could be broken, Germany's status in Europe could be restored, only after all Germans had been reconciled to fight for the common goal. Civil war split the German people into two races, and with such a split no comeback was possible.

In this milieu the vision of a dictatorship rallying the military and the proletarian forces was in the air. The Communist intelligentsia,

---

[4] Ernst von Salomon, *Die Geächteten* (Berlin, 1931), p. 163 ff.

looking around for effective instruments of action, were attracted to this activist nationalist youth, in type and behavior so distinct from the conservative German trade-unionist.

In Hamburg the Communist Party was led by two old socialist militants, Dr. Heinrich Laufenberg[5] and Fritz Wolffheim. During the war, in their courageous fight against the Social Democratic bureaucracy, they had accused the Reich and its socialist defenders of predatory expansionism. In 1915 they published a pamphlet denouncing German imperialism. But in 1918, the effects of the defeat were felt earlier and more palpably in Hamburg, Germany's port to the world. Germany's trade was ruined, the docks were idle, and the Hamburg workers were the first to grasp the economic truth later expressed by Hitler: Export or die.

In October 1919, Laufenberg and Wolffheim visited Karl Radek in Berlin-Moabit, where since the January days he had been a state prisoner. They proposed a policy to him for which they had coined the term National Bolshevism. Following the peace of Versailles, they argued, Germany will sink lower even than after the Thirty Years' War or during the Napoleonic era. The German people will be irrevocably lost if we do not create an organization that coalesces the energy of the nation into one firm entity. We must reconstruct at home and break the foreign chains; the organization to do this can only be the proletarian dictatorship. The power of the German people, though profoundly shaken by four years of war and by the shameless treason of the Social Democrats, is yet strong enough—if the fight is a fight for bare life, a fight for the genuine interests of the entire people—to make true Bismarck's words and to rouse up Germany armed to the teeth from the Baltic to Lake Constance.[6]

Radek was very much interested and discussed with the two men from Hamburg the implications of their proposals. Their ideas had some relevance to Radek's own policy, developed with Bukharin during the Brest-Litovsk negotiations, that Russia should carry a revo-

---

[5] Laufenberg, well known as the author of an erudite history of the Hamburg Social Democratic Party, died in 1932. Ernst Niekisch, a Social Democrat who promoted National Bolshevism, wrote his obituary: "In 1919, Laufenberg already thought in terms of continents."

[6] Heinrich Laufenberg und Fritz Wolffheim, *Revolutionärer Volkskrieg oder konterrevolutionärer Bürgerkrieg?*, Erste kommunistische Adresse an das deutsche Proletariat (Hamburg, 1920).

lutionary war to Europe. Russia plus Germany should bring the Bolshevik message to the Channel and throw the British and American armies into the Atlantic. Meanwhile Radek's aggressiveness had changed to something like despair. He feared the success of the interventionist armies, especially during the Yudenich offensive against Petrograd. He paced restlessly up and down his cell and expected decisively bad news any minute. It seemed to him an audacious way out to come to an understanding with a portion of the German army and in opening a new phase of the German war to save revolutionary Russia by a grandiose diversion. In 1918 Radek had wanted to continue the war against Russia's then main enemy, Germany, which would have been equivalent to a silent agreement with the Entente. Now that France, Britain, and, in the background, the United States were the main enemies of Russia, Radek conceived a possible alliance with defeated Germany against the West.

At first, Laufenberg and Wolffheim won a substantial following in the Spartakusbund, which after the death of Liebknecht and Luxemburg and the arrest of most of its other outstanding leaders was again in a period of confusion and disorganization. In 1919 there was no regular contact between Radek in his cell and Lenin's Politburo. When Radek returned to Moscow in January 1920 and made his report, Lenin flatly rejected National Bolshevism as a crying absurdity.

Lenin versus National Bolshevism

The Versailles negotiations shook the young Weimar Republic to its weak foundations. No group in Germany wanted to be responsible for signing the treaty. The Ebert cabinet, fearful that the Reichswehr, whose support of the government was in any case half-hearted, would mutiny if they signed, were panicky at the thought that the Baltic troops would return and arrest the Social Democratic government as traitors to the Fatherland. Hectically, and in secret, Ebert sought the advice of the military hierarchs. Noske, convinced that the best generals would resign if the treaty was signed, threatened his own resignation. "If the generals resign, the army will disintegrate. Without troops, the Reich could not be kept in order." [7]

---

[7] E. O. Volkmann, *Revolution über Deutschland*, p. 301.

Ebert appealed to Hindenburg as the supreme military authority. On June 17, 1919, Hindenburg replied: "If hostilities are reopened, we are not militarily equipped to retake Posen in the East and protect our frontiers. In the West, in view of the Entente's numerical superiority and its ability to encircle both our flanks, a serious attack would leave us hardly any hope for success. A successful end to our operations is most questionable, but as a soldier I must prefer an honorable death to an ignominious peace." [8]

Hindenburg's empty gesture did not dispel the confusion. Several generals, among them Märcker, felt that if Noske, a Social Democrat, were the dictator of Germany and the head of the army, it would be possible to revivify the will of the German people to fight; it would be possible to refuse this infamous peace and begin the war again. This other version of National Bolshevism lasted three days. On June 20, Gröner wired Ebert to sign the treaty and blew up all phantasmagoria.

The Moscow Politburo undoubtedly knew of this internal convulsion in the Reichswehr. The first thin threads between the Red Army and the German General Staff were spun in this period, in spite of the continuing civil war; but to weave these threads into a new thick carpet, which would cover over the antagonism between revolutionary Russia and capitalist Germany with a military alliance, was quite a different operation. In his unambiguous rejection of this policy, Lenin used as his personal target not its advocates in his own Politburo but the relatively unimportant Laufenberg and Wolffheim. Lenin developed his criticism into a positive proposal for a foreign policy of the revolutionary German working class, in which the new uncertainty of defeated Germany in Europe, realistically analyzed, was the starting point.

> Finally, one of the undoubted mistakes of the "Lefts" in Germany is their stubborn insistence on non-recognition of the Versailles Peace. The more "solidly" and "importantly," the more "determinedly" and categorically this viewpoint is formulated (by K. Horner, for instance), the less sensible it appears. In the present conditions of the international proletarian revolution, it is not enough to renounce the crying absurdities of "National Bolshe-

[8] Volkmann, p. 282.

vism" (Laufenberg and others), which has gone to the length of advocating a bloc with the German bourgeoisie for war against the Entente. One must understand that the tactics which do not concede that it is essential for a Soviet Germany (if a German Soviet republic were established soon) to recognize the Versailles Peace for a time and to submit to it, are fundamentally wrong. From this it does not follow that the "Independents" were right in putting forward—at a time when the Scheidemanns were in the government, when the Soviet government of Hungary had not yet been overthrown, and when there was yet a possibility of a Soviet revolution in Vienna in support of Soviet Hungary— in putting forward *under these circumstances* the demand to sign the Versailles Treaty. At that time the "Independents" temporized and maneuvered very clumsily, for they more or less accepted responsibility for the Scheidemann traitors, they slipped, more or less from the viewpoint of the merciless (and most cold-blooded) class war against the Scheidemanns to the "classless" or "above-class" viewpoint.

At present, however, the position is obviously such that the German Communists should not tie their hands and promise positively and without fail to repudiate the Versailles Treaty in the event of the victory of Communism. That would be foolish. They must say: the Scheidemanns and Kautskyists have perpetrated a series of treacheries; they obstructed (in part, directly ruining) an alliance with Soviet Russia and with Soviet Hungary. We Communists will do all we can to *facilitate* and *pave the way* for such an alliance; at the same time, we are by no means obliged to repudiate the Versailles Treaty immediately. The possibility of repudiating it successfully depends not only on the German but also on the international success of the Soviet movement. This movement has been hampered by the Scheidemanns and Kautskyists; we shall further it. Therein lies the crux of the matter; that is where the fundamental difference lies. And if our class enemies, the exploiters and their lackeys, the Scheidemanns and Kautskyists, missed a number of opportunities to strengthen both the German and international Soviet movements, to strengthen the German and international Soviet revolutions, the blame will fall upon them. The Soviet revolution in Germany will strengthen the international Soviet movement, which is the strongest—and the only reliable, invincible, omnipotent bulwark—against the Versailles Peace and against international imperialism in general. To put liberation from the Versailles Peace absolutely and unconditionally and immediately in the forefront *before the question* of liberating other countries oppressed by imperialism from the yoke of imperialism is petty bourgeois nationalism (worthy of Kautsky, Hilferding, Otto Bauer and Co.) and is not revolutionary internationalism. The overthrow of the bourgeoisie in any of the large European countries, such as Germany, would be such a gain to the international revolution that for its sake one can, and must if necessary, tolerate a *more prolonged existence of the Versailles Peace.* If Russia by herself could endure the Brest-Litovsk Peace for several months to the advantage of the revolution, it is not impossible for Soviet Germany, in alliance with Soviet Russia, to endure an even longer existence of the Versailles Treaty to the advantage of the revolution.

The imperialists of France, England, etc. are trying to provoke the German Communists, they are laying a trap for them: "Say you will not sign the Versailles Treaty!" And the Left Communists, like children, fall into the trap laid for them instead of maneuvering skillfully against the crafty and, *at the present moment,* stronger enemy, instead of telling him: "Today we shall sign the Versailles Treaty." To tie one's hands beforehand, openly to tell the enemy, who is now better armed than we are, whether and when we shall fight him is being stupid, not revolutionary. To accept battle at a time when it is obviously advantageous to the enemy and not to us is a crime; and those politicians of the revolutionary class who are unable "to maneuver, to compromise" in order to avoid an obviously disadvantageous battle are good for nothing.[9]

After the signing of the Versailles Treaty in the summer of 1919, a reaction set in in the Spartakusbund against Hamburg National Bolshevism. The factional strife on the political issue was poisoned, for at the same time Laufenberg and Wolffheim rebelled against the centralism of Pieck's leadership. The revolt against the successors to Luxemburg and Liebknecht, who had taken advantage of the underground status of the party to establish a bureaucratic rule, spread throughout almost all Spartakist branches. Laufenberg and Wolffheim were expelled, and their splinter group disintegrated quickly. But this first phase of National Bolshevism left a deep imprint on the party and endured, stimulated by Radek's continued interest and activity.

---

[9] V. I. Lenin, *"Left-Wing" Communism: An Infantile Disorder* (New York: International Publishers, 1934), pp. 56–58.

The Weimar Republic and the Comintern Are Founded

The first rapprochements between the activists of the two camps, however, were without immediate results. The military leaders were too close to their anti-labor past, to the traditions of Bismarck and Wilhelm II, which had implanted in them irrepressible hatred of the internal enemy. Thus the German army marched again, this time not in enemy country but in the homeland, covered by the authority of the Republican government. It beleaguered the strongholds of the workers' resistance (Bremen, for instance, was besieged three days before it surrendered), marched through the countryside, with the old splendors and the old banners, invaded towns and industrial regions as it had invaded the towns and regions of Europe. Thus, General Märcker, later one of the leaders of the Kapp putsch, became known as the Conqueror of Cities.[10] The army followed the rules of war. Soldiers marched in in Indian file, taking protection against snipers, seized the major buildings of the town, raided the workers' quarters, arrested Social Democrats and Communists by the hundreds, summarily executed them by the score, closed down the workers' press, administered towns and regions under martial law. When their orders had been carried out, the army marched off and the civilian administration came back, but into a changed atmosphere.

This civil war was waged three years, running parallel with the one in Russia. Each camp came to know the other better and better, and to hate the other better and better. The workers, in spite of their repeated defeats, were not really beaten; the Freikorps, in spite of their repeated victories, were not really successful.

During the civil-war years, 1918–1920, the alliance of the army with the former high Reich bureaucracy and big business went on as though drafted by old Marx himself. This social reality extinguished the first wave of National Bolshevism in the ranks of the younger generation. The National Bolshevist ideologues were isolated, in a milieu filled with economic conflict. The unfinished German Republic was swept by a wave of mass strikes, despite a joint committee to preserve civil peace set up by the German Federation of Labor (ADGB) with the

---

[10] Ernst von Salomon, *Nahe Geschichte* (Berlin, 1936), p. 89.

Manufacturers Association (*Reichsverband der Deutschen Industrie*) under Carl Legien and Theodor Leipart.[11] The Berlin uprising was only one major episode of the civil war, in the words of Ernst von Salomon, "the model for the Reich. Germany became the field of operations of the Freikorps, where battles of varying scope developed." [12] From Hamburg to the Lake of Constance, in Bremen, Essen, Stuttgart, Brunswick, Saxony, there were frequent clashes between the Workers' Councils and the regrouping army. "Everywhere the Workers' and Soldiers' Councils have taken the initiative in administering local affairs, after the principle *J'y suis, j'y reste.*" [13] The socialist workers were with the revolutionaries, but everywhere these were in a minority among the political leaders. Everywhere they were weak in leadership, ineffective in organization, and debilitated by internal quarrels. On the other hand, the military had under their command amazingly few troops and comparatively poor equipment.

Both the army and the revolutionaries regarded the Ebert government as a caretaker regime, supplanting the old system but leaving the door open to other developments. Ebert therefore hurried the elections for the Constituent Assembly, to give his cabinet a new, Republican legality. On January 19, 1919, in this atmosphere of civil war and utter disintegration, the election was held; 44 per cent of the electorate cast a ballot for a socialist republic, and expected its imminent realization. Ebert chose Weimar for the first session of the German parliament; in spite of the army's victory in January, in spite of the defeat of the Spartakusbund and the Shop Stewards' Committee, Berlin was still not safe enough. General Märcker, the organizer of the Landesjäger Freikorps, protected Weimar against a possible revolutionary coup. "Weimar was encircled at ten kilometers distance; all roads situated in this circle were secured by groups of officers and non-commissioned officers with full equipment. . . . Villages and industrial hamlets in Thuringia were unfriendly toward our troops." [14]

---

[11] Leipart survived the Nazi regime and in 1946 was in Berlin promoting the Socialist Unity Party. Legien died on December 26, 1920.

[12] *Nahe Geschichte*, pp. 28–29.

[13] Gen. Maj. Ludwig Märcker, *Vom Kaiserheer zur Reichswehr: Geschichte des freiwilligen Landesjägerkorps. Ein Beitrag zur Geschichte der deutschen Revolution* (2nd edition, Leipzig, 1927), p. 109.

[14] Märcker, p. 91 ff.

During 1919, the civil war in Germany represented a repetition of the initial stage: government and Freikorps troops marching into the industrial regions and liquidating the administrations of the Workers' and Soldiers' Councils. General Märcker, the Conqueror of Cities, the commander of only one of the Freikorps groups marching about Germany, notes in his memoirs the following actions: occupation of Gotha on February 17; a week of serious fighting, February 27–March 3, in Halle; occupation of Magdeburg, April 9; occupation of Brunswick on the same date, when the local rule of Independent Socialist Sepp Oerter came to a quick end; action against Leipzig, May 7–30, with sorties against Eisenach and Erfurt.

In March 1919 fighting was resumed in Berlin. Rumors were circulated that sixty policemen had been killed in Lichtenberg.[15] Later it was known that these rumors were false, but meanwhile Noske ordered a general house-to-house search for weapons. The quarters of the Volksmarine Division were surrounded and after a short fight occupied. Twenty-four sailors were manhandled and killed out of hand. Artillery was used. Planes crossed over the city, and new rumors were circulated that they would bomb the workers' suburbs. The Reinhardt Regiment, and especially one Oberleutnant Marloh, became notorious for their brutal handling of the revolutionaries. More than two hundred were summarily executed.

But in spite of the Spartakists' defeat, the spring of 1919 brought rising revolutionary hopes in Europe. On March 2, the First World Congress of the Communist International convened in Moscow. Its manifesto reflects best the moods, the hopes and the illusions, of the crusaders for world Communism. The Communists felt themselves the legal heirs to all revolutionary traditions of the nineteenth century; they specifically related their organization to the Communist Manifesto of Marx, issued in 1848. The First International had deteriorated in the Franco-Prussian War of 1870–1871, the Second in the war of 1914. A new and still more bloody war would be unavoidable if imperialist society were not supplanted by Communism.

There were thirty-two delegates present, but they did not represent parties comparable with the old labor organizations. The young Com-

---

[15] Compare the account in *Die Wahrheit über die Berliner Strassenkämpfe* (Verlig *Freiheit*, USPD daily, Berlin, 1919).

munist groups had won neither strength nor political experience. Rumania, Switzerland, Czechoslovakia, and Belgium were represented only by sympathetic elements of their Social Democratic parties.

Shortly before her death, Rosa Luxemburg had selected two delegates to attend the congress, Hugo Eberlein and Eugen Leviné. Only Eberlein reached Moscow, where he defended Luxemburg's point of view that the time was not ripe for the foundation of a Communist International. The Austrian delegate, Steinhardt, flamboyantly announced the imminent revolution in German Austria.[16] Eberlein, without information on the Austrian situation, wavered; he did not vote Yes to the formation of the Comintern, however, but abstained. Thus, in the founding document of the Communist International, the signature of the most important country for the expansion of the revolution was missing.

The Bavarian Council Republic

On April 7, 1919 civil war crystallized into the proclamation, in Bavaria, of the one German council republic. Of all the German *Länder,* Bavaria was the least integrated in the Reich. Prussian centralism was abhorred. Bavaria, outside the main path of the battles, had suffered relatively little from the war, but large groups of the middle class very early developed a pacifist attitude. Loyal to their own Wittelsbach dynasty, the Bavarian burghers felt no tenderness for the Hohenzollern Wilhelm II. When the defeat brought disaster to the Reich, Bavaria was shaken by a centrifugal tremor.

Independent Socialist Kurt Eisner, the first Republican premier, ruled Bavaria with a Social Democratic cabinet. Bavaria had relatively little large-scale industry; the city population was engaged principally in handicraft and small business. There was one big plant in Munich, the Maffey factory, and another erected by Krupp during the war, and Nuremberg, Fürth, Augsburg, and Schweinfurt had some industry.

---

[16] Karl Steinhardt, whom I knew very well, was a Hamburg printer who came to Vienna at the beginning of 1918. Under the influence of the Bremen Radicals, he joined our student group. On November 14, 1918, after the incidents at the Austrian parliament, we were arrested together and released after a few weeks in prison. Steinhardt survived twenty years of purges; he was installed in the first city administration when the Red Army marched into Vienna in 1945.

The Bavarian Social Democrats, weaker than in the Reich, had a rather large fringe of intellectuals and artists but relatively little contact with the peasantry.

Under these circumstances the mere existence of a socialist government antagonized important sectors of the population, excited by the news of civil war in other parts of the Reich and the crisis in Central Europe. On February 21, on his way to the Landtag, Eisner was assassinated by Anton Graf von Arco auf Valley, a twenty-one-year-old lieutenant in the Royal Bodyguard, member of one of the oldest noble families of Bavaria, accepted in the Thule Society, an exclusive monarchist club. An hour later the Landtag was opened by Eisner's colleague, Social Democratic Minister Ehrhart Auer, with a memorial speech. One Lindner, a butcher by trade, a member of the Workers' Council, shot and wounded Auer in the Landtag; he blamed the Social Democrats, "the murderers of Luxemburg and Liebknecht," for the assassination of Eisner. In the riot that followed several shots were exchanged and two men were killed—Oesel, a deputy of the Center Party, and a Major von Jahreis, a member of the General Staff in the gallery.

Munich was in a state of extreme agitation. Eisner, the pacifist socialist, was carried to his grave by an ecstatic following. A wreath was placed at the site of his death; the main portal of the Landtag was decorated with pictures and flowers. It was feared that Eisner's assassination was the prelude to a planned monarchist coup, that officers and students would eliminate the socialists from the administration by violence and proclaim a dictatorial rule in Munich. "The assassination of Eisner was regarded as the result of a great bourgeois conspiracy of officers and students." [17] During Eisner's funeral church bells were rung throughout Bavaria.

A few days later anarchist Erich Mühsam proposed to the Munich Workers' and Soldiers' Council that they proclaim a socialist republic. This proposal was adopted by 234 votes to 70, with the Spartakists voting against it. A government was formed, composed of Social Democrats, Independent Socialists, and anarchists. Despite their weak parliamentary representation, the USPD was influential among the

---

[17] Escherich-Heft, *Der Kommunismus in München.* Dritter Teil: *Dem Bolschewismus entgegen* (Munich, 1921), p. 10.

Munich workers and the Social Democrats had to compromise with them.

The first Bavarian council government has always been depicted as a half-crazy adventure of literati and intellectuals.[18] The bulk of the government was composed of representatives of both socialist parties, led by visionaries who believed religiously in the imminence of humanitarian socialism. All of them later proved to be serious militants, who suffered loyally for the cause they had adopted.

At the head of this group was Gustav Landauer, a cultured humanitarian anarchist, the author of a series of essays on Shakespeare, Hölderlin, and the French Revolution. He visualized socialism as an anti-autocratic coöperative. Landauer was an outspoken individualist, a defender of socialist morality, an opponent of terror and violence against the class enemy. Erich Mühsam, the other anarchist writer in the cabinet, had a following among intellectuals and young workers.[19] Ernst Toller, the third writer in the government, was in 1919 a young man uncertain in his politics. He also was what the Germans call an ethical socialist, a man who embraces socialism for its spiritual and moral values. Toller committed suicide in the United States, to which he escaped during the fascist era, depressed by the contrast between his socialist faith and Communist reality. The fourth outstanding figure of this group, Silvio Gesell, Minister of Finance, was also an anti-bureaucratic type. He was a follower of Henry George, a defender of a physiocratic money and land reform designed to give

---

[18] Compare the contemporary pamphlet written under the pen name Paul Werner by Paul Frölich, a Right-wing leader of the Communist Party expelled in 1929 for Bukharinist deviations. Werner represents the Bavarian Council Republic as a farce, opposed throughout by the Spartakusbund as an adventurist folly. He hardly mentions the events in the neighboring countries; for the Spartakusbund the Hungarian Soviet Republic, like that in Bavaria, was anathema, and its reports on them were as sparse as possible.

"The Bavarian Soviet Republic began as a farce. It ended as a tragedy. It was not created by Communists but was the product of the perplexity and intrigues of socialists in the government, of anarchistic Don Quixotes and opportunist Independent Socialists." (Paul Werner, *Die Bayrische Räterepublik: Tatsachen und Kritik*, Petrograd, 1920, p. 15.)

[19] Mühsam remained loyal to his ideas after his release from the Schönfeld Fortress, in which he was imprisoned for five years. In the Hohenstein concentration camp in 1933, the SS-guards forced him to sing the "Internationale" and killed him in the middle of a verse. His wife escaped to Russia, where she was arrested.

the peasant a new freedom and independence. The author of a book and various pamphlets on this subject, Gesell expressed his horror of the centralized state in picturesque terms. "The state is good enough," he said, "to carry our mail, sweep our streets, polish our boots, and perform similar minor tasks. But it should not interfere in the higher spheres of human life." However, in the utopian style characteristic of the Munich milieu, he proposed that state bakeries be set up throughout the land, to produce free bread for everyone, and not only bread but pastries and whipped cream.

The Bavarian Peasant Bund was represented in the cabinet by Kübler. Another member was Social Democrat Ernst Niekisch, a public-school teacher who later became well known as a National Bolshevik and an author. He published an aggressive anti-Nazi book [20] and suffered because of it a life sentence in the Brandenburg-Görden penitentiary from which he was liberated after Berlin's fall.

"The Foreign Minister" of this cabinet, Dr. Franz Lipp, sent two telegrams, one to Berlin and one to Moscow, which characterize best the spirit of the Bavarian revolutionaries. Jealous of its local prerogative, Bavaria had preserved after the foundation of the Reich its ambassador to Berlin, who in this period was Dr. von Preger. Lipp sent him the following telegram:

> The *opus primum nec non ultimum* of Mr. Preuss on the German constitution will never be binding law for Bavaria, for I cannot sacrifice the special rights of Bavaria, won by Bavarian blood at Wörth and Sedan; therefore I command that you immediately hand your resignation to Count Brockdorff-Rantzau. [21]

To Moscow Dr. Lipp broadcast the following:

> The proletariat of Upper Bavaria happily united. Social Democrats plus Independent Socialists plus Communists welded together as into one hammer. Liberal bourgeoisie completely disarmed as agents of Prussia. Bamberg seat of the fugitive Hoffmann, who has taken with him the key to my ministry toilet. Prussian policy, with Hoffmann as its lackey, aims to cut us off from Berlin-Leipzig-Nuremberg and from Frankfurt and the Essen coal region. At the same time they paint us to the Entente

---

[20] Ernst Niekisch, *Hitler—ein deutsches Verhängnis* (Berlin, 1932).
[21] Quoted in Werner, *Die Bayrische Räterepublik*, p. 77.

as bloodhounds and plunderers. The hairy gorilla hands of Gustav Noske, meanwhile, are streaming with blood . . . We want peace for all time. Immanuel Kant's *Perpetual Peace,* 1795, Theses 2–5. Prussia wants an armistice only to prepare a war of revenge.[22]

This government was unable to take the military measures necessary to defend its brand of socialism. As a first step, they tried to reorganize the University of Munich, center of monarchist student conspiracy. April 7 was proclaimed a national holiday, to celebrate the inception of the new regime. The town was painted in red; the masses were jubilant. The German revolution, in spite of its bitter defeats, was still young and full of hope, sure of the imminence of socialism, sure that the majority of the German people had only to proclaim it to breathe life into the aspirations of two generations.

This cabinet did not break up Bavarian institutions. The civil servants were kept on and assured of the benevolence of the new regime. A revolutionary tribunal of twenty-eight judges was set up to block new plots and assassinations.

However, the reality of the situation in Bavaria and in Germany soon unveiled its ugly features to the Munich enthusiasts. The German working class did not stand up and by its sheer weight crush its opponents. The convulsions that were destroying its vital forces continued. On April 5 the Spartakusbund called on its members to follow Communist discipline and abstain from coöperating in any way with the new cabinet.[23] Social Democrat Schneppenhorst, War Minister of the new cabinet, deserted Munich and went to Bamberg, where a counter government proclaimed its loyalty to Ebert. The Social Democrats of Bavaria were deeply shaken by this move; a secret plebiscite on April 11 of 7000 party members resulted in an even split for and against the Council Republic.

After the first twenty-four hours of enthusiasm, an uneasiness set

---

[22] Volkmann, *Revolution über Deutschland,* p. 223, quoting a document in the Reich archives. The theses of Kant are the following: "2. No state having an independent existence, whether it be small or great, may be acquired by another state through inheritance, exchange, purchase, or gift. 3. Standing armies shall after a time be entirely abolished. 4. No national debts shall be contracted in connection with the foreign affairs of the state. 5. No state shall interfere by force in the constitution and government of another state."

[23] Werner, *Die Bayrische Räterepublik,* p. 144.

in among the Munich workers, the march of the Freikorps throughout the Reich disquieted the Workers' Councils. However, the workers, being Bavarians, believed that Berlin would not dare invade Bavaria. But on April 13 the Munich garrison revolted, arrested several
members of the government, and transported them to the jail in
Erbach. This changed the mood profoundly; the Landauer cabinet
fell, and a Communist cabinet was installed.

It has often been asked in Communist literature why the party let
itself be forced into a policy that from the onset it judged disastrous.
Very simply, the Communists could not resist the drive of the Munich
workers, who, irritated after the garrison coup, wanted to defend
Munich.

At the head of the new group were Eugen Leviné, Max Levin,
Victor Axelrod. Leviné was not the personal emissary of Lenin and
Trotsky he was rumored to be, but one of many Russian revolutionary intellectuals who had fled from Tsarist Russia to a German university. He was a Russian who had embraced German culture; he
was a German of Russian origin.

Leviné was born in 1883 in St. Petersburg, son of a rich Jewish
merchant. Russian Jews, as Jews everywhere before 1933, admired
German culture. Eugen went to a German school in St. Petersburg
and afterwards to Heidelberg and Wiesbaden, where the many young
Russians formed a national and revolutionary fraternity. Leviné
went back to Russia in 1905, participated in the revolutionary struggle, was arrested and sent to the Schlüsselburg Fortress. He escaped
to Germany, was extradited to Russia and banished to Siberia, where
he worked in a lead mine. Again he escaped, and came back to Germany, his second homeland, via Tibet and Turkestan. He got his
doctor's degree in the summer of 1914 in Berlin and in 1915 was
drafted as a naturalized citizen. In the army he served first as interpreter in Russian prison camps and then in the infantry. At the end
of the war, he was employed in one of the war agencies in Berlin,
where he met the new residents of the Soviet Embassy. A member
of the Social Democratic Party, he joined the USPD and later the
Spartakusbund.

During the first months of the revolution, Leviné was active in the
Rhineland, Brunswick, and Saxony. He arrived in Munich in March

1919, in popular regard the personification of Bolshevism. Leviné had never been a member of the Lenin party nor a pupil of Leninist discipline.

The second Russian Bolshevik on the Munich scene was of the same grain. Max Levin was born in Moscow in 1885, also a son of a Jewish merchant. Arrested in the 1905 revolution, he escaped to Zurich, where he studied science. Here he came in contact with Lenin and met other members of the Bolshevik group, but he did not become a professional revolutionary. Levin went to Germany, became a German citizen, and continued his studies in science. Before the outbreak of the war, he was drafted into the infantry, and he participated in combat duty until 1918. In November of that year he went to Munich and as a Spartakist became president of the Soldiers' Council.

Another figure of interest in the new group was a young sailor, Rudolf Eglhofer, who had participated in the 1917 Kiel mutiny. Together with Reichspietsch and Köbes, he received a death sentence, which was later commuted to life imprisonment. Freed in 1918, he went to Munich.

The new leaders realized that all chance of survival depended on the immediate organization of military defense, which alone could prolong the Munich episode until the movement outside Bavaria gained enough momentum to comprise industrial regions. Eglhofer was charged with organizing a Red Army. The life span of the Bavarian Council Republic was too short, however, to permit the molding of the 20,000 workers he loosely formed into guerrilla brigades into anything like a regular army. His forces were reinforced by Russian prisoners of war from the nearby camp at Puchheim—a fact widely used in Berlin propaganda.

In a few days grim reality ended the short festival. There were three centers—Munich, with its Red Army; Bamberg, with the Social Democratic government constantly calling on the workers to desert the putschists; and Ingolstadt, where Noske's troops gathered to prepare the march on Munich.

In the camp of the revolutionaries there was increasing confusion and dissension. The USPD accepted Spartakist leadership, but reluctantly. Toller in particular resisted, and time was lost in negotiating with him; he finally resigned to take a military command. He defeated the Reichswehr troops at Dachau—an episode displaying military talents unexpected in the young Toller, and stimulating to the Munich revolutionaries. In the meantime, Colonel von Epp, organizing burgher guards, student volunteer corps, and Freikorps, got reinforcements from all sides, especially from Heidelberg and Tübingen. The Munich revolutionaries remained isolated; virtually no reinforcements from the Reich appeared. In the first days, however, the Red Army had local successes. Several fliers deserted the government troops. The revolutionaries were hopeful; there was unrest in all Germany, especially in neighboring Saxony.

But the Munich group was unable to attract the Bavarian peasantry and middle class to its side. At the beginning the countryside had remained indifferent, but now it was deeply disquieted by the Munich-Berlin war being fought on its soil. The USPD began to waver, and Toller proposed peace negotiation with Social Democrat Hoffmann. But as Hoffmann sided openly with Noske, and Noske sided openly with the old army, no reconciliation was possible.

On April 13, in the Luitpold Gymnasium, a group of workers killed ten prisoners, members of the Thule Society, which was considered the center of the counter-revolutionary conspiracy. Among the ten was one woman, Hella Gräfin von Westarp. The government had not ordered the execution of these persons as hostages, but it was so reported, and this incident of the civil war was utilized to the utmost to stigmatize the council cabinet as terrorist.

On May 1 the army entered Munich, preceded by a battalion of Social Democratic volunteers. Retaliation began, and out-terrored the terror of the Bavarian revolutionaries. Eglhofer was killed, as were many other Red Army prisoners. Landauer was manhandled and, after a summary court martial, executed. The workers' quarters were raided and the Freikorps men behaved in their usual manner. There was another episode, counterpart of the one in the Gymnasium. According to an eye witness, watching the executions at the Stadelheim prison:

> The moment a prisoner showed his face at the window, the soldiers shot at it. They did not want the others to see the summary executions in the prison yard. Thus thirty people were shot. I myself saw it. This was on Sunday, May 4, at 7:30 in the eve-

ning. The day before, several men had been shot in the street as
a demonstration. Two women went to the corpses and wept bitterly, "My darling, my poor darling." Then a soldier cried, "Take
the women, they belong to them." Thus they also came to
Stadelheim, hair down and in disorder; first came a Capucine
monk, praying, and after him the women. With "Jesus" on their
lips, they died under the salvo. The Capucine said to the soldiers, you should be ashamed. The soldiers laughed. They un-
dressed the bodies; they sought especially the shoes of the dead.
They took the rings from the fingers of the dead, and took their
watches.[24]

The Munich episode made a strong impact on the Bavarian middle
class, and increased their horror of the revolution and the revolutionaries. Bavaria became the *Land* with a perpetual state of emergency,
which hampered all attempts at socialist organization. The Communist Party went underground. Leaders not killed in the first days
were sentenced by civil courts to long prison terms—including the
leaders of the first cabinet, Toller, Mühsam, and the others. Leviné
was condemned to death on June 3 and executed a few days later.

For every German socialist, Munich became synonymous with reaction. Many a Munich socialist had to flee the city, and in most cases
the Berlin Social Democratic police protected these refugees. Without the civil war in Germany, Munich would never have become the
birthplace of the Hitler movement.

The Hungarian Soviet Republic

Isolated in a stable Europe, the Bavarian experience would have
been the farce, the tragi-comedy, it was termed by most contemporaries. The Bavarian Council Republic must be viewed against the
background of both continuing civil war in Germany and unrest
throughout Central Europe, Italy, and the Balkans.

From the first moment of the Russian revolution, Bolshevik propaganda had found an especially fertile ground among the prisoners of
Austria-Hungary, who became yet more eager after the downfall of
the Hapsburg monarchy. The returning prisoners found in their
new fatherlands neither economic nor political stability. All the

---

[24] Report of Wilhelm Creowdy, friend of Count Arco-Valley, quoted in Werner,
Die Bayrische Räterepublik, p. 110.

internecine irritations—the result of the Hapsburg art of playing one nation against another to the benefit of its own difficult equilibrium— survived the monarchy.

The Hungarian war prisoners produced a relatively important group of Communist neophytes, among whom Béla Kun rapidly won a reputation. Kun was born in 1886 in Szilágy-Cseh, in Transylvania, that disputed and troubled border country between Hungary and Rumania. Son of the village notary public, he graduated from the Gymnasium, and became a journalist and an employee of the workers' sick-benefit society in near-by Kolozsvár (Klausenburg), where he joined the Social Democratic Party. When the war broke out, he was drafted into the 21st Honvéd Regiment of Kolozsvár. Taken prisoner by the Russians in 1916, he was put in the camp at Tomsk, in Siberia.

Here he rapidly became popular among his camp comrades by his fervent socialist propaganda and his anti-Hapsburg attitude. When the revolution broke out he went to Moscow and, with his intimate friend Tibor Szamuély, organized a Hungarian Communist group.[25] In November 1918 Kun arrived in Budapest with the passport of an army doctor bearing the name Eugen Sebestyen. The Russian Red Cross mission, in Budapest under the terms of the Brest-Litovsk Treaty, assisted him in his first endeavors. With him came a group of former Hungarian socialists—Julius Alpari, Vladislav Rudas, Béla Szántó.

The Hungarian Communist Party was founded on November 21 and, in the insecure atmosphere of Budapest, rapidly won a growing influence. On February 21, 1919, after demonstrations and street riots, the Communist leaders were arrested and the Communist press closed down. In the following weeks the government rapidly disintegrated, under the pressure of Rumania and Czechoslovakia, who demanded the cession of border territories.

On March 21, the Hungarian Social Democratic leaders visited Béla Kun in his prison cell and asked the Communists to enter the government. In the prison, an inter-party agreement was signed, based on the following three points: (1) a Hungarian Soviet Republic

---

[25] In 1918 the Socialist Party of Great Britain published a compilation of the articles Kun had written for *Pravda* during that year: Bela Kun: *Revolutionary Essays* . . . (London, 1918).

was to be proclaimed in which both socialist parties, Social Democrats and Communists, would share governmental responsibility; (2) a revolutionary army was to be created immediately, to defend Hungary against Rumania and Czechoslovakia; (3) the Social Democrats and Communists were to merge into a united Socialist Party. This about face of the Social Democrats followed from their despair at maintaining alone the independence of Hungary against its greedy neighbors. On the same day that they visited Kun in jail, the cabinet received an ultimatum from the Entente, delivered by the French Colonel Vyx, demanding the immediate withdrawal of Hungarian troops from the Czech, Yugoslav, and Rumanian borders. The Hungarian socialists hoped for Russian protection and the elimination of their main enemy, Rumania, by Russian troops.

In this period, despite the weakness of the Bolshevik regime, hemmed in by interventionist armies, the appearance of the Red Army in Central Europe was considered an imminent possibility by both camps, revolutionary and counter-revolutionary alike. The turnabout of the Hungarian Social Democrats in twenty-four hours had shocked the West. From one day to the next, Paris, London, Berlin expected a similar move from the Social Democrats in Austria, who were in every respect in a much stronger position. Austria had neither a native Freikorps nor an occupation army; its new frontiers were secure; the Hapsburg collapse had left a social vacuum in which the Social Democratic Party was the only organized force. It was the only labor party in Europe that, by a mere declaration and completely without terror, could have taken power.

In reporting to the First Comintern Congress that revolution in Austria was imminent, Steinhardt had been somewhat inadequate. The Communists had less influence there than anywhere in Germany. The leaders of the Austrian Social Democrats stubbornly resisted any slip from the middle way they had chosen; compared with the Italian or the Hungarian socialists, their closest neighbors, they represented a moderate wing. They kept to this middle road by skillful maneuvering among their own members, who watched the development of the Russian revolution with increasing enthusiasm and demanded the adoption of Russian methods in Austria. Throughout the country, workers' councils were elected. In contrast to what happened in Germany, the traditional labor organizations did not fight these councils but attempted to absorb them. Every speech of a Social Democratic leader in Austria began with an attack on Noske and Ebert and ended with a solemn declaration of sympathy with Lenin and Trotsky. If the Bolshevik method could not be applied in Austria, it was only because the country was too weak, too dependent on foreign help.[26]

The Austrian Marxist school, led by Otto Bauer and Max Adler, had developed a theory of when democratic methods might be supplanted by the proletarian dictatorship. This would come about only if, after the proletariat had won a majority by parliamentary procedure, it was violently opposed by a reactionary minority. In this period the Austrian Social Democrats had the support of almost half of the electorate and hoped to get a majority in the near future. Their program of moderate socialism, however, was illusory in the political convulsion that shook all the Hapsburg-successor states.

The Hungarian Communists waited impatiently for the revolution in Austria. A group of propagandists and organizers were sent to Vienna, among them curious types calling themselves anarchists or anarcho-syndicalists. Of these a former Budapest lawyer, Ernst Bettelheim, gained a certain notoriety; he was the first in Europe to attempt to provoke a mass revolt by sabotage. On April 18 his group set fire to the Austrian parliament, and on the same night the Hungarian Communists attempted a coup d'état, but even most of the Austrian Communists resisted their effort, certain that the Social Democratic workers would not be led into action by such methods.

The labor movement was seized by a deep unrest: to join or not to join the Hungarian Soviet Republic; whether to form a bloc with Hungary in order to expand the socialist enclave into Italy and into Germany. The Social Democratic leaders had their hands full quelling uprisings in the party against its moderation. Nothing helped them more than the infantile and adventurist intervention of the Hungarian Communists in Vienna, which hindered much more than it helped the growth of solidarity among Austrian workers.

The Hungarian Soviet Republic had a short life, from March 21 to

---

[26] Cf. Karl Tomann and Elfriede Friedländer [Ruth Fischer], *Ist Deutsch-Oesterreich reif zur Räterepublik?* Reden auf der 2. Reichskonferenz der Arbeiter-räte Deutsch-Oesterreichs, 30 Juni 1919 (Vienna, 1919).

August 1, 1919. The Communist Party, inexperienced and lacking cadres, antagonized both the middle class and the peasants by a series of mistakes—especially the decree of April 4 by which all estates exceeding 100 *joch* were to be formed into producers' coöperatives. This socialization of the land was later termed a fundamental error by Lenin, who was trying to find a *modus vivendi* with the peasant majority in Russia. He watched with concern the wavering policy of the new Hungarian Socialist Party and suggested to Kun that he not abandon the independent organization of the Communist cadres. Kun rejected this advice, and this dispute was later the center of a wide discussion in the Comintern.

On June 24, a counter-revolutionary revolt broke out in Budapest, led by officers of the former Hungarian army. The revolt was quickly quelled, but it weakened the resistance to the invading Entente armies. At the end of June the Hungarians had a partial success against the Czechs, and for a few weeks there was a Slovak Soviet Republic. By a compromise reached at the beginning of July, the Hungarians evacuated Slovakia in exchange for a promised evacuation of the Hungarian territory occupied by the Rumanians. But the Rumanians continued to advance. On July 29 they crossed the Tisza River at Szeged, the key to Budapest. A counter offensive of the Hungarian army ended in a rout, and the Soviet government collapsed immediately after. On August 1 the Communists resigned, and the trade-unions set up a government, which a few days later was taken over by bourgeois parties.

Béla Kun, Eugen Varga, György Lukács, Mátyás Rákosi, among others, fled to Vienna, where they were interned in a special annex of the Steinhof lunatic asylum. On July 15, 1920, on a train of the Red Cross mission, they left for Russia, where they were well received by the Bolsheviks as the only Communist group in Europe with an important revolutionary experience of their own. They soon became integrated into the Russian party machine and got assignments in the state administration.[27]

---

[27] Béla Kun, especially, participated actively in the civil war and then became a close collaborator of the Comintern Presidium. In the summer of 1937, at the height of the great purge, Kun was arrested. Another political prisoner was with him in the military prison of Lefortovo, where he saw Kun returning from an investigation, raising his fist to the heavens in a silent gesture of despairing protest. It was not Vyshinsky's policy to allow important non-Russian Communists even the highly

Mussolini on the Horizon

In 1919 there was a revolutionary wave in the industrial centers of North Italy, the result of disappointment and economic difficulties following the end of the war and influenced by the Russian revolution.

In 1919–1920 the Socialist Party numbered 300,000 members, the trade-unions 2,000,000. The party had 156 deputies in the Chamber and a majority in 2022 village and town councils, including those in

restricted forum of the witness stand, and Kun was shot some time during 1937 behind closed doors.

Eugen S. Varga, the Minister for Economy of the Hungarian Soviet Republic, became the leading Soviet economist, who for twenty years analyzed the trends of capitalist economy for the Politburo. He was until January 1948 a member of the Soviet Academy of Sciences and editor of the *Journal for World Economics,* Moscow.

Toward the end of the Second World War, Varga had accepted "an assignment from the All-Union Communist Party to make an objective study of the effect of the war on capitalist economies and on their economic outlook in the post-war period. . . . He reported his conclusions in a monumental book that was circulated for a year only as a party document for use in guidance in formulating foreign policy. His conclusions were that objective analysis compelled him to adopt positions on the post-war relationship between the Soviet Union and the Western democracies that in every instance were the complete opposite to what are now basic tenets of the Communist Party line" (*New York Times,* January 25, 1948).

Julius Alpari was the founder of the first modern Communist press correspondence, the well known *Inprecor.* Mátyás Rákosi, Josef Pogány, Béla Vago, and many other Hungarian Communists became agents of the Comintern in Western Europe; under the name John Pepper, Pogány was the Comintern representative to the United States during the early twenties. György Lukács became a leading Marxist theorist, specializing in literary criticism.

The defeat of the Soviet Republic engendered a poisoned environment, in which factional strife developed to such a point that the Russian state authorities intervened in 1920 and arrested the dissenters. Cf. Vladislav Rudas, *Abenteurer- und Liquidatorentum: die Politik Béla Kuns und die Krise der K.P.U.* (Vienna, 1922).

In this struggle for survival, Mátyás Rákosi, the key figure in the Communist-dominated Hungarian government set up in 1945, came to the top of the heap. He had begun his Comintern career with errands to Western Europe during the early twenties; in both the Levi crisis in Germany and the Serrati crisis in Italy, he became notorious in socialist circles for the crude directness with which he carried out the Moscow directives. In 1925, together with Béla Szántó, another official of the Hungarian Soviet Republic, Rákosi returned illegally to Hungary, where he was arrested and sentenced to fifteen years' imprisonment by the Horthy government. He served his full sentence, and in 1940 he was to have been tried again, this time for his participation in the 1919 government. But the German-Soviet pact was then in effect, and the Hungarian government exchanged Rákosi for a group of Hungarian flags that had been taken to Moscow by the Tsarist army that had helped crush the Kossuth uprising in 1848. From his prison in Szeged, he was taken to Budapest police headquarters, where he signed a pledge never to return to Hungary; then he walked down the steps, entered the automobile from the Soviet Embassy that was waiting for him, and went off to the Moscow-bound train.

most of the urban centers.[28] After a loss during the war, the Socialist Party, the coöperatives, and the trade-unions gained converts; large and small municipalities were completely dominated by Socialists. The local proletarian dictatorship gained momentum and spread to the countryside. Even in those rural districts where it had been reformist, the Socialist movement in this period took a revolutionary turn.

The distinctive feature of Italian Socialism was its large influence among the peasants, especially among the farmhands in the Po plain. The farm tenants of Central Italy, originally conservative, joined in the agrarian revolt. There was a tradition of syndicalist direct action in North and Central Italy. Local communes, run by Socialists, continued to impose local taxes from the landowners. Employers were forced to deposit money as a guarantee that they would carry out the agreements the unions forced them to make. Finally many of the landowners fled their estates and sought refuge in the cities.[29]

In Bologna, the local dictatorship of Nicola Bombacci struck panic. In Turin, Antonio Gramsci, a native of Sardinia, developed a new theory of the factory council. During the struggle for power, *gli consigli di fabbrica* (factory councils) would be the instrument of a combined political economic struggle, and later they would be the nuclei out of which socialist society would grow. Gramsci had joined the party as a student and became editor of the *Avanti* ("Forward") in Turin. As a leader of the Communist wing in the Socialist Party, he founded the paper, *L'Ordine Nuovo* ("The New Order"). The occupation of the Turin factories was led by him and others like him. Arrested in Rome in November 1926, he spent long years in jail, where he died in the middle thirties from tuberculosis. His name and life have become part of the Italian Communist legend.

This momentous movement was dispersed because it lacked an energetic leadership. The Italian Socialist Party, one of the most humanist and idealist of the entire European family, had a pacifist tradition. All Italian Socialists admired the Russian revolution and its leaders, Lenin

[28] Ivanoe Bonomi, *From Socialism to Fascism: A Study of Contemporary Italy* (London, 1924), p. 36.
[29] Cf. A. Bordiga, "The History of Fascism," *The Labour Monthly*, London, February-March 1923, Vol. IV, pp. 93–99, 172–183.

and Trotsky, and despised Noske and Ebert as traitors. But they were unable to solve their own perplexing problems.

During 1920, the Italian party discussed affiliation to the Comintern at length and formed various wings. The mores of the Italian party did not permit the militants to expel their comrades merely because they were "reformist opportunists," and it was this issue of expulsion that formed the focus of the internal struggle. While the Socialists argued and wavered, an energetic socialist renegade arose, Benito Mussolini. All that he had learned in the movement, he applied to organizing the counter movement. Self-confident, of plebeian origin, with a wide knowledge of the Italian working class, he coördinated the militant elements, who were disgusted with the passivity of the old-generation leaders.

In Moscow, Lenin was perturbed by Mussolini's appearance. This renegade, he recognized immediately, was a precursor, a new word in counter revolution. Urgently he sent messages to Milan, Bologna, Turin, Rome, imploring the comrades to separate themselves from the temporizers and regroup the cadres for militant action.

All the various Italian party groups sent delegates to the Second World Congress in August 1920 to come to a settlement with the Comintern leadership on the Twenty-One Conditions.[30] G. Serrati, the leader of the Center group, defended his opposition to a split by pointing out that no machine had yet been invented to divine the thoughts of the Right-wingers, whose rhetoric was revolutionary enough. Lenin tried to come to terms, but without avail; the quibbling in the party went on.

When the delegates returned to their homeland, a spontaneous mass movement broke out, with new and unexpected forms. In September 1920, some six hundred thousand strikers occupied the factories, particularly in Turin and Milan. This plant occupation, this gesture toward workers' ownership, was expected by everyone in and out of Italy to develop into full-scale civil war. The government, intimidated by the scope of the action, let the movement peter out without opposition and by this wise policy saved itself. For lack of coördination and more fundamental aims, the strike resulted in no more than a small rise in

---

[30] See p. 140 ff., *infra.*

wages and a vague promise for workers' control of production, which was never put into effect. In April 1921, at its convention in Leghorn, the party split over the Twenty-One Conditions, with a small Communist majority. Serrati still firmly refused to sanction the expulsion of the Right; in 1924, his organization joined the Comintern by entering the Communist Party. But in these months the party had lost its stamina; the defeat of the syndicalist workers in Northern Italy invigorated Mussolini's bands in formation.

Thus, with the defeat in Hungary and Italy, the European revolution came to an anticlimax. If the Italian and Austrian socialists, with their formidable and well-trained organizations, had crossed the thin line that separated their declarations of principles from action, Hungary might have been the starting point of a Central European revolution. For a historic moment, the initiative for the transformation of the continent shifted from Berlin to Vienna–Budapest–Milan and was lost.

The defeat of the Bavarian Council Republic did not end the civil strife in Germany. The struggle between the Freikorps and workers' groups was so turbulent in industrial centers, particularly in Berlin, that for the better part of 1919 the Ebert cabinet preferred to remain in the quiet middle-class town of Weimar. Here, on August 11, 1919, the new constitution was adopted.

German Communists Underground

Shortly after the Hungarian defeat, in September 1919, the Spartakists held an underground party convention in Heidelberg. Just as Ebert had chosen Weimar as safer than Berlin, so the Spartakists selected a Southern town. Even so, the delegates had to change every day the place of their assembly and the name of the organization they pretended to be. This facilitated neither discussion nor democratic procedure.

Characteristically, the Spartakist convention did not survey the defeat in Central Europe and its implications for European socialism. These men, just emerged from battles in Berlin, Munich, Bremen, were blind to the inevitable invigoration the Freikorps movement would derive from the events in Hungary.

The defeat had torn the party into two conflicting wings. In the entire picture there was not a single positive feature. The best leaders were dead, hundreds of others arrested, other hundreds fled from their home towns, where they were best known and could organize with the best results. Newspapers and periodicals were semi-legal. And, above all, there was a general feeling of disorganization, of rudderless confusion. The fundamental controversy between Luxemburg and Liebknecht on the probable development of the German Republic continued in a scurrilous and distorted form among their successors. It centered around three major issues. The first, the liquidation of National Bolshevism, as represented by Wolffheim and Laufenberg, had been settled in substance before the convention, but its aftermath loaded the discussions with animosity. The second and third issues were the "trade-union question" and the "parliamentary question," from now on items on the agenda in every crisis in the German Communist Party.

The Left opposition, led at this time by Willi Münzenberg, proposed abstention from the Weimar parliament—a demonstrative gesture to indicate to the working class that a parliament elected in the middle of a civil war had no claim to democratic legitimacy. Participation in the elections would indicate that the Communists accepted the status quo created by the Freikorps. As always with the German Communists, this political problem was clouded by dogmatic verbiage.

The same argument was put forward in the discussion of the trade-union policy. Accepting union discipline, maintaining the laborious union routine, limiting union policy to the wage struggle, would indicate no less that the Communist Party accepted the new status of labor in the Weimar Republic. Legien and the trade-union bureaucracy, who had been the staunchest supporters of the war, were bound to Ebert, and Ebert to the army. It was, therefore, impossible to develop revolutionary cadres within the trade-unions. The individual worker was conditioned by the intimate tie that bound him, first of all, to his union. Communist followers and sympathizers had to be extricated from the stifling influence of "trade-union cretinism," which had brought the German labor movement to its present desperate state.

The bitter disappointment in the trade-union bureaucracy was so intense that even Paul Levi, one of the most moderate of the Spartakist leaders, a man well versed in the intricacies of German parliamentarianism, also advocated boycotting the trade-unions. Karl Radek, from his prison cell, intervened in August in favor of participation in both the elections and the trade-unions. Levi then reversed his position and corralled a majority behind Radek's platform. The delegates had no time even to read the new program. Under the pretext of conspiratorial precaution, the opposition was not informed of the place of meeting of the last session. Reformist Communism started by violating elementary party democracy. The substantial opposition was mechanically cut off from the convention. It split from the party and formed the KAPD (*Kommunistische Arbeiterpartei Deutschlands*— Communist Workers' Party of Germany), which lined up with the Dutch Communist Herman Gorter, author of an *Open Letter* to Lenin opposing his concept of the party and its relation to the working class.[1] In Berlin, where the Communists numbered some 12,000, the majority left the party, most of them joining the KAPD. After his return from Heidelberg, when Wilhelm Pieck spoke to the remaining loyal members (I was present at the meeting), he counted 36 heads. The figures were similar in Hamburg and Essen.

Starting from a criticism of traditional political action, the KAPD investigated all the problems of organizing the socialist society. It emphasized the necessity of forming class organizations, transcending both party and trade-union lines, to check any trend toward a party monopoly and State Party dictatorship. The "shop steward" was placed in opposition to a communist party striving for a monopoly of power. This tendency was in the tradition of German radical socialists, who had attacked the powerful Social Democratic machine that through two decades of sacrifice and devotion they themselves had built up.

In the fall of 1919 there was a resurgence of strikes in Berlin. Resistance to the Ebert cabinet flamed up on every occasion. The deep-rooted hostility of the Berlin workers crystallized around even slight incidents.

The electrical workers, led by one of them, Wilhelm Sylt, struck and cut off the city's power. Factories and public transport were paralyzed. Sylt was willing to resort to sabotage—even blowing up the central power stations. During the thirty years of German trade-unionism the workers had been trained by their union leaders in moderation, never to disrupt the economy to such an extreme degree. The Berlin and

---

[1] Cf. Bernhard Reichenbach, "Zur Geschichte der KAPD," *Archiv für die Geschichte des Sozialismus und der Arbeiterbewegung* (Leipzig, 1928), XIII, 117–140.

Prussian authorities reacted to the threat by organizing Technical Emergency Squads (*Technische Nothilfe*), composed of engineering students. In the following period, these Teno auxiliaries became one of the most hated, though ineffective, of the anti-labor organizations.

Wilhelm Sylt, a quiet and discreet man, an intelligent and highly skilled worker, rapidly gained authority. Within a few months after the withering away of the Shop Stewards' movement, the Berlin factories produced a new type out of the same milieu. Sylt was neither a politician nor an orator; he was eager, not to coin formulas, nine, ten, or fifteen planks of a political platform, but to find effective measures against the military.

The electrical workers raised again the question of the status of the shop stewards and factory councils in the new German Republic. Article 165 of the Weimar Constitution granted them only a limited "share in management," in order to stimulate production and maintain industrial peace. At a turbulent demonstration before the Reichstag building on January 13, 1920, protesting this limitation, several participants were killed or wounded. After it, the Bannmeile Decree, forbidding demonstrations in the center of the city, was passed. The *Betriebsrätegesetz* (law on factory councils), implementing Article 165, marked the end of any hope organized labor had had to share political and economic power in the new state on equal terms with the entrepreneurs. The function of the trade-unions and their representatives, the factory councils, in defending rights already acquired and raising the workers' living standard presupposed a free-enterprise economy of continuing recovery and stability. This new law was intended to bring to a close the tumultuous struggle for workers' management and to adapt the councils to a capitalist economy.

The Officers' Rebellion

Now that the councils had suffered a setback, the military hoped to push their newly won advantages against the whole of organized labor, as a preliminary to a complete restoration of pre-war Germany. The revolt of the army against Ebert, known as the Kapp-Lüttwitz putsch, was prepared under the eyes of the government. The rebellion found a ready ferment in the conditions of the Versailles Treaty, which stipulated the reduction of the army from 400,000 to 200,000 and finally, by July 10, 1920, to 100,000 men. Of 24,000 old army officers only 4,000 could be included in the new Republican army, the Reichswehr, and the rest had to look for a place in the precarious civilian life of the hated Republic.[2] So radical a reduction of the officer corps endangered the schemes of the General Staff, and they combined a fight against it with a crusade against the prosecution of the Kaiser and some eight hundred other personages as war criminals.

From the Republic's first days the Freikorps officers had intended to set up a military dictatorship at the first possible moment. At the end of 1919 they circulated a pamphlet entitled *Reflections on Dictatorship* among their troops. In March 1920, one portion of the General Staff, in alliance with the Freikorps commanders, decided to strike decisively. On March 10 General Walther von Lüttwitz appeared in Ebert's reception room with a written ultimatum demanding the immediate transfer of power of the Social Democratic government to neutral experts, that is, high civil servants of the Imperial Reich. The Reichstag was to be dissolved, and there would be elections for a new National Assembly under the auspices of the army-established cabinet. Ebert was to resign; a plebiscite would elect a new Reich president. Delivery of war matériel to the Entente was to be stopped. Another most important point was the purge of the Reichswehr: the small group of generals convinced that the army was best served by cooperation with the Social Democrats was to be dismissed.

The conspirators offered to make Noske dictator. One morning he found a copy of *Reflections on Dictatorship* on his desk. One chapter was entitled "The Person." "A dictator, whose task is to save what can yet be saved, must be a personage popular in the broadest circles . . . Anyone looking over the outstanding men of the country will hit on one name as self-evident—Noske."[3] Shortly before the uprising, this offer was renewed orally in the name of the conspirators by Hauptmann Pabst,[4] whom Noske calls the real organizer and chief of the Garde Kavallerie Schützen Division. In this at-

---

[2] "This clause [of the Versailles Treaty] was another source of danger to the Republic not yet well established. Its fulfillment meant that several hundred thousand young men would be thrown into the streets without the possibility of finding a situation in civilian life." Otto Braun, *Von Weimar zu Hitler*, p. 85.

[3] Gustav Noske, *Von Kiel bis Kapp*, p. 196.

[4] E. O. Volkmann, *Revolution über Deutschland*, p. 322.

tempt to combine the restoration forces with a proletarian mass leader, we find the first and most striking example of a new trend of the German counter revolution, the incorporation into one totalitarian-state apparatus of elements of both labor and the successors to the Imperial Reich. Noske declined; he knew that he personally, disconnected from the Social Democratic organization, would join the generals alone, without influence. Noske was, and remained, a loyal member of the Social Democratic Party; for all its tragic errors, German Social Democracy did not produce a Mussolini.

At first Ebert did not believe that the threat was serious and remained peacefully in Berlin. On the morning of March 13, a so-called "Marine Brigade" under the command of General von Lüttwitz marched into Berlin. It had been stationed in Döberitz, in the environs of the city; it was led by Captain Hermann Ehrhardt, a *Landsknecht* leader who had gained stature in the Baltic borderland war.[5] The men sang as they marched into Berlin:

> Hakenkreuz am Stahlhelm,
> Schwarzweissrotes Band;
> Die Brigade Ehrhardt
> Werden wir genannt.

(A swastika on our helmet, and a black-white-red band. We are called the Ehrhardt Brigade.)

Ehrhardt surrounded the government buildings and proclaimed the overthrow of the Ebert cabinet. Wolfgang Kapp, a high-ranking civil servant of the German National People's Party, and General von Lüttwitz were declared the heads of the new government.

Ebert called General von Seeckt and Major von Schleicher to the Reich Chancellery to work out a plan to expel the rebels. Seeckt and Schleicher coolly declined. They would never agree to a fight of

---

[5] Another Marine Brigade, under one Löwenfeld, was stationed in Silesia. Although composed exclusively of officers and sergeants, these troops sought to capture some of the glamour that the navy retained in German folklore with their self-given name of Marine Brigade. Following the Versailles stipulations, the Allied control authorities had demanded their dissolution; the new Reich navy, which had a permitted strength of 15,000, wanted to incorporate the brigades. Cf. Rudolf Mann, *Mit Ehrhardt durch Deutschland: Erinnerungen eines Mitkämpfers von der 2. Marinebrigade* (Berlin, 1921).

The *Landsknechte* were rough fifteenth-century soldiers often engaged in free-booting.

Reichswehr against Reichswehr; such fratricide would destroy Germany. They proposed to come to terms with the rebels. Ebert finally realized that if he did not leave Berlin at this moment he would not survive the crisis. The government fled to Dresden, but here the Reichswehr garrison was considering arresting Ebert's cabinet as rebels against the new government. So they fled again, this time to Stuttgart; in the South there was a better chance for resistance to the Berlin dictatorship.

Carl Legien

In this moment of extreme danger to the Republic, in which his alliance with the generals turned against Ebert, the German Federation of Labor decided to intervene along a line fundamentally contradictory to all its traditions and behavior. They called a nationwide general strike against the rebels. A joint committee was formed to direct the strike, in which all labor organizations, the Communists included, took part.

This was perhaps the most complete political general strike in a modern industrial country. German economy was brought to a standstill. From one hour to the next, no train ran, there was no gas, no electricity, only a limited water supply. The rebels had excellent artillery and machine guns, airplanes, well-trained and reliable troops, a well-conceived strategic plan for the conquest of Germany. But against the power of organized labor they were paralyzed; no army can function in a vacuum.

On the second day of the putsch, General Gröner tried to mediate between the Ebert government and the Kapp group, but without avail. Kapp and Lüttwitz capitulated after three days. When the General Staff realized the depth of their defeat, they made their peace with Ebert. He returned to Berlin; the Social Democrats called off the strike; and Seeckt and his associates remained at their posts of command—Ebert could not risk breaking with the army forces.

The central figure of this general strike was fifty-nine-year-old Carl Legien, the organizational genius of the German Federation of Labor. On March 13 he remained in Berlin; according to his vehement criticism the Ebert cabinet also should have remained to lead the resistance. The old legalist went underground and, indifferent to the good possibility of losing his life, from his underground head-quarters he directed the *Generalstreik*.

Carl Legien's story is most revealing for the character of the German labor movement. With his lifelong friend and biographer, Theodor Leipart, he had worked in his youth as a lathe operator in Hamburg. In creating the federation of German trade-unions, he overcame only with great difficulty, on the one hand, the tradition of localism, the result in part of the craft structure from which German industry had started, and, on the other, the ambition of the party leaders, who in the nineties jealously fought the competition of the trade-union or-ganization. In founding the *Generalkommission,* Legien coalesced into one powerful national body the splintered local guilds.

For thirty years, as an inveterate defender of gradualism, he fought first Bebel and Auer and later Luxemburg and Liebknecht. He de-veloped the technique of the economic strike into a highly precise instrument for bargaining, a knife to be applied only by skilled sur-geons and only with infinite precautions and in case of utter emer-gency.[6] Legien's political religion can be summed up in his often-quoted slogan against the revolutionary Social Democratic wing: *Generalstreik ist Generalunsinn* (A general strike is general nonsense).

Legien was the staunchest supporter of the war and the aspirations of the Reich. "In a letter to Jouhaux in November 1914, he wrote that it was thoroughly understandable that after the outbreak of the war the workers in France no less than in Germany sided with their Fatherland."[7] Ludendorff and Hindenburg honored Legien for his patriotism and invited him many times to their headquarters; he was photographed at their side. By these actions he attracted to his person a really virulent hatred.

Legien advocated the expulsion of Liebknecht from the party; for the organizer of disciplined millions, Liebknecht's break of Social Democratic discipline was unpardonable. In 1917, defending his pro-war policy at the metal workers' union convention, Legien de-manded that the abscess be cut immediately, before the entire body became infected. He emphasized that if the party had followed his

---

[6] Cf. Carl Legien, *Das Koalitionsrecht der deutschen Arbeiter in Theorie und Praxis* (Hamburg, 1899).

[7] Theodor Leipart, *Carl Legien: Ein Gedenkbuch* (Berlin, 1929), p. 100.

advice and expelled Liebknecht, it would have avoided the split. "Party discipline must be maintained at any price."

Now the aging union leader suddenly realized that the alliance with the military was leading to the extermination of organized labor. It was the nationalistic, prudent old trade-unionist who at this moment made the most audacious political proposals. When the Ebert cabinet returned to Berlin, Legien, contemptuously pointing to Ebert and Noske, declared that without the intervention of the unions they would be dead men. He also had his ultimatum to lay before them.

> After the government's return, Legien demanded in the name of the Central Strike Committee the elimination from office of the Ministers Noske, Heine, Oeser. He demanded further that the Trade-Union Federation be decisive in the reconstruction of the government, have the key role in economic and social-political affairs.[8] All those who had collaborated with the putschists should be strictly punished; all Reich and *Länder* police troops should be thoroughly purged of anti-Republican and dubious elements. Until these demands were carried out, even though the Kapp rebels had capitulated, the general strike would continue. It was an exciting parley that took place on March 19 between Legien's trade-union delegation and the Reich cabinet. It lasted the whole night, and the well-known agreement was reached only at the dawn of March 20.[9]

The Social Democratic leadership stigmatized Legien's ultimatum as blackmail, and in the end the politicians won the upper hand. In

---

[8] Even during the first period of the Weimar Republic, the Social Democratic Party was ordinarily a minority in the cabinet. It had a majority during three and a half months in 1919, the period when the Versailles Treaty was signed, the Constitution adopted, the Reichswehr organized. In early 1919 and 1920, it had parity.

Chancellor	Cabinet Installed	No. of Ministers	No. of Social Democratic Ministers
1. Scheidemann	Feb. 13, 1919	14	7
2. Bauer 1	June 21, 1919	13	7
3. Bauer 2	Oct. 2, 1919	14	7
4. H. Müller 1	March 27, 1920	14	7
5. Fehrenbach	June 21, 1920	13	0
6. Wirth 1	May 10, 1921	13	4
7. Wirth 2	Oct. 26, 1921	13	5

[9] Leipart, *Carl Legien*, p. 117.

the same night the trade-unions approached the USPD to ask whether they would enter a labor coalition; the USPD negotiated with the Communist Party to determine whether it would support the new cabinet. Legien was unable to overcome the opposition of the Social Democratic politicians, who feared that such a labor cabinet would stimulate the revolutionary movement to new vigor. The Left wing of the USPD, on the other hand, also opposed the leadership of Legien; the deep-rooted conflict between nationalist and pacifist socialists could not be healed so easily. During this same night Wilhelm Pieck and Jakob Walcher promised the loyal opposition of the Communist Party to such a labor government.

During the Kapp putsch the Communist Party, debilitated by the Heidelberg split, reached new depths of passivity. The Politburo, led by August Thalheimer, analyzed the biggest mass strike Germany ever saw as a fight between two counter-revolutionary wings, Kapp and Ebert. The Communists were told by their Politburo not to support the Ebert government against Kapp. When this manifesto of the Central Committee, sent by special couriers, reached the local organizations, many of them burned it. Paul Levi was in prison; when he was released a few days later, he quickly adjusted Thalheimer's line. The policy of the Communist organizations throughout the Reich, however, reflected this initial weakness and confusion. Only months after the expulsion of the KAPD, this line of Thalheimer produced another opposition within the party, led by Berlin and Hamburg, which called itself the Left.

The Kapp putsch, this episode in the long fight between the forces of the restoration and German labor, illustrates the impasse of German socialism. Legien's belated proposal was the only reasonable and effective policy; a militant trade-union government would have quelled Nazism before it could have developed the strongholds it had already won. But Legien's own past handicapped him in his attempt to make such a decisive turn.

Red Partisans in Germany

The united action of all labor organizations had brought the subterranean revolutionary torrent to the surface. The putsch of the hated Reichswehr was an injection to all radical groups, convinced since 1918 that a showdown between the workers and the forces of reaction was unavoidable. But this time the workers did not discuss various platforms on how to dissolve the army, but armed themselves for resistance to the putschists.

This was particularly so in the Rhineland and the Ruhr, where the commanding officer was Generalleutnant Freiherr von Watter; his Reichswehr troops worked closely with the Freikorps Lichtschlag. One typical Lichtschlag incident of 1919 is symbolic. The Freikorps had surrounded a conference of worker delegates in Werden, near Essen, and had shot into the meeting hall. All fled into the open, where the shooting was continued. The Freikorps took dozens of prisoners, led them through the town, spat on them, beat them, called them *Schweinehunde,* and shot them as they marched. From a victory of the Kapp rebels, the workers expected a regime punctuated by hundreds of such incidents. As Severing put it in his memoirs, "where workers and soldiers collide, blood flows." [10]

When Legien called the general strike, he was answered in this region with the formation of workers' battalions, calling themselves the Red Ruhr Army. They expected hourly the invasion of Watter, who was in open sympathy with the Kapp rebels, and who had rallied his troops around his headquarters in Münster. Severing reports that his attempt on the day of the putsch to get Watter's unambiguous declaration of loyalty to the Ebert-Bauer cabinet was unsuccessful. The Freikorps were streaming into the Ruhr. On March 14 the Freikorps Lichtschlag, under Hauptmann Hasenclever, were beleaguered in the small town of Wetter by worker guerrillas, who disarmed them. Fighting developed in the entire area and was especially intense in Dortmund; it spread rapidly from the Ruhr to Wuppertal, to Remscheid, Elberfeld-Barmen. Workers seized arms in Bochum, stormed Essen.

These guerrilla groups were made up not of peasants entrenched in the woods but of workers organized around their plants and establishing their battalions and divisions parallel with the numerous in-

---

[10] Carl Severing, *1919/1920 im Wetter- und Watterwinkel; Aufzeichnungen und Erinnerungen* (Bielefeld, 1927). Severing reports that the investigation committee of the Prussian Diet later stated that the commander, Lieutenant Thiel, had gone beyond his authority.

dustrial hamlets, small towns, and cities of the industrial region. The formation of these battalions was greeted with enthusiasm; Social Democratic and Catholic workers alike joined in the movement to throw Watter and the Freikorps out of the Ruhr, to march to Berlin, to arrest Kapp and Lüttwitz, to establish a workers' government, to crush the military conspiracy once and for all. In a few days this loosely knit guerrilla army began to work out means of closer coordination. In various key points local leaders arose. Virtually the entire population was sympathetic, supported them with all the means at their disposal; and in the end this improvised army was estimated by its opponents at about 50,000 men.

The Red Army reached its greatest maturity in the Ruhr, but there were similar trends in Saxony and Thuringia, in Southern Germany, and in the industrial centers of the North and the Baltic area. At the time of the Kapp putsch, I was returning to Berlin from a party convention in Durlach and was stranded by the rail strike in Leipzig. The organization of the Leipzig workers went along the same lines as in the Ruhr, except that there the Social Democratic machine put more obstacles in the way of the organizers. The city was full of news about the organization of the Chemnitz workers, who would march to Leipzig and unite to encircle Berlin.

Chemnitz was the strongest organization of the Communist Party, but, like all others, during the putsch it was out of touch with the Central Committee in Berlin. Heinrich Brandler, leader of the Chemnitz Communists, acted quickly and effectively in the city proper; workers' councils were set up, and all persons who might support Kapp were disarmed and arrested. The councils occupied the City Hall and prepared the city for its defense. But apart from these security measures, no action was taken; no action outside the city proper was even considered. In Mittweida, a small town near Chemnitz, the engineering students sympathized with the Kapp rebels; but when they barricaded themselves in their school building, they were not attacked—to spare bloodshed.

Near Chemnitz, in Falkenstein, Max Hoelz organized his guerrilla troops.[11] With offensive spirit, they tried not only to defend their

---

[11] Max Hoelz, one of the most interesting leaders of German Communism, acted outside conventional labor tradition and discipline. Son of a farmhand, born

home town against a possible attack but to spread throughout the region. Brandler maneuvered skillfully to avoid any inroad of the Hoelz troops into his peacefully organized Chemnitz district. A few days after the putsch, Hoelz was solemnly expelled by the Chemnitz Communists for lack of party discipline. "We herewith solemnly declare that we reject the activities of Hoelz, who has attempted to substitute himself for mass action. By these activities Hoelz and his comrades have put themselves outside the party; the party can live only when the entire membership adheres to its program." [12]

In effect, the Chemnitz Communists marked time and thus prevented the fusion of the Saxon partisans. The isolated Leipzig resistance movement was quelled in the same moment that Ebert returned to Berlin. On March 18 the general strike was called off in Saxony, and General Senfft von Pilsach signed an agreement with two Social Democratic ministers, Schwartz and Lipinski, giving the Reichswehr a free hand in disarming the worker snipers still resisting.

Effects of the Putsch

The Kapp putsch was depicted by all contemporary observers as the revolt of an insignificant army caucus at the fringe of the regular army, without political or military importance. In fact, the officers' rebellion was decisive in the life of the Weimar Republic; it facilitated

---

in 1889 in the poor Vogtland, in Saxony, he did not join any labor organization before 1914. He returned to Germany from England shortly before the outbreak of the war and participated as a foot soldier in active duty on the Western front. In 1918 he organized the unemployed in Falkenstein, his home town, and a few months later joined the USPD. By his activist initiative, he soon became popular in the entire region. During the Kapp putsch, he won Reich-wide fame by his talented organization of workers' brigades. Arrested in 1921, he was condemned to life imprisonment, of which he served seven years. Released in 1928, he became for a time a celebrated figure of Communist propaganda and went to Moscow.

In the Soviet Union, he soon had serious difficulties with the authorities. In May 1933 a party order sent him to Nizhniy-Novgorod, where he was killed by the GPU. His funeral was made an occasion for party mourning; André Marty and Fritz Heckert were his pallbearers. This murder of a well-known and well-beloved Communist leader, a top secret in Comintern circles, contributed much to the disintegration of Communist cadres in Hitler Germany. (Cf. Max Hoelz, *Vom "Weissen Kreuz" zur Roten Fahne: Jugend-, Kampf-, und Zuchthauserlebnisse*, Berlin, 1929; Karl I. Albrecht, *Der verratene Sozialismus: Zehn Jahre als hoher Staatsbeamter in der Sowjetunion*, Berlin, 1939.)

[12] Heinrich Brandler, *Die Aktion gegen den Kapp-Putsch in Westsachsen* (Berlin, 1920), p. 59.

considerably the subsequent victories of the counter-revolutionary forces. It was a revolt of the entire army against the Republic, a campaign planned in two movements. First, the rebels in Berlin were to paralyze the Ebert cabinet. Seeckt would await the result of this coup, and if it had been successful the entire Reichswehr staff would then have gone over to the dictator.

On the other hand, the Red Army in the Ruhr could be called an army only metaphorically. There was no staff of military experts, there was no regular equipment, there was not even competent political coördination of all the dispersed worker battalions. But in spite of these fundamental weaknesses, the *levée en masse* in the Ruhr aroused panic among the professional soldiers trained in the Imperial army. The blast furnaces and the mines in Dortmund, Bochum, Gelsenkirchen, the metal works in Essen, the textile works in Elberfeld-Barmen and Krefeld, were the natural units of this army; but enthusiasm, initative, organizational experience were its real force. Beginning as a defensive against the invasion of the hated Freikorps, it rapidly transformed itself into a dynamic crusade against the Reichswehr. The General Staff quickly recognized its miscalculation. They had hoped that the fearful time had past when "there was a plethora of officers without soldiers and masses of soldiers in whom the last remnants of discipline had completely vanished." [13]

It was exactly this unfolding resistance in the Ruhr that brought about the realignment between the Reichswehr and the Ebert cabinet. The artist of this arrangement was Generaloberst Hans von Seeckt, since 1919 the creator and defender of the new German army. Seeckt, a military delegate to Versailles, had added his name to a statement protesting the signing of the treaty. His original concept for the reorganization of the army had been the division of the troops into "large" and "small" Reichswehr brigades, the large ones for the fight on the border, and the small ones for combating the internal enemy. On Seeckt's initiative, General von Lüttwitz had been designated to lead the fight within Germany. Seeckt had good contacts with the Freikorps and the Black Reichswehr divisions—troops not authorized by the Versailles Treaty.

---

[13] Generalleutnant a. D. von Metzsch, "Seeckts Beispiel als Soldat und Mensch," *Generaloberst von Seeckt, Ein Erinnerungsbuch,* p. 63.

When Ebert returned to Berlin, Seeckt kept the upper hand in all matters concerning the rebellious Reichswehr troops. He maneuvered with the greatest care not to come in conflict even with Captain Ehrhardt, to whom he wrote on March 22, 1920, that he recognized the excellent discipline of Ehrhardt's Marine Brigade . . . "and I thank you for accepting my command. I am convinced that I can rely completely on the 2nd Marine Brigade and its commander in the bitter fights before us with the armed Spartakist terror. I give you my personal guarantee that the warrant allegedly issued for your arrest will not be valid as long as the Marine Brigade is under my command." [14]

Seeckt's reference to the Spartakist terror concerned the Ruhr. The Reichswehr found there an excellent opportunity to change its partial defeat into a success, to carry on its internal warfare, and so to consolidate its position in the government, which had been endangered by Legien's policy in the general strike. The Reichswehr action in the Ruhr was a well-planned counter blow to block the way to a labor government, aimed at the Social Democrats no less than at all other labor groups.

Several Social Democrats of high rank and influence tried to avoid the clash between the army and the workers. On March 23–24 a conference took place in Bielefeld, the gate to the Ruhr, convoked by the unions, the three workers' parties, and the workers' defense battalions. Carl Severing, Reich and State Commissar for Westphalia, and Otto Braun, premier of the Prussian government, took part as representatives of the Ebert cabinet. The Communist Party was represented by Wilhelm Pieck. [15] The local workers' organizations intended to coördinate the defense squads throughout the Ruhr into a single regional defense corps, to repulse the probable repetition of the Kapp putsch and by its very existence counterbalance the Freikorps, the Black Reichswehr divisions, and the numerous other secret counter-revolutionary partisans. The Bielefeld joint declaration put a stop to this initiative.

Trade-union representatives talked the workers' delegates into

---

[14] Berthold Jacob, *Wer?, Aus dem Arsenal der Reichstagsbrandstifter* (Strasbourg, 1933).

[15] Paul Merker, in *Deutschland, sein oder nicht sein?* (Mexico, 1944), I, 64, gives a detailed analysis of the Kapp events, but is silent concerning Pieck's signature to the Bielefeld agreement, which was bitterly attacked by his own followers.

limiting themselves to a local workers' defense corps, a kind of auxiliary police. The representatives of the Ebert government solemnly promised that if the compromise was accepted the Reichswehr would not invade the Ruhr. A joint statement was accepted, known as the Ten Points of Bielefeld. But Ebert's Chancellor, Social Democrat Hermann Müller, was too weak to resist Seeckt's continued pressure. With story after story of the Ruhr terrorists circulating in Berlin, Seeckt got what he wanted—a governmental order to send the Reichswehr into the region. On March 28, Hermann Müller tore up the Bielefeld agreement and sent an ultimatum to the Ruhr workers for the immediate and complete dissolution of all workers' defense corps and the immediate surrender of all arms. General Watter, the Kapp rebel,[16] and the Freikorps Lichtschlag reinstated the authority of Berlin in Essen. Carl Severing accompanied him as civil adviser. The Freikorps had a heyday.

The Reichswehr was most eager for this action, for it gave the army an opportunity to regain control of the zone demilitarized by the Versailles Treaty. The Entente Commission in Paris gave its permission to have the troops enter the 50-kilometer neutral zone, and on April 3 the invasion began. Then, as a reprisal for this violation of the Versailles Treaty, on April 6 French troops occupied Darmstadt and Frankfurt am Main. General Degoutte, their commander, openly criticized the cruelty of Watter's officers.

Watter's troops took their full revenge.

> When the troops marched into Fröndenburg, cheers to the Emperor were heard, in which officers and some of the troops joined . . . Officers and men felt themselves again in Imperial Germany. In Buer and Bottrop arrested workers were maltreated if they refused to sing *Heil Dir im Siegerkranz* [the Imperial anthem]. . . . This attitude of the troops towards the representatives of the working class was the less understandable because the trade-unions and the Social Democrats did everything they could to assist the Reichswehr in carrying out their difficult task.[17]

---

[16] "In Münster we negotiated with Reich and State Commissar Severing and the commander of the troops, General Watter. The latter did not impress me favorably. He made ambiguous statements, and it was difficult to nail him down to clear, definite tactics." (Braun, *Von Weimar zu Hitler*, p. 96.)

[17] Severing, *1919/1920 im Wetter- und Watterwinkel*, p. 207 ff.

The Reichswehr established military courts, which with perfunctory formality sentenced dozens of local leaders to death or long terms of imprisonment. A part of the Red Ruhr Army continued to fight. A revolutionary committee was set up in Mühlheim with headquarters in Gelsenkirchen. A member of the KAPD, Gottfried Karusseit, signed himself commander-in-chief of the Western Sector of the Red Army; in the Prussian Diet, Pieck characterized him as a petty bourgeois gone wild. There were skirmishes in the whole region—in Wesel, in Gelsenkirchen, in Dortmund. There were wild rumors everywhere: Lenin spoke at the market place in Dortmund.

The Supreme Court was very clement toward the Kapp rebels. Of all the conspirators only the former Imperial police president of Berlin, von Jagow, was convicted; he was sentenced to five years of "honorary" confinement.

The Ruhr offensive reëstablished the shaken authority of the Reichswehr. The general strike had made possible the survival of the Ebert cabinet, and the trade-unions got nothing in return; the army had rebelled against the Ebert cabinet, and in return was sent to clean up the Ruhr. The final balance sheet of the Kapp putsch was favorable to the army.

The coöperation between Noske and Lüttwitz had been so intimate that, principally under Legien's pressure, Noske was forced to resign as Minister of War. His resignation marked the end of an era; it was the collapse of Ebert's alliance with the General Staff and finished the Social Democratic attempt to control the Reichswehr. Noske was succeeded by the Wurttemberg Democrat, Otto Gessler, whose efforts in the Reichstag to further rearmament were perfectly coördinated with Seeckt's far-reaching plans.

Within the Reichswehr, labor's easy victory in the general strike resulted in deep and enduring convulsions. The establishment of a military dictatorship pure and simple was recognized as an unrealizable goal. The Imperial generals cooled toward their radical fringe, the Freikorps captains and lieutenants; Seeckt especially resisted the tendency of the radicals to push him into the role of a military dictator. On the other hand, Seeckt cleansed the Reichswehr of Social Democratic interference. When Ebert asked him whom the Reichswehr really supported, he replied, "The Reichswehr, Herr Ebert, backs me." Seeckt's reorganization of the Reichswehr was under the cover of Weimar legality and in the face of opposition from its Black divisions. Soon after he became Chief of Staff following the Kapp putsch, several officers demonstratively walked out of a conference at which he was presiding.

The Kapp putsch was decisive in the development of German Communism. Until this time, the Spartakists had been an isolated minority. The German worker, grown up in the spacious building of the million-member party and the million-member trade-unions, looked down on the Spartakists with the contempt of the experienced organizer; they were intellectuals, outsiders. Until March 1920, there was no substantial influx of USPD members into the Spartakusbund. Among the German workers the prestige of the Moscow Bolsheviks was incommensurably greater than that of their German followers. The Kapp putsch stimulated new impulses in the USPD. After a two-year experience with Lüttwitz, Seeckt, Watter, Ehrhardt, the workers were convinced that these men would not be disarmed by well-rounded formulas; they had lost their hope that the Social Democratic government would act against the open and secret rearmament of the restoration. The mood prevailing in the spring of 1920 was, "We need an organization able to cope with the excellently organized Freikorps and their allies in the army"; and it was at this moment that the Comintern stepped in.

The Second World Congress

In spite of the primary importance of Germany in the Bolshevik concept of the world revolution, the actual relations between the two organizations, the Russian Communist Party and the German Communist Party, were casual and intermittent during the period of the Russian and German civil wars. After Joffe and Bukharin had been expelled from Germany and after Radek, with only a few weeks of participation in German Communist affairs, had been arrested, there was no important Bolshevik to take a part directly in the early development of the German Republic.[18]

---

[18] In 1919, the Comintern established at Berlin a West European Bureau, organized by J. Thomas with the assistance of M. G. Bronski, which limited its activities to propaganda. It published excellent material but did not intervene in the life

Despite its ambiguous aftermath, the quelling of the Kapp putsch by the trade-unions had rekindled hopes in Russia that Germany would find her way back to a socialist path. The Russian civil war had aroused widespread sympathy among European labor, and now that the war had reached a successful conclusion with the definitive defeat of the Tsarist generals, this sympathy tended to deepen into closer solidarity and to broaden out among more strata of the working class; Left pro-Soviet wings were sprouting in all socialist parties. The year 1920, moreover, marked the high point of membership in trade-unions throughout Europe. In the spring of 1920, there developed against this background the Polish-Russian war, which in part was a continuation of the Russian civil war and in part reflected the determination of the border states not to permit the westward expansion of the Russian revolution that the new mood of optimism presaged. During the next months, Moscow dreamt of abolishing this reactionary block on the road to Germany, which had just demonstrated anew its revolutionary strength.

The collapse of the three oppressor nations, Tsarist Russia, Germany, and Austria-Hungary, gave Poland the national independence it had been seeking for not quite 125 years. In the new Europe that sprang up after 1918, Poland's dominant interest was to guarantee the permanence of her independence. Thus she leaned on the Entente for the protection it offered against "the Colossus of the East," and Pilsudski mapped out a plan to detach the Ukraine, the weakest flank of Bolshevik power, and attach it to a Polish-led alliance that would block the westward march of Communism. Between defeated Germany and weakened Russia, with French aid, with the Ukraine under its control, Poland would become the pivot of Eastern Europe. The tension on the uneasy Russian-Polish border suddenly heightened into war; Pilsudski attacked the Ukraine and reached Kiev in May 1920.

---

of the German party. As early as 1920 the *Rätekorrespondenz* (Council Correspondence) and the *Russische Korrespondenz* (Russian Correspondence) published all the important Russian documents in the German language. Yet it was only with difficulty that couriers could be sent to and fro. Important matters were arranged by letter or occasionally by telegraph; between the Berlin group and the Moscow center there was no direct telephone connection. In this early period these technical difficulties made Russian political opinion on German events available in general only after the critical moment had passed, when it was primarily of theoretical interest.

Pilsudski's leap to Kiev electrified Russia; it renewed the nationalist resistance to dismemberment born in the civil war. The Russians recaptured Kiev much quicker than Trotsky, the commander in chief, had anticipated, and the Poles sued for peace. At this point Trotsky wanted to accept the peace offer, which meant that the Red Army would not cross the border into Polish territory; in part he was motivated by the weakness of his troops, but in part his reason was political rather than military. He did not want to carry the Bolshevik message on the points of the bayonets of an invading army; he did not want to disturb the painful equilibrium of the border states in an anti-Soviet direction. But opposed to Trotsky were all of the various party factions, with Lenin at their head. Lenin carried the Central Committee with him, and even such conservatives as Rykov joined him in demanding that the Red Army push on to Warsaw and beyond. Warsaw was the gate to Europe; the Red Army's entry into Warsaw would mark the end of Russia's isolation. In support of Lenin, Bukharin and Radek resurrected their theory of the revolutionary offensive.

The Russian counter offensive, beginning in June 1920, shook the front from the Dvina to the Russian border. A provisional revolutionary Polish government was set up, with its headquarters in Bialystok, composed of Julius Marchlewski, Felix Dzerzhinsky, Felix Kon, and Joseph Unschlicht. Pilsudski received French reinforcements under General Weygand, along with more munitions and more money. The Red Army's defeat before Warsaw was due, however, only in part to these French reinforcements; in great part it resulted from the attitude of the Polish workers and even of Polish Communists. These had been instructed to welcome the invading Red Army with an insurrection, but they had received this order with lukewarm enthusiasm and they carried it out falteringly. Polish workers and peasants remained passive, or if they acted they very often acted with Pilsudski; they preferred the status they had in the new Polish state to the possibility of a proletarian dictatorship, which would have become in actuality a renewal under different circumstances of the submission to Moscow that had just been broken.

> The war was popular [two leading Polish Communists write] among broad strata of the [Polish] people, first of all because by

the war Poland might realize its dream of reconstruction within its historical frontiers; second, because the Entente, Poland's "benefactor," wanted it and supported it with weapons, munitions, flour, lard, and raw materials; and then because the war offered possibilities of enrichment to the civil servants, the officers, policemen, businessmen, and their many followers.[19]

During the Russian-Polish war, there was throughout European socialist parties a renewed and intensified interest in the Comintern, which reached its height in Germany at the time of the Second World Congress. The slow and painful development of the German Communist Party had been in sharp contrast with the opportunities offered by the violent crisis of the Weimar Republic. Lacking experienced leaders, and with the weak cadres further debilitated by acrimonious internal discussions, on which the whole interest of the sectarian grouplets and factions focused, the party did not take advantage of the possibilities for activity in the dissension between Ebert and his military allies.

In Lenin's view, the split of the KAPD from the German Communists was a symptom of this immaturity. In his pamphlet *"Left-Wing" Communism: An Infantile Disorder* (the same in which he discussed National Bolshevism and the Versailles Treaty), he lifted the confused debate at the Heidelberg convention to a general political evaluation of the Weimar Republic. He defended the majority decision against the KAPD, but his premises and conclusions had another emphasis than those of Paul Levi and Karl Radek. When they rejected the KAPD "putschists," it was with an emotional undercurrent of passionate hatred. Levi thought it possible to avoid all clashes with the military by skillful maneuvering and held the Communist military counter organization in contempt. In its intimate circle, the Levi group never tired of blaming the Shop Stewards and Liebknecht, who in their view had fallen into the trap of the military

---

[19] E. Brand and H. Walecki, *Der Kommunismus in Polen: Drei Jahre Kampf auf vorgeschobenem Posten* (Hamburg, 1921), p. 42.

According to Trotsky, "One of the reasons for the extraordinary proportions which the catastrophe before Warsaw assumed was the conduct of the command of the southern group of the Soviet armies, operating in the direction of Lvov. The chief political figure in the Revolutionary Military Council of this group was Stalin. Stalin wanted, at whatever cost, to enter Lvov at the same time that Smilga and Tukhachevsky entered Warsaw." (*My Life,* p. 458.)

provocation and were therefore responsible for the rout of the German Communists. In Levi's early speeches—for example, that at the Third Party Convention in Durlach in February 1920—he interpreted the civil war as being in its last stage; by his analysis, after this stage—the initial phase of socialist illusions—the Communist Party would win over the bulk of the Social Democratic workers by its correct policy. His aim was the formation with Communist coöperation of a socialist government, which, supported by a majority in the Reichstag, would be able to introduce far-reaching social reforms and to curb the counter revolution by constitutional procedure. In the KAPD Levi sensed the powerful element in the German working class that held his policy unrealistic and impossible; he strove not only to expel the KAPD from the Comintern but to create an attitude that would outlaw from the German labor movement, once and for all, all adventurists, putschists, Blanquists, Bakuninists—in a word, all who did not believe in the stability of the Republic. In this fight, Levi referred constantly to the tradition of Marx, who had waged a merciless fight to outlaw Mikhail Bakunin, the great Russian anarchist, from the First International.

Under Lenin's auspices, and in the face of Levi's opposition, the Second World Congress, meeting in August 1920, created for the KAPD a special status of sympathizer membership. Its delegates to the congress were accepted by the Moscow steering committee. The same attitude was adopted by the first two congresses toward other activists in the labor movement, toward the IWW in the United States and similar groups throughout the world. Paul Levi and the Spartakist Central Committee, who never accepted this policy toward the Ultra-Left, were consistently defeated in their constant demand that they be expelled.

Lenin's decision to defend, with qualifications, the Ultra-Left wing of the Comintern was based on two major points. First, the repercussions of the expulsion of syndicalist and anarchist groups would tend toward a deformation of the Communist parties into purely parliamentary machines. Second, in spite of his rejection of syndicalist concepts within his own party, Lenin did not want to introduce the same disciplinary methods into the Comintern, for such a transfer to the increasingly heterogeneous Communist parties would stunt and pervert them. In the specific case of Germany, moreover, Lenin had broader arguments for his point of view; his interpretation of the German situation, despite many similiar formulations, differed fundamentally from that of Radek and Levi.

Lenin's characteristic attitude of constructive criticism was to be seen most clearly in his evaluation of the Kapp putsch, and especially in his appreciation of Legien's counter move. In his criticism of the German party's statement on the putsch, Lenin begins by pointing out that its offer to support the socialist government that Legien proposed was "perfectly correct from all points of view of basic premises and of its practical conclusions." [20] Its premise, he continued, was that there was no possibility for a dictatorship of the proletariat under the leadership of the Communist Party. The promise to be a loyal opposition to a socialist government would have as its practical result the exclusion of bourgeois parties from the new government after the Kapp putsch had been crushed. "Undoubtedly these tactics in the main are correct," he wrote, for such a socialist government may reverse the trend in Germany.

In this pronouncement Lenin met Legien half-way. The fight against the German counter revolution was not limited to struggling for a proletarian dictatorship, Russian style, but could be conducted by a labor government, German style. There was another point of contact between the two: their common distrust of Social Democratic politicians, their doubt whether these would break their alliance with the army and its illegal appendages and their defenders in the Reichstag, the bourgeois parties. Lenin the revolutionist and Legien the organizer might have met in the statement that the situation in Germany cannot be fundamentally changed by a mere regrouping of political parties into a new cabinet. The wrath of Legien against the politicos, translated into Leninist phraseology, became, "The Scheidemanns do not and cannot go beyond the bounds of bourgeois democracy, which in its turn cannot be but a dictatorship of capital."

---

[20] Lenin, *"Left-Wing" Communism: An Infantile Disorder*, p. 87 ff. Lenin dated the original edition April 27, 1920; on May 12, he added several appendices dealing with later developments in Germany, Italy, and Holland. Appendix II criticized the German Communist Party's statement on the Kapp putsch, which had appeared in the *Rote Fahne* of March 26. The pamphlet was published simultaneously in Russian, German, English, and French on June 20.

The Communist half of such a joint government, therefore, could not submit to Social Democratic discipline, which would confine it to purely parliamentary methods. The German counter revolution was too strong and too well organized to be dealt with by these methods alone. To renounce resistance to the Freikorps and the Black Reichswehr would bind the workers and give all the advantage to the anti-Republican forces, which would tolerate a parliamentary regime exactly as long as it needed it to prepare another coup.

Lenin's analysis of the Kapp putsch might have become the starting point for a German Communist policy *sui generis,* which would have discarded both the immaturity of its early years and the conservatism of its Social Democratic forebears. Lenin's initiative, however, never bore fruit; it came just when the defeat in Poland marked the end of hope of an expansion of the revolution and the beginning of an inevitable decline in Russia. The German Communist mass party, born at the eve of this decline, lost the youthful virility of the Spartakusbund and, without ever having been an important revolutionary force, adopted the decrepitudes and the mannerisms of the Russian party in decline.

Zinoviev at Halle

In March 1920 the USPD convention had elected four delegates to negotiate at the Second World Congress for its affiliation to the Comintern. Two were for affiliation, Walter Stoecker and Ernst Däumig, and two against, Wilhelm Dittmann and Artur Crispien.[21] They were met with the Twenty-One Conditions for affiliation of new parties, which aimed unambiguously at the most precise coördination of Communist parties with the Moscow center. The relation of the Central Committees to the Comintern Presidium, the control of the Communist press, the nomination of parliamentary deputies, the for-

---

[21] *Der zweite Kongress der Kommunistischen Internationale: Protokoll der Verhandlungen vom 19. Juli in Petrograd und vom 23. Juli bis 7. August 1920 in Moskau* (Hamburg, 1921), p. 781. The fifth delegate mentioned, Schiller, did not play an important role. All four of the men listed in the text were Reichstag deputies. Stoecker died in a concentration camp during the Nazi regime. Däumig died on July 5, 1922. Dittmann survived the Hitler regime and is living in Switzerland. Crispien died in Switzerland in January 1947.

mulation of all major issues in the various fields of Communist activity—all were stipulated with a maximum of detail and imposed with a maximum of authority.[22]

Over the years, Communist parties have been increasingly controlled from Moscow, and it has become standard to make a mechanical identification of this later product with the international formed on the

[22] "The Second Congress of the Communist International rules that the conditions for joining the Communist International shall be as follows: 1. The general propaganda and agitation shall bear a really Communist character, and should correspond to the program and decisions of the Third International. The entire party press should be edited by reliable Communists who have proved their loyalty to the cause of the proletarian revolution. . . . All periodicals and other publications . . . are subject to the control of the Central Committee. . . . 2. Every organization desiring to join the Communist International shall be bound systematically and regularly to remove from all the responsible posts in the labor movement (party organization, editorship, labor unions, parliamentary factions, coöperatives, municipalities, etc.) all reformists and followers of the 'Center,' and to have them replaced by Communists. . . . 3. Communists shall everywhere create a parallel illegal apparatus, which at the decisive moment should be of assistance to the party in its duty toward the revolution. . . . 4. Persistent and systematic propaganda and agitation must be carried on in the army, . . . [if necessary] illegally. . . . 5. A systematic and regular propaganda is necessary in the rural districts. The working class can gain no victory unless it possesses the sympathy and support of at least part of the rural workers and the poor peasants. . . . 6. Every party desirous of affiliating to the Third International shall renounce not only avowed social patriotism, but also the hypocrisy of social pacifism. It shall systematically demonstrate to the workers that without a revolutionary overthrow of capitalism no international arbitration, no talk of disarmament, no democratic reorganization of the League of Nations, will be capable of saving mankind from new imperialist war. 7. Parties desirous of joining the Communist International must recognize the necessity of a complete and absolute rupture with reformism and the policy of the 'Centrists.' . . . The Communist International cannot reconcile itself to having such avowed reformists as, for example, Turati, Modigliani, Kautsky, Hilferding, Hillquit, Longuet, MacDonald, and others entitled to consider themselves members of the Third International. . . . 8. Every party desirous of belonging to the Third International must denounce without reservation all the methods of 'its own' imperialists in the colonies, supporting not in words only but practically a movement of liberation in the colonies. . . . 9. Every party desirous of belonging to the Communist International shall be bound to carry on systematic and persistent Communist work in the trade-unions, coöperatives, and other organizations of the working masses. . . . 10. Any party belonging to the Communist International is bound to carry on a stubborn struggle against the Amsterdam 'International' of yellow-dog trade-unions. . . . 11. Parties desirous of joining the Third International shall be bound to inspect the personnel of the parliamentary factions, . . . to subordinate them to the Central Committee of the party. . . . 12. All the parties belonging to the Communist International shall be formed on the basis of the principle of democratic centralism. . . . 13. The Communist parties of those countries where Communist activity is legal shall clean

basis of the Twenty-One Conditions. That one developed out of the other is true, but to identify them is a distortion, for it neglects the contrast between the characters of Lenin and Stalin and the different political climates in which the two men lived. Lenin's concept of a functioning Comintern was based on the premise that the Russian monopoly of power and ideology would be temporary, soon to be supplanted by victorious socialist movements in technologically advanced countries. Then the immature Communist International would overcome its initial perversions, the result in part of its Russian origin, and grow up into a higher type of international labor organization.

It was not the question of centralization alone, however, that became the content of the conflict between an important group of the USPD, led by Rudolf Hilferding,[23] and Lenin, but the question of who should

---

out their members from time to time, in order systematically to free the party from petty-bourgeois elements that have penetrated into it. 14. Each party desirous of affiliating to the Communist International shall render every possible assistance to the Soviet Republics in their struggle against all counter-revolutionary forces. . . . 15. Those parties that have stood for the old Social Democratic programs shall as soon as possible draw up a new Communist program in conformity with the special conditions of their country and with the resolutions of the Communist International. . . . 16. All the resolutions of the congresses of the Communist International, as well as of its Presidium, are binding for all parties joining the Communist International. . . . 17. Each party desirous of joining the Communist International shall bear the following name: Communist Party of such and such a country, Section of the Third International. . . . 18. All the leading organs of each party are bound to publish all the most important documents of the Presidium of the Communist International. 19. Parties that have joined the Communist International or are desirous of doing so shall convene within four months of the Second Congress of the Communist International a special convention to discuss these conditions. . . . 20. Parties that are at the present time willing to join the Third International but have not so far fundamentally changed their tactics shall take care that not less than two-thirds of their committees are composed of comrades who have made an open and definite declaration prior to the convening of the Second Congress in favor of affiliation to the Third International. . . . 21. Members of a party who reject in principle the conditions and theses of the Third International are liable to be excluded from the party. . . ." (*Protokoll des zweiten Kongresses*, pp. 388–395.)

[23] Rudolf Hilferding, born in 1877 in Vienna, joined the socialist movement as a student and became one of the staunchest supporters of Victor Adler, the founder of the Austrian Social Democratic Party. In 1902, at the age of 25, he was an important contributor to Kautsky's *Neue Zeit*, especially on problems of Marxian economics. August Bebel called him to Berlin in 1906, where for a year he lectured at the party school; when the police interrupted this activity with a threat to expel him, he was succeeded by Rosa Luxemburg. He then became foreign editor of the *Vorwärts* (1907–1915). In 1910 he published his major work, *Finance Capital (Das Finanzkapital: Eine Studie über die jüngste Entwicklung des Kapitalismus)*, on which Lenin based a good portion of his study of imperialism.

lead the new mass party. For a time the Hilferding group, wavering, debated whether they could not find a compromise; they wished to remain at the head of the United Communist Party. But that was just what Lenin wanted to prevent. He wanted the Hilferding-Dittmann-Crispien policy eliminated from the revolutionary German organization. "What would you do if they accepted your Twenty-One Conditions?" Zinoviev was asked. "We would find a twenty-second," he replied.

In this discussion the Russian Communist Lenin and the German Communist Levi, despite apparent agreement, confronted each other with fundamentally different points of view. Lenin attempted to continue the revolutionary efforts outside Russia and to ready the young parties for a period of severe and complex struggles, in which they would have to transform themselves into the leading forces of their respective countries and lead the fight against the counter revolution through a maze of unexpected and dangerous problems. When he counseled the German Crispien or the Italian Serrati, Lenin never failed to stress the imminence of the counter-revolutionary coups. A crisis was pending in both countries; Mussolini was active rallying his partisans.

> How does Crispien speak of terror and violence? [Lenin demanded]. "These are different things," he says. Perhaps you can so differentiate in a sociological text, but not with regard to practical politics, especially not with regard to the German situation. We must apply violence and terror against groups that act like

---

In the party discussions about imperialism and war, Hilferding belonged to the Marxist Center group, of which Kautsky was the principal figure. On August 3, 1914, Hilferding was one of the fifteen Social Democratic Reichstag deputies who opposed voting for war credits. During the November days Hilferding was one of a group with Kautsky, Haase, and Dittmann in the moderate wing of the USPD; he became an editor of *Freiheit* ("Freedom"), the party's chief organ. For two months in the decisive fall of 1923, as Stresemann's Finance Minister, he drew up plans of currency reform. From June 1928 until December 1929, he was again minister in the cabinet of Hermann Müller; he was forced to resign by the pressure of Reichsbank President Schacht. Hilferding was the usual principal reporter to party conventions; he edited the party's theoretical monthly, *Die Gesellschaft* ("Society"). At the end of March 1933 he escaped over the Danish border and settled in Switzerland until 1938. In that year he joined the party's National Executive Committee in Paris, where it had fled from Prague. In the fall of 1941 he was delivered to the Gestapo by Vichy authorities; he died in a Paris prison a few days later, either a suicide or killed by the Gestapo.

the German officers in assassinating Liebknecht and Rosa Luxemburg, against people like Stinnes and Krupp, who monopolize the press. Of course, it is not necessary to anticipate and to declare that we will apply terror in any case, but if the German officers and Kappists, if Krupp and Stinnes remain as they are, then we must apply terror.[24]

Levi tried to belittle the importance of the decision to be taken and to present the Twenty-One Conditions as a mere formality, as an entrance fee that the USPD could easily pay.[25]

But the Twenty-One Conditions represented an abstraction of revolutionary discipline that did not correspond to the reality even of the Russian party, and less of the other Comintern affiliates. The discussion in the USPD was carried on for many months; its central point was how to organize a militant party. This was only the starting point; all the questions of the Russian revolution were, for the first time, brought to large worker audiences and compared and collated with their own experiences since 1918. It was not a discussion where a standpoint could be accepted or rejected on academic grounds; decisions had consequences in the lives of the disputants. For each and every one, acceptance or non-acceptance of the Twenty-One Conditions was a deadly serious matter; the workers discussing the affiliation or non-affiliation to the Moscow center correctly interpreted their decision as one determining the revolutionary policy to be carried out immediately after a regrouping of their cadres.

Thus, in spite of the form of the discussion, which referred to the relation between the Russian center and the Communist parties, the fight within the USPD was essentially concerned with Germany. These USPD workers did not want to sacrifice their old Social Democratic habits of party life but to eliminate a hesitant and weak leadership. The internal development of the Russian party, its transformation, already beginning, into a monopolistic State Party, was veiled to its associates in Germany as well as to its organizers in Russia; the

---

[24] *Protokoll des zweiten Kongresses*, p. 349.

[25] Levi, who had a liking for literary allusions, quoted for his future colleagues the verses:

> *Amor, der dich liebt und peinigt,*
> *Will dich selig und gereinigt.*

(Eros, who loves and tortures you, wants to have you blessed and purified.) *Ibid.*, p. 362.

Independent Socialists accepted the Twenty-One Conditions as the premise of their reorganization to fight against the restoration forces.

The USPD split at its convention in Halle, October 12–17, 1920. The current for affiliation with the Comintern had in the meantime gained such momentum that the German government did not dare to deny Zinoviev, its chairman, permission to enter the country. Halle, center of the machine and chemical industry, was the background for a duel between Zinoviev and Hilferding, who was supported by Russian Social Democrats, Abramovich, Martov, and others, who had just in this year settled down in Berlin. The USPD Left looked on these men as enemies of the Russian revolution, not to be trusted. Russian and German elements were mixed in the discussion in strange and distorting proportions; the complexity of the problems involved was never clear to the rank and file. Among German workers knowledge of Russia was rudimentary.

Zinoviev arrived in Halle accompanied by A. Lozovsky, at this time representative of the Profintern, the Communist trade-union international. Zinoviev spoke German fluently but with effort; for many years he had lived in Switzerland but he had never been active in a German organization or lectured in the language. When he mounted the platform, he found before him a divided convention. The hostile group comprised almost half, and they were disposed to heckle him. He spoke for four hours; he began hesitatingly and with an insecure small voice, hunting for appropriate terms and seemingly intimidated by his excited audience. But in the course of his speech he won over the majority. For the delegates who fell under Zinoviev's spell, the details of the organizational procedure disappeared behind the major issue of revolutionary policy in Germany. Affiliation to the Comintern was decided by 236 votes to 156.

In the sweep for the Moscow policy in 1920, a peculiar shift of emphasis took place, already indicating the deterioration in Russia. In 1918 the Bolsheviks, able to destroy the bourgeois state machinery and replace it with the local power of soviets, had fascinated the German workers. But by 1920 the vision of the workers' councils had faded. The Red Army became the major fruit of the revolution, and with its rise the state plan supplanted the council concept. The German workers, unfamiliar with living conditions in Russia, accepted

Planned Communism naïvely and enthusiastically, with all the bias toward organized society inbred in German labor. The state plan was in fact much better fit for German economy than Russian, but Russia was presented to the Halle convention as a country in which the socialist ideal of an economy of abundance organized by the state was in the process of realization, as a country in which poverty and want were disappearing.

Zinoviev felt this current, a current that swept through all, Social Democrats and Independents alike. He wrote a little pamphlet on his sojourn entitled *Twelve Days in Germany:* "We have a way out, a hope. We go forward to the complete elimination of money. We pay wages in commodities. We introduce trolleys without fares. We have free public schools, free, if temporarily poor, meals, rent-free apartments, free lighting. We are realizing all this very slowly, under the most difficult conditions. We have to fight ceaselessly, but we have a way out, a hope, a plan." [26] These were magic words.

At this Halle conference, Ernst Thälmann appeared for the first time as a political figure, leading the Hamburg delegation and speaking for the Comintern wing of the USPD. Thälmann represented a substratum of the organization, the unskilled or semi-skilled workers, uncertain in Marxist theory, at a disadvantage with the trained party politicians, distrusting the party bureaucrats, but full of energy and initiative. It was this group, and not the party theorists gathered around Hilferding and Abramovich, that decided that the USPD should join with the Spartakusbund and form the United Communist Party. The split brought the majority of the USPD to the Comintern; the minority stagnated another year and a half between the United Communist Party and the Social Democratic Party, and then went back to the latter at the Nuremberg convention on September 22, 1922.

After a last short session of the now defunct Spartakusbund, the unification took place in December 1920, in Berlin, in an atmosphere of ambiguity and obscurity. The Independent Socialists tolerated the Spartakists as a most disagreeable but unavoidable appendage of the Comintern. The Spartakist intellectuals accepted the welcome but very rough raw material, which needed much polishing before it

---

[26] Gregory Zinoviev, *Zwölf Tage in Deutschland* (Hamburg, 1921), p. 74.

could be brought up to their high-class brand of Marxism. Thus, the two groups entered the new party from different premises; the life of the German Communist Party between 1920 and 1923 was filled with clashes between these currents. The Spartakist leaders were jubilant over the long-desired possibility of building up a mass organization able to compete with the Social Democrats in propaganda and parliamentary influence. The Independent Socialist workers, coming from a mass organization of just this type, strove for exactly the opposite, for the formation of an elite party able to organize the fight. Between 1918 and 1920, the USPD had won with a minimum of effort a maximum of parliamentary influence; in these years, for example, the percentage of the electorate supporting the party rose from 6 to 17. In 1920 there were 103 USPD deputies in the Reichstag, as compared with 278 deputies of the Social Democratic Party and only two of the Communist Party. In spite of these easy victories, the party had been defeated at every crucial point.

The unification convention, in contrast to the simplicity of the preceding Spartakist gatherings, already reflected the new propaganda methods transferred from Moscow to Berlin. The large meeting hall in the *Lehrervereinshaus* in Berlin's Alexanderplatz was elaborately decorated with a wealth of red cloths draped over pictures of Lenin and Trotsky, of Liebknecht and Luxemburg, of Zinoviev. Communist sergeants at arms were posted at all the doors. There was an artistic frame of classical music and revolutionary poetry. The USPD delegates, mostly workers from the bench, were disgusted by the new official pomp; they had looked forward to a sober analysis of the German situation, concrete proposals on what to do next. Paul Levi gave them instead a speech on the economic situation of the world, in which a wealth of statistics was combined with varied news of events in Asia and in the Anglo-American world, and which ended with the bombast, "Enter, ye workers of Germany, enter [our new party], for here are thy gods." I watched workers from Essen and Hamburg leaving the conference hall; they could express their disgust with this rhetoric only by despoiling some of the nice decorations with their plebeian spit, a symbol of the growing cynicism among certain strata of German workers, a weak reflection of the basic doubts prevailing in the Workers' Opposition groups in Russia.

Chapter 6 · The Road to the New Economic Policy · · · · · · ·

Throughout the Russian civil war and for some years afterward there was a strong current toward local power, toward decentralization, toward workers' control of factories and regional armies, toward a federation of independent national units. This was the original October trend, which would be defeated only after it had fought a gradually losing fight within the party, successively as the Workers' Opposition, the Military Opposition, the Trade-Union Opposition, all of which had their origin in an attempt to establish coöperative socialism on a local basis.

Nationalization of Industry

As they had first recognized and then fostered the peasants' seizure of the land before and during the revolution, so after it the Bolsheviks conceded for a period the workers' seizure of factories. The industrial revolution that was to shake Russia over the next three decades had begun slowly, with a decree on November 14, 1917, concerning workers' control. The old proprietors, still in physical and juridical possession of their property, were to continue production under workers' councils, which were given the right to control production plans and conditions of labor. But this scheme never worked. A series of individual expropriations set in; a red flag flying from a factory indicated that the workers had taken it over and were managing it. Socialism was not felt to be equivalent to the expropriation of private ownership, which was only an essential precondition; nor was the coördination of managers, engineers, and other experts under the control of workers' organizations considered socialism. The first step toward a socialist economy was the collective management by the producers themselves. As applied for instance to the railroads, this would mean that they would be controlled by those actually working on the trains and in the shops, and not by an expert appointed from the outside, even though he might be a trade-unionist or even a former railroad worker.

These attempts at workers' management were soon blocked by the general poverty and the disintegration of the economy. Large modern plants, isolated units in an agrarian country, were not a sufficient industrial base for the small workers' elite to revive and direct production. In May 1918 the All-Russian Congress of Economic Councils opposed the spontaneous expropriation of single factories: the disrupted capitalist economy of Russia needed a more cautious transition to socialist forms. The Bolshevik Party labeled as syndicalist any attempt of the workers to interfere in production. Under the pressure of the German armies in the Ukraine, compulsory measures were intensified. On May 30 martial law was declared in the cities in the Soviet zone. On June 11 committees of poor peasants were set up to facilitate the requisitioning of grain; they continued the agrarian revolution by dividing up the land of the wealthier peasants among themselves. Soon they were joined by bands of armed workers, groups of about seventy-five armed with two or three machine guns, who began to requisition stored grain. For the countryside, these detachments became the personification of War Communism.

On June 28, a decree was passed ordering general nationalization of industry. All factories with a capital of more than one million rubles were confiscated, as well as smaller plants in certain industries—mining, textiles, tobacco, glass and porcelain, cement. The immediate reason for this decree was political, to combat the pressure of victorious Germany; the German army in the Ukraine was advancing to the Don, and if its successes continued the Russian entrepreneurs hoped to regain their status in their factories. In anticipation, many of them transferred their titles to German companies, some of which were set up only for this purpose.

Larin, who was at this time in Berlin on a commercial mission, on the 25th [of June] telegraphed to Lenin that there was a likelihood of the German Ambassador in Moscow lodging a claim with the Soviet Government that certain important Russian enterprises were now owned by German citizens and were accordingly to be exempt from any nationalization decree. Faced with this danger of an important part of Russian industry passing into German hands, the Council of People's Commissaries hastily within the space of forty-eight hours prepared and passed the new decree, while Vesenha [Supreme Council of National Economy] at an all-night sitting drew up a list of the enterprises to which the decree should apply. The result was that the decree appeared in *Izvestia* on the very morning on which, in all probability, Count Mirbach was preparing to deliver his diplomatic note.[1]

Thus the first general nationalization decree was a product of both the civil war and the war with Germany, a strong political gesture without economic content. Most of the important industrial regions were cut off from Moscow—the Ukraine, the Don Basin, the Caucasus—the main industrial centers in this period, the principal reservoirs of vital food stocks and raw materials, of grain, coal, iron. More than half of the transport system was in enemies' hands, which in a country of Russia's continental size laid waste the other part. All economic measures were taken under the spur of military expediency, and as the Red Army gained the lost provinces, within their ruins was created the skeleton of a centralized economic administration. The greater the economic difficulties, the more stringent were the compulsory measures resorted to.

The year 1919 was one of military victories, gained at the cost of increasing want, in food, in raw materials, in production of all kinds.[2] In March 1919 the food situation was so serious that compulsory measures for its distribution by coöperatives were intensified, which meant in substance that the rationing system was made stricter. City populations were forced into coöperatives and were divided for rationing into three categories: workers, their families, and the former ruling classes. For the workers and employees of state enterprises, including the families of soldiers, rationing was alleviated by supplemental dis-

---

[1] Maurice Dobb, *Russian Economic Development Since the Revolution* (London: G. Routledge and Sons, Ltd., 1928), pp. 59–60.

[2] The following table gives the percentage of the production of various items

tribution from canteens and bonuses in goods; they were also given their lodging and fuel free, as well as, in theory, telephone, gas and electricity, transport. At the end of this period Russian economy was divided into two unequal halves: a rigidly controlled state economy, functioning poorly and granting only a bare minimum living wage to its workers, and an enormous disorganized agricultural sector.

Capitalism had been displaced, not by a planned economy but by economic anarchy, on which shaky foundation were raised the centralized bureaus. The roots of the structural change in Soviet economy, which matured only in the post-NEP period, are all to be found in the civil war. The two main features—the utter disruption of the economy, and the contrast between the small controlled market with the much larger black market—are the characteristic features of all Europe following World War II.

By the beginning of 1920 the civil war had about come to an end.

---

during the first half of 1920 as compared with six months' production during a peace-time year, 1913 or 1914:

Colors, varnishes, etc.	2.2
Paper and cardboard (includes Ukraine)	15.2
Rubber goods	1.7
Glass	13.0
Matches	16.0
Tobacco	17.7
Spirits, 40°	10.0
Sugar (includes Ukraine)	9.0
Coal (includes Ukraine and Siberia)	25.0
Naphtha (includes Caucasus and Emba)	33.0(?)
Platinum	33.0
Gold (in Siberia)	12.0
Iron ore (includes Ukraine)	12.0
Cast iron (includes Ukraine)	2.4
Iron and steel (includes Ukraine)	4.0
Cotton thread	20.0
Cotton goods	3.3
Sowed flax	50.0
Potash	0
Nitric acid	0
Flour	18.0
Mineral fertilizer	0
Soap and candles	2.8
Pencils	1.2

(From a report of Larin in *Pravda*, November 14, 1920, cited in K. Leites, *Recent Economic Developments in Russia,* Oxford, 1922, p. 146.)

On January 26 the Entente blockade was abandoned. The result of this political amelioration, however, was not a loosening but a further intensification of economic control, a steady movement toward increased state economy. Total nationalization was decreed on November 29, 1920, when all plants with mechanical power employing five or more workers, or without mechanical power and employing ten or more workers, were nationalized.

With the trend toward nationalization, there was a tendency to abolish money. By a decree of April 30, 1920, all wages were to be paid in goods; in February 1921, six weeks before the inception of the NEP, taxation in money was abolished. The trend was in part an indication of the Bolshevik desire to establish a moneyless economy, and also the result of the breakdown of the currency system and the substitution of barter. On October 6, 1917, according to the figures of the State Bank, there had been 16.2 billion rubles in circulation; by May 1918 this had increased to 41 billion, and by the end of 1918 to more than 230 billion.[3]

The Red Army and the Party

During these years of travail, Trotsky grew from one of the revolutionaries to a national leader, second only to Lenin in stature and fame. It was he who organized the Red Army, the most efficacious instrument both in repelling capitalist intervention and in shaping the young Soviet state. The Russia that emerged from the civil war was the Russia of Lenin and Trotsky.

The Fourth Congress of the Soviets, March 15–17, 1918, appointed Trotsky Commissar of War, head of the Red Army that had been authorized by the Central Committee a month before. After the fall of Simbirsk, it was decided that Trotsky should go to the Volga front. On August 7, not knowing that Kazan had in the meantime fallen to the Czechoslovak legionaries, he left Moscow in a train hurriedly assembled during the night, from which, during the next two and a half years, he organized the Red Army. The train of the *Predrevoyensoviet* (the Chairman of the Revolutionary Military Soviet) went to

---

[3] Four different kinds of ruble were circulating in these years: Tsarist rubles, Duma rubles, Kerensky rubles, and Soviet rubles. As the inflation developed, both their purchasing power and the relative value of the four changed rapidly.

"Samara, Chelyabinsk, Vyatka, Petrograd, Balashov, Smolensk, Samara again, Rostov-on-Don, Novocherkask, Kiev, Zhitomir, and so on, without end . . . One of the notes to my military books mentions 36 trips, with a total run of over 105,000 kilometers." [4]

In organizing the Red Army, Trotsky frequently came into conflict with local workers' units. In the first phase of the revolution, in each town, in each army unit, on each battleship, workers or soldiers or sailors had risen and established the power of their soviet. "These detachments frequently had to wage minor wars. Enjoying as they did the sympathy of the masses, they easily became victorious. They received a certain tempering, and their leaders a certain authority." These local military units, organized around the industrial units of the area, were coördinated with the workers' councils. They established a local power based on local armies, which might have been able to develop their own administrative and organizational methods even against the Moscow center. "In the beginning," Trotsky writes, "not only provinces but even region after region had its own Council of Peoples' Commissars with its very own Commissar of War."

Against this localist principle of military organization Trotsky waged a two-year fight in the name of military efficiency.

> Accustomed to easy victories, the guerrilla detachments . . . displayed their worthlessness; they did not have adequate intelligence sections; they had no liaison with each other; nor were they ever able to execute a complex maneuver. Hence—at various times, in various parts of the country—guerrillaism met with disaster. It was no easy task to include these separate detachments in a centralized system. The military ability of the commanders was not high, and they were hostile to the old officers, partly because they had no political confidence in them and partly to cover up lack of confidence in themselves. [5]

Trotsky introduced the severest military discipline.

> I issued an order which was printed on the press in my train and distributed throughout the army: "I give warning that if any unit retreats without orders, the first to be shot down will be the

---

[4] Trotsky, *My Life*, p. 414.

[5] Trotsky, *Stalin: An Appraisal of the Man and His Influence*, edited and translated from the Russian by Charles Malamuth (New York: Harper and Brothers, copyrighted 1941, issued 1946), p. 298.

commissary of the unit, and the next the commander. Brave and gallant soldiers will be appointed in their places. Cowards, dastards and traitors will not escape the bullet. This I solemnly promise in the presence of the entire Red Army." [6]

Late in 1918, for the first time, a Communist military commissar, one Panteleyev, was court-martialed on Trotsky's specific orders and shot for "violation of military duty." This incident aroused a violent opposition, in which almost all the party leaders joined. Stalin used it in his fight against Trotsky; Bukharin, "a Left Communist and therefore opposed to the employment of 'generals'," had an article published in *Pravda* intimating that Trotsky shot "the best comrades without a trial. . . . The centralized army was proclaimed to be characteristic of the imperialist State and in its place the opposition advocated the system of guerrilla detachments." [7]

Opposition to Trotsky's military measures led to serious internal party strife, which Lenin moderated. He made the party realize that it owed the salvation of the revolution and the country to Trotsky's military genius; on the other hand, he countered the centralization of the army by means of greater control of its commanders by the party. The term "Military Opposition," used by party historians and Trotsky alike to denote this faction, is inadequate to characterize the fundamental schism between party power and army power, united under Lenin's command. This conflict is a major element in Stalin's rise, for Lenin protected him against Trotsky's extreme hostility. The improvization of a modern army from scratch, brilliantly carried out by a Bolshevik newcomer, created in the decisive first three years of the new state a permanent and dangerous friction between the two new cadres in formation, the Red Army officer corps and the party organizers.

When it took power, the Bolshevik Party was less centralized than any of its Western Social Democratic counterparts; it comprised loose units of men inexperienced in organizing, administering, and governing. The abundant verbalization on party discipline was in striking contrast to the actual conditions of party life in revolutionary Russia. Local groups, made up principally of new members, were cut off from

---

[6] Trotsky, *My Life*, p. 401.
[7] Trotsky, *Stalin*, pp. 299, 303.

the center by the civil war and had to act largely on their own. Long-distance telephone, cables, airplanes, were at the disposal of only the highest layer of the party. Rail communications, frequently interrupted by the war, took days and, to the remote provinces, weeks. Even party literature was curtailed by the scarcity of paper.

Under these conditions there was a gusto in the Bolshevik units for independence and a constant revolt against the military discipline imposed by the state of emergency. Fighting against "petty bourgeois anarchy," Trotsky built up the Red Army with thousands and later tens of thousands of old Tsarist officers. This integration of old-regime officers into the army of the revolution aroused suspicion among the party organizers. Nurtured in the lessons of the French Revolution, the Bolsheviks watched the amazing performance of their commander-in-chief with constant remembrance of Napoleon Bonaparte. Trotsky is undoubtedly right when he reports in his memoirs the rumors and intrigues against him in Moscow during the two and a half years he commanded the front from his mobile train. Lenin worked for a compromise and repeatedly tried to fill up the higher ranks of the new army with reliable party members; the conflict is illustrated in an anecdote that Trotsky relates.

> During our reverses in the East, when Kolchak was approaching the Volga, . . . Lenin wrote me a note: "What if we fire all the specialists and appoint Lashevich as commander-in-chief?" Lashevich was an old Bolshevik who had earned his promotion to the rank of a sergeant in the "German" war. I replied on the same note: "Child's play!" [8]

The process had gone much too far to be reversed. Later when Lenin again discussed the situation on the front during one of Trotsky's rare visits to Moscow, Trotsky gave him the details about the reconstruction of the army.

> "You ask me," I said, "if it would not be better to kick out all the old officers. But do you know how many of them we have in the army now?"
> "No."
> "Not even approximately?"
> "I don't know."

---

[8] Trotsky, *My Life*, p. 447.

"Not less than thirty thousand."

"What?"

"Not less than thirty thousand. For every traitor, there are a hundred who are dependable; for every one who deserts, there are two or three who get killed. How are we to replace them all?" [9]

As organizer of the Red Army, Trotsky asked for and got increasing control over all available manpower. He was in charge of the rail system, whose reorganization was *the* prerequisite to the mobility of the army. His later program to fuse the trade-unions into the state administration must be put against this background. Rigid labor discipline was installed in all sectors connected with the army, and this decisively changed the climate in the factories. The vanguard of Bolshevik workers suffered this change with clenched teeth as an unalterable but temporary condition to survival, but they did not accept this military discipline of labor as the socialist economy for which they had overthrown Tsarism and capitalism. Trotsky's reorganization of transport was again under the authority of Lenin, who supported him against resistance from all sides and in particular against that crystallizing in the party into various forms of "Workers' Opposition," the first organized resistance within the party to the State Party regime.

Democratic Centralism

An early group of this opposition, calling themselves Democratic Centralism, was led by Valerian V. Ossinsky, in 1918 chairman of the Supreme Council of National Economy, and Timofei V. Sapronov, who submitted an oppositionist platform to the Eighth Party Congress in March 1919. "The hierarchy of the officials follows the old style," they declared. "The party and the soviets are degenerating into a bureaucratic system. One single man, Lenin, holds all the strings of power in his hands." Their attack was directed particularly against three party institutions set up by the Eighth Congress. Zinoviev, undoubtedly with the endorsement of Lenin, proposed that the Central Committee delegate certain of its duties to three smaller committees, the Political Bureau (Politburo), the Organizational Bureau (Orgburo),

---

[9] Trotsky, *My Life*, p. 447.

and the Secretariat. Stalin was the only man from the beginning a member of both the Politburo and the Orgburo.[10]

Ossinsky and Sapronov broadened their criticism of party organization to a general demand for democratization of the Soviet state. They asked for democracy not only in the party and in the soviets but also in the state administration and in industrial management. Their key demand was the separation of party and soviets, which was equivalent to a demand for the legalization of several parties. Another member of the group, Vladimir M. Smirnov, centered his attack on the too rigid organization of the army.

During the civil war the internal party conflict was buried under the common will to survive; from March 1919 to March 1920, the party doubled.[11] The new members were mostly workers, who brought with them immense reserves of energy and élan. In this period the revolutionary wave was still rising, and the sacrifices these workers were willing to endure decided the fate of the Soviet state on the

---

[10] Cf. Trotsky, *Stalin,* pp. 345–346.

[11] The membership figures of the Bolshevik Party are given below in Column 1 according to the *Bolshaya Sovetskaya Entsiklopediya,* XI, 531, and in Column 2 according to the *History of the CPSU:*

	1	*2*
Beginning, 1905	8,400	
Beginning, 1917	23,600	40 to 45,000 (p. 183)
April 1917	40,000	80,000 (p. 188)
August 1917	200,000	240,000 (p. 196)
Beginning, 1918	115,000	270,000*
Beginning, 1919	251,000	
March 1919	313,766	313,766 (p. 232)
Beginning, 1920	431,400	
March 1920	611,978	611,978 (p. 240)

* The Seventh Party Congress, March 1918, "was attended by 46 delegates with vote and 58 delegates with voice but no vote, representing 145,000 Party members. Actually, the membership of the Party at that time was not less than 270,000. The discrepancy was due to the fact that, owing to the urgency with which the congress met, a large number of the organizations were unable to send delegates in time; and the organizations in the territories occupied by the Germans were unable to send delegates at all . . . At the Seventh Party Congress the name of the Party was changed to the Russian Communist Party (Bolsheviks)—R.C.P. (B.)" (*History of the Communist Party of the Soviet Union (Bolsheviks),* ed. Commission of the Central Committee of the CPSU (B), New York: International Publishers, 1939, pp. 218–219.) It is common knowledge that the anonymous *History of the CPSU (B)* was written by Stalin himself. Together with his *Problems of Leninism,* it is the definitive statement on the matter, the text in all Russian schools, widely translated and propagated abroad.

battlefield. Parallel with the upsurge of revolutionary enthusiasm, there was a growing desire for another type of party and state organization.

The Eighth Party Congress, March 1919, rejected as incorrect the interpretation of Democratic Centralism, but it did not eliminate Ossinsky and Sapronov from key posts in party and soviet work. The oppositionist leaders included some of the great figures of the civil war, and their popularity as worker-Bolsheviks lasted into peace time. The growth of the group was such that they were able to get control of the Ukraine—one of the most important provinces.

The natural antagonism between the Moscow center and the Ukraine, and the rapid change of local power there during the civil war, had made this the province where anarchist, anti-centralist tendencies found most response among the population. Nationalist aspirations were welded together with anarcho-syndicalist movements shaped by the peculiarities of their Ukrainian origin. Nestor Makhno, the most important of several anarcho-syndicalist peasant leaders, established a type of peasant commune in the Southern Ukraine, where he fought continually during 1918–1919. His attitude toward the Kremlin and the Red Army command was ambiguous. He was not at all an instrument of the Whites, nor was he disposed to submit to Muscovite control; he attempted to maneuver a degree of regional autonomy between the two dominant forces. In the early twenties the Red Army crushed his partisan bands, but the Makhno movement has remained a Ukrainian legend.[12]

At the Fourth All-Ukrainian Party Conference meeting in March 1920, the Democratic Centralism group won a majority in the Central Committee. The Ukrainian Communists elected this anti-centralist faction in the hope of reducing Moscow's interference to a minimum. This fusion of national resistance with the anti-state group in the Bolshevik Party was correctly interpreted by the Politburo as a most dangerous symptom and was quickly quelled; by Moscow's order the Sapronov Central Committee was disbanded.[13]

---

[12] Cf. P. Arshinov, *Die Machno-Bewegung, 1918–1921* (Berlin, 1923).

[13] Sapronov and his group combined their fight for collective management and soviets independent of the State Party with one to protect the Ukrainian peasant from rigid measures of the Moscow center. Thus, in the later exegeses of party history, the Bolshevik worker Sapronov appears as an agent of the kulaks:

Another group, calling themselves Workers' Truth, were led by Alexander A. Bogdanov, a Bolshevik veteran and theorist. He developed Sapronov's analysis to the thesis that the socialist character of the Russian revolution was completely destroyed. The group demanded democracy, by which they meant freedom of political organization and the elimination of the Communist Party's control of the state.

A third group, called the Workers' Opposition, with a program essentially the same as those of Democratic Centralism and Workers' Truth,[14] was led by Alexandra Kollontai and Alexander G. Shlyapnikov. The group gained importance during 1920–1921.[15]

"At the Fourth All-Ukrainian Conference a group of supporters of 'Democratic Centralism,' led by Sapronov, came forward as the political exponents of the ideas of certain groups within the Party which had succumbed to the direct influence of petty-bourgeois and kulak elements. They emphatically opposed the independent organization of the poor peasants, the formation of Committees of Poor Peasants in the Ukraine. Yet without such organization, it would have been impossible to expropriate the land of the powerful class of Ukrainian kulaks, it would have been impossible to carry out in the Ukrainian villages the socialist revolution which had been effected in the Russian villages in the summer and autumn of 1918.

"By fighting against the socialist revolution in the Ukrainian countryside, the Sapronov group acted, in effect, as the agents of the Ukrainian kulaks" (N. Popov, *Outline History of the Communist Party of the Soviet Union*, New York: International Publishers, II, 87).

[14] Alexandra Kollontai, *Die Plattform der Arbeiteropposition* (Berlin, 1921).

[15] Cf. Ciliga's report of meeting the survivors of the various groups in Russian prisons and isolators, where he spent 1929–1934: Anton Ciliga, *The Russian Enigma* (London, 1940).

Sapronov, exiled to Siberia in the late twenties, did not appear at the big show trials. He survived at least till 1940, when friends in Paris received intermittent short personal messages. According to reports from Paris, he was among a group of oppositionists killed in 1941, after the outbreak of the German-Russian war. Bogdanov died in 1927 of natural causes. Smirnov disappeared during the purge period of the thirties. Ossinsky appeared as Vyshinsky's witness against Bukharin in the 1938 trial.

One of the most gifted of these Workers' Oppositionists was Alexander G. Shlyapnikov. Born in 1884, he entered the Social Democratic Party in 1900, as a boy of sixteen. After having participated in the 1905 revolution, he was sentenced to two years of prison. Between 1908 and 1914 he lived abroad. A metal worker, he spent his time organizing the trade-union; in 1917, he became a leading figure in the Petrograd soviet. In April 1917 he became chairman of the Metal Workers' Union and for a short period Peoples' Commissariat for Labor. In 1924, in order to remove him from Russia, he was sent to the Paris embassy; from there he came several times to Berlin to confer with Maslow and me. Between 1926 and 1929, he was again in Russia as president of the Metal Import Board. In 1930, at the time of the purge of the Trade-Union Opposition, he disappeared from sight.

Alexandra M. Kollontai, the member of the Workers' Opposition best known abroad, has lived a different life from all the others. Born in 1872, she entered the Social Democratic Party in 1899; on several occasions she was its representative to

War Communism and the Trade-Unions

Lenin had linked the War Communist economy to the improvement of the country's technical equipment by coöperation with revolutionary Germany. His "Electrification plus soviets are socialism" meant a high level of technical development combined with a full unfolding of a workers' democracy. Lenin was so much concerned with the technological level as an inalienable premise to council democracy that he called the first step of such an electrification plan "the second program of our party." The Eighth Congress of Soviets, December 22–29, 1920, adopted an electrification program, which was bound to one for the reconstruction of industry. The year 1920, which marked the virtual close of the civil war, was also the climax of a trend toward planned centralized economy.

One aspect of this trend was the proposal to use large-scale labor armies. The peasants' sons were not to be sent home to the countryside, where misery and starvation prevailed, but were to work as labor battalions wherever manpower was needed. During the civil war, following Lenin's appeal, volunteer labor brigades (called *subbotniki*, from the Russian word for Saturday) cleared roads and maintained railroad lines. Now this method was to be extended; the disrupted Russian economy was to be conquered by the same man, Trotsky, and with the same methods that had proved so efficacious in defeating the enemy. It was planned to militarize labor completely, if temporarily; not only was the Red Army to be maintained and transformed into a labor army, but it was to be enlarged through a draft of peas-

---

international women's congresses. In 1915, she joined the Bolsheviks, and Lenin sent her to the United States to organize support for his view among socialists. She returned to Petrograd in March 1917 and was arrested after the demonstration in July. She became a member of the Bolshevik Central Committee and of the Central Executive Committee of Soviets, and People's Commissar for Social Welfare. In 1920, she became vice-president of the International Women's Secretariat of the Comintern. In 1922, in order to remove her from Russia, she was sent as a staff member to the Oslo embassy, and the next year she became Soviet representative to Norway. In 1926, at the height of the campaign in Russia against the Workers' Opposition groups, she was sent still farther off, to Mexico. I saw her on her way there in Berlin, and she was depressed and unwilling to continue "the hopeless struggle." Since then, she has become a loyal follower of Stalin; she has been rewarded with a long series of diplomatic posts and, in 1933, the Order of Lenin.

ant workers. On January 15, 1920, the first labor army was formed out of the Third Red Army Corps, followed soon afterward by two others.

Three months later, with the verve of a great revolutionary tribune, Trotsky defended the project. Of the 1,150,000 industrial workers, he said, only 850,000 were working. "Where are the 300,000? They have gone away. Where to? To the village? Perhaps to other industrial occupations. Perhaps they are busy with speculation. Thus, in a military sense, as against 800,000 workers there are 300,000 deserters." Like soldiers, workers must be forced to do their duty. The trade-unions have an enormous task to mobilize the workers, but it is a different matter with the peasants because there is no trade-union apparatus to carry out the militarization of the village.

We must first, Trotsky continued, concentrate on the production of the means of production. "Only then, when we have the means of production, can we go over to the production of consumers' goods directly for the masses." Once having overcome the initial poverty, economic development will proceed by leaps and bounds, overtaking capitalist development. Important branches of industrial and home economy, for example, will be electrified without passing through the steam age.

"The bourgeois axiom" that compulsory work is not productive is correct only if free voluntary labor is compared with the feudal system. It is true that productivity of the labor armies is low and was at first even lower. Thirteen to fifteen soldiers, sometimes as many as thirty, cut only as much timber as three to four men before the war, or as much as one man in the northern provinces. But men of the first labor armies who had to cut timber spent a good portion of their time with transport; many of them did not know how to chop down a tree or cut it up, and there had been no instruction and no tools. "These circumstances are sufficient to explain the low productivity of labor."

We must draft a minimum number of peasants, and try to replace militarization by the concept of the duty of labor. However, we must fight against deserters with the methods of the army. "We cannot wait until every peasant and every peasant woman understand. We must compel everyone to stand at the place where he belongs . . . If there is unified party consciousness and party will, we will fulfill the greatest task in world history."[16]

Enthusiastically the planners, Larin, Kritzmann, and others,[17] enlarged this proposal to a general scheme for the reconstruction of Russian industry by militarization of all labor. This plan to reconstruct Russia by labor armies never materialized. In practice it amounted to using a portion of the army for such emergency tasks as the clearing of roads and railroad tracks and various reconstruction projects. Already in disintegration because of the continued "desertion" of peasant-soldiers, the plan ended completely with the installation of the NEP.

In this concept of state economy, there was no place for worker management and shop stewards. At the head of each of the new state enterprises was a single manager, in most cases a technician. In the

---

[16] Trotsky, "Ueber die gegenwärtigen Aufgaben des wirtschaftlichen Aufbaus," speech to the Ninth Party Congress, April 1920, *Russische Korrespondenz*, Berlin, July 1920, No. 10, pp. 11–19.

[17] Mikhail Alexandrovich Lurye, born in 1882, joined the Social Democratic Party in 1901 under the name Larin and the Menshevik faction in 1906. In exile in Stockholm during the war, he studied the German war economy; in articles in newspapers and economic journals in Russia and abroad, he contrasted German efficiency with the muddle in Russia and cited the war economy of Germany as the first practical effort to build a collective economy.

In 1917, Larin joined the Bolsheviks and returned to Russia. Overflowing with new ideas for the organization of Russian economy, he contributed to the concepts of the State Planning Commission, the Supreme Council of National Economy, the change of the old Tsarist administrative regions into units based on the economy, the Soviet monopoly of foreign trade. Partly because he was a newcomer to the party, partly because his rich fund of uncoördinated concepts was based on dogmatic schemata with little regard for the realities of Russian economy, Larin soon came to be considered as insufficiently serious. Lenin in particular opposed him and called the schemes of him and Kritzmann "tedious scholasticism, sometimes literary and sometimes bureaucratic." For Lenin, the Goelro—the plan for the electrification of Russia—was the only "scientific" one; his closest collaborator in economic matters was the Old Bolshevik, G. M. Krzhizhanovsky. With the installation of the NEP, Larin was eliminated from all influence. He continued to write articles on economic matters and died in Moscow in 1932.

One of the most fascinating larger works of this period, which develops economic theory into its philosophical implications, is L. Kritzmann, *Die heroische Periode der grossen russischen Revolution* (Berlin, 1929). See also V. P. Milyutin, *Die Organisation der Volkswirtschaft in Sowjet-Russland* (Berlin, 1921), *Sozialismus und Landwirtschaft* (Hamburg, 1920); I. Larin and L. Kritzmann, *Wirtschaftsleben und wirtschaftlicher Aufbau in Sowjet-Russland, 1917–1920* (Hamburg, 1921).

early period these specialists were subordinated to Communist commissars, whose duties referred not only to labor relations but to production plans proper. The new period of war economy had been opened with a mighty drive against workers' interference with production; the state manager had to be fully empowered to direct the enterprise. In this period trade-union membership became compulsory.

Parallel with the opposition of Bolshevik workers to the party rule, there was resistance in the trade-unions, which numbered in this period about three million members. Once poverty and civil war had made one-man management the rule, the question became who would designate this man—the party, the army, or the unions. The program of the Workers' Opposition groups [18] had had a wide response, but it was becoming obvious that now Lenin and the party would resist a return to the collective management of the early revolution. Russian trade-unionism announced its claim, to counter Trotsky's and the party's.

In contrast to the Western labor movement, Russian unions were a young organization. Under the Tsar, their growth had been handicapped by long underground periods. This is not to say that the Russian working class went into the revolution without experience in mass organization. Since the turn of the century, and particularly in the period around 1905, there had been a mass of educational societies, sick-benefit groups, cultural organizations, and especially coöperatives —all groups that served more or less as a school for trade-unionism. Immediately after the February revolution, unions were organized on a nationwide scale in the millions, in contrast to the hundreds of thousands in the party. Beside its proletarian core the party included peasants, intellectuals, and civil servants; but the unions were much more limited. More than any other Russian organization, their growth indicates the growth of economic awareness in industrial centers during these years. Throughout civil war they were bound to the party and army in intimate relation, but the influence of the Mensheviks was greater in the unions than in other Soviet institutions.

---

[18] "Workers' Opposition groups" here include not only the group of Shlyapnikov and Kollontai, but also the two previous factions, Democratic Centralism and Workers' Truth, and various other groupings expressing part of a general ideological trend against the monopoly of the State Party.

The proposals of the various Workers' Opposition groups were the topic of general discussion in 1919–1921. The union organizers demanded that they be given the task of managing industry; this in their view was the specific role of trade-unions in a socialist society. The fact that the unions were already centralized and disciplined would avoid the disadvantages of localism; on the other hand, that they represented a far broader stratum than the party would give them, in this key position, a role of counterbalancing its monopolistic aspirations. Though this trade-union platform and that of the Workers' Opposition group can be separated in party histories, in practice they were often supported by the same group of men.

> This faction was headed exclusively by the "Left" Communists of 1918—Ossinsky, Sapronov, Maximovsky, V. Smirnov and others. They used the same arguments against one-man management, against industrial armies, against the militarization of individual branches of industry as were used by the "Left" Communists two years earlier against the establishment of strict discipline in mills and factories, against the abolition of "the full power of the local authorities," against the creation of a strong centralized state apparatus, in fact against the proletarian dictatorship.[19]

The platforms of both the Workers' Opposition and the trade-unions were intended as a counter-plan to Trotsky's labor army and the party dictatorship. The discussion reached a culmination in the proposal of Shlyapnikov for a congress of producers, which would be the real government of the country. In a buffer group, Bukharin proposed the milder compromise that trade-union nominations to economic and administrative posts be binding for the Party. This "trade-union question" was the topic around which the Ninth Party Congress, in March–April 1920, revolved; the discussion reached its apex in November, at the Fifth All-Russian Trade-Union Congress.

The principal opponent of the unions was Trotsky, who wanted to transform them into a branch of a militarized economy.

> In the system of War Communism in which all the resources are, at least in principle, nationalized and distributed by government order, I saw no independent role for trade-unions. If industry rests on the state's insuring the supply of all the necessary

---

[19] Popov, *Outline History of the CPSU*, II, 91.

products to the workers, the trade-unions must be included in the system of the state's administration of industry and distribution of products.[20]

The trade-unions, under Mikhail P. Tomsky, fought this scheme. In retrospect, it might be said that such a fusion of trade-unions into the state apparatus would have reduced the unions to a labor front of the State Party, but in Trotsky's concept it was meant, partially at least, to counterbalance the dominance of the party in the state apparatus by strengthening his own apparatus. As leader of an army-labor combination, Trotsky would have had the key position in the party and in the state. Despite the bitterness of the dispute at this time between Trotsky and the Workers' Opposition, all the oppositionist groups alike hoped to shift power from the party to broader organizations. "The resemblance of the platform of the 'Workers' Opposition' to Trotsky's platform was that, while Trotsky spoke of turning the trade-unions into organs of the state, the 'Workers' Opposition' spoke of trade-unionizing the state." [21]

Against both oppositions, Lenin defended the party monopoly. He rejected the claims to trade-union management that Shlyapnikov and Tomsky put forward as an anarcho-syndicalist deviation, which meant that in his opinion they were incorrect in general and in particular unsuitable in the present disruption of Russian economy. Only much later did it become a basic tenet of Stalinism that anarcho-syndicalists had to be mercilessly liquidated as traitors to the working class. Lenin fought for the centralized power of the party, but always with a full consciousness of the dangers to the original concept of soviet democracy involved in the use of compulsory measures. This comes out most clearly in his opposition to Trotsky's plan of transforming the trade-unions into state labor organizations. For Lenin, the principal task of the unions was not to administer but to form a link between the governmental bodies and the broad masses, and to act as schools of Communism and economic management. This very limited concept did not allow the unions to share in the state power, but on the other hand Lenin defended the independent role of unions in the Soviet state as representatives of their class interests, imperative in a state still

---

[20] Trotsky, *My Life*, p. 464.
[21] Popov, *Outline History of the CPSU*, II, 116.

far removed from even the first phase of realizing its goal of a class-less workers' state. This argument followed from Lenin's life-long belief that trade-unionism is one of the three organic forms of prole-tarian struggle—the economic, the political and the theoretical. But it was not an answer to the problem, which grew in the next months to unmanageable proportions. The State Party, isolated, splitting be-tween its workers' and administrators' wings, estranged from the broad masses, suffered the growing hostility of the entire country and drifted toward catastrophe.

The Kronstadt Uprising

On March 1, 1921, following a strike wave that was most severe in Petrograd, the general unrest came to a climax in the fortress of Kronstadt, before the gates of Petrograd. The sailors and the garri-son called a citizens' meeting, which was attended by 16,000 people. Kalinin spoke in vain against the program this meeting adopted, which became the rallying point of the opposition in the country. The Kronstadt sailors formulated an alternate answer, imbued with the October spirit, to every major problem. They represented conflicting tendencies and groups—the multitude of dissatisfied peasants, the mid-dle class, the intellectuals, the organized counter-revolutionary nuclei, but also the opposition of the workers to state regimentation.

The Kronstadt program, made up in substance of the following points, has become increasingly relevant after twenty-five years of party dictatorship.

(1) New elections by secret ballot with full freedom of agitation in the pre-election campaign "among workers and peasants."

(2) Freedom of speech and press for workers and peasants, for an-archists and Left socialists.

(3) Freedom of assembly for labor unions and peasant organizations.

(4) Liberation of socialist and anarchist prisoners.

(5) Elimination of the practice by which the party has representa-tion in all Soviet institutions; no party should be given special priv-ileges in the propagation of its ideas and state support for such pur-poses.

(6) Abolition, in particular, of the corresponding party commissars in the army.

(7) Equality of rations for all who work, with the exception of those employed in trades detrimental to health.

(8) Abolition of Communist guards in mills and factories; where guards are necessary, the shop units should designate them from the ranks of the army and the factory workers, according to their judgment.

(9) Full freedom for peasants with regard to their land, on the condition that they manage it with their own means and without employing hired help.

(10) The right of craft production by one's own effort.[22]

The Bolshevik Party declared that the White Guardist General Kozlovsky was behind the Kronstadt uprising and therefore no compromise was possible. On March 7, at the order of the Politburo, Trotsky began the bombardment. Kronstadt was taken after ten days of battle, waged during the Tenth Party Congress. Between the 1st and the 17th of March, several regiments of the Petrograd garrison and of the sailors of the port were disarmed and sent to the Ukraine or the Caucasus. Arrests and executions throughout Russia followed. At the height of the mutiny, the fiftieth anniversary of the Paris Commune of 1871 was celebrated in Moscow.

Lenin had given Trotsky the order to take the Kronstadt fortress under artillery fire, but he realized that this first large-scale uprising against the state power, one so near the industrial and political center of Russia, Petrograd, marked the end of the old course. Lenin had held the party together by a series of compromises, by continuous realignment of conflicting groups. He had compromised with Trotsky on the question of army structure. He had tempered the opposition of the party organizers, led by Stalin, against Trotsky. He had tolerated the state planners, but had not permitted the fusion of the trade-unions into the state. He could not let the fortress Kronstadt fall into the hands of a group hostile to the party, but he also could tolerate the dangerous experiments with the Russian peasantry no longer. At this hour, Lenin gained his full stature and retook the reins of the party into his hands. A peasant economy cannot be industrialized by military and therefore terrorist measures. The dictatorship in Russia

---

[22] Emma Goldman, *My Further Disillusionment in Russia* (New York, 1924), pp. 67–68.

was based on two classes, and Lenin intended that this alliance be maintained. Following the Kronstadt uprising Lenin returned to his original concept of the transformation of Russian economy, which was as different from the reality of war economy as from the program of the state planners.

On March 8, the Tenth Party Congress assembled in Moscow. Recognizing how close the party was to a breakdown of its power, the delegates rallied around Lenin as the one man who might yet save them.

Under the slogan, "Give us back free trade," Lenin said, the country was in revolt against the Bolshevik dictatorship. The peasant masses and the urban middle class hoped that by overthrowing the rigid regimentation of the State economy they would be able to find a way out of their misery and poverty by the restoration of market relations between town and country. It was the protest of the small producer against an inefficient state industry. The rebellion reflected more, however, than the resistance of the petty bourgeoisie; it had deeply affected the proletariat and had spread to the factories of Moscow and the provinces. Lenin commented on "the ferment and discontent" lately manifest among non-party workers; at meetings recently held in Moscow, "it was evident that they were transforming 'democracy' and 'liberty' into slogans that would lead to the overthrow of Soviet power."

Lenin called on the working class not to abandon the State Party in the hour of its greatest peril. He advocated the strongest measures against dissidents; the Tenth Party Congress proscribed party factions, a step that later gave Stalin a starting point for his own methods.

In the midst of the country's turmoil, however, in terms that today seem shockingly polite and moderate for Communist polemics, Lenin discussed as much as attacked Shlyapnikov's views on Communist society, drawing on Engels to substantiate his point. He rejected the program of the Workers' Opposition as unrealizable under the conditions of want, and in a land where the peasant population would predominate for many years. The shortest period, he declared, in which large-scale industry can be organized sufficiently to make the worker the central figure of Russian economy is ten years, but he accepted this "anarcho-syndicalist" proposal as an opportunity for an interchange of opinion among party members on this principled question.

> But if a comprehensive discussion is necessary, let us have it, by all means; we shall find the people who will quote in detail the whole of our literature. And if it is necessary and appropriate, we shall raise this question internationally, for you have just heard the report of the representative of the Communist International and you all know that a certain deviation towards the Left exists in the ranks of the revolutionary international working-class movement. The deviation about which I have just spoken is the same as the anarchist deviation of the KAPD in Germany, the fight against which was clearly revealed at the last congress of the Communist International.

Lenin pleaded with Shlyapnikov for patience.

> A year or two of relief from famine, a year or two of regular supplies of fuel, so that the factories may function, and we shall receive a hundred times more assistance from the working class, and far more talent will arise from its ranks than now. No one has any doubt about this, nor can there be any doubts.

Lenin summed up this statement by declaring that the propagation of Shlyapnikov's program was incompatible with membership in the Communist Party, but added that "scientific research" on it should not be abandoned.

> If Comrade Shlyapnikov, for example, in addition to his recently published book on his experiences in the revolutionary struggle in the underground period, writes a second volume in his leisure time during the next few months in which he will analyze the concept "producer," we shall all be pleased.

Lenin analyzed the background of the crisis: The demobilization of the peasant army was releasing hundreds of thousands of "broken men" who could not find work, whose only trade had become war; the result was often banditry. "The demobilization created an incredible number of insurgent elements throughout the country." The proletariat is a small minority, while the peasants remain the overwhelming majority. "We could not demonstrate [to them] the superiority of large-scale production in practice, because this large-scale production has been destroyed." The area under cultivation, the means of production, and the yield have diminished; there is "absolute starvation" in the towns. The petty-bourgeois elements are arousing the peasantry against the workers, and that is more dangerous than Denikin, Yudenich, and Kolchak together.

Lenin ended his report with the lapidary words, "Owing to the economic situation, the Soviet power is shaking."

Lenin proposed to announce "that very evening over the radio to all parts of the world that the Congress of the Government Party has substituted a tax for the food quotas and has thus given a stimulus to the small farmer to enlarge his farm." He referred to a law dated October 30, 1918, introducing taxation in kind, which had remained a dead letter. The kernel of Lenin's New Economic Policy (NEP) was not taxation in kind alone, nor even the security given the peasant by ensuring him a fair return for his labor, but the return to a limited market system and the creation thereby of a changed political atmosphere in the country.

The utopian period was over. In Europe the trend was obviously towards regaining social equilibrium after the post-war crisis, and, despite all the emphasis on the world revolution, the Bolsheviks were not counting on rapid changes in Asia. "During the past three years we have learned to understand that banking on an international revolution does not mean calculating on a definite date . . . That is why we must be able to coördinate our activities with the class relationships in our country and in other countries, in order that we may be able to maintain the dictatorship of the proletariat for a long period and remedy, if only gradually, all the misfortunes and crises which have befallen us." [23]

---

[23] Lenin, reports to the Tenth Congress of the Russian Communist Party (Bolsheviks), March 1921, *Selected Works,* English edition (Moscow, 1937), IX, 83–130.

Chapter 7 · The United Communist Party · · · · · · · · · · ·

In the first phase of its reorganization after the convention in December 1920, there was transferred to the ranks of the United Communist Party of Germany the disenchantment of the Independent Socialists who entered it. After having freed themselves with so much turmoil from their reformist tradition, they heard with bewilderment the message of the New Economic Policy that from now on Russian Communists would be good merchants and salesmen. The Levi-Radek group in the German party greeted the new line with enthusiasm. To them the NEP was the password to an equally sharp turn in German policy. Paul Levi hoped for an authorization by Lenin to adapt the NEP to Germany, so that the party could participate in a Social Democratic government by developing the new party as a pressure group. The USPD neophytes were outraged by this proposal; it seemed to them a gross perversion of the tasks of the party and a dangerous misconception of the situation in Germany.

Karl Radek had come to Germany immediately after the unification, to set the party on this new course. In an Open Letter published on January 6, 1921, he proposed the united action of the workers' parties to shift the burden of the reparations "from the shoulders of the proletariat to the shoulders of the bourgeoisie." This Open Letter, intended to lead the Communist leaders straight into the ministers' chairs, was a complete about face from Luxemburg's political abstentionism.

The United Communist Party expected to get a half million dues-paying members, a figure that was never reached. By March 1921, just before a new split, there were 300,000 to 350,000 members, and after this the membership declined to about 200,000. The reorganization combined traditional Social Democratic features with new forms creeping in from Moscow, with the scientific manipulation of the masses as the major object.

A special department for trade-union work was created at Communist headquarters, modeled after the pattern of the central board of the German Federation of Labor. Specialists followed closely the inside developments in all the various trade-unions and organized parallel groups of experts to guide the Communists in the unions. Another department, directed by Edwin Hörnle,[1] was created to specialize in Communist propaganda and organization in rural areas. The mentality of the Communist Party of 1922–1923 is nicely illustrated by the various pocket calendars published during the period. One of these [2] begins, on its first page, as follows:

To Be Filled In Immediately

This book belongs to ....
Address ....
Membership number: Party ....
                   Union ....

For each of the days of the year, there is a space to be filled in, as follows:

Meeting ....
Caucus (or committee) meeting ....
Reporter ....
Result ....

It is a curious publication for a party clandestinely preparing for the seizure of power.

In accordance with the Twenty-One Conditions for entrance into

---

[1] In 1947 Deputy for Agricultural Reforms in the Russian-occupied zone of Germany.

[2] *Taschenkalender der KPD, 1923* (Berlin, 1922).

the Comintern, special attention was given to building up an underground organization parallel to the legal party. In 1920 the underground section had been composed mainly of military detachments of the old USPD cadres, together with party sympathizers. They called themselves *Der Apparat* (The Apparatus); their "general staff" was headed by Ernst Däumig and Emil Barth. The members of this well organized group held in contempt the military organization of the Spartakusbund, with which they later united. The Russian specialists considered all these German underground organizations worthless and undertook a reorganization; the *Apparat* was smashed and many an Independent Socialist eliminated. Whenever resistance groups independent of the party developed, their activities were officially condemned and banned for party members.

During 1918–1920 the Spartakusbund had been mainly an underground organization, but of a different type from the various new "divisions for special tasks." The underground activities of the Spartakusbund were born in the fight against the Freikorps; they were independent of the Moscow state apparatus and Moscow advisers. Technically they were weak and ineffective, but in spirit they maintained in underground life all the specific features of their socialist origin. The Russian agents in the German labor movement introduced new elements, tried to adjust the defense corps built up for the protection of the movement to the purposes of the Russian state, which wanted a secret service organization on German soil.

The new apparatus was streamlined; the M-Group (military apparatus proper), intended to train cadres of Red soldiers, was organized as a skeleton army. The men got basic training, sometimes under Russian officers, made secret maneuvers and night marches, and learned how to use hand grenades and light artillery. Access to the arms, hidden in caches, was permitted only to the leaders, men trusted by the liaison to the Russian secret police.

All the leaders of the Central Committee were anxious to gain personal influence within these military groups and allocated to them large portions of the party budget, always promising them still more. Yet at the same time there was a tug of war between the military apparatus and the Central Committee, who considered these preparations for civil war out of date. It gradually transformed the M-Men into study groups on military theory, with their sole active role the protection of party meetings. This met stiff resistance from the USPD workers, who demanded on the contrary more help in the acquisition of weapons and the care of those already acquired and hidden. There were many incidents in the course of these clandestine maneuvers, and for reasons of conspiracy the men arrested as a result were denied open party support. The leaders of the legal party, on the other hand, were protected by laws of parliamentary immunity and, in cases of the arrest of other leaders, by noisy party campaigns.

Another secret apparatus began to gain weight in the internal life of the party, the N-Group (*Nachrichten*—intelligence). This was better equipped and had a larger staff of politically trained leaders and larger funds at its disposal. The N-Men began to take over tasks that had been assigned to the M-Men, for instance, the protection of important party meetings or of Russian agents passing underground through Germany. Research groups were established. Small bands of five to ten men armed with revolvers and hand grenades were assigned to special duties. A subdivision, the Z–Group (*Zersetzung*—disruption), entered hostile organizations masked as their adherents and thus gained influence and information from the inside. Groups groomed for disrupting army and police formations were bound to the party by scrupulously concealed contacts. T-Groups (*Terror*) were singled out for sabotage missions and the liquidation of traitors.

Thus, from the beginning of the United Communist Party there was a sharp split of policy on all party levels. The series of incidents in 1921 most inadequately called the March Action, in which these groups were active for the first time, has won a certain prominence in Comintern history; it became the hub of an involved discussion on questions of revolutionary tactics and of the interference of the Russian secret service agents in the German labor movement. Lenin, Trotsky, Zinoviev, Radek, Bukharin, but not Stalin, took part in the discussion, which broadened into a general survey of Communist strategy.

The March Action

In the months preceding the Kronstadt revolt, March 1921, an action in Germany to divert the Russian workers from their own troubles

had been concocted by a caucus of the Russian party, centering around
Zinoviev and Béla Kun. Levi's reports had grossly exaggerated the
forces of the new German party; according to them a few incidents
would suffice to bring about the same lineation of forces as during
the Kapp putsch. Kun and A. Guralsky, a former member of the
Left Poale Zion,[3] a man with experience in the underground Polish
labor movement, were sent to Berlin in February 1921 with a secret
mandate from the caucus probably not endorsed by the Politburo.
They started their offensive in the Mansfeld coal region in Central
Germany where there was constant conflict between the miners and
the Prussian police detachments.. Following an uprising in Mansfeld,
conditions would be ripe for a general strike; this would lead to a
socialist government, which by its sheer existence would inject new
life into the discouraged and rebellious Russian workers.

The new M- and T-Groups were assigned to provoke the Freikorps,
in order to set the unions in motion. Several bombs were exploded in
Breslau and Halle; several other bombings planned for Berlin did not
materialize. Hugo Eberlein, who had had experience in sabotage in
Upper Silesia, was put in charge; following this unhappy assignment
the rank and file gave him the nickname *Hugo mit der Zündschnur*
("Hugo with the Quick-match").

The strike was complete only in Mansfeld and parts of Thuringia
and Saxony. For a few days Mansfeld resembled the Ruhr during
the Kapp putsch. Max Hoelz left the Vogtland, joined the Mansfeld
guerrillas, and organized the Hoelz guards. The scattered workers'
forces could not fuse themselves into a unit, mainly because the Leuna
workers, armed and able to organize a full division, locked themselves
inside their factory and awaited the offensive of the Reichswehr.

There were partial strikes in the Ruhr and in Berlin. Independent
of the Mansfeld action, there were local strikes and riots throughout
restive Germany. The Mansfeld uprising, however, was too localized
to crystallize these diverse activities into a countrywide general strike.
Compared with the Kapp putsch, the March Action turned out to be
a minor episode.

The reprisal was much more effective; side by side with the police,

---

[3] A Jewish socialist party founded in 1901 in Russia. In 1922 the Left wing
joined the Comintern.

the Reichswehr attacked. Workers' villages were shelled with artillery. An armed train arrived from Wurttemberg; students from Göttingen made a special raid on the town of Sangerhausen, in the Halle region. The guerrillas destroyed rail tracks, bridges, and stations, blocking traffic almost completely for a week. Villages and small towns changed hands several times. During the raids on workers' quarters, some fifty to sixty workers were killed. Some of the prisoners were beaten by Reichswehr soldiers and forced to shout in the streets "Long live the Reichswehr!" [4]

Some of Levi's friends—organizers of the Berlin metal workers union, Paul Malzahn and Paul Neumann—had toured the city's factories and called on the workers to abstain from striking in support of the Mansfeld strikers. In an outburst of indignation, the party demanded the immediate expulsion of Levi and these strike-breakers.

At this climax of the party crisis, Lenin intervened. He gave energetic support to Levi at the Third World Congress, meeting in July-August 1921, on whose agenda "the German question" was an important item. The German delegation, led by August Thalheimer and Paul Frölich, presented a carefully prepared thesis on "the revolutionary offensive"—a theory that the working class could be moved only when set in motion by a series of offensive acts. Lenin rejected this theory. He did not openly attack the Zinoviev-Kun caucus for their activities in Germany, but in his support of Levi's polemics against them there was an implied but obvious opposition to their tactics.

Levi turned his campaign against the March Action into a bitter crusade against Zinoviev as Comintern Chairman; this attempt to oust Zinoviev Lenin adamantly rejected. At first the congress supported the German delegation in its brief for the March Action. Lenin fought against this offensivism and won his point, with certain qualifications. The March Action was declared one step forward —which was ambiguous because it was associated in every Communist's mind with the remainder of the title of a Lenin pamphlet

---

[4] A committee of the Prussian Diet again investigated the brutalities of the Reichswehr and the police. According to Communist estimates (*Taktik und Organisation der revolutionären Offensive: Die Lehren der März-Aktion,* VKPD, Berlin, 1921), some 7000 men were arrested, of whom hundreds were sentenced to long prison terms. Apart from whether this figure is exact, the reprisals were indeed harsh.

—and two steps back. The ambiguity protected the authority of the party against Levi, but attempted to integrate his criticism in its policy. Lenin read into the theses of the congress large portions of Levi's criticism, but, by discarding all illusions on the possibility of a peaceful development of the Weimar Republic, he gave them a different emphasis.

In his report to the congress on world affairs, Trotsky presented the new orientation of the Politburo to the perspective for world revolution. The post-war crisis had been mastered by the capitalist powers, which had been able to reëstablish a political and economic equilibrium. From this premise, Trotsky asked for a sharp change of Communist policy to digging in, to concentrating on the building of mass parties; the era of world revolutionary expansion had definitely come to a standstill. Trotsky presented his report as party spokesman, but his interpretation emphasized to an extreme degree the stabilization of capitalism. Without a basically different analysis of the situation, Trotsky on the one hand and Lenin and Zinoviev on the other differed substantially concerning the continuity of the stabilization and the possibility of further action by the Communist parties. The nuance of this difference between Lenin and Trotsky consisted in a more or less cautious interpretation of not only the stabilizing but also the de-stabilizing factors. Trotsky's analysis was regarded as closer to Levi's than to Lenin's.

I was present at many closed party meetings where Lenin's defense of Levi was bitterly resented. He was called an opportunist, a Right-winger; the expected disciplinary measures against Béla Kun and his group were considered unwarranted. In this fever of emotional indignation against him, a sober evaluation of the political consequences of the new tactics he proposed was lost. The Left wing of the party became more and more incensed at this protection of Levi. In the acrimonious discussion that developed, the March Action and Levi's opposition to it were quickly pushed aside and the emphasis shifted to the future policy of the party.

Around Levi there was a multitude of conciliatory groups; they all accepted Levi's policy and blamed Levi's insubordination. It became clear after a while that Levi was developing from his criticism of the March Action and its abortive terrorism a general reëvaluation of Communism in Germany, soon to become a principled opposition to Bolshevism. His emphatic rejection of putschism was based on his belief that Germany could return to normalcy if labor did not provoke the enemy class. Stressing the difference between Russia and the West, he attacked Bolshevism for its Asiatic character; he called the Russian agents in Germany the mullahs of Khiva and Bokhara. Lenin had accepted Levi's break of discipline as a measure necessary for correcting the party policy, but when he saw the drift of his general analysis, he dropped him, as the Bolsheviks say, completely and absolutely.

The March Action had a serious effect on the new party in Germany. Paul Levi, who had painted the prospects of the unification in splendid colors, published a pamphlet, *The March Action: What Is the Crime?*, attacking the putschists in the party. Among other important leaders, two deputies to the Reichstag joined in his protest, Clara Zetkin and old Adolph Hoffmann, a typical socialist pacifist. (Years before, he had formulated "Ten Commandments for Free Thinkers," and his nickname in the party was "Ten-Commandments Hoffmann.")

On July 8, 1921, at the German-Russian border on her way to the Third World Congress, Clara Zetkin had had her papers on the March Action confiscated by the Prussian police, undoubtedly with her tacit agreement. The partial support the Levi group received from Lenin left them in a quandary whether to seek to regain control of the party or to split and form a new group. When they decided that their defeat was certain, the Social Democratic *Vorwärts* published, on December 25, the material seized from Zetkin six months earlier. Two more Reichstag deputies, Kurt Geyer and Wilhelm Düwell, left the party; some time later, two more followed, Ernst Däumig, the one-time leader of the Shop Stewards' Committee, and Marie Wackwitz.[5]

---

[5] During the Second War, Geyer was in London, the leader of a pro-British group of German refugees associated with Vansittart.

About the same time as these associates of Paul Levi, but independently, a prominent leader of the Left wing, Dr. Ernst Reuter-Friesland, also quit the party. With a socialist-pacifist background, Reuter had been taken prisoner on the Eastern front; when the revolution came in Russia, he sided with the Bolsheviks and helped to organize support for them, particularly among the Volga Germans. About the turn of the year 1919–1920 he returned to Berlin and entered the Spartakusbund. After the unification with the USPD in December 1920, he was elected by the Left wing as the first Political Secretary of the new Berlin-Branden-

These dissidents gathered around a periodical that Levi began to publish, *Unser Weg* ("Our Way"), and founded the KAG (*Kommunistische Arbeitsgemeinschaft*—Working Committee for Communism).[6] In January 1922, twenty-eight high party functionaries, expelled by the Central Committee for circulating *Unser Weg,* joined Levi's splinter group. Levi edited Rosa Luxemburg's pamphlet on the Russian revolution and made it the cornerstone of his propaganda against the Bolsheviks. Clara Zetkin, who had encouraged Levi, remained in the party; posing as *the* intimate friend of Rosa, who had known her innermost thoughts, she became the official mouthpiece of the Comintern in fighting this pamphlet as a distortion.[7]

---

burg organization. In this period I worked together with him at Münzstrasse, 24 and learned at first hand of his unusual organizational talent. During the March crisis Reuter opposed Levi and after his exit was elected General Secretary of the Central Committee. With his knowledge of Russian, it took him only a few months in this key spot to become convinced that there was nothing to be done to combat the growing Russian influence; at the end of 1921 he quit the party and entered the Social Democratic organization.

For a time he was editor of *Vorwärts;* then he became a member of the City Council of Berlin and later the city's Commissioner for Transport Services, a post in which he demonstrated his administrative talent in modernizing its transit system. He left Germany after Hitler came to power; from 1935 to 1946 he was in Ankara as adviser to the Transport Minister of the Turkish government. When he returned to Berlin in 1946, he was elected mayor of the city but was not allowed to take office. He became the key figure of a bitter fight between the Social Democratic Party and the Soviet occupation authorities.

According to a *New York Times* dispatch dated July 10, 1947, "Today's *Tägliche Rundschau,* the Russian Military Government's official paper for Germans, carried a long interview with General [Alexander G.] Kotikov in which he opened the record to the Russian objections to Dr. Reuter, renegade Communist. General Kotikov accused Dr. Reuter of being anti-Soviet, having a 'pretty dark and dubious' record in Turkey from 1935 to 1946 and being considered by the then German Ambassador to Turkey Franz von Papen, 'useful for Hitler Germany.'

"In addition, General Kotikov said, Dr. Reuter is unqualified for his City Council post. He said that the Social Democrats who elected Dr. Reuter had known the Russian position but precipitated a city crisis by electing him nevertheless. As for the Russian right to veto an elected official, General Kotikov pointed out that General Lucius D. Clay subscribed to this principle."

[6] The Communist youth organization was particularly influenced. "The party has many senile habits. At the party meetings, they smoke and drink."

At the end of 1922 there was a different trend in the youth movement. In Berlin a Communist group, Awakening Youth, was founded; a party report (*Bericht über die Verhandlungen des III. (8.) Parteitages der Kommunistischen Partei Deutschlands,* Berlin, 1923, p. 118) describes this movement as "aiming at direct interference with meetings and demonstrations of the reactionary groups by small youth squadrons composed of 25 or 30 activists and militant young people."

[7] In 1922 Levi's group entered the USPD, now led by Hilferding, and with it reëntered the Social Democratic Party in September of that year. Levi was elected

A German NEP?

The decisions of the Third World Congress stimulated another passionate discussion on the degree of capitalist stabilization. After Levi's exit another old Spartakist, Ernst Meyer, former editor of the Social Democratic *Vorwärts,* became the chairman of the German Politburo. Meyer, also a close disciple of Rosa Luxemburg, was a refined intellectual, deeply interested in art and literature, a subtle and complex personality. His high standing in party circles was based on his devotion to the cause, but he was absolutely incapable of personal intimacy with the proletarians in his own party.

Ernst Meyer, stimulated and supported by Karl Radek, repeated Levi's thesis that the NEP marked the definite end of an era, which meant in German terms that the civil war was over. The German revolution has petered out, he declared; the German Republic will adjust to the new conditions and fight for a new status in post-Versailles Europe; its policy will revolve around the lightening of the reparations. German Communists have to reorient their basic policy and concentrate on organizing a united front with all labor and middle-class groups to shift the taxes for reparations from these classes to big business and the large landowners. Meyer went one step further than Levi. Adapting the Russian formula to Germany, he proposed "taxation in kind," by which he meant the government would administer heavy industry in order to pay reparations debts. The workers would be guaranteed high wage standards and an extensive social security program, and all additional profits would be turned over by the government to the Reparation Commission. The Communist slogan, "Seize 51% of all real values," covered bank assets, stocks and bonds, as well as real estate, factories, mines, and so on. This state control of all key industries, introduced as a means of paying reparations, would finally result in a socialist state economy, making superfluous a violent overthrow of the government.

Social Democratic Reichstag deputy from Chemnitz and as such coördinated the Left elements of the party throughout the Reich in a loose grouping. He tried incessantly to change the course of the Social Democratic Party, which he came more and more to consider disastrous. He died in 1929 by jumping out of a window during an attack of fever and was mourned by many socialists as a brilliant personality and a sincere fighter against German militarism.

Meyer called his program the German NEP,[8] which could be realized before the seizure of power by the Communists—that is to say,
without the seizure of power. The NEP, he maintained, is the decisive phase of socialist transformation; War Communism and expropriation were fundamental errors that should never be repeated. Not
only the economic program of the NEP was to be imitated, but the
social and cultural restorative measures were a healthy and inevitable
reaction against "the spirit of 1917."

On the eve of the Fourth World Congress of the Comintern, in
November 1922, about three thousand delegates of the Berlin party
assembled in the *Kliems Festsäle* to formulate a program in strong
opposition to Ernst Meyer's German NEP. I was elected delegate to
the Comintern congress, with the explicit assignment of opposing
this program there. The convocation and its deliberations were completely in accord with the party's constitution, but the assembly's
aggressive attack on Comintern policy was used by Meyer as a pretext to propose to the Presidium that it take disciplinary measures
against the rebellious Left wing. The Left leaders, in the words of
the Central Committee, were anti-Bolshevik; their expulsion would
emphasize that the NEP was obligatory for all of the Comintern.
Ernst Meyer's group in the party called themselves the Conciliators,
indicating a will to bring the Levi group back in. As a first step,
they tried to get Lenin to consent to expel the Left wing by exposing
their contacts in Berlin and Moscow with the Workers' Opposition
groups.

After the Tenth Russian Party Congress, Shlyapnikov, Lutovinov,
and Myasnikov had been sent to Berlin on various trade missions,

---

[8] In 1946 in Berlin the Radical Democratic Party, calling itself a bourgeois-labor
party, resurrected Meyer's 51% seizure of industry. On July 8, in its application for
a license, it submitted to Allied Headquarters a program rejecting Marxism and
therefore the Social Democrats, for "this party is headed by men who did not
accomplish any progressive reforms before 1932." By a political combination of the
middle class with labor, the Radical Democrats want to promote an economic
system in which the important enterprises would be state-controlled, with 49% of
the stock in the hands of private capital. Controlled capitalism, they declare, has
shown its capabilities in the United States.

This program was implemented by demands for social reforms, including the
expropriation of estates larger than 620 acres, trade-union development without compulsory membership, uniform schooling up to nine years, religious instruction of
youth by the churches (*New York Times*, July 9, 1946).

principally in order to eliminate them for a while from Russian party life. They all got in touch with the Berlin Communists, the center of the Left opposition in the German party, as well as with the dissident Communists, the KAPD. A friendship sprang up between them and the Russian-born Arkadi Maslow, the leader of the Berlin Communists. In secret sessions at the home of Arthur Rosenberg, later the historian of the German Republic, they reported on the workers' situation in Russia. They asked the Berlin organization to continue with all its energy to fight against state regimentation, the State Party, and the degeneration of Communism, to build up its Left wing as independently as possible. About these contacts between the Russian and German Left, the underground organization had certainly delivered ample reports to the Russian Politburo.

The Conciliators had had a partial success; they got Lenin to write a letter to the Seventh Convention of the German party, in Jena, August 1921, recommending the temporary elimination of Maslow from German party life. In this letter Lenin, in reviewing the Levi crisis, tried to counteract the tendency toward splintering the party and to remold the groups into a new unit. "It would be a good thing if the German party sent Maslow and two or three of his overzealous supporters and comrades-in-arms who obviously do not wish to support the 'peace treaty' [by which was meant the Comintern arrangement between the Right and Left wings of the German party] to Soviet Russia for a year or two." [9] The Right wing expected the party convention to take a corresponding decision to enforce Lenin's suggestion. But the convention rejected it by an overwhelming majority, and against the will of the delegates Lenin did not take any further action. The Right wing continued, however, to intrigue for the physical elimination of Left leaders by sending them to Russia; for them stringent measures against the Workers' Opposition groups in Russia meant as a counterpart the cutting off of this syndicalist wing of their party. Since they were not able to effect that by democratic party procedure, they appealed to the power of the Russian state via Comintern channels to do it for them.

Lenin had taken rigid measures against the Workers' Opposition

---

[9] Lenin, "A Letter to German Communists," August 14, 1921, *Selected Works,* English edition, X, 296.

groups and, as the outstanding leader of the party, carried the responsibility for them, attracting to his person the hatred of the opposition. It was in this period that he became the object of attack by Left Communists throughout the world. But in spite of his strong rebuttal to the Workers' Opposition, he held the door of the party wide open to them; during and after the Kronstadt crisis his attitude reflected his consciousness of the implications of the social and party split and the responsibility of the party in it. Lenin's ambiguous attitude towards the Workers' Opposition has proved to be quite an inadequate amelioration of the stern party discipline he imposed, but it must be put against the revisionist fury that seized the party and the Comintern during the first year of the NEP and the constant pressure on Lenin to enforce rigid measures against the Comintern Left.

Discussion with Lenin

I arrived in Moscow in November 1922, a few weeks after Mussolini's march on Rome, as Berlin delegate to the Fourth World Congress. From the day of my arrival I was stigmatized as an anti-Bolshevik, who would probably be expelled and in the interim should be treated accordingly. Radek and Bukharin tried to save me, to convince me to drop my opposition to the Central Committee and to accept their interpretation of the situation in Germany. By Radek's analysis, Germany's civil war had ended with the defeat of the proletariat. The collapse of the German bourgeoisie was not in sight; on the contrary, German bourgeois rule was gaining continuously and considerably in strength. Along with other Left delegates, from Hamburg and the Ruhr, I opposed this suggested policy and asked for a hearing of our views.

A meeting was arranged between the Russian delegates, in fact the Politburo, and the German delegation. The German crisis was considered so important that Lenin, already very sick and no longer actively participating in every-day affairs, headed the Russian delegation, composed also of Zinoviev, Bukharin, Trotsky and Radek. The meeting took place in one of the salons of the Kremlin, near St. Andrew's Hall, where the congress was in session. This appearance of Lenin created a sensation among the assembled delegates. The mood of the foreign Communists was turned towards a conciliatory policy abroad, and the German Left delegates were unpopular at the congress. Our expulsion was expected as a result of this conference, and if Lenin had proposed it he would have easily gained a large majority for the motion. Stalin was not present; at this time he remained aloof from Comintern matters.

Lenin, ill and pale, sat between Zinoviev and Trotsky and listened attentively to Ernst Meyer's thesis on the consequences of the Russian NEP on German Communist affairs. Meyer was supported by a delegate from Bremen, Karl Becker, an intimate friend of Radek, originally a member of the International Socialist group, which had always been regarded by the Bolshevik Party as their next of kin in Germany.

Meyer and Becker, using Leninist terminology, developed their program for a German NEP and summed up their political conclusions with the demand that immediate punitive measures be taken against the Left. As a minimum, its leaders should be eliminated from office by exiling them to Russia. The Berlin and Hamburg organizations should be thoroughly purged and reorganized, by the authority of the Lenin Politburo and with the assistance of its special agents. Significantly for the later transformation of the party, the Spartakist leaders, as soon as they were unable to get their policy accepted by democratic party procedure, opened their drive for Reformist Communism by seeking Russian state intervention in the life of their party, contrary to the Comintern mores of the time.

Karl Liebknecht and Rosa Luxemburg had fought all their lives against the discipline imposed by the National Executive Committee of the Social Democratic Party. But before 1914 the strongest measure that Ebert and Scheidemann could take against them was their expulsion, which could not be effected without the consent of the local branch. As party members, the oppositionists had access to the press; Radek, for example, was for years the editor of various party dailies. Liebknecht was a Reichstag deputy. The oppositionists all got important party positions if they won the support of the rank and file. Before 1914 the Social Democratic bureaucracy could not assign bothersome oppositionists to a task in Siberia; Luxemburg had won permanent residence in the country by the simple device of a formal marriage with a German national. When Ernst Meyer, Rosa's disciple, asked Lenin to eliminate Maslow from Germany because of his Russian origin, he introduced a new element into German Communism.

I defended the arguments of the Left: The Left opposition of Berlin and Hamburg endorsed the NEP as necessary for Russia, because it adjusted the methods of socialist transformation to an agrarian economy and to the current political situation in Europe. But the NEP did not eliminate the concept introduced by the October revolution [10] of workers' management in a workers' state. If this vision of transforming capitalism into a socialist society was to be stigmatized as a fundamental error, to be replaced on a world scale by the NEP, a concubinage of capitalism with state capitalism, then the founding of the Comintern had been an error that should be corrected by its immediate dissolution.

In Germany, to accept such a program of gradual transformation would be unrealistic and dangerous. Our task could not be limited to the furtherance of a list of labor demands but had to focus action against the counter revolutionaries, who had continued their regrouping without a break and were almost ready for another coup. If we destroyed the militant spirit of our young Communist organization, we would but pave the way for the restoration of German imperialism. We rejected the erroneous and mechanical application of the NEP to Germany; it had no direct bearing on our present and pressing tasks.

At this point Lenin spoke and surprised the meeting with a firm rebuttal of Meyer's defense of Leninist principles. The specific conditions, he said, that made the NEP the only correct policy for Russia were not duplicated in the more advanced West. He emphasized the immaturity, the lack of organizational experience of the Russian proletariat, and repeated once again that the fight against the counter revolutionaries was immeasurably harder in Germany than in Russia but that socialist realization would be incommensurably easier. There was nothing new in Lenin's analysis; he had interpreted the German situation in the same terms time and again. But the audience was surprised by his resolute reaffirmation at this time of his long-standing evaluation of the strength and method of the German counter revolution.

---

[10] On February 8, 1918, the Russian calendar was put forward thirteen days to make it conform with the Gregorian calendar in general use in the West. What had been the February revolution began by this new system on March 8; what had been the October revolution on November 7. Throughout this book, specific dates are given in the revised calendar, but references to "the October revolution" have been so written, both to maintain the emotional content of the phrase and to avoid confusion with the November events in Germany.

Lenin's speech implied the rejection of all disciplinary action against the Left. This rejection of state intervention into German Communist affairs should be considered in conjunction with one of the last speeches he made on the Comintern, at the same Fourth Congress. In his summary of five years of the Russian revolution, Lenin closed with a commentary on Comintern methods. Our resolutions on the organizational structure of the Communist parties and on the methods and content of our work, he said, are almost thoroughly Russian. That is to say, everything is taken from Russian conditions. That has a bad side. It is too Russian not because it is written in Russian but because it is thoroughly permeated with the Russian spirit. Foreigners are not able to understand these decisions; they are not able to carry them out. "I have the impression that we made a big mistake with this resolution, namely, that we ourselves have blocked our road to further success." [11]

Following Lenin, Zinoviev defended the Berlin and Hamburg Left against the Right wing, as did to my surprise Radek and Bukharin, too. Lenin had again intervened to amalgamate the various elements of the German party. On his initiative the Comintern had made a serious attempt in 1919 to coöperate with the anarcho-communists. In 1921 Lenin had tried to conserve the Right-winger, Paul Levi, in the party. In 1922, at the Fourth World Congress, Lenin intervened for the third time and opposed the expulsion of the Left, which he had severely criticized on several occasions. At all crucial points, Lenin's intervention in German Communist affairs presents an attitude directly opposed to that of his successor Stalin. Lenin nursed the cadres of German Communism so carefully because he took with deadly seriousness the threat of the German counter revolution. Again, as so often in the past, the sponsor of iron party discipline stood for an application of this discipline with careful consideration of every alternative revolutionary policy.

Lenin's compromise worked out poorly in Berlin. It did not relieve the tension between the Left and the Central Committee, which prepared the next party convention in such a way as to create the conditions for a sharp turn towards Reformist Communism and to purge the party of all oppositionist elements.

---

[11] Lenin, report delivered at the Fourth Congress of the Communist International, November 13, 1922, *Selected Works,* English edition, X, 320–333.

2.

NATIONAL BOLSHEVISM

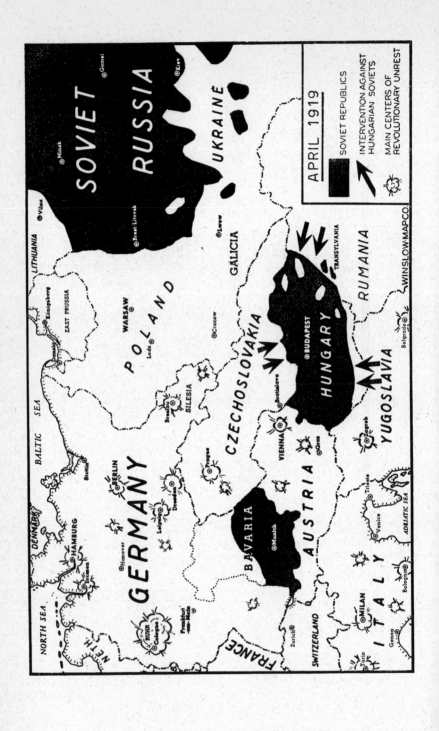

APRIL 1919

SOVIET REPUBLICS

INTERVENTION AGAINST
HUNGARIAN SOVIETS

MAIN CENTERS OF
REVOLUTIONARY UNREST

SOVIET RUSSIA

UKRAINE

LITHUANIA

Gomel

Kiev

Minsk

Vilna

Brest-Litovsk

Lwow

GALICIA

Konigsberg

EAST PRUSSIA

WARSAW

POLAND

Crscow

SILESIA

Breslau

Lodz

Danzig

Stettin

BALTIC SEA

TRANSYLVANIA

RUMANIA

BUDAPEST

HUNGARY

Bratislava

CZECHOSLOVAKIA

Belgrade

YUGOSLAVIA

Zagreb

Graz

VIENNA

Prague

Dresden

Leipzig

BERLIN

Hanover

GERMANY

DENMARK

HAMBURG

NORTH SEA

RUHR
Cologne

Frankfurt
Main

BAVARIA

Munich

AUSTRIA

Trieste

Venice

ADRIATIC SEA

Zurich

SWITZERLAND

FRANCE

NETH.

ITALY

MILAN

Bologna

Genoa

Turin

WINSLOW-MAP CO.

As stipulated by the Versailles Treaty, Upper Silesia was to decide by a plebiscite whether to join Germany or Poland, and the date of this plebiscite was set for March 20, 1921. In the early spring of 1921 Polish guerrillas under Korfanty[1] penetrated Upper Silesia, in the region around Gleiwitz and Ratibor, which was considered German. Frei-korps troops, reinforced by Bavarian auxiliaries, entered the area with the silent acquiescence of the German government,[2] and a minor war developed between the two irregular forces, complicated by constant strikes of the Upper Silesian miners and the activities of the Social Democrats and trade-unions. The miners, among whom there were many Poles, did not welcome the Freikorps; and the Communist Party in the region, reflecting this view, did not oppose Korfanty. However, the result of the plebiscite was a German majority of 717,122 against a large Polish minority of 483,514. After the plebiscite, the Allied Control Council divided Upper Silesia into three zones, one each to Poland and Germany and one under its control.

Meeting in London, the Reparation Commission (Repco) notified

---

[1] Wojciech A. Korfanty was a deputy to the Reichstag from 1903 to 1918 as representative of the Polish minority in Upper Silesia. In a statement at Brest-Litovsk, Radek cited Korfanty as the one who typified the real spirit of Poland in the German Reichstag (Russia, Ministerstvo Inostrannykh Dyel, *Livre Rouge,* Commissariat du Peuple pour les Affaires Étrangères, Moscow, 1920, p. 17).

[2] The Upper Silesia campaign has always had a place of special honor among the Freikorps. See, for example, Arnolt Bronnen, *Rossbach* (Berlin, 1930).

the German government on May 5 that it had changed the form of the
payment stipulated by the Versailles Treaty. The total debt was set at
132 billion gold marks, to be paid at the annual rate of two billion gold
marks plus a 26 per cent levy on German exports. All legislation concerning taxation was to be subject to Repco review, and a Repco representative was to be stationed in Berlin. A first payment of one billion
gold marks had to be made within 25 days. If this new proposal, which
came as the climax of a year of wrangling between German and Allied
representatives, was not answered within six days, the Ruhr would be
occupied; two months before, on March 8, French troops had occupied
the three cities of Duisberg, Düsseldorf, and Ruhrort. In Germany this
latest proposal was called "the London Ultimatum." [3]

Reparations in Kind

The Freikorps campaign against Korfanty intensified the distrust of
the Berlin cabinet in Paris and London. This, together with the London
Ultimatum, provoked a government crisis. Chancellor Fehrenbach, of
the Center Party, resigned, to be succeeded by Dr. Joseph Wirth, also
of the Center Party but further Left.

On May 11, the Reichstag voted 225 to 172 to accept the London
Ultimatum. The opposition comprised three Right parties—the German
National Peoples' Party, led by Count von Westarp; the German
People's Party, led by Stresemann; and the Bavarian People's Party,
the name of the Center Party in Bavaria—and the Communists. Communist Deputy Wilhelm Könen [4] rejected the ultimatum as a starvation
sentence for the German people. He accused the Union of German
Industrialists of manipulating the rising inflation so as to compensate
themselves for their loss by reparations payments.

To pay the reparations in kind stipulated by Versailles, all Leftists
demanded taxation in kind. The German Federation of Labor, the
Social Democratic Party, and the already disintegrating USPD offered
a series of bills in the Reichstag aiming at a juster distribution of the

---

[3] Cf. Reparation Commission, Publication No. 5: *Report on the Work of the
Reparation Commission from 1920 to 1922* (London, 1923); John W. Wheeler-
Bennett and Hugh Latimer, *Information on the Reparation Settlement* (London,
1930); Heinrich Schnee and Hans Draeger, ed., *Zehn Jahre Versailles* (Berlin,
1929), vol. I.

[4] In 1947, a leading figure of the Berlin Socialist Unity Party.

reparations burden. Implicit in all these proposals was a demand for stronger state control of heavy industry. The Union of German Industrialists, through its leader, Hugo Stinnes, vehemently opposed this trade-union plan and demanded on the contrary that the ownership of the German railway system revert from the state to a private corporation to be specifically formed for this purpose. This control of freight charges would have concentrated still more economic power in the hands of the industrialists' union. The trade-unions answered with a campaign in which taxation in kind, the nationalization of the mines, and state monopoly in foreign currency were combined with slogans for the state control of trusts. The government, vacillating between these two organized groups, sought a way out of the dilemma through a loan from the Bank of England, but in vain. Maneuvering to delay the reparations payments, the German government declared: "First loans and then payments and a balanced budget."

On January 11, 1922, there was a conference of the Supreme Allied Council in Cannes. Walther Rathenau, Minister for Foreign Affairs, had obtained from London a delay in payments, but with strengthened control measures; at Cannes he expressed "the will to fulfill the reparations obligation to the degree possible," and this speech, vociferously opposed by all the nationalist organizations, was one of the factors that led to his assassination the following June. But even Rathenau did not fully accept the Repco's demands. Meanwhile the inflation developed apace; the mark stood at 650 to the British pound.

One conflict led to another. Reich Chancellor Wirth resisted all demands for Allied control of taxation as incompatible with German sovereignty. And in Paris, Premier Poincaré and Loucheur, a leading spokesman for French heavy industry, steadfastly rejected this policy of the German government. Inside the Repco, the French, in continual disagreement with the British and Belgian representatives, succeeded in sharpening the already severe wording of the commission's statements. Acrimonious notes from the Repco were answered by acrimonious notes from the Reich government.

Germany's difficulties with her reparations debts brought her closer to Russia, another debtor nation under constant Allied attack, particularly by France, for its abrogation of Tsarist debts. On April 10, 1922, at Britain's initiative, a conference was called at Genoa to discuss the problem of war debts; both Germany and Russia were invited to attend. During the period immediately preceding the conference, the Foreign Offices of the two debtor nations had come closer together. Radek, in Berlin during these months, had excellent relations with both such men as Brockdorff-Rantzau, who typified the pro-Russian tendency among the monarchists, and Rathenau, who represented the same bias among German Republicans.

The Soviet delegation to Genoa was made up of Foreign Commissar George Chicherin, Maxim Litvinov, and Christian Rakovsky. Rathenau arranged a brilliant reception for them in Berlin, which Radek attended, at which a treaty of friendship between the two nations was drafted. When the conference convened in Genoa, Rathenau and Chicherin met secretly in the near-by town of Rapallo and affixed their signatures to this treaty. The news of this alliance deprived the Genoa Conference of any meaning.

By the Treaty of Rapallo the two governments promised to undertake in the most benevolent spirit to assist each other in alleviating economic difficulties. Both parties renounced war claims and pre-war debts. The Soviet government was recognized de jure.

In Germany the Treaty of Rapallo was welcomed by practically everyone, including the Western-minded Social Democratic Party, whose spokesman in the Reichstag called it "a surprise jump towards a new active German policy." The nationalists were jubilant that Germany was again able to have treaties on its own without the consent of the victors. In the words of Stresemann's German People's Party, "We must after all welcome the conclusion of the German-Russian treaty, in spite of some objections, as a symptom of the resurrection of Germany's activity."

The speaker for the German Communist Party declared, "The Rapallo Treaty is as yet nothing more than fine phrases, which have at present no real meaning." [5] The treaty was as great a surprise to the rank and file of the party as to the Allied representatives at Genoa. Except for a few intimate friends of Radek (perhaps Brandler), no one was informed of the negotiations. A feeling of uneasiness crept into the party; the Communists linked this Russian-German alliance to the

---

[5] Fritz Schwahn, *Von Ebert bis Hindenburg: 10 Jahre deutsche Republik* (Leipzig, 1928), p. 29.

regressive process of the revolution since the Kronstadt uprising. Russian Communism was too overwhelming an authority to be openly attacked for its foreign policy, but an undercurrent of distrust came to the surface as a demand that this treaty be separated from the policies of the Comintern. The expelled Communist Left, the KAPD, openly attacked this policy as a Russian capitulation to the German counter revolution, and they found a ready response among Communist Party members.

At Genoa, Germany was asked several times to balance its budget. Just after the end of the conference, on June 24, members of the Organization Consul [6] killed Rathenau in the streets of Berlin-Grunewald— a violent demonstration by the nationalists that they would not tolerate any other settlement of the reparations debt than complete abrogation. The German Federation of Labor called a protest strike and big demonstrations, in which the Communist Party joined in. Stinnes, speaking for German heavy industry, opposed any compromise with the Repco and tried to bring the conflict to a head. The mark stood at 1650 to the pound; by July 1, it had climbed to 2000, and a week later to 2500.

In August of the same year a new conference was held in London. Poincaré accepted a moratorium, but only against further production pledges, which would mean tariff barriers between the occupied and non-occupied zones of Germany, the exploitation of state forests and Reich estates by the Allied Control Committee, the seizure of the coal mines and administration of them by Allied experts. No definite solution was reached; tension grew between France and Britain. In the fall of 1922 the Reich government called a meeting of the Allied experts

---

[6] Known also as the Organisation Escherich, or Orgesch; a conspirational military group famous for its Fehme activities. The three murderers, Techow, Kern, and Fischer, were captured in Thuringia. Two committed suicide. Ernst von Salomon, who helped to arrange the assassination, was arrested with Techow and sentenced to five years.

On June 4 this same Consul group had tried to poison Scheidemann with prussic acid. After 1933 its head, Friedrich Wilhelm Heinz, became one of the leaders of the Reich Union of German Writers. The opening lines of one of his poems run:

> Abteilung Knack hält Jahresschau
> Und schmunzelnd zählt man die Genossen,
> Von Liebknecht bis zu Rathenau,
> Die man gekillt und abgeschossen.

(The Division of Toughs has its annual review and, smirking, checks off the comrades, from Liebknecht to Rathenau, that have been killed and shot.)

in Berlin and tried to work out a new compromise. Through all German proposals ran the phrase, "First loans and then reparations payments."

On October 28, Mussolini's March on Rome added a strong note to Europe's disintegration. The mark stood at 35,000 to the pound.

In November 1922 (while the Fourth World Congress of the Comintern was in session), the Wirth government resigned. The Social Democratic Party refused to enter a coalition with the German People's Party, whose leaders were demanding the abolition of that cornerstone of trade-union policy, the eight-hour day. Wilhelm Cuno, former managing director of the Hamburg-American Line, became Chancellor. On December 9 a new conference was called in London, to which Britain, Belgium, and Italy sent delegates. The German government presented its plan, which again was a demand for substantial foreign credits.

On January 2–4, 1923, a new conference, new discussions. As early as November 21, 1922, the French cabinet had completed detailed plans to occupy certain parts of the Rhine-Ruhr area and had assembled a French administrative staff to insure the transfer of reparations coal. This plan was part of a larger concept. Supplementing the Saar, Luxemburg, Belgium, Poland, and Czechoslovakia, whose industries were largely under French control, the Ruhr would make France the largest coal producer in Europe; in effect, this arrangement would mean that the coal and iron ore mined under French control would surpass Britain's output.

The custom of the German government of delivering ten per cent less than stipulated had been tolerated by the Repco and become normal procedure. But at the January conference Poincaré made an issue of a ten per cent difference in deliveries of coal and telegraph poles and repeated his demand for immediate occupation of Bochum and Essen and for Allied control of the Ruhr mines. Poincaré's proposal was opposed by the British representative, Bonar Law, who favored a simultaneous settlement of reparations and inter-Allied debts, with a sizable reduction in the amount of Germany's obligation. The French and the British were unable to reach an agreement, and on January 4 the British representation walked out of the conference. This act, Poincaré declared, restored to France her full freedom of action, and on January 11

French and Belgian troops began to occupy the whole of the Ruhr.[7] The mark stood at 50,000 to the pound, and from this day on its fall was ever more precipitate; by the end of January, it stood at 250,000 to the pound.

On January 12, President Ebert urged the German people to resist the occupation. On the same day a prominent leader of the Rhine Social Democrats, Wilhelm Sollmann, spoke in Bonn to the reunited Social Democrats, inciting them to resist with all their force this criminal violation of the German people's rights.

The Reichstag met on January 13, its flag at half mast; Reich Chancellor Cuno appeared, surrounded by the premiers of all the German states. The Social Democrat Paul Löbe, president of the Reichstag, and Hermann Müller-Franken, leader of the Social Democratic parliamentary group, protested in the name of the German workers against the Ruhr occupation; Stresemann spoke in the name of all bourgeois parties. The extreme nationalists demanded an immediate break of diplomatic relations with France and the expulsion of the Reparation Commission from German territory. The Communist deputy, lacking detailed instructions but following the party line just formulated in a Comintern manifesto, said, "In this hour of attack from without, we must attack our bourgeoisie from within." With a solemn ceremony, the Reichstag adopted, against Communist opposition, a measure calling for "passive" resistance by 284 votes to 12, with 16 abstentions.

One hundred thousand French and Belgian troops marched into the Rhine-Ruhr. Essen and Gelsenkirchen were occupied on January 11 and 12, 1923, and on January 14 the German government issued a White Book detailing the atrocities allegedly committed. A week later the French army was in possession of all exits from the Ruhr by railway and canal, and by the end of the month control was established. There were minor incidents—shooting in Düsseldorf and Bochum. Courts-martial began; the burgomaster of Dortmund was arrested on January 17. On January 27 coal operators were arrested, among them Fritz Thyssen, after a tumultuous occupation of his plant at Hamborn.

---

[7] The occupation took place under the guise of giving protection to an engineering commission going into the Ruhr to supervise the delivery of reparations coal. The military action was based on Article 248 of the Versailles Treaty and Articles 17 and 18 of its Appendix. Later a long dispute developed between British and French jurists on the proper interpretation of these articles.

Cuno sent Thyssen a message praising his loyalty and protesting the arrest of the mine directors. The government promised to recompense the mine owners for loss of profits; it guaranteed relief benefits to the miners if they would strike against the occupation authorities and threatened to jail those who refused to strike, designating their work as coöperation with the enemy, high treason against the Fatherland.

The nationalists reacted violently. On January 26 General Ludendorff issued a call to arms. Ex-officers began open military training of large groups of youngsters. The Citizens' Militia and the Orgesch, which had toned down their activities, reappeared provocatively. Black Reichswehr groups sent many saboteur squadrons into the Rhine-Ruhr, encouraged by the Reich government. The monarchists and counter revolutionaries of all varieties preached the *levée en masse*.

The French occupation authorities decreed the following measures: confiscation of all coal and taxes, establishment of tariffs between occupied and unoccupied Germany, military command of important rail centers. When the German Security Police were expelled from the Rhine-Ruhr, the British press began to speculate on the danger of Communism in the area, a danger that the French occupation could not suppress without the assistance of the police, a trained anti-Communist contingent. The Berlin cabinet, in spite of its patriotic united front with the Ruhr workers, took care to emphasize the imminence of this peril.

Germany, an Industrial Colony

In their first years, German Communists had no more detailed foreign policy than the establishment of a socialist state and the subsequent coöperation with Russia and other socialist states in a European socialist union. As a palpable force in German life, they were impelled to adapt their principles to the realities of German life in the setting forth of a domestic policy, but their foreign policy was limited to vague formulas. Even National Bolshevism, as formulated in 1919 by Wolffheim and Laufenberg, had made the seizure of power by the working class a precondition to their defense of Germany. Though they emphasized the unification of the army with the working class in a joint defense of the Fatherland against the West, the dictatorship of the proletariat was still the basis of national resistance.

During the Polish-Russian war in August 1920, however, Paul Levi, one of the few Reichstag deputies of the Spartakusbund, had announced a new program with the slogan, sensational at the time, "Alliance with Soviet Russia," and offered Communist support to any German government that would accept this policy. He offered, in fact, civil peace in exchange for an alliance with Russia. This speech was directly inspired by Karl Radek, and was attacked by the Berlin organization of the party.[8]

Levi's speech was timed with secret negotiations between Radek and, on the one hand, Victor Kopp,[9] then a Russian representative in Berlin, and Count Ernst zu Reventlow on the other. Reventlow wrote:

> A change in the mood of the masses seems to be taking place under the terrible pressure of the times. The idea of the struggle of the masses, as used today by radical elements, must not be directed against our own people. These ideas must be transformed and directed against the real enemies of the working class, against the Entente, which has bound the proletariat in chains of slavery. Important symptoms, indicating a decisive change of mentality and ideas, are already evident.[10]

Colonel Bauer, assistant to General Ludendorff and one of Radek's major contacts, was in Budapest, to neutralize the anti-Bolshevik government in Hungary in case of a German-Russian alliance.

To explain these contacts with the German army and the German secret service, a theory was worked out in Moscow headquarters. One of its main advocates was Professor Eugen Varga, who under the name E. Pawlowski developed a theory on reparations in a series of pamphlets.

Germany can fulfill the stipulations of the Versailles Treaty, he wrote, only by increasing her industrial output, which would enable her to increase her exports. The surplus of exports over imports could

---

[8] Cf. Report of a Communist Party meeting in the *Kommunistische Arbeiterzeitung*, KAPD weekly (Berlin, August 1920).

[9] In 1918 Kopp had been a member of Chicherin's Commissariat for Foreign Affairs. In 1925, he became Ambassador to Japan, and later he was Soviet Minister to Sweden. Cf. Grigory Bessedovsky, *Revelations of a Soviet Diplomat* (London, 1931).

[10] *Deutsche Tageszeitung*, Berlin, August 31, 1920.

be paid into the reparations fund. But this increased production is possible only with foreign credit, which the Entente will not grant except against production pledges. The result of these pledges will be that the Entente will take over all the major production lifelines in Germany—railroads, the control of the budget—and will thus make Germany completely dependent on British and French imperialism. (The United States did not seriously intervene in German affairs until 1924; hence Varga's attack was directed against Britain and France.) The German worker will work for British and French imperialism under the control of German managers, who will share the profits with their foreign superiors. Thus Germany will be transformed into a colony of British and French imperialism, working as much as India or Indo-China for the profit of the City and the Bourse. Until now colonies have been backward agrarian countries with slight industrial development. The main profit of the British Empire comes from areas forced to accept British-manufactured commodities in exchange for raw materials and agrarian products. Germany will be the first of a new type of colony; its highly developed industry will be incorporated in its entirety into the British industrial system.[11]

From this beginning of Varga-Pawlowski the theory was developed in a series of articles and pamphlets by Bukharin, Radek, and Thalheimer. The Profintern—Communist trade-union international—under A. Lozovsky took up the theme; its pamphlets on the reparations problem emphasized that the burden of payments fell on the German worker.[12]

This theory contained nothing that seemed to contradict the interests of German Communists. In their opinion, the German worker had a double burden, capitalist accumulation in his own country and payments enforced by the peace treaty. Wages and taxes were linked with the reparations payments, it was true; but the only policy acceptable to them would have been to pay the reparations bill out of the industrialists' profit margin instead of the workers' pay envelopes. In the

---

[11] In March 1947, Professor Eugene Tarlé, of the Soviet Academy of Sciences, revived Varga's theory; all plans for the industrial rehabilitation of Western Germany he dubbed a design to make Germany an industrial colony of the West—"industrial feudalism."

[12] Cf. Z. Leder, *Das Reparationsproblem, die Gewerkschaften und die Arbeiterklasse* (Berlin, 1924).

midst of the economic disintegration, there were new investments in heavy industry and increased profits.

In the main, the theory of Germany's transformation into an industrial colony of the West was fabricated to implement the Treaty of Rapallo. In 1922–1923 Varga, Bukharin, and Radek were discovering a new role for the German bourgeoisie, which they changed from the class enemy to a victim suffering almost as much as the German workers. A national front of all classes against the Entente was imperative. The theorists of "the industrial colony, Germany," tried to direct the German labor movement in all its wings—Right, Left, and Center, trade-unionist and Communist—into new channels. But five years of civil war had convinced the activist minority of the working class that democratic socialism was possible in Germany only after all the nationalist and militarist organizations preparing to lead the country into a war of revenge had been wiped out. In shifting the emphasis of the class hatred from its historical object—the German bourgeoisie in all its personifications—to the Entente, the theorists perverted the labor movement of Germany, and consequently of Europe. They aggravated the intellectual and psychological confusion that was the prime condition for the growth of totalitarian ideologies and organizations.

This revision of Leninist class policy went further than the limited German problems. According to Lenin's concept, the necessity of temporary blocs with hostile groups was always subordinated to the general strategy of the European revolution. Lenin defended Brest-Litovsk and later agreements of the Soviet government with bourgeois states as temporary compromises necessary to win time. Alliances between the workers' state and bourgeois states, however, should never in his view supplant the solidarity and international organization of the working class of all countries. Thus, a theory of the revolutionary character of the German bourgeoisie substituted for this concept a Communist foreign policy based entirely on power politics. The alliance between Russia and the German bourgeoisie was urged as necessary for the defense of Russia against future invasions from the West; in case of war, such an alliance was considered more realistic than one between Russian and German workers. Thus, the abandonment of the concept of a workers' revolution in Germany, not only at present but in fact for the whole post-Versailles period, was a fundamental revision of

Lenin's analysis of the balance of class forces in Germany. The rank and file of the German party understood the implications of this policy only vaguely. Varga-Pawlowski and Radek presented their ideas to the young Communists as clever proposals for better propaganda. The party discussions revolved around problems of democratic or dictatorial Communism and the party's relation to the trade-unions. For loyal party members all inquiries into Soviet foreign policy were taboo. A critic who asked pointed questions on this subject was quickly strait-jacketed. In intimate party circles, in the Left caucus, the industrial-colony theory was condemned bitterly and sharply; by general consent, however, these opinions did not appear in the Comintern press, which at this time gave much space to internal discussions.

Chapter 9 · Karl Radek · · · · · · · · · · · · · · · · · ·

Karl Radek was born Karl Bernardovich Sobelsohn in 1885 in Lvov, Galicia (Austrian Poland). As a young student in Tarnov, he joined the Polish Socialist Party (PPS), the nationalist wing of the Polish labor movement. Quite early, however, he was attracted to the Marxist group, the Social Democratic Party of the Kingdom of Poland and Lithuania, and between 1904 and 1908 he was most active in it. "From the age of fourteen, he has been connected with various workers' movements—first in Galicia, and then as a spirited member of the Social Democratic Party."[1]

Karl was educated in Vienna and Bern. In 1908, he left his native Galicia and went to Germany, where, under the pen name of Parabellum, he became contributing editor to various Social Democratic newspapers, the *Leipziger Volkszeitung* and the *Bremer Bürgerzeitung*. In Bremen he animated a small radical group composed of younger party members in opposition to the party leadership. August Thalheimer, editor of the Göppingen party paper, published his anti-nationalist articles.

In 1912 a "Radek case" appeared on the agenda of the German party convention in Chemnitz. There was a motion to expel him, ostensibly for personal reasons; he had irritated the party bureaucracy by his constant attacks on their nationalist policy. He was pictured as a bad character. He had borrowed an overcoat (or, by other versions, a pair

---

[1] Karl Radek, *Portraits and Pamphlets* (London, 1935), p. xii.

of trousers) from a comrade on a cold winter night and had not returned it immediately. On the basis of this and similar trifling episodes,
it was implied that he was a thief. The petty bourgeois of the party
made a pompous ado about this "unsocialist" behavior; and in protest
against this smear campaign, Parabellum had adopted several years before a new pseudonym, K. Radek, which to a Pole suggested the word
kradziez, theft.

Luxemburg and Radek were members of both the German and the
Polish parties, and this incident in the German party was a reflection
of a split the same year in the Polish one, in which Luxemburg led one
faction and Radek the other. Luxemburg had been supported by most
of the national leaders and Radek by the Warsaw organization, including Walecki, Unschlicht, and Hanecki. Lenin was disposed to
favor the Warsaw group.[2]

The National Executive Committee of the German party held that
it was unnecessary to expel him since he had never been accepted as
a member. This reduction of his status to that of an intruder made it
unnecessary to investigate the charges against him, which otherwise
would have been required by the party constitution. While the case
was pending, the Göppingen local gave Radek an additional membership in order to protect his status.

The party convention decided against Radek; in the words of its
Grievance Committee:

> Fifteen comrades in Bremen have protested against the ad-
> mission of Radek into the party, but according to the party con-
> stitution individual members have not the right to grievances of
> this kind. Therefore, it is proposed to refer the matter to the
> National Executive Committee. In any case, it has to be deter-
> mined whether a comrade expelled from another party of the
> International is eligible for membership, whether it is possible
> for us to review his expulsion, or whether this has to be done by
> the International.

The delegate Anton Pannekoek defended Radek. Rosa Luxemburg,
behind the scene of the convention, sided with the convention against
Radek, whom she heartily disliked, as did Clara Zetkin and almost all

---

[2] Cf. Lenin, "The Split in the Polish Social Democratic Party," *Sotzialdemokrat*
(Marx-Engels Institute reprint, Moscow, 1934), January 1, 1913, No. 30, p. 15 ff.

the other associates of Luxemburg. The president of the party convention, Noske, supported by delegate Ebert, ruled against a discussion
on Radek's status. As a result, the affair was referred to the National
Executive Committee and never officially concluded.

Radek, waiting nervously in Chemnitz for the decision, wrote to the
party convention:

> Not able to answer in person the attacks made against me on
> the floor of the convention with regard to the affair at Göppingen,
> I wish firmly to state that I was a member of the Leipzig organ-
> ization from 1908 to 1911 and that I fulfilled all my party duties.
> All statements to the contrary are false; I will welcome the oppor-
> tunity to clarify the matter before the investigating committee of
> the Bremen local.[3]

This affair was not a small episode in Karl Radek's life. It was a
painful offense for him to be deprived of membership in the German
party, the highest type of Social Democratic organization. He had
been outlawed not only by the Right wing, Noske and Ebert, but by
the undisputed leaders of the Left, Luxemburg and her friends. Rosa
was everywhere respected as the personification of socialist morality,
the model of exemplary behavior in the socialist way of life; that she
had joined in the move to expel him marked Radek among most of
the Social Democratic radicals as an immoral person.

In Radek's character structure, this incident contributed substantially
to his insecurity, the scintillations of his political stand. He told me the
story over and over again, varying the details but always emphasizing
the injustice, magnifying the importance of the affair, citing it as an
example to the younger generation of dirty party intrigue.

In the Ranks of the German Revolution

Radek continued to be politically active in Germany until 1914. In
1915, he avoided being drafted into the Austrian army by taking refuge
in Switzerland, where he came in contact with Lenin's group.

In April 1917 Radek's name was on the list of Bolsheviks traveling
to Russia through Germany in "the sealed car." There was an under-

---

[3] *Protokoll über die Verhandlungen des Parteitages der Sozialdemokratischen
Partei Deutschlands.* Abgehalten in Chemnitz vom 15. bis 21. September 1912
(Berlin, 1912), p. 515.

standing, however, that as an Austrian citizen he could not go to
Russia, which was still at war with Austria. Lenin and his group proceeded to Petrograd; Radek accompanied them as far as Stockholm,
where he remained with the task of organizing international contacts
for the Bolsheviks. He was given the mission of combating the anti-
Leninist tendencies in the Zimmerwald grouping and preparing the
way to an independent international organization.

He worked at this time with Angelica Balabanoff, who reports on
their collaboration in her memoirs. "We despised Radek personally
and considered him a vulgar politician." [4] Apart from the personal
antagonism that would naturally arise between two such contrasting
personalities, this judgment was based on political differences. Balabanoff was trying to organize an international grouping independent of
the Moscow center, and Radek was working for the opposite.

Radek took no part in the October events but immediately thereafter
went to Petrograd and, for the first time, formally joined the Bolshevik
Party and wrote various articles for *Izvestia* under the name Viator.
Immediately after his arrival from Stockholm, Radek was charged by
Chicherin with the direction of the Central European Division of the
Commissariat for Foreign Affairs, which meant principally the organization of propaganda among war prisoners. The first committees
of German, Austrian, and Hungarian prisoners of war were formed
in the camps. He sponsored a Liebknecht Brigade among the Germans
in the Siberian camps, organized huge mass meetings in Moscow,
where delegates from the camps declared their allegiance to the October
revolution.

Radek was a member of the Russian delegation to Brest-Litovsk,
where he was the expert on the Polish question. General Hoffmann's
staff was especially incensed by the aggressive attitude of the Pole,
Radek, whom they regarded as their subject. The revolutionary journalist antagonized the German generals. Radek, whose personality had
matured, became a notorious figure. With a sense of irony, he dressed
and behaved in such a fashion as to exaggerate his physical peculiarities; he was the bizarre apostle of Bolshevism, whom any reporter
could recognize on sight as the little man with the huge head, with

---

[4] Angelica Balabanoff, *My Life as a Rebel* (London, 1938), p. 188.

his beard encircling his clean-shaven face like a monkey's, his pro-
truding ears, his spectacles, his pipe held between tobacco-stained teeth.
Hurrying along the street, an English cap on his head, he carried a
bundle of newspapers with the *London Times* on the outside. Under
this mask was a man engaged to his marrow in the struggle of the
new society in Russia and the effort to expand it westward.

Back in Russia, Radek initiated together with Bukharin the violent
attack on Lenin's Brest-Litovsk policy. As one of the editors of the
journal of this wing, *The Communist,* he developed a program of revolutionary war against German imperialism. Lenin attacked him frequently and vehemently, calling him a lamentable Leftist who avoided
responsibility. This fight against Lenin's peace policy marked the peak
of Radek's revolutionary enthusiasm. He later accepted Lenin's view,
but the experiences of the civil war made pessimism his dominant
mood, broken for a few weeks during the Polish campaign of 1920.
This basic pessimism concerning the future of Communism was a facet
of Radek's personality obvious to anyone who knew him intimately.

After the expulsion from Berlin of the official Russian diplomatic
delegation—Joffe, Bukharin, and Rakovsky—in November 1918, Radek
was sent to Germany as head of a party mission. At Vilna, at the instigation of the German Republican government, the mission was stopped
and only Radek succeeded in getting through.

In Germany he took part in the founding convention of the Spartakusbund in December 1918. Here he met Rosa Luxemburg again;
their relations were cold and impersonal. Not only the long history of
past differences in Poland and Germany separated them, but also their
attitudes toward Liebknecht, Ledebour, and Müller, whose participation in the activities of the Shop Stewards' Committee Luxemburg
regarded as putschism.

After the Bloody January week in Berlin, on February 4, Radek
was arrested, but only on a charge of registering under a false name.
Attempts were made to kill him. Two months later, while he was
still in prison, in order to give him the protection of at least nominal
diplomatic status, the Soviet government appointed him Ukrainian
envoy to Berlin; this was in the middle of the civil war in the Ukraine,
long before the Kremlin could be assured of eventual control of the
area. In addition, the Russians arrested several persons as hostages;

and in January 1920 Radek was released in exchange for, among others, Georg Cleinow, Heinz Stratz,[5] Dr. Brendel.

The year Radek spent in prison was not too uncomfortable. Immediately after his arrest, the General Staff took the matter in hand; Radek was much too precious a contact between them and the young Bolshevik government to be killed off by some exalted Freikorps leader. Secret orders were issued to spare him, and he was given special privileges in his cell—in striking contrast to the treatment given other Communists. Jogiches had been arrested in February 1919 and was killed a few weeks later, shot in the back under the pretext that he had tried to escape. Just as surely as Radek was spared by special order, this murder, like that of Liebknecht and Luxemburg, had been arranged. Radek was given an especially large cell where he could receive friends; he had a secretary, and was even allowed to get in touch with the Moscow government. His messenger to the outside world was Karl Moor.[6]

At this time I was in Berlin, getting my first lessons in conspiratorial technique. Radek, having heard of my Austrian experiences, wanted to see me and sent Moor to bring me to him in the Moabit prison. Moor, to my great surprise, took me to the Bendlerstrasse headquarters of the General Staff, where all doors opened before him as if by an electric eye. An officer gave me a pass, whose name, civil status, and description were palpably faked; and with this pass I had access to

---

[5] Cf. Heinz Stratz, *Drei Monate als Geisel für Radek* (Berlin, 1920). In this pamphlet Stratz reports his arrest in Kiev on July 29, 1919, where he had remained after the withdrawal of the German army as executor of the German Artists' Home, set up during the German occupation. "It was difficult to liquidate the estate, for because of the nationalization of houses no one wanted to take on a new lease." Released for exchange on October 28, 1919, he wrote his pamphlet immediately after his return to Berlin and dated it December 27.

Cleinow also wrote a pamphlet after his exchange: *Bürger, Arbeiter, rettet Europa! Erfahrungen im sterbenden Russland* (Berlin, 1920).

[6] Karl Moor died at the age of eighty in Berlin in 1932. Son of a high-ranking Austrian officer, he was educated in Nuremberg. He broke with his family and became a friend of Liebknecht and Ledebour. Later he went to Switzerland, where he took the name Karl Moor (the hero of Schiller's *Die Räuber*). One of the founders of Swiss Social Democracy, he participated in many international congresses.

He met Lenin in Geneva, and often gave the Bolshevik organizers help from the considerable fortune he had inherited. After 1917 he went to Russia, from where he was sent to Europe with special assignments for the revolutionary government.

Radek's cell three times a week. I took full advantage of it. This prison cell became for me a classroom, where I got my lessons in advanced Communism. The episode in the Bendlerstrasse headquarters, the friendly contact between Moor and the officers in the midst of the German civil war, were burned into my memory. They gained significance as time went by and Radek's peculiar mission to Berlin became more apparent.

From the Moabit prison, Radek took an active part in the formation of the German Communist Party. He saw all the leaders and many of the militants in his prison cell, where he received an amazing number of visitors, three times a week, from two to six in the afternoon. He favored his old friends of the Bremen *Arbeiterpolitik* group, of whom Charlotte Kornfeld (widow of Johann Knief, one of the most talented leaders of the group, who had died in 1918 of tuberculosis) was charged with the responsibility of publishing Radek's collected articles of the period preceding the World War.[7] He was very eager to have these German articles in print again, to reëstablish his reputation as an old Social Democratic militant.

From his prison cell, Radek intervened in the party discussion concerning the program of the first National Bolsheviks, Wolffheim and Laufenberg. In the summer of 1919 he intervened again in the trade-union discussion preceding the underground Spartakusbund convention in Heidelberg. I smuggled a letter to Paul Levi out of the prison and took it to the convention.

Radek had other visitors than his party comrades. Ludendorff's adjutant, Colonel Bauer, visited him regularly, as did not only other officers but such key industrialists as Felix Deutsch, who was connected with Walther Rathenau. Another visitor was Professor Otto Hötzsch.[8]

The Central Committee of the newly formed German Communist Party was not officially informed of these contacts between Radek and the General Staff, but two or three of his intimates, such as Paul Levi

---

[7] Karl Radek, *In den Reihen der deutschen Revolution, 1909–1919,* introduction by Paul Frölich (Munich, 1921).

[8] Otto Hötzsch, an authority on Eastern Europe, was Reichstag deputy for the German National People's Party. He was president of the German Society for East European Studies and editor of *Osteuropäische Forschungen* and of *Osteuropa, Zeitschrift für die gesamten Fragen des europäischen Ostens.* In 1946 he was in Berlin, coöperating with the Russian authorities.

and August Thalheimer, undoubtedly knew about them. Many political figures of the Weimar Republic were glad to have the opportunity of seeing Radek and discussing German policy with him. He played his double role adroitly—he was the representative of the Russian Politburo on the one hand, and on the other he made himself the envoy of the Russian state on a semi-official diplomatic and military mission to the German government.

Radek's role in the Russian party was insecure. He was a member of its Central Committee, and later as its delegate a member of the Comintern Presidium, but he was not in the Politburo of the Russian Communist Party. He was a consultant on foreign affairs, a kind of gifted interloper, a journalist. From the Russian angle, these activities were relatively unimportant, too slight for Radek's driving ambition. He longed to have a first-class role in forming the decisive plans, made in the Politburo by men in control of important branches of the party.

To improve his unsatisfactory status in the Russian hierarchy, Radek tried to build himself up as the leader of the German Communists. He knew the German labor movement well; he was thoroughly convinced that there was no better expert for Germany in Russia. The decisions of the Russian Politburo concerning Germany were not based automatically on Radek's reports, although often during the early period he was the only direct contact to the German party. His shortcomings, his journalistic approach, his impressionistic evaluations of men and facts, were well known, especially to Lenin; and often enough Radek's proposals were not accepted, or were considerably modified. His conversations with German officers in 1919 were regarded as a minor detail in working out Soviet policy and of slight weight for the development of German Communism.

Radek, however, was more involved in all the details of German Communist policy than any Russian leader. Between 1918 and 1921 he frequently went to Germany. He knew hundreds of militants personally, traveled a good deal in Germany, wrote party documents. His speeches and articles were reprinted in German editions by the Communist publishing house in Hamburg. They were at this time textbooks for militants; they were read intensively and taken seriously by other political groups as well, which saw in them the direct presentation of Moscow's point of view and hence considered them more authoritative than the writings of German Communists.

After Luxemburg's death, in spite of the long-standing differences between her and Radek, most of her intimate friends came under his influence. Clara Zetkin, Paul Levi, August Thalheimer, Jakob Walcher, Heinrich Brandler, all endorsed the leadership of Karl Radek, already the representative of the powerful Russian party and a valuable contact to Moscow.

As early as October 1919, in the letter to the Heidelberg convention, Radek wrote in a pessimistic mood:

> The world revolution is a very slow process in which more than one defeat must be expected. I have no doubt that in every country [Russia!] the proletariat will be forced to construct its dictatorship several times and will several times see the collapse of this dictatorship before it will finally win.[9]

Radek was thoroughly convinced that for a long period to come the Spartakusbund would not be able to do more than organize and propagandize.

> In 1918–1919 the party consisted of several thousand workers, and the Spartakusbund had the role of holding back the working class and preventing unnecessary clashes.[10]

In all of his early pamphlets and speeches, Radek emphasizes his main idea: the impossibility of doing more than propagandizing in 1918–1919, the impossibility of developing the Communist forces in an open fight. However, he had a feeling of how the German worker reacted to this Communist passivity; he constantly reiterated that the workers no longer trust any political leaders and since the defeats of 1919–1920 regard them all as traitors. He sensed the dangerous disillusionment prevalent among activist workers.

> The German revolution saw the discredit of one party after another. It demonstrated how revolutionary phraseology meant nothing; the Communist Party has first to win back the confidence of the workers in the process of revolutionary struggle.[11]

---

[9] Karl Radek, *Zur Taktik des Kommunismus: Ein Schreiben an den Oktober-Parteitag der KPD* (Berlin, 1919), p. 5.

[10] Karl Radek, "Der Weg der Kommunistischen Internationale," a speech at the Third World Congress, reprinted in *Bibliothek der Kommunistischen Internationale* (Hamburg, 1921), XVIII, 34.

[11] *Ibid*, p. 44.

In his pessimism he emphasized that the proletarian dictatorship in
Russia would not be able to withstand the offensive of world capital;
he interpreted every event as the approaching climax to the fated experiment. Radek's offer to the trade-unions and Social Democratic
Party for a common fight against the reparations was based on this
analysis. After the unification of the USPD with the Spartakusbund
into the United Communist Party, December 1920, he looked forward
to a change in the attitude of the trade-unions.

> The Social Democratic workers are full of democratic illu-
> sions. They still hope that they can improve their situation within
> the framework of capitalist society, and they regard the Com-
> munists as the conscious splitters of the proletarian movement.
> If the Communists had not split the working class, if the prole-
> tariat had remained united, it would have won a majority in the
> Reichstag and everything would be all right. . . .
> It is clear that in this situation we cannot count on spontaneous
> unorganized movements in Germany unless the masses are shaken
> through and through by external events. Ten million workers
> are union members. They look up to their leaders; they listen to
> their slogans. . . . Communist strategy must be to convince these
> broad masses of workers that the trade-union bureaucracy and
> the Social Democratic Party not only refuse to fight for a work-
> ers' dictatorship but also do not fight for the most basic daily
> interests of the working class.[12]

In an *Open Letter* dated January 8, 1921, Radek had developed the
tactics of a united front with the trade-unions.

> We have worked out these tactics within several factory groups,
> trade-unions, and local organizations for the past two years. . . .
> The fight of the Communists against other parties shall never
> become a fight of one section of the proletariat against another.[13]

After Levi's exit Radek praised Thalheimer and Brandler as genuine
emanations of the revolutionary spirit, able to lead the party to greater
successes.

---

[12] Karl Radek, *Soll die Vereinigte Kommunistische Partei Deutschlands eine
Massenpartei der revolutionären Aktion oder eine zentristische Partei des Wartens
sein?* (Hamburg, 1921), pp. 21–22.
[13] *Ibid.*, p. 25, 33.

Bloc with Brandler and Thalheimer

All the leading men of the Russian Politburo nursed their personal connections with selected groups of foreign Communists. Lenin and Zinoviev were particularly interested in Germany; Trotsky, who spoke a fluent French and knew France particularly well, was the expert for French and Spanish revolutionary movements. Radek, himself outside the intimate Bolshevik circle, fervently admired Trotsky's brilliant personality and his military genius. In 1923, in the confusion during the last year of Lenin's life, when the impending fight between Trotsky and the Troika—Stalin, Zinoviev, and Kamenev—was being prepared, Radek lined up with Trotsky. He tried to bring the Brandler group into his orbit, a major link in a chain of Trotskyist strong points throughout Europe. Trotsky and Radek hoped that a moderated German Communist Party would help to counterbalance the growing influence of the Bolshevik center by giving support to the non-Bolshevik elements integrated into the Russian party after 1917. The strengthening of Trotsky's status was to be coördinated with Radek's German policy; access to the key positions in the old-type trade-unions and coöperation with the Social Democrats would have reinforced Trotsky's position, and with it the position of Radek, in the Russian Politburo.

During all of 1922 Radek, traveling between Berlin and Moscow, concentrated on jockeying for a united front with the Social Democratic Party. He hoped to supplement it by one on an international scale. Responding to Radek's suggestion, Fritz Adler, the Austrian socialist, convoked a conference of the three internationals at Berlin. Adler headed an independent international group, composed mainly of the Austrian Social Democratic Party and the Independent Labour Party of Great Britain, whose position on most questions was somewhere between those of the Socialist and Communist internationals. Lenin had called it the Second and a Half International. From his intermediate position, Adler intended to act as a conciliator and reunite the working class of the world into one organization. As delegates to this Berlin conference, the Comintern sent, in addition to Radek, the following: Bukharin, from the Russian party; Clara Zetkin, from the German; L. O. Frossard and Alfred Rosmer, from the French; Warski, from the Polish; Stojanowits, from the Yugoslav; Bohumil-

Smeral, from the Czech; and Katayama, from the Japanese. A Committee of Nine was elected, composed of three representatives of each international,[14] but it passed away within a few months.

This tentative rapprochement between Western socialists and Russian Communists, which in any case had produced nothing more fruitful than a heated discussion, came to a definite end with the trial, in Moscow, June 1922, of the Left SRs. Vandervelde, the Belgian Social Democrat, an expert on Russian affairs, and Kurt Rosenfeld, a Social Democratic deputy to the Reichstag, were admitted to the trial as attorneys for the defense. The Social Revolutionaries were sentenced to long terms, and the Comintern began a campaign for punitive measures against the "social traitors," in which the drive for labor unity was drowned.

For Radek the Berlin conference had been an important step forward. He hardly believed in the possibility of immediate unification, but in his view a program of world labor unity was a prerequisite to the legalization and stabilization of the Communist parties in the West. Lenin and Zinoviev, on the other hand, criticized Radek's position severely. In one of the last articles he wrote on Comintern affairs, entitled "We Have Paid Too Dearly," Lenin made the point that in the Berlin conference Vandervelde and his friends had been given a platform from which to propagandize against Soviet Russia.

Radek did not abandon his campaign for an international united front. Under his influence, the German Central Committee issued a slogan, "Convoke an international world congress," leaving it equivocal whether it should be a repetition of the discussion between the Second and Third Internationals or should attempt to fuse the trade-unions of the world into a new organization. Throughout Germany at the end of 1922, there was active propaganda for such an international world congress; comrades from the French, British, Czech, Swedish, Polish, Russian parties took the floor and helped to popularize the slogan. This was another aspect of the concept of a World NEP. If a common policy of democratic reforms could be effective then a reunification of the two internationals was correct.

---

[14] *The Second and Third Internationals and the Vienna Union.* Official Report of the Conference between the Executives held at the Reichstag, Berlin, on the 2nd April 1922 and the Following Days (London, 1922).

An attempt was made at the Fourth World Congress, November 1922, to clarify the issues of the united front, to answer the question recurrent in every Communist party—what is a labor government?— to mold the dogmatists of the young Comintern parties toward a flexible and realistic application of Communist theory. Radek's interpretation of a united front in Germany, however, was not to be included.

> The Communist International must take into consideration the following possibilities:
>
> I. Pseudo-labor Governments
>   1. A liberal workers' government, such as existed in Australia or may soon emerge in Britain.
>   2. A Social Democratic workers' government, such as that in Germany.
> II. Real Labor Governments
>   1. A government of workers and poor peasants, such as may develop in the Balkans, Czechoslovakia, etc.
>   2. A workers' government with the participation of the Communists.
>   3. A genuine proletarian workers' government, which in its pure form can be realized only by the Communist Party.[15]

The designation of the British Labour Party as "pseudo" did not, in this case, indicate that it should not be given qualified Communist support. It had long been axiomatic with socialists that Britain, as well as Germany, the seat of Continental industry, would make a major contribution to Europe's transformation into a socialist commonwealth. The Bolsheviks did not exclude the possibility that here the overthrow of the bourgeoisie might be achieved by the mere massive weight of the organized workers. In 1923, when Ramsay MacDonald became Britain's first socialist Prime Minister, Lenin criticized his government sharply, but he never shared the illusion of the first British Communists that they could eliminate the Labour Party and seize power alone. In Lenin's eyes, the role of the party in Britain was to act as a ferment, to stimulate the development of the British Labour Party. Two years earlier, Lenin had argued against the ultra-Lefts of the English party, who had rejected as reformism the use of parliamentary methods.

---

[15] *Protokoll des Vierten Kongresses der Kommunistischen Internationale: Petrograd-Moskau vom 5. November bis 5 Dezember 1922* (Hamburg, 1923), p. 1017.

The British Communists *should* participate, *should,* from
within Parliament, help the masses of the workers see the results of a Henderson and Snowden government, should help the
Hendersons and Snowdens to defeat the combined Lloyd Georges
and Churchills.[16]

But in Germany, the denotation of the Social Democratic government as "pseudo" was intended to forestall Communist participation in it. Germany was not Britain, for at least two reasons. The
Communist Party of Germany was not a propaganda sect, with
slight possibility of growth; it was an already meaningful party whose
real importance lay in its potential during the developing crisis. In
Germany, moreover, the counter revolution had demonstrated—in the
Kapp putsch and in the activities of the Freikorps generally—that it
was not to be defeated by the methods of Social Democracy. Aggressive nationalism was rising, and it was imperative to oppose to it a no
less determined party of socialism. In the words of the Second World
Congress:

> Belated German parliamentarism—an abortion of the bour-
> geois revolution, in itself an abortion of history—this parliamen-
> tarism suffers in its infancy from every illness peculiar to senile
> decay. The most democratic Reichstag of the Republic of Ebert
> is powerless, not only before the Iron Marshal Foch, but even
> before the Stock Exchange machinations of their own Stin-
> nesses, as well as before the military conspiracies of their war
> clique. The German parliamentary system is a void space be-
> tween two dictatorships.[17]

The workers organized in the Social Democratic Party, it was clear,
would make up the resistance to growing nationalist reaction. The
directive of the Fourth World Congress did not prohibit collaboration with the Social Democrats; the Stalinist policy of "social fascism"
would appear only in 1928–29. Nor did it prevent the possibility of a
joint government between Communists and Left Social Democrats.
What was proscribed was the entrance of a Communist party into any
Social Democratic government as a minority tail to a passive Social
Democratic majority.

---

[16] Lenin, *"Left-Wing" Communism: An Infantile Disorder,* p. 64.
[17] *The Capitalist World and the Communist International.* Manifesto of the
Second Congress of the Third (Communist) International (Moscow, 1924), p. 16.

Radek was opposed to this Comintern concept for Germany. For him, there were two broad alternatives in the German future: military nationalism or trade-unionism; and it was his master plan to combine the two into one. The difference in stature between him and Lenin was too great for him to risk open opposition; therefore his line was a zig-zag between his own policy and Lenin's.

In November 1922, when Radek returned to Berlin with Ernst Meyer, he maneuvered with his old Spartakist friends to supplant Meyer with someone closer to himself, in order to carry out his united-front policy. For following Lenin's intervention, and after meeting Zinoviev at the congress, Meyer seemed unwilling to build up a disciplined Radek faction in Germany.

Radek chose Heinrich Brandler, a Spartakist veteran and leader of the Chemnitz branch. Brandler had been born in 1881 in Warnsdorf, in the Sudeten. He lived and worked all his life in Chemnitz but never became a German citizen and could not be elected to the Reichstag. A worker in the building trade with long experience in the union movement, he joined the Social Democratic Party, whose Chemnitz branch was in the Left faction, and became one of Luxemburg's disciples. He joined the Spartakist opposition in 1916 and was regarded as one of the group's founders. Brandler was well known and liked among the Chemnitz workers of both parties, but his political experience was limited to this provincial corner. He despised the newcomers to the party, who had not earned their spurs through years of routine laborious tasks. A Communist without years of training in the Social Democratic Party before 1914 was without value in Brandler's eyes, not to be trusted. The destructive tendency of the young post-war generation was for him a disquieting and incomprehensible phenomenon. He had an immense pride in the German working class as he had known it, and a self-respect as a leader in it. The power of the new Russia impressed him, but he was also convinced that the Russians were unable to understand either the German worker or the peculiar factors of German politics. The German revolution would avoid certain features of the Russian; it would be non-violent, without terror, destruction, and chaos, which were due to the backwardness of Russian labor. German socialist economy would immediately function smoothly, would be highly productive.

The new crop of activists, Blanquists, Bakuninists, putschists, did nothing but destroy the slow steady work of the party organizers and should be eliminated from the movement at any cost.

Brandler had a much firmer hand than the refined intellectual Ernst Meyer. With Brandler, Radek would be able to get a group of trade-unionists into the key party posts, able to carry out a down-to-earth policy. It was a delicate operation to put Brandler in command; his reputation in the party was under fire. He had opposed Max Hoelz during the Kapp putsch, and he was held mainly responsible for the passivity of the Chemnitz organization during the general strike that broke it. Moreover, when he was taken into court following the putsch, he defended himself in legalistic rather than political terms, for which act he was made miserable over a long period by the party ideologues.[18]

At Brandler's side Radek put his old friend from Göppingen, August Thalheimer, whose trade was Marxian philosophy and who was intended to serve as Brandler's brain. Zetkin was to be the galleon figure of the group, and Fritz Heckert and Jakob Walcher, two energetic unionists, Brandler's adjutants. With such a combination, Radek hoped to get a solid support for Trotsky as Lenin's successor and to further weaken Zinoviev in the Comintern.

During 1923 Radek's maneuvering with Brandler against Zinoviev became hectic. He arranged and rearranged his German policy, adjusting its zig-zag to the varying needs of the Soviet Foreign Office. The defeat in Germany and the defeat of Trotsky in the Russian party eliminated Radek from the Comintern.

At the Fifth World Congress, July-August 1925, Zinoviev summed up the "ten differences between us and Radek":[19]

(1) A different evaluation of Paul Levi's desertion at the Third World Congress.
(2) A different attitude toward the Left dissidents in Germany, the KAPD.

---

[18] Compare the pamphlet that Brandler issued after the trial: *Der Hochverrats-Prozess gegen Heinrich Brandler vor dem ausserordentlichen Gericht am 6. Juni 1921 in Berlin* (Berlin, 1921).

[19] Gregory Zinoviev, *Speech in Reply to the Discussion of the Work of the ECCI* [Executive Committee of the Communist International], delivered June 26, 1924; published by the Press Bureau of the Fifth World Congress (Moscow, 1924), pp. 20–24.

(3) The open letter to the trade-unions, written by Radek and Levi on January 6, 1921. "Some comrades, including Bukharin and myself, were against this letter. Lenin intervened and settled the dispute."

(4) Policy regarding the Berlin conference of the three internationals.

(5) On the Norwegian question and the case of Martin Tranmael.[20]

(6) Attitude toward the Left wing of the German party. "I was quite sure that we had to come to an agreement with the Left at all costs."

(7) On the question of workers' governments.

(8) On the theses of the Leipzig convention.

(9) On the question of taxation in kind.

(10) On the questions before the conference of September 1923, dealing with the preparation for the seizure of power in Germany.

From the very beginning of the German revolution, once his Brest policy had lost out, Radek did not share the view of Lenin and Trotsky that under the pressure of events the bulk of the Social Democratic workers would be molded into a force powerful enough to transform German society. In his estimation, the Communist minority had to be trained to manipulate the Social Democratic majority— by coöperation, infiltration, disintegration, reconsolidation. By these measures a civil war would be avoided, or reduced to a few skirmishes forming a background to a revolution directed from above, by which the labor government would build up a monopoly of legality for itself. Radek is much more the forerunner of the Machiavellian tactics that later became standard in the Comintern than Lenin or Trotsky; for these, it was a fundament of revolutionary tactics that the proletarian party openly declare its program and openly fight for it.

Radek's tedious elaborations concerning workers' government in Germany represent the shift from the golden age of Bolshevism, when the assumption that the revolution would expand into Europe formed the basis of all political thinking, to the following transitional period,

---

[20] The Norwegian question concerned the federalist tendencies of the Norwegian party, which rejected the intervention of the Moscow Executive Committee in internal party affairs. One of its leaders, Tranmael, ignored invitations and orders to go to Moscow, but was not expelled. Cf. Bukharin's report on this matter, *Protokoll des Vierten Kongresses*, pp. 955–956.

when maneuver became the main strategy. Zinoviev's no less tedious exposition of the various species of labor government was an attempt to reconcile two irreconcilable epochs by a formula. In this discussion lie the roots of Comintern policy of the following periods; the small beginnings of Radek and others developed in the middle thirties into the People's Front and during World War II into the Democratic Front. The Communists in Germany who supported Radek did so not in the expectation that they were making the Russian Politburo an offer to dominate the German party, but out of a conviction that the transformation of German society was the task of the mother party, the Social Democrats, and not of the Communist minority.

In September 1922, when the Hilferding wing of the USPD returned to the Social Democratic Party, Radek regarded these Left socialists, who had proved unsuitable for use in the Communist Party proper, as channels into the center of the mass party of the German workers. But in 1923, when the Social Democratic Party was rapidly losing strength under the double pressure of the inflation and the French occupation, Radek shifted his principal attention to the possibility of manipulating the rising nationalist forces. The united-front policy in 1922 and the Schlageter policy [21] in 1923 are two sides of the same counterfeit coin—two attempts to win a Communist victory by delegating the task to another organization manipulated from behind.

From 1924 on, Radek was estranged from German Communism. He became the dean of the Sun Yat-sen University in Moscow, and studied China and Chinese Communism fervently. In the lull between Trotsky's defeat in 1923 and the renewed struggle in 1926, Radek remained loyal to his faction, in contrast to Brandler. [22] In 1926, when Zinoviev and Trotsky united to attack the rising Stalin, Radek was reconciled with Zinoviev and became during the next two years one of the most aggressive leaders of the Zinoviev-Trotsky bloc. [23]

---

[21] See Chapter 13, *infra.*

[22] Compare Radek's letter to Zetkin, *infra,* p. 509, note 9.

[23] Radek was expelled from the Russian party at its Fifteenth Congress, in December 1927. Sent into exile, he returned to Moscow in 1929, having capitulated to Stalin. He was restored to party membership and again worked as a specialist on foreign affairs, writing for *Pravda* until 1937. In that year he was a defendant in the Moscow trial and sentenced to ten years' imprisonment. Rumors that he was still alive and politically active under cover reached the outside world from time to time. His role in the trial will be analyzed in another study by the author.

The Communist Party of Germany represented a form of organization new in Europe, the first of its type, whose many other versions grew to maturity only after the Second World War. It integrated features adapted from the manipulative machinery of the Russian State Party into a European labor organization. Its organizational skeleton in 1922–1923 is very interesting, for aspects of both the parent democratic labor organization and the subsequent police party are found in it; during this period neither form was dominant. The structure of the party was farthest removed from that of Lenin's Jacobin fraternity of professional revolutionaries. Its paid functionaries had a surface resemblance to their counterparts in the Social Democratic Party, but the ever closer relation to the Russian party began to transform these German labor bureaucrats into Russian functionaries.

Organization Report for 1922

The party report for the year 1922 reflects the ambition of the German Central Committee to cover the same range of activity as the Russian. Special departments had been organized in municipalities and coöperatives; among women, youth, and children; for education and recreation, work among farmhands and peasants, aid to Soviet Russia; for legal aid and material help to prisoners and their families.

The party had a press service and thirty-four daily newspapers, including fifteen reprints with only the masthead changed. Its many magazines included: *Die Internationale, Kommunistische Parteikor-respondenz, Der Kommunistische Gewerkschafter, Der Kommunis-tische Genossenschafter, Der Kommunistische Landarbeiter, Der Pflug, Die Kommunistin.*[1] During 1922 the Central Committee had issued thirteen leaflets, whose political trend is indicated by a few of their titles: March, *Confiscation in Kind or State Bankruptcy;* April, *Genoa, the German-Russian Treaty, and the World Workers' Congress;* July, *Proletarian United Front or Coalition with the Bourgeoisie?* Leaflets were issued in either a large edition of four million copies (reduced in September 1922 to 1.8 million) or a small edition of 1.4 million copies (reduced to half a million). Books and pamphlets were published in inelegant formats. Translations from Russian authors were just beginning to appear; during 1922 the party published a vol-ume of Dostoyevsky's short stories.

Following the March Action, some 6000 party members had been arrested, of whom about 1500 were held for a week or two and then released without trial. Of the 4500 who were tried, 500 were acquitted and the remaining 4000 were sentenced to a total of 3000 years' imprison-ment. Legal aid for such cases was arranged through the *Juristische Zentralstelle* (Central Legal Agency), and support of their families was organized through the *Rote Hilfe* (Red Aid). Receipts of the Red Aid during 1922 totaled 9,881,428 marks, its expenditures 8,444,800 marks.

Aid to Soviet Russia was also organized through a separate body. In 1922, 27 municipalities gave important sums or sponsored chil-dren's homes in the Soviet Union. Tools and clothing valued at eight million marks were collected by young people and children. An issue of "workers' bonds" raised two million marks. The organization had its own illustrated weekly, *Sichel und Hammer* ("Sickle and Ham-mer"), whose first edition was 130,000 copies. Russian films were shown and the proceeds went to Russia. A Russian violinist, Soemus, accom-panied by a choral group that gave political recitations, toured the country.

---

[1] "The International," "Communist Party Correspondence," "The Communist Trade-Unionist," "The Communist Coöperator," "The Communist Farmhand," "The Plow," "The Communist Woman." The two magazines designed for cir-culation among peasants, *Der Kommunistische Landarbeiter* and *Der Pflug,* had both been suspended during 1922 for lack of interest and funds.

Propaganda among peasants was relatively inefficient. During this period, farmhands split from the trade-union created after November 1918, and organized an independent Communist-controlled union. The party's Rural Division organized agrarian commissions and issued a model contract. Small peasants were approached with a special calendar combining agricultural matters with propaganda.

The Women's Secretariat organized housewives' committees to control prices, particularly in the coöperatives. Its high point was the celebration on March 8 of each year of an International Women's Day.

There were two magazines for youth, both edited by Edwin Hörnle —*Das proletarische Kind* ("The Proletarian Child") for youngsters, and *Der Junge Genosse* ("The Young Comrade") for adolescents; the latter was issued in an edition of 30,000 copies. An international conference of Communist children's organizations was organized in Berlin on September 16–18, 1922.

One specialty of the children's and youth groups was organizing ceremonies, following Social Democratic tradition, to replace religious confirmations, baptisms, weddings. A pamphlet, *The Fire,* was dedicated "to young Communists on their way into life at the occasion of their confirmation," at the age of thirteen. It contained poems, some by Max Barthel,[2] pictures of Luxemburg and Liebknecht, and such quotations from their books as the following:

> Long is the way, it will take many hundred years, but the way is straight before us and we sing our Red Freedom song, startling and terrifying as the danger of war.

The Division for Instruction and Recreation embraced the following subdivisions: education of the party proper; agitation in workers' educational, sport, and cultural societies; work among artists, writers, musicians, and artistic presentation (already!) of party meetings and conventions; school policies and teachers' movements; youth and children; intellectuals. The party was particularly active among teachers and organized both an independent teachers' union and Commu-

---

[2] After 1933 Barthel went over to the Nazis and continued to write poetry under Hitler. He was friendly with Radek, visited him in 1919 in his prison cell in Moabit, dedicated a volume of verse, *Utopia,* to him. He was also a friend of Willi Münzenberg, the founder of the Communist Youth International.

nist groups in the official one. Communist students in the universities were organized in *"Kostufras"* (Communist student fractions).

Work concerned with education was carefully planned. The Remscheid and Bochum branches were called to order for founding a Free People's University instead of participating in the schools organized by the respective city councils. In Frankfurt am Main, on the other hand, the workers' academy organized by the city was declared inadequate for Marxists.

The Central Committee had organized two party schools, with a combined body of seventy-four pupils. The curriculum included economic theory, the history of the German and Russian revolutions, the agrarian program, Marxism. There were also seven district schools and four traveling party teachers, serving groups in sixteen districts and seventy-eight locals.

During the latter part of 1922, the Communist Party of Germany was gaining in influence and membership. In the third quarter of 1922 it had 218,555 members;[8] this contrasts with a membership figure of a year earlier, just after the March Action, of 180,443. Over the same period the Social Democratic Party became weaker, in spite of unification with the Hilferding wing of the USPD.

The influence of the party was, of course, greater than this core of disciplined membership would indicate. In many districts where, according to the complaint of the Central Committee, not a single Communist could be found, the party was none the less given important support in elections. The electoral return in general was often twenty to forty times the number of members in a district.

---

[8] Of these 191,845 were men; 26,710, women. These figures were tallied only after payment of dues, which during a period of rising inflation was not always regular; the actual membership was somewhat larger. In September 1922 the most important of the 28 party districts were the following:

	Branches	Members
Berlin-Brandenburg	220	24,908
West Saxony	73	11,610
East Saxony	73	3,580
Halle-Merseburg	235	23,374
Thuringia	243	15,147
Wasserkante (Hamburg District)	90	23,206
North Rhineland	159	18,525
South Rhineland	138	19,309

The party was strongest in Berlin, Hamburg, and the Rhineland—
in membership and also in the degree of influence its adherents had
attained. In these and the other key industrial centers, the mood of
the civil war persisted. In Central Germany, on the other hand, the
atmosphere was different. USPD locals had gone over intact to the
Communists, and they felt themselves masters of the party. These
workers were scattered in small shops throughout the many industrial
villages of this area—in the machine and textile factories of Saxony
and the glass, optical, toy, and textile shops of Thuringia. In many
of these small towns and villages, the Communists had gained substantial local influence, with substantial representation in town councils and other local institutions. They were bound to the Social Democrats by the intimacy of life in a small community; members of the
two parties coöperated without friction in local trade-unions and in a
mass of local committees and sport and cultural clubs. In this area,
the Communists had a feeling of self-assurance; the civil war was in
the past, and the sins of Noske and Scheidemann could be forgotten
with it.

In 80 town councils throughout Germany the Communists were in
an absolute majority; in 170 others they had a plurality. More than
6000 town councillors were registered members of the Communist
Party. A special party agency for municipal affairs (*Kommunalpoli-
tische Abteilung*) coördinated these activities.

Local successes seemed even more important when contrasted with
the Reichstag, where, following the defection of Paul Levi and his
associates, the official party faction lacked two of the fifteen deputies
needed to propose legislation. Accordingly, whenever the Communist
Party of Germany wanted to offer a bill to the Reichstag, it had to
approach two members of the hostile Levi group to ask them to make
up the necessary quorum.

In the trade-unions the Communist Party had 997 organized groups;
400 union officers were party members; 60 local union councils had
Communist majorities. But nationally Communist influence was relatively slight. At the Leipzig Trade-Union Convention in June 1922,
only 90 of the 694 delegates were Communists.[4]

---

[4] More than half of the Communist delegates were from the Metal Workers'
Union, the others from the building trades, the civil service, railroads, transport.

Red Bloc in Saxony and Thuringia

It was the intention of the party leaders to develop the local successes from town to state governments, and in January 1923 a convention was convoked in Leipzig to discuss this policy.[5] Paul Böttcher, editor of the Communist daily there, had sketched the advantages of the policy a year before.[6] Under his direction, the Leipzig party set about to create an appropriate atmosphere for the convention: delegations of workers were to come to it and demand that the party

---

The party dominated several smaller unions, splinters off the traditional German Federation of Labor. In Chemnitz, for example, some 22,000 expelled building workers had founded an independent union. Some 16,000 seamen, or more than half of all those on German ships that could be organized, were in the Communist-led *Deutscher Schiffahrtsbund,* which was of particular use to the party for conspirational assignments abroad. Jan Valtin, author of *Out of the Night,* came out of this milieu.

A different kind of organization was *Die Union der Hand- und Kopfarbeiter* (Union of Workers of Brain and Brawn), an attempt in the tradition of the International Workers of the World at uniting manual and office workers into one big union. Three-quarters of its 100,000 members were in the Ruhr. This union was a member of the Profintern, and Moscow did everything possible to combat its anarchist and federalist tendencies; these were specifically condemned as "dangerous" at the union's convention, in Essen in October 1922.

[5] A survey of the convention's staff members is of interest. Many of them have survived as functionaries in Soviet-occupied Germany.

Martha Arendsee, during World War II a member of the Free Germany Committee in Moscow, now in the Socialist Unity Party in Berlin.

Paul Böttcher, expelled in 1929.

Heinrich Brandler, expelled in 1929.

Fritz Heckert, died in Moscow, 1935.

Bernhard Könen, during World War II in the Free Germany Committee in Moscow, now in the Socialist Unity Party in Berlin.

Arkadi Maslow, expelled in 1926, died under ambiguous circumstances in Havana in 1941.

Wilhelm Pieck, during World War II a leader of the Free Germany Committee in Moscow, now the head of the Socialist Unity Party in Berlin.

Werner Scholem, see page 440, note 3, *infra.*

Walther Ulbricht, during World War II a leader of the Free Germany Committee in Moscow, now second in command of the Socialist Unity Party in Berlin.

Hugo Urbahns, expelled in 1926, died in Stockholm in January 1947.

Jakob Walcher, expelled from the party in 1929, active in the Council for a Democratic Germany in New York during World War II, now returned to Germany and active in the Socialist Unity Party.

Ernst Wollweber, staff member of Soviet Military Intelligence in Germany, probably killed by the GPU in Moscow in 1936.

Clara Zetkin, died in Moscow, 1934.

[6] Paul Böttcher, "Sozialdemokratisch-kommunistische Regierung," *Die Internationale* (Berlin, May 14, 1922) vol. IV, No. 21, pp. 471–476.

enter the state governments; any new electoral victories were to be announced; the successes in the local trade-unions were to be contrasted with the lack of influence of the party in the big industrial centers.

In Berlin, Karl Radek, with Heinrich Brandler and August Thalheimer, prepared the statement of policy for the convention. It had to be carefully drawn, for participation of Communists as ministers in state governments conflicted with every theory and policy of international Communism as it had developed up to that time. Radek had to avoid a comparison with the discussion at the beginning of the century, when the entrance of the French socialist, Alexandre Millerand, into a bourgeois cabinet had been debated throughout the International.

There were 219 delegates at the Leipzig convention. The Right wing was represented by Halle-Merseburg, Thuringia, Erzgebirge-Vogtland, West Saxony, East Saxony, Wurttemberg, South Rhineland, Lower Rhineland, and Baden; the Left opposition by Berlin-Brandenburg, Wasserkante (the Hamburg District), Hessen-Frankfurt, Middle Rhineland, and Lusatia. The political dichotomy of the party had a geopolitical background. The Communists "in power" in the hamlets and towns of Central Germany underestimated the force of the counter revolution; the Communists of the great industrial regions held in contempt "the democratic illusions" of their comrades in socialist Thuringia and Saxony.

The discussion on whether or not Communists should participate in the governments of Saxony and Thuringia was essentially one on the character of the Social Democratic Party. Was this party indissolubly bound to the German counter revolution? Or could either the party as a whole, or as a minimum a Left faction of it, be won over to "a workers' policy"; and if so, how could this be achieved?

According to Radek and Brandler, the Social Democratic Party was the Left wing of the bourgeois bloc. The task of the Communists was to win it over to form the Right wing of a workers' bloc. This could be done by forming a united front with such Left Social Democrats as Dr. Erich Zeigner,[7] minister in the Saxon government, who

---

[7] Dr. Zeigner survived the Nazi regime; he was elected mayor of Leipzig in 1946. He has collaborated completely with the Russian occupation authorities.

in opposition to the policy of the Social Democratic leadership in Berlin would be sympathetic to a coalition cabinet with the Communists. As a beginning, it was decided that the program of this united front should be: drastic measures of social reform, formation of trade-union committees to control production, formation of *Proletarische Hundertschaften* (Red Hundreds) for the military defense of the working class.

A Red Bloc in Saxony and Thuringia would be the model for the Reich, a focal point for all German labor. But this concept of a Red Bloc of Central Germany—a cliché in the Communist press of the period—was based not on the intrinsic strength of the Communist Party but on its ability to infiltrate and manipulate the Social Democratic Party. In the city councils of Leipzig and Dresden, the two key cities of "Red Saxony," the Social Democrats had an overwhelming majority and the Communist Party was weak.[8]

In general throughout Saxony and Thuringia, old Social Democratic functionaries, integrated into the Socialist Unity Party, form the bulk of the present administration.

"Today the city of Leipzig is harnessed by a control apparatus, composed of two presidents, ten executive secretaries, twenty divisional secretaries, and about sixty other party employees . . . Among the special divisions created are those for politics, culture, agitation and propaganda, cadres and information (a security service with a special spy net), economics, finance, none of which is inferior to their oppressive Nazi Party predecessors. In each of the city's thirty-two boroughs, the party has a system of street and house representatives, coördinated by a paid secretary . . . Of the 80,000 members of the Socialist Unity Party in Leipzig, more than 200 are party employees, working in two central party buildings and twenty borough branches . . .

"Zeigner and the other Social Democrats in the administrations of Saxony, Mecklenburg, and Brandenburg, are without influence. The Ministers of the Interior, for Economy, the police chiefs of both the states and other political divisions, are all Communists. The few Social Democrats remaining in the police administration were removed after the Truman speech [recommending a loan to Greece and Turkey]; for example, Police President Kurt Krippner in Zwickau, Vice-president Eger in Chemnitz, Vice-president Hennig in Leipzig, Police Chief Schönfeld in Grimma, all of whom have been active in the working-class movement for thirty years and victims of fascism." (*Sopade Informationsdienst*, Social Democratic Party, Hanover, May 13, 1947.)

[8] In the election of November 5, 1922, in Saxony, 268,000 Communist votes had elected 10 deputies to the state parliament, as compared with 1,000,000 votes and 40 deputies for the Social Democrats. Opposed to this so-called proletarian majority of 50 deputies, there was a bourgeois minority of 46 deputies (8 Democrats, 19 German People's Party, and 19 German National People's Party).

In the election of October 16, 1921, Berlin had lost its proletarian majority. A combined Left faction of 110 councillors (21 Communists, 43 Independent Socialists, and 46 Social Democrats) was opposed by a bourgeois group of 115, of which the strongest component was the German National People's Party.

In Berlin and the other major industrial areas, the ratio of Communist voters to Communist Party members was much higher than in Saxony. In these areas, moreover, the party had significant strength in the factory councils, which offset to some degree its comparative electoral weakness.

One of the principal differences between Left and Right Communists was their interpretation of the relation of factory councils to trade-unions. For the Left, the councils were a movement of genuine independent worth, to be supported in competition with the trade-union apparatus. For the Right, they were rather a pressure group, to be used to force the reluctant unions to open their doors to the Communists. Radek and Brandler proposed the formation of "factory committees for the control of production," but through regular union channels. A united Social Democratic–Communist union movement would be the base for a Reich workers' government. Current Communist slogans often began *"Der ADGB muss . . ."* (The trade-union leaders must . . .).

But important as these differences between party factions were, the whole discussion was principally a deliberate diversion from what the Left considered the most urgent business of the day. The pending Ruhr crisis was not on the agenda; it was to be dealt with only under the general head of foreign policy. Since the signing of the Treaty of Rapallo, nationalist circles in the German army and government had sharpened relations with the Reparation Commission, vacillating between pressure and provocation. The delegates came to the Leipzig convention well aware that something decisive was brewing there.

During the preparatory meetings of the convention, the Ruhr and Rhineland were occupied by French and Belgian troops. The proposal of the Left to recognize this fundamental change in the German scene by making the Ruhr crisis the main convention topic was defeated by a narrow margin, and instead of a serious discussion there was a public meeting on the question, with Clara Zetkin as the party speaker. This incident aggravated the feeling between the factions: the Brandler group spoke of the exploitation of the Ruhr incident by the Left to push its adventurist policies, and the Minority was infuriated by the Right wing's persistent refusal to deal adequately with the most pressing problem facing the party.

The emphasis of the convention was insistently returned to the ques-

tion of whether Communists should enter the state governments of
Saxony and Thuringia. In the middle of her report on the Fourth
World Congress, Clara Zetkin was interrupted by the news that under
Communist pressure the Saxony state government had resigned. In an
attempt to heighten the emotional appeal of this local Communist victory. Albert Stolzenburg, the acting chairman, arranged to show the
delegates lantern slides concerning the incident. He read the accompanying report:

> Dresden, January 30, 1923. In the session of the Saxony Landtag
> . . . Minister Lipinski denounced the illegal work of the Commu-
> nist Party. . . . Comrade Böttcher asked that the formation of the
> government in Saxony be the task of the whole working class.
> "We want a factory-council congress . . . which shall decide on
> the formation of the workers' government."

Böttcher, with Stolzenburg and Pieck, was one of the three co-chairmen
of the convention. After the "renewed stormy applause" had subsided,
Stolzenburg continued:

> Comrades, you have expressed your enthusiasm over this event.
> I want you to join with me in three cheers. Long live the revo-
> lutionary proletariat of Saxony! Long live the German revolu-
> tion! Long live the world revolution!

"The delegates cheer enthusiastically," the convention proceedings continue, "repeating these exclamations, and then stand up and sing the
Internationale." But immediately after this self-congratulatory exhibition a motion by Maslow to remove Stolzenburg as convention chairman was defeated by only a narrow margin.

Zetkin's report shows that the servile Russian patriotism that was to
become endemic in the Comintern already had strong beginnings in
this period. She describes her feelings on crossing the Russian border:

> Take off your shoes! The soil on which you are standing is
> holy soil. This soil is hallowed by the revolutionary struggle, the
> revolutionary sacrifices of the Russian proletariat (Stormy ap-
> plause) . . .
>
> > *Du musst herrschen und gewinnen,*
> > *Oder dienen und verlieren,*
> > *Leiden oder triumphieren,*
> > *Amboss oder Hammer sein.*[9]

---

[9] *Bericht über die Verhandlungen des III. (8.) Parteitages der Kommunistischen Partei Deutschlands,* Abgehalten in Leipzig vom 28. Januar bis 1. Februar 1923 (Berlin, 1923), pp. 268–277.

["You must rule and win or serve and lose, suffer or triumph, be anvil or hammer." These verses from Goethe were the standard declamatory finale of party speeches.]

Until then, it had been the tradition in the Comintern that minority groupings in any Communist party have proportional representation on its Central Committee, these members to be chosen by each oppositional faction. Radek and Brandler broke with this tradition and, over protest of the Left, gave it inadequate representation; moreover, they themselves selected those Left-wingers who in their opinion were most amenable to compromise. This procedure, following the failure to issue a party statement on the Ruhr invasion, brought the convention to the verge of a split. To protest the infringement of its constitutional rights, the Left decided not to participate in the election of the Central Committee. A Central Committee thus elected would not have the confidence of the largest party locals—those in Berlin, the Ruhr, Hamburg.

Karl Radek saw that he had gone too far. At a secret night session, of which there is no record in the convention proceedings, he proposed a compromise by which four delegates of the Left opposition would be elected to the Central Committee. Supported by Vasil P. Kolarov,[10] Radek posed as the Comintern's neutral arbiter, but he maneuvered successfully to prevent the election of the Left leaders, Thälmann and Maslow.

Only the loyalty of the Left to the Comintern prevented a split. The Minority delegates were convinced that the Right wing would again muff its chance and lead the party to another defeat. After the secret night session, the new Central Committee was publicly elected,

---

[10] He was fraternal delegate to the convention from the Communist Party of Bulgaria. Born in 1877, Kolarov had joined the Social Democratic Party of Bulgaria in the 90's. In 1903, he joined the *Tesnyak* ("narrow") group, the Left wing that later affiliated to the Comintern; two years later became a member of its Central Committee and in 1919 its General Secretary. In the years before and after the war, he was the usual delegate of the Bulgarian party to international conferences, including Zimmerwald and Stockholm. In 1920, he was arrested together with Dimitrov. In 1921, Kolarov became a member of the Comintern Presidium; the next year he was chosen as his party's representative to the international. A leader in the 1923 insurrection in Bulgaria, he went after its collapse to Moscow, where for a time he was director of the International Agricultural Institute. In 1945, he reappeared in Bulgaria, where he is today one of the important leaders of the Communist Party.

but the Left denoted its dissatisfaction by abstaining from voting. The
Majority voted for Minority candidates, who received votes approxi-
mating the total possible number of 219; but Majority candidates were
elected by votes ranging from 166, for Brandler, the new party leader,
to 112, for Ulbricht. Arthur Ewert, the Minority representative whom
Radek chose, got only 163 votes, for the Left was convinced that he
would soon be won over to the Majority.[11]

Radek had been informed that the Soviet Foreign Office hoped to
exploit the French-German conflict in a manner contradictory to Comintern policy. Not merely the Communists but most Social Democrats
and unorganized German workers as well would have vigorously opposed even temporary collaboration with German nationalists and the
German government against France. Openly to propose such a policy at
a Communist Party convention would have been an invitation to revolt.
A discussion on the Ruhr occupation, however, could only have led
either to a more or less explicit avowal of National Bolshevism, or to
binding the party to a contrary policy. The Soviet Foreign Office
wanted above all a flexible hand in Germany, a hand that could co-
operate to any degree that seemed desirable with the German cabinet
concerning the Ruhr occupation; and Radek was, among other things,
its liaison to the German government.

Hence it was necessary to divert the energy of the convention into
other matters, such as trade-union tactics or participation in the state
governments of Saxony and Thuringia. These problems, thus isolated
from the main flow of European politics, were reduced to provincialism.
At the time neither faction realized fully that they were discussing a
side issue, nor precisely why the main problem facing the party was
not permitted to appear. Thus, Radek concentrated his effort on the
question of a united front and workers' government.

> The struggle for the united front leads to the conquest of the
> old proletarian mass organizations, such as trade-unions and co-

---

[11] Ewert did indeed go over to the Right during 1923. In 1928, as a leader
of the Conciliators, he rebelled against the party along with Hugo Eberlein and
Gerhart Eisler (alias Hans Berger) and was banned from Germany. Assigned to
Brazil, he participated in the putsch of Carlos Prestes there. Ewert was confined
in an insane asylum; in 1946 he was released into a private nursing home. His wife
was in a Nazi concentration camp and is reported to have died there.

operatives. These instruments of the working class, which the tactics of the reformists have transformed into tools of the bourgeoisie, become again by this struggle weapons of the proletariat. The class struggle must now be waged for the defeat of the bourgeoisie. . . .

A workers' government is neither the dictatorship of the proletariat nor a peaceful parliamentary development toward it. It is rather an attempt of the working class within the framework of bourgeois democracy, and at first with the methods of that democracy, to develop through proletarian mass organizations a workers' policy. The proletarian dictatorship, on the other hand, is a conscious blasting of the democratic framework; it blows up the democratic state apparatus and replaces it completely with proletarian class organizations.[12]

Immediately after the Leipzig convention the Politburo of the Russian party intervened and declared the Leipzig theses to be "incorrect." A reformist path to socialism by a coalition of the two working-class parties was formally rejected as a "Right deviation." This criticism, however, in spite of its extensive presentation, was intended more as an emollient to the party crisis than as a serious investigation of the major questions of German policy; it was based in fact on the conflict in the Russian party.

Zinoviev watched the German Right with a suspicious eye; it was linked via Radek to Trotsky. On the other hand, the Brandler faction continued its efforts to expel the Minority, to stigmatize it as wreckers of the party. A split would have brought with it, however, the danger of exposing the clandestine contacts between the Russian government and German nationalist circles. Moreover, a Communist mass party was most desirable as a Russian pressure group, as a reserve for developing a possible alternative line in the future. As the conflict between the Central Committee and the Left wing developed, the Politburo tried to act as conciliatory arbiter.

Thus the Politburo's intervention had two main objectives, to keep the line of the German party fluid, and to prevent a split. The proposal of the Ruhr Communists to seize local power was rejected, but with a kind of pat on the head for their revolutionary zeal. This was in con-

---

[12] *Parteitagsbericht,* Leipzig convention, pp. 417, 420.

trast to the crusade of the Berlin Central Committee against adventurist putschists, but it was a difference only in emphasis. The deepening economic crisis was reflected throughout Germany in unrest, demonstrations, hunger riots; and it was obvious that the German Left spoke for a portion of the German working class. The Central Committee should learn to handle the rebels more skillfully.

After the Kronstadt uprising in March 1921, Lenin hoped—but failed—to get a workable compromise among the conflicting elements in the Russian Party [1] and in the country. The impact of the Workers' Opposition groups can best be measured by the dimensions of the Party purge from March 1921 to March 1922. "Altogether, nearly 170,000 persons, or about 25 per cent of the total membership, were expelled from the Party as a result of the purge." [2]

Following the Tenth Party Congress, in March 1921, the newly elected Central Committee removed N. N. Krestinsky, L. P. Serebryakov, and E. A. Preobrazhensky (the last a collaborator with Bukharin in the writing of many Communist texts), who had been elected at the previous congress a year before as the three-man Secretariat. They were considered too lenient toward the oppositionist groups in the Party; later all three were involved in anti-Stalinist factions. The new Secretariat comprised V. M. Molotov, E. Yaroslavsky, and L. M. Mikhailov; and it was this trio that carried out the purge of the Workers' Opposition. Following the Kronstadt revolt the later adju-

---

[1] From this point of the narrative on, the word *Party* is capitalized when referring to the Russian institution, in order to indicate that it has become the sole instrument of power in the state—the State Party.

[2] [Joseph Stalin], *History of the CPSU*, p. 259. N. Popov (*Outline History of the CPSU*, II, 150) gives an even higher figure: "Two hundred thousand members—almost one-third of the Party membership, if we reckon that 730,000 members were represented at the Tenth Party Congress—were eliminated from the Party . . . Certain excesses were committed during the purging in the provinces."

tants of Stalin begin to play an important role for the first time—such men as A. Andreyev, S. M. Kirov, V. V. Kuibyshev, N. A. Uglanov.

After the end of the civil war, the army lost its predominant place in Soviet life to the advantage of the Party apparatus. However, Trotsky, the organizer of the army, had become the most popular leader among the Russian people generally, more popular than Lenin, the Party leader. He had miraculously saved Russia from dismemberment and destruction by the invading powers. To the masses, he was Trotsky the Victorious, Trotsky the Savior. In Russia the enthusiasm of the youth focused on him, and to the outside world his power seemed unlimited and his command over Russia's army and economy without parallel. But in the Party Trotsky's position was less secure. During the two and a half years he traveled about the front in his commander's train, his rulings had been in constant friction with the Party; his attitude toward Party interference was irritable and contemptuous. He attracted to him, none the less, all the forces in the Party opposed to the Moscow center, for he was the alternative candidate with the best chance of success.

Lenin's attitude toward Trotsky was complex and changing. He regarded it as one of his major tasks to integrate so powerful a figure in the Party and state leadership, and in many of the political issues Lenin and Trotsky were joined against the smaller figures opposing them. He did not, however, want to let Trotsky get into the pivotal position either in the Party or in the Comintern.

Stalin Becomes General Secretary

The Central Committee decided to coördinate the Party groupings at all costs, and this was the principal point on the Eleventh Party Congress agenda in March 1922. It was decided to strengthen the Secretariat of the Party by reducing two of the three men to the rank of assistants to one General Secretary. Joseph Stalin was delegated as General Secretary on the second of April 1922. At this time, Stalin was undoubtedly Lenin's choice for the post; in part because Stalin was also the choice of the Party bureaucracy, who wanted a strong man not only against the class enemy, but also against the Workers' Opposition and any encroachment on the Party apparatus by Trotsky.

In 1922, Stalin had a good reputation in the Russian Party. He was an intimate pupil and friend of Lenin, he was an "Old Bolshevik," he came from the rank and file, he had lived in Russia during the exile, he neither was nor wanted to be a brilliant writer, theorist, or orator. He was a matter-of-fact organizer with a down-to-earth pragmatism, with vitality and energy, not a socialist tribune in the European style. More than Trotsky, more than Zinoviev or Bukharin, Stalin was the representative of the Party functionary, the Bolshevik organizer. He was known by the upper brackets of the hierarchy; on the Central Committee he managed a thousand Party affairs with skill, seeking and sometimes finding a common denominator between the Party organizations in the provinces and the center. Since the Party cadres wanted him to be General Secretary Lenin had no serious political or personal reason to force another choice.

On May 26, Lenin suffered his first attack of arteriosclerosis; the Party leadership kept it secret from the membership. Lenin, who had always been concerned with the health of his comrades, had himself been an inexhaustible source of vitality. Now his sickness was so serious that whether he would ever return to work was not known. Jockeying for his succession began immediately. Just because Trotsky was the heir apparent, the top ranks of the Party united against him, and this was the historical opportunity in the making of Stalin.

Kamenev took over Lenin's chairmanship of the Politburo. He and his alter ego, Zinoviev, acted as the political brain of the Central Committee. In this period, they treated Stalin with a certain hauteur, intending to make him their instrument in coördinating the Party. Of the younger men, Bukharin supported Zinoviev and Radek, Trotsky. Zinoviev was leader of the Petrograd branch and Kamenev of the one in Moscow; commanding the Party in the two capitals of Russia, they believed themselves certain of a majority at all conventions.

For a while Stalin was content to follow the law of political primogeniture and let Zinoviev set the line. He concentrated entirely on two organizational tasks: the coördination around him of provincial branches, making full use of the natural antagonism between the capitals and the provinces; and the coördination of the Orgburo, the Central Control Commission, and the Cheka[3] under his command.

---

[3] The name Cheka was taken from the initial letters of *Chrezvychaynaya Kommissiya* (*Extraordinary Commission*). Founded on December 20, 1917, it was

The Central Control Commission was the body that supervised, punished, and purged the Party membership, and its function was interwoven with that of the Cheka. Each province had its own Control Commission, directly responsible to the one in Moscow; this network comprised a counterbalance to the Party, more dangerous than the Party itself, because it operated secretly and by police methods. In the name of Party and state security, a Control Commission could eliminate any undesirable member from the Party and put him outside Soviet legality. Stalin used the post-Kronstadt purge to play with these two instruments of power, Party and Control Commission, and to see that all men not in accord with him in the Party hierarchy were eventually subordinated or expelled. Four of the seven members of the collegium of the Central Control Commission became the fundament on which Stalin built his power. One of these was Stalin himself, self-appointed delegate of the Orgburo, and the other three were his men—M. F. Shkiryatov, G. A. Korostelev, and M. K. Muranov.

All these activities of Stalin were in part veiled to the other leaders, and the part that was seen was not appreciated at its full value. Unrelentingly he kept pointing out the danger of Trotsky, and with this before the other leaders' eyes he maneuvered skillfully to get his steps approved. During 1922 Trotsky's participation in the Politburo was reduced to a mere formality. All questions were decided in secret sessions of its membership minus Trotsky; and the same procedure, urged as a necessary safety measure against a possible coup, was adopted in the provinces against Trotsky's supporters.

In August 1922, a few months after the Eleventh Party Congress, the Twelfth Party Conference was called to review the relation of the

---

reorganized successively under the names GPU (*Gosudarstvennoye Politicheskoye Upravleniye*—Political Directorate of the State), OGPU (*Obyedinyonnoye GPU*—United Political Directorate of the State), and NKVD (*Nar-Kom-Vnu-Del, Narodnyi Kommissariat Vnutrennikh Del*—People's Comissariat for Internal Affairs). In late 1946, it was divided into the MVD (*Ministerstvo Vnutrennikh Del*—Ministry of Internal Affairs), whose chief function is regulating the forced-labor industrialization, and the MGB (*Ministerstvo Gosudarstvennoy Bezopasnosti*—Ministry of State Security), which corresponds to both intelligence and counter-intelligence and functions also outside the Soviet Union. This frequent change in name of the state police reflects both its periodic shake-ups and a desire to engender confusion. Note the trend, indicated by the successive names, from "Extraordinary" through "United" to "Ministry of the Interior."

Party to the working class. On the agenda were a revision of the Party constitution, the task of the trade-unions, the task of the coöperatives, the question of anti-Soviet parties under the New Economic Policy; and on every point the decision taken was intended to strengthen the monopoly of the Party. "Tried and trusted" Communists were to be implanted in the unions in order to eliminate "the mutual alienation and antagonism between Communist trade-union leaders and business managers." The Trade-Union Opposition in the Party, almost completely beaten, made another attempt to gain a limited freedom of movement in at least one field. They urged the separation of workers' coöperatives from the State coöperative center, the *Centrosoyuz.*

The Party control of factory canteens, medical aid stations, nurseries, sanatoriums, was one of the most effective means of keeping workers under control, for the amount of food allocated to a factory became proportional to its Party patriotism, to its subservience to Party dictates. In full retreat, the trade-unions fought a last-ditch battle on this modest issue: to separate the workers' very livelihood from the strict control of the Secretariat. Stalin recognized that even so limited an autonomy would endanger his rise to power and answered the demand with a firm No. "We have to strengthen the state trading organizations," the conference replied. In a hypocritical defense of the NEP, autonomous workers' coöperatives were rejected because they would alienate the peasant coöperatives and, by the standard argument, "would thereby facilitate the activities of all kinds of bourgeois anti-Soviet elements."

If you distrust the state trade organization, the trade-unions were answered, you distrust the State Party. And if you distrust the Party, you are the enemies of the country; you have joined the bourgeois counter revolution.

> Taking advantage of the economic difficulties of the country which affected the conditions of the working class, the Social Revolutionary and Menshevik Parties attempted to carry on anti-Soviet agitation and propaganda to the effect that the Soviet government had ceased to be a working-class government, that it was degenerating and deserting to the side of the bourgeoisie, that the working class had to carry on its own policy independent of the policy of the Soviet government. This anti-Soviet agitation met with a certain response among individual elements in the Party who were

weak and unstable, particularly from among the former "Workers' Opposition." [4]

Slowly recovering from his stroke, Lenin recognized that at best he would never resume the full load he had carried. Stalin, who had been acceptable to him when he was under his own political control, became a problem. On his sickbed Lenin felt the repercussions of the purge, the throes of the post-Kronstadt crisis; and he began to revise his concept of the State Party monopoly. His speech at the Fourth World Congress, for example, warning European comrades not to imitate Russian methods mechanically, was an outgrowth of the Party purge. In his disappointment with Stalin, Lenin overcame his estrangement from Trotsky. The two top leaders, one removed from control by sickness and the other by intrigue, achieved a rapprochement.

Lenin's Testament on Party Leadership

Lenin had returned to work for a short period, but on December 16 he suffered a second stroke and it was clear that his active life was over. The struggle for succession entered its acute phase. During his final illness, Lenin watched the crisis grow in the Party leadership; for him, continuity of the collective leadership was of paramount importance.

Deeply concerned, Lenin had had many discussions over the question of his successors during 1922 with all of his political intimates. Everyone on the Politburo was carefully analyzed, his strengths weighed against his weaknesses. The danger of a split, and with it the destruction of the Party and of the Comintern, was the major factor in all decisions.

Trotsky remained first on the list of possible successors. He had strong support among the state administration, the army hierarchy, the Party intelligentsia; in the Comintern the French party favored Trotsky's candidacy. He also had strong opposition in the Comintern; in 1922, when Radek boosted Trotsky as the coming man, he got a lukewarm response in Europe. Trotsky was feared for his too strict discipline, for his rigid intervention from the top; at this time no one regarded him as a Party democrat.

---

[4] N. Popov, *Outline History of the CPSU*, II, 169.

Lenin wanted neither Trotsky nor Stalin nor any other individual as the leader of the Russian Party after his death. He did not want a personal leadership; he did not regard any one of the top Bolsheviks as capable of leading the Party alone. In particular, he feared the elimination of Zinoviev from his post as head of the Comintern.

In the eyes of the Party, Zinoviev had many weak points. His attitude toward the October uprising, though never brought up in this period, detracted nevertheless from his reputation as a "stalwart revolutionary." [5] His regime in Leningrad, where the Workers' Op-

---

[5] At the two decisive sessions of the Central Committee during which the coup was mapped out, on October 20 and 23, 1917, Zinoviev and Kamenev had opposed Lenin's stand that the Bolsheviks should attempt to seize power by an armed uprising. Their opposition was based on two points—first, that the Bolsheviks should not attempt to take power alone, for if they succeeded with this narrow base they could hold it only by means of terror, and would thus destroy the growth of proletarian democracy; and, second, that the international situation was not favorable enough. On October 24, they made their view known to the most important regional committees of the party, and on October 31 they published a statement in the Menshevik newspaper *Novaya Zhizn* advocating a coalition government of all socialist parties. Lenin proposed expelling them for breach of party discipline, but this was never carried out because they were supported in their view by substantial strata of the party, including several other members of the Central Committee, among them A. I. Rykov, V. P. Nogin, and V. P. Milyutin.

On November 17, ten days after the uprising, these five men—Zinoviev, Kamenev, Rykov, Nogin, and Milyutin—resigned from the Central Committee with a statement protesting the policy of the new government: "The Central Committee of the SDLP (B) passed a resolution on November 14 negating the agreement it had with the other parties represented in the Workers' and Soldiers' Soviets on the formation of a soviet government . . . With tremendous effort we managed to get the Central Committee to pass a revised resolution, which could have become the basis for the formation of a soviet government. But this new resolution was followed by a series of acts by the leading group of the Central Committee, which has thus clearly shown that it is resolutely determined not to permit the formation of a government by soviet parties but to maintain at no matter what cost to the workers and soldiers the exclusively Bolshevik government. We cannot take the responsibility for this disastrous policy of the Central Committee, which is being carried out against the will of a preponderant part of the proletariat, who long for a speedy close to the sanguinary struggle between the various groups of the democracy. Therefore, in order to have the right to publish our opinions and to ask the workers and soldiers to support our slogans, we resign our functions in the Central Committee. Long live the government of the soviet parties!" (Quoted in Lenin, *Sämtliche Werke,* XXII, 616.)

The split was healed after a few weeks, and the men reëntered the Central Committee. Neither Lenin nor Zinoviev clung to the memory of their crucial difference at this, the most decisive moment of Bolshevik history; their reconciliation was complete. In 1923, however, Trotsky used the incident in his fight against Zinoviev and Kamenev, who with Stalin formed the Troika (cf. Chapter 17, *infra*). When the Troika split asunder, Stalin adopted this line of polemics, and it has

position was especially strong, attracted to him many criticisms from
the rank and file. And finally, the general unpopularity of the Comintern organization among the Russian Party hierarchy, who were
tired of its constant defeats and never-ending internal convulsions,
was reflected in their attitude toward its representative on the Politburo. The fate of the Soviet state, the affairs of the Russian Party,
were discussed with relative freedom in the Comintern and criticized
with ignorance and crude naïveté, while the responsible Russian leaders, the Party bosses in the provinces, the managers and administrators,
were bound by strict discipline to silence on many questions. The poor
reputation of the Comintern did not enhance Zinoviev's position, but
on the other hand a good portion of his strength in the Politburo
was based on his authority in an international organization not completely under the control of the Russian apparatus. From the beginning Stalin feared that Zinoviev would be able to organize his "foreigners" against the General Secretary.

A week after his second stroke Lenin dictated a letter to the Central
Committee on the question of leadership, which was later designated
as Lenin's Testament. According to Trotsky, who is undoubtedly
most accurate:

> The so-called testament was written at two periods, separated by
> an interval of ten days: December 25, 1922 and January 4, 1923.
> At first only two persons knew of the document: the stenographer,
> M. Volodicheva, who wrote it from dictation, and Lenin's wife,
> N. Krupskaya. As long as there remained a glimmer of hope for
> Lenin's recovery, Krupskaya left the document under lock and key.[6]

It was more than a year later, not long before the Thirteenth Party
Congress, which met in May 1924, that Krupskaya handed the letter
to the Secretariat of the Central Committee. At this time Krupskaya
was closest to Zinoviev, who had known of the document at least since
Lenin's death on January 21, 1924. The Testament is strongest in
his support, and he wanted it made public to help him in his struggle
against both Stalin and Trotsky, who from different angles were cor-

---

become an important part of the Stalinist legend that Zinoviev and Kamenev began
their betrayal of Lenin and the Bolshevik Party as early as 1917.

[6] Trotsky, *The Suppressed Testament of Lenin* (New York: Pioneer Publishers,
1946), p. 14.

nering him in the Politburo. What he feared most was an alliance between Trotsky, the army organizer, and Stalin, the Party organizer, against himself, the Comintern organizer. But Stalin—in such matters a master of sophistication and subtlety—blocked the reading of the letter before the congress; as a compromise, it was read to a meeting of the congress seniors, the leaders of the provincial delegations, where members of the Trotskyite opposition, including Trotsky himself, for the first time heard it read.[7]

---

[7] The existence of the Testament was first made known to the general public on October 18, 1926, when Max Eastman sent the text of it to the *New York Times*. He reprinted it in his book *Since Lenin Died,* and Trotsky, in the middle of a struggle to get legal status for the Opposition within the Party, acceded in the demand of the Stalinist faction that he denounce this attack. He did it in such a way, however, as to confirm Eastman's statement that such a letter did actually exist and had been discussed by certain of the delegates to the Thirteenth Party Congress. "Eastman asserts in several places," Trotsky wrote, "that the Central Committee has 'concealed' from the Party a large number of documents of extraordinary importance, written by Lenin during the last period of his life. (The documents in question are letters on the national question, the famous 'will,' etc.) This is a pure slander against the Central Committee. . . . Comrade Lenin has not left any 'will'; the character of his relations to the Party and the character of the Party itself excluded the possibility of such a 'will.' The bourgeois and Menshevist press generally understands by the designation of 'will' one of Comrade Lenin's letters (which is so much altered [in Eastman's version] as to be almost illegible), in which he gives the Party advice on organization. The Thirteenth Party Congress devoted the greatest attention to this and the other letters and drew the conclusions corresponding to the situation obtaining. . . . Whatever Eastman's intentions may be, this piece of botched work is none the less a tool of counter revolution and can solely serve the ends of the incarnate enemies of Communism and of the revolution." (*Inprecor,* English edition, Vienna, September 3, 1925, Vol. V, No. 68, pp. 1004–1006.)

Two years later, when the fight in the Russian Party had developed to such a point that Stalin felt it incumbent to reply to the frequent references to Lenin's Testament, he too wrote an article in *Inprecor.* "The Opposition raised a cry—you heard it, all of you—that the Central Committee of the Party was 'keeping Lenin's "Testament" concealed.' . . . It has been proved over and over again that nobody has concealed or is concealing anything, that Lenin's 'Testament' was addressed to the Thirteenth Party Congress, and that this 'Testament' was read to that Party congress. That the Party congress resolved unanimously not to publish the Testament, among other reasons because Lenin himself did not wish or demand its publication. . . . It is said that in the 'Testament' in question, Lenin suggested to the Party congress that it should deliberate on the question of replacing Stalin and appointing another comrade in his place as General Secretary of the Party. This is perfectly true." (*Inprecor,* November 17, 1927, vol. VII, No. 64, pp. 1428–1434.) Stalin referred to and even quoted the Testament in his fight against Bukharin in 1929; compare the speech he delivered at the April session of the Central Committee, Stalin, *Selected Writings* (New York: International Publishers, 1942), p. 116, where the stenographic record of the July 1926 plenum (Russian edition, Part IV, p. 66) is cited.

The full text of the Testament follows.

By the stability of the Central Committee, of which I spoke before, I mean measures to prevent a split, so far as such measures can be taken. For, of course, the White Guard in *Russkaya Mysl* (I think it was S. E. Oldenburg) was right when, in the first place, in his play against Soviet Russia he banked on the hope of a split in our party, and when, in the second place, he banked for that split on serious disagreements in our party.

Our party rests upon two classes, and for that reason its instability is possible, and if there cannot exist an agreement between those classes its fall is inevitable. In such an event it would be useless to take any measures or in general to discuss the stability of our Central Committee. In such an event no measures would prove capable of preventing a split. But I trust that is too remote a future, and too improbable an event, to talk about.

I have in mind stability as a guarantee against a split in the near future, and I intend to examine here a series of considerations of a purely personal character.

I think that the fundamental factor in the matter of stability—from this point of view—is such members of the Central Committee as Stalin and Trotsky. The relation between them constitutes, in my opinion, a big half of the danger of that split, which might be avoided, and the avoidance of which might be promoted in my opinion by raising the number of members of the Central Committee to fifty or one hundred.

Comrade Stalin, having become General Secretary, has concentrated an enormous power in his hands; and I am not sure that he always knows how to use that power with sufficient caution. On the other hand, Comrade Trotsky, as was proved by his struggle against the Central Committee in connection with the question of the People's Commissariat of Ways and Communications, is distinguished not only by his exceptional ability—personally, he is, to be sure, the most able man in the present Central Committee—but also by his too far-reaching self-confidence and a disposition to be far too much attracted by the purely administrative side of affairs.

These two qualities of the two most able leaders of the present Central Committee might, quite innocently, lead to a split, and if our party does not take measures to prevent it, a split might arise unexpectedly.

I will not further characterize the other members of the Central Committee as to their personal qualities. I will only remind you that the October episode of Zinoviev and Kamenev was not, of course, accidental, but that it ought as little to be used against them personally as the non-Bolshevism of Trotsky.

Of the younger members of the Central Committee, I want to say a few words about Bukharin and Pyatakov. They are, in my opinion, the most able forces (among the youngest) and in regard to them it is necessary to bear in mind the following: Bukharin is not only the most valuable and biggest theoretician of the party, but also may legitimately be considered the favorite of the whole party; but his theoretical views can only with the very greatest doubt be regarded as fully Marxian, for there is something scholastic in him (he has never learned, and I think never has fully understood, the dialectic).

And then Pyatakov—a man undoubtedly distinguished in will and ability, but too much given over to administration and the administrative side of things to be relied on in a serious political question.

Of course, both these remarks are made by me merely with a view of the present time, or supposing that these two able and loyal workers may not find an occasion to supplement their one-sidedness.

December 25, 1922

Postscript: Stalin is too rude, and this fault, entirely supportable in relations among us Communists, becomes insupportable in the office of General Secretary. Therefore, I propose to the comrades to find a way to remove Stalin from that position and appoint another man who in all respects differs from Stalin only in superiority—namely, more patient, more loyal, more polite, and more attentive to comrades, less capricious, etc. This circumstance may seem an insignificant trifle, but I think that from the point of view of preventing a split and from the point of view of the relation between Stalin and Trotsky which I discussed above, it is not a trifle, or it is such a trifle as may acquire a decisive significance.

Lenin

January 4, 1923

This letter was written, again, to combat "so far as such measures can be taken" the split that anti-Soviet forces, personified here by the *Russkaya Mysl* ("Russian Thought"), were banking on. The Party, resting on an alliance between two classes, the workers and the peasants, might one day be pulled apart by a fight between them. Lenin discusses, rather, the more immediate danger rising from "considerations of a purely personal character." "A big half" of the danger of a split is the relation between Stalin and Trotsky.

Lenin is first of all disquieted by the enormous power that the General Secretary has concentrated in his hands. "I am not sure that he always knows how to use that power with sufficient caution." Ten days later, this formulation is strengthened: "I propose to the comrades to find a way to remove Stalin from that position and appoint another man who in all respects differs from Stalin only in superiority . . ." But Trotsky, according to Lenin, represents the same danger from another angle. "The most able man in the present Central Committee" has a "too far-reaching self-confidence and a disposition to be far too much attracted by the purely administrative side of affairs." Lenin classes "the two most able leaders of the present Central Committee" together as being both, if not equally, dangerous; in the leadership of either there would be an overgrowth of organizational power, a possible deformation into personal dictatorship. As a counter measure, Lenin proposes that the Central Committee be increased to fifty or a hundred, emphasizing the necessity for a larger collective control.[8]

In the final paragraphs of the Testament Lenin gives a critical evaluation of the other important members of the Politburo, and it is noteworthy that Zinoviev and Kamenev are the only ones who are not criticized for their current attitude. He mentions the October episode only to emphasize again that it should not be used against them. That is most characteristic of Lenin's attitude toward them in 1922.

Already during Lenin's lifetime, the leadership that would succeed him had been established—the Troika,[9] consisting of Zinoviev, Kamenev, and Stalin. This uneasy alliance, formed out of a fear of Trotsky, was never a going concern, and in the coming years Zinoviev would shift back and forth between Stalin and Trotsky in a vain search for a combination of political leaders able to resist the various dangerous currents and undercurrents. For him, as Lenin's

---

[8] Between the Sixth and the Eleventh Party Congresses—that is, from the first congress after the revolution to the date of Lenin's proposal—the size of the Central Committee varied slightly around twenty-five. Over the same period the number of candidates was increased from one to nineteen. (*Bolshaya Sovetskaya Entsiklopediya*, XI, 539–540.)

[9] A common metaphor in Party language; the original meaning is a team of three horses or the vehicle pulled by it.

disciple, the continuity of the rule of the proletarian elite was bound
to the continuity of Bolshevik leadership.

Lenin's Last Political Statement

During the first two months of 1923, by an intense effort, Lenin
dictated a series of five articles to give his final word of advice on the
Soviet society. These last articles suffer from a certain obscurity, caused
in part by the fact that they were written in Party language to the
Party membership; Lenin did not want to incite non-Party workers
against it.

One of these articles, entitled "How We Should Reorganize the
Workers' and Peasants' Inspection,"[10] suggested that the recently
formed inspection committees, made up of the rank and file of Russian workers and peasants, should be fused with the Central Control
Commission, the supreme Party court. This fusion would have weakened the bond of the Commission to the secret police and given non-
Party "cooks" control over the policy and mores of Party members.

In a second article, "Better Fewer, but Better,"[11] Lenin attacked
the inflated bureaucracy as costly and ineffective.

> The situation in regard to our state apparatus is so deplorable,
> not to say outrageous, that we must first of all think very carefully
> how to eliminate its defects, bearing in mind that the roots of these
> defects lie in the past, which, although it has been overturned, has
> not yet been overcome, has not yet passed into a culture of the
> remote past.

Lenin's concern was not merely with the relation of the state bureaucracy, growing in power and corruption, to the working class, but also
with the possible split between the Soviet state and the peasantry.

> We must strive to build up a state in which the workers retain
> their leadership of the peasants, retain the confidence of the peas-
> ants, and, exercising the greatest economy, remove every trace of
> superfluity from our social relations.
> We must reduce our state apparatus to the utmost degree of

---

[10] Lenin, *Selected Works*, English edition, IX, p. 382 ff.; completed January 17,
1923.
[11] *Ibid.*, IX, p. 387 ff.; completed February 9, 1923.

economy. We must remove from it all traces of superfluity, of which so much has been left over from Tsarist Russia, from its bureaucratic capitalist apparatus.

The criticism in these two was completed in another article, "On Coöperation," [12] in which Lenin took up the attack by the Workers' Opposition, which had been outlawed only months before, and carried it to a startling climax. It was not enough to build barriers from below against the Cheka's encroachment on the Party's functions; what was needed was to supersede the State Party with other forms of organization.

> Not everyone understands that now, since the October Revolution, . . . the coöperative movement acquires absolutely exceptional significance. . . . We have accomplished the overthrow of the rule of the exploiters, and much that was fantastic, even romantic, and even banal, in the dreams of the old coöperators is now becoming the most unvarnished reality. . . .
> The power of state over all large-scale means of production, the power of state in the hands of the proletariat, the alliance of this proletariat with the many millions of small and very small peasants, the assured leadership of the peasantry by the proletariat, etc.; is not this all that is necessary in order from the coöperatives —from the coöperatives alone, which we formerly treated as huckstering . . . —is not this all that is necessary in order to build complete Socialist society?

Thus, at the dawn of the State Party era and with the estrangement and hostility growing between the state hierarchy and the people, Lenin demanded that the Soviet society be built in the main on coöperatives of all producers—an old formula loved by syndicalists and utopian socialists but regarded by the Bolshevik Party as a ridiculous requisite of another century. These formulations of Lenin were a response to the program of the semi-legal Workers' Opposition, whose principal figure in this period was Gabriel Myasnikov.[13]

---

[12] *Ibid.*, IX, p. 402 ff.; completed January 6, 1923.

[13] Myasnikov had already been expelled from the Party before the Eleventh Congress, in March 1922. His program was essentially the same as that of the Sapronov-Shlyapnikov groups, except that his demand for political democracy was broader. "Myasnikov . . . went so far that he advocated freedom of press for all—from the monarchists to the anarchists" (N. Popov, *Outline History of the CPSU*, II, 156).

Lenin Breaks with Stalin

At the beginning of 1923, after Lenin's second stroke, Stalin tightened the screws. In the process of welding the Control Commission to the Cheka, he gave the second more weight. In these months, he began his file on Party leaders, listing their weak points, their errors, their reaction to the zig-zag of the revolutionary struggle. This dark cabinet of Stalin, with full records on every Party functionary and prominent Comintern figure, was the base on which his control of the Party was built.

Lenin, deathly sick, could not grasp the full impact of this new

---

After his expulsion, he was sent on a trade commission to Berlin where he met Maslow and the other leaders of the Left wing of the German party and of the Left dissident party, the KAPD. Here they were given a very discouraging picture of the state of the Russian working class. Stalin got reports on these meetings, and he recognized this contact between the Russian Left and the German Left as a dangerous symptom. The Myasnikov group, driven underground by the Cheka in 1923, continued to organize a countrywide Workers' Opposition. In 1927 Myasnikov himself escaped via the Persian border and reached Paris after 1933.

Myasnikov was a metal worker by trade, a native of the Urals. In 1939, when I last saw him, he had adjusted well to life in a Paris factory despite his rudimentary French. At the beginning of the war, he took a refresher course and graduated as an engineer.

During 1928–1929 Myasnikov wrote a book against the Russian State Party, *Victory and Defeat of the Russian Proletariat*, of which only a few chapters have been published in little Left magazines (*Europäische Monatshefte*, Paris, February 1939, pp. 12–16). When Soviet Russia was in greatest danger, he wrote, in the time of the civil and interventionist wars, there were several soviet parties. This multi-party system did not at all weaken the defense of Soviet Russia but on the contrary strengthened it. The coöperation of the bulk of the Russian people, expressed in their various political organizations, produced the enthusiasm necessary to carry them through this difficult period. When the danger of foreign intervention was over, the bureaucracy destroyed the exchangeable parts of the state machine and established its one-party rule. But, he continued, the working class is not monolithic and can not be represented by a single party. It is a heterogeneous class and needs a multi-party system of representation. The rule of the bourgeoisie functioned well in their prime with a multi-party system; bourgeois society granted freedom of press, freedom of speech, freedom of organization. There was a constant change of the men in power, and the contrast between government and opposition parties made the system more flexible. The danger of being overthrown has never been overcome by a totalitarian party, but empirically by the art of government. The bourgeois class knew to what limit it could grant democratic rights and where a danger to its continued rule began. The Party dictatorship excludes the working class from participation in government; it is a deformation into a monopoly of power that in the end will be deadly to both Russia and the international socialist movement.

In 1946, friends in Paris tried to find out what had become of Myasnikov. He had been taken to Russia in a Soviet plane—voluntarily, according to rumor. His French wife, however, has so far not had a word from him.

police control of the Party, but he learned enough of it to be profoundly alarmed. As Lenin became weaker, Stalin became bolder; and as Stalin, in his "rude" fashion, reached out for personal power, Lenin revised the opinion he had set down of him in his Testament, which was essentially that he should share power in the government equally with Trotsky. Of the issues in late 1922 and early 1923 that brought the relations between Lenin and Stalin to the breaking point, the most important was that of Georgia.

The independence of the Republic of Georgia, then governed by Mensheviks, had been recognized by Moscow in May 1920. In February 1921, however, on the personal initiative of Stalin, to whom the rule of his native province by the Mensheviks was unbearable, the Red Army occupied it; in July Stalin entered Tiflis in the role of a conqueror. The Mensheviks were expelled from the government and driven into exile, but the peasants in the countryside and the workers and intellectuals in Tiflis strongly resisted the Muscovite sovietization. Even the Georgian Bolsheviks proposed that Georgia remain an independent republic, bound to Moscow by friendship but not subject to its domination. This separatist tendency was ruthlessly crushed by Chekists, acting under G. K. Ordzhonikidze, Stalin's agent in Georgia. The Georgian Bolsheviks tried to get a hearing before the Central Committee in Moscow, where they were hampered by Stalin and Dzerzhinsky, who managed to keep Lenin from hearing the full story. Sensing how deep the split was, however, Lenin collected data independently and decided to intervene in behalf of the Georgian Bolsheviks. Contrary to all Party custom, he wrote a letter on March 6 over the heads of the Politburo to the Georgian branch, as follows:

> To Comrades Mdivani, Makharadze and others (Copies to Comrades Trotsky and Kamenev).
> Esteemed Comrades:
>   I am with you in this matter with all my heart. I am outraged by the arrogance of Ordzhonikidze and the connivance of Stalin and Dzerzhinsky. On your behalf I am now preparing notes and a speech.
>
>   With esteem,
>   Lenin [14]

---

[14] Trotsky, *Stalin,* p. 361.

According to Trotsky, Lenin wrote another letter on the same day, to Stalin, breaking off all personal relations with him.

> Kamenev . . . had just been to see Nadyezhda Konstantinovna Krupskaya, at her request. She told him in great alarm: "Vladimir has just dictated to his stenographer a letter to Stalin saying that he breaks off all relations with him." The immediate cause of this was of a semi-personal character. Stalin had been trying to isolate Lenin from all sources of information, and in this connection had been very rude to Nadyezhda Konstantinovna. "But you know Vladimir," Krupskaya added. "He would never have decided to break off personal relations if he had not thought it necessary to crush Stalin politically." [15]

Three days after these two letters were dictated, on March 9, Lenin suffered his third and most serious stroke, which made any political activity impossible for him. In the panic that struck the Politburo, the Georgian question was disposed of summarily and everyone concentrated on the one dominant issue: the question of successorship.

Between Lenin's second and third strokes, Zinoviev's position in the Politburo had become more and more difficult and entangled. As long as there was a hope for Lenin's recovery, the Troika represented itself as a caretaker directory. As it became more likely that their rule would not be ended by Lenin's return, their relations with each other wore thin on the issue of the post-Lenin composition of the Politburo. Zinoviev was supported solidly by Kamenev and Bukharin, passively by Tomsky, and more and more ambiguously by Stalin. "The bloc with Zinoviev and Kamenev restrained Stalin . . . They never transgressed certain limits." [16]

With Lenin removed from active participation, Trotsky's stature was increased. Just before the Twelfth Party Congress, the Politburo adopted his statement on the task of industry, with certain amendments added stressing the need for Party leadership over the state apparatus. Even Stalin gave evidence that he recognized Trotsky's new status. There was a discussion as to who should take Lenin's

---

[15] Trotsky, *My Life*, p. 485. Trotsky's account of this letter is consistent in his other works; cf. *Stalin*, pp. 374–375, and *The Real Situation in Russia* (New York, 1928), p. 308, where he cites corroboratory evidence from testimony by M. I. Ulyanova, Lenin's sister, and a speech of Zinoviev.

[16] Trotsky, *Stalin*, p. 394.

place at the congress as political reporter for the Central Committee, and "Stalin was the first to say, 'The Political Report will of course be made by Comrade Trotsky.'"[17] Trotsky politely refused and proposed instead that the General Secretary make the report. Zinoviev, tightly cornered between the two, managed to get a majority for him to give the report.

The Twelfth Party Congress, the first composed of delegates elected under the control of Stalin's Secretariat, convened in Moscow on April 17, 1923. When Zinoviev delivered his report, he was surrounded by what Trotsky terms "virtually oppressive silence," an indication that from now on the Party would be governed not by political leaders but by the organizers.

In his organizational report, Stalin centered his attention on the necessity of building up the apparatus of the proletarian dictatorship. The driving motor must be without question the Party, which must guide the state apparatus with such "levers and transmission belts" as the soviets, the Young Communist League, coöperatives, trade-unions. Zinoviev and Kamenev, respecting their alliance with Stalin, were silent on this interpretation of the role of the Party, but it was attacked by Trotsky and by an anonymous platform circulated by a Workers' Opposition group. To implement the report, the boundaries of the country's administrative regions were redrawn so as to give the Party greater local power. As an ironic postscript, the congress merged the Control Commissions with the Workers' and Peasants' Inspection Committees, in accordance with Lenin's proposal, placing V. V. Kuibyshev at the head of the reorganized Central Control Commission. By this move the Inspection Committees were killed, body and idea; nothing could indicate how little relevance Lenin's last articles had to the growing incubus of Party power than this formal acceptance of his suggestion. The membership of the Central Control Commission was raised from seven to fifty, with ten candidates —with all posts filled by Stalin's intimates, and its newly defined function transformed it into a special GPU for Party members.

Two oppositionist groups, Workers' Group and Workers' Truth, were under attack at the congress and immediately afterward. They

---

[17] *Ibid.*, p. 366.

had dared to establish contacts abroad and were accused of organizing a Fourth International. A. A. Bogdanov, the leader of Workers' Truth, circulated a declaration that the proletarian dictatorship existed only in name, having been destroyed by the State Party after the civil war. In the summer of 1923, both of these groups were formally expelled.

At the congress, the hidden struggle between Zinoviev and Stalin came out in the fight over the Georgian question. The support that Zinoviev and Bukharin gave the Georgian delegates in their demand for broader local autonomy was harshly rebutted by Stalin, who spoke at length on the dangers of "local chauvinism." With the growing power of the Party, the national resistance became a vital issue in all of the border provinces; between the Great Russian centers, representing principally workers' organizations, and the national minorities in the agrarian regions, there was a natural antagonism, which the General Secretary exploited in order to purge the deviators and to build up his regime. Shortly after the Twelfth Congress, the Central Committee called a special conference to deal with the national rebellions in various regions. At the beginning of the year, S. M. Kirov had been sent to Azerbaijan to strengthen the centralized control there. The results in carrying out the new policy had been poorest, the conference decided, in Turkestan. " 'I consider that the Ukraine is the second weak point of the Soviet power,' said Comrade Stalin." [18]

The Twelfth Party Congress, without changing the formal balance in the Politburo, raised Stalin from one of three to the position of first power. Zinoviev returned to his Comintern office burdened by the Party crisis, which he knew had not run its course, and concentrated on keeping it secret from the Comintern. One of his first tasks was to consult with the German comrades who had come to Moscow for guidance and arbitration. The developing struggle for control of the Russian Party was the milieu in which the German delegates, in a decisive paroxysm of their country, sought assistance for the final blow against the German bourgeoisie.

---

[18] N. Popov, *Outline History of the CPSU*, II, 190.

The French occupation authorities had set a sentry house between Hamm and Dortmund to mark the line between occupied and unoccupied Germany. All trains halted there, and all passengers got off to be inspected. It was easy to enter the occupied zone by trolley, bus, or bicycle, or on foot, but beyond this sentry house a German policeman or a German army detachment had no power. Hundreds of thousands of miners and metal workers were unemployed in the occupied zone, and the small dole they were given by the German government lost its purchasing power from day to day. The time of most of the inhabitants was spent at meetings and demonstrations.

Passive Resistance

The Berlin cabinet answered the occupation with a call for passive resistance. During January and February 1923 Ruhr-Rhine industry was largely paralyzed. Trains were stalled and wires cut; in reprisal the French fined cities and arrested burgomasters. After some weeks, however, these government-inspired activities diminished rapidly. Already in January, after the arrest of several coal-mine managers, Berlin was unable to organize massive protest strikes. The government threatened, on this occasion and several times later, to jail the miners who continued to work. On March 4, President Ebert announced heavy punishment for any aid given the French, including work in

the mines or on the railroads. On March 18, he spoke in Hamm, gate-
way to the Ruhr, to urge that resistance be continued.

Rising living costs stimulated the workers to demand increases in
wages and relief, and at the end of March, bands of unemployed demonstrated throughout the Rhine-Ruhr for price control. Frequently
they marched to the city halls to present their demands: higher relief
payments, free coal, milk for children, winter clothing, free medical
attention, a special bonus to cover the increase in rent. The Berlin
cabinet was alarmed; so was the Board of the German Federation of
Labor. French troops were in constant conflict with rioters; in Buer-
Recklinghausen tanks were used against them.

The attitude of the industrialists was ambiguous. In general, they
welcomed the propaganda of the nationalists, who presented the French
occupation to the workers as a danger to their vital interests; but the
mine-owners had little confidence in the national discipline of their
workers. At the end of January, the Berlin stock market called for a
United States protectorate of the area. At the same time that the
workers were forced into passive resistance, many entrepreneurs reno-
vated or enlarged their plants. Among the workers, rumors never
ceased about secret negotiations between the Ruhr industrialists and
the Comité des Forges, about a secret understanding between the Cuno
cabinet and the British government. On March 20, the miners' trade-
union, disquieted by the unrest, appealed to the cabinet to come to a
settlement.

Paris hoped that the separation of the Rhine-Ruhr from Germany
might be made permanent by the formation of an independent
Rhenish republic. Literature against the German government, even if
seditious, was tolerated, or to some extent favored. General Degoutte
of the French army coöperated with the separatist leaders. But the
organizations were weak; their leaders—among others, Joseph Matthes,
Adam Dorten, and Joseph Smeets—were not taken seriously. Smeets,
however, was severely wounded by nationalist partisans in one of the
numerous clashes between the groups. The average Ruhr worker
viewed the "independence" of a French-sponsored Rhineland with
a certain scepticism, but he had no more enthusiasm for the German
nationalists. He remembered too well the punitive expedition of the
Freikorps and the Reichswehr under General Watter. Unpopular as

the French were, the hatred of the Reichswehr was such that the average Ruhr worker preferred the French occupation to what he called the German occupation.

German nationalist propaganda in the Ruhr, moreover, ran head on into the internationalist spirit that had developed among the workers there. During the twenty-five years before the war, the mining industry had developed much faster than the native population. Agents were sent to the agrarian regions of Germany and Eastern Europe to hire miners; many sons of poor peasants or farmhands, one million between 1895 and 1900, left their homes and streamed into the Ruhr. In the area around Gelsenkirchen, one could find East Prussians, Poles,[1] Russians, Italians, Hollanders, Slovenes and other South Slavs. This multi-national group met nationalist propaganda with stony indifference. One of the main items of nationalist agitation was the Black Disgrace, as the presence of colored French troops was termed, which left the workers unmoved.

State power had been weakened in the occupied zone, and the occupation army did not set up an administration of its own. The German police and administration had been withdrawn; Berlin had no apparatus to implement its repeated warnings and manifestos.

Die Essener Richtung

During this period the Berlin organization sent me as liaison to the Rhine-Ruhr, and I was very active in the region between Hamm and Cologne. The party militants had only contempt for the separatist leaders, Matthes and Dorten, and rejected any coöperation with them. Their interest was focused on the possibility of expropriating heavy industry, a powerful incentive around which Communist, Social Democratic, and Catholic workers rallied. "Let us not wait any longer to throw out the owners of the plants and the mines. Let us install factory councils to coördinate all Rhine-Ruhr industry and end this

---

[1] There were some 1177 Polish societies in the Ruhr in 1913. In 1905, when the Polish immigration reached its peak, the 10,000 Polish workers of Gelsenkirchen were served by a Polish bank, Polish churches, Polish-speaking clerks in department stores, Polish coöperatives, and a Polish newspaper, the *Wiarus Polski* ("Polish Grenadier"). (Eberhard Franke, *Das Ruhrgebiet und Ostpreussen: Geschichte, Umfang und Bedeutung der Ostpreusseneinwanderung;* Volkstum im Ruhrgebiet, Vol. I, Essen, 1936, p. 20.)

fraudulent passive resistance of the corrupt Berlin cabinet. We can produce coal without orders from Berlin. Let us establish an independent Rhine-Ruhr economic unit." To them the center of the revolutionary action was in the Rhine-Ruhr, not in Saxony and Thuringia. "If instead of standing idle at the pit-heads, we go in and set up our own administration, the population of the area will support us. We will rebuild our proletarian militia and a strongly organized Rhine-Ruhr will lead the German revolution."

Thus, the plans of three years before were being revived. A Rhine-Ruhr Workers' Republic would become the base from which a worker army would march into Central Germany, seize power in Berlin, and crush once and for all the nationalist counter revolution. This plan developed in part outside the party, born of the opportunity, the hunger, and the memory of the days of the Kapp putsch. In part it was pushed by the Ruhr Communists, who were supported by Hamburg, Berlin, Upper Silesia. Finally, after many secret meetings, it was decided to convoke a regional party convention, in Essen on March 25, 1923, to draft a program for the seizure of the factories and the seizure of local power.

The Essen convention was divided into two almost equal factions. The delegates from the Krupp Works and metal plants of Essen were Right-wingers; those from Wanne, Gelsenkirchen, Bochum, Dortmund, Buer, among them many miners, were eager to seize local power. The Ruhr was the only region in Germany where there were syndicalist groups of importance.

The convention debates focused on Cuno's policy of passive resistance, with which the party acted in silent agreement; the Left proposed action against the government. Collusion with nationalist elements, based on a policy of binding Germany to Russia in a continental bloc against the West, would result only in re-aligning the counter-revolutionary forces against the German workers. Radek's program—"strict disobedience of the occupation authorities, work stoppage in all military-occupied plants"—was thus opposed by the Left, but no one dared to attack the Russian Politburo openly for his policy.

The Left's demand that the miners be taken over by the workers was made in an atmosphere seething with rumors that they would be seized by the French army. Poincaré had threatened to take over the Ruhr industry on April 1, ten days after the Essen convention, and this threat enlivened its proceedings. This possibility was also under constant discussion in the Reich cabinet and in the board of the German Federation of Labor. Stimulated by the Cuno cabinet, the trade-union leaders had repeatedly declared that in such a case they would call a nationwide general strike, a more powerful one than that against the Kapp putsch, for which they expected solid support from all the nation. The Left, sceptical of the trade-union leaders' promised general strike, declared that the Communist Party should not join in a government-ordered strike to preserve Ruhr property in the hands of the bourgeoisie but should transform it into a proletarian strike, "to crush all fascist tendencies, to overthrow the Cuno government, and to establish a Revolutionary Workers' Government." The Left presented its view in a statement designed to rally the party around the Ruhr Communists and to change fundamentally the course of the party:

> The Ruhr occupation has so aggravated the process of disintegration of the capitalist economy in Germany that the situation of the German bourgeoisie is hopeless. The economic burden of the passive resistance adopted by the Cuno cabinet is felt most severely by the German proletariat, which has to bear the total cost of the Ruhr occupation. . . . In view of the military and political weakness of the German bourgeoisie, the active resistance proposed by nationalist circles is now impossible. The propaganda and the preparations of the nationalists are the framework of the counter revolution, with which they are preparing a bloody fight against the proletariat. The methods of fascism are the political forms by which the bourgeoisie will enchain the proletariat. . . . The historic task in this situation is to save the German proletariat from endless gray enslavement by fighting for political power. Thus the unity of proletarian Germany will be preserved against all imperialisms.[2]

At this moment, Clara Zetkin, member of the Comintern's Executive Committee, stepped in, sent by Radek and the Central Committee. In a solemn and pathetic exhortation, she warned the Ruhr Commu-

---

[2] Resolution of the Opposition at the Essen convention, March 25, 1923. *Bericht über die Verhandlungen des IX. Parteitages der Kommunistischen Partei Deutschlands,* Abgehalten in Frankfurt a. M. vom 7. bis 10. April 1924 (Berlin, 1924), p. 132.

nists to avoid a repetition of the adventurist policy that had brought the party to disaster in the past. The situation of the Ruhr workers, squeezed between the competing imperialisms of France and Germany, she depicted as hopeless. It was imperative to avoid adventurism. The party should concentrate its energies on fighting the runaway inflation. In spite of Zetkin's prestige, the stand of the Left gained considerable support in the party. Radek, seriously alarmed, telegraphed to Moscow, and in response to his request the Executive Committee of the Comintern sent the Ruhr Communists a formal rejection of their program. Any Rhine-Ruhr uprising against the Cuno cabinet would be openly disavowed by the Comintern, and the rest of the German Communists would be instructed not to coöperate.

Die Essener Richtung—the Essen line—began to fight for support in the Reich. The Berlin and Hamburg branches were already behind it, and others might be won over. The Russian Politburo, apprehensive over this disturbance of its foreign policy, called the two factions to a conference, to meet in the Kremlin in May.

The Krupp Incident

On March 31, six days after the Essen convention, there was an incident at the Krupp plant there, the noisiest of a series of clashes between French troops and German industrialists. When the Engineering Commission arrived at the plant, they were met with a prearranged ceremony of passive resistance. Called out by the factory sirens, the 53,000 workers were ordered to stop work for half an hour and assemble in the yard. These workers depended on the plant's trucks for transport of their food and the payroll; and when they learned that the Commission intended to requisition the trucks for French army use they began to demonstrate, gathering around the plant garage on Altendorfer Strasse, climbing to the roofs of neighboring buildings. Nationalist agitators made speeches to incite the workers against the French; they tried to start them singing patriotic anthems, but without success. In the clash that developed between the demonstrators and the troops, thirteen workers were killed and forty-two wounded.[3]

---

[3] "Krupp vor dem französischen Kriegsgericht," *Süddeutsche Monatshefte* (Munich, June 1923), Vol. 20, No. 9, p. 88 ff.

A few days later the owner of the plant, Dr. Gustav Krupp von Bohlen und Halbach, was arrested, together with a group of his managers. The Berlin cabinet built up Krupp as a national hero, who had made a courageous stand for Germany's honor. Leaflets were distributed showing Poincaré sitting down to a dinner, served on a silver platter, of a roasted German child. Nationalist propaganda reached new heights, but the Ruhr workers had not had time to lose their bitter hatred of the Black Reichswehr left over from its expedition of 1920. Minister of Defense Gessler had found it necessary to speak in the Reichstag to deny charges that he was sponsoring Freikorps preparations for armed uprisings against the French in the Ruhr. A few days after the Krupp incident, a meeting of the Essen factory councils energetically rejected joint action with the industrialists and voted to resist independently.

On April 13 the workers of Mühlheim stormed the town hall, having besieged it for a day, and took over the administration. The tension in the town was such that the French refrained from intervening immediately. Ignoring the directive of the Comintern, the Mühlheim local of the Communist Party began to organize "workers' power." They distributed food from the storehouses, organized a workers' militia, sent fraternal delegates to neighboring industrial cities. News of the Mühlheim uprising excited the whole region.

Berlin accused the French of tolerating and even protecting the Communist uprising. The Cabinet's formal request to send back the Security Police from Berlin was granted. The Communist militia retreated to the Mühlheim Rathaus, from which German police expelled them on April 21. Ten were killed and seventy wounded.

Again the party's Central Committee sent instructions to the Essen local to cease these putschist adventures. Party members taking part in them were threatened with expulsion, and in some cases this threat was carried out. But the tide of unrest continued to rise, and it reached its high point in May.

On May 9, Krupp was taken to prison in Düsseldorf, and nationalist propagandists glorified his martyrdom. A sabotage group dynamited a bridge in Essen; nationalist agitators swarmed all over the region. The French fined the city of Essen and sent one strong protest after another to the Berlin Cabinet. Finally the Berlin police were forced to arrest Friedrich Wilhelm Heinz, a staff member of the Organization Consul.

One of the nationalist heroes was Leo Schlageter. He culminated his sabotage of the occupation by blowing up a rail line near Düsseldorf. Taken prisoner by the French, he was tried by a military court and executed on May 26. One of dozens, his case is particularly interesting because Radek was later to glorify him as "a courageous soldier of the counter revolution [who] deserves to be sincerely honored by us, the soldiers of the revolution."

At the end of May heavy fighting broke out in the Ruhr. On the 27th, there were thirteen killed in clashes at Bochum and Gelsenkirchen between "fascists" and "Reds." In Dortmund and Gelsenkirchen food stores were seized. The Gelsenkirchen miners stormed the police headquarters and, as a joyous symbol of their fight against Berlin, made a large bonfire of the police records. The Cabinet again asked permission to send in Security Police, and again General Degoutte granted it. After several days of fighting, the Security Police, led by Reichswehr officers trained for civil war by experts who had studied the experiences of 1918–1920, drove the workers out of their Gelsenkirchen stronghold. In Bochum, after heavy fighting, they arrested the Communist Committee.

By the end of May 500,000 miners and 120,000 steel workers were on strike; they remained in the mines and factories, so that even the managers could not proceed with their administrative duties. On May 30 the strikers returned to work; they had obtained a fifty per cent rise in pay, but their other demands had been rejected.

This series of riots and strikes indicated the strength of the unrest. Lacking any directive force, these largely spontaneous movements remained local incidents.

Conference in Moscow

I returned from Essen to Berlin, charged by the Ruhr Communists with putting pressure on the Central Committee for a change of policy. At the *Rote Fahne* headquarters, I saw Radek, who was awaiting the latest news to give his personal finishing touch to the next day's editorial. At an informal meeting of the Politburo, at which Heckert and Pieck were present, I again defended the initiative of the Ruhr

Communists and again proposed giving them new instructions. Radek exploded with indignation. He pictured the party's forthcoming annihilation in the gloomiest colors, and threatened with expulsion all who opposed his support of passive resistance.

In May I went to Moscow as one of the Left delegates to the secret conference of the German factions called by the Russian Politburo. The other delegates were: representing the Right, Paul Böttcher and Heinrich Brandler; representing the Left, Arkadi Maslow and Ernst Thälmann. The Russian delegation was made up of Trotsky, Radek, Bukharin, and Zinoviev.

Brandler's Central Committee would have preferred to avoid this conciliatory conference; it had hoped to expel the Left wing before Moscow could interfere. But the invitation could not be declined. After a week's discussion, the Russian Politburo achieved a compromise. The Leipzig program of "winning over the Social Democratic Party from the Left wing of the bourgeoisie to the Right wing of the labor movement" was solemnly condemned. All groups agreed in a general way that the revolutionary crisis in Germany was developing, that it was necessary to "intensify" the struggle for power, particularly in the Rhine-Ruhr.

The Moscow politicians found it easy to manipulate the Left wing, who were more concerned with fighting Brandler's moves to expel them than with the real issues of the joint statement. Thus, the Leipzig formula was rejected but Brandler's proposal that Communist ministers enter the state governments of Saxony and Thuringia was accepted by the Russian Politburo. The Rhine-Ruhr occupation was discussed, but not thoroughly; and, once again, the question of National Bolshevism was not brought up. However, Brandler's demand that the Russians bar Maslow's return to Germany on the pretext of a party investigation was refused. As a gesture of reconciliation, four Left-wingers were added to the Central Committee by coöptation, a compromise that no one liked.

The crisis in the German party was by no means healed. The division of the German party into hostile factions, based on the surface entirely on a different interpretation of the current situation in Germany, was a reflection more fundamentally of the struggle for Lenin's succession, which was at its height at the time of the May conference.

Lenin was dying, and Stalin had not yet consolidated his power as his successor.

Radek Banks on a Reichswehr Coup

During the Ruhr occupation the relation between the German and Soviet governments became so friendly that Radek could install himself officially at the Berlin Embassy, 7 Unter den Linden. Here he received journalists and political personages without restriction or supervision; he also had at his disposal a room in the building of the Soviet Trade Delegation, which he often used for his conversations with Reichswehr representatives.[4] Radek went back and forth between Unter den Linden and the *Rote Fahne* office, 225 Friedrichstrasse, as freely as he was accustomed to walk from his Kremlin apartment to the office of *Pravda*. For him, in those days of early spring 1923, Berlin was almost another Moscow.

The Reichswehr's preparations for an armed conflict with France ran counter to the anti-militarist spirit of Social Democratic and Communist workers, whose "studied malice" toward the Reichswehr is described by a contemporary nationalist politician as follows:

> In the police headquarters of Dresden there used to be a special State Intelligence Division for years, which was engaged in spying on the Reichswehr with studied malice. Not only troop movements by rail or road were watched, but the most incidental details. For this spying, the railroad factory councils and the trade-union organizers, official and unofficial, collaborated with specially delegated police officials, linked with forces in and outside Saxony.

---

[4] In 1923, Yuri C. Lutovinov, a leader of the Workers' Opposition, was assigned to the Berlin office of the Soviet Trade Legation in order to sever his relations with other Russian oppositionists. According to Bessedovsky (*Revelations of a Soviet Diplomat,* p. 100), Lutovinov was sent to Berlin to check Victor Kopp's muddled financial affairs. One day a group of German officers called there and asked to see the successor of Karl Radek for the usual conversations; he refused to receive them. Later that year, when Lutovinov returned to Moscow, Radek had the impudence to accuse him of seeking contacts with fascists. Lutovinov pushed his way into a session of the Politburo and threatened Radek, and after this scene the affair was dropped.

Lutovinov had entered the Bolshevik Party in 1904 at the age of seventeen. A metal worker by trade, he devoted his main energy to trade-union work and after 1917 became a member of the boards of the Metal Workers' Union and of the All-Russian Trade-Union Council. In May 1924, in despair over the degeneration of the Party, Lutovinov committed suicide.

Thus, the strength of troops on maneuvers, the types of armament, and the type and purpose of maneuvers or special training courses were observed; they spied on officers traveling alone, on Reichswehr men whether in uniform or civilian clothes. Railroad tickets were examined and the destination noted; baggage was searched. The flights of army carrier pigeons were observed and their flying time noted. Alterations in railroad timetables were examined to determine to what extent these changes might be in the interest of the Reichswehr. Officers' canteens and even their recreation halls were spied on. Barracks were watched day and night. Even the license numbers of civilian automobiles that stopped at military headquarters were noted and the names of their owners checked.[5]

The extreme nationalist group around the German People's Party of Freedom (*Deutsch-Völkische Freiheitspartei*) was organizing secret military activities, and, according to Zeigner's report to the Landtag, it was backed by the Cuno government. He exposed a secret covenant between General von Seeckt and Carl Severing, Social Democratic minister in the Prussian cabinet.[6]

Zeigner and Richard Lipinski, another Saxon Social Democrat, sent Reich President Ebert frequent notes of concern over the increasing secret rearmament.

During the Reichstag recess from July 7 to August 8, 1923, the tension between Saxony and the Reich developed into open fight. Dr. Zeigner maintained a provocative crusade against the Ruhr resistance and, to the delight of the French, violently denounced the Reichswehr. There was actually an exchange of diplomatic notes. The president of Saxony further sharpened the antagonism between his government and that of the bourgeois Reich Chancellor, Dr. Cuno, . . .

Dr. Zeigner could not do enough to vilify the Reichswehr. These denunciations, so pleasing to the French, . . . created an impossible situation.[7]

---

[5] *Sozialdemokratie Kommunisten*, Flugschriften der Deutschen Volkspartei, No. 46 (Berlin, 1924), pp. 13–14.

[6] Court record concerning the Black Reichswehr, quoted in Paul Merker, *Deutschland, sein oder nicht sein* (Mexico City, 1944), I, 87, and in Kurt Caro and Walter Oehme, *Schleichers Aufstieg: Ein Beitrag zur Geschichte der Gegenrevolution* (Berlin, 1933), p. 156.

[7] Albrecht Philipp, *Sachsen und das Reich* (Dresden, 1924), pp. 6, 13. Philipp was a Reichstag deputy of the German National People's Party.

Radek's knowledge of the Black Reichswehr activities was incomparably greater than that of such socialist pacifists as Zeigner. Assisted by a staff of experts and military attachés, he had access to military intelligence reports of the Red Army, which were not available, of course, to the German Communist leaders. When the Cuno government struck against the Ruhr Communists, Radek exerted pressure for his policy of civil truce by threatening the Cuno Cabinet:

> The government knows that, because of the dangers arising from French imperialism, the German Communist Party has been silent about many things. The government, which is responsible for the deeds of its agents, is becoming by these deeds unsuitable for international negotiations. . . . If the government does not stop its provocative campaign against the Communist Party, we will break our silence.[8]

This indirect public acknowledgment of collaboration with Cuno created alarm and confusion in the party. The *Kommunistische Arbeiter-Zeitung* ("Communist Worker's Gazette"), the organ of the anti-Bolshevik dissident communists, in an attack on Radek's dealings with the nationalists, proposed that the Communists change the name of their party to the National Bolshevik People's Party of Germany.

One issue of the *Rote Fahne* was published with the following rimed headline:

> Against Cuno and Poincaré,
> On the Ruhr and on the Spree.

Radek came to the office the following morning and fired the two men responsible for it (one of whom was Gerhart Eisler, alias Hans Berger) for "neglect of duty." The headline was changed to:

> Against Cuno on the Spree;
> On the Ruhr against Poincaré.

In the army and in the Black Reichswehr, a possible alliance with Russia was the basis of endless discussions on the war of revenge. These secret dealings between the general staffs of the Red Army and

---

[8] *Die Rote Fahne*, May 27, 1923.

the Reichswehr got a distorted confirmation in the last public show trial in 1938. N. N. Krestinsky, long-time Soviet ambassador to Berlin, was one of the defendants. After confessing to having joined the illegal Trotskyite group in 1921, he continued:

> A year later I committed a crime— . . . the agreement I concluded on Trotsky's instructions with General Seeckt, with the Reichswehr in his person, about financing the Trotskyite organization in exchange for services of an espionage nature which we undertook in this connection to render the Reichswehr. . . . Trotsky argued that our line in foreign policy coincided with that of Germany at that period, that Germany was in a state of ruin after the war, and that in any event, in view of the existence of revenge sentiments in Germany with regard to France, England and Poland, a clash between Germany and Soviet Russia in the near future was out of the question. . . . Since 1923 the agreement with Seeckt was carried out mainly in Moscow, and sometimes in Berlin. . . .
>
> VYSHINSKY: . . . I want to get more precise information on one question. You said that in the winter of 1921–1922 you evolved your calculations on the German Reichswehr.
>
> KRESTINSKY: The plans to utilize the German Reichswehr for criminal Trotskyite purposes appeared in the spring of 1922.
>
> VYSHINSKY: Did your Trotskyite organization maintain contact with Seeckt even before 1921?
>
> KRESTINSKY: There was a contact with him of which I do not want to speak at an open session [this is probably an allusion to the Polish-Russian war of 1920]. . . . It was not a contact of a Trotskyite nature.
>
> VYSHINSKY: If you please, we shall not speak of everything in open session. But something may be said right now. In the first place, who was Kopp?
>
> KRESTINSKY: Generally speaking, Kopp was an old Menshevik. . . .
>
> VYSHINSKY: You say that in July 1920 this same Kopp established contact with Seeckt. . . .
>
> KRESTINSKY: It was Seeckt who got in touch with Kopp. . . .
>
> VYSHINSKY: . . . While he was the representative of the Red Cross in 1920, Kopp had contact with General Seeckt. Is that true?
>
> KRESTINSKY: Yes.[9]

---

[9] *Report of the Court Proceedings in the Case of the Anti-Soviet "Bloc of Rights and Trotskyites,"* Moscow, 1938, p. 262 ff.

Radek had not been permitted to testify on this matter at his trial, a year before

The truth behind this frame-up is simple. During 1922–1923 liaison between the general staffs of the two armies was made by order of Trotsky, Commander in Chief of the Red Army. This was done, however, following the foreign policy worked out by the Politburo and first of all by the General Secretary. Moreover, the Reichswehr itself often took the initiative and got in touch with the Red Army staff. Vyshinsky's garnishing, however, that Seeckt financed Trotsky with large amounts of gold is one of the monstrosities that make the trials what they are.

The secret discussions of a German-Russian alliance became more concrete in 1923, following the appointment late in 1922 of a pro-Russian German diplomat, Ulrich Graf von Brockdorff-Rantzau, to the post of Moscow ambassador. Brockdorff had long sympathized with the Soviet government. In April 1917 he had favored free passage for Lenin through Germany to Russia. And after the Bolshevik victory in November, he very quickly envisaged the possibility of a Russian-German continental bloc against the West. In December 1918 the Council of People's Deputies appointed him State Secretary for Foreign Affairs. Two months later he became Foreign Minister in Scheidemann's cabinet, a post that he resigned in protest over the signing of the Versailles Treaty. He withdrew from public life and worked in silence for a pro-Russian German foreign policy. In 1922, with his friend, Ago Freiherr von Maltzan zu Wartenberg und Penzlin, director of the Eastern Division of the Foreign Office, he drafted the Rapallo Treaty, and both men regarded this as one of their major achievements.

Radek discussed directly with the men near the Cuno cabinet Russia's attitude toward a renewed war between France and Germany and promised benevolent neutrality, including the support of the war by German Communists. He ground out many editorials, organized

---

Krestinsky's. "Tell us briefly of your past Trotskyite activities," was Vyshinsky's strict order. In contrast to the other defendants, Radek sketched over the first ten years in as many lines of testimony and developed in detail only his Trotskyite activities of the thirties. Thus Radek, a leading member of Trotsky's faction in 1925–1927, was kept silent about this period, while Krestinsky, at best a sympathizer with the group, had to go back to 1920 in his confession. Radek's role, as cast by Vyshinsky, was different, and he did not want to involve him too deeply in a matter of high treason. (Cf. *Report of the Court Proceedings in the Case of the Anti-Soviet Trotskyite Centre*, Moscow, 1937, p. 82 ff.)

sessions of the Central Committee, intervened in the distribution of party posts by the Orgburo. For Radek, the disintegration of the Weimar Republic was a golden opportunity to accumulate political laurels and build himself up as a leader of the first rank in Russia. He counted on a complete break between Germany and France, with a localized war between the Reich and the Rhine-Ruhr occupation troops, in which Britain, for many reasons, would not interfere. He considered the German military forces capable of throwing back the French army, thus isolated, and in the course of the war a Reichswehr-Communist bloc could get the upper hand.

At the time of the Genoa conference, April 1922, in order to lay the groundwork for a possible German-Russian coöperation, Radek had begun publishing articles in Russian newspapers attacking France as a servant of British capital. In his semi-official status in Berlin, he visited the Foreign Office in Wilhelmstrasse, and made a trip to Prague, where he contacted officials of the Czech government and tried to weaken its ties to France.

> Some time ago [Ernst Troeltsch writes] I spoke to Mr. Radek at a party; he was here [in Berlin] for a short visit between Genoa and Moscow, having given his promise not to propagandize. He emphasized the nationalism of the Soviets, which regard as completely logical the so-called testament of Peter the Great, as well as the need for uniting Communists and extreme nationalists in Germany for the final struggle against Western European capitalism. He spoke uninhibitedly, with the manner of a statesman who can afford to be sincere, to introduce new and somewhat crude manners into politics. He has asked the best counter-revolutionary writers of Germany to visit him to discuss this problem, but the response has been rather ambiguous. He has also spoken with officers of the Schupo [German police group]. . . .
>
> A professor belonging to the German National People's Party, whom I heard speaking to Radek, agreed with him completely. For both of them, this was the path to the future. German Social Democracy they both condemned as being petty bourgeois and pacifist at any price; moreover, it understands nothing of the art of governing.[1]

---

[1] Ernst Troeltsch, *Spektator-Briefe: Aufsätze über die deutsche Revolution and die Weltpolitik, 1918/22* (Tübingen, 1924), pp. 269–270.

During these years, the discussions between Radek and nationalists were kept secret, especially from the party. Opposition was feared from all sides, from Social Democratic and trade-union circles, and from groups within the nationalist and Communist camps. Some news of course leaked out. Later I sat with Count zu Reventlow in the Reichstag Committee for Foreign Affairs and, assuming that I was in accord with Radek's policy, he told me many details of their collaboration.

Reventlow himself publicly acknowledged his contacts with Radek in defending his policy of collaboration with the Communists against nationalist critics. In 1924, when as a result of the Dawes Plan National Bolshevism had temporarily subsided, he published a pamphlet called *Nationalist-Communist Unity?* In this he wrote that during 1918–1919 there had been a danger of a united front of both socialist parties with the Communists, which could have destroyed all nationalist organizations. In this period he was against the Spartakusbund, but things changed at the time of the Russian war against Poland.

> When the Red Army was marching on Warsaw, I was in favor of coöperating with it, from our German point of view, in order together to crush the Polish state. At that time we had enough organized troops and matériel at our disposal.[2]

The Schlageter Speech

After years of secret discussions with German nationalists, Radek at last openly proposed a united front between them, the army, and the Communist Party. In June 1923, at a meeting in Moscow of the Enlarged Executive Committee of the Comintern, Radek delivered a speech under the title "The Comintern's Fight against Versailles and the Capitalist Offensive."[3] Intended as a reply to a recent speech of Lord Curzon in London, Radek's talk was designed to sharpen the

---

[2] Graf Ernst Reventlow, *Völkisch-kommunistische Einigung?* (Leipzig, 1924), p. 10. In his books written after 1924, and particularly after Hitler took power, Reventlow played down his policy of German-Russian collaboration but never completely discarded it. In his works, National Socialism had a strong sprinkling of what may be called proletarian socialism.

[3] Karl Radek, *Der Kampf der Kommunistischen Internationale gegen Versailles und gegen die Offensive des Kapitals* (Hamburg, 1923).

British-French antagonism; Poincaré had to be isolated to give Germany a chance to prevail over France in a renewed conflict.

> England fears the growing air power of France [Radek declared]. She is attempting a policy of provocation in Paris, thereby encouraging French imperialism to smash its head against the wall of German resistance. German coal mines united with the iron ore of Brieux would form the basis of French control of Europe up to the Beresina.

On the other hand, Radek blamed the German bourgeoisie for not recognizing their real interests. The Russian Politburo, and Radek as well, of course knew of the secret German-British feelers concerning the Ruhr, and the possible rearrangement there was a nightmare for the Russian Foreign Office.

> The German bourgeoisie are like a pack of hyenas fighting each other for a piece of the corpse. As a class they have a great world political interest in the liquidation of the Versailles Treaty, but because each clique of German capitalism thinks only of its next immediate profit, the class as a whole is helping Poincaré to victory.

If you German bourgeoisie capitulate to France, Radek exclaimed pathetically, then you are doomed. The coördination of German and French trusts, this unity with French capitalism, is delivering your Fatherland to the enemy.

> The policy of all capitalist powers will lead to the destruction of Europe. The old continent marches not toward stabilization, but to great battles. . . .
> The defeat of the German bourgeoisie on the Ruhr is already certain, but not formally completed. They are not able even to capitulate.

In Radek's view, Europe would probably see a prolonged crisis, in which general destruction would break down all possible stabilizing trends. In this disrupted atmosphere, Radek feared a regrouping of forces into a united front against Russia. "The menace of war is greater than in 1914. Soviet Russia is now in great danger."

This phrase, Soviet Russia is in danger, is Radek's leitmotif. Independent action, he insisted, on the part of the various Communist parties is no longer possible; all must now forego all other tasks to unite on one prime objective, the defense of the state where workers' power has been achieved. By this analysis, a German revolutionary movement would be dangerous, would be contrary to the interests of Soviet Russia. To build a protection belt around Soviet Russia, it is necessary to coöperate with German nationalists and the German army, and to this end the German party has to be curbed.

> The German government tried to provoke a Communist uprising in the Ruhr, but thanks to the cold-blooded German Communist Party this plan was not realized.

To make this policy palatable to the German Communists, Radek alluded to the bloody defeats of the civil war and posed as a mentor who would shield the German party from a repetition of that destruction.

> The German bourgeoisie has tried to lie about the Ruhr strike and present it as a Ruhr revolt. It wants the German working class to suffer another brutal defeat.

The German Communist movement, Radek continued, is completely incapable of overthrowing German capitalism. Its role is that of a prop to the foreign policy of Soviet Russia, according to the needs of the moment. Europe organized under the leadership of the Bolshevik Party and fighting with the military skill of the German army against the West; that is the perspective, the only way out.

> We were and we are convinced that the European Continent will be capable, if the working class is victorious, of fighting the Anglo-Saxon blockade, and even the submarines and airplanes of the Anglo-Saxon capitalist world.

A few days later, at the same meeting of the Comintern's Executive Committee, Clara Zetkin spoke on the new phenomenon of "fascism," which since Mussolini's seizure of power in Italy had been a matter of deep concern for the Comintern. This new type of mass movement disquieted the Communists because Mussolini had been able to attract large strata of the working class. Following Zetkin's speech, Radek took the floor, to deliver a panegyric on the nationalist hero, Leo Schlageter, whom he called the "Wanderer into the Void." [4] He

---

[4] *Der Wanderer ins Nichts* was the title of a contemporary novel by Friedrich Freksa, a nationalist extremist. The hero is a Freikorps soldier killed in the fight against the Spartakusbund.

began in a high emotional key:[5]

> I can neither supplement nor complete the comprehensive and
> deeply impressive report of our venerable leader, Comrade Zetkin,
> on international Fascism. . . . I could not even follow it clearly,
> because there hovered before my eyes the corpse of the German
> Fascist, our class enemy, who was sentenced to death and shot by
> the hirelings of French imperialism, that powerful organization
> of another section of our class enemy. Throughout the speech of
> Comrade Zetkin on the contradictions within Fascism, the name
> of Schlageter and his tragic fate was in my head. . . . Schlageter,
> a courageous soldier of the counter revolution, deserves to be sin-
> cerely honored by us, the soldiers of the revolution.

Radek continued with a biography of Leo Schlageter in which all
the counter-revolutionary military groups in which he had fought
the revolutionary workers' movement were carefully enumerated.
Schlageter, he recalled, had been a soldier in the Baltic volunteer
corps that stormed Riga.

> We did not know whether the young officer understood the
> significance of his acts. Social Democrat Winnig and General
> von der Golz, the commander of the Baltic troops, knew what
> they were doing. They sought to gain the friendship of the Entente
> by performing the work of hirelings against the Russian people.
> . . . Schlageter's leader, Medem, later admitted that he marched
> through the Baltic into the void. Did all the German Nationalists
> understand that?

Schlageter had also participated in the Ruhr campaign under General Watter, who for the miners was the personification of evil. Radek
told how Schlageter had fought in Watter's expedition, in order to
emphasize that the Communists would coöperate even with those
who had made up the murder squadrons against the Spartakusbund
at the time of the civil war.

> Against whom did the German people wish to fight: against the
> Entente capitalists, or against the Russian people? With whom
> did they wish to ally themselves: with the Russian workers and
> peasants in order to throw off the yoke of Entente capital or for
> the enslavement of German and Russian peoples?

---

[5] All quotations from this speech are taken from the original Comintern translation, published in *Labour Monthly,* quasi-official organ of the Communist Party
of Great Britain (London, September 1923), Vol. 5, No. 3, p. 152 ff.

Schlageter is dead. He cannot supply the answer. His comrades in arms swore there at his grave to carry on his fight. They must supply the answer: Against whom and on whose side?

This speech set a new tone in the Comintern, and particularly in the German Communist Party. In their polemics against such Social Democratic theorists as Karl Kautsky, Lenin and Trotsky had argued that a Red terror against the White terror of the counter revolution would be inevitable. The necessity of wiping out the counter-revolutionary squadrons, the murderers of Karl Liebknecht and Rosa Luxemburg, the assassins of hundreds of workers, was one of the popular "new" ideas transforming the legalist-minded Social Democratic worker into a revolutionary.

Now Radek discovered that these Whites were made up of honest patriotic masses.

We ask the honest, patriotic masses who are anxious to fight against the French imperialist invasion: How will you fight, on whose support will you rely? The struggle against Entente imperialism is a war, even though the guns are silent. . . . If the patriotic circles of Germany do not make up their minds to make the cause of the majority of the nation their own, and so create a front against both Entente and German capital, then the path of Schlageter was a path into the void. . . .

If the honest patriotic masses did not heed Radek's call to unity, if the nationalists did not form a united front with the workers, then

Germany . . . will be transformed into a field of bloody internal conflict, and it will be easy for the enemy to defeat her and to destroy her.

Radek referred to the darkest hour of Germany's past, in 1806, after the Battle of Jena, when the young Prussian state lay helpless before the advancing armies of Napoleon. He referred to the heroes of young German nationalism, Gneisenau and Scharnhorst, the predecessors of the Freikorps organizers. These German nationalists and their leaders, Clausewitz and Freiherr von Stein, had found a refuge in Tsarist Russia and had waged a war of liberation from Russian soil. In exorcizing these venerated ghosts of German freedom, Radek crusaded for the necessary alliance between the Soviet power and German nationalism.

The powerful nation cannot endure without friends, all the more so must a nation which is defeated and surrounded by enemies. . . . If the cause of the people is made the cause of the nation, then the cause of the nation will become the cause of the people. . . . We believe that the great majority of the nationalist-minded masses belong not to the camp of the capitalists, but the camp of the workers. . . . We are convinced that there are hundreds of Schlageters who will hear [this truth] and who will understand it.

So striking a change in the Communist line was not of course made by Radek alone; his speeches expressed the result of internal discussions in the Politburo. At this time the strict discipline of the Russian Politburo in the Comintern had not yet been weakened, and very little information leaked out concerning these secret discussions. Through personal contact with Zinoviev and Lutovinov, I had more information on the matter than other German Communists, but it, too, was only partial.

Radek had been assigned to make the Schlageter speech because of growing Soviet-British tension in the Near East.

National Bolshevism in Turkey?

In its first phase, the Bolshevik seizure of power in November 1917 had seemed to favor the further expansion of British interests in the Near East.

In 1919 the British held the Caucasus and Turkestan. General Denikin was about to expand from his monarchist stronghold at the Caspian Sea; his squadron was manned by British sailors. His volunteer army, supported by the Kuban and Terek Cossacks, had gradually consolidated its position in the Northern Caucasus. After the collapse of Germany, the French fleet entered the Black Sea with transports intended to supply Denikin. Several divisions of French troops were landed in the Crimea and at Odessa. Two years later all these attempts had failed. The British were particularly concerned by the progress of Soviet policy in the Near East, where the situation looked more and more threatening. Persia, Afghanistan, and the neighboring countries were in an antagonistic mood; Turkey was in revolution.

In May 1919 Turkish territory was occupied by Greek troops under

French, British, and Italian auspices, and the partition of the country was apparently an immediate danger. Mustapha Kemal Pasha, a general, rallied a considerable part of the army around a program of national liberation and, with his troops reinforced by peasant rebels, called the country to rise against the Osman dynasty. His military coup swiftly broadened into a social upheaval against the antiquated and oppressive regime, whose heavy taxes and corrupt administration were notorious. The movement gained such momentum that Kemal was able to set up a revolutionary counter parliament in Ankara, the Great National Assembly, to oppose the Osmanian dynasty in Constantinople. From Ankara, Kemal marched triumphantly to Constantinople, and the Sultan abdicated.

In the first phase, the Kemalist revolutionaries coöperated with the Russian Communists; Soviet Russia was the first to recognize the Ankara government. After returning from his Zurich exile in 1917, Lenin had immediately attacked the Kerensky government for continuing the imperialist policies of Tsarism:

> It has not even published the secret treaties of a frankly predatory character (concerning the partition of Persia, the robbing of China, the robbing of Turkey, the annexation of East Prussia, the annexation of the German colonies, etc.) which, as everybody knows, bind Russia to Anglo-French imperialist and predatory capital. It has confirmed these treaties concluded by Tsarism which for several centuries robbed and oppressed more peoples than did all the other tyrants and despots, Tsarism which not only oppressed but also disgraced and demoralized the Great Russian people by transforming it into an executioner of other peoples.[6]

Repeatedly, the Soviet government declared its annulment of the secret Russo-British treaty concerning the partition of Persia and Turkey.

Under the auspices of Stalin, then in the Commissariat for Nationalities, a Turkish Communist Party had been founded on July 25, 1918, made up principally of Turkish prisoners of war in Russia. It had never developed into an independent force, for Kemal did not want a

---

[6] Lenin, "The Tasks of the Proletariat in Our Revolution," April 10, 1917 (the so-called "April Theses," a general statement of policy which reversed the Bolshevik policy after Lenin's return to Russia), *Collected Works* (New York, 1929), Vol. XX, Book I, p. 131.

Communist party in Turkey. He preferred his own brand of revolutionary nationalism; on his initiative, a National Communist Party was founded in 1920 in Ankara, which emphasized the social content of Islam as a more perfect form of socialism than Western Marxism. The Great National Assembly, Kemal told the peasants, would realize communism together with the national liberation of Turkey.

In Moscow this new type of peasant Bolshevism was the basis of speculations on the possibility of a similar development throughout the Near East, by which peasant communism would be integrated with the rising movements for national independence. Radek especially was enthusiastic about such a possibility. Already in 1919, while in the Moabit prison, he had received Talaat Pasha, a Turkish nationalist, and in January 1920 he invited Enver Pasha, another Turkish leader,[7] to Moscow.

In 1920, at the height of these hopes for a peasant revolution in the Near East, the Comintern called to Baku the First (and only) Congress of the Peoples of the Orient. The Politburo sent Zinoviev, Béla Kun, and Radek. The fulcrum of the congress discussions was the rise of Kemal and the weakening of the British Empire that, it was hoped, would follow. Radek, later describing the ceremony to his German friends, recalled half proudly, half satirically, how the 2000 colorfully garbed delegates threw their swords into the air. Zinoviev spoke to them in words that were being repeated in Communist circles all over the world:

> We call you, first of all, to a holy war against British imperialism. We will throw a firebrand against its rulers; we will make life miserable for those brazen-faced British officers, lording it over Turkey, Persia, and India.[8]

A proclamation of the congress, signed for Turkey by one Comrade Süphi declared, "Rise, ye peasants of Anatolia, for the Holy War under the banner of the Comintern!"

From then on Baku was the center of Soviet propaganda among

---

[7] Enver Pasha, one of the first of the Turkish nationalists to get in touch with the Bolsheviks, followed a policy of his own apart from Kemal. After repeated attempts to form a Pan-Turanian movement in Russian Central Asia, he disappeared — probably was killed — in Tadjikistan (upper Bokhara) in 1923.

[8] Cf. *Protokoll, Erster Kongress der Völker des Ostens,* in Baku, am 1. September 1920 (Hamburg, 1921).

the Moslems. Radek was proud to be the spokesman for the Turks in the Comintern; through his instigation, passages on "the young peasant people of Turkey" were included not only in all its decisions but even in the theses of the Leipzig convention in Germany.[9]

Entrenched in Istanbul, the new Turkish name for the old capital, Kemal established a new form of dictatorship. Throughout the country, he adapted the Communist party structure and discipline to his own conditions and organized his People's Party, based in the main on officers' groups, which ruthlessly suppressed all opposition to the new state and its party. He introduced his famous series of reforms, all intended to modernize the state administration and to Westernize education and mores; industrialization was stimulated only later, in the thirties. With the consolidation of his power, Kemal cooled toward Moscow, and the old Russian-Turkish antagonism, which for a short period had disappeared behind the collaboration between the two revolutionary movements, came again to the fore. The Communist Party was frequently driven underground and the national revolutionary, Kemal Pasha, rapidly became notorious in Comintern circles for his cruel methods of suppression.

Because of the rebellion of Kemal, the Sèvres peace treaty between Turkey and the Entente had never been carried out and the status of the Dardanelles remained uncertain. On November 20, 1922, Britain called a conference at Lausanne to discuss all pending questions with the new Turkish government and other interested powers. The Turkish delegates broke off the conference in February 1923; a few months later Sir Anthony Rumbold, former High Commissioner in Constantinople, reconvened it and offered a draft proposal more in line with Turkish demands. This rapprochement between Turkey and Britain alarmed the Kremlin, particularly since it was accompanied by a new stiffening in Soviet-British relations.

---

[9] "In the Versailles Treaty and the other peace treaties, world capital attempted both to burden the proletariat, by increased exploitation, with the cost of the war and of capitalist reconstruction, and to squeeze the 'vanquished' states in favor of the victorious states. This senseless plan could not operate, partly because it was materially impossible, partly because it was forcefully opposed by the masses of the oppressed peoples. The Turkish peasants destroyed the Treaty of Sèvres with weapons in hand because this treaty menaced their national existence." (*Bericht über die Verhandlungen des III. (8.) Parteitages der Kommunistischen Partei Deutschlands*, p. 409.)

Ever since the Bolsheviks had seized power, there had been a tension between Russia and Britain, reflected in and often aggravated by a series of incidents. Early in 1923 diplomatic correspondence concerning several of these "incidents" began to pile up. On April 10, Lord Curzon, in demanding information on Russia's seizure of a British trawler, the *James Johnson,* called the Soviets "pirates." On May 6, one Hy Slogett, a member of the British mission charged with protecting the ship, was shot, allegedly accidentally, by Soviet police who were chasing robbers. The episode was the topic of an excited debate in the House of Commons. In a note of protest, Britain gave Russia ten days in which to comply with her demands for compensation and the cessation of hostile propaganda and political affront. The incidents continued: another trawler, the *Lord Astor,* was captured by a Russian gunboat off the coast at Murmansk; a British warship was sent to prevent Russian interference with British ships outside the three-mile limit.

On May 10, V. V. Vorovsky, the Russian delegate to the Lausanne conference, was assassinated by Maurice Conradi, a White Russian émigré. For years after, the case was to be the basis of disputes and litigation between Russia and Switzerland.

Everyone in the Kremlin expected a definite break with Britain. On May 11, Radek made an impassioned speech in memory of Vorovsky; Trotsky spoke aggressively against British provocations. The Politburo nervously awaited further complications. A series of diplomatic notes was exchanged between the Kremlin and the British Cabinet. Partially yielding to British pressure, Russia promised to reduce her legation personnel in the Near East. Britain, on the other hand, denied that she had been intervening in Asiatic Russia.

The Lausanne Treaty, recognizing the new Turkish state, was signed by twelve powers on July 24, 1923, and settled the status of the Dardanelles. Turkey was granted practically all the demands that had previously been denied, particularly territory up to the 1914 borders, including Smyrna, Istanbul, and Eastern Thrace.

A Russian-German Bloc

Radek's Schlageter speech was intended as a demonstrative gesture to threaten Britain with the possibility of a Russian-German bloc, able to counterbalance Britain's realignment with Turkey. When Turkey deserted Russia's fight against the victors of Versailles, this gave more weight to the Soviet policy of supporting Germany just in the process of breaking the treaty.

Radek had transmitted his secret instructions not to the German Central Committee, but to the head of the German Politburo, Heinrich Brandler, and his more intimate group. Brandler's policy also required that the German revolutionary movement be bridled, so from quite different premises he and the Russian Politburo came to the same practical conclusion. When a year later Zinoviev accused Brandler and Thalheimer of passivity during the 1923 crisis, of not having prepared the struggle for power, they correctly replied that all the instructions they received from the Politburo during this first period of the Ruhr invasion had stressed prudence and a united-front policy. This program Brandler had followed loyally, for he agreed with it.

The details of the instructions given by the Russian Politburo to Brandler during the Schlageter period have never been divulged by Brandler or Thalheimer. When in 1931, Trotsky, already in exile, attacked the German party for its "National Communism," for its collusion with the rising Nazi movement, he referred to Brandler's policy of 1923. Thalheimer replied:

> Of course we foresaw in January the possibility of a revolutionary situation developing out of the Ruhr occupation. But we also reckoned with another possibility, namely a compromise between German and French capitalists, which then really took place. This second alternative was formulated especially by Radek in the *Rote Fahne*. . . .
>
> The Executive Committee of the Comintern foresaw a revolutionary fight for power neither in January nor even in June. In June there was a meeting of the Enlarged Executive Committee, at which no word was said about a revolutionary fight for power lying ahead. This meeting revolved around the British-Russian tension, on which Radek reported officially, and the increased danger of war between Soviet Russia and Britain. The Comintern Chairman, Zinoviev, reported on the question of the united-front policy, and he too did not consider the question of the fight for power of immediate relevance.[10]

---

[10] August Thalheimer, *1923—Eine verpasste Revolution? Die deutsche Oktoberlegende und die wirkliche Geschichte von 1923* (Berlin, 1931), p. 20.

Radek was supported by "the brain of Bolshevism," Nikolai Bukharin, whose status in the Comintern and in the German party was unique. Neither a statesman nor a journalist, he was not obliged to carry the weight of responsibility. Bukharin was the theorist, the man who after Lenin's death would spread his ideas. His books popularizing Marxism and Leninism were the textbooks of young Communists, who followed his *ABC of Communism* with an advanced course from his *Historical Materialism*. Among all the Russian Communists, Bukharin was held in highest esteem by the leaders of the Second International, especially by those with "Centrist" or "Austrian Marxist" leanings. In the eyes of young Communists, Zinoviev was the manipulator of Party affairs, Radek a half-suspect politician, Trotsky the leader of the Red Army and of the Russian state, Stalin a Party administrator; but Bukharin was the enlightened leader in abstract Communist theory, a man without an enemy in the whole of the Comintern.

As a theorist, Bukharin presented National Bolshevism more clearly and more aggressively than Radek. As early as November 1922—that is, on the eve of the Ruhr crisis in Germany—he proposed a policy of blocs with the bourgeoisie.

> There is no principled difference between a loan and a military bloc. I affirm that we [i.e., the Soviet state] are now strong enough to make a military alliance with a bourgeois state, in order to crush one capitalist country with the help of another. . . . In a country that has concluded such a military alliance, it is the duty of our comrades to help such a bloc to victory.[11]

To all but a very few of the delegates to the Fourth World Congress, Bukharin's speech seemed an abstract speculation on far-distant possibilities, and almost no one associated these theoretical statements with the actual situation in Germany. In an article published three years later, howover, Bukharin referred to public manifestos of "supreme bodies of the Soviet power" declaring its sympathy with "defeated and subjugated" Germany. A national united front between the Communist Party and the bourgeoisie for the defense of the German Fatherland against Entente imperialism had not been, Bukharin emphasized, at all excluded.

---

[11] *Protokoll des Vierten Kongresses der Kommunistischen Internationale* (Hamburg, 1923), p. 420.

> When Germany, defeated and subjugated, reduced to the status of a semi-colonial country, resisted the imperialism of the victorious Entente, in manifestos, declarations, etc., the supreme bodies of the Soviet power publicly declared their sympathy. At this time, the Communist Party considered defending the German Fatherland against the imperialism of the victorious Entente.[12]

This was echoed by Bukharin's follower, Eugen Varga:

> There were two different lines of struggle. One line was the proletarian revolutionary line, and the other was a bourgeois one. The Communist Party of Germany worked toward the revolutionary line, by which passive resistance would have been led by a workers' government. This government, by appeals to the working masses and the petty bourgeois masses of France, would have disintegrated the French united front against Germany and would have built up national resistance as a joint mission of all the German people with the proletariat of the world. . . .
>
> Shortly after the defeat of Germany, there was a rapid colonization by the Entente, correctly characterized by the *Echo of Paris* as Balkanization.[13]

At the Fifth World Congress this concept of Soviet-bourgeois blocs was restated in the discussion of the Comintern program, on which Bukharin was the main reporter.

Of all the members of the Russian Politburo, Zinoviev was the most hesitant, unenthusiastic, ambiguous, in carrying out this policy of National Bolshevism. He wrote many articles and pamphlets on the problems of 1923, but he never went so far as Bukharin. His analysis of the German situation after the Versailles Treaty was of course in accord with the general Comintern line, but he did not attempt to reinterpret the role of the German bourgeoisie. He emphasized rather the necessity of winning over the middle class and the peasantry.

For the young German Communists, however, the intervention of Bukharin and Radek was decisive. It reversed the trend that the early Comintern had represented and returned to the spirit of labor patriotism, which had led the working class to the support of the Kaiser

---

[12] *Inprekorr*, No. 130, January 1926.

[13] E. Pawlowski [Varga], "Die Niederlage des bürgerlichen Deutschlands im Ruhrkampf," *Die Kommunistische Internationale* (Petrograd, 1923), No. 26, pp. 96–106.

during the war. The current of nationalism in the German working class had been broken by the growing influence of international Communism. For the Communist internationalists, the chief enemy was not the Entente but the German military, the General Staff, the Freikorps, the Black Reichswehr, and such of their key supporters in big business as Stinnes, Thyssen, Klöckner. The National Bolshevism of Radek and Bukharin disturbed this process and, within German Communism, created a new current of German nationalism.

The new policy engendered strife and controversy in the party. In the intimate circles of the Left wing, it was rejected as dangerous for the further development of Communism in Germany.

August Thalheimer, the acknowledged theorist of the German party, was charged by Radek with presenting the new policy to the members. In his zeal, he went even further than Bukharin at the Fourth World Congress. He buried the German proletarian revolution, which had been finally defeated in the civil war of 1918–1920. He presented the Cuno government as fulfilling the task of the socialist revolution. An erudite student, Thalheimer based this surprising interpretation of Cuno on an analogy with Bismarck.

> At least temporarily, and against its own will, the German bourgeoisie is revolutionary in its foreign policy, as it was at the time of Bismarck (1864–1870), and for analogous reasons. The collapse of the German bourgeois democratic revolution in 1848 forced the Hohenzollern dynasty to take over the tasks of the German bourgeois revolution.[14]

Solidly backed by Bismarck, Thalheimer explained to the young Communist generation the dual role of German big business. The war in the Ruhr, which has the support of Cuno, Stinnes & Company, has a twofold character. To the extent that it is a national resistance movement of a disarmed and exploited people against the imperialist oppressor, it is "objectively revolutionary."

Could Germany be regarded as a "future imperialist power"? "Today that is not the case." Germany, defeated and disarmed, menaced by dismemberment and economic and political enslavement, can be considered a future imperialist power from only a "purely theoreti-

---

[14] August Thalheimer, "Die grundsätzlichen Fragen des Ruhrkampfes," *Die Kommunistische Internationale,* 1923, No. 26, pp. 107–110.

cal angle." "Today Germany is not the subject but the object of imperialist policy."

Thalheimer's article, translated into other languages, caused a worldwide stir in Communist circles. Two Czech Communists, working with the German opposition, attacked this revision of Communist theory. Alois Neurath's question, "What is the objective of Comrade Thalheimer's policy?" was answered by no one. "Thalheimer neglects giving the conclusion that follows from his thesis." Neurath gave Thalheimer the excuse of not knowing what he was doing.

> It is clear to what consequences such theses must lead [Neurath wrote]. The German proletariat must first of all support the fight of the German bourgeoisie against "French imperialism." It must "temporarily" conclude a pact for civil peace with Cuno, Stinnes & Co., perhaps not explicitly but in fact. . . . It is a dangerous beginning to give way before the mood of those sections of the working class beginning to be influenced by nationalist and chauvinist currents.[15]

Along with this article, Zinoviev printed another on the same subject by Joseph Sommer, another Czech. He had encouraged Neurath and Sommer to write their polemics against Thalheimer. Thus the two editors of the magazine, the big Russian leaders, played a game of chess, Radek using Thalheimer as his pawn and Zinoviev the two Czechs.

Forerunners of Nazism

Radek's speech on Schlageter had a tremendous response in Germany. Young Communists, young nationalists, officers, nationalist philosophers, literati, all began to discuss "the Schlageter line." Communists built up small groups in which nationalists and socialists met to discuss the necessity of a united German front against France.

The German Politburo, in agreement with Radek, instructed party organizers on how to carry out the Schlageter policy. One of its circulars, for propagandizing among nationalist officers, read: "One has to speak with officers very courteously and amiably, to address them by the title 'Your Excellency.'" Party branches were instructed to

---

[15] Alois Neurath, "Eine verdächtige Argumentation," *Die Kommunistische Internationale*, 1923, No. 26, pp. 110–113.

organize student groups,[16] nationalist youth circles, all kinds of "bourgeois" contacts. "Concentrate the fire of propaganda on the Schlageter line," was the party order. Remmele, a Communist deputy, spoke in Stuttgart and was greeted by "enthusiastic applause from fascists and workers."[17] Communist speakers declared, "The time is not far off when the *Völkische* and the Communists will be united."[18]

Radek himself took the lead and in July 1923 issued a special edition of the *Rote Fahne* under the title "Germany's Way," in which he, Reventlow, and Arthur Moeller van den Bruck discussed the future of National Bolshevism. Radek's speech on Schlageter was given the front page. Reventlow's weekly, *Reichswart* ("Guardian of the Reich"), answered Radek's proposal at length. Moeller van den Bruck discussed National Bolshevism in his magazine *Gewissen* ("Conscience"). A month later, on August 22, the *Rote Fahne* published another article by Reventlow entitled "One Part of the Way," and a rejoinder by Paul Frölich. "Whoever comes to us without intrigue," Frölich wrote, "will find us ready to march at his side." Solemnly, Reventlow asked Frölich about the possibility of German-Russian coöperation, which had seemed to him most feasible at the time of the Polish-Russian war. "Do you believe that this occasion has passed forever?" "No, I don't believe so."

The collapse of 1918 had marked the historic end of one brand of German nationalism, that of the conservatives and monarchists. The revolution of 1918 gave birth to a new type of German nationalism and imperialism, which, years later, would shake the world under the name of National Socialism. The Nazis had thousands of forerunners, with various faces and voices. Before Hitler came to power, many other forms of German neo-nationalism were tested. Within these amorphous pre-forms of National Socialism, the floating ideas of the messianic fanatics began to settle on Pan-Eurasia.

Moeller van den Bruck was a representative forerunner of Nazism, "the well-known counter-revolutionary writer" mentioned by Troeltsch.

---

[16] At a meeting of Berlin University students organized by the Berlin party branch, I was the speaker. The attitude of the nationalists against capitalism was discussed, and I was obliged to answer some anti-Semitic remarks. I said that Communism was for fighting Jewish capitalists only if all capitalists, Jewish and Gentile, were the object of the same attack. This episode has been cited and distorted over and over again in publications on German Communism.

[17] *Die Rote Fahne*, No. 183, Berlin, August 10, 1923.

[18] *Berliner Tageblatt*, No. 69, February 9, 1924.

In Imperial Germany his principal interest had been in esthetics and literature; he had translated Dostoyevsky. After 1918 he gathered a circle of young nationalists about him; it was he who coined the phrase "The Third Reich." By his political concept, the nations of the world were divided into two classes, the Haves and the Have-nots. Germany was the proletarian among nations. And he declared that Germany could transform her defeat in the war into a victory if she won the revolution that would enable her people to wage total war.

Moeller-Bruck and other advocates of German nationalism were magically attracted to the "mysterious" phenomenon of the young Russian Soviet power. Russia, defeated in 1918, had been forced by Germany to sign the Treaty of Brest-Litovsk, so similar to Versailles. She had withdrawn from the Entente and was quite isolated in the arena of world politics. But in spite of this, Russia had begun to emerge out of its wreckage and suffering as a mighty power in the East, organizing a new army and developing a spirit of aggressive militancy.

German nationalists were very sensitive to the fact that in the Comintern, as contrasted with the League of Nations, the language of official procedure was German. They compared the moderation of Minister Erzberger at Versailles with the bold intransigence of People's Commissar Trotsky at Brest-Litovsk.

In 1919, marching against the Bolshevik arch-enemy in Riga, sudden doubt had befallen Ernst von Salomon, the young *Landsknecht* soldier of the Freikorps:

> What are we doing here in this torturous darkness? Behind us no people, no Reich. Over there, a tremendous new force in the making, an emphatic will, a unique belief that with an iron hand molds this horde of illiterate peasants and workers into soldiers and gives to those fallen outcasts a soul and a religion. . . . Beyond the border arises an amorphous but growing power, standing in our way, which we half admire and half hate.[19]

---

[19] Ernst von Salomon, *Die Geächteten,* p. 66. During World War II Ernst's brother, Bruno von Salomon, was active in the *National-Komitee Freies Deutschland* (National Free Germany Committee) in Mexico City, a branch of the Moscow committee founded in 1943 by the Communist Erich Weinert; Freiherr von Einsiedel, Bismarck's great grandson; and General Walther von Seydlitz, commander of the VI German Army at Stalingrad. The two leading members of the Mexico City committee were the Communist trade-unionist Paul Merker and the scion of a German feudal family, Arnold Vieth von Golssenau, who under the name Ludwig Renn is known as a Communist writer. Both Merker and Renn returned to East Germany in 1946.

The split in the German people created by the civil war was so deep, the class hatred so bitter, that it was impossible to reorganize a popular army and prepare a war of revenge. If national salvation depended on a war against the West, it could be achieved only after ameliorating the social strife in the country and Germany's relations with Soviet Russia. Thus, Radek's proposal to Reventlow, based on the interrelation between revolution and national liberation, fell on fertile soil. Against imperialism, army and people must coöperate, and against the West, the German and Russian governments had to reach an understanding. Radek was very clear about this impasse of German nationalism and about the type of person to whom he addressed his appeal. In one of his reports, he wrote, "Germany is a map of all forms of civil war: . . . secret organizations, the Fehme, groups for political assassination; from passive resistance, the typical action of oppressed Oriental peoples, to open civil war. . . . Germany is a murderers' den."

Since 1918, beginning with the murder of Liebknecht and Luxemburg, the assassination of opponents had become a permanent feature of German political life. When the Fehme included among its victims two Reich ministers, it set high marks in its regime of terror. Matthias Erzberger, Finance Minister, had signed the Treaty of Versailles; and Walther Rathenau, Minister for Foreign Affairs, tried to carry out its terms. The Fehme killed both, Erzberger in August 1921 and Rathenau in June 1922.[20]

Clandestine traffic of ammunition and weapons was common in most

---

[20] Erzberger wrote in his memoirs that on the day when the Reichstag ratified the Versailles Treaty "members of the Reichswehr attempted to kill me but failed. A few days later an attempt was made to bomb my office at the Finance Ministry. A hand grenade wrecked the room in which I was supposed to be sleeping. On the occasion of the third attempt to kill me, at Moabit, I was visibly protected by the hand of God; I was only slightly wounded . . ." (Matthias Erzberger, *Erlebnisse im Weltkrieg,* Berlin, 1920, p. 383.) The fourth attempt, on August 26, 1921, was successful. On a walking trip in the Black Forest, Erzberger was shot with twelve bullets, the traditional death for a traitor.

On November 25, 1946, in Freiburg im Breisgau, Heinrich Tillessen, Erzberger's assassin, was tried before a German court for this twenty-five-year-old crime and acquitted on various juridical grounds, among them that the general amnesty of 1933 was applicable. In announcing the judgment, the court said that as a mature man Tillessen had severed himself from his deed and was now a man of high moral character. In any case, the assassination had been motivated, in the words of the court, by his exalted patriotic desire to lead Germany to a better future. The *Tribunal Général* in Rastatt, the juridical supervisory authority of French-occupied Germany, protested the judgment and demanded a new trial. (Cf. *Neue Züricher Zeitung,* December 4, 1946.)

German organizations, from the Reichswehr, which had storage centers hidden from the Reparation Commission's control, to the Black Reichswehr and Communist Party, which trafficked in rifles and ammunition and cached them. These "traveling rifles" circulated all over Germany. A type of expert arose, with an excellent knowledge of the weapons available on the black market. These experts, nationalist and Communist, met in the same beer gardens, in the towns and villages most suitable for conspiracy against the Repco and the police. All over the country, the Schlageter policy resulted in many personal contacts between Right and Left hunters of rifles and machine guns, and there were many curious incidents. Writing of such an expert on the Communist side, Walter Zeutschel, a contemporary observer, notes: "He got the weapons from various contacts and friends in fascist circles, who gave him a relatively cheap price for large quantities."[21] The same rifles were often sold several times to the party's Central Committee; rifles, if only hurriedly inspected, are rifles.[22]

The liquidation of corrupted comrades—a Communist Fehme—developed naturally out of this milieu. Zeutschel also tells of a plan by which a girl was to lure a traitor into a trap—a small church near the public park of Friedrichshain in Berlin. There he was to be knocked unconscious with a sandbag and then injected with a poison.

The Communist underground, on the other hand, continued its traditional clandestine activities; sabotaging the army and the police, terrorist reprisals against terror detachments of the nationalist extremists. These actions were separate from the diplomacy between Radek and German counter revolutionaries. On street corners, the German workers of the rank and file fought with knives and revolvers and an occasional rifle against "the fascist bandits." In all parts of Germany there were riots and clashes, and many an unknown victim

---

[21] Walter Zeutschel, *Im Dienst der kommunistischen Terror-Organisation* (Berlin, 1931), p. 71.

[22] Traffic in cached arms was general in Europe after World War II as well. Typical of the situation is this anecdote from France. Minister of the Interior Édouard Depreux conceded the truth of the frequently rumored secret stores of arms. At the beginning of March 1947 a man in possession of forty machine guns, grenades, and other arms was arrested; he was a member of both the Gaullist Union and the *Francs-Tireurs et Partisans,* a Communist guerrilla band. These arms were sold to the highest bidder, and in the enveloping fog of false papers, of false accusations and counter accusations, it was well-nigh impossible to trace them. (Cf. *New York Times,* March 18, 1947.)

fell in this setting of civil war. These Communist workers did not quite know what was going on in the higher brackets of the party hierarchy, although they were somewhat disquieted by the strange theoretical formulations of their leaders. All branches of the party brought pressure on the Brandler Committee to fight rising fascism more energetically. Reports streamed in about the increasing armament of Nazi groups, about the intense preparations of their organizations, about the need to fight them more vigorously and more effectively. In this year of 1923, the average rank-and-file Communist instinctively concentrated his attention and energy on this fight against rising Nazism. He was not so much interested in parliamentary combinations in Saxony and Thuringia, and he was completely indifferent to historical analyses of Bismarck and of the objectively revolutionary role of Cuno and Stinnes.

Brandler began to write violent articles against the fascists and to instruct party editors in the same vein. *"Schlagt die Faschisten, wo ihr sie trefft"* ("Beat up the fascists wherever you meet them"), he wrote in the *Rote Fahne.*

A "fighting-day" against fascism was prepared for July 29, 1923, called, according to Zinoviev's report to the Fifth World Congress, over Radek's opposition. Sponsored and encouraged by Zinoviev, it was the result of the increasing dissatisfaction of the rank and file with a party policy of collusion with the fascists and passivity.

3.

THE COMMUNIST
UPRISING OF 1923

NORTH SEA

HAMBURG

Wilhelmshaven

Groningen

Oldenburg

Bremen

NETHERLANDS

Amsterdam

Hanover

The Hague

Arnhem

Münster

Bielefeld

GERMANY

Gelsenkirchen

Bochum

Essen

Dortmund

Hamm

RUHR

Duisburg

Hagen

Kassel

Krefeld-Urdingen

Elberfeld-Barmen

Düsseldorf

Antwerp

Remscheid

München-
Gladbach

Solingen

BELGIUM

Brussels

Cologne

Liége

Aachen

Lille

Bonn

RHINELAND

RHINE

Koblenz

Frankfurt-
am-Main

Hanau

Wiesbaden

Offenbach

Mainz

Darmstadt

LUX.

Trier

Ludwigshafen

Mannheim

SAAR

Saarbrücken

FRANCE

Karlsruhe

LORRAINE

Nancy

Stuttgart

Strasbourg

Ulm

ALSACE

Freiburg

WINSLOW·MAP CO.

RHINE-RUHR, MARCH 1923

ALLIED OCCUPATION
UNDER THE
VERSAILLES TREATY

OCCUPIED BY ALLIED
ARMIES IN MARCH 1923

Basel

Zurich

SWITZERLAND

AUSTRIA

The Ruhr crisis was approaching its climax during the spring and early summer of 1923. Inflation disrupted economic life; the banks quoted the official foreign exchange rates only twice weekly, and bootleg traffic in money reached unprecedented heights. The German Finance Minister was inundated by requests from entrepreneurs for permission to print their own "emergency currency," and city councils did begin to issue such currency to pay their civil servants. In June the mark stood at 0.5 million to the British pound, in July at 1.5 million, in August at 120 million.

The lower middle class, most heavily hit, was uprooted. "Business as usual" was a farce, particularly for small tradesmen and peasants, who received valueless paper marks for valuable commodities. Thus, despite a good harvest, the farmers held back their crops, and aggravated the already dangerous food shortage in industrial areas.

This disruption of economic life endangered the legal structure of the Weimar Republic. Civil servants lost their ties to the state; their small salaries had no relation to their daily needs; they felt themselves in a boat without a rudder. Police troops, in sympathy with the rioting populace, lost their combative spirit against the hunger demonstrations and closed their eyes to the sabotage groups and clandestine military formations mushrooming throughout the Reich. Hamburg was so tense that the police did not dare interfere with looting of foodstuffs by the hungry masses. In August, large demonstrations of dock workers in the Hamburg harbor led to rioting. "Parts of the police," Zeutschel wrote, "are regarded as unreliable; they sympathize with the working class."[1] The Cuno cabinet itself contributed to the weakening of legality by sponsoring the Black Reichswehr and instigating sabotage in the Ruhr.

Civil War in Gestation

The separatist movements in the Rhine-Ruhr and Bavaria got a new upsurge. General Ludendorff, feeling that the decisive moment lay ahead, was very active in Munich. He continued to give the monarchists qualified support but began to ally himself with the burgeoning *Militärorganisation der Deutschsozialen und Nationalsozialisten* (Military Organization of German and National Socialists)—as the Nazi movement was then known. For the first time since 1918, the Hohenzollerns, exiled to Holland, had serious hopes of being recalled, following the collapse of the Weimar Republic. They sent hundreds of messengers into the German provinces, revitalizing their contacts with army and business circles.

During these early months in the summer of 1923, Hitler's name began to be known outside Munich. The Bavarian cabinet was in open revolt against the Reich, and a proclamation of Bavarian independence seemed possible at any moment. The French government sponsored this Bavarian separatism; some French liaison men even contacted the Hitler organization.[2]

During July, Rhine-Ruhr separatism also reached a peak. Rumors were spread that one of its leaders, Joseph Smeets, would apply to the League of Nations for recognition of a Rhenish Republic. The trade-unions, including those in the Rhineland, threatened to oppose such a proclamation with another general strike. The Catholic clergy of the Ruhr and Rhineland petitioned Pope Pius to use all means at his disposal to prevent the separation of Rhine-Ruhr from the Reich.

On July 13, Captain Ehrhardt, awaiting trial for high treason for his participation in the Kapp putsch, escaped from the Leipzig prison.

---

[1] Walter Zeutschel, *Im Dienst der kommunistichen Terror-Organisation*, p. 10.

[2] Some details of these contacts were revealed early in July at the trial for high treason of Professor Georg Fuchs, a dramatic critic, and Hugo Machhaus, a composer-conductor. Cf. Georg Fuchs, *Wir Zuchthäusler: Erinnerungen des Zellengefangenen Nr. 2911* (Munich, 1931).

Hitler celebrated this "national deed" in a mass meeting in Munich, followed by a series of demonstrations in honor of the old army. Ludendorff proclaimed his new slogan, "With God for the People and Liberty," in contrast to the monarchist cry, "For God, Kaiser, and Fatherland." He also began a drive for a memorial statue to honor "the national martyr," Albert Leo Schlageter.

In this atmosphere, seething with rumors of the impending return of the Kaiser from Holland and of the Bavarian conspiracy and the threatened separation of the Rhineland from the Reich, the working class became rebellious. The trade-union leadership became panicky, fearing a situation beyond their control. They incessantly (for example, on May 25 and June 1) urged the Reich cabinet to come to a settlement with France. The Social Democratic Party pointed out in weekly statements that the currency problem "must be solved," and the cabinet regularly promised to solve it. The National Association of German Import and Export Trade, however, protested against all planned control of foreign exchange as a danger to free enterprise.

Wages and salaries lost all relation to economic reality. The Cuno cabinet wanted taxes based on gold; the Social Democrats demanded a capital levy on "real values"; the workers continued to demand the nationalization of heavy industry, thus threatening the very existence of the cabinet. Communists actually occupied a coal mine near Zwickau for a few days. They announced that they would operate it, but were quickly ousted by the Central Committee. Bread riots became commonplace: in Berlin, Dresden, Frankfurt am Main, Mannheim, Cologne.

Meanwhile, the French tightened their control of the Rhine-Ruhr. The city of Barmen was heavily fined; chemical works in Bochum were occupied; mines near Essen and coke ovens on the Rhine-Elbe Canal were seized. At the beginning of August, the Inter-Allied High Commission ordered that mines in the occupied zones be seized, following the failure to deliver reparations coal. Nationalist sabotage groups intensified their activities. In the first days of August, when hand grenades were thrown at French troops in Düsseldorf, the chief of police was arrested. The nationalists answered with renewed bombing in the town. The French made arrests and imposed heavy sentences but were not able to stop the saboteurs. During the same weeks there were similar incidents in Essen and many other points.

By the end of July, the Cuno Cabinet was on the verge of collapse. In Germany and abroad, its resignation was regarded as imminent, and it was not supposed that its successor could be just another parliamentary combination. A revolutionary change was expected, in fact was regarded as overdue.

Reformist Communism lost its grip on the party's rank and file. During the summer of 1923, the provincial organization came into the hands of more radical elements, young workers who had been sent into the front lines at the age of sixteen. They had returned, married, remained penniless. At sixteen, they had tossed hand grenades; at seventeen, they had made peace demonstrations; at eighteen, they had participated in strikes and civil war. The march of Bavarian fascists on Red Saxony was an impending peril. Daily raids of fascist organizations in workers' neighborhoods raised feelings to fever pitch. The malaise increased. The outbreak of large-scale hostilities was expected daily, and industrial centers were bitter against the dangerous passivity of all the responsible leaders.

The average Communist began to concentrate his energy more and more on the organization of military formations. The party's security service (*Ordnungsdienst*) had been superseded by Red Hundreds, shock troops composed of energetic militants; and for the rank and file of the party, the task of the hour was the immediate extension of this military program. The Red Hundreds had been designed to draw non-party sympathizers into action in support of the party. Trade-unionists and members of the Center Party, Free Masons and zealous Catholics, were all made welcome in their ranks. They adopted the names of the factories with which they were affiliated—for example, the Siemens Hundred, or the Borsig Hundred.

The antagonism in the German party became most acute around the problem of organizing the Hundreds. For the party membership, the Red Hundreds idea was a reappearance of the workers' councils of 1918 in the new situation, and it sensed that in these armed and locally organized units it might find the means to slip out from under the discipline of Berlin and Moscow. Brandler's slogan, "A and B Government" (*Arbeiter- und Bauern-Regierung,* Workers' and Peasants' Government), found a weak response among Left Communists. The Central Committee, on the other hand, tried to deflect the Hundreds into organs of mere propaganda. In Saxony and Thuringia, Right-wing Communists tried to establish models of Reformist Communist policy and focused their activity on *Kontrollausschüsse,* committees of housewives and unemployed, consumers' committees to fight the inflation. These committees were coördinated with factory councils, and it was intended that both organizations become permanent economic advisory boards to the state government. In organizing these two groups of all-worker committees, into which the middle class and peasantry could be drawn, the Right-wingers hoped to create the mass base for a parliamentary workers' government in Saxony and Thuringia. By the practical results of such positive measures, this provincial model would attract the majority of trade-unionists to this policy and thus create a premise for a parliamentary workers' government of the Reich. The intention was to legalize these various wildcat committees; the factory councils were to be integrated into an *Arbeitnehmer-Kammer,* a permanent advisory board dealing exclusively with labor questions, later to be stabilized by legislation. Thus, the Reformist Communists also wanted to adapt the council concept, but in accordance with their interpretation of the Ruhr crisis.

The control of the police by Social Democrats hampered the development of Red Hundreds in Saxony and Thuringia. The provincial governments did not want to aggravate their conflicts with the Reich cabinet by tolerating a wild Hundreds movement, and in these states the Hundreds became an auxiliary organization to the regular police, coöperating with them against black marketeers. There the Hundreds never attained the momentum they gained in the lawless region of the occupied Rhine-Ruhr.

The first Zeigner government, formed in Saxony at the end of March 1923, was based on a majority of Social Democrats and Communists, but did not include Communist ministers in the cabinet. Shopkeepers were in constant fear of looting and riots and constantly petitioned the state authorities concerning their untenable situation. Business organizations complained to the Reich cabinet about conditions in Saxony and the danger that plants would be wrecked by sabotage. The Control Committees held regular conferences with the Zeigner cabinet, but never won any status, since Saxony's government had no power to interfere in the Reich economy. These committees,

with the impossible task of controlling runaway prices, never got farther than organizing protest meetings and attempting, by joint action
against individual grocers, to set some limit to rising prices. All the
hectic activity of the committees resulted in only one achievement—
an amnesty to political prisoners and petty thieves.

The Left Communists in Hamburg and Berlin viewed this coöperation between the Zeigner cabinet and the Control Committees and
factory councils as only a brake on the revolutionary potentialities of
the factory-council movement. Saxony's Communist-backed Social
Democratic government seemed to them more a hindrance than a help
in forming a united front of trade-union and Communist workers
against the Cuno cabinet. In Berlin and Hamburg, the Hundreds and
Control Committees expanded considerably, but in these two major
industrial regions the authorities averted even the forms of interference
from below. Here the wildcat activities of the "organized unorganized"
developed into minor street-fighting.

In East Prussia, a Communist-led strike of farmhands quickly grew
to palpable proportions, involving 120,000 participants. This strike
added a new element to the complex picture of Germany in transition;
heretofore farmhands had been silent, without influence on events.
Since 1918, the official trade-union of farmhands had gone through a
major crisis. One of the first acts of the Ebert government had been
to proclaim the right of farmhands to organize, which they had not
had in Imperial Germany. The Farmhands' Trade-Union grew to be
one of the strongest in Germany; in 1920, it had 860,000 members. In
1923, its membership had fallen off to 150,000. Various oppositionist
farmhands' unions were founded—for instance, the Farm and Forest
Workers of Germany, which held two Reich conventions during this
period. *Völkische* groups also began to fight for influence among the
farmhands.

The strike was violent in the Marienwerder and Pillkallen regions,
where shots were fired at the police and the Teno auxiliaries sent to
protect the big landowners. Industrial workers responded with great
sympathy; there were common meetings and joint groups of city and
farm workers. The strike in East Prussia was followed by weaker
movements in Mecklenburg, Pomerania, Brandenburg, Magdeburg,
Hessen-Kassel, and the vicinity of Leipzig. In Magdeburg, when the

Social Democratic police president arrested the strike committee he was opposed by the Social Democratic rank and file. The farmhands of Magdeburg called for solidarity from the workers there, who responded with a strike of their own. At Goldberg, in Mecklenburg, the farmhands seized weapons from nationalist caches and marched to the houses of the big estate owners, threatening to arrest them and seeking to uncover more hidden weapons of the nationalists.

In the city councils, the Communist and Social Democratic deputies were under strong pressure from the unemployed and the poorest strata of the workers. A wave of petitions demanded free milk for children, community canteens, the distribution of clothing and coal, a rent moratorium. More than three hundred municipal councils, in which were some seven thousand Communist deputies, passed motions granting these demands. The attempts of Reich officials to interfere in these local activities were usually without result. Rotthausen, a small municipality near Essen, granted its inhabitants one sweeping relief measure after another, and the Prussian government sent a representative there to prevent "socialism"; he got rid of the Communist administration by incorporating the town into the city of Essen.

Factory Councils versus Trade-Unions

The inflation brought the trade-unions of Germany to the greatest crisis since their formation. All wage policies of "trade-unionism as usual" were made meaningless by the economic disruption.

Since 1918, Germany had seen two kinds of strikes: the wildcat strikes characteristic of the civil war, and the official trade-union strike, begun only after mature reflection and along prudent constitutional lines, following the tradition developed by Carl Legien at the end of the nineteenth century. The unions had increased their authority by leading these strikes, with careful preparation, to repeated victory, which after 1918 was due largely to their coördination with the Reich and state governments. Now, the status the unions had achieved over long years was nullified in a few months by the 1923 inflation.

A specific effect of the inflation on trade-unions concerned their local organizers, the bulwark of conservative labor policy in the factories. Those local leaders were workers from the bench, distinguished by special skill in their trade but representative of the average worker in behavior and thought. They were moderately paid, but enjoyed certain advantages in sickness and disability insurance, and looked forward to an old-age pension after decades of service. Inflation swept away not only the purchasing power of their wages, but also their dream of security, and the bulk of the small trade-union organizers themselves began to advocate revolutionary change. At the beginning of 1924, when the storm had passed, the official bulletin of the German Federation of Labor summed up the experience thus:

> The German government got extraordinary powers to quell uprisings but applied these powers entirely against Left putschist movements. Republican workers were indignant that the military apparatus was used to remove the Saxony government from office, to suppress Social Democratic newspapers, and to install a dictatorial regime in Thuringia, while the armed Ehrhardt bandits continued undisturbed. . . . Some hundreds of thousands, part of those millions won since 1918, dropped out because want destroyed their belief in the trade-unions.[3]

For the trade-unions the status of factory councils became of increasing importance. In their past effort to minimize the importance of the councils, the union bureaucrats had won a major victory by subordinating them to the official trade-union organization, but the struggle between the councils and the union organizers had never completely ceased. With the inflation, the factory councils began to take the lead again in presenting workers' demands to the entrepreneurs. Salaried union organizers, who had tried to maintain this activity under their exclusive control, were supplanted by volunteer council leaders, who were trusted more.

In open competition with the trade-unions, the factory councils started to organize regional and local conventions. This duel reached a climax with the election of the Committee of Fifteen, comprising factory-council delegates from all over the Reich, with its headquarters in Berlin.

It is characteristic that the term *soviet* was carefully avoided, partly because it had fallen into disrepute through the weak and inefficient organization of the councils in 1918, partly because of the increasing criticism and distrust of the Russian model. Whenever Communists

---

[3] "Ein Schwarzes Jahr" ("A Black Year"), editorial in the *Gewerkschafts-Zeitung* (Berlin, 1924), XXXIV, 1.

tried to launch the slogan of German soviets, they met stiff resistance among the workers. The factory councils consciously sought to enhance their reputation by representing themselves as the successors to the *Betriebsobleute,* the genuinely German factory organization, by tying themselves to the tradition of the movement that, during the last year of the war, had prepared the overthrow of the Imperial government.

For the first time since 1918, a workers' organization outside the political parties and trade-unions became increasingly popular. Concurrently, the unions lost ground; the membership of the German Federation of Labor, 7.8 million at the end of 1922, fell during 1923 to 5.7 million.[4]

Strike in the Money Press

Inflation made the normal strike for wages meaningless. The money crisis decreased all trade-union struggles considerably.[5] In the critical

---

[4] *Gewerkschafts-Zeitung,* XXXIV, 400.

Of the 18 million Germans classified as employed at the end of 1922, 14,260,000 worked under a collective contract. Of these 12,500,000 were organized in one of the following: the German Federation of Labor (ADGB); the Christian unions; the Hirsch-Dunckers, a union founded by two men named Max Hirsch and Franz Duncker in competition with the Social Democratic unions; and the AfA-Bund (*Allgemeiner freier Angestelltenbund*), the white-collar union.

German Federation of Labor (ADGB)
Membership in 1922–1923

Year	Quarter	Membership	Gain or Loss Number	Gain or Loss Percentage
1922	I	7,810,133	+58,544	+0.8
	II	7,883,906	+73,773	+0.9
	III	8,068,938	+185,032	+2.3
	IV	7,821,558	−247,380	−3.1
1923	I	7,427,638	−393,920	−5.0
	II	7,287,049	−140,589	−1.9
	III	7,039,059	−247,990	−3.4
	IV	5,749,763	−1,289,296	−18.3

[5] The strikes and lockouts during the inflation were as follows:

Year	Number Strikes	Number Lockouts	Participants Strikes (000 omitted)	Participants Lockouts (000 omitted)	Working Days Lost Strikes (000 omitted)	Working Days Lost Lockouts (000 omitted)
1899–1913 *	1,885	229	406	61	5,291	2,716
1919	3,682	37	2,725	32	32,464	619
1920	3,696	114	1,916	91	15,444	1,311
1921	4,093	362	1,818	202	22,596	3,278
1922	4,348	437	2,241	220	23,383	4,351
1923	1,878	168	1,752	119	11,014	1,330

* Average. (*Gewerkschafts-Zeitung,* XXXIV, 392.)

period of inflation, fights had to be short ones for after a few days their object was without substance. During 1923, the number of strikes without result was considerably higher than in the years before; many fights had to be abandoned before a settlement could be reached.

With the rising inflation, the Reich Printing Office could not issue paper money rapidly enough. Auxiliary printing shops were installed; the Reich Bank promised paper money enough for all by August 4. The same week the paper money crisis was brought to a climax by the Communist cell in the Reich Printing Office. These printers, ordinarily models of conservative restraint, decided to take Germany's fate into their hands and to hit the Cuno cabinet in its most vulnerable spot— the money press. They struck, with the deliberate intention of over- throwing the Cuno cabinet, of lighting the signal for a nationwide rebellion. As the printers had anticipated, their action paralyzed the state machinery. The reserve of paper money was absorbed in a few hours; no wages could be paid, either to civil servants or to anyone else.

The printers' act instigated a mass strike on August 10, which rapidly assumed civil-war forms. All Berlin traffic ceased; limited amounts of gas and electricity were supplied for emergency use only; power plants were closed, cutting off power to important parts of German industry.

Under the pressure of the Berlin workers, an emergency conference of the city's Trade-Union Council was convoked in order to delib- erate on whether to endorse the strike, which was already complete in the Berlin area. With such an endorsement by the capital's Trade- Union Council, the German Federation of Labor and Social Demo- cratic locals throughout the Reich would have given the strike their full support, bringing about the longed-for united front of the working class into one powerful revolutionary movement; but the endorsement was withheld. The socialist parties were invited to send representatives to the Council session, the Communist Party for the first time; this extraordinary step was in itself an indication of the trade-unionists' mood. Otto Wels, Paul Hertz, and Rudolf Breitscheid were present for the Social Democratic Party; and Ottomar Geschke, Fritz Heckert, and I for the Communist Party. It was a dramatic session; the destiny of the German working class, and of Germany, hung once again in the balance. The discussion was impassioned. Gustav Sabath, a typical old Berlin trade-union leader, and with him the entire group of veteran union bureaucrats were on the verge of supporting the strike. They were restrained by the Social Democrat Wels, the political leader. Thus, as during the Kapp putsch, the trade-union leaders were again better able to judge political events and take effective action than the Social Democratic Party. These pupils and disciples of Carl Legien had his faults, but also his horse sense and administrative ability. If the union leaders had supported the strike, the successor to Cuno would have been a trade-union man; Germany would have had a trade-union government, backed by militant workers able to face all the consequences this implied.

On August 10, the Communists in the Reichstag moved a vote of no confidence. On the 11th, Cuno resigned. Now the strike in Berlin spread like wildfire: to Central Germany, the Wasserkante, the Rhineland, Stuttgart, Upper Silesia, Thuringia, East Prussia. It was comparable only to the strikes of 1919–1920. There were riots in many towns; on August 11, thirty-five workers were killed and a hundred wounded in Hamburg, Gelsenkirchen, Krefeld, Aachen, Leipzig, Dresden, Ratibor. On August 12, food riots took place at Hanover, Rotthausen, and Gelsenkirchen, and thirty more demonstrators were killed. On the same day, Gustav Stresemann formed a new cabinet with four Social Democratic members, among them Rudolf Hilferding as Minister of Finance.

Foreign observers agreed that the threat of a social revolution in Germany was imminent, that the next few days would bring final decisions. Paradoxically, the only group convinced that Germany could not proceed toward revolution was the Central Committee of the Communist Party. The factory councils, determined to go forward, met stubborn resistance from their Communist leadership. The Brandler Central Committee was frightened by the dynamism of the movement, which upset all its Reformist Communist time-tables for organized progress within the framework of the Weimar Constitution. If the strike continued, it would obviously develop into a civil war, which would not end merely with the replacement of the Stresemann government by still another parliamentary combination.

With the beginning of the strike, the Central Committee had left the party headquarters in Rosenthalerstrasse in the care of a few minor officials and retired to one of its underground headquarters. This senseless performance—no one would have risked, in the midst of the strike, touching the Central Committee of the Communist Party—only hampered contact between the capital and the provinces. The Central Committee delegated Fritz Heckert to direct the strike from Berlin, with instructions to limit it to economic demands and to bring it to an end as quickly as possible. Brandler insisted on breaking the strike, since it was not officially endorsed by the German Federation of Labor. The Berlin organization, in sharp conflict with Brandler, wanted to coördinate the many local strikes into a movement against the Cuno cabinet. During the initial phase, the Left argued, the trade-union leaders would withhold formal approval, but in fact approve and yield later. This discussion of how to win official trade-union support was based on contradictory interpretations of the entire political crisis.

Local party committees waited for orders from Berlin. They wanted to avoid isolated clashes with the army until the weapons supposedly at the disposal of the Central Committee had been distributed. This concept of military discipline and coördinated action of the revolutionary workers' movement was firmly rooted in the Communist rank and file. The party believed that the Central Committee, with the help of Russian money and the Russian state apparatus, had cached tremendous reserves of weapons and ammunition and that they would gain access to these hidden arsenals only at the moment of the order from supreme Moscow and Berlin headquarters. The Brandler group had circulated impressive statistics in the party concerning weapons already acquired, as well as fantastic rumors about promises of immediate military help by the Red Army. In August 1923, however, Brandler sent his couriers into the Reich not with the go-ahead signal but with confidential orders to the contrary. To the Berlin Committee, he pictured the situation in the Reich in the darkest colors, emphasizing minor difficulties.

On August 13, the Central Committee issued a formal order to end the strike the next day, since its major object—the resignation of the Cuno government—had been attained. Against the resistance of the majority of Berlin factory councils, this party intervention brought the strike in the capital gradually to an end. Elsewhere, for another week, the strike wave jumped from one corner of Germany to another, and on a local scale violent resistance continued for quite a while. Brunswick workers, for instance, threatened "to seize the government," and in the Ruhr and Rhineland, the mines and metal industries were shut down by a renewed wave of strikes on August 20.

President Ebert's designation of Dr. Gustav Stresemann to form a new four-party coalition government had been intended to counter the threat of Communism in Germany. Immediately after he took office, Stresemann warned the Communists that his government would oppose violence with all its power. He urged the press to help in combating Bolshevism. Severing, the Prussian Minister of the Interior, issued an order suppressing the Committee of Fifteen for its "futile attempt at a general strike."

The strike had unexpected results for Radek's policy; the National Bolshevik experiment came to a sudden halt. Stresemann arranged with the British to end the passive resistance in the Ruhr and, with the help of British arbiters, to reorganize the reparations payments. The Moscow Politburo knew of this immediately. A year later, Stresemann told a convention of his party that for more than a year he had consistently followed the same foreign policy. "This policy began during the Ruhr fight and it led toward London."

The turn of German foreign policy was dictated by the fear that, with the inflation spiral out of control, the revolutionary situation in the Ruhr would infect the rest of the country and give momentum to the latent civil war, in which the Communists could easily overthrow the government. Stresemann's evaluation of the prospect for German Communism was nearer to reality than Brandler's. Characteristic of Stresemann's general attitude is his description of a meeting of the National Liberal Women, a conservative nationalist organization of Imperial Germany, which took place one or two weeks after the November revolution:

> At this meeting, there was no cognizance of the 9th of November. There I firmly opposed the lack of civil courage prevailing at that time and the destruction of everything that, until that day, was regarded as sancrosanct. There we toasted the Old Germany and we sang the *Deutschlandlied,* and that in the city of the People's Commissars and the Revolution.[6]

---

[6] "Nationale Realpolitik," speech of Stresemann at the Sixth Party Convention, German People's Party, Dortmund, November 14, 1924, *Flugschriften der Deutschen Volkspartei,* No. 56 (Berlin, 1924), p. 36.

Fear of Bolshevism was a major factor in weakening the pro-Russian policy of the first Cuno cabinet. In Moscow, on the other hand, the consequences in Europe of a British-German coalition seemed so serious that the Politburo leaders interrupted their holidays in the Caucasus and returned to the Kremlin. A conference of the Executive Committee of the Comintern was convoked. In a sharp turn, the Politburo decided to organize the uprising in Germany, to put a staff of several thousand military experts at the disposal of the German party, to accord it unlimited financial help. A definite time-table was set. For the first time, General Secretary Stalin used his new authority to intervene in German affairs.

Zinoviev, Bukharin, Trotsky, and Stalin had been absent from Moscow during the better part of the decisive months of July and August, 1923, exchanging their views as usual by telephone and letters. Kuusinen and Radek, in temporary charge of Comintern affairs, had carried out the policy of discouraging the German Communists, in accordance with the secret orders of the Politburo. During the summer, the Cuno strike had intensified the differences between Zinoviev and Stalin in their interpretations of the German situation. Zinoviev, and with him Bukharin, had recommended street demonstrations against the fascists. That the Russian Politburo was divided on this specific matter was communicated to Brandler, who, by the very fact of these conflicting opinions, felt encouraged to brush aside all opposition to his own cautious line.

Under the influence of the news from Germany and constant pressure from the German Left wing, Zinoviev became less and less certain that the Politburo's decisions on Germany had been based on an adequate grasp of the situation. In the Russian delegation to the Comintern, he spoke to Bukharin, Kuusinen, and Pyatnitsky, attempting to win them over to support a change of policy. (O. V. Kuusinen, a Finn, was not a member of the Russian Politburo, but in the Comintern he was a de facto member of the Russian delegation, with the same weight as, say, Radek or Bukharin in making important decisions.) Any progress in Germany, however, would have shifted the advantage in the Russian faction fight to Zinoviev, as Chairman of the Comintern, by drawing the wavering groups in the Party hierarchy to him. Stalin acted. In a letter to Zinoviev and Bukharin, he took a most vigorous stand against any encouragement to German militants:

> Should the Communists (at the given stage) strive to seize power without the Social Democrats? That, in my opinion, is the question. When we seized power, we had in Russia such reserves as (a) peace, (b) the land to the peasants, (c) the support of the great majority of the working class, (d) the sympathy of the peasantry. The German Communists, at this moment, have nothing of the sort. Of course, they have the Soviet nation as their neighbor, which we did not have, but what can we offer them at the present moment? If today in Germany the power, so to speak, falls, and the Communists seize hold of it, they will fall with a crash. That in the "best" case. And at worst, they will be smashed to pieces and thrown back. The whole thing is not that Brandler wants to "educate the masses," but that the bourgeoisie plus the Right Social Democrats will surely transform the lessons—the demonstrations—into a general battle (at this moment, all the chances are on their side) and exterminate them. Of course, the fascists are not asleep, but it is to our interest that they attack first; that will rally the whole working class around the Communists. (Germany is not Bulgaria.) Besides, according to all information, the fascists are weak in Germany. In my opinion, the Germans must be curbed, and not spurred on.[1]

This letter of Stalin is without doubt an accurate presentation of the official Politburo line until Stresemann turned toward Britain.

Bulgaria Is Not Germany

The Bulgarian crisis to which Stalin referred indicates how differently the Politburo judged the situation in the Balkans from that in

---

[1] *Arbeiterpolitik* (Leipzig, February 9, 1929); quoted in Trotsky, *The Third International After Lenin* (New York, 1936), pp. 322–323. This letter was reproduced by the Brandler opposition in 1929, just after their expulsion, to answer the charge that in 1923 it had consciously and against the advice of the Russian Politburo sabotaged the German revolution. In 1927 Zinoviev had read the same letter into the official Party report at the plenum of the Central Committee and Central Control Commission. He was also defending himself at this time against the accusation of having been responsible for the German defeat in October 1923.

In the official textbooks of Party history, this letter is suppressed: the Stalin group is presented, for instance, by N. Popov and Y. Y. Yaroslavsky, as having encouraged the German Communists.

Germany. At the Lausanne conference in May 1923, Curzon had succeeded in weakening the link between the Turkish nationalist movement and the Soviet Union. This masterpiece of diplomatic skill ended further Russian infiltration into the Near East, and the change in the political scene in Turkey was reflected in the Balkans and especially in Bulgaria.

The government there was headed at this time by Alexander Stamboliyski, the leader of the Agrarian Party. Son of a peasant, he had studied agronomy in Germany. In 1915, when he was a deputy in the Sobranye, the national parliament, he was sentenced to life imprisonment for his opposition to King Ferdinand's pro-German attitude. After Bulgaria's defeat in the World War, Stamboliyski became Prime Minister and signed the Treaty of Neuilly with the Entente powers in 1919. Born and bred in Bulgaria's terrorist tradition, he ruled the country with an iron hand, ruthlessly discriminating against the townspeople. "Sofia, that Sodom, that Gomorrah, may disappear," he declared; "I shall not weep for her." He formed an Orange Guard of peasants to protect his Green dictatorship against uprisings. The Communist Party, like all workers' organizations, was semi-legal, but Stamboliyski maintained cordial relations with Soviet Russia. Following the line set in November 1922 by the Fourth World Congress of the Comintern, the Bulgarian party under Georgi Dimitrov cautiously avoided sharpening the conflict between the restless country and the government.

Georgi Dimitrov, born in 1882 near Sofia, was one of six children of a small-handicraft man who later became a factory worker, all of whom participated in the revolutionary movement of their country. One of his brothers, Constantine, was killed during the Balkan War of 1913; another, Nikola, took part in the Russian revolutionary movement in 1905 in the region of Odessa, was arrested and exiled to Siberia, where he died in 1917. The third brother, Todor, died in a Bulgarian prison in 1925. Both of his sisters were no less active; even his old mother appeared in Comintern performances when needed.

The Bulgarian socialists, natives of a country that had suffered Turkish occupation for five centuries, were contiguous with the Russian terrorists. At the turn of the century the Social Democratic Party had split in two—the so-called "Broad" or revisionist socialists and the

"Narrow" or doctrinaire socialists. In 1903, the year the split was consummated, Dimitrov founded a printers' union; from 1904 to 1923 uninterruptedly, he was general secretary of the Bulgarian Federation of Trade-Unions, in which capacity he traveled about and learned the country thoroughly. He traveled in other Balkan countries as well, particularly in Rumania, and helped from afar to organize the Bulgarian and Macedonian emigration in the United States. From 1913 on, he was also deputy to the Sofia municipal council, the regional council, and the Sobranye.

The party split was reflected in the trade-unions, and Dimitrov could not be moved by either Trotsky or Christian Rakovsky or Carl Legien, all of whom went to Bulgaria in an effort to bring the factions together. He was determined not to yield an inch to the Broad group. The reformists appealed to the trade-union international, which in 1913 convoked a special conference with the Bulgarians to Budapest, but without avail.

In 1919, the Narrow socialists entered the Comintern. The Bolsheviks had a high regard for this well-disciplined Marxist party, with a similar background and development, and gave the Bulgarians a status almost equal to their own in the early work of building the international. From the beginning, Dimitrov was the most prominent of the many Bulgarians used as missionaries and agents to other countries. A tall, rather handsome man, cold, he was regarded as an excellent organizer but a zero in matters of political theory.[2]

---

[2] The career of Georgi Dimitrov has been one of the most illuminating facets of Comintern history, a key to many difficult problems. During the twenties he became the Comintern's principal organizer in the Balkans, always a major concern of Soviet foreign policy, with his headquarters shifted periodically from Yugoslavia to Vienna and Berlin. During these years, he gained in stature and ended as one of the very few non-Russians—Kuusinen is another—with a power in the Comintern almost equal to that of the Politburo members.

At the beginning of the Nazi regime, on March 9, 1933, he was arrested in Berlin as a Comintern agent. Together with his Bulgarian assistants, Blagoi Popov and Vasil Tanev, the German Ernst Torgler, and the Hollander Marinus van der Lubbe, he was accused of having set fire to the Reichstag. The duel in the courtroom between Göring and Dimitrov was a spectacle that the whole world watched with fascination. Both the Nazi and the Stalinist propaganda machines were put in high gear, and behind the mountains of fanciful lies and half-truths, it was difficult at the time to discern what was happening. At the climax, however, one blunt fact protruded through the elaborately contrived mask: after having been hounded for three months in a Nazi court, Dimitrov was extradited to Russia.

While the trial was running its course, I met two of the important witnesses in

On June 9, 1923, the Stamboliyski cabinet was overthrown by an army coup ignited by Macedonian terrorists but led by Professor Alexander Tsankov, who, discreetly encouraged by certain British advisors, had formed the Democratic Entente, comprising the urban bourgeoisie, the intelligentsia, the Social Democratic Party, and the League of Active Officers (patronized especially by King Boris III, well known for his pro-German and anti-Bolshevik sympathies). Dimitrov and his party continued to follow the directive of the Comintern. The Bulgarian Communists remained neutral in the conflict between Tsankov and Stamboliyski; any other position than this passivity would have been "adventurist putschism." Thousands of Stamboliyski's followers were

Paris—Wilhelm Pieck, who at this time was eager to speak to Maslow and me, and Maria Reese, a Communist Reichstag deputy and the intimate friend of Torgler. (Later she returned to Germany and became a Nazi sympathizer, but this fact does not impinge on her creditability; she was getting the full details from Torgler's lawyer, with whom she was in almost daily contact.) Independently, both told me the same story, that before Dimitrov stood up in the courtroom to make his courageous peroration, he knew of the secret arrangement between the GPU and the Gestapo that he would leave it a free man. The other two Bulgarians were included in the arrangement, but Torgler and van der Lubbe were not. Pieck and Reese were both much concerned with this fact, but from different points of view. Pieck, knowing that Torgler had been abandoned by the Politburo, was fearful that he might see through the combination and make a statement in the courtroom baring the secret deal between the two state police forces. When I saw him, therefore, Pieck was busy arranging for a refugee from underground Germany to arrive in London with the startling message that Torgler was a traitor to the anti-fascist cause. Maria Reese's reaction, of course, was quite different; she later wrote a pamphlet breaking with Communism but with only vague allusions to the deal, since she hoped to save Torgler's life and did not want to antagonize the Gestapo. Pieck's courier did go to London and delivered his message in a loud stage whisper, but since Torgler never revealed the arrangement by which Dimitrov was saved, the charge against Torgler was allowed to peter out. Van der Lubbe was executed, and the other four defendants acquitted. "Torgler heard without visible emotion the announcement of an acquittal, which carried no prospect of freedom. Dimitrov, Popov, and Tanev showed neither relief nor gratification but quietly resumed their seats." (Douglas Reed, *The Burning of the Reichstag,* London, 1934, p. 331.) When Bulgaria refused to accept its three nationals, Russia made them Soviet citizens and Dimitrov, Popov, and Tanev were sent to their new fatherland in a plane.

After this triumphant return to Moscow, Dimitrov became the No. 1 Anti-Fascist Martyr and shared the leading place in the Comintern with Dmitri Manuilsky. At the Seventh World Congress in 1935, the one that set the People's Front policy, Dimitrov was acclaimed almost as noisily as Stalin himself. After Russia's victory over the Nazis, he was returned to his native land of Bulgaria, which he has since ruled in the best terrorist tradition, but his future is not bounded by this corner of the Balkans. He has remained especially close to the German Communists and all their Free Germany emanations. If there is to be a Stalinist United States of Europe, one of its principal officers may be Georgi Dimitrov.

arrested and he himself was assassinated after a three-day hunt; there were riots and skirmishes between revolting peasants and the new government. The Communist Party suffered increased persecution, and Dimitrov had to go underground.

Behind the scenes it was obvious that the change of the political picture in Bulgaria was closely connected with that in Turkey, and the Russian Politburo, feeling the pressure of the tightening British security belt, immediately threw all principles about "adventurist putschism" overboard as far as the Bulgarian Communists were concerned. Dimitrov and his friends were called to Moscow, and at the same June session of the Comintern Executive Committee at which Radek made his touching appeal to the honest nationalist masses of Germany, the Bulgarian Communists were severely criticized for their opportunist errors. The same Radek who opposed an anti-fascist demonstration in Berlin as too dangerous for the strong Communist Party of Germany, argued vigorously against the passive attitude of the Bulgarian Communist, Vasil Kolarov. The Bulgarian party had underestimated the peasantry, had defended Macedonian autonomy within a Balkan federation, and had thus been responsible for a serious defeat.

> We are of the opinion [Radek said] that the coup d'état in Bulgaria represents a serious defeat of our party. We like to hope that it will not be an annihilating defeat. But it is certainly the greatest defeat a Communist party has ever experienced. . . . The Bulgarian party endeavors not to understand its defeat but, on the contrary, to adorn it. We have before us the appeals of the Bulgarian party; they are the sorriest feature of the whole defeat. We have the appeal of June 9, the appeal of the 15th, and a whole series of articles. The party defended the following standpoint: Two cliques of the bourgeoisie are fighting; we, the working class, stand aside and we hope and demand that we will be vouchsafed freedom of the press and all sorts of good things.[3]

Without consulting any other Comintern parties, the Russian Politburo ordered the Bulgarian Communists to prepare a military counter blow. A group of military advisers selected by the intelligence service of the Red Army was sent to Bulgaria under various disguises. The

---

[3] Karl Radek, "Der Umsturz in Bulgarien," *Die Kommunistische Internationale,* No. 27 (Hamburg, 1923), pp. 115–120. The text reads: "We have the appeal of February 9, the appeal of the 15th . . ."; but this is obviously an error.

Bulgarian party was given a large fund to organize an uprising in early fall. In the view of Radek, one of the instigators of this Bulgarian plot, its goal should be not a Bulgarian soviet republic but the return of the Agrarian Party to power. Reinstalled with the aid of the Bulgarian Communists, after a bloody battle with the Tsankov regime, the Agrarians would be dependent on Communist support. Their government, compelled to adopt a friendly attitude towards Soviet Russia, would block British influence in the Balkans and the Near East. For the Russian Politburo, the Bulgarian uprising was not the beginning of a new European wave of Communist revolution but a prop to Russian influence in the Balkans.

In the middle of August, Dimitrov reported to Moscow that he foresaw the possibility of definite action at the end of September; this message coincided with the unexpected Cuno strike in Berlin. Reviewing reports of the strike movement and the growing unrest in all parts of Germany, the Politburo compared them with reports on the preparations for the Bulgarian coup d'état.

Secret Session in Moscow

Only weak echoes of the Russian Party crisis and the imminent action in Bulgaria were heard in the Berlin Communist headquarters, which was engrossed in the German situation to the virtual exclusion of anything else. Brandler, fearing that if the sharp division in the Russian Politburo became known in the German party, this would hinder him in carrying out his policies, carefully kept all information that Radek sent him within his own intimate circle. The Left was not interested in Trotsky, who for them was primarily a close friend of their arch adversary, Karl Radek.

During the summer of 1923, several members of the Workers' Opposition, among them Shlyapnikov, came to Berlin and conferred secretly with the Berlin opposition. They reported on the situation within the Russian Party and the Comintern in the darkest colors. In the opinion of these Russian oppositionists, it was necessary to prepare a split; under the leadership of the Russian Politburo no revolutionary action in Germany would be possible. The Left was not disposed to split the party in the midst of the general crisis, but plans were made for intimate coöperation among the various Left oppositionist groups within the Comintern. Popov's statement in this regard is quite correct.[4]

The Brandler group was of course informed on the secret conference between the Russian and the German Left-wingers. They reported it to the Russian Politburo and asked for the immediate removal of Maslow, the Berlin party leader, who had organized the clandestine contacts. Without Maslow, the Berlin organization would be easier to handle.

In Moscow, Stresemann's pending rearrangement with Britain had brought Stalin over to support a turn in German Communist policy. Every one of the Russian leaders was now eager to come out as a promoter of the German revolution—Zinoviev, Bukharin, Trotsky. Only Radek did not give up his own line. By a decision of the Politburo, Zinoviev, as Comintern Chairman, called the German leaders to Moscow to confer in a special meeting of the Comintern Executive Committee. The conference, devoted principally to military strategy rather than politics, went on during September and the first week of October —coinciding with the Trotsky crisis in the Central Committee. Only five parties other than the Russian—the French, Czech, Polish, Bulgarian, and German—were represented, and these mostly from the staff at Comintern headquarters. This was no conference for propagandistic purposes; behind closed doors the Russian Politburo debated with the German delegation the details of the planned uprising.

When Brandler arrived in Moscow, he got the shock of his life. He found it plastered with slogans welcoming the German revolution. Banners and streamers were posted in the center of the city with such slogans as "Russian Youth, Learn German—the German October Is Approaching." Pictures of Clara Zetkin, Rosa Luxemburg, and Karl Liebknecht were to be seen in every shop window. In all factories, meetings were called to discuss "How Can We Help the German Revolution?"

Brandler arrived first, at the end of August, followed by several of his staff. However, the Brandlerites had to warm their feet for several weeks before the arrival of the Russians, who were involved in their own Party crisis. Brandler used this time to prepare, with the support of Kuusinen and Radek, an investigation committee against

---

[4] See N. Popov, *Outline History of the CPSU*, II, 192.

Maslow. Only then, after Brandler had finished his preparations, were the Left leaders also called to Moscow, partly to participate in the debate but mainly to give Radek the possibility of holding Maslow and me back in Moscow after it.

Brandler had gone to Russia certain that his policy would be continued. His proposals were all intended to exploit further the economic crisis for Communist propaganda and to reach a united front with the Left wing of the Social Democratic Party, especially in Saxony and Thuringia, culminating possibly in the participation of the Communist ministers in a coalition cabinet.

Immediately after Brandler's arrival, Karl Radek told him of the about face of the Politburo. Brandler felt himself cornered; in the intimate circles of his devoted friends, he discussed the possibility of open rebellion against this "idiotic adventurist course." At home in Germany, however, the party had been held to a moderate Brandler line only by the support Brandler had been given by the Executive Committee of the international. Once the party learned that he was no longer thus backed, he would have no hope of holding it. If he attempted an open revolt, he would be thrown out by his own friends; his Central Committee was composed of irresolute characters who fought the Left but were nevertheless very much under its influence. They criticized Brandler constantly and hamstrung his attempts to establish an alliance with the Social Democratic Party. Brandler knew that his men would desert him immediately and organize a new faction if he opposed the Russian proposals.

Therefore, he decided to compromise. He accepted the Russian line "in general." He did not object to characterizing the situation in Germany as "revolutionary." On the contrary, driven by his temperament and his ambition, he completed the political picture held by the Russians with distorted and inexact descriptions of the situation in Germany, presented with the intention of characterizing his own followers in Saxony and Thuringia as more revolutionary than the others. Behaving like the leader not of the whole party but of his own faction, he described the two states in such fashion that the Russians were given the impression that the Communist Party already had a key position there.

Saxony and Thuringia, according to Brandler, were completely in the hands of the Red Hundreds. The Hundreds, moreover, were armed—a most important point. In an article in *Pravda,* for instance, Brandler described the Thuringian workers living in scattered industrial hamlets like a kind of Caucasian tribe. The Thuringian workers, he intimated, all had their rifles hidden behind their kitchen stoves. If the party were to give the signal, they would rise to be formed into military units in a minute. In Saxony, industry is almost completely under control of the workers, he said. And, in addition to that, a powerful network of consumers' groups, composed of all strata of the population, had effectively organized the economic life of the state. This fanciful presentation was ardently seconded by Walther Ulbricht, the ambitious Thuringian organizer.

I remember these reports very vividly. Could the Russian Politburo be taken in by such distortions, or were they merely pretending to adopt Brandler's views? The Left wing was forced to be less "revolutionary" than Brandler and to modify his picture with a more sober survey. Today, I think that to a certain extent even Zinoviev, and certainly Trotsky, who did not know the German situation in detail, were impressed by Brandler's phantasmagoria. Brandler had a certain status among the Russians as a German trade-unionist and Communist, as a person with a good mixture of revolutionary élan and down-to-earth sense.

In any case, the Russian Politburo got the impression that an armed nucleus existed in Germany that could be developed by energetic intervention from the outside. Since an uprising had definitely been approved, the matter of the armed kernel, willing to fight, was of major importance. At this time no one would have proposed an uprising without organized armed groups willing to go ahead.

There was general unanimity concerning the Ruhr situation. "The slogan of the Red Hundreds was effective only in the Ruhr district, where it had such a reality that the Red Hundreds were growing like mushrooms, with tremendous speed."[5]

The Brandler group's report of serious symptoms of growing disintegration in the Reichswehr was correct so far as the relations between it and the Communist apparatus were concerned. But the picture was again distorted when these contacts were presented as in-

---

[5] August Thalheimer, *1923: Eine verpasste Revolution?*, p. 19.

cluding Communist leadership of the Reichswehr opposition. The various pro-Russian groups of the Reichswehr, far from accepting the the leadership of the German Communist Party, had formed links with Russian Communist politicians principally with an eye to getting a military alliance, or at least political support from Russia, in a war against France. The Reichswehr did not want to be transformed into a German Red Army; it wanted to exploit the Communists, by means of vague promises that the party would have a changed status in an army-governed Germany, becoming a transmission belt to the Soviet government. This pro-Russian tendency in the Reichswehr, moreover, was blocked by a stronger group, which aimed at exterminating the Communist Party and establishing a military dictatorship unhampered by socialist and pacifist quibblers. In the September conference, however, Brandler's presentation implied that a group of the Reichswehr would be willing to fight under Communist command, neutralizing the other part of the army. And it was assumed that this portion of the Reichswehr would accept a larger Communist influence in Germany in exchange for a Russian alliance against the Versailles Treaty.

Also, the possibility was taken into serious consideration that important groups of officers would come over to the Communist side in the course of events. Hans von Hentig, a member of a conservative family, was a major contact with the Reichswehr for the Brandler Central Committee. Through his brother, a diplomat who remained in the service after Hitler took power, Hentig had valuable inside information. As organizer of the party's military apparatus in Thuringia, he was charged with buying weapons. Together with the Russian expert, Skoblevsky, and others, he mapped the plan for the uprising. The two Hentig brothers are typical, in different ways, of the conservative elements that came under the influence of Russian Communism via German National Bolshevism.

Communist propaganda pictured the economic situation, as always, in terms of complete collapse of the capitalist system in Germany. However, before the turn in September, the prevailing school of thought in the Russian Party was inclined to consider the European capitalist economy as on its way to recovery. On the very day the Communists entered the Saxony government, the leading economist of the Comintern, Eugen Varga, expressed this opinion as follows:

The first period of economic stabilization in Germany begins with August 15. The workers had achieved through their mass movement an adjustment of their salaries to the increasing prices. . . . The introduction of a sliding wage scale under the pressure of general strike made the continued inflation of the mark superfluous. At the end of August, a whole series of plans for the creation of a new stable currency appeared.

Social Democratic workers had a waiting attitude, they expected stabilization.[6]

On September 11, definite news reached Moscow that German-French negotiations had begun. This was decisive. Zinoviev was able immediately to get a decision from the Politburo to push forward the uprisings in both Bulgaria and Germany. He was still opposed by Radek and Varga, but he had the support of Trotsky and Bukharin. Trotsky, the internationalist, was certain that a change in Europe would be reflected in a favorable turn in the life of the Russian Party.

Dimitrov was sent a message to go ahead at the end of September, and the beginning of October was proposed for Germany. But when Brandler was asked to fix a starting date, he met the proposal with stubborn resistance. Even after the reversal of policy, he had expected nothing more definite than a general directive, in whose vague terms he would still have found ample room to maneuver. Zinoviev did not want to issue a specific order to the German delegation over their objection, both because this was contrary to the Comintern mores of that period and because of his own attitude before the Bolshevik revolution of November 1917.

A scholastic discussion ensued, a most bizarre introduction to the events in Germany, around the question of whether Marxists can set in advance the date for a revolutionary uprising, and, in particular, whether such a date could now be set in the case of Germany. Trotsky, in the midst of his political struggle within the Russian Party, proposed a time-table of events up to a climax on the 7th or 9th of November. Without over-emphasizing these historical dates, he pointed out the value of such symbolism for mass mobilization. Brandler, panicky over Trotsky's proposal, threatened the Politburo with his immediate departure. He did not say, of course, that he was against

---

[6] A. Pawlowski [Varga], *Vor dem Endkampf in Deutschland* (Hamburg, 1923), pp. 42, 47.

the whole action: he reiterated that it was impossible to set a date, that such an arbitrary date would have disastrous consequences for the party and for his own relation to the Left. Zinoviev, the compromiser, found a way out. Solemnly, he asked Brandler whether he objected on "principled grounds." That, of course, Brandler denied. In principle he was "for the revolution." Trotsky's proposal to set a date was dropped, not on "principled grounds," but with the argument that the German Communists should themselves fix the time of the uprising. But since it was hoped that the Bulgarian uprising, expected to start in the very near future, would prove a considerable stimulus to the German revolution, it was decided that the uprising should take place in the next four to eight weeks.

After this incident, another fog-bound discussion started. Should the German comrades or should they not organize "soviets"? Both Left and Right agreed that factory councils, which had played the key role in the Cuno strike, should be developed into the pivotal organizations. The two wings had different reasons for their attitude, but for one moment they were in terminological agreement. Both Zinoviev and Trotsky advocated the election of soviets, with a broader range of activity than that of the factory councils already in existence. Radek opposed this proposal vehemently, and from his point of view correctly, for the development of a soviet movement would, by its very nature, have compelled him to carry out the decisions of the Comintern more than he wanted to. The final decision to support the factory councils gave him and Brandler much more possibility of avoiding definite commitments.

Meanwhile, Dimitrov and Koralov had left Sofia and set up a secret headquarters in Northwest Bulgaria, selected for its better communication facilities with Moscow. They organized a "Committee for Revolutionary War," distributed arms to peasants' and workers' groups, and mapped out a plan with experts of the Red Army's General Staff. According to Comintern legend, the uprising was defeated mainly by treason, which gave the government advance warning and enabled it to prepare against the partisans. Actually, however, the country resisted being absorbed into the Soviet orbit, and, moreover, the Bulgarian party could not shift quickly enough from the united-front policy to armed action. After being routed by government troops, about a thousand guerrillas slowly withdrew into Yugoslavia. In spite of this unsuccessful ending, the action was for Dimitrov an important step up to his later brilliant Comintern career.[7]

In Moscow, news of the Bulgarian defeat reinforced the pessimism of Radek and Brandler, but Zinoviev and Trotsky regarded it as a temporary setback, which would be corrected by a favorable development in Germany. The discussion at the conference turned now to technical preparations; in small sub-committees the general strategic plan of the German uprising was sketched out. After a short preliminary period of intense propaganda, the Communist Party was to enter the governments of Saxony and Thuringia. In these governments, the Communists would concentrate all their energies on arming the workers; their task would be to organize an army of proletarian units, based on the Red Hundreds in factories and industrial villages. After this brief preparatory stage, a general uprising would be declared by the Red governments of Saxony and Thuringia, which would give other regions immediate armed help in their fight against the counter revolution. The Red Army of Saxony would march to Berlin, and the Thuringians to Munich, the centers of the counter revolution, and during its march the Red Army of Central Germany would rally around itself all forces willing to overthrow the government.

The new government would not be composed entirely of Communist leaders, but would include Left Social Democrats, trade-unionists, and National Bolshevik officers. Its domestic policy would be directed towards the immediate socialization of heavy industry only; small business and the peasantry were not to be antagonized by state intervention. The big landowners of East Prussia, Pomerania, Meck-

---

[7] The Comintern has never denied its role in the 1923 Bulgarian uprising. On the contrary, in the Stalinist history of the glorious revolutionary past, quite a few pages are devoted to this action in the Balkans. "The uprising of the Bulgarian workers and peasants against fascism and for a workers' and peasants' government broke out on September 23, under the leadership of the Communist Party. As plenipotentiary of the Central Committee of the Communist Party of Bulgaria, Dimitrov took a leading part." (Stella D. Blagojewa, *Dimitroff, Aus dem Leben eines Revolutionärs* (Moscow, 1934), p. 50.)

On November 23, 1933, at the Reichstag-fire trial, Dimitrov boasted of his role in the Bulgarian events. "I am proud of the heroic September uprising. My only regret is that at that time I and my party were not yet real Bolsheviks. For this reason, we were not able successfully to organize and lead this historic popular revolt, at whose head stood the proletariat." (*Ibid.*, p. 51.)

lenburg, and Upper Silesia would be expropriated and their land divided among poor peasants.

Blueprint for a German Red Army

The conference decided to carry out this plan with the maximum of technical and military preparation. The political implications seemed less important than counterbalancing the resistance expected from parts of the Reichswehr and the counter-revolutionary corps by organizing as many Red military formations as possible. The Central Committee of the German party and even its Politburo were regarded as too large for such a task. A committee of seven members was to have dictatorial powers, entitling it to appoint comrades to posts over the heads of the elected regional committees; and the disposition of funds was given into the hands of Brandler, assisted by Pieck and Eberlein.

In the actual military force, the Red Hundreds would be supplemented by the M-Apparat and the intelligence service of the Red Army. Since the Red Hundreds were semi-legal and with only rudimentary liaison, their staff was considered unfit for command posts. The secret military groups of the German party, on the other hand, were a small but highly disciplined band of shock troops, led by men who had gained some military experience either in the Imperial army or during short training periods in Russia. Before 1923, however, the military training of foreign Communists in Russia had been sporadic and ineffective, and the conference made the major decision of assigning several hundred Red Army officers to lead these clandestine military groups of the German party. Many of these were not Russian, but Austrian, Hungarian, Serbian, Polish, or other foreign Communists who had fought in the civil war in Russia and later entered the Red Army; as Central Europeans, these were felt to be more suitable. The transfer of these officers was entirely through Russian channels; assigned to their posts, the men proceeded to them in various disguises and then reported exclusively to their Russian superiors, the residents of the OMS in the Russian Embassy.[8] This multinational group of Communists sent

---

[8] "The heart of the Comintern is the little known and never publicized International Liaison Section, known by its Russian initials as the OMS (*Otdyel Mezhdunarodnoi Svyazi*). Until the purge got under way, the OMS was headed by

to Germany in September 1923 can well be compared with the International Brigade in Spain thirteen years later, of which indeed it was an abortive form.

Finally, there was a group of Russian military intelligence agents. They maintained contact with the military apparatus of the German party but remained apart from it, receiving their orders directly from the Red Army staff in Moscow. Their principal task was liaison to the oppositionist officers of the Reichswehr. Walter Krivitsky, one of the chiefs of this department, was sent to Berlin, where he organized the three secret services of the German party. Concerning his mission, he writes:

> When news reached our department of the French occupation of the Ruhr, a group of five or six officers, including myself, were ordered to leave at once for Germany. . . .
>
> We at once created three types of organizations in the German Communist Party; the Party Intelligence Service working under the guidance of the Fourth Department of the Red Army; military formations as the nucleus of the future German Red Army, and *Zersetzungsdienst,* small units of men whose function was to shatter the morale of the Reichswehr and the police.[9]

[Ossip A.] Pyatnitsky, a veteran Bolshevik, trained during the Tsarist regime in the practical business of distributing illegal revolutionary propaganda . . . As the chief of the OMS he became in effect the Finance Minister and Director of Personnel of the Comintern." (W. G. Krivitsky, *In Stalin's Secret Service, an Exposé of Russia's Secret Policies by the Former Chief of the Soviet Intelligence in Western Europe,* New York: Harper and Brothers, 1939, pp. 51–52.)

One of the most important OMS residents in Berlin, Mirov-Abramov, was executed in 1937, accused of having sent Trotsky large sums of money given to him by Yagoda, then chief of the GPU. Mirov-Abramov was never a Trotskyite; he was a Comintern technician who knew too much.

[9] W. G. Krivitsky, *In Stalin's Secret Service,* pp. 38–39. Krivitsky was especially interested in the organization of terrorist groups and had a certain respect for them. This contrasts sharply with his contempt for almost all legal Communist organizations. These groups were composed of good, fanatically devoted militants, according to Krivitsky.

"I recall a meeting of one of these groups on a September evening in the city of Essen, shortly before the Communist uprising. I recall how they came together, quietly, almost solemnly, to receive their orders. Their commander announced tersely:

" 'Tonight we act.'

"Calmly they took out their revolvers, checked them for the last time, and filed out one by one. The very next day the Essen press reported the discovery of the body of a murdered police officer, assassin unknown. For weeks these groups struck swiftly and effectively in various parts of Germany, picking off police officers and other enemies of the Communist cause." (*Ibid.,* p. 43.)

With this officer corps as a center, a skeleton of a regular army was set up in the plan, with not only a general staff but artillery officers, machine-gunners, a signal corps, and so on. Special commissions of the military apparatus were assigned to buy all the weapons and munitions available on Germany's well-stocked black market. Gathered in secret regional headquarters, these weapons would be distributed a few days before the coup. Larger groups of German Communists would undergo the four or five weeks of basic military training, which included maneuvers of several days to train them for prolonged night marches and guerrilla fighting. In this schedule for maneuvers, the courier service—including a chain of bicycle and motorcycle riders, radio operators, and carrier pigeons—would act to transform the skeleton groups rapidly into a mass army.

Any Reichswehr officer willing to join the embryonic Red Army would be most carefully considered. He would immediately be assigned to the actual fighting and entrusted with higher posts of command, but surrounded by reliable comrades. If a Reichswehr officer offered his services, unless there was definite proof that he was acting as a spy, he would be questioned by Russian experts and attached to the regional staff; and this fact would be made known to his comrades in the Reichswehr. The enigma in the plan remained the German Reichswehr. How would the army react? Would the officers again take the lead and rally the various illegal military formations, welding them into a unit to crush the military organization of the workers? In Berlin the Reichswehr would have all the advantages in the initial stage. The plan designated Saxony and Thuringia as the starting point of the fighting partly because there were no Reichswehr contingents of importance in these provinces. That a mass army could here be quickly organized seemed self-evident and beyond discussion. Berlin, symbol of the German Reich, surrounded by Brandenburg garrisons, was regarded as one of the most difficult points to take but also the most decisive one. All organizations in the Reich were to be given strict orders to await the signal from Saxony.

Trotsky gave his wholehearted authority and support to the military preparation of the German revolution. He helped with technical advice; he was interested in many minor details. Several times he discussed with Brandler the military complications of the coming struggle; for a time at least, Trotsky considered Brandler the right man for the job. There was a good, almost warm, relation in these weeks between the two men, who shared a dislike for Zinoviev, the opponent of Brandler in the Comintern and of Trotsky in Russia.

The leading Left-wingers were convinced that all these military preparations were valueless. They knew that the military apparatus was a dilettante organization, the hideout for many members estranged from the real life of the party, who would prove weak in a moment of emergency. They were inclined to believe, moreover, that the favorable moment had passed after the Cuno strike, that the workers now felt that the compromise with Great Britain would help the German economy out of its impasse. Even so, if the conflict was now to be sharpened, the accent had to be on the political action, on the expansion of the activities of factory councils, on intensified mass propaganda and mass organization for a Communist solution of the German crisis. A coalition cabinet in Saxony and Thuringia, I was sure, would not stimulate Berlin or the Ruhr, unless it was followed by, for instance, occupation of factories by workers' committees, open military organization in all industrial centers, armed demonstrations, and, finally, the formation of dual government—regional and Reich committees of factory councils, proclaiming their aspiration to rule Germany from now on. The Reichswehr could be crushed only by such an array of revolutionary labor organizations, to which the various secret party apparatuses would be of additional help, no more and no less. Cut off from the unfolding of a revolutionary mass movement, these military groups could produce nothing more than isolated riots, easily crushed by the authorities.

During the discussion, Brandler was constantly pondering on a workable counter plan, which could be effected, he knew, only after eliminating the criticism of the Left leaders, who were much better able to follow his devious policy than any Russian observer. Thus, Brandler accepted the Comintern program on the condition that the two outstanding Left-wingers, Maslow and I, be held back in Moscow. There was a conflict around this point in a subcommittee of the Russian Politburo. Trotsky was willing to accept Brandler's stipulation; according to Kuusinen,[10] after a bitter fight Zinoviev was

---

[10] "A Misleading Description of the 'German October,'" *The Errors of Trotskyism.* Communist Party of Great Britain (London, 1925), pp. 350–351.

able to get only a small majority for his compromise proposal, by which I would return to Berlin and Maslow would remain in Moscow. According to the German party constitution, Maslow could not be held back against the will of the Berlin organization, which, having sent him solely as a delegate to the conference, was loudly demanding his return. The most convenient means of detaining him was to bring him before a committee to investigate some obscure points in his personal history, after which his immediate return to Berlin was promised. Against such a procedure very little could be done, for insinuations of this kind against high party functionaries had to be brought before the International Control Commission.

On Brandler's insistence, another curious procedure was decided on. The Politburo selected Vasily Schmidt—a close friend of Tomsky, the chairman of the trade-unions—to be my personal advisor in the coming battle of the Berlin Communists against the counter revolution. Schmidt's presence was meant to guarantee the military discipline of the Berlin organization; whenever we differed, he would have the last word, in the name of the Russian Politburo. He was one of the four Comintern delegates sent to Germany during the revolutionary upheaval; the others were Radek, who headed the group, August Guralsky-Kleine, and "General" Alexis Skoblevsky.

Brandler left Moscow on the 9th or 10th of October. As I left the Kremlin, I saw Trotsky bidding farewell to Brandler, whom he had accompanied from his residence inside the Kremlin to the Troitzki gate—an unusual gesture of extreme politeness. There they stood, in the sharp light of an autumn afternoon, the stocky Brandler, in his unpressed civilian suit, and the elegant Trotsky in his well-cut Red Army uniform. After the last words, Trotsky kissed Brandler tenderly on both cheeks in the usual Russian manner. Knowing both men well, I could see that Trotsky was really moved; he felt that he was wishing well the leader of the German revolution on the eve of great events. With juvenile contempt, I watched this emotional farewell. In the bitterest of moods, I passed through the gate, fully convinced that we were running towards disaster.

With false passports, Schmidt and I traveled together via Eydtkuhnen into East Prussia. I had the feeling that the frontier guards of Latvia, Lithuania, and even Germany had been informed that an important Russian dignitary would pass there incognito and should be treated with special consideration.

On our trip, we of course discussed the German situation. Schmidt was a simple, agreeable fellow, a Russian trade-unionist and a good organizer, but of the utmost naïveté in all matters of foreign policy. Not particularly interested in German affairs, he had never studied the country and knew only what he had read in some recent reports. He questioned me especially about trade-unions. When I gave him the usual party report, counting on my fingertips the oppositionist factions we had in the unions, he shook his head. "Bad, very bad," he said; "unions should not be split." He asked similar disarmingly innocent questions about other German matters, including even geography, but the question that most startled me was, "What is the USPD?"

One of the party's various secret offices was in the back room of a small dairy on Hauptstrasse in Berlin-Schöneberg, where the Berlin organizational secretary, Hans Pfeiffer (nicknamed "Kartothekovich" because of his love for indices), sat with his files, busy with sordid routine work. Here I installed Schmidt comfortably, and here he spent the better part of his Berlin sojourn. He attended, of course, all meetings of the Berlin committee, but with his rudimentary German he could follow their proceedings only with difficulty.[11]

Total Mobilization of the Party

When I arrived in Berlin in the middle of October, I found the attitude of the party completely changed. The German Politburo had not waited for the decision of the Moscow conference to reach it. Already in the middle of September, a substantial group of Russian advisers and technical experts had arrived in Germany, of whom one of

---

[11] Vasily V. Schmidt, born in 1886, entered the Bolshevik Party in 1905 and devoted his principal energy to the organization of metal workers in St. Petersburg. From 1918 to 1928 he was People's Commissar for Labor and secretary of the All-Russian Trade-Union Council; for a period he was vice-president of the Council of People's Commissars. In 1930, because of his association with Tomsky, he was demoted from trade-union work and became vice-president of the People's Commissariat for Agriculture. In 1933, because of his continued association with the Right bloc, he was removed from all posts and demoted to economic work. In 1938, he was mentioned by Vyshinsky in the Bukharin trial as one who had helped Tomsky in his oppositionist conspiracy. He did not appear at the trial, however, or since then, and it is probable that he was killed during the purges.

the most prominent was General Skoblevsky.[12] He was an invisible member of the Directorium, made up officially of the seven members of the German Central Committee who had been designated to lead the revolution. One of his main assistants was Hans Kiepenberger, who was in charge of disruption in army, police, and monarchist units.

---

[12] With the German Communists, Margies and Felix Neumann, he was a defendant in the so-called Cheka Trial, in Leipzig, February–April 1925. In preparation for the 1923 uprising, "the German Cheka" had planned assassinations of, among others, General von Seeckt and Hugo Stinnes.

With boyish pride, Heinz Neumann (not related to Felix, but also involved in these plots) has told me how he spent many mornings observing Seeckt's regular walk through the Tiergarten, trying to judge the best place for an ambush. It should not be surprising to find even such a man as Seeckt, who until his death advocated coöperation with the Red Army, the object of a GPU plot. Among the highly political Russian agents operating in Germany, there certainly was opposition to collaborating with the Reichswehr, and Seeckt was regarded as the officer who would offer most effective resistance to a Communist coup. The Berlin branch may have been encouraged to organize a *provokatzia,* a provocation, for solving political problems by terror was already a favorite method among the men of the secret apparatus. The T-Group organized by Felix Neumann, however, actually carried out only one murder, that of the barber and former party member, the "traitor" Johann Rausch.

In 1925, relations between the Red Army and the Reichswehr were very cordial, and the danger of a Communist revolt seemed to have passed. The trial, therefore, was more a farce than a serious investigation. The court and the newspapers collaborated in confusing the issues and in emphasizing those minor details of the German Cheka that made the whole affair seem ridiculous. Skoblevsky was accused of having received $200,000 to purchase explosives, dumdum bullets, poison bacilli, bombs, and other munitions.

The trial is one of the very few objective proofs that an important group of Russian military experts was sent to Germany in 1923. Most of the evidence was dismissed by the average German citizen as mediocre melodrama, but even some of the most fantastic details were accurate to the letter. Heinz Neumann has told me how he and his GPU friends experimented with cholera bacilli. They fed impregnated cabbage leaves to rabbits, but with their amateurish technique the germs died and the rabbits ate and grew fat. Threatening notes to adversaries were actually signed "The League of Red Cats"; this kind of dadaistic kitsch was popular among the children of the *Proletkult.* (Cf. Dr. Arthur Brandt, *Der Tscheka-Prozess,* Berlin, 1925.)

Margies and Felix Neumann received long prison sentences. Margies became a party martyr, but Neumann, because he had reported some details of the organization, was condemned by the Communist apparatus as a spy and a traitor. After his release from prison, he disappeared into obscurity. Skoblevsky was sentenced to death, but he was never executed. He was exchanged for Karl Kindermann and Theodor Wolscht, two German students who had been defendants in a trial in Moscow parallel with that of the German Cheka.

Together with a third student, Max von Ditmar, a native of Estonia, these two young men had gone to Russia with letters of introduction to Lunacharsky and Krupskaya from, among others, Theodor Liebknecht and Oscar Cohen, a lawyer and a member of the USPD. In a letter to Dzerzhinsky, Kindermann confessed that

The political and military activities of the party were strictly separated. All party members fit for military service were drafted by their locals and assigned to special tasks. In order to protect the party staff against untimely arrests, some ten thousand functionaries were ordered to leave their homes, to see their families only occasionally, and to live in underground quarters. The shock troops of the Red Hundreds were quartered in part in dormitories; the secret stock of arms was taken to local caches, from which they could be quickly distributed. The M-Apparat procured military maps of all the regions considered important, on which were marked the public buildings to be seized. Surprise attacks on police and Reichswehr barracks were sketched. As a final touch, the Directorium designated the assembly points for the Red Hundreds of Berlin, Saxony, and Thuringia.

These preparations, of course, were not of equal intensity throughout the Reich. In the industrial centers, and in the strongpoints of Communist organization, they had real scope, drawing in many Social Democrats. There was a remarkable harmony between Communist and Social Democratic workers with regard to their common military defense against monarchists, Hitlerites, fascists, counter-revolutionaries. Since the summer of 1923, "everybody" in Germany expected a monarchist or a fascist putsch in Bavaria, which fact redounded in broad sympathy among the people for the Communist preparations for military resistance. The Ruhr occupation, the inflation, and this daily expected fascist coup in Bavaria had abraded the four-year-old constitutional procedure to a thin façade. The masses wanted a military organization to pit against the professional military skill of their adversaries.

The party membership gave sincere and whole-hearted support to

---

they had plotted to assassinate Stalin, Trotsky, Zinoviev, and Dzerzhinsky himself. According to the indictment, the three defendants (as well as a fourth, a certain Baumann, who was not present at the trial) were members of the Organization Consul. Heinz Neumann, who was twenty-three years old at the time, testified at the trial as an expert on this and other fascist groups in Germany.

After this Moscow trial, Kindermann led an adventurous life. Some years after he and Wolscht were exchanged for Skoblevsky, he published a book on his experiences in Moscow, *Zwei Jahre in Moskaus Totenhäusern: der Moskauer Studentenprozess und die Arbeitsmethoden der OGPU* (Berlin, 1931). In 1938 he went as a Nazi agent to Tokyo, where he was arrested by the American occupation authorities on October 29, 1945.

these military preparations. Never before had the will for action been so general among German Communists; on every previous occasion when military action was asked of them, the rank and file had been divided. In March 1921, for instance, substantial groups of the most valuable elements of German Communism had resisted an "adventurist" policy. Before 1923, the fear of the showdown with the cruel and expertly led counter revolution had curbed the best and most conscious elements of the German labor movement. In September and October 1923, the situation was reversed. The official promise of the Russian Politburo to support the German uprising was enthusiastically regarded as decisive. The many Russian comrades in Germany, the unlimited funds (mostly in American dollars), the professional methods of preparation, produced confidence that Russia's assistance this time was secured.

Such a typical white-collar worker as Ernst Torgler, prototype of conservative prudence, bade farewell to his family, left his home in the middle-class Berlin suburb of Karlshorst, and slept for weeks in a community dormitory awaiting The Day. On my return from Moscow, I had been surprised to see the change of attitude towards "putschism" in Torgler and others like him. These sober German workers were under a spell of revolutionary ecstasy.

The Directorium lived in a fear that their preparations would be brought to a sudden stop by armed state intervention, a misgiving that at the height of the inflation was quite baseless. When the Left urged that the daily spontaneous demonstrations and strikes all over Germany be strongly supported, they were answered by pointing out that first we needed another few weeks to be militarily ready. Hans Pfeiffer declaimed, for example, "Comrades, under no circumstances should we proclaim a general strike. The bourgeoisie would find out what we are planning and would destroy us before we start. On the contrary, let us soften down our spontaneous movements. Let us hold back our groups in the factories and the unemployed organizations so that the government will think that the danger is over. And then—after they are lulled into an illusion of complete safety—let us strike in one night, quickly and decisively, arrest the government, storm the Reichswehr barracks, and ring the knell of the last battle." I called this kind of strategy "the conspiratorial revolution," to be realized by a small group and presented to the working masses the next morning as a surprise.

When Brandler returned from Moscow, his first decision had been to move his headquarters from Berlin to Dresden, the capital of Saxony. This step, it was explained to the party, was necessary to rally the Saxon workers around it, but actually the withdrawal of the Central Committee from Berlin was intended to facilitate Brandler's policy of restricting the Communist action to a local experiment and avoiding its development into a nationwide uprising.

There was no longer any opposition in the party to entering the Saxon cabinet. Now the party accepted "Communist ministerialism" as helpful in building a bastion for the military organization, and only a few organizers of the Berlin branch did not believe that these Russian plans would prove workable. Ernst Thälmann, the figurehead of the Left, until September 1923 a stubborn opponent of Communist participation in a Social Democratic government, had returned from Moscow with a new enthusiasm for the strategy.

The small advisory group of the Russian Politburo had correctly evaluated the strength of the Reichswehr troops that the Saxon revolutionaries would have to face as no more than a fraction of the 100,000 men in the Reichswehr. How much support these troops would get from the illegal Black Reichswehr units would depend on how the flux of national upheaval would be resolved. If the workers' troops struck first and were able to gain control of important points quickly, many potential supporters of the nationalist forces would be immobilized or would even be drawn into the revolutionary forces. The task of the Communist ministers, therefore, was to arm some fifty to sixty thousand Saxon workers, and Brandler promised that these munitions would be distributed promptly.

During the year 1923 the German cabinet had secretly encouraged the reorganization of the German army and had granted funds to various nationalist corps. It was one of Germany's open secrets that, thinly disguised as labor battalions, renascent armies had been maneuvering on the big estates of East Prussia and Brandenburg. These Black Reichswehr units used modern equipment, including artillery and airplanes, and in this respect the Red Hundreds were not comparable. But in the general breakdown of German society, Moscow was gambling that many Schlageters would join the Communist revolutionaries.

The young officers of the Black Reichswehr were in conflict with one part of the General Staff, many of whose members were inclined to accept Stresemann's compromise with Britain and France. Even von Seeckt, though before and after 1923 he was a staunch supporter of collaboration with Russia, at this moment also considered a compromise with the West, in order to stem the Communist avalanche.

In Bavaria, the Reichswehr, coöperating with the Bavarian cabinet minister Gustav von Kahr, was openly preparing a military revolt against Berlin. Beginning in Saxony and Thuringia by crushing the socialists there, the troops would march to Berlin, arrest the cabinet, and, for the salvation of the Fatherland, set up a military dictatorship. Von Kahr and his circle would have been satisfied with a greater independence of Bavaria from the Reich, but Ludendorff was fighting for a Greater Germany and considered Munich only as his *place d'armes*.

His plan got no official encouragement from Seeckt's headquarters, but important Reichswehr politicians wavered toward it.

Brandler in the Saxon Cabinet

The leadership of the trade-unions and of the Social Democratic Party was torn between their fear of a Communist uprising and the rebellious mood of their own rank and file, who did not believe in the promised stabilization. The Social Democratic hierarchy was not at all the iron phalanx that it appeared to the Communist leaders. These men were also seized by the confusion and indecision that had embraced all strata of German society. Was it really possible to stabilize the currency? Would the awaited foreign loans materialize? Would Britain permit Germany to reënter the world market as her competitor? Would it be possible to find a workable compromise with France?

Hilferding's finance policy in particular was challenged by the Social Democratic leadership. Concerning this, Otto Braun writes:

> The Social Democratic Reich Finance Minister, Hilferding, stopped the note press. He had many plans for the stabilization of the mark and for the creation of a new currency, but he did not come to a quick decision. One day Stresemann came to me in complete despair and insisted: You must influence your party friend Hilferding to make a decision on the question of currency. He does not progress beyond deliberations, but meanwhile we are perishing. . . . When Stampfer writes, "Hilferding was without doubt the most erudite Finance Minister the German Reich ever had," I agree with him. However, in this period that was a fatal mischance. For, as Goethe says, it is not enough to now how, one must also use the knowledge; it is not enough to want, one must also act.[1]

Every group of industrialists or politicians had its own plan. The circle around Louis Hagen, the Cologne banker, for instance, wanted to create a Rhenish currency, which the wiseacres called the Louis d'Or.

On September 26, the Reich President had announced the official end of passive resistance and at the same time promised wages in gold. This promise was not kept; the inflation kept rising to ever dizzier heights, to billions and trillions of marks to the dollar.[2] In these months

---

[1] Otto Braun, *Von Weimar zu Hitler*, pp. 126–127.

[2] On October 21, a day when throughout the country Germany's collapse reached a crisis, the mark was quoted officially at 40 billion to the dollar; unofficially

newspapers reported daily the number killed and wounded in hunger strikes. On September 29, the government had declared a state of emergency, which enabled it to intervene through the Reichswehr in practically every branch of civil life.

On October 1, the Black Reichswehr garrison at Küstrin, near the Polish border, revolted under Major Ernst Buchrucker and had to be subdued by Prussian police troops. This premature outburst of the new putsch in preparation was the nationalists' answer to what they considered a betrayal—the ending of passive resistance to the Ruhr occupation and the tentative negotiations with France surrounding it. Also in the first week of October, there were clashes in Düsseldorf between the police and the French-sponsored Rhineland separatists. The expected outbreak of civil war on a larger scale spurred the efforts of the German government to come to terms with British and French experts.

On October 3, the Stresemann-Hilferding cabinet was regrouped by replacing the Social Democratic Minister of Finance by a representative of the German People's Party, Dr. Hans Luther. At the end of November, Stresemann was replaced as chancellor by Wilhelm Marx, of the Center Party, but still retained the portfolio for Foreign Affairs.

All eyes were fixed on the sizable German Communist Party, with its enormous Moscow shadow. The disruption of German society was such that a successful Communist uprising seemed probable. Only the resistance of the Social Democratic Party now stood between the old Germany and a new society. The inflation had sapped the Social Democratic organizers of their self-confidence; from one day to the next they feared the reactionary coup d'état, which once consummated would leave them no exit. Of all German political leaders, few counted more on the possibility of stabilization than Radek and Brandler.

In Saxony, the Zeigner cabinet was in a delicate situation. It was responsible for peace and order, but the clashes between unemployed and police troops had developed on several occasions during September

---

it was selling as high as 60 billion to the dollar. The effort to stabilize the mark passed through several stages. In August, over the protest of Finance Minister Hilferding, the cabinet had adopted the proposal of the banker and Reichstag deputy Karl Helfferich (who for a short while after Mirbach's assassination had been Germany's representative in Russia) and instituted the so-called *Roggenmark* (rye-mark), whose value was based on the price of grain. Then, beginning in September, the value of the mark was tied to that of real estate, and this so-called *Rentenmark* lasted until the gold standard was reëstablished after the Dawes stabilization.

to large-scale riots. The Saxon police force included many Social Democrats among its members, in some places a majority. Many Social Democratic workers hoped that in the end the Saxon police would help them fight the Bavarian nationalists, but whenever a Social Democrat in police uniform wounded or killed a comrade wearing the rags of the unemployed, socialists reacted to the incident with indignation. Thus, the Zeigner cabinet received an unceasing flow of complaints, while the Communist Party was given wide support for its demand that demonstrators not be molested, that those arrested be released, that the police officers involved be dismissed and replaced by militant socialists.

Under this pressure, the Zeigner cabinet resigned. After the revolt of the Black Reichswehr garrison at Küstrin, the apparent imminence of a Bavarian putsch made Zeigner ready to accept Communist participation in the government. On October 10, three Communists—Heinrich Brandler, Paul Böttcher, and Fritz Heckert—entered the new Saxon cabinet, and a few days later Karl Korsch and Albin Tenner entered the cabinet of Thuringia. As the new head of the state chancellery, Brandler employed as his secretary Gerhart Eisler, who hoped that by becoming a state employee he might get German citizenship.

With Communists in the government, everyone expected immediate radical measures—state control of large industry, sharp price control, the organization of public works, the confiscation of big estates, substantial state help to the unemployed, and, most important, the formation of workers' battalions. The Communist ministers, on the contrary, tried their best to limit their program. Brandler wanted to win over the Social Democrats and the trade-unionists, not so much the rank and file as the conservative and unimaginative middle brackets, the rock on which Social Democracy was built. This stratum of small functionaries, characteristic of the inner structure of the whole German labor movement, was best typified in Saxony, the old strongpoint of socialist radicalism. Enamored of legal procedure, these honorable labor bureaucrats lacked the vision for the great change that was necessary; with their provincial eyes they could not see the transformation through which Germany had passed since 1918. They clung to a concept of a "balance of forces," in which a well-organized labor movement would have its well-defined place.

Brandler and his friends were as though hypnotized by this class;

they wanted to prove, first of all, how respectable Communist ministers could be. Brandler made himself familiar with administrative procedure and began to draft proposals for decrees to augment relief allowances to the unemployed and to improve labor relations. Heckert and Böttcher called various conferences to discuss economic measures, all of which remained strictly routine: increase of the dole, price control, improvement of the labor market. Heckert proposed distributing the carp of the royal lakes to the unemployed, a measure whose inadequacy aroused irony among the hungry workers. In Thuringia, Tenner opened an energetic campaign not against the Nazis but against muskrats, which were a nuisance to the local farmers.

When Berlin received the news that Communists had been taken into the Saxon and Thuringian cabinets, Germany's fever rose several degrees in the breasts of Stresemann and Seeckt. Zeigner attempted to counter this reaction in a public appeal to the Reich cabinet, addressed in particular to the Reichswehr Minister, Dr. Otto Gessler. Zeigner asked for measures against the monarchist "traitors" in the army. "We are not fighting here for any provincial aims," he said in substance. "Saxony fights for the very existence of the German republic, which can be smashed by the onslaught of the Bavarian reactionaries." The Social Democratic Party, burning in the same fire of disintegration as every other German institution but still tied to its long tradition, was pushed to the Left by this strong appeal from Erich Zeigner, one of its most prominent representatives; and this shake-up was reflected in nationalist circles, whose trend toward social radicalism was driven forward. During the rising inflation, the nationalist movement had already stripped off its heritage from conservative bourgeois pre-war nationalism. The specific characteristic of National Socialism—its imitation first and later assimilation of Left radicalism—has its origins in these months, so decisive for the development of German society under the Weimar Republic.

Saxon industrialists appealed to Berlin for protection from rioting and Red threats.[3] On October 14, Reich President Ebert, invoking Article 48 of the Constitution,[4] assigned General Adolf Müller to

---

[3] Verband Sächsischer Industrieller, *Denkschrift über den Terror der Arbeiter zur Erzwingung von Lebensmitteln oder Lohnerhöhungen* (Dresden, 1923).

[4] "If a state does not fulfill the duties obligatory under the Reich Constitution and Reich laws, the Reich President, with the help of the armed forces, may order its compliance.

institute a "Reich Executive" in Saxony and Thuringia, which meant that these two states would be occupied by the Reichswehr, whose rule would supplant that of the elected local governments. Müller, expecting serious resistance from the populace, hesitated almost a full week before beginning to assemble the requisite troops. Ebert's proclamation of a Reich Executive against Zeigner, a fellow Social Democrat, was opposed not only in the party but even in the higher brackets of the administration. Otto Braun, then premier of Prussia, reports that he was against the measure, which he characterized as a violation of the Constitution.

> In my opinion, applying Article 48 of the Constitution in this way against legally elected ministers was a very dangerous precedent, which could bring disaster in the future. My friend Ebert, with whom I discussed the matter privately, did not agree with me. . . . Even so, I remained of the opinion that from the beginning one has to keep to constitutional methods. Ebert was angry and we parted somewhat estranged.[5]

The provincial police were put under the command of the Reichswehr, which ordered them to be "energetic" against demonstrators. The resulting clashes, especially in Chemnitz and Dresden, were so impressive that Berlin began to waver and considered recalling Müller.

From Moscow, the Politburo watched the developments in Germany

---

"If public security and order are, or are threatened with being, seriously disturbed, the Reich President may take such measures as are necessary for their reëstablishment, if necessary with the help of the armed forces. To this end he may nullify, completely or in part, the constitutional rights stipulated in Articles 114, 115, 117, 118, 123, 124, 153 . . .

"These measures may be annulled only at the demand of the Reichstag. In case of danger, a state government may take provisional measures . . . [but] these measures may be annulled by the Reich President or the Reichstag."

[5] Otto Braun, *Von Weimar zu Hitler,* p. 133. Braun continues: "In the late summer of 1932, after the Reich Executive against the Prussian government, I heard from the mouth of Hindenburg a bitter confirmation of my 1923 prophecy. 'What do you want?' he said. 'Your deceased friend Ebert took much more stringent measures against the Saxon government than I have taken.' This was not factually correct, . . . but I had to admit the formal juridical analogy."

During the long fight between the Reich and the Social Democratic Party, Kaiser Wilhelm had boasted that with one lieutenant and ten men he could disperse the Social Democratic phantom. Two generations of socialist workers enjoyed laughing at this empty bombast. Then, on July 20, 1932, the Kaiser's boast became an actuality; Carl Severing, the last Social Democratic president of Prussia, was removed from office by two police officers.

with intense interest. Radek, feeling that he could not handle the situation without help, asked for instructions, and in the name of the Executive Committee Zinoviev replied with a telegram ordering resolute armed resistance to the Reichswehr invasion:

> We interpret the situation thus: The decisive moment will come in not more than four, five, or six weeks. We therefore consider it necessary to occupy immediately every position that can be useful. We believe that, under the given circumstances, the purpose of our entrance into the Saxon government must be put into practice. If the Zeigner group is willing to defend Saxony effectively against the Bavarian fascists, we must enter. Immediately, fifty to sixty thousand men must be armed. Ignore General Müller. Same attitude in Thuringia.[6]

The Chemnitz Conference

From Berlin, Müller issued a proclamation to the Saxon people, co-signed by Gessler, Ebert, Stresemann, and Seeckt. The signature of Ebert indicated the support of the Social Democratic Party leadership, which he controlled. Müller was preparing his troops for the march into Saxony; Nazi groups made inroads over the Saale River from Bavaria into Thuringia; with the entire economy shattered by inflation everywhere, demonstrations, food riots, and strikes reached a climax. When would the first shot be fired, and from which side? In a showdown between "monarchists" and Communists, a decisive part of the Social Democratic Party and the trade-unions would desert Ebert and join in the battle. At this moment, on October 21, a conference of factory councils convened in Chemnitz.

The Social Democratic Party sent fewer delegates than it was allowed, for Right-wing elements, following Ebert, wanted to minimize the importance of the conference. As its composition indicates,[7]

---

[6] *Parteitagsbericht*, Frankfurt convention, p. 30.

[7] The representation to the conference was as follows:

Factory delegates	140
Local trade-union councils	102
Coöperatives	26
Action committees	15
Unemployed committees	16
Communist Party	60
Social Democratic Party	7
Independent Social Democratic Party	1

(August Thalheimer, *1923: Eine verpasste Revolution?*, p. 26.)

it was intended as one more routine labor conference, and the delegates had been chosen for their knowledge of economic matters rather than for their political acumen.

Behind the scenes, Communist organizers worked feverishly. Radek was in Chemnitz; so was Skoblevsky, and with him his large staff of technical experts. Just before the conference opened, the Directorium met to discuss Zinoviev's telegram, Müller's imminent march into Saxony, and the projected arming of sixty thousand Saxon workers. The telegram had deflated Brandler's boasting; now was the time to produce the arms he had been speaking of. The large stocks in police barracks would soon be under Reichswehr control; heavy arms, even machine guns, could then be taken only by force. The Communist Party would be able to distribute only its own stock of arms, which was in fact poor enough. Thus, the weapons available to the workers depended on the scope of the action, on the energy and audacity with which it was organized, on whether the Communists could succeed in stimulating the masses to take their enemy's arms. But that was just the type of decision that, at any price, Brandler wanted to avoid. Thus it was resolved that a general strike should be declared in Saxony as a protest against the Reichswehr invasion, to see what reactions there would be in the Reich.

Brandler, the principal Communist delegate to the Chemnitz conference, asked it to proclaim the general strike. His speech was not inspiring; his manifest opinion that a general strike at this moment was an adventurist gamble sounded through his rhetorical appeal to arms. Brandler's background, his reaction to the Moscow conference, were well known to his Social Democratic colleagues. The split in the Russian Politburo, the lessened authority of Trotsky, the final sickness of Lenin, and, finally, the shadow of the Bulgarian defeat hung over this unhappy gathering in a provincial corner of Germany.

Brandler's speech was followed by an icy silence. Everyone knew that a general strike against Müller would open a new phase of civil war. Some at least of the Social Democrats had the illusion that Müller would not act against Zeigner but would march through Saxony to fight the fascists in Bavaria. The conference wavered. It would have been possible to lead its members out of this mood of panic, but not by rhetoric alone; at every important turning point there are hesitations of this kind to be overcome. The doubts of the Social Democrats at Chemnitz, moreover, were completely justified: it was a stupid plan to load the weight of a collision with the Reichswehr entirely on the shoulders of the Saxon workers. Successful action was possible only if led by the key centers of proletarian strength—by Hamburg, Berlin, the Ruhr—where from the first moment of mobilization of their forces the socialists could have held the advantage. In every one of these regions the Communist Party was stronger than in Saxony, and its choice of this state was interpreted by the Social Democratic delegates as an attempt to spare the Communist cadres.

In the moment of indecision that followed Brandler's speech, Ernst Graupe, a minister in Zeigner's cabinet, stood up and threatened to bolt the conference together with the other six representatives of the Social Democratic Party if Brandler's proposal was accepted. This was the crucial moment. Even without Graupe, Brandler could get a majority for the general strike, but it would have meant fighting the issue through the Social Democratic branches of all Saxony—not the optimum beginning of a civil war. A small committee was elected to deliberate on the possibility of a general strike, and with this second-class funeral Brandler's motion was buried.

On October 23, two days after the conference in Chemnitz, General Müller entered Dresden, the capital of Saxony, without difficulty. In Meissen, Zwickau, and Pirna, he met resistance. Shots were fired at the soldiers, obstacles put in the way of the marching troops. In Freiberg, the masses attacked the Reichswehr with naked hands. Thirteen were killed, many wounded. The troops occupied all public buildings and all strategic points. Communist newspapers were suppressed, hundreds of rank-and-file members arrested. It was not yet Nazi terror, but the arrested men were beaten, handcuffed, isolated with a diet of bread and water.

On October 27, Berlin demanded the immediate resignation of the Zeigner cabinet, which insisted on its legal rights and refused to resign. The Stresemann cabinet appointed Dr. Karl Heinze, of the German People's Party, as civil commissioner for Saxony, and General Müller arrested Zeigner. The Communist ministers promptly went underground and left for Berlin. Spontaneous attempts to organize a protest strike failed, and the Reichswehr occupied the rest of Saxony without difficulty. Thuringia was occupied only a month later, on November 13, by General Paul Hasse.

When Dr. Heinze took over as administrator of Saxony, he began to negotiate with the Right Social Democratic group led by Dr. Karl A. Fellisch. In a talk to the Saxon Diet, Heinze gave his personal word that the troops would be withdrawn. General Müller remained, however, and the new Fellisch cabinet worked until the end of November under Reichswehr occupation.

Zeigner was charged with malfeasance: his wife had accepted a goose sent by some village admirer. Zeigner had not even known that the roast goose he had eaten on a certain Sunday was a gift, but this ridiculous affair, in a vicious campaign of calumniation, was blown up into "bribery of a state official." A few day later, Zeigner was released, only to be jailed again on November 21, this time charged with high treason.

Thus the "workers' governments" of Saxony and Thuringia came to a lamentable end. After nine months of heated and complicated discussion, after three Moscow conferences, the contribution of the Communists to the Saxon and Thuringian administrations had consisted in weak propaganda and futile palliatives. The Communist movement was at that time immeasurably stronger than the Nazi organization, which was confined mainly to Bavaria and numbered only fifteen thousand members.[8] The heirs of the militant tradition of the Spartakus uprisings, with such experienced advisers as Radek, Zinoviev, and Trotsky, should have been able to take the lead in Germany's catastrophic situation. Seen from the inside, however, the Communists were an insufficiently organized group of panic-stricken people, torn by factional quarrels, unable to come to a decision, and unclear about their own aims. Six years after the Russian revolution, the flames had burnt so low that they could not ignite even Red Saxony.

Fiasco in Hamburg

On October 22, the same week that the Chemnitz conference began and Müller entered Dresden, an uprising had started in Hamburg, an isolated fight of a handful of militants. The evening before the Chemnitz conference, the Central Committee of the Communist Party had

---

[8] Cf. Konrad Heiden, *A History of National Socialism* (London, 1934), p. 89.

gathered couriers from all parts of Germany there to await the signal
for the revolt. The Moscow decision had been clear, and the Central
Committee had accepted it; Zinoviev's telegram had been equally
definite, and Brandler had not rejected it. That Brandler would base
the future action of the party exclusively on the decision of the Chemnitz conference was a development that the waiting couriers had not
foreseen. Brandler's announcement that the fight was called off, that
a retreat was unavoidable, stunned them, but they obeyed and scattered
to carry this message to the groups awaiting their return.

One courier, however, had already departed. Hermann Remmele,
a member of the Central Committee, had taken the train for Hamburg,
and with him Ernst Thälmann, a delegate to the conference from
Hamburg.[9] With the message that the day for action had arrived, they
reached the city towards six in the evening and ordered the immediate
mobilization of the party. All party buildings were closed to non-
members and sentinels were posted before the entrances. The Red
Hundreds were called to their rallying points. The meetings were
quiet. No exhortations, no speeches.

The leading committee, with Thälmann as commander in chief,
ordered a demonstration the same evening as a decoy. Women and
children gathered at all the points known as Communist strongholds
with the task of diverting the police patrolling them. In accordance
with the party preparations of the last two months, the Hamburg
Communists concentrated on military action. No strike was called, no
statement of political aims prepared. The plan centered around the
acquisition of weapons. The police barracks were to be attacked at
dawn, the officers and men arrested, and their arms distributed to the
Red Hundreds.

During the night the Red Hundreds were gathered; they brought
with them enough food for two days. Former soldiers got command
posts. The groups were poorly armed; fifty men had three revolvers
and two rifles. Though the Communists had been fed for months on
fairy tales about the technical military preparations for the great coup,
they obeyed and remained together.

---

[9] Remmele had an unhappy end. In 1932 he wrote a eulogy of Soviet Russia,
but he could not swallow the Moscow line of 1933 that the Nazi victory had been an
"orderly retreat" of the Communist Party. He was killed in 1937 by the GPU.

At 4:15 in the morning, the assigned hour, about ten police stations were attacked. Some sentinels were killed but on the whole the bloodshed was slight. Most of the stations the Communists took by surprise; they arrested the policemen and distributed several dozen rifles. The principal target, however, the station in Von Essen Strasse in the borough of Barmbeck, which had a stock of machine guns, though it was attacked with a strong force under the command of a former officer, Hans Botzenhardt, was not taken—a major setback.

In the meantime, the counter order of the Central Committee reached the city by another courier, but Thälmann and the other leading Communists were out fighting. For twenty-four hours the courier tried in vain to find contacts.

The fighting began to develop. The police forces from the stations the Red Hundreds had taken returned from central headquarters with reinforcements. In Schiffbek, a workers' quarter, they tried to penetrate with armored cars, at first unsuccessfully. They met the same resistance in Barmbeck, a slum suburb, with many terraces and courtyards, irregular little streets and queer corners, where the population was solidly on the side of the Communist rebels. The police did not enter this dangerous area but surrounded it with a force of a thousand men.

> Spontaneously trees were cut, paving stones were torn up, trenches dug out. . . . Within an hour, more than fifty barricades were erected in Barmbeck. Without the support of the workers' population, the Communists could not have defended themselves against the police. The revolutionaries never had more than eighty rifles and twice as many revolvers. . . . Every window, every roof, every corner, was dangerous for the police. . . . Every terrace, every projecting wall, every house, every passageway, was cover for the revolutionaries.[10]

The Hamburg workers were not hostile to the Communist rebels; this time the police fought alone, without reinforcement by Social Democratic workers. In the dockyards and in the harbor, work was slowed down.

The Hamburg rebels fought under the illusion that all Germany was fighting, that Russia would soon intervene. Many Hamburg Com-

---

[10] Walter Zeutschel, *Im Dienst der kommunistischen Terror-Organisation*, p. 23.

munists who had emigrated to Russia because they were wanted by
the German police were now back.

> The comrades were eagerly asked, "How are things in Russia?
> Do we get support from them? Are the comrades ready?" They
> answered, "The plans to overrun Poland are ready in the desk of
> the General Staff. The garrisons at the border have been re-
> inforced. Reserve troops have been called up in secret. . . . The
> Red Fleet is ready to go to sea. Transport ships with weapons and
> ammunition for Germany are being made ready to sail." [11]

In Moscow, the Komsomol had formed special auxiliary corps destined
exclusively for Hamburg.[12]

On the second day Communist circles were swarming with encouraging rumors. The Red Fleet was entering the harbor. The Russian
army had invaded Poland. The Communist squads were in good
spirits; they were certain that they could get the upper hand in
Hamburg.

Meanwhile the second courier had finally reached Botzenhardt,
Thälmann, and the other leaders. They learned that the Chemnitz
conference had been a bluff, that Hamburg was fighting alone. Since
the decision to retreat had been endorsed by Radek and Skoblevsky,
the fabulous stock of arms would not be distributed. The group around
Thälmann did not have the heart to convey this news to the Communist foot soldiers, and the fighting went on for several days.

---

[11] Zeutschel, p. 26.

Zeutschel's little book is one of the very few participant reports of the Hamburg
uprising. He was twenty years old in October 1923, an unemployed construction
worker, and under the alias Burmeister a member of the illegal apparatus of the
German party. As commander of a group under Botzenhardt, he participated in
the attack on the Von Essen Strasse police station.

In 1924, Zeutschel was arrested by the Prussian police for his connection with
the assassination by a T-Group of a farmhand who was supposed to have handed
over hidden weapons to the fascists. Sentenced in the so-called "Little Cheka Trial,"
he was freed after four years by an amnesty. After working for one year as contributing editor of the Communist daily, the *Hamburger Volkszeitung*, he left the
party.

Im Dienst der kommunistischen Terror-Organisation is a crude compilation of
personal souvenirs, mixed with self-pity and bizarre political statements. In 1931,
when the book was published, his principal grievance against the party was still
that it did not publicly acknowledge the activity of the terror groups; the terrorists,
he complains, had been deserted by the party bureaucrats.

[12] *Post factum*, on November 7, Moscow students demonstrated, carrying a banner with Nikolai Bukharin's words, "We throw our books into a corner and take
up rifles to help our German brothers."

As abortive as the uprising was, the Hamburg Communists had seized more weapons in a few hours than they got from the Central Committee. The Brandler Committee had bought and stored arms but, for fear that local groups could not be held in, had not distributed them.

At the end of the second day of fighting, secret orders were given to the top leaders of the Red Hundreds to retreat the following day. A third day of street fighting followed, with decreasing energy and resistance, and at the end of that day the groups were disbanded. Guns were thrown away or hidden. Some hundreds of Communists were arrested; several other hundreds fled, mostly to Berlin.

In the Stalinist legend as it was later fabricated, this uprising was represented as the result of the unusual ability and clearsightedness of the Hamburg Communists. They had indeed shown courage, but their action was none the less an ill-prepared and poorly led affair. The localized street fighting was in contrast to the big words of the complicated party resolutions, to the money and manpower with which the party had prepared the German October. During those three days proletarian Hamburg waited for further developments, and there, as in Saxony, everything depended on audacious and well-considered initiative. Events in Hamburg, the second largest city of Germany, would have weighed infinitely more than the decisions of a conference in provincial Chemnitz.

The Kahr-Ludendorff Plot

In August, it had become apparent that Moscow's policy for Germany was beginning to make a turn, that German Communists, until then held back, might be spurred on. Stresemann, who still had no means in sight of overcoming the general breakdown, attempted to stabilize his cabinet in preparation for this expected Communist move by adding to it four Social Democratic ministers, and this act had been received both inside his party and among extreme nationalists, especially in Bavaria, with animosity. Field Marshal von Ludendorff, who had gone to Munich some months before, watched the maturing crisis and decided that the time had come for another putsch.

Since the summer of 1919 Munich had become the rallying point of all the bitterest opponents of "the November Republic." When Captain Ehrhardt broke out of the Leipzig prison in the spring of 1923, it was to Munich that he fled; and the Berlin government did not risk arresting him there again. It was at Munich that Adolf Hitler appeared for the first time on the Reich horizon.

This early Hitler is a curious product, blending all the cross currents of old and new Germany, which in the uncertainties of the year 1923 were beginning to crystallize into a definite form. With one foot in the old pre-war conservative camp and the other among the forces of social radicalism, he felt his way to a means of coalescing the two into a party sufficiently powerful to overthrow the November Republic. In these first beginnings, we find in an undeveloped state all the characteristics of later National Socialism—the combination into one policy of the dynamic aspirations of the German workers with the no less dynamic aims of German imperialism, and the consequent fervent appeal to every class—the workers and the captains of industry, the army and the peasantry, the middle class. In his drive for power, he built an organization adapted from the model of the Bolshevik State Party via the example of Mussolini, the carrier of this virus in Europe; and on this trunk he grafted features from the old Prussian army, whose tradition of discipline he admired as the incarnation of the German way of life.

Despite his rapid rise, in this period Hitler was still no more than an appendage to Ludendorff. Ludendorff did not want to attempt another merely military putsch in the manner of Kapp and Lüttwitz but to base it on a friendly government in Bavaria. He formed an alliance with Gustav von Kahr, a conservative of the old school, whose first interest was to free Bavaria from the domination of Berlin, the symbol of Prussia in the old Germany and of the Reds in the new.

On September 26, the Bavarian cabinet declared a state of emergency and appointed Kahr as State Commissar with dictatorial powers. General von Lossow, commander of the Reichswehr troops in Bavaria, was openly sympathetic to him. Both Munich and Berlin watched to see what reaction there would be from the workers' parties, in particular from Communist headquarters. After several weeks passed without any important action from the Communist Party,

Lossow pledged allegiance to von Kahr's government, which act constituted treason to the Stresemann government.

This was no Bavarian separatist movement;[13] on the contrary, Ludendorff and Kahr, "the trustees for the German people," declared that the true welfare of the Reich was now being guarded in Munich. But they still hesitated before the final step, a march through Thuringia and Saxony to Berlin. They feared Red resistance, and they were waiting for support from the Reichswehr in Berlin. This hope that they would find backing in the North was not without a basis, for Seeckt and the others were wavering toward openly supporting Ludendorff and if it came to the point of pitting Reichswehr against Reichswehr they would undoubtedly have gone over. When Stresemann sent Müller into Saxony and Hasse into Thuringia, he was playing with the feeble hope that in case of serious danger to the Reich these troops could also be used against the Bavarian mutineers. But if these troops were sent against Lossow, the probability was that they would not fight him but join with him and together march on Berlin. Then Ludendorff would have had another Kapp putsch, but on a much larger scale, with the civilian authorities isolated again from the military and helpless before their advance. The easy dispossession of the Zeigner cabinet added fuel to the conspiracies and pushed the Reichswehr in Berlin closer to Munich. The inflation, the disrupted economy, the loss of Germany's status in European economy, were reflected in the Reichswehr as in all German institutions, and the General Staff was also beset by indecision. Compared with the incidents in 1918–1920, the token resistance in Saxony and Thuringia amazed Seeckt by its inefficiency; the plot that Ludendorff was hatching looked temptingly easy of fulfillment.

It will be decided this week whether the nationalist extremists dare to join the issue [Stresemann declared on November 5]. The Reich government has sufficient Reichswehr troops at Coburg. If the Reichswehr fails, these extremists will be victorious. Then we may have a dictatorship of extreme nationalists. I am leading a dog's life. If these gangs manage to push their way into Berlin, I shall not go to Stuttgart [as the Reich government had done at

---

[13] However, during these same fateful days, a Rhineland Republic was proclaimed; this weak offspring of French policy lasted only a few days.

the time of the Kapp putsch]. I shall remain where I have the right to be, and they can shoot me there if they wish to.[14]

On the evening of November 8, Kahr, still hesitating, made a speech to his followers in the Bürgerbräuhalle in Munich. Hitler, whose role as a radical vanguard of the bloc was to override the waverings of his associates and push them forward, marched in at the head of his storm-troopers and enforced the proclamation of a new national government, whose members, including Hitler, were hastily chosen and immediately announced. General Lossow was to be Reichswehr Minister; Colonel Seisser, the chief of the Bavarian police, was to be the Reich Minister of the Interior; Ludendorff was to command the troops that would march on Berlin. This government, pulled out of Kahr with forceps, never developed beyond this forced birth and died the same night. Kahr was not willing to admit his parentage of this beerhall foundling, and when he returned from the demonstration he met with his intimates and decided to act against the Hitlerite extremists, if necessary with police force, rather than bring the division of the two Reichswehr wings to a head. Thus Kahr was the Brandler of the nationalists, the man who held his extremist wing in tow and prevented decisive action. The civil war, whose hot lava was bubbling over the top, receded once again.

There was also a nationalist counterpart to the Hamburg uprising. On November 9, when Ludendorff and Hitler found themselves betrayed by Kahr, they decided to override him by a direct appeal to the masses. At the head of their followers, they marched to the Feldherrenhalle, the monument to the glory of the old army, where they were easily dispersed by police troops.[15]

Thus the apathy of the Communists facilitated the rearrangement between Stresemann and the rebellious Bavarian Reichswehr. Not only did Stresemann and Seeckt emerge from the crisis with greater authority, but for a moment the waning status of Ebert, who against

---

[14] Quoted in Arthur Rosenberg, *A History of the German Republic,* p. 215.

[15] After the Nazis took power, the site of this nationalist gesture became a national shrine. In the trial that ensued from the incident, Ludendorff was freed (the court ruled that he had been at the scene by accident), and Hitler was sentenced to nine months of "honorary" confinement, during which he wrote *Mein Kampf.*

Hitler was able to avenge this betrayal after he came to power. Kahr was murdered during the bloody purge of June 30, 1934, and his body was thrown into the Dachau moor.

the advice and over the protest of his most intimate Social Democratic associates had backed their move against the Communists, was re-established. Until the very last moment, Ebert and Stresemann had not been sure of Seeckt's support. Once again, the destiny of the German Republic was decided in an emergency night session. In the night of November 9, the fifth anniversary of the Kaiser's abdication, Ebert risked for a second time charging Seeckt with restoring the authority of the Reich against the mutinous Reichswehr, this time against Lossow in Bavaria.

> On the night of November 9 [Otto Braun writes], immediately after it got the news from Munich, the Berlin cabinet convened. Curiously enough, I was called belatedly, although I lived directly across Wilhelmstrasse from the Chancellery. When I arrived at the excited session, it had already been decided to transfer executive power, on the basis of the state of emergency that had already been declared, to Seeckt, Commander in Chief of the armed forces.
>
> Stresemann did not understand my objection to this choice. Ebert also was annoyed by my reminder of our agreement that in case of the declaration of an emergency executive power should remain with a civil body. In Prussia, he said, the military would act only in agreement with the civil authorities; in Bavaria only a man with military authority, such as Seeckt had, could bring the Reichswehr to terms. It may be that he was not completely wrong in this. Nevertheless I could not refrain from calling his attention to the fact that it had been just this Mr. von Seeckt who, with his stand that Reichswehr does not fight Reichswehr, had made resistance to the Kapp rebels impossible.[16]

On November 22, after the defeat of the Communists in Saxony and of the Hitler putsch in Munich, Seeckt ordered the dissolution for the period of the emergency of the Communist Party. The situation was sufficiently pacified for him to order the withdrawal of the Reichswehr from Saxony the same day. It was the first time that the Communist Party was outlawed on a national scale; during the years of civil war, it had frequently been semi-legal or illegal, but this state had always been restricted to a certain area, particularly Bavaria, or to a period of days or weeks. The Seeckt decree was carried out in many areas by Social Democratic police, and they often executed it with relative

---

[16] Braun, *Von Weimar zu Hitler*, p. 135.

clemency. The party continued to function but called its meetings and demonstrations under transparent disguises. Its deputies in both the Reich and the state parliaments continued to hold office; they could see their electors and they held caucus sessions. No one expected the state of emergency to continue for more than a few months; the prohibition had a provisional character.

Despite this clemency, which contrasts with similar measures of our own day, Seeckt's order was a new and disquieting feature of Weimar democracy. It was a litmus for determining the efficacy of dictatorial methods, and the reaction of the labor movement to them. The German Communist rank and file found much sympathy among the bulk of the trade-unionists, in spite of the many differences between them, for their struggle to continue their organization was in the tradition of the German labor movement during Bismarck's time. The outlawing of the party deepened the bitterness among the Communists; it ratified their defeat in the civil war and marked the end of a period.

With the Hamburg defeat and the outlawing of the German party, all the secret military activity came to a halt. The military advisers from the East disappeared, and party life was reconstructed by the Central Committee around agitational tasks, "as usual." Its order calling off the secret mobilization of the party was met with a passionate outburst of scorn and distrust. For months the little man of the party had lived outside his normal circle, had made sacrifices to his belief that tomorrow, or the day after, he would take his post in a completely transformed German Republic. The rank and file, drilled in the tenet that lack of "correct leadership" had hindered the establishment of a workers' republic, turned as one man against the party's leader, Brandler. Russia was far away. The problems of the Russian Party were a topic of intellectual discussion but had nothing to do with everyday German problems. The culprit was closer home. Brandler and his lieutenants had spent the past months exciting the party members, exhorting them, promising them, ordering them; and thus he became the target of the general disappointment.

Zinoviev, himself endangered by the German defeat, encouraged this attack from afar. In ambiguous political statements, which did not single out Brandler by name, he promoted the disintegration of his caucus in the party. During the decisive days that Brandler was a minister of Saxony, a "Centrist group" was in formation. Members of his staff criticized him incessantly, wrote him on October 17, for instance:

Things cannot go on as they are now. You are using valuable
time in petty quarrels with Social Democratic bastards in the
government behind closed doors. . . . Our entrance into the
cabinet has only one aim, to reinforce tenfold the new revolutionary courage of the masses and to organize our forces.[1]

Thus Brandler was made the scapegoat, and criticism of his policy
and person grew out of all proportion to the role he had played; even
to this day, though he has remained the principal butt of Stalin's historians in their explanation of why the German October was defeated, Brandler has attacked the Comintern and especially Zinoviev
but has never exposed the Russian Politburo's contribution to the rout
of German Communism. He has every right to feel himself unjustly
treated.

In his defense, Brandler pointed out, correctly, that he had never
really accepted Moscow's plan for the uprising.

I resisted the decision to enter [the Saxony cabinet] until the
last moment. . . . An entrance into the government should not
have been made without the preparations that I have summed up
here, which were not made because of the decision of the Executive
Committee [of the Comintern]. To my regret, I finally agreed to
this decision, believing that I could handle things in my way. As
I saw it, there was no basis for an uprising in November or even
for resistance to the Reichswehr invasion. . . . We would not have
got away, as in Hamburg, with a small number of victims; we
would have been decisively defeated. For the non-Communist
workers, with all their sympathy for us, would not have participated in the street fighting in Saxony any more than they did in
Hamburg. There have been situations when we began to fight
even though things looked much more hopeless than in October.
But in 1918–1920, it was a different story.[2]

This diplomatic statement after the coup manqué did not calm
the party masses. The constant frustration the German worker had
suffered with his leaders, trade-unionist and Communist alike, was
later skillfully exploited by the Nazis in their drive against the labor
bureaucrat—*gegen die Bonzen.* "The Mecklenburg branch told the
Berlin comrades to hang Brandler upon the nearest tree. The Commu-

---

[1] *Parteitagsbericht,* Frankfurt convention, p. 276.
[2] *Ibid.,* pp. 246–247.

nists in East Prussia threatened him with the same fate if he ever went there . . ."[3]

Trotsky Breaks with the Politburo

The news of the German catastrophe and the revolt of the party against Brandler reached Zinoviev, who was responsible for Comintern policy, at a most crucial moment. In these last months of 1923, a multitude of factors disrupted the Politburo to the breaking point. The prolonged illness of Lenin confused the relations of the leading politicians to a degree that has never been adequately analyzed. The internal weakness of the Party and its strained relation to all other strata of the country made the question of whether the leader would die or return to his post dominant in all calculations, combinations, and intrigues. The position of Zinoviev, and with him of Kamenev, had been inflated during the few weeks of hope that the German Communists would be successful. Now the reaction was strong. Zinoviev had to consider seriously whether he would survive or be carried away by the wave of indignation over the ill-conceived and poorly executed action in Germany.

Economic conditions had been improved by the New Economic Policy, but not enough to create a balance between industrial and agricultural production, which continued to manifest the disparity termed in Party jargon "the scissors." The low level of agricultural production following the war had continued, culminating after a bad harvest in the summer of 1921 in a famine in the Volga basin. (Lenin had made an appeal for help to the United States, which had been answered with the Hoover Mission.) But with the NEP—and a good harvest in 1922—there had been a considerable improvement. Industrial recovery still lagged, however, and this disproportion was aggravated by an inflation to the disadvantage of the peasant consumer. At the end of 1922, the state bank issued notes called *chervontsi,*

---

[3] Walter Zeutschel, *Im Dienst der kommunistischen Terror-Organisation,* p. 25. Jean Valtin (*Out of the Night,* New York, 1941, p. 58) reports that Ruth Fischer approached a T-Group with the request that they give Brandler a beating. The story is inaccurate so far as I am concerned. Luise and Eva Schneller, the two girls Valtin mentions, were members of the Brandler faction; and in the fall of 1923, when I had only the authority of the Berlin branch behind me, they would not even have listened to such a proposal. The anecdote is, however, typical of the T-units, which all over the Reich were brewing similar plans.

which represented gold equal to the content of the pre-war ten-ruble coin. Chervonets rubles were issued, however, only in large denominations, and for all small transactions the inflated paper rubles had to serve. Thus two moneys ran through the country, one guaranteed and the other subject to continual depreciation by inflation. During 1923 the inflation of the paper ruble not only got out of control but affected the value of the chervontsi, which depreciated by about a quarter from January to October. This rapid price increase deprived the peasant market of industrial commodities. Moreover, the state trusts hoarded commodities, not wanting to exchange these real values for inflated rubles. Thus the greater agricultural production under the NEP was not compensated, and again the peasants decreased the amount of land under cultivation. "The peasant was beginning to be in as bad a position as he had been under 'war communism.' "[4] Groups of peasants, for example the cotton growers of Turkestan, began to demand payment in chervonets rubles.

Even apart from monetary difficulties, industry was unable to fulfill the peasants' demand for agricultural implements and consumers' goods. The progress of crafts and small enterprises brought limited results, but heavy industry was far below the pre-war level and the country had dire need of all types of commodities. According to the official historian of the Russian Party, "The national economy was progressing too slowly to absorb unemployment."[5]

There were two schools of opinion in the Party on how to remedy this economic crisis. One of these was inclined to attribute all shortcomings to the backwardness of the country, and expected improvement only from further tightening state control and state planning. The other felt that there was already too much centralization of control in state trusts and syndicates and demanded that state organizations be curbed, so that the peasant market could breathe more freely. This suggestion was opposed by the already large group of industrial managers, who saw in any weakening of state control a direct threat to their hierarchical status. The program of concentrating industry, already advocated by the Twelfth Party Congress in 1923, was pushed harder.

---

[4] Maurice Dobb, *Russian Economic Development since the Revolution*, p. 233.
[5] [Joseph Stalin], *History of the CPSU*, p. 264.

In fact, all strata of Russian society were dissatisfied with the results of the NEP: the Party, which feared that it was losing its grasp on the economic apparatus and control of the peasants and strove on all levels to conserve its dictatorial control; the peasants, who had expected not only more consumers' goods but also more freedom of movement; the state bureaucracy and the Soviet intelligentsia, who were uneasy over the forms of life under the new economic conditions, who also wanted more freedom from the Party apparatus; and finally the workers, who bitterly compared the increased discipline in the Party and trade-unions with the relative freedom of the NEP-men.

The various outlawed groups of Workers' Opposition, removed from the higher brackets of the Party, gained new strength among the rank and file. With Lenin's disappearance, Trotsky was the lonely and imposing opponent of the ruling hierarchy, and all the various oppositionists in the country turned toward him, hoping that a man of his stature would be able to fight the Party monopoly. Although he was still military commander, Trotsky was already losing the implements of military power. It was becoming clear to the country that the danger of dictatorship did not come from the army alone, that the Party hierarchy was already more dangerous. Now it was an advantage to Trotsky that he was a non-Bolshevik, a newcomer in the Party, a revolutionary statesman who had joined the Bolshevik Party as an almost isolated socialist intellectual; that although he had been a founder of the new state he was not accepted by the ruling hierarchy. The Workers' Opposition came out in support of Trotsky against the Politburo. The Democratic Centralism group made a formal bloc with him, and the various other groups, including many who had been opposed to Trotsky on the question of organization of the army and trade-unions, supported the Opposition.

In the first phase of this new resistance movement, it concentrated on how to heal the disrupted economy of the country. Its platform included a number of proposals for remedying the inefficient organization of state industry. "The gist of this policy was to enforce commercial accounting of the most vulgar bourgeois kind . . . disregarding political considerations." [6] But the new point that raised an imme-

---

[6] N. Popov, *Outline History of the CPSU*, II, 196.

diate storm of protest in the Party was a proposal known as "commodity intervention," that is, free trade with the capitalist world, which was indeed an audacious idea with far-reaching implications for the Party monopoly. Its premises were that the industrialization of Russia would be a long process; that the state industry was too weak for this task; that without substantial imports of both machinery and consumers' goods, Russia would not be able to reach economic equilibrium. Abolition of the state monopoly in foreign trade and stimulation of NEP trade with the capitalist world would have eased the tension in Russia and in the end weakened the monopoly of the Party. First of all, it would have given the peasants incentive for larger production— the goods the workers could not supply them—and thus without coercive methods contributed to the transformation of Russian economy into one of farmers' coöperatives. During his later temporary alliance with Stalin, Bukharin developed similar concepts on peasant economy, for the crux of the relation between the Party and the country was precisely the method of industrializing the peasant economy.

In implementing the NEP, the Trotsky Bloc of September 1923 went one step farther and demanded greater Party democracy. In justifying the demand, Trotsky tried to destroy the myth of the infallibility of the Old Guard. He addressed himself especially to the student and youth organizations, which were in ferment against the older Party generation, and polemized against it with the obvious analogy of the degeneration of the old guard of the Second International. His demands, however, did not go farther than a democratic and rejuvenated Party regime, to be achieved not by juridical definitions of Party statutes but by a return to "collective initiative, to the right of free and comradely criticism without fear—the right of organizational self-determination." He desired that everyone should feel that from now on no one would dare to terrorize the Party. This weaker edition of the earlier formulations of the Workers' Opposition was bound to the term coined by this group, "workers' democracy," but its essence was different.

In the 1923 Trotskyite Bloc, the Workers' Opposition and general dissatisfaction in the country were the driving force. It was enlarged by the integration of a substantial group of state administrators, who, even though many were Party members, resented the increasing encroachment of the Party apparatus. All the concepts of workers' democracy in a revolutionary period, carried out by soviets and trade-unions, had failed. Now there was a new attempt to build up an independent state apparatus, which would include the Party as its executive branch, and not vice versa. "It is necessary to regenerate and renovate the party apparatus, and to make it feel that it is nothing but the executive mechanism of the collective will." [7] This rebellion of the state organizers against the party found its expression in the formation of various rebellious Party caucuses.

A series of troubling incidents took place, which only the posthumous book by Trotsky begins to explore. Lenin's break with Stalin in this period was symptomatic of the growing general fear that not Trotsky but Stalin might be the counter-revolutionary Bonaparte who would kill the Bolshevik Jacobins. Zinoviev had felt this danger at the Twelfth Congress, where although he was the political reporter he was aware of the new power of the Stalin machine for the first time.

> Zinoviev . . . wavered between two plans: (1) to reduce the Secretariat to its former status of a subsidiary of the Politburo, by depriving it of its self-aggrandized appointive powers; and (2) to "politicalize" it, which meant establishing a special collegium of three members of the Politburo within it as its highest authority, these three to be Stalin, Trotsky and either Kamenev, Bukharin, or Zinoviev. Some such combination, he felt, was indispensable to offset Stalin's undue influence.[8]

Zinoviev renewed this effort in September 1923 and met with his caucus in a grotto near Kislovodsk, a famous Caucasian watering place. He invited among others G. K. Ordzhonikidze, one of Stalin's best friends, and charged him to take a personal message to Stalin promising that the Secretariat would not be touched if Stalin agreed to coördinate it better with the Politburo. As a compromise, of which nothing ever developed, he suggested that three members of the Politburo be included in the Orgburo to control the Secretariat. Back in

---

[7] Trotsky, *The New Course*, New International Publishing Co. (New York, 1943), p. 93.

[8] Trotsky, *Stalin*, p. 367. This text is a transcription from Trotsky's notes by Charles Malamuth, the book's editor. I was in Moscow during these months and can confirm this report.

Moscow, Zinoviev attended several sessions of the Orgburo and Trotsky stayed away, thus indicating his refusal at this time to give Zinoviev support against Stalin.

In September 1923 Trotsky demonstratively walked out of the plenary session of the Central Committee and on October 8 he submitted to the Party the Statement of the Forty-Six: because of the incorrect leadership of the Central Committee the country was going to ruin. Among the high Party dignitaries who signed it were G. L. Pyatakov, E. A. Preobrazhensky, N. I. Muralov, V. V. Ossinsky, and T. V. Sapronov. A few days later, before his departure for Germany, Radek addressed a separate letter to the Central Committee in which he declared his solidarity with the Statement of the Forty-Six but in terms more deferential to the Politburo. All these incidents were hidden from the Comintern.

At this moment, Russia received the news of the German defeat.

> The approach of the events in Germany set the party aquiver. . . . The critical revision of the internal regime of the party was postponed by the anxious expectation of what seemed to be the imminent showdown in Germany. When it turned out that this showdown was delayed by the force of things, the party put the question of the "new course" on the order of the day.[9]

The old course to which this was opposed was the Party regime since the Kronstadt uprising, set at the Tenth Party Congress and made yet more rigid at the Eleventh and Twelfth Congresses. The fight against the Workers' Opposition was eliminating the Party rank and file from all participation in the making of policy. The Stalin Secretariat, under pressure, promised a rejuvenation of Party democracy, which meant in substance an offer to compromise with the Opposition. In Moscow, Petrograd, Baku, Kiev, this apparent weakening of the Politburo's grasp strengthened during the first phase the force of the Opposition. The disappointment in Russia and the disappointment in the Comintern fused into one, which rapidly endangered not only Zinoviev but also the new General Secretary, Stalin, who was not at all sure that from his place behind the scenes he could bring the Party rebellion under his control.

---

[9] Trotsky, *The New Course*, pp. 13–14.

On November 7, Zinoviev issued a statement for Party democracy. At the same time the fight against Trotskyism began, with all the devices of dogmatic exegesis against deviationists. In this fight Stalin cautiously induced Zinoviev and Kamenev to commit themselves while he remained in the background. But the two halves of the Troika, united only by their common fear of Trotsky, each tried to come to an understanding with him against the other. Trotsky's articles, published under the title *The New Course,* had found such a response in the Party that it seemed that he had only to step on the platform to lead it against the Politburo. In his defense Trotsky touched the core of his case against the dogmatic Leninists, that his role in the founding of the new state was a better guarantee of loyalty than citations from pre-1917 Party history.

> I came to Lenin fighting, but I came fully and all the way. My actions in the service of the party are the only guarantee of this: I can give no supplementary guarantees. . . . Does the whole of Leninism lie in docility? [10]

This language, already bold, opened a Trotsky wedge into all Party branches. The Moscow organization, for example, was divided approximately in half, and in the beginning a majority undoubtedly was with the Opposition. At the climax of the campaign, however, Trotsky suddenly disappeared from the open battle and declared himself too sick to continue the discussion. The confusion in the oppositionist camp was enormous; the Party bureaucracy fought with greater ferocity, and by large transfers of opponents from Moscow to other areas the group of shrewd Party organizers won the day. During this time, Trotsky writes,

> Stalin was evidently thinking up a maneuver with the aim of making peace with the Opposition at the expense of his allies. . . . He made obvious overtures to me, displaying an utterly unexpected interest in my health. . . . Without breaking with his allies, of course, Stalin carefully protected for himself the road of retreat to the Opposition. [11]

According to Trotsky, Zinoviev could answer Stalin's threat only by going to Petrograd for support and bringing into the Party campaign

---

[10] Trotsky, *The New Course,* p. 57.
[11] Trotsky, *Stalin,* p. 387.

his own shock troops, distributed by automobiles to wherever Trotsky had a majority. As is evident in this narrative, if Trotsky had gained one or two more locals, Stalin would have shifted sides.

In Trotsky's *My Life,* published in 1930 and written much more dogmatically than his later book, the reader comes to a curious paragraph. In the midst of reporting the decisive 1923 crisis, Trotsky takes three pages to describe the pleasures of duck hunting. He gives a portrait of a certain duck hunter, who is interested only in shooting birds in swamps. Because of him, Trotsky got wet feet and came down with an attack of influenza, followed by "some cryptogenic temperature," which kept him away from Party life for several months.

But, despite the campaign against Trotsky, no one at this time thought in terms of eliminating him from the state leadership. What they all wanted was to prevent him from becoming the state dictator and to force him to share the power.

> Kamenev was asking the "old Bolsheviks," the majority of whom had at some time left the party for ten or fifteen years: "Are we to allow Trotsky to become the one person empowered to direct the party and the state?" . . . Much later, in 1925, Bukharin said to me, in answer in my criticism of the party oppression: "We have no democracy because we are afraid of you." [12]

After the Opposition was virtually crushed, the secret offers to Trotsky for a compromise were publicly confirmed. On December 5, in an empty statement on the new course, the Central Committee reaffirmed its promise of Party democracy. In a Stalin-inspired Politburo statement published in *Pravda* on December 18, the supposition that there had been any attempt to eliminate Trotsky from the most active participation in Party and state affairs was labeled as a malevolent invention. As if by accident, a letter from Zinoviev's Petrograd branch appeared the same day with a similar statement.[13]

Trotsky did not appear at the Thirteenth Party Conference, January 16–18, 1924, where a statement of policy, based on Stalin's report, explicitly rejected the two key demands of the Opposition, namely, economic concessions "to international imperialism," with the aim of

---

[12] Trotsky, *My Life,* pp. 488–489.

[13] Boris Souvarine, *Staline, Aperçu Historique du Bolchévisme* (Paris, 1935), pp. 322–323.

strengthening business relations with foreign capital, and permitting factions within the Party. Trotsky's policy was characterized as a deviation from Leninism, but no organizational measures were taken against him. He decided that his influenza made a sojourn in the sunny South necessary and on January 18 departed for Sukhum. As Lenin's death was expected from one week to the next, this trip is one of the most puzzling incidents in the whole complex picture. The simplest explanation is the most probable: that Trotsky, following a common Party custom, removed himself from the site of the factional struggle in order to give his opponent enough of an advantage to facilitate a reconciliation.

On January 21, Lenin died. Here the student of the period cannot avoid considering the possibility that Trotsky may have had a secret understanding with the Politburo that he would not return to Moscow. The normal procedure would have been to hurry back immediately, not only for the funeral, at which Trotsky's silhouette should have been seen by the Russian people, but for the subsequent distribution of key posts and the first political decisions after Lenin's death. Both of Trotsky's books describe his absence as necessitated by circumstances, but it is evident that he did not want to return to Moscow. He got the news about Lenin's death on January 21 at the Tiflis station. He cabled to Stalin to ask when the funeral would take place, and upon receiving the answer that it would be the following Saturday he decided that he could not reach Moscow in time and continued his trip to Sukhum.

It is impossible to close this narrative on the Trotskyist Opposition in the fall of 1923 without mentioning Trotsky's suspicion that Stalin may have poisoned Lenin. His posthumous book, written after Yagoda confessed in the 1938 trial that he had poisoned unwanted comrades, deals extensively with the matter. H. G. Yagoda, a druggist by profession, had worked in the GPU for sixteen years, including the whole period of Lenin's illness. In 1933 Stalin accorded him the Order of Lenin; in 1935 he made him General Commissar of State Defense—honors indicative of the continued and intimate relation between the two men. Yagoda was tried along with four Kremlin physicians, charged with the murder of Maxim Gorky and of two members of the Soviet government. Trotsky considered it possible that under Stalin's orders Yagoda did poison Gorky, for if the world-famous Russian poet had objected to the execution of so many veteran Bolsheviks, this type of elimination would have been the most comfortable. Thus, Trotsky reconstructed from the trials a series of incidents. In his agony, Lenin had asked for poison several times. As Party Secretary, Stalin had the organization of Lenin's household under his control and in particular the GPU men designated for Lenin's security; thus, it was physically possible for him to get poison into Lenin's medicaments or food. Even dying, Lenin was an obstacle to Stalin's plot. The interesting aspect of this narrative is not solely whether it is true but the atmosphere it conveys. Two years later, it became the obsession of the oppositionist leaders that they would be killed by poison or by an operation ordered by Party physicians.

The Maslow Commission

Maslow, still held back in Moscow, attended a good dozen of decisive Party meetings. When, at the beginning of December 1923, the German delegates arrived in the midst of the intra-Party turmoil to get advice from the leaders of the world revolution, he reported his observations to them. The students, the youth, important groups from the Moscow factories, attacked the Politburo most aggressively, pointing out that there was no remnant of democracy left in the Party, in the trade-unions, or in the soviets. In rebuttal, the speakers of the Politburo openly threatened their opponents with state measures. Behind doors it was reported that the Stalin Secretariat had sent this and that oppositionist to remote corners of Central or Northern Russia. These were not arrests, but assignments to which no objection was possible. Disobedience would have been followed by expulsion from the Party, expulsion by arrest, and arrest by deportation. In conversations with the Workers' Opposition representatives during the summer months before the final crisis, we sometimes naïvely felt that our Russian comrades were exaggerating. Their statement that all Soviet democracy had been destroyed after the Kronstadt uprising was attributed to bitterness resulting from too rigid Party discipline and personal frustration. Their judgment on the Party, however, we accepted as more or less correct, for the status of the Opposition in it was manifestly weakening.

For many reasons, Maslow and I were not able to accept Trotsky's point of view. All of his points concerning democracy were artificially limited to the narrow field of Party legality; he ignored the major issue of the relation between the Party and other Soviet organizations. The temporary alliance between the Workers' Opposition groups and Trotsky had been made in spite of their continued distrust of his autocratic methods. Hidden behind discussions about the new and the old generation, about the lessons of October, about nuances in the interpretation of Party history before 1917, the real issue was the persistence of terrorist measures, which had outgrown their original function of combating the counter revolution.

Several Russian friends of Maslow, especially Lutovinov, reacted to Trotsky's sudden withdrawal as a most alarming symptom. Trotsky's "flight to Sukhum," as it was called among the oppositionists, was correctly interpreted as an attempt to avoid drastic measures against him. Discussions began to include what shrewd steps were best to avoid expulsion from the Party and deprivation of Soviet legality. If Trotsky went to Sukhum, the others associated with him in his caucus had to fear a less voluntary transfer to a less healthful climate. His flight, his silence, were understood as meaning "Attention, danger ahead!" For he could, and he should, have risked more than his more vulnerable supporters.

The atmosphere of the shifting and reshifting Russian factions and groupings was duplicated in the Comintern. Reports in Moscow that there was an important and increasing revolt in the German party against Brandler added another large element of instability. Neither Zinoviev nor Stalin could afford, particularly at this moment, to risk a break-away of the most important party of the Comintern, and both changed their attitude toward the German Left from patriarchal condescension to genuine consideration. Zinoviev, however, wondered how long the Left Communists would remain in the Comintern, tied to a Russian State Party visibly in transformation.

During September and October Maslow was treated almost like an outcast; he was on the verge of losing his party status completely. In November, the atmosphere suddenly changed. Ossip Pyatnitsky, the Comintern treasurer, personally visited him and asked ceremoniously whether he had everything he wanted; did Comrade Maslow have enough winter clothing for the Moscow climate? Maslow had already bought a lambskin coat at the Sukharevka market, and declined state help in solving his personal problems.

Arkadi Maslow was an interesting figure of German Communism for the simple reason that he was a Communist of Russian origin but not a Comintern agent. That a Russian should have a decisive influence on German policy without having first passed through the Bolshevik Party and been endorsed by its Central Committee was more than an anomaly; it was for the Russian leaders an insupportable negligence of the etiquette of discipline, an indication of too great independence. From the beginning of his activity in the German party, therefore, Maslow aroused more interest in Moscow than the native leaders.

During the convulsions of the Politburo in September and October, the committee charged with investigating Maslow's past was in session. Its chairman was Joseph S. Unschlicht, an important GPU chief intimate with Dzerzhinsky, and its other members were Peter I. Stuchka, a Lettish GPU agent; Felix Kon, a member of the International Control Commission; Adolf Warski and Mme. Vera Kostrzewa, two Poles, both close friends of Brandler; and Clara Zetkin. Several other European Communist parties also delegated members; for instance, Boris Souvarine took part in the early phases of the investigation. Trotsky was represented by Pyatakov. The Berlin organization, instructed to choose representatives for Maslow's defense, had sent Werner Scholem and Max Hesse to Moscow. A large majority of the committee were Maslow's political enemies. As a minimum the committee would make it impossible for Maslow to be elected to the German Central Committee; as a maximum he would be assigned to Northern Russia.

The committee began to work immediately after my departure from Moscow in September 1923. It had no material for investigation: there were no documents to study, no witnesses to hear, no evidence to examine. It was not even possible to formulate the accusation correctly; taken out of the context of rumors it became very vague. Therefore, the committee decided to study Maslow's life from childhood on in every detail. Since Maslow was a young man and in 1923 had no biography of interest, this investigation also came to a dead end. After three months, the committee formulated a condemnation of Maslow's behavior in the following way: when arrested in 1922, he had told the Berlin police that he had come to Germany on a sailboat from Denmark and thus given the impression that he had been sent by the Comintern. He had thereby compromised the Russian Party. For this misdeed he was deprived of his party functions and assigned to Northern Russia for a minimum of a year. If during that period he showed ardor and loyal obedience to Comintern authorities, his case would be reconsidered by the International Control Commission and he might then be sent back to Germany.

Thus, not only had the key figure of the German Left been eliminated during the decisive weeks of the uprising, but he and the political tendency he represented were maligned. It was a short step from the insinuation that Maslow had been in the pay of Severing to the deduction that the whole Left was a provocative movement organized by the Social Democratic police. Though everyone in the highest Russian and German circles knew that there was not the slightest figment in Maslow's past on which to hang this tale, it was investigated with straight faces, just as later the Moscow show trials were carried out, in order to help enforce a political line. But in this period GPU manipulation was still in a nascent state, and everyone concerned felt uneasy, especially Radek, who had been principally responsible for suggesting "If we could open Severing's secret files—" He paid me a dozen visits only to assure me of his friendship and trust in Maslow, who needed only to have his record cleared of unreasonable doubt to fulfill the party career for which he was destined.

Berlin, Hamburg, the Ruhr, had reacted both with great interest and with deep indignation to Maslow's enforced residence in Moscow. Maslow had much better relations with the average party member than the leaders of the older generation—Brandler, Heckert, Thalheimer. He had studied music at the Dresden Conservatory, and physics under Einstein and Planck. He was an unusually gifted writer, with a knowledge of the language and literature of half a dozen countries. He spoke well, with a minimum of oratorical effect. He understood machinery and spoke with the workers at the bench in their language, about their jobs, as if he were a member of their crew. In contrast to the intellectuals who ran the party, he could take an automobile apart, if he had to, and put it together again. In Hamburg, aided by his knowledge of the sea, he got on well with the sailors. The crude, mechanical elimination of such a man at a critical period underlined for the rank-and-file German worker as nothing else could have done one aspect of the Russian machine to which he was tied.

The personnel of the investigating committee had been decided by Stalin's Secretariat, and Zinoviev did not risk interfering in it but carried out the decision in the Comintern. Zinoviev treated Maslow in a friendly fashion, consulting with him often on German politics, but he did not dare to speed up his case. When Brandler's boast that, with Maslow removed, victory would be certain proved to be the soap bubble it was, it was apparent that a great injustice had been done. Stalin, who had fabricated the plot, rushed in to rectify the wrong and posed as a leader who can see no injustice done without himself interfering.

In the Politburo, Stalin proposed that he be substituted for Un-schlicht as chairman of the committee for the conclusion of the investigation. He transformed the committee into a political forum, in which the German Right and Left discussed the abortive uprising. After having set the stage, he took the floor and made a strong speech both for the Left in the German Communist Party and for Maslow. "Maslow is the very best element we could find in Germany," Stalin said. "He combines all the qualities that will give us a real revolutionary leader. If we had had fifty Maslows in Germany, a victory would have been certain and Germany and Russia would have been saved from the onslaught of the counter revolution."

I was present at the last session of the investigating committee, when Stalin, in a bid for the leadership of the Comintern, took the floor to defend Maslow. He was full of moral indignation about the way the Comintern (read Zinoviev) had handled the matter. He was for greater Party democracy, for more independence of the Comintern parties from the Moscow center. He hinted that this was not to be achieved under the present Comintern leadership. Before and after the session, he invited Maslow to several private talks at which he embroidered these topics. With this speech the committee was practically adjourned. Maslow was not "an agent of Severing," as had been insinuated. Not only could he return to Germany freely, but he was once again an eligible candidate to the German Politburo and could be elected to replace Brandler.

The intervention of Stalin in the Maslow commission was a blow to Radek and Brandler, who had counted on the indecision of the Comintern to get their own point through. As always, Stalin's move was a shrewd balance—the result of a careful study of the various forces and personalities in the party—and it is a good sample of his flexibility. That Maslow had been prevented from taking part in the decisive October events had been understood in the German party as a clear indication that Brandler had the support of Politburo.

Stalin's change of attitude had been motivated also by the reaction in Russia to the German defeat. The Politburo and the General Secretariat, it was obvious, had fatally underestimated the importance of the developments in Germany and their influence on the Russian Party and on Russia. In the fall of 1923 it was evident in Moscow that the German disaster was a major turning point in post-war Europe. The formal dissolution of the German party dotted the i's, made it clear that the prolonged civil war had come to a close with all the trump cards in the hands of its opponents. The Russian rank and file also reacted with unexpected vehemence; the Leningrad and Moscow Communists understood that Lenin's concept of a European October had suffered final and irrevocable disaster. The passivity of the German Communists contrasted with the traditions of the Russian civil war, in which personal courage, initiative, and partisan fighting against an often overwhelmingly strong opponent had been decisive. Russian Communists and Russian workers felt isolated in a hostile capitalist world; even the German party, which had been presented to them as a model of revolutionary efficiency, had proved an unreliable and stupid ally.

Thus every Russian politician had to reconsider his German policy. Trotsky concentrated his attack on Zinoviev's personal responsibility for the German disaster; Zinoviev defended himself by involved dogmatic expositions of the historical background of "Trotskyism." Stalin sponsored the fight against Trotskyism, since for the moment Trotsky was his most dangerous competitor in the Politburo, and prepared his fight against Zinoviev. All three knew that the German disaster had isolated the Russian revolution for a long period, that a new policy of retreat was imperative, that the Comintern was a corpse. However, appearances had to be saved.

In January 1924 the Russian and German Communists convened in the Kremlin to "draw the lessons" from the German events. Zinoviev was exhausted from the maneuvering with Stalin and the fight with Trotsky, whose position was already so endangered that, in order to avoid sharpening further his relations with the Politburo, he preferred once again to remain absent from the meeting. Trotsky's opinions were, however, represented by Radek, who supported the Brandler wing. The meeting got into action slowly and clumsily. All delegates had arrived at the end of December but had to wait for the Russian Politburo to settle its German policy.

On my way to Moscow I saw another instance of the incongruity between the illegal status of the German Communists and the uninterrupted relations between Russian and German state authorities. I was wanted by the police, and could not travel under my own name. I had made a thousand public speeches in all parts of Germany, and a warrant for my arrest, probably with my photograph, had been sent to all frontiers. I had quarreled several times with Mirov-Abramov, the OMS resident in the Russian Embassy, because I feared that the GPU was arranging for my arrest by furnishing an inadequate false passport. Nevertheless, I passed the frontier at Eydtkuhnen without trouble. The agent of the Berlin political police exchanged a few words with the Russian diplomatic courier whom Mirov had designated to accompany me as a guarantee of my protection, and then did not so much as look at my false passport. The dissolution of the Communist Party had not broken the police-to-police contacts.

Talks with Stalin

When I arrived in Moscow, Stalin invited me to a private interview. I saw him several times, together with Maslow. They spoke in Russian, without an interpreter, which gave Maslow an advantage over other Germans. In my conversations with Stalin, Maslow acted as interpreter.

To our surprise, Stalin was well informed on the details of German party organization, but he was much less able to grasp the implications of German policy. We were both startled by the attitude of this man, so different from that of the other Russian leaders we had met. Even a private discussion with Zinoviev, for example, was at this time largely an exchange of diplomatic phrases; he was visibly under pressure. In our relative ignorance of the Russian Party crisis, Maslow and I often left Zinoviev's Kremlin apartment exchanging sarcastic comments on the cheap tricks he had used to cover his frank opinions. Nevertheless we felt that inside this Party strait-jacket there remained a man with a genuine interest in building up a labor organization in Germany, who shared our hope that a Communist victory in Germany would create for the Russian Party the atmosphere for a new start. We thought Zinoviev's methods inadequate, but we recognized his sincere respect for the German working class and his no less sincere concern for the future of Germany. Discussions with Radek or Bukharin invariably had another aspect. Radek spoke always of the latest zigzag of foreign policy, and with Bukharin we would most probably be drawn into a discussion on complicated Marxist theory.

Stalin was different from all these: he dealt entirely and thoroughly with the implications of the internal party structure. His entire experience had been organizational; his whole energy was devoted to coordinating. His discussion of organization and groupings was not haphazard but directly related to a concept of how to arrange them best for power, of what hierarchical pile reached highest. At this period, we could see no more than the surface of this attitude, but that was enough to puzzle us. We reacted no more favorably to his military uniform, to his highly polished boots, to his transparent intention of building himself up as a military leader.

At this time I was myself principally an organizer and just for this reason I was especially shocked by his advice on how to hold power in the party. In November 1921, in the midst of the Levi crisis, I had been elected chairman of the Berlin branch. It was a most unusual step to put a young woman in command of the largest party organization in the Reich, and the Berlin Communists elected me to this post in part because of my youth, because they distrusted the old leaders and wanted to avoid building up an organization that would become an instrument of power in the hands of a few. I was not only young and not only a woman; I was an Austrian citizen who had come to Berlin only in 1919. My nomination aroused much opposition; the

Central Committee did all it could to block my election. In this period, my "machine" consisted of a group of enthusiastic supporters of Maslow's policy strengthened by my own excellent relations with the Berlin rank and file.

During the first years after my arrival from Vienna, I had worked as a party writer. My nomination in November 1921 was a surprise to me, a spontaneous reaction of the delegates against the Central Committee. But once installed in the Berlin headquarters, 24 Münzstrasse, I set to work enthusiastically with a small staff, consisting of half a dozen paid party organizers and another half dozen clerks, which guided the several thousand volunteers who gave all their spare time and energy to building up the party. No salaried functionary could vote in the regional council unless he was elected, and his salary was more an obstacle than a help to his candidacy. The Berlin organization's funds came entirely from membership dues and occasional drives, and there was always enough of a surplus to enable us to pay our share to the Central Committee. The membership not only insisted on the most accurate auditing of the books but jealously guarded its right to control voluntary functionaries as well. There were regional conventions at least twice a year, and conferences of smaller areas more frequently. The rules existed in order to facilitate a process by which the leaders represented accurately the will of the collectivity. During 1921–1923, the unity of will was so organic in the Berlin organization that only a minimum of tricks was necessary to hold it together; it was not I that guided the organization but the organization that guided me.

Thus we met, Stalin, the shrewd and experienced organizer of tens of thousands of salaried employees, including the state police, and I, the naïve and inexperienced representative of a democratic workers' organization. It was not the function of the various national leaders, Stalin declared, to give in to their rank and file but rather to join the leading group in the Comintern on the basis of a workable compromise, which would enable us all to handle the party mass more easily.

Maslow and I saw Stalin again in the first days of January. That the Communist cause had suffered a final setback in Germany was not mentioned, nor the future policy under such changed circumstances. Instead, we went over the regrouping of the underground Communist cadres, and Stalin showed an amazing capacity to grasp every German organizational detail, however apparently insignificant. He stressed the necessity of relating the illegal party apparatus to every legal ramification, the branch organizations in the trade-unions, the nuclei in the factories. And he emphasized the importance of women's, youth, and children's organizations; he showed a significant interest in the interrelation of the various secret apparatuses with the party. The party's inexperience in conspiracy he criticized severely, and he stressed the necessity of a relentless effort both to improve the technique and to enlarge those parts of the organization that would remain secret even if the party was again made legal. The utmost care was to be used, he emphasized, in covering the contact between the secret branches and the Russian Party.

On January 8, A. Lozovsky reported on the trade-union question. It was one of those meetings where no one really listens, since nothing new could possibly be said on the subject. Everyone agreed that we ought to have influence in the trade-unions and that we did not have it. In the midst of this meeting a messenger came and asked Maslow and me to follow him unobtrusively.

We were led to a modest apartment in the Kremlin, the one-story house assigned to Stalin; previously he had received us at Party headquarters. We met him in the dining room, furnished in a shabby middle-class style with a large table, half a dozen chairs, a telephone. We both knew that this secret meeting in this unusual place was not intended merely to continue our previous discussions. The atmosphere of personal feud and distrust hung heavily over the room; Stalin spoke hesitatingly at first, not knowing how far he could go. These walls would hear many more conversations with top-ranking party bureaucrats during 1923, 1924, and 1925, as he built up his apparatus within the apparatus. Stalin could open party jobs and state jobs, give influential assignments in Russia and abroad, and very often "responsible party tasks" combined with substantial material advantages—apartments, automobiles, country residences, special medical care, jobs for the members of the family. We, on the other hand, wanted something he could not give us—success of the Communist cause in Germany.

Stalin developed a thesis of "Bolshevik discipline," which consisted, said he, in absolute confidence among the leading staff members of the organization. He had tried, so he maintained, to overcome the dissension in the Russian Party resulting from the Trotsky crisis and to recreate an iron guard of leaders who would coöperate without words or theses and be bound together by the necessity of unalterable self-defense. We would soon return to Germany, and he wanted to find out whether we would be reliable enough to be accepted into the inner group. As Stalin continued to ponder about certain weaknesses in human characters, pointing obviously to Zinoviev (for the Trotsky question seemed to be already settled by the Party discussion), the meaning of this excursus on Bolshevik discipline became clear enough. We were seeking an evasive answer—one that would neither attract the hostility of Stalin nor commit us to deserting Zinoviev—when our conversation was suddenly interrupted. Zinoviev and Kamenev appeared, paying an informal visit to Stalin.

It came out later that the Secretariat had assigned them to attend a certain Party meeting at the time of our visit to Stalin. They did not want us to be alone with him, however, and had left as soon as they heard that we were to be taken to him. Zinoviev and Kamenev began to tell inept stories about the meeting; their laughter was artificial, the atmosphere tense and nervous. Maslow and I got away as quickly as possible.

Outside we exchanged a few words summing up our impression that the continued submission of German Communism to the Politburo would be disastrous and would end in catastrophe. Both of us were convinced that we had to build up an independent party organization which, without breaking the official tie to the Comintern, would be able to find an independent policy in which internationalism was not merely a cover for unending sacrifices, for determining German policy by the day-to-day course of the Russian State Party.

During these weeks Maslow and I had many conversations under more normal conditions with all the other Russian leaders, especially with Bukharin and Radek. What I remember best is that they all had an air of nervousness about them, that they all avoided coming to any definite conclusion concerning the importance of the German defeat, which was presented as one more setback; after a period, it was said or implied, the party would be back again, continuing its fight as usual. In contrast to Lenin's habit of turning corners so sharply that their angles stuck into the consciousness of everyone concerned, there was a general agreement to befog the meaning of the defeat both for Germany and for Russia.

One of our most interesting discussions was with Mikhail Tomsky, the leader of the Russian trade-unions. Tomsky stood somewhat apart from the factional struggle, identifying himself neither with Trotsky nor with Zinoviev nor with Stalin. After the conflict over the trade-union question, he had been assigned to Turkestan for a period to eliminate him from activity in the center. After his return, he kept his dissatisfaction with the Party's labor policy to himself, but became the center of a group of trade-union leaders who continued the fight to change the relation between the unions and the Party. Even more than before, they wanted to be rid of the Party monopoly, to strengthen the union's independent role.

Tomsky was especially interested in the organization of the German factory councils and the part they played in the Cuno strike. He was fascinated by this German experience, for in this industrial country he expected the proletariat to have a much greater weight than in his native peasant Russia, where the soviets had easily become one wheel in the Party's political machinery.[14]

My Russian advisor, Schmidt, had returned to Moscow some time before me and at Radek's instigation had written an unfavorable report on the Berlin organization. But in the Russian Party Schmidt sided with Tomsky's trade-union group. Because of his growing friendship with Maslow, Tomsky induced Schmidt to tear up his report and write a favorable one, and he arranged a meeting at which Maslow spoke on the potentialities of the factory-council movement. Several hundred leaders of the Moscow unions discussed his report on this new form of proletarian organization. Stalin's Politburo, in a counter move, sent to the meeting Lozovsky and Jakob Walcher, who attacked Maslow's anarcho-syndicalist views and defended the classical Communist concept of trade-unions as necessarily tied to the party.

---

[14] Mikhail P. Tomsky had been a member of the Party since 1905. Sentenced to a term of hard labor under the Tsar and later exiled, he returned after the February revolution. From 1917 to 1929 he was chairman of the All-Union Central Council of Trade-Unions; he was elected to the Central Committee of the Party in 1919. From 1920, he was head of the Trade-Union Opposition, which allied itself with Bukharin and Rykov in 1928–1929. He committed suicide on August 22, 1936, driven to despair by the climax of Stalin's terror regime during the dekulakization.

On January 11, finally, the official session of the Comintern Presidium took place. There were present Zinoviev, Bukharin, Radek, Pyatnitsky, and some technicians of the Russian Party; Dimitrov and two or three other Bulgarians; Warski, Walecki, and Kostrzewa from the Polish party; and for the German party, Brandler, Walcher, and Clara Zetkin for the Right wing; Remmele, Pieck, and Könen for the Center; Scholem, König, Max Hesse, Maslow, and Fischer for the Left. Five statements on the German events were prepared for discussion: Zinoviev's, the Center group's, another presented by Zinoviev for both himself and this group, Brandler's defense presented by Radek, and a Left platform.

Reporting as representative in Germany of the Executive Committee of the Comintern, Radek said that he had been one of four such (Radek, Guralsky, Skoblevsky, and Schmidt), who had acted on all questions by unanimous agreement and had signed all reports. These delegates had not taken part in the Chemnitz conference, but had participated behind the scenes in the meetings of the Central Committee. What did we find in Germany in October 1923? asked Radek.

> The strategic plan of the party, accepted here by the Executive Committee in the conferences of September and October, broke down. It started from the following basic idea: the proletariat would march in Saxony to defend the workers' government, in which we would participate; the proletariat would try to exploit the state power in Saxony to build a wall in this closely organized proletarian region between counter revolution in Bavaria and fascism in the North. At the same time, the party would intervene all over Germany and mobilize the masses. . . . The comrades in the government were not able to arm the proletariat; they had only 800 rifles in Saxony. . . . I agreed to drop the plan for an uprising in Saxony because the united front with the Social Democratic workers could not be achieved. However, I proposed proclaiming a general strike.[15]

Radek had opposed, he added, Ruth Fischer's proposal to combine a general strike in Berlin with the mobilization there of Red Hundreds and the armed units of the party. "My proposal was strike without

---

[15] *Die Lehren der deutschen Ereignisse* (Hamburg, 1924), pp. 5–6.

uprising," he said, "and that was rejected, on October 26, 1923, by the small committee of seven members of the Central Committee."

Actually, a few days later this Directorium reversed its decision and in substance accepted Radek's proposal. It decided that the party should call a nationwide protest strike but avoid armed fighting; but the party locals did not call the strike, or did so only partially and ineffectively. Radek's advocacy of a peaceful strike was an alibi and not a policy, for even he realized that in October 1923 the Communists could not have called a general strike as a mere demonstration.

Fascism has triumphed over the November Republic, Radek said. "In Germany the November Republic was dead in the hearts of the working people. No rabbit would stand up to defend it." This was an implicit defense of his Schlageter policy. Drawing a middle line between his friends Trotsky and Brandler, Radek stated that it would have been wrong to set a date for the uprising in Moscow but that a date should have been set. In the discussion that followed, I recalled that in September Walther Ulbricht had reported in Moscow that it would be superfluous to arm the Thuringian workers, since in Thuringia everybody already had a rifle. I also quoted Guralsky, representative of the Central Committee at the September conference, who boasted on his way back from Moscow that in three days we would have power in Saxony and set our army on the march towards Berlin.

The center of the dispute shifted to the responsibility for the telegram sent by the Comintern to the German party proposing that it ignore General Müller and arm the Saxon workers. Zinoviev faced the joint opposition of Radek, the Poles, and the German Right, who tried to make him personally and exclusively responsible for this "political folly." Zinoviev had acted in accordance with the decision of the Russian Politburo, but he could not say this in his defense for he had to maintain the fiction that the Comintern represented the collective will of all the parties and was not a branch of one. Every delegate to the session knew of the fight in the Russian Party, and those who attacked him but not the Politburo hoped thus to come out of the struggle with a gain for themselves.

> ZINOVIEV: The telegram was decided on in the presence of Brandler.
> WARSKI: What an error! What an illusion!

ZINOVIEV: The representative of the German party gave us those figures—fifty to sixty thousand [workers already armed and easily to be mobilized in Saxony].

PIECK: The party never learned of this decision.

ZINOVIEV: The telegram was decided on in the presence of three German and three Russian comrades. How did we anticipate that our decision would be carried out? As an episode in the civil war, and we emphasized this in the text. . . .

BRANDLER: I did not agree to this telegram.

ZINOVIEV: I bear the greatest responsibility for the entrance into the government. Brandler was undecided. He said "I don't know whether that has been sufficiently prepared," but he gave in. . . . Compare our telegram with the speeches of the ministers. . . . A commission composed of Zinoviev, Kolarov, Clara Zetkin, whose emendations were accepted, wrote a letter to the Central Committee [expanding the proposal in the telegram].[16]

Zinoviev then tried, but vainly, to return to a discussion of policy. He polemized against Radek's conclusion that fascism had been victorious over the November Republic. He was interrupted by constant heckling; his opponents were more comfortable discussing the responsibility of the Comintern Chairman than policy in Germany. Trotsky was defended in his absence by Warski, who referred to a letter from the Polish Central Committee to the Russian Politburo in support of Trotsky. The German Right, however, did not join in on this crucial question; Brandler hoped that by deserting Trotsky he might work out a compromise. Radek, on the other hand, attacked Zinoviev and defended Trotsky aggressively; Zinoviev's reply, alluding to a speech by Radek before the Moscow students, was interrupted by an uproar and almost broken off. Thus the deliberations continued, distorted by the convulsive struggle in the Politburo.

When Zinoviev started analyzing the development of the German party, Pieck shouted, "Who gives a damn for the development of the party? A mass party that was formed by a shotgun marriage!" Zinoviev warmly defended Brandler; he should not be sacrificed. From now on, a majority of the Center, with a minority representation of the Left and Right, should lead the party. Zetkin replied in the name of the Right wing that in the final vote they would accept Zinoviev's resolution.

---

[16] *Die Lehren der deutschen Ereignisse*, pp. 60–62.

The Polish delegation produced another letter from their party to the Russian Politburo, this one dated January 21, 1924, the day Lenin died, defending Radek and expressing concern about the state of the Executive Committee without Lenin and with Trotsky's authority endangered. The Poles asked that the Russian Party guarantee that even the possibility of eliminating Comrade Trotsky from his leading Party and state positions was unthinkable. Again Zetkin, Pieck, and Brandler remained silent, thus paying for their posts in the new German Central Committee. In deserting Trotsky, until then their recognized Comintern leader, the Right facilitated Stalin's silent manipulations.

The German defeat has been discussed in the Russian Party and the Comintern for the last twenty years.[17] Though a Western mentality finds this labyrinth of dogmatic feuds difficult to thread, the complicated struggle for power within the Russian hierarchy can be understood only after the interrelation between Russian and German party affairs has been raveled. In 1931, when the fate of Germany was again in suspense, Thalheimer tried to regain the good graces of Stalin by denying that the German Right had sided with Trotsky in 1923. He declared:

> The Executive Committee of the Comintern reëvaluated the Germany party only in *December* 1923. Only now are we able to state the reasons and the date of this turning point. . . . How did it come about that after having approved essentially our strategy, Zinoviev and the Executive Committee executed a turn of 180 degrees?
>
> The following is the context: On December 13, 1923 (if I am not wrong), Comrade Radek made a speech in a big party meeting in Moscow, intervening in the debate about Trotsky. If the majority of the Russian Central Committee turned against Trotsky,

---

[17] In the official Party histories, Stalin has made the most of Trotsky's temporary alliance with Brandler. Popov writes, for example:

"The broadest masses of the workers and petty bourgeoisie were in the mood for revolution, but the opportunist leadership of the German Communist Party, which was headed by the Luxemburgists Brandler and Thalheimer, proved absolutely incapable of utilizing the situation which had arisen, let themselves be taken in tow by the 'Left' Social Democrats, and thus enabled the German bourgeoisie to extricate itself from the acute political crisis.

"In spite of the fact that the Trotskyists maintained factional contact with the Brandler group, they attempted to saddle the Central Committee with the responsibility for the crass opportunist errors of the Brandlerists." (N. Popov, *Outline History of the CPSU*, II, 196.)

he declared, not only he *but all the leaders of the German and French Communist parties, the principal parties of the West, would turn against the majority of the Central Committee.* That was on December 13. Some days later Zinoviev sent a letter to the Central Committee of the German Communist Party in which he changed his policy completely. . . . The real reason for this change was the *panic* in the leadership of the Russian Communist Party, originating mainly with Zinoviev, who took Radek verbatim and believed that the German Central Committee would support Trotsky against a majority of the Russian party leadership. That was the reason for the change. It had nothing to do with the events in Germany or in France or in the Comintern proper. It was simply *the consequence of a maneuver in the internal Russian factional fight.* We learned of this speech of Radek's only much later. The campaign, the fire against us, etc., etc., had been going on for a long time when, at the time of the Fifth World Congress, we learned the real cause of the turn. Radek's statement, moreover, had been invented. No one had authorized him to say that we would fight on Trotsky's side if he was attacked. When we first got the news of the fight around Trotsky, we said: Before we can judge this, we have to know the facts behind the fight. I wrote an article in the *Internationale* as soon as we got the facts *against Trotsky's point of view.* Therefore, it was not our real attitude toward the Russian party crisis that resulted in the turn, but the fiction of such an attitude.[18]

This colored presentation is a fabricated post-crisis defense, garnished with servile observations on Stalin's lucid analysis of German politics. In reality, every participant in the committee in Moscow during January 1924 knew exactly what he was selling and what he was buying. In 1924, Thalheimer and his group hoped that at the suggestion of Zinoviev and Stalin they might be coöpted into the German Central Committee, even if a majority of the party was opposed to them. The German Right, therefore, sold Trotsky to Stalin's Politburo and to Zinoviev's Comintern Presidium and was paid with encouragement of the Right cadres and with jobs in the party's secret services and the Profintern, the Red trade-union international.

The fight between Trotsky and the Politburo was during its first phase mainly a fight over the Old Guard's desire to preserve their prerogative of power. In spite of his brilliant achievements during the

---

[18] August Thalheimer, *1923: Eine verpasste Revolution?*, p. 11.

October revolution and in all his later state functions, Trotsky had remained outside the Party hierarchy. Lenin had introduced this relationship but had also tried to find the mean between the two poles, the Old Guard and Trotsky. When the old Party leaders, Stalin and Zinoviev, combined against Trotsky, Radek's support was logical, for Radek was even more an outsider.

The alliance of Stalin and Zinoviev seemed to have brought under control the Party crisis arising from Lenin's approaching death. During this period Marxism as an interpretation of history was transformed into scholastic dogma. In the attack on Trotsky in 1924 the fundamentals of Stalinism were produced: a mythus of Bolshevik Party history. As an absolute monarch derives his just power from God, so the power of Stalin, as Lenin's rightful heir, follows from the infallibility of Bolshevism.

Neither Zinoviev nor Bukharin, in participating in the fight against Trotsky, intended to expel him from Soviet legality. Many Trotskyites, however, were transferred to assignments far away from the political centers of Moscow and Leningrad; high-ranking Trotskyites—for instance, Rakovsky and Pyatakov—were eliminated from Party positions and assigned to high state or diplomatic functions, and the small fry were mercilessly eliminated. This was Stalin's great opportunity, and he used it to the fullest extent. Zinoviev did the talking against the Trotskyites and Stalin the organizing. The Secretariat got its men into all important party posts.

Lessons of October

After the Fifth World Congress, in August 1924, Trotsky decided that he could no longer be silent and had to strike back. He started a second series of discussions by publishing Lessons of October,[19] a pamphlet attacking the Troika but with the main fire directed against Zinoviev. Trotsky denies the relevance of the pre-October Bolshevik tradition; the October experiences, he states, had opened a new period of development. In this analysis of the Russian and German Octobers he drops his unreliable German partners, Brandler and Thalheimer.

---

[19] The pamphlet appeared first in October 1924, written as an introduction to a projected two-volume collection of Trotsky's writings during the first year of the revolution, entitled *1917*.

It was nonsensical, according to Trotsky, to represent the Party as a consistent unit, as always being the same. The Party before 1917 had consisted of a few thousand elite staff members; because of Lenin's unique qualities as a leader, it had remained a living and democratic organization in spite of his highly centralist principles. By 1923 the Party had grown into an organization of half a million members; never before was a state led by a disciplined mass organization of such scope. The fusion of this mass Party with the new state apparatus was an entirely new phenomenon that should be analyzed without dogmatic prejudice. This collective body of half a million members monopolized political and economic power in a country of 160 millions and maintained it by terrorist measures. By 1923, the attempts to create a soviet democracy had failed. During the short first period, 1917–1919, under civil-war conditions, the soviets had been representative bodies and a responsible part of the government. By now they had deteriorated into administrative divisions of the State Party, a deadwood stage for platform speakers, decorative settings for propaganda performances, or, as Stalin correctly defined them, auxiliary organizations to carry the word of the Party to the masses. The prohibition of Party factions at the Tenth Party Congress, in March 1921, reflected the withering away of Party democracy. Trotsky justifies it in his pamphlet as an emergency and temporary measure essential in the critical moment of the Kronstadt uprising. But since then the fight against factionalism had been intensified to a point where all internal Party life suffocated.

In *The New Course,* written a year before, Trotsky had demanded the legalization of groups and factions and especially a greater opportunity for influence by the youth. Youth, by its rebellious nature, would bring an oppositional element into the State Party and thus counterbalance the power of the Old Guard. *The New Course,* however, did not touch the crucial problem of soviet democracy. In accepting the premise of total power for the State Party and in limiting his fight to one for another Party constitution, Trotsky had estranged the various Workers' Opposition groups, who were convinced that the State Party had to be deprived of its monopoly and that only a system of several parties could form the necessary counterweight to the increase of totalitarian dictatorship.

Lessons of October attacks an even narrower question, that of the

Party leadership. Trotsky desired first of all to destroy the authority of Zinoviev and Kamenev, whom he regarded as the most noxious personifications of the Lenin legend. Since Lenin personified the 1917 revolution, Trotsky wanted to destroy their identification with the Lenin of October. He linked their "desertion" in 1917 with Zinoviev's lack of leadership in the German October. But the purpose of Trotsky's proof that the Old Guard was fallible was only too obviously to propose himself, and during 1924 the Old Bolsheviks united to rebut Trotsky's attack. Polemics against Trotsky in this period include articles not only by each of the Troika but also by Sokolnikov, Kuusinen, and Krupskaya, Lenin's wife, who seldom participated in intra-Party discussion.[20]

Trotsky's counter myth was that the criterion of present policy was the behavior of its proponent in 1917. Thus, though it contains a pertinent analysis of party structure, *Lessons of October* missed the crucial problem of the period. In Russia the Bolsheviks had seized power, and the problem was how to combat the monopoly of the Bolshevik Party without again leading the country to ruin, dismemberment, and collapse; how to overcome without terrorism the resistance of the peasantry to industrialization of the country and modernization of agriculture. That was the task of the generation of 1924, to plow below the problems that had been dealt with in *The New Course,* to draft a program for an elimination of the Party monopoly and for the establishment of a new form of democratic society, to develop Lenin's vague suggestions of 1917 into concrete formulas for a functioning workers' democracy.

With regard to Germany in 1924, Trotsky's *Lessons of October* was equally irrelevant, for it fostered the dangerous illusion of German Communists that they could seize power soon if only they would thoroughly "Bolshevize" their party. What they needed in 1924 was rather a thorough shake-up, to help them realize that the time for the Jacobin coup d'état had passed, that for a period their task was to regroup all forces for the militant defense of the Weimar Republic.

Lessons of October was not an effective weapon in the fight against Stalin's rise. As a competent interpretation of the German events of

---

[20] *The Errors of Trotskyism,* Communist Party of Great Britain (London, 1925).

1923, however, it remains of great value. The turning points in the history of the German Republic were grasped more clearly by Trotsky than by any other contemporary. That is true of his analysis for 1933 as well as 1923; his three pamphlets on the German situation,[21] written in Istanbul just before Hitler came to power, represent a correct and succinct presentation of the German crisis of 1932, fully confirmed by Hitler's victory and its consequences.

In 1924, however, Radek and Brandler's evaluation of the situation seemed much more realistic than the bold *post factum* interpretation of Trotsky. The Right Communists had the men of common sense on their side. The split in the labor movement, the stubborn refusal of either the Social Democratic politicians or the strongest organized force in Germany—the trade-unions—to participate in preparing an uprising, seemed to justify the Communist retreat. An uprising would have meant sailing with an organized minority into the torrent of spontaneous mass actions, counting on organized labor to join in. Brandler's point of view, in spite of the personal conflict between him and Zinoviev, resembled that of Zinoviev and Kamenev in their opposition to the 1917 uprising. Radek and Brandler were afraid not only of beginning a civil war with a minority but also, as Zinoviev had stated in November 1917, of "maintaining a purely Bolshevik government by means of political terror."

Against these fears, Trotsky emphasizes the maturity of the revolutionary situation in Germany in October 1923 and the consequent likelihood that the Communist initiative would be broadened into a people's movement:

> We witnessed in Germany the classic demonstration of how it is possible to miss a perfectly exceptionable revolutionary situation of world historical importance.

(At the Comintern conference in January, this same assertion had been attacked by Stalin not for its content but for its contradiction of declarations by Pyatakov and Radek, Trotsky's friends.) The Politburo, Trotsky hints, had never seriously prepared the full support of a German revolution by Soviet Russia:

---

[21] *Germany—the Key to the International Situation* (December 1931); *What Next? Vital Questions for the German Proletariat* (September 1932); *The Only Road for Germany* (April 1933).

It is indispensable for us to have a concrete account, full of factual data, of last year's developments in Germany. What we need is such an account as would provide a concrete explanation of the causes of this most cruel historic defeat.

The German retreat had been defended by enumerating the overwhelming forces of the Communists' adversaries, by emphasizing the risks involved. The probable extermination of the Communist Party had been put in the forefront, a disaster of such scope that all sacrifices were justified to avoid it. Trotsky attacks this thesis by a comparative analysis of the Russian October revolution. "You underestimate the strength of our enemy," all opponents of the October insurrection had said, "and exaggerate our own forces." Petrograd was the decisive strategic point. Here were concentrated 5,000 officer cadets, splendidly equipped and organized, eager to fight. Petrograd was the headquarters of the army, its garrison was reinforced by Cossack regiments and further by artillery deployed around the city. It was also possible that important bodies of troops from the front would join the Petrograd garrison against the revolutionaries. All these forces, Trotsky writes, could be evaluated beforehand in a way that made insurrection seem impossible. In their calculations, the German comrades

> meticulously added [to the strength of the bourgeoisie] the forces of the Reichswehr and the police; then they reduced the whole to a round number (half a million and more) and so obtained a compact mass force armed to the teeth and absolutely sufficient to paralyze their own efforts. No doubt the forces of the German counter revolution were much stronger numerically, and at any rate, better organized and prepared than our own Kornilovites and semi-Kornilovites. But so were the effective forces of the German revolution.

There were, Trotsky rightly points out, important differences between Russia and Germany. The specific weight of the proletarian centers in Germany were unparalleled on the Continent; only in England was there a similar distribution of the proletarian population.

> The proletariat composes the overwhelming majority of the population in Germany. In our country, the question—at least during the initial stage—was decided by Petrograd and Moscow. In Germany, the insurrection would have immediately blazed in scores of mighty proletarian centers. On this arena, the armed

forces of the enemy would not have seemed nearly as terrible as
they did in statistical computations, reduced to round figures. In
any case, we must categorically reject the tendentious calculations
which were made, and which are still being made, after the debacle
of the German October, in order to justify the policy that led to
the debacle. . . . Never tested in the fire of insurrection, these
forces would have seemed immeasurably more terrible than they
proved in action. . . . Passive fatalism is really only a cover for
irresolution and even incapacity for action, but it camouflages itself
with the consoling prognosis that we are growing more and more
influential. . . . What a gross delusion! The strength of a revolutionary party increases only up to a certain moment, after which
the process can turn into the very opposite.

This passive fatalism of the German party in 1923, Trotsky propheti-
cally predicted, would have certain consequences:

> The hopes of the masses change into disillusionment as a result
> of the party's passivity while the enemy recovers from his panic
> and takes advantage of this disillusionment. We witnessed such a
> decisive turning point in Germany in October 1923.[22]

That is exactly what occurred. The enemy took substantial advantage
of the disillusionment of the radical elements in Germany. For the
fatalistic passivity of the Communist leadership was not reflected only
among the party's rank and file; millions in Germany had awaited
the Communists' initiative. Sympathy with Communism in Germany
had transcended working-class circles. The intelligentsia and the universities; large strata of the proletarianized middle class, uprooted by
the inflation; groups of young officers; and even substantial numbers
of farmhands and small peasants, suffering terribly in the inflation, had
partly feared, partly hoped for a turn toward a decisive change. It was
only later, after Stalin's Russia had definitely turned to national socialism, that the Germans eventually chose their own brand.

The repercussions of the German defeat on the international Communist scene cannot be overstated. They were particularly incisive in
Italy, where Mussolini had just begun to consolidate his power. The
Italian working class, if it had not lost its initiative through the defeat
in Germany, might still have got rid of him.

---

[22] This and the four quotations just preceding are from Trotsky's *Lessons of
October,* translated from the Russian by John G. Wright . . . (New York: Pioneer
Publishers, copyright 1937), pp. 23, 69–72.

In Germany, the bitterness was reflected in intense party strife, which had a deep demoralizing effect on the rank and file. The German worker was not merely the man of tradition, overprudent at decisive turning points, that he was pictured by Marxist social scientists. There were, it is true, the conservative, slow-thinking, tradition-bound socialist workers, who had grown up in the mass party before the war and learned there to go forward step by step with the utmost caution. But there was also the young generation, largely ex-soldiers without links to the prewar past, with the soldiers' contempt for civil legality, who wished to change German society from top to bottom. The impotence of the old party leaders, Communists included, enabled the Nazis to exploit this polarization in the working class and build up a plebeian mass party.

The cadres of German restoration were composed of all classes, in the first phase elements mainly of the army, land-owners, and expansionist industrialists, who were joined during the inflation by frustrated intelligentsia and petty bourgeois and finally, during the depression of 1929–1933, by substantial groups of workers. The restoration movement thus involved important strata of all classes, but its driving force was the desperate elite of the old Imperial groups, who wanted to regain, at any cost and by any means, Germany's lost status. This goal was incompatible with Germany's geopolitical and population resources and could be attempted only by over-emphasis of coördination and centralization. The function of Nazi terror was to overcome these shortcomings; its specific forms were the result of both the civil war and the high technological standards of the country.

If German labor had acted to prevent this German Imperial restoration when it first began to develop, it would have purified the European organism by annihilating its most dangerous sorespot. Trotsky and the Communist Left were correct in their warning that such an opponent could not be crushed with democratic procedures.

German labor, at the head of the German Republic in 1923, would have been faced with a dangerous and complex task. A civil war in that year could not have avoided terrorist measures. In the process of defeating the well-organized and brutal opponent, German labor would have established a dictatorial government and prevented the development to its maturity of the phenomenon known as Nazism. It is my conviction, however, that in 1923, before German labor had lost its internationalist and humanitarian tradition, before its organizations had been corroded from within, its dictatorship would have been a historical episode. Germany would have found an equilibrium in a return to democratic government.

In the eyes of contemporary observers, the Hitler putsch was even less mature and more adventurist than the Communist uprising in Hamburg, but it gave Adolf Hitler status. Until November 1923, Hitler had been a provincial crackpot, unknown outside Bavaria; the monarchist conservatives and even the extreme nationalists had not regarded him as a serious political figure. His attempt to seize power at the peak of the political and economic crisis gave him a nationwide hearing; he gained popularity because he attempted to change the course of the German Republic fundamentally. Hitler presented nationalism in a proletarian disguise and thus captured the imagination and energy of the masses. In 1923, National Socialism won the first round in the battle against International Communism, which had definitely proved its impotence. When the great depression of 1929 set in, the Nazis were already a length ahead.

4.

THE PERIOD
OF TRANSFORMATION

Among the famous lithographs of Käthe Kollwitz, there is one entitled *Germany in 1923—and in Spring 1925*. The first half shows a German working-class woman, sitting in deep sorrow with her head hidden in her hands; the eyes are closed in exhaustion, the lines around the thin mouth express bitterness and despair. In the second half, the same woman is shown in the same pose, but her eyes are open; half incredulous, half curious, she blinks again into the light; her mouth is fuller, and some of the lines have disappeared. Käthe Kollwitz, without ever having been a member of the Communist Party, was one of its venerated People's Artists, and these lithographs represent the moods of the time.

Despite the apparent victory of the Berlin cabinet against both extremes, the Communists in Hamburg and the Nazis in Munich, its position in domestic and foreign affairs remained both complex and insecure. The quelling of the Hitler putsch had not quelled the nationalists and the Black Reichswehr. With the rearrangement between Seeckt and the Bavarian Reichswehr, Munich was retained as the *place d'armes* of the anti-Weimar contingents. In the army and its illegal fringes, dictatorial aspirants were legion, and they regarded the breathing spell that the Seeckt-Kahr agreement had given Berlin as a temporary surcease, during which they could prepare their next coup. With their many sympathizers in high influence, the nationalist conspirators much more logically than the Communists could regard their defeat as a strategic withdrawal.

The success of the Berlin cabinet in its negotiations with the British, who agreed that reparations should be decided by pourparlers and that the occupation of the Rhine-Ruhr should come to an end, relieved only the greatest pressure on the Reich. For the French continued to occupy the area and continued to press for their permanent control of the Ruhr. France planned to become the organizer of the Continent up to the Vistula. British reparations proposals were intended, on the one hand, to block these French aspirations and, on the other, to draw Germany westward from a possible alignment with Soviet Russia. With this French–British–Russian rivalry, German industry felt able to demand again that loans precede reparations payments; it hoped that through this maze of conflicting interests it might find a path to the restitution of Germany's power.

An American Offer

At the end of 1923 a really powerful competitor of British policy in postwar Europe appeared for the first time, the United States. In response to the isolationist wave that flooded the country after 1918, the Senate had rejected President Wilson's proposal to enter the League of Nations. The United States had borne the principal burden of financing the war and had come out of it with every European nation her debtor. For her, reparations were directly linked to the repayment of Allied war debts.

Germany, in spite of her defeat, was still industrially the most advanced country in Europe, and with foreign loans her economy could be rehabilitated in a short time. Since 1920, German economists had emphasized this situation in numerous memoranda, based on surveys and concluding with proposals for intensified production. Reparations could be paid only after foreign loans had enabled Germany to buy raw material abroad and to rebuild her industry, thus giving her the possibility of producing the necessary surplus. Moreover, German experts kept pointing out that reparations payments had to be flexible, varying with the changing economic situation in Germany. This demand for flexible annuities, based on sound economic reasoning, became a major weapon of the German government for the revision of the Versailles Treaty.

In the fall of 1923, at the peak of the political crisis in Hamburg,

Munich, and Dresden, President Coolidge accepted the suggestion of Secretary of State Hughes that the reparations problem be submitted to an investigation by nonpolitical experts. On December 7, this committee of experts was selected, with General Charles G. Dawes, later Vice-President, as its chairman. By the end of the year, "the Dawes Plan" was being tentatively drafted, corresponding in its main features to the proposals made by various German experts during the past years. Its essence was that reparations were to be paid from economic profits, especially export surplus, and not from a transfer of capital. No definite amount was stipulated for the total sum of payments. The enormous fixed annuities were replaced by sliding annuities corresponding to the output of German economy. For the first period German economy would be given a relative respite to enable it to produce the surplus goods required for delivery abroad, during which period the first substantial American loans would create the basis for later payments. From September 1, 1924, to August 31, 1925, Germany had to mobilize 200 million gold marks, to which would be added a loan of 800 million gold marks from the United States. In the first reparations year, Germany's payments would begin with one billion gold marks and reach not a minimum nor a maximum but a "normal" annuity of 2.5 billion gold marks in 1928–1929. The reparations agent in Berlin was empowered to stop payments to Germany's creditors in case of renewed economic and financial crisis. On the other hand, the Allies could get higher annuities if German business prospered. This sliding reparations scale was an immediate stimulus to German industry, but the Dawes Plan tied the German economy to the American business cycle.

The American experts had accepted Poincaré's idea of production pledges, but in an American way. For to the French government production pledges were another term for the seizure and annexation of the most industrialized and richest region of Germany; France's demand for the internationalization of the Ruhr after World War II repeats the French policy of 1923. The American proposals, on the other hand, were all based on economic considerations. The production pledges consisted in a system of safeguards, comprising together a firm control of Germany economy. As a first security guarantee, an independent company, controlled by representatives of the creditor states, was set up to administer the government's rail system. Their representation in the board of the Reichsbank transformed it, too, into an institution independent of the German cabinet. Around these two key measures there was built an array of guarantees equivalent to a control of the Reich budget, such as mortgages on customs receipts and taxes on transportation.

In Germany the Dawes Plan met violent opposition from an articulate minority; it would result in the "colonization" of Germany, in its "Balkanization." (Control of banks and railways was indeed the classic method of guaranteeing loans to Turkey, to the Balkans, to China.) Nationalist sentiments were antagonized by the direct intervention in domestic affairs. Workers and employees in state institutions feared that the foreign experts would lower their wages and salaries. However, the nationalist opposition, except in the Right wing of the German National People's Party and in groups and grouplets around the extreme Right parties, was shadow-boxing. The top figures of big business and the Reich administration accepted the Dawes Plan as the best way back into the world market. Since an immediate change in the relationship of forces in Europe was excluded, and since the restoration of German industry was the premise to Germany's future, the Dawes Plan was endorsed by the majority of conservative parties and organizations.

Its staunchest supporters were the trade-unions and the Social Democratic Party, which criticized only those portions affecting the wages of their followers. In general, they welcomed the intervention of American capital, for they wanted a safeguard against a renewed economic and political crisis in the 1923 style.

The Dawes Plan made a strong impression on the Moscow Politburo. The Russian experts, among them Eugen Varga, studied all its details and saw in it a confirmation of their theory of the "industrial colony, Germany." The implications for Soviet Russia of this direct American intervention in German economy were of the utmost importance. Of all the consequences of the Dawes Plan in Germany, the Russian Politburo was interested in only one—how it would affect Soviet policy. There was no conference to build up a workable Comintern policy based on the profound change the Dawes Plan introduced in Europe. A fundamental revision of an important portion of the Versailles Treaty demanded a corresponding change in German Communist policy, based both on the unbroken power of the forces of restoration and the place that Germany had to find in the new balance between Europe and the United States. The influx of Left revolutionary phraseology, the result of the October defeat, well served Moscow's policy of avoiding commitments in Germany, of refraining from analyzing the implications of the Dawes Plan.

Thus the Dawes Plan was interpreted only as a new instrument for the encirclement of Russia, for the preparation of German intervention under British sponsorship. The German party was instructed to fight the plan without qualifications. These instructions were superfluous, for the Communist Party, rank and file and leadership alike, were united at this period in their opposition to all intervention from the West. The Russian Politburo, fearful of loosening or breaking its relation with German military circles and Moscow-oriented nationalists, emphasized not only the economic consequences of stabilization but also its broader prospects for Germany's future. Shall Germany become a dagger in Britain's hand directed against Moscow? Which way can Germany go, towards London or towards Moscow? Germany cannot stay in the middle of the road, and will be crushed if she does not make her choice in time. The Dawes Plan is, in spite of its more flexible formulations, an economic Versailles, which will enslave generations of Germans to Wall Street and the City; a combination of Germany with Russia, on the other hand, would free her finally from Western domination and colonization. Communist pamphlets, leaflets, propaganda meetings, speeches in the Reichstag, as well as more specialized propaganda among the Reichswehr officers and nationalist circles, all went under the headline "London or Moscow." [1]

Manuilsky's Mission to Berlin

On March 1, 1924, the state of emergency under which the Communist Party had been banned since October 1923 was cancelled, and General Seeckt was replaced by Minister of the Interior Karl Jarres (later, in the 1925 elections, the nationalists' candidate for the presidency). With this transfer, party life was eased and the return to its former status prepared.

The membership figure of the Communist Party had decreased

---

[1] Cf. *London oder Moskau?* Reichstag speeches by Ernst Thälmann and Ruth Fischer (Berlin, 1924).

from 267,000 in September 1923 to 121,394 in April 1924, reflecting principally the loss of revolutionary cadres repelled by the party's apathy. The party press reached perhaps twice the membership. During the illegal period, party literature, disguised as something else, had been distributed to provincial units by parcel post.[2] The greatest success was a song book, of which 300,000 copies were printed. In Essen, the French occupation authorities confiscated all literature in the party bookshop. "In several cities, such as Bremen, the police burned the literature in the open market place."[3]

During this illegal period, the Russian Politburo watched with concern the growing anti-Moscow trend in the German party. In 1922, Zinoviev had sent August Kleine-Guralsky to Berlin. Still under the discipline of the Russian Party, he had been elected to the German Politburo at the Leipzig convention. In October 1923 he deserted Brandler and was the driving spirit in the formation of a Center group, comprising principally Hermann Remmele, Wilhelm Könen, Walther Ulbricht, Walther Stöcker. A Central Committee made up in the main of this group would have been an excellent front for Moscow control. As its actual chairman, and with his membership in two parties, Guralsky would have been in a position to carry out Moscow's manipulation of the German party with the greatest of ease. To have Guralsky as the leader in fact of the German party was a pet idea of Zinoviev during this period, but when it became obvious that this plan could not be realized, other measures of disciplining it were considered.[4]

At the suggestion of the Stalin Secretariat, the Politburo had assigned a strong man, Dmitri Z. Manuilsky, to help Zinoviev. This assignment was one of the major instruments by which Stalin penetrated Zinoviev's Comintern. Until that time, Manuilsky had served only on Russian

---

[2] For instance, in December 1923, 154 parcels and 380 smaller packages were sent out; in January 1924, 364 parcels and 639 smaller packages; in February, 377 parcels and 74 smaller packages. During this illegal period the Red Aid, with 120 lawyers on call, handled 6,600 cases. The military authorities often arranged to have Communist organizers taken into protective custody.

[3] *Bericht über die Verhandlungen des IX. Parteitages der Kommunistischen Partei Deutschlands.* Abgehalten in Frankfurt a. M. vom 7. bis 10. April 1924 (Berlin, 1924), p. 64/46.

[4] After having passed through various phases of Party grace and disgrace, including a temporary attachment to the Zinoviev opposition, Guralsky was sent to Latin America, probably to Brazil, in the middle thirties.

Party missions; he had no qualifications for a foreign assignment. Until 1923, only outstanding Russian Communists, whether in theory or in international experience, had been delegated to the Comintern. Real authority had been vested in such figures as Bukharin and Trotsky; foreign Communists taken into Comintern service met stiff resistance from the Communist parties, as did, for example, Mátyás Rákosi in Italy during the Serrati-Levi crisis.

Stalin's introduction of Russian Party methods into the Comintern can be well illustrated by the person of Manuilsky. The son of a Ukrainian village priest, he had joined the Bolshevik faction of the Social Democratic Party in 1904 as a student in the St. Petersburg University. He participated in the Kronstadt revolt in 1906, was arrested and deported, escaped from Russia. Until 1917 he traveled about Europe, particularly in France, where for years he was a salesman. In 1909 he joined a dissident group and wrote some articles against Lenin in the *Vperyod,* a sin that was a weapon in the hands of the General Secretary. When he returned to Petrograd in 1917, he at first joined a group between the Bolsheviks and the Mensheviks; he was close to Trotsky in the period and, according to Trotsky, warned him against joining with Lenin. He did, however, join the Bolsheviks later in 1917.

In the summer of 1919, the Party sent him to the Ukraine, where he remained till 1923. In the Ukraine, with its special problems of nationalist and Workers' opposition, Manuilsky found his place on the side of the Party apparatus. In this hot spot, this man of the Orgburo acquired a flexible adaptability, and as from his excellent vantage point he observed the rising power of the Stalin Secretariat, he maneuvered to be on the winning side.

He was sent in 1920 as Comintern agent to France, officially as head of the Ukrainian Red Cross. Deported from France, he became People's Commissar of Agriculture in the Ukraine and Secretary of the Ukrainian Party. In 1924, he headed a Comintern mission sent to Germany, comprising members of the secret branches, formally under Comintern jurisdiction but in fact bound by a secret arrangement to Stalin.[5]

---

[5] During the two decades of the Stalin Comintern, Manuilsky remained a leading figure. He and Georgi Dimitrov are the men best versed in the intricacies of the world-wide apparatus; according to reliable informants, Manuilsky remained head of the Comintern after its "dissolution." In 1945–1946, a member of the Russian

When I met Manuilsky, first in Moscow and later in Berlin, I encountered a type of Russian Communist new to me. What struck me most was his outspoken cynicism. His interest in Communist theory was limited to its use in manipulation. He lived in Berlin as one of a set of bohemians, rather easy-going in personal matters, but interested only in intrigue and with a cold contempt for anyone who accepted the Communist International on the basis of its avowed aims and principles. German Communists liked Manuilsky no better than he them; the gap between their clumsily serious but passionate devotion and his cold irony left no room for friendship. He treated the German comrades like a group of over-enthusiastic and bothersome infants, who were forever intruding into grown-up problems, the ones he discussed with his own circle of Russian agents to which no foreigner had access.

Manuilsky had a larger staff than Radek before him. He settled down in Berlin, took various apartments, and sent private observers to all provincial branches, whose reports were forwarded by him to Moscow; the German party did not know even of their existence. His uninterrupted stream of visitors represented all groups and grouplets; they discussed the party crisis with the Comintern representative, who listened benevolently to their complaints. He made himself the confidant of the party intellectuals, helping them also in their personal difficulties by adding them to his payroll in press or information assignments or by recommending them to Moscow headquarters for political jobs in Russia or abroad. In this first period of his German activities, however, Manuilsky got poor results. The German party, still dominated by the moods and wishes of its rank and file, remained in unbridled rebellion against Moscow, though it was never able to articulate it adequately. Manuilsky's reports to Moscow followed a pattern: the German party was drifting away; if the Left was allowed to get control of the party leadership, it would lead the party away from the Comintern. But too strict measures immediately would result only in strengthening the anti-Moscow trend. He asked for a period of time to penetrate into and organize the German party.

Central Committee, he was Ukrainian delegate to the UN conferences in San Francisco and New York.

Manuilsky's first major test came at the Ninth Congress of the German party, which convened at Frankfurt am Main at the beginning of April 1924. The Frankfurt police knew, of course, that the meeting of the Sport Club, or whatever Hugo Eberlein had called it that day, was actually a Communist Party convention. But the game was played on both sides and everything went quite smoothly. In critical moments, however, the technical staff assigned to protect the meeting with shock troops could cut discussion short by announcing the danger of a police raid.

The spirit of this Frankfurt convention was best expressed in the antagonism of the rank and file to the trade-unions, which were held responsible for the 1923 defeat. Again, as in 1919 and 1920, the question of Communist participation in the unions was discussed. Convinced that the unions had lost the confidence of the German working masses for good, many delegates felt that the party was wasting its energy in supporting these decaying institutions and would do better to build up independent Communist-dominated unions. While the convention was in session, an All-German Committee of Revolutionary Trade-Unionists was being organized, comprising both the independent unions and representatives of Communist fractions in the regular trade-unions. In spite of their relatively small membership, the independent unions were of immense help to both the legal and the underground organization of the Communist Party.

The proposal to concentrate on building up independent unions gave the Russian leaders a welcome opportunity to intervene in German affairs. According to traditional Leninist doctrine, leaving the trade-unions was a serious political error. In an open letter to the Frankfurt convention, Zinoviev warned against this brand of ultra-Leftism and added some remarks on the danger of anti-Bolshevism. He singled out for attack Boris and Samosch.

Boris and Samosch were the party names of two young men who had emigrated from Russia after the revolution. In the party paper, *Roter Kurier,* they had expressed doubts concerning the socialist character of the Soviet state. Together with a third young theorist, Rolf Katz, they investigated the relation, in a time of revolutionary ebb, between

Soviet foreign policy and Comintern policy. The New Economic Policy, a partial restoration of private enterprise, linked Russian economy to the world market; and Soviet foreign policy, compelled to adapt itself to Russian economy, had to aim at amicable relations between Russia and her capitalist neighbors. Such a policy of compromise was bound to come in conflict with the interests of the non-Russian revolutionary parties. Therefore, Boris and Samosch concluded, the Comintern organization should be disconnected from the Soviet state. Its headquarters should be shifted from Moscow; all political and organizational ties between the two should be cut; Communist parties should renounce Moscow's financial support and carry out their policy without considering the changing necessities of Soviet foreign policy. The Russian Party should be one member of the international, with equal rights, but without dominating it by state power.

These proposals of Boris and Samosch, young men with little influence, aroused a storm of protest from the Moscow Politburo. If the German Left tolerated anti-Bolshevist ideas of this color, Zinoviev said, it would be "hopelessly lost to the world revolution." Zinoviev pointed to their national origin; every Russian not under the discipline of the Russian Party but a member of another branch of the Comintern was as such highly suspicious. This Zinoviev letter, one of several interventions by the Russian Politburo behind the scenes, angered the Left delegates. The estrangement between the Moscow Politburo and the German Communists was palpable. The Politburo, it was evident, would not tolerate any independent tendencies in the German party and would prefer splitting the party to such a development. Boris and Samosch had no following at the Frankfurt convention. But the German Communists in general were too much involved in their own quarrels, in the fight of their various groups for power, to be able to investigate Russian policy thoroughly, or the NEP, or their implications. In secret sessions of the Left, however, many delegates from Berlin, the Ruhr, Hamburg, and the Palatinate proposed resisting Moscow's tutelage. In confidential replies to Zinoviev and to Stalin, the faction denied Zinoviev's accusation and expressed their concern about the hostility of the Politburo toward the German Left. The German Left leaders, at this time Thälmann, Maslow, and Fischer, got a mandate to fight such interference energetically and to secure the independence of the party from the Russian Politburo.

The political decisions of the Frankfurt convention were not at all adequate to the urgent political tasks created by the Dawes Plan. The party concentrated on learning the lessons of the struggle for power and sought a foolproof formula to make certain that this passivity would never be repeated. The phrases repeated in the convention's documents concerned methods of organizing for power, of seizing power. These slogans rapidly became absurd, in view of the change in both Germany and Russia, and the Frankfurt decisions were open to just criticism. But, balancing to some extent this gross inadequacy of the Left, there was another aspect of the party turn. With vigor, with enthusiasm, the rejuvenated cadres threw themselves into reorganizing the party, into reasserting Communist policy. For a time, German Communists believed that it was possible for them to shape their own destiny.

At the Frankfurt convention Manuilsky concentrated all his effort on controlling the composition of the Central Committee. According to party rule, the Central Committee had to be made up in accordance with the strength of the various factions among the delegates. The Left majority gave the Center more representation than the number of its delegates entitled it to and also included Clara Zetkin and Wilhelm Pieck for the Right.[6] But Manuilsky was unable to maneuver the election of Brandler, Thalheimer, or Walcher, which he wanted not in support of their policy but to get better foci of disintegration. The Left majority got control of the entire party and its apparatus at Frankfurt—the most complete shift of staff, from Central Committee to local organizer, since the founding of the Spartakusbund. Party property, newspapers, buildings, funds, changed hands.

After the Frankfurt convention, Manuilsky and his subordinates returned to Moscow and reported on the poor results of their mission.

---

[6] Brandler's Right wing, with only 11 delegates out of 118, was not entitled to a single man on the new Central Committee. Of the 118 delegates, 81 had entered the Social Democratic Party or the USPD before the outbreak of the war, 18 during the war, and 19 after the beginning of the revolution; 12 had been members of the Spartakusbund and 84 members of the USPD; 96 had been in a trade-union before 1919. (*Parteitagsbericht*, Frankfurt convention, pp. 399–400.)

The disappointment in Moscow was great; later, Zinoviev reported to the Comintern Executive Committee:

> First of all I must sincerely admit that the German Left Communists have conquered the party against the will of the Executive Committee. This is the first and last case of this kind that I know of in the entire history of our international. These circumstances prove that the German Left had considerable strength at this time; at least in the first period it took over the party against the will of the Comintern. The Executive Committee could do nothing but accept this fact and maneuver in the expectation that a nucleus would take form within the Left nearer to us. There was no other way out. Brandler or the Left: that was the choice at that time. All the more or less healthy proletarian elements went with the Left, for the Right leadership had been bankrupt. Unfortunately, our attempt to form a Center group had no success; this Center group soon disappeared.[7]

Frankfurt increased the heat between Stalin and Zinoviev. The decisions of the Politburo against the German Left, given to Zinoviev as the Comintern Chairman to carry out, were intended in part to estrange him from the German party, at this period the Comintern's strongest party outside Russia. Among the top Russian leaders, Zinoviev was regarded as the representative of internationalism. A Left German Communist Party, a trouble-breeder that would make difficulties for Russian foreign policy, might still by its very existence strengthen Zinoviev's influence in the Politburo in spite of his public criticism of it. However, as the overwhelming majority of the German party backed the new leadership, Stalin decided to wait and see.

Just before the convention, Stalin and Zinoviev had sent separate handwritten letters to Maslow and me by Max Levin.[8] He told us about

---

[7] *Protokoll: Erweiterte Exekutive der Kommunistischen Internationale,* Moscow, February 17 to March 15, 1926 (Hamburg, 1926), p. 501. Cf. V. Lominadze, leader of the Russian Young Communist League, in *Rote Fahne,* July 4, 1926, where he discusses the strength of the ultra-Left in Germany, Poland, and Italy: "The leadership of the German Communist Party went over to the ultra-Left—Maslow, Ruth Fischer, Scholem, Katz—against the will of the Comintern. However, the Comintern had no choice at this time." In the subsequent party discussions and in the press, it has frequently been said that Moscow "installed" the Left leadership in 1924.

[8] After the breakdown of the Bavarian Council Republic, Levin had found asylum in Moscow, where he worked at Comintern headquarters and devoted most

the tension between Stalin and Zinoviev and stressed that both of them were anxious to remain on the best of terms with the Left leaders of the German party. Neither Maslow nor I had reacted to Stalin's private letter, nor to Manuilsky's many suggestions that we coördinate better with the Russian General Secretariat. Only much later did I realize that in rejecting these offers of Stalin's we had entered a danger zone. With his power machine rolling forward, Stalin could not tolerate two such uncoöperative persons in Berlin, a key spot in Comintern politics. Maslow in particular aroused his resentment, for instead of the eternal gratitude Stalin felt was due him, Maslow paid him back with distrust and a drive for independence. By the shrewd rules of politics as Stalin played it, such open-faced contempt for a powerful adversary, who offered himself as a protector, was unpardonable. It was hardly possible to call us to Moscow for another investigation; some other device had to be found to eliminate us from the direction of the German party.

In the first Reichstag election after the inflation, on May 4, 1924, the Communist Party showed a large gain, from 15 seats, filled before its unification with the USPD in 1920, to 3,700,000 votes and 62 seats. The Social Democratic Party, on the other hand, got a warning—the severest loss since November 1918, a drop from 171 deputies to 100. The Democrats also lost heavily, returning with 28 instead of 38 seats; Stresemann's own party, the German People's Party, returned with 45 as compared with 44 seats. The German National People's Party, under Admiral von Tirpitz, on the other hand, elected 95 deputies as compared with 67; with the additional 36 seats of such extreme nationalist grouplets as the *Deutschvölkische Freiheitspartei* (German People's Party for Freedom), it represented the major German trend after the inflation crisis, which fact demonstrated the insecurity of the Republic's victory over Hitler and his followers. On the morning after the election, German and foreign observers noted this swing to the extremes, Left or Right ("Tirpitz and Ruth Fischer were the victors"), and these symptoms of continued German unrest were only one more argument to support the Dawes Plan.

---

of his time to studies on the relation between Marxism and science. In 1937, after years of secret confinement, he was executed without a formal accusation or trial, for the crime of having been a personal friend of Zinoviev.

Immediately after the election, I was sent to the convention of the British Communist Party. It was customary to exchange fraternal delegates to all important party sessions and conventions, but with the growing monopoly of the Comintern's official intervention, this had become increasingly a mere formality. Playing with a bigger fire than it knew, the new German Politburo set itself the task of building up contacts independent of Moscow with other parties of the West; the German Left began to make European Communist policy.

I traveled to London under an assumed name and there met the official Comintern delegate, D. Petrovsky, who worked in the Communist Party of Great Britain under the name Bennett. He also had a staff, but smaller than Manuilsky's, of advisers and technicians. I met also Ellen C. Wilkinson, who had just left the Communist Party, and John Walton Newbold, with whom I discussed German policy. I met Harry Pollitt, C. Palme Dutt, William Gallacher, all of whom showed more interest in the German party than in the good advice of Bennett. Bennett and I traveled together to Manchester, where the convention took place. After my few words of greeting to the delegates, the police came to arrest me, but me alone. Bennett remained undisturbed. The police, however, politely waited for me in the lobby, and this gave me the opportunity to escape in the dress and with the papers of one of my English friends. After this incident I disconnected myself from the Comintern representative and traveled, without his knowledge, to Liverpool and from there back to Germany. When I boarded the train in Cologne, I saw in the newspaper that Maslow had been arrested some days before in Berlin.

Immediately I wired to a devoted comrade to meet me in Hanover and conduct me into Berlin by a devious route. I lived underground in Berlin until the Reichstag opened and I was protected from arrest.

On the train from Hanover to Berlin, we discussed Maslow's arrest. We were convinced that the Moscow apparatus had discarded the relative inefficiency of Comintern discipline and had this time acted in collusion with the Berlin police. Maslow had been arrested on his way out of a session with Comintern representatives, protected by special agents. He was the only one arrested, although at this period he was relatively unknown to the Berlin police. One of the detectives fabricated a small riot on the pretext that a pickpocket was in the group; Maslow was taken to the police station and arrested for having conspired to overthrow the German government in October 1923, when he was detained in Moscow.

On June 17, 1924, the Fifth World Congress of the Comintern convened in Moscow. Since Communist activities and prospects in Europe were in such a state of ebb that the Comintern had lost its attraction for Russian Communists, Zinoviev needed an impressive demonstration to regain his position in the Russian Politburo.

The Fifth World Congress reflected the indecisiveness, the restlessness, the secrecy that hung over the Comintern in this period. No progress had been made by the Comintern in any country, and the congress reflected this stalemate. While the congress was in session in Moscow, special GPU troops suppressed an uprising in Georgia about which the delegates were kept in complete ignorance. About this uprising Popov writes:

> The change for the worse in the state of feeling among individual sections of the rural population had already been manifested in the early autumn of 1924 by a number of serious symptoms.
>
> The first of these was the August insurrection in Georgia. This insurrection, which was suppressed in a few days, was the result of provocation by foreign imperialists and was organized by the Mensheviks with money supplied by these imperialists. It was supported by the former nobility and part of the petty bourgeoisie. But a small part of the peasantry also manifested a sympathetic attitude towards the insurrection. Particularly dangerous was the fact that this attitude was manifested in the poor, semiproletarian districts of Georgia (Guria and Mingrelia).[9]

---

[9] N. Popov, *Outline History of the CPSU*, II, 225.

A few weeks earlier Zinoviev had reported at the Thirteenth Party Congress, held in May 1924, on the dangerous tensions in the country:

"Foreign observers are very much concerned about whether we intend to continue the NEP. British and German newspapers have expressed their inquietude. In Belgrade, the *Novoye Vremya,* a newspaper of White Russian émigrés, writes: 'If the NEP stops, then we propose to organize a VEP' [that is, a Pan-Russian pogrom]. The Mensheviks lament the expulsion of speculators from Moscow, the strict regulation of state trade, the augmented rights of the GPU, the political trials in Kiev, Leningrad, and Stavropol, the rejection of new concessions, and the allocation of houses and apartments along 'class lines.'" (*Inprekorr*, No. 91, June 9, 1925, p. 1240.)

The Fifth World Congress interpreted the European situation imprecisely; an ambiguous concept of relative capitalist stabilization hampered a resolute change of Communist policy. In an involved discussion on the character of workers' governments, the term was accepted as a "synonym" of the dictatorship of the proletariat. This terminological device was meant to open the way, without any explicit statement, to eventual participation in Balkan or Central European governments.

This new attempt to expand into the Balkans by way of "workers' and peasants' governments" was the result of the deliberations against the "Industrialists." The revolution, it was argued, has failed in Europe's industrial country par excellence, Germany, and France and England have obviously no impending revolutionary crisis. But can we not seize power in the unstable Balkans, where the bulk of the population is made up of peasants? These Balkan peasants, who would obviously not be attracted by the promise of a dictatorship of the proletariat, might support a workers' and peasants' government, friendly to Soviet Russia. The term *synonym* was necessary both to distinguish this policy from the recent unhappy experiences in Saxony and to mask the change by presenting it as identical with early revolutionary concepts. This urge to build a continued unbroken tradition, this habit of never calling a turn a turn, is a main feature of Stalinist dogma.

But the concept of a peasant government in the Balkans reflected also the groping for a rearrangement between Communists and peasants in Russia. Under the NEP—that is to say, in an agricultural country with a limited free market—the peasantry needed a more direct political voice than the Communist Party afforded them. The committees of poor peasants had been an instrument of class struggle in the villages, which during the civil war had acted somewhat as agents of the urban-based Communist Party. The fight between the rich and the poor peasants had never been resolved. Could not a committee of poor and middle peasants, increasingly independent from the Party, both finish this fight in the village and represent the peasants in state and national bodies? This new policy had far-reaching implications. The Krestintern, an attempt to unite various peasant organizations into an international under the auspices of Moscow, had been organized in 1923, and its second congress was in preparation. In 1924, Zinoviev proposed forming non-Party peasant groups in the soviets—nuclei of a possible future Soviet peasant party.

> The atmosphere at Moscow was not cheerful. The failure of the German revolution had created a feeling of melancholy not very far removed from despair. It was realized that the last card of a historical epoch had been played. Who was to blame? Radek, head of the Comintern [!], was naturally the scapegoat. Trotsky's partisans used the word "funk"; it was sheer cowardice, they said, not to send the cavalry that had been ready so long through the Polish Corridor. . . . The party manifestly tended towards serious internal struggles.
>
> The Comintern had to change its tactics. The "Industrialists" seemed to have lost much ground after the German fiasco. They returned to their discussions of social revolution, which was to come by way of the Balkans and Italy, centering on the peasant classes. It was again proposed to form a "Krestintern," or International of Peasants, as an auxiliary to the Comintern.[10]

One major topic of the Fifth World Congress was the fight against Trotskyism. All brother delegations, aping Zinoviev's statements, appeared on the platform declaring their unbroken and unbreakable loyalty to "Leninist principles." This parade was intended to bolster the weak position of Zinoviev's Comintern against the "liquidators," those, that is, who wished to abolish this useless institution, this hindrance to the establishment of good relations with the capitalist states. Thus, Zinoviev used the fight against "Trotskyism" in part to defend the Comintern against the opposition in the Russian Party.

The discussions did not reflect the real strength of the Trotskyite group in the Comintern. Each Russian faction feared an alliance between each of the other opposing groups and Trotsky's; all the members of the Politburo watched jealously to see that everyone conducted a sufficiently vehement campaign against Trotskyism. From behind the scenes, through the decisions of the Russian Comintern delegation, Stalin pushed Zinoviev into the forefront of the anti-Trotskyite campaign. Zinoviev threw the ball back, hoping that the endorsement of his anti-Trotskyite theses by the "highest world authority" of the Communist parties would make a Stalin-Trotsky alliance impossible.

---

[10] Grigory Bessedovsky, *Revelations of a Soviet Diplomat*, p. 68.

Thus, the Fifth World Congress was an arena for the struggle between the various groups in the Politburo; it had no other meaning and it had little authority.

On June 14, when Trotsky appeared with Stalin and Zinoviev at Lenin's tomb, he received an enthusiastic ovation from the assembled crowds. However, since his policy at this period was silent withdrawal, he did not interfere in the debates and tolerated patiently the rhetorical tirades on Trotskyism produced by the Congress.[11] Trotsky was accused of various past and present deviations from Leninist doctrine, all of which related to differences between Lenin and Trotsky before the 1917 revolution—differences which had lost their relevance under the new condition of a State Party in power. The campaign against Trotskyism at the Fifth Congress was a dull affair—"mustard after dinner," as the Russians say. To accuse Trotsky of "counter-revolutionary" or "bourgeois" inclinations was still unthinkable. The campaign was intended to bar him from the first place in the Politburo, but not to exclude him permanently from the collective leadership of the Party or the Comintern, or to question his "revolutionary honor."

Stalin's appearance at the Congress was characteristic of this phase in his struggle for power. He let the flow of speeches and the numerous meetings of the delegations pass by without taking part. Scrutinizing the behavior and personality of the delegates, he selected certain ones for private conversations in the Russian Party headquarters, ordinarily forbidden to Comintern delegates. He organized a personal correspondence with observers in the European parties, who would report directly to him as the organizer of the Russian Politburo. There was not a word of criticism of Zinoviev by any member of the Russian Comintern delegation; that would have been against Russian Party protocol, which regarded even the slightest crack in the façade of Russian unity before "foreigners" as a major crime. However, Stalin succeeded in creating the impression that Zinoviev was not the real boss.

At this Fifth World Congress, Stalin became known to Comintern

---

[11] "Trotsky, who was invited to attend the Congress and state his views, refused to appear, hypocritically pleading Party discipline as his reason. Party discipline, however, did not prevent him at this very time from delivering a report on the international situation at a congress of veterinaries—a report which radically differed from the line of the Comintern and the Party." (N. Popov, *Outline History of the CPSU*, II, 213).

delegates for the first time. He glided silently, almost furtively, into the salons and corridors around St. Andrew's Hall. Smoking his pipe, wearing the characteristic tunic and Wellington boots, he spoke softly and politely with small groups, assisted by an inconspicuous interpreter, presenting himself as the new type of Russian leader. The younger delegates were impressed by this pose as the revolutionary who despises revolutionary rhetoric, the down-to-earth organizer, whose quick decision and modernized methods would solve the problems in a changed world. The men around Zinoviev were old, fussy, outmoded.

I had ample opportunity to observe the effects of this wooing. I headed a group of some forty German delegates who were interested almost exclusively in the best defense of their own national interests. The fireball among them was Ernst Thälmann, the new chairman of the German party. He especially attacked Zinoviev for the German defeat; with infantile insistence, he plodded for the most Left formulation of each thesis. He was so outraged by my acceptance of the "synonym," by this betrayal of the principles of our party and caucus, that he sat with his back to me during the following sessions. Everyone in the Russian Party, however, flattered Thälmann, seriously considering every crude suggestion. Heinz Neumann, one of the younger delegates, was enthusiastic about Stalin. With Maslow in the Moabit prison, he was one of the few among us who spoke Russian, and whenever Stalin appeared he followed him like an admiring puppy that had found a new master. Stalin took a liking to this fledgling and used him as a sounding board, not only among the Germans, for Neumann was a polyglot and could speak with most of the European delegations in their native tongue.

At the end of the congress, Thälmann, Maslow *in absentia,* and I were elected as new members to the Comintern Presidium.

The German delegates to the Communist World Congress returned —their pockets filled with resolutions on workers' governments—to a Germany where the question of the hour was the acceptance or rejection of the Dawes Plan.

The Reichstag Accepts the Dawes Plan

In the statements of the Marx-Stresemann cabinet, the Dawes Plan was called "the road of the great sacrifice," thus meeting half way the "second Versailles" that Helfferich, the nationalists' economist, termed it. On the other hand, Stresemann emphasized that the Dawes Plan would offer the only solution to the reparations problem and that, if the Reichstag approved it, it would finally lead to the "liberation of our brothers on the Rhine and in the Ruhr." All the nationalist groups in Germany knew that he was right.

The Social Democratic Party also supported coöperation with the United States enthusiastically. The Social Democrats were so concerned with the violent nationalist propaganda against the Dawes Plan that they intended, if it was rejected by the Reichstag, to initiate a plebiscite for its acceptance. Arthur Crispien, a former Independent Socialist and a radical in speech and behavior, well known for his rhetoric on "scientific socialism," greeted the Dawes Plan as a capitulation of the capitalists to the masses.[12] The trade-unions added to these rhetorical flourishes more sober observations on the necessity of a just distribution of the Dawes burdens.

Of all political parties in Germany, the Communist Party attacked the Dawes Plan most aggressively. Demonstrative conferences of the German, French, and Belgian parties were called to emphasize the united front of Western Communists against this plan to encircle the Soviet Union. In the spring of 1924 Stresemann was not certain that he had the necessary quorum for his policy in the Reichstag. In a session of the Committee for Foreign Affairs, he even made the Communist Party a vague offer of amnesty (there were still thousands of Communists in prison) if they would vote for the Dawes Plan.

Seeckt feared the repercussions of this violent Russian propaganda. On May 29, he made a speech on a Russian plot and Communist subversive movements. The Social Democrats chimed in; on June 3, Reichstag President Paul Löbe made a statement against "the Communist plotters."

Dr. Arthur Rosenberg and I were the Communist members of the Reichstag Foreign Relations Committee at this time. A large group of General Staff officers emphasized in hearings before the committee that the Dawes Plan would weaken neither the traditional friendship between Russia and Germany nor their spiritual alliance against the Versailles Treaty. These declarations were mainly designed for the Communist committee members, to report to Moscow. In public,

---

[12] *Sozialdemokratischer Parteitag, 1924: Protokoll* (Berlin, 1924), pp. 43–50.

however, such nationalists as Count zu Reventlow tried to blur their previous collusion with the Communists.

In August 1924, the Dawes Plan was finally accepted in the Reichstag by 248 votes to 175; the opposition comprised the German National People's Party and its satellites, and the Communist Party.

The general agent for reparations, S. Parker Gilbert, made his headquarters in Berlin. For five years, the Dawes Plan worked admirably and precisely. Between September 1924 and July 1931, the date of the Hoover moratorium, Germany paid 10,821 million gold marks. The creditors were delighted by the prompt and full payments; the safeguards functioned well; and the size of the annuities was fixed at a generous rate, to the advantage of Germany's creditors. It was, of course, inherent in the plan that exports should become the basis of German recovery. Without exports, no surplus production for reparations was possible.

> Germany's capacity to meet reparations obligations depended on these foreign loans. . . . These foreign loans gave to Germany such an impetus in the years 1924–1929 that she was able to raise enormous taxes and also the reparations amounts . . . The whole plan was intended to be transitional until Germany could stand on her own feet again. The continuation of reparations payments depended, however, upon the uninterrupted inflow of foreign money and upon the avoidance of crises.[13]

The Dawes Plan, Brook continues, inspired Germany "with the great example of the United States," and furthered the process, already characteristic of German industry, of merging it into a few giant undertakings. It had "started much later than the British industry, and therefore was from the beginning adjusted to working on a larger scale (fewer furnaces working, but more output)."

Agriculture and industrial production increased as well as purchasing power, in spite of the heavy taxation. German banks fostered a policy of expansion, based on higher figures of savings deposits and on the general feeling of the economic boom. With the rising exports, revenue income increased and foreign debts decreased slowly. Exports

---

[13] Warner Frederick Brook, *Social and Economic History of Germany from Wilhelm II to Hitler, 1888–1938* (London, 1938), p. 174.

were mainly of coal and iron ore; chemicals—dyes, potash, nitrogen; manufactured goods—optical goods, paper, machines. With the rising production, transport showed a corresponding improvement. Canals and waterworks were greatly enlarged; there were new steamers and locomotives; the Reich road system was expanded. Automobile production and traffic took a spurt upwards. One of the most characteristic features of this general trend was the development of public utilities—electric and gas works, transport lines, municipal housing projects, schools, sport arenas, swimming pools, public parks, theaters.

The Dawes Plan initiated a period of recovery unparalleled in scope and intensity, similar to the promoters' era of the 1870's. Rationalization of industry, orientation of Germany's economic and technological policies, were molded on America's pattern. It was the re-discovery of America, a pilgrimage to the "American economic miracle." [14]

The mere fact that the reparations agent residing in Berlin had the decisive word in regard to Germany's finances and especially the stability of the Reichsmark inspired the capitalist world with such confidence that Germany became the principal area for investment from all parts of Europe; British, Swiss, and Dutch money was added to the stream of dollars. American bankers frequently preferred public utilities as an investment, since cities and states were considered safer than private enterprises. Thus, under the Dawes Plan, American private enterprise sponsored collective and community enterprises in Germany.

On October 20, after having struggled to gain a majority with difficulty, Marx-Stresemann dissolved the Reichstag, with the avowed intention of crushing the extremists. The Communist deputies had immunity only as long as the Reichstag was in session. On July 5, in violation of this law, the police had searched the lockers of the Communist deputies to the Reichstag and the Prussian Diet; and the moment the Reichstag was adjourned, they received orders to arrest, among others, Ruth Fischer and Ernst Thälmann. [15] We had to go underground, but we considered our Berlin underground quarters insecure because they were known to the GPU agents, who were in col-

---

[14] Gustav Stolper, *German Economy, 1870–1940* (New York, 1940), pp. 176–178.

[15] Cf. *New York Times*, October 22 and 29, 1924.

lusion with the Berlin political police. For a while a group of the Politburo went to Prague.

A favorite pastime at German party discussions in this period was comparing longer and shorter perspectives of the revolution, a longer with a shorter preparatory period for the seizure of power and the transformation of the Weimar Republic into a German Soviet Republic. Armed with the science of Communist dogma, the naïve rank and file believed that they were able to predict accurately the time necessary for their struggle for power. The next opportunity, the imminent new crisis of the Republic, would find the German Communists with a reorganized, a "Bolshevized," party, the guarantee for seizing power, and would bring the long civil war to a victorious end. A more realistic analysis met with bitter emotional resistance from the rank and file, who regarded pessimists as potential traitors to the Communist cause. All Russian leaders, Right, Left, and Center alike, though they differed in their proposals for Communist policy, catered to their German followers with "short revolutionary perspectives." This permanent state of revolutionary crisis, moreover, made a much stricter party discipline necessary and permitted the Politburo much more direct intervention in German affairs.

In Germany, the Dawes era began with the slogan *Bürgerblock-Regierung*—Government by a Bourgeois Bloc. Bourgeois parties had been divided into two wings: the Center and Democrats, which had entered Social Democratic governments, and the others, which had remained in opposition. The *Bürgerblock* slogan was intended to break this interclass alliance and to make a clear cut between bourgeois parties and labor camp. The bulk of the civil servants were still men held over from the pre-1918 monarchist regime, and it was an important aim of this proposed coalition to break up the strongholds of the Social Democrats, especially in the Prussian administration.

In the few months between April and October there had been important changes in the European political scene. MacDonald's cabinet in London came out for a rearrangement with Germany, for arbitration in international affairs, for gradual disarmament. In France, Pacifist Herriot succeeded Poincaré. The League of Nations was reanimated by these changes of policy in Britain and France. Europe turned its face towards the West—towards Britain and France, and increasingly towards the United States—and hoped for Western reconstruction and the conservation of Western civilization.

As the year 1924 drew to its close, it seemed that the postwar crisis had been overcome. By accepting the Dawes Plan, Europe had apparently begun a gradual revision of the Versailles Treaty, which would make possible both a reconstruction of German industry and a rearrangement of Germany's political relations with the world. Germany had not yet entered the League of Nations, but this step was due once the Dawes Plan had proved its effectiveness. Enthusiasts began to write about the era of peace, in which all European nations would gradually become a federation that would coöperate harmoniously with Anglo-America.

Russia's shadow on Europe became thinner; its isolation behind the barrier of anti-Soviet states from the Baltic to the Black Sea, "from sea to sea," seemed to have become a permanent feature of postwar Europe. The heavy loss of the German Communist Party in the Dawes election, December 7, 1924, illustrated this trend. The party dropped almost a million votes, and the *Deutschvölkische Freiheitspartei* returned 14 deputies instead of 32. Von Tirpitz's German National People's Party, however, gained half a million votes. Unexpectedly, the largest gain (from 6,609,000 votes in the May election to 7,886,000 in December) was made by the Social Democratic Party, which thus returned almost to its pre-1923 force.

This Social Democratic victory was like an electric shock to the Moscow Politburo. For Moscow, the success of the Dawes Plan and Germany's imminent entrance into the League of Nations were manifestations of a new balance of power, of a British-German alliance against Soviet Russia. If "the new intervention," the British-German war on Russia, that obsessed the Politburo materialized, in its estimate the Social Democratic Party would help to mobilize the German working class for it. Thus, the campaign against the Versailles Treaty was intensified; and only those German parties or politicians that maintained unwaveringly their opposition to Versailles, their opposition to a rearrangement with the West, were courted—no matter what their views were on domestic German policy. This continuation of the Schlageter policy of 1923, veiled in anti-capitalist rhetoric, was coupled with a new directive to intensify efforts to disintegrate the Social

Democratic Party and the trade-unions by means of a united front with them. These two Moscow directives were in contradiction and tended to cancel each other out; Moscow, frantic over the superiority of the Social Democratic forces, demanded immediate results from both. The German Communists, still with a will of their own, resisted these contradictory instructions and faltered after a policy of their own, suitable to the situation in Germany as they judged it. Thus the prime concern for Moscow became a better coördination, a complete subordination, of the German party to its policy; the "Bolshevization" of the German Communist Party was on the order of the day.

During the first period of the Dawes stabilization, the polarization of German society increased: an aggressive Right, whose bands were fighting in the streets of every industrial town, whose pressure group in the administration was striving to eliminate the Social Democratic newcomers, on the one side, against an embittered working-class minority fighting a losing battle on the other.

Monarchist Resurgence

The nationalists intensified their monarchist propaganda, not so much in order to restore the Hohenzollerns as to revivify the ideology of a strong Germany among the masses. "Republic" stood for weakness and "monarchy" for strength. The Hohenzollern princes appeared at various ceremonies in honor of the war dead; veterans' associations celebrated uninterruptedly one German Day after another, glorifying Germany's former status in the concert of world powers and deploring her present shameful indignity. This resurrection of monarchist propaganda was well received, being reflected in increased membership in all the various leagues, clubs, bands in which monarchist sympathizers were organized.

The open civil war of 1918–1923 simmered down to a state of latent civil strife, into episodes between labor organizations and the reactionaries. The Stahlhelm (Steel Helmet), now in the forefront of paramilitary organizations, had been founded in Magdeburg as an association of front soldiers "against mutiny and revolution" by a reserve officer, Franz Seldte, who had been in Berlin on furlough on November 9, 1918. Hindenburg and Field Marshal von Mackensen were honorary members. The organization was divided into cells, broader circles, youth groups, and children's groups (*Kernstahlhelm, Ringstahlhelm, Jungstahlhelm, Kinderstahlhelm*); its especially militant group was called the *Scharnhorst-Bund,* after the partisan leader against the Napoleonic invasion. The *Nationale Bund Deutscher Offiziere* (National League of German Officers), the most imperialist-minded group of the old army, was affiliated, as was the *Deutsche Offizier-Bund* (German Officers' League).[1]

During all the years of the Weimar Republic, there was much ado around the question of the German flag. The Reichstag had supplanted as the Reich flag the black-white-red of Imperial Germany by black-red-gold, the colors of the 1848 revolution. The flag of the merchant marine had remained black-white-red, with the new colors in one corner. By another decree, President Ebert had added ten other Reich flags, which varied combinations of the two tricolors with iron crosses, recalling the glorious days of the World War. On May 15, 1926, a final decree would instruct the embassies and consulates to use the old Imperial flag only. The parliamentary struggle that preceded this decree was accompanied by a "flag war," in which one party destroyed the flag of the other, and this fight around symbols played a considerable role in forming the anti-Republican cadres. In the frequent incidents between "monarchists" and "Communists," the extreme Right had more armed groups at its disposal, and the Left frequently suffered heavy casualties. Social Democrats and Communists alike fought the monarchists, and the victims were from all organizations.

On May 11, 1924, there had been a day-long street battle in the industrial center Halle an der Saale, a Communist stronghold. A Communist mass meeting in the People's House was attacked by Stahlhelm formations. The police interfered only at the end of the battle by firing into the crowded meeting hall. Six were killed, nine seriously wounded.

---

[1] Hermann Martin, *Zehn Jahre Stahlhelm* (Leipzig, 1929).

One of the issues the offensive against the Social Democrats made use of was l'affaire Barmat. The five Barmat brothers were Polish Jews who had emigrated to Holland, where through various enterprises they tried to make deals with every one of the new forces in Europe. In 1917, for instance, they attempted to offer Trotsky a relief committee; during 1918 they tried to do business with the Ukrainian Rada. In March 1919, they got contacts to various Berlin Social Democrats, particularly to Ernst Heilman, deputy to the Prussian Diet, for whom they arranged some writing assignments in Holland (at, incidentally, only fifteen guldens per article). Through these contacts, they got visas to Germany and established regular business relations with various Reich offices, especially the Prussian State Bank and the *Preussische Seehandlung,* for the import of foodstuffs. As a price for these contracts, they donated some 15,000 to 20,000 marks to Social Democratic newspapers, founded a children's home in Pirna, and paid various individuals commissions. Gustav Bauer, Social Democratic deputy and Reich Chancellor for a short time, got a large percentage; Fritz Ebert, Jr., son of the Reich President; Police President Richter of Berlin; and the above-mentioned Heilman received smaller percentages. These facts came to light before an investigating committee of the Prussian Diet and led to Bauer's resignation as deputy and his expulsion from the party.[2]

With the shady business transactions of the Barmats as a starting point, a vicious campaign was waged against the corruption in the Social Democratic Party. In fact, the party had in general appointed honest administrators to all branches of the civil service; one of its real virtues was precisely this honest administration, which compensated to some degree for the party's weaknesses.

Another incident took outsize proportions in the nationalists' campaign against the Republic. A man named Emil Gansser had published an open letter in the *Mitteldeutsche Presse,* a small nationalist newspaper, in which he charged President Ebert with high treason for his participation in the munitions workers' strike in January 1918. Ebert sued for libel, and the trial, which had been postponed several times,

---

[2] Berlin *Vorwärts,* January 7, 1926. See also Dr. Joseph Kaufhold, *Der Barmat-Sumpf* (Berlin, May 1925); Karl Radek, *Die Barmat-Sozialdemokratie* (Hamburg, 1925). Kaufhold was a member of the investigating committee of the Prussian Diet.

was finally begun on December 9, 1924, two days after the elections, under *Landgerichtsdirektor* Bewersdorff in Magdeburg. In defending his action, Ebert stated that he had participated in its steering committee only in order to limit the strike. A group of witnesses testified that his policy had been motivated by patriotism, that he had really wanted to support the war effort wholeheartedly. Not his motives but his deeds decided his responsibility, the court held, basing its judgment on an 1889 decision by which a man had been sentenced for arson in spite of his intention to put the fire out. "The investigation proved that at the strike meeting the assembled workers heckled Ebert with insults and that he responded to these remarks by demanding that the strike be continued," according to a contemporary anonymous pamphlet.[8]

The editor was convicted of using libelous language, but the judgment was no more than a formal exoneration of Ebert; in fact, it amounted to a judicial acknowledgment of his guilt—his guilt, it must be noted, of supporting a strike outlawed under the Hohenzollern monarchy, which had been succeeded by the Weimar Republic, of which Ebert was the president. If the Hohenzollerns returned, Ebert would be a criminal, and this case indicated that even without their return the judges, most of them remaining in office from the Imperial regime, did what they could to interpret the rule of the law according to pre-Weimar standards.

Another warning to the Republicans was the precarious position in the Prussian Diet of Otto Braun's cabinet. With the Social Democratic administration supported by only the Center and the Democrats, Braun had a narrow majority. If the Communists had joined in supporting the administration in its fight against the monarchists, the Republican majority would have been considerably enlarged and the Social Democratic cabinet more secure.

This "Prussian question" was especially thorny for the Communist Party. It held Social Democratic Minister Severing, in command of the Prussian police, responsible for protecting the reactionaries in street battles, suppressing Communist demonstrations, killing demonstrators. To the Communist rank and file, "Social Democrat" meant

---

[8] "A" [Adolf Stein], *Eberts Prozess* (Berlin, 1925).

the cop who beat him up, not the fellow worker at the bench. On the other hand, the Communist deputies to the Prussian Diet might have been able to exert enough political pressure to sever the Center and Social Democrats from their nationalist associates. With such a policy in Prussia as the starting point, a political alliance in the trade-unions and the municipal councils could have developed, eventually pushing the Social Democrats towards a more militant defense of their organization and the Weimar Republic.

The precondition to such a turn, however, would have been a demonstrative disconnection from Moscow's foreign policy and a sober analysis of the fundamentally changed situation. Instead, the Communists were occupied with the Bolshevization of the party, with the discussion on long or short perspectives, with propaganda for the revolution. In a speech to the Chemnitz branch, Arthur Rosenberg, at this time a leading member of the German Politburo, declared that after the party's defeat in the December 1924 election, parliamentary influence was utterly meaningless for German Communism, which between two waves of the revolution had as its unique task the guarding of a revolutionary spirit and organization. German Communists, Rosenberg said, didn't give a damn if they lost one or two million votes in this parliamentary monkey business.

"Defense of the Republic"

Into this party atmosphere, Maslow, still in prison awaiting trial, projected a proposal for a new policy, "defense of the Republic." For this time, early in 1925, this was a bold swing from the revolutionary phraseology of the Frankfurt convention to a realistic appreciation of German politics. Faced by the developing capitalist prosperity and the vigorous offensive of German nationalism, Maslow suggested that the Social Democratic Party be offered a complete realignment of the socialist forces in the ganglia of its influence, the Reich administration and the Prussian Diet—a proposal profoundly different from boring within the trade-unions, which was the content of the traditional Comintern united-front policy.

The Communist policy of defense of the Republic should be based, according to Maslow's proposal, on a fight to dissolve the Black Reichswehr and the Fehme and to destroy the Wilhelmian influence in the Reich and Prussian administrations. Ultimately, the Republicans must disband and disarm the Reichswehr; and in its place, to defend the Weimar Republic against restoration, groups of armed citizens, trained for a few months, would take over the function of the professional army and police. In several letters from his prison cell to the Central Committee, Maslow insisted that the question of Reichswehr versus People's Militia be the basis for rearranging the relation between the Social Democratic Party and the Communists. Such a goal could be reached, however, only through several phases of political activity, of which the first was a fundamental change in the attitude of the Communist Party.[4]

This proposal was made not in the middle thirties but at a time when the Nazi movement was not yet fully developed, when a total Nazi victory was as far outside any calculation as Stalin's State Party regime. In proposing a militant Republican policy at this crisis of the Weimar Republic, Maslow abandoned all his group prejudices and tried to push the Communist Party to the fore in its defense. For the German Politburo, the usual Communist united-front campaigns were linked to the party's prestige; the Social Democrats should first refrain from attacking them, and then the Communists would discuss terms. Maslow's proposal was not only above this question of prestige but much broader than the usual demand for a strike in common. Maslow wanted to offer a political alliance not only to the Social Democrats but to the Center, a party of both Catholic workers and Catholic petty bourgeois, and this step outside the labor front was at once the most original point of his platform and the most attacked.

Manuilsky viewed Maslow's policy with uneasiness. If the German party accepted this concept, an independent German Communist policy might develop, which would interfere with Russian foreign political maneuvers and, in particular, affect the plans to collaborate with German nationalists. Russia's prime interest, to establish a barrier against a Western European bloc, conflicted with the essential task of the German Communists in this period, which was to integrate all anti-imperialist forces. The German Central Committee, therefore, found itself with a most delicate problem. The party's policy could

---

[4] Cf. Arkadi Maslow in the *Funke,* Berlin, March 25, 1925. The *Funke* ("Spark"), named after Lenin's *Iskra,* was an internal party bulletin.

not continue to be a repetition of revolutionary phraseology of fading significance, but a resolute change of policy met stubborn opposition from one section of the rank and file, discreetly encouraged by the Moscow Politburo. An "Ultra-Left" opposition was formed, led by Arthur Rosenberg and Werner Scholem and supported by large proletarian groups in Berlin's Wedding, the Ruhr, and Southern and Western Germany. It accused Maslow of the opportunistic sin of "coalition policy," which meant in the language of German socialists a policy of collaborating across class lines, as, for example, with the Imperial government in a vote on war credits.

The disruptive forces both in the Communist Party and in the Reich generally came to a focal point around the issue of the presidential election. The seven-year term of Fritz Ebert, the Republic's first president, was approaching its end, and the campaign to elect his successor exposed behind the thin façade of the Dawes stabilization the new alignment of the actual forces in Germany.

The obvious candidate for the monarchists was Field Marshal Paul von Hindenburg, but they hesitated about taking so audacious an offensive. Admiral von Tirpitz, prototype of the German monarchist, had taken the lead in 1924 with his German National Peeople's Party, which he had maneuvered so well that even in the December 1924 election, when all the extremist parties had lost heavily, his party had gained half a million votes. Under the Weimar Constitution, if there was not an absolute majority for a presidential candidate on the first vote, there was a run-off election; in this case, with some six or eight candidates running, the first vote would certainly not decide the election. Thus the monarchists sought a way out of their quandary by nominating Minister of the Interior Karl Jarres, a civilian of moderate monarchist color, who was more acceptable to the anti-militarist mood of the industrial centers. His role as a trial kite was obvious, however, for the campaign for Hindenburg was already in full swing.

The Social Democratic Party intended to run Ebert for a second term, but on February 28, just one month before the election, he died. This was a serious loss, for the candidate the party substituted, Otto Braun, the Premier of Prussia, did not have nearly as much prestige in the country at large.

Thälmann a Presidential Candidate

The Communist Party put up as its candidate Ernst Thälmann. Wilhelm Pieck, in the name of the Right, had first timidly proposed the nomination of Clara Zetkin. This was rejected by an overwhelming majority of the party, for many reasons, the most important of which was that she was an outspoken Right-winger. After this, Thälmann had been the obvious choice. He was the symbol of Left Communism; he was a proletarian by origin and popular in the party. The German Politburo selected him because of his status within the party as the personification of the revolutionary German worker.

Maslow, in line with his general proposal of defense of the Republic, demanded that Thälmann's candidacy be withdrawn and that the party support a Republican candidate, provided he accepted the following program: that all dynastic properties and war and inflation profits be confiscated; that all members of former ruling houses be expelled from Germany; that all monarchist officers, judges, and civil servants be removed from office, and that judges and civil servants be elected; that church and state be completely separated; that the withholding tax on wages be abolished and supplanted by a tax on large incomes; that the legal protection of the eight-hour day be more rigidly defined and enforced; that there be freedom of press, organization, assembly, strike, demonstration; that there be political amnesty. All these demands were explicitly formulated so that they could be realized within the framework of the Weimar Constitution; they were not a socialist program, but rather a means to complete the bourgeois revolution and destroy completely the Imperial remnants. They were attacked by the Ultra-Left faction as Brandlerite, and in truth they were similar to Brandler's program of 1923; but they were offered not during the revolutionary upsurge of the previous five years but in a period of defeat, when socialists had to look to defense.

The preliminary vote was on March 29, 1925, with the results noted in the table on page 420. (The candidates are listed from Left to Right and grouped into the blocs that contended in the run-off election.) At first glance, the decisive feature of this tally seems to be that the sum of the votes for the three candidates of the People's Bloc was a definite plurality, almost a majority. But the amazing aspect of the

Ernst Thälmann, Communist Party	1,871,815	7.0%
Otto Braun, Social Democratic Party ..	7,802,497	29.0%
Dr. Willy Hellpach, Democratic Party	1,568,398	5.8
Wilhelm Marx, Center Party	3,887,734	14.5
People's Bloc	13,258,629	49.3%
Dr. Heinrich Held, Bavarian People's Party	1,007,450	3.7%
Dr. Karl Jarres, German National People's Party and German People's Party	10,416,658	38.8
General Erich Ludendorff, Nazis	285,793	1.1
Reich Bloc	11,709,901	43.6%

election was not this but the very large vote for Jarres, some two and a half million more than his runner-up. The total of votes for the People's Bloc was larger, but the cohesion within the Reich Bloc, already on this first vote with three candidates running, was very much greater.

After the results were announced, the monarchists decided that the tide had definitely turned in their favor; they posted Hindenburg as their candidate in the run-off election. In this delicate balance, the stand of the Communist Party could have been decisive. Once again, Maslow urged that Thälmann's candidacy be withdrawn, and once again his proposal was attacked as opportunism.

I was in Moscow at a session of the Comintern Presidium when the news of Hindenburg's candidacy arrived. Zinoviev was taken aback: if it was possible to nominate Hindenburg, the regrouping of the monarchist forces in Germany must have reached a danger point. Independently of Maslow, Zinoviev proposed that the Communist Party support Braun against the candidate of the Imperial regime. Reichstag deputy Iwan Katz, the leader of the Ultra-Left group in Hanover, was at this time the permanent German delegate to the Presidium. Ever since the days of the Spartakusbund, Katz recalled, the Social Democrats had been the butchers of the working class; it would be an outrage to demand that the Communist Party, many of whose members had been killed by a combination of monarchists with Social Democratic police, give its support to Otto Braun.

In an interval between the long and heated debates, I had a discussion with Zinoviev. The results of the preliminary election, he pointed out, made a complete change in German Communist policy imperative. If we support Otto Braun in the election, we support neither him personally nor his policy; we defend the Social Democratic workers and the Republic against the murderous intentions of the extreme Right. "Isn't that the policy of the lesser evil?" I asked. This traditional Social Democratic slogan had always been the butt of Communist ridicule. "Why should we always be for the greater evil?" Zinoviev replied.

Stalin abstained from taking a stand on this issue, vital as it was for both Germany and Russia. It was Zinoviev who took the matter to the Comintern Presidium, which in its session of April 2, 1925, discussed the Hindenburg candidacy.

> ZINOVIEV: In the name of the Russian Politburo and the German delegation, I want to defend the following tactical proposals. We cannot at all accept the point of view that the choice, Republic or monarchy, is immaterial to us. . . . Bourgeois democracy is generally much more favorable than monarchy for our class struggle, even if this democracy is a very poor one. . . . We started with the perspective of an imminent fight of the proletariat against bourgeois democracy. . . . The moment the revolutionary wave declines, the difference between bourgeois democracy and monarchy is of greater importance. The monarchist candidate in Germany has received eleven million votes. . . . The monarchist danger is not so much that the Hohenzollerns may return; it is a more complicated "monarchist" danger, but it is a danger.
>
> We all know that Social Democracy is no serious obstacle to monarchist restoration; it is itself semi-monarchist. We saw that already in the speeches of Scheidemann during the November days, and we see it now in his memoirs. The Social Democrats were the last to desert the monarchy; the Social Democrats are bad Republicans—bourgeois, petty bourgeois Republicans, and very bad ones. It is most unlikely that they will be able to protect the Republic. The situation is like this: the Social Democrats got eight million votes, we got two million, the nationalists eleven million. The so-called Republican Bloc has thirteen million votes, the monarchists eleven to eleven and a half million; everything hangs by a thread. If a monarchist candidate is elected, the Social Democrats and the bourgeoisie will try to hang the responsibility on us. . . .
>
> The greatest danger is that broad strata of the working class

will be estranged from us. . . . I believe that our slogans must be very simple; only the most popular demands should be put forward. . . . In the first election, we tested our own forces; in the run-off election, we must take into account the final result. . . . You can learn these tactics by rereading Lenin. . . .

Emotionally one can object to electing the cursed Otto Braun. Would we vote for Ebert if he were alive? Of course, we would—against Jarres. As a workers' party, we cannot say that Social Democracy and the bourgeoisie, in every matter on which we have to take our political stand, are enemies on the same level. We must decide whether the issue is between bourgeois democracy and monarchy. . . . Only Communists are true Republicans to the end.

You tell me that the *Vorwärts* will be jubilant: the revolution has come to an end. . . . We can answer them soberly: you say that the world revolution has been called off. Now you can accept our proposals for common action even more easily.

RUTH FISCHER: I find Zinoviev's proposals completely correct . . . [though] I do not underestimate the difficulties of these tactics for our party. . . . The period of immediate revolutionary struggle has come to an end in Germany; it is this difference between 1923 and 1925 that is not understood by our comrades.

KATZ: Our comrades see in the Ebert-Barmat party the worst enemy of the working class, a corrupt group of the bourgeoisie. . . . The danger of monarchy is not stronger than in the past. Last year the monarchists were much more influential; last year Hitler and Ludendorff would have polled millions of votes. Jarres is a typical representative of big business. . . . The consequences of these tactics will be terrible; the party will break up.

ZINOVIEV: We live encircled by enemies. We need brains; if we lose, the working class will have to bear the capitalist yoke twenty-five years longer. In Britain we voted for MacDonald; people like Engels and Lenin had studied the English question for decades to find a road in Britain. You don't understand what kind of enemies we have. . . .[5]

In Berlin, the proposal of Zinoviev and Maslow to withdraw the party's candidate in the run-off election was rejected by the German Central Committee under the influence of Thälmann, who liked the role of presidential candidacy. Thälmann had many qualifications for the job. His home town was Hamburg, Germany's largest harbor, which bred internationally minded radicals among its workers. Here, before and during the World War, "Teddy" Thälmann had been an

---

[5] *Die monarchistische Gefahr und die Taktik der KPD* (Berlin, 1925), pp. 6–11.

unskilled worker on the docks; he won recognition from his fellow workers for his militancy against the Kaiser's imperialist dream of world conquest. During the civil war his name became known to the anti-militarist workers of the Wasserkante, the northern seacoast of Germany. He led Hamburg's USPD delegation to the Halle convention in 1920, and was one of the most ardent promoters of the split. In the fight between the Left and Right within the Communist Party, he quickly became one of the leaders of the Left.

Ernst Thälmann was not the usual socialist leader. In the Social Democratic Party unskilled workers were rarely elected to key posts; men of Thälmann's type were kept to the lower ranks, even of the Spartakusbund, whose hierarchy was composed of intellectuals like Paul Levi and trade-unionists who had left the shop in their youth like Jakob Walcher.

Thälmann was a big man and rather stout. As a youth, he had gone to sea in the merchant marine, and he still retained the rolling gait of a sailor. He had had a poor education, and Marxist terminology and foreign expressions were always a struggle for him; but his wide experience and excellent political instinct helped him from the beginning of his career. He was a very emotional orator, shouting, sometimes almost incoherently, and tearing off his white collar—a gesture that was invariably greeted with cheers. He won his audiences, however, by the seriousness of his convictions and the passion of his arguments. His hatred of the "generals"—of Hindenburg and Ludendorff —and his irreconcilable opposition to the regrouping of German imperialist forces were beyond question.

The Russian Politburo recognized early both the strong and the weak points of Thälmann's character. Masters of political psychology, the Russian leaders knew exactly how to utilize his personality, his vanity concerning his proletarian origin, his distrust of intellectuals, his ambition. There was another Left leader in the Hamburg organization, Hugo Urbahns, a country teacher by origin—big, blond, stubborn, stiff, very much the type of the North German. Between the "learned" Urbahns and the "proletarian" Thälmann, there was an unquenchable antagonism which Radek exploited to the utmost, flattering the plebeian Teddy against the intellectual Urbahns.[6] In Sep-

---

[6] Hugo Urbahns died in January 1947 in Stockholm, where he had lived since 1933.

tember 1923, for example, there was one of the rare joint sessions of the Russian Politburo and the German delegation to the Comintern, to discuss preparations for the uprising. Thälmann delivered a report that made Maslow and me blush; he addressed the Russian leaders in the style of a street meeting, yelling with his usual agitational crudity. Stonily, the Russians suffered for more than an hour without interrupting his rhetoric; after he had concluded, Radek stood up, apparently deeply moved, and thanked Germany's best proletarian son for his wonderful report.

The Red Front Fighters' League, founded at the end of 1924, elected Thälmann as its first *"Führer."* The League had a double purpose: to protect workers' organizations, meetings, clubs, and living quarters against attacks by nationalist terror groups, and to counteract the "front spirit" sponsored by the monarchists through the Stahlhelm and the many other veteran organizations flourishing throughout Germany. In 1924, there were no National Socialist workers; worker stood against nationalist, and vice versa. After a difficult beginning, the League rapidly developed into a mass organization; parading in uniform and military discipline appealed to Communist and Social Democratic workers alike. The choice of an appropriate Red Front uniform was for a time the hobby of Thälmann and one of his intimates of this period, Willi Leow.[7] Activists, who often disliked routine assignments from a party or trade-union, were more easily won over to such an organization.

The Russian Politburo helped create a legend around Thälmann, the German proletarian revolutionary, setting him over against the old leaders and the new intellectuals. Stalin especially took an immediate fancy to him at their first meeting in Moscow in 1923. Thälmann was given the honorary title and the uniform of an officer of the Red Cavalry, and he took a childish pride in wearing it. Very early, various Russian institutions, children's homes and the like, were named after him. His nomination as presidential candidate, in particular, gave a boost to the Thälmann legend, which has many features in common with the Hitler myth. Before that, Thälmann was a party figure; after it, he became Germany's best known Communist leader. Even later,

---

[7] Leow, for a long period an outstanding Red Front leader, was sentenced to death in Moscow in 1934 for corruption and embezzlement of party funds.

when it was obvious how disastrous the policy had been, the failure of the party to support a Social Democratic candidate in the 1925 election was never strongly condemned, for Stalin shielded Thälmann and covered any action that had been his responsibility.

Thälmann's candidacy had an important influence on the life of the party, demonstrating the limitations to hierarchical manipulation. Thälmann was now a Communist figure of national proportions, and the Russian Politburo had to consider him to a certain degree; Stalin put great effort into winning him over during the ensuing Comintern crisis. Later, as his weaknesses became more apparent, his authority became a burden to the party. The legend lived on, however, and because of his popularity attempts to get rid of him by various oppositionist wings always failed.[8]

The Communist campaign was a great success. The meetings, ending in riots with the monarchists, were unusually well attended and enthusiastic. There was a particularly tumultuous riot in Halle on the eve of the election; the same day a Social Democrat was killed in Berlin. The Communist rank and file was in high spirits at the aggressive hostility between the extreme Right and the extreme Left; it felt itself at the helm of the anti-monarchist movement. Of course, the party did not expect to get Thälmann elected president, but it was excited by its success in rallying a relatively large group of close adherents around undiluted Communist slogans. For many members this kind of success ranked higher than any possible electoral returns, and the party as a whole was able to overlook for the moment the fact that in the preliminary vote Thälmann had suffered a further loss of one million votes from the election of December 1924.

The Social Democrats, on the other hand, were in a dilemma after the enormous vote for Jarres. Ebert, first president of the Weimar Republic, had had enough authority to rally the Center Party behind him, but Otto Braun, Premier of Prussia, did not have it. Unwilling to risk an uneven fight, the Social Democrats decided to support Wilhelm Marx, the Center Party candidate, in the run-off election; and

---

[8] At the beginning of 1933, just after the Nazis took power, Thälmann was arrested, and he spent the following decade in various prisons and concentration camps. He was killed in Buchenwald in September 1944, according to official reports by an air raid on the camp factories, according to camp inmates by the Nazis themselves.

after this Thälmann felt even more justified in stubbornly retaining the Communist candidacy. On the other hand, the Social Democrats made no attempt to overcome the deadlock in the labor camp.

In the run-off election, which took place on April 26, 1925, there were thus three candidates—Hindenburg, Marx, and Thälmann. The results were as follows:

Hindenburg (Reich Bloc)	14,655,641	48.3%
Marx (People's Bloc)	13,751,605	45.3
Thälmann (Communist Party)	1,931,151	6.4

Thus, the People's Bloc and the Communists together polled a majority, but Hindenburg, as the candidate with the largest vote in the second election, became president of Germany.[9]

The Reich Bloc Is Stabilized

After the election the mood in the Communist Party changed to bitterness. At a meeting of the *Zentralausschuss* (the Central Committee with additional elected delegates from provincial branches) on May 9–10, 1925, the various factions clashed violently over the post-election policy. The Left proposed supporting the People's Bloc in the Reichstag and particularly in the Prussian Diet. The Right opposed this but was willing to accept a united front with the Social Democrats and the

---

[9] Paul Merker, in arguing against the allegation that the Communists opened the door to power for Hindenburg by running their own candidate in the run-off election, makes a rather cumbersome point around the fact that the Bavarian People's Party, the Right wing of the Center Party, deserted Marx for Hindenburg. "If these Catholics had been loyal to the chairman of their brother party and their co-religionist, his victory would have been certain . . .

"To hinder the election of Hindenburg, the Communist Party . . . declared its willingness to renounce its own candidate in the run-off election if the Social Democrat Otto Braun was the candidate. That was a decision of extraordinary importance for the period, demonstrating that the German Communist Party wanted to bridge the gap between it and the Social Democratic masses. Otto Braun, supported by Communists, Social Democrats, the Center Party, and the Democrats, would have won; and his victory would have precluded the election of Hindenburg. The Social Democratic Central Committee did not accept this proposal, though their party, the strongest party of the Left, was entitled to propose Braun's candidacy. With the Center and the Democrats, it formed the so-called 'People's Bloc,' which made Reich Chancellor Dr. Wilhelm Marx its candidate." (*Deutschland, sein oder nicht sein*, I, 118–119.)

Merker does not mention the fact that the Communists delayed making their proposal to support Braun until after the Social Democratic Party was already committed to support Marx, and thus made of it an empty, if face-saving, gesture.

trade-unions, without the bourgeois Center Party. The Ultra-Left wanted no alliance with any group. Manuilsky gave the Zinoviev-Maslow policy formal support; watching the disintegration of the Left into several factions with an experienced eye, he conceived a plan to take advantage of this division. In the involved discussions on the danger of an opportunistic line, the rank and file's distrust of Communist policy is strikingly reflected.

ERNST MEYER [representing the Right Opposition to the Central Committee; ordinarily a speaker who weighed his proposals carefully, but here indulging in sheer demagogy]: Maslow's proposal is opportunistic, too near the concept of bourgeois democracy. . . . We must, for instance, ask whether we should demand the elimination of reactionary civil servants by the election of soviets.

RUTH FISCHER: The candidacy of Hindenburg is symptomatic of the new course of the bourgeoisie. It is wrong to say that the German bourgeoisie has just made an error, is confused. Hindenburg's candidacy is a program, a plan for restoration on a new basis. The bourgeoisie hopes to maneuver with the Entente against Russia.

DECISION OF THE PARTY CONFERENCE: The election of Hindenburg as Reich President does not mean that a part of the bourgeoisie has rebelled against the reparations policy; on the contrary, it is meant to quell the nationalist opposition of the petty bourgeoisie and to unite the bourgeois opposition to the Dawes Plan. . . . German stabilization depends entirely on American credits. The parties of the Reich Bloc therefore also recommend that Hindenburg remain loyal to the Dawes program. . . . At the same time, the bourgeoisie obviously intends by the election of Hindenburg to increase the pressure on the working masses for reparations burdens. A new series of terrorist attempts can be seen, such as the bloody clashes in Halle, the death sentence in the Leipzig trial [the Cheka Trial], a renewal of fascist activities, and even the trial against the *Reichsbanner* organization.

For the moment, the bourgeoisie has resigned itself to its dependency on Entente imperialism, but it has not at all decided to renounce finally an imperialist policy of its own. It will try to regain an active foreign policy, to reconstitute a position of imperialist power for Germany (entrance into the League of Nations, colonial mandates, guarantee pact). . . . This "national policy" is in fact a British imperialist policy. . . . The line between Right and Left parties is not delineated; the barriers between the parties are not very clear. The monarchist counter revolution is in progress. . . .

In this epoch of imperialism, concentration of capital and the general elimination of free competition correspond to a concentration, on the political level, of state power in the hands of a strong government, whose reactionary tendency will increase with the crisis of imperialism. This trend . . . produces a series of phenomena that can be called fascism.

In the principal point in dispute, the Communist policy in the Prussian Diet, the anti-Thälmann forces were able to get a small majority for their view:

In a situation in which our party is an arbiter between the Right and the so-called Left, it is permissible, and even under certain conditions mandatory, to make a Left coalition against a Right coalition.

From the discussion on this resolution:

RUTH FISCHER: The turning point since October 1923 was the Hindenburg election; it was a test for the party, which has not proved equal to its task. . . . The Communist workers' distrust of any change of tactics is a serious obstacle to improving party activities.

Hindenburg is the candidate of England; the Dawes Plan is an American-British plan, but with enough advantages to the French bourgeoisie to be at the same time a French plan. The trend towards a monarchist restoration, which began not in recent months but on November 9, 1918, has been considerably increased since the defeat of October 1923.

ARTHUR ROSENBERG: There is no distinction possible between the two blocs; they both represent big business, and the Communists cannot defend one big-business group against the other without definitely losing their revolutionary morale. If the resolution to support a Left cabinet in the Prussian Diet is accepted, the Communist Party would be compelled to vote for the police budget. We should then vote for the salary of Lieutenant Pietzger, the police commandant in Halle. This is something absolutely new in Comintern policy, in contradiction to the resolutions and decisions adopted by all its world congresses and executive committees. "Peasants are no playthings," and the Communist Party no more. The umbilical cord to the bourgeoisie must first be cut, and then we can group around us small peasants and the intelligentsia. But it is impossible to achieve the coöperation of working class and bourgeoisie.

HANS WEBER [from the Palatinate, leader of another Ultra-Left faction]: If this policy is continued, Communists would finally be asked to vote for the black-red-gold flag.

WERNER SCHOLEM [in the name of another Ultra-Left group]: The Communist Party cannot accept the police budget in the Prussian Diet.

Representatives of the other European parties supported the proposals of Zinoviev. The Austrian representative stated that the Austrian Communists considered themselves a part of the German party. The French representative pointed out that the policy of the German party had done considerable harm to the cause of the French Communists; the Hindenburg election had increased the French distrust of Germany.

Someone reported on the great excitement in the factories. Hindenburg's election had not been expected; there was sharp criticism among the workers that the Communist Party had not recognized the seriousness of the situation. Then Thälmann announced to the session that the following day the Social Democrats would plaster all Germany with posters showing Hindenburg riding to power on Thälmann's shoulders. (In 1932, when the Social Democrats supported Hindenburg against Hitler, this post-election slogan of "Hindenburg on Thälmann's shoulders" would be turned against them.)

RUTH FISCHER: Anyone listening to this discussion would believe that this conference is taking place outside space and time.[10]

The election of Hindenburg marked the end of the civil war and closed the first of three formative phases of the German counter revolution. During the second phase, from this election till 1928–1929, there was an attempt to restore Imperial Germany and to bring back the Hohenzollerns or their proxies. The third phase, from the American depression to the Nazi accession, saw monarchism supplanted by new forms of power politics.

The alliance during 1918–1923 between the army's General Staff and the Social Democratic Party had been based on common fear

---

[10] *Die monarchistische Gefahr*, p. 44 ff.

and mutual distrust. In this period the weakness of the Ebert regime gave the Freikorps, the Jacobinites of the counter revolution, the role of catalyst in the process of revolution or counter revolution. In both their form and their behavior, the Nazi *Schutzstaffel* and *Sturmabteilung* (SS and SA, Security Guard and Storm Troopers) were linked directly to the Freikorps and can be understood only from this base. After the Kapp putsch, the Freikorps movement had come to a standstill; the Communist uprisings of 1921 and 1923 were quelled mainly by police forces. As Salomon puts it, "The Freikorps had been exhausted; Severing's police, and behind them the Reichswehr, took their place." With Hindenburg's election, the Freikorps temporarily lost their importance; they retreated to the background of German life to await the end of the Dawes stabilization, and then reappeared in their new forms of SS and SA.

In 1923, the danger of a revolutionary uprising was eliminated, and the nationalists no longer had to fight a defensive battle. They concentrated their efforts on regaining control of state administration, temporarily lent to the Social Democrats as caretakers over a difficult period. After 1923, the nationalists felt themselves strong enough to transform the state by legal procedure; they instituted a coördinated campaign to build up enough popular support to make this transformation possible by a plebiscite.

The 1925 election was the first German plebiscite, and no one knew how the German people would react to this direct appeal to them. Hindenburg was presented as a man whose brilliant career during forty years of peace in Imperial Germany would guarantee the same stability. Now the loyal servant of kings and emperors became the supreme authority of the German Republic. Hindenburg was a myth; he was Father Hindenburg, the Savior. He was the incarnation of non-partisan Germany, the Germany outside the warring political organizations.

Hindenburg never denied his unwavering loyalty to the Hohenzollern dynasty. His study was full of various souvenirs of the Hohenzollern regime: flags, curiosities of the period of Frederick the Great, golden laurels, marble statues of the Emperor.

> Each January 27 Hindenburg sent the Emperor birthday greetings . . . During the presidential campaign, Hindenburg received

an enormous number of letters. Some asked when he thought the next European war would break out and what he would recommend as the best protection against air raids and gas attacks.[11]

The army felt an enormous increase in its prestige as a result of the unexpected ease with which Hindenburg won the election. Under the Constitution, the president had enough power and a sufficiently long term of office to build the basis for the far-reaching development of the army's policy. In this period everyone counted on the continuation of the prosperity that the Dawes stabilization had brought. With continued stability, Hindenburg would be able to restore Wilhelmian Germany, whether with or without Wilhelm, by a gradual transformation of Weimar institutions back into those they had in part replaced. Thus, in jurisdiction, in administration, in education, in philosophy, the election of Hindenburg revitalized the ideas and forces of the old, gave them new courage and new hope of reconquering the new. German labor, which had not had time in the seven years of the Republic to develop new forms, was more and more driven into the defensive. Now that the Field Marshal was at the head of the state, the army moved up with him, to lead national policy.

The Hindenburg election made a tremendous impression outside Germany. In France the general nervousness was increased, and the military intensified its struggle for armaments. The British tendency to coöperate with Germany was given a push forward, now that it was definite that Germany had been stabilized on the middle road. The new post-Versailles states on Germany's borders were alarmed. In the United States, where a strong interest had developed in rebuilding Germany under Dawes's auspices, the appearance of the Kaiser's Field Marshal after a few years of the democratic Republic was an enigma, another evidence that the maze of European politics was hopeless. On the one hand, Hindenburg was welcomed everywhere as an indication that the revolutionary tide in Germany had been definitely stemmed, that a new era of stabilization had begun. On the other hand, his election strengthened the antagonisms between the big powers of the world and signaled the renewed danger of war.

---

[11] Dr. Gerhard Schultze-Pfaelzer, *Wie Hindenburg Reichspräsident wurde* (Berlin, 1925), pp. 23, 14.

The Hindenburg election shook the German Communists to a new awareness. The Left Central Committee issued a call for a party convention the following July in order to have it decide on Maslow's policy of defense of the Republic. During the pre-convention discussion in the provinces, Maslow's supporters won a substantial majority, and it was evident that, for the first time, a leadership would be returned to office twice in succession. Only after it received this renewed mandate from the party would the Left be able to realize the policy of defense of the Republic and get results.

Meanwhile, the German Left continued to seek contacts with other European parties independent of both the Comintern and the Moscow Politburo. Delegations had been sent to Britain, Norway, France, Poland, to consult with the parties of those countries on common problems, and these relations were viewed with suspicious anger by the Stalin Secretariat. Later, in branding the German Left as anti-Bolshevist, Moscow cited these consultations as the nucleus of a Fourth International, the result of Maslow's Western orientation.

It was now evident even outside Russia not only that there was a fight between Trotsky and the Politburo but that the one between Stalin and Zinoviev was sharpening. The attitude of the Communist Party of Germany, the largest unit of the international outside Russia and in the center of Europe, was vital to all the Russian antagonists. If the German Left was stabilized by being reëlected, Stalin feared that Zinoviev would regain so much of his lost prestige that Stalin's grasp on the Comintern and even his own Party would be loosened.

The Russian intervention against Maslow—his retention in Moscow in October 1923 and the suspicion that his imprisonment in Berlin had been arranged by the GPU—had strengthened his status in the German party. It felt that he had been treated unfairly; German Communists liked the idea of being led by a man who, though German in education and experience, was sufficiently at home in Russia to be able to combat the frequent interventions of the Moscow Politburo with some measure of success. The years that Maslow spent in the Moabit prison were perhaps the most active period of his life. Through a wide correspondence, he observed party life closely and wrote incessantly, sending articles to explain and defend the new policy not only to all the party newspapers and branches but to other organizations in Germany and abroad. His influence grew, and with it the possibility of an independent German party and around it an independent grouping of Western parties.

Stalin received one unfavorable report after another from Manuilsky and his other observers in Germany. Their import was clear: act now. If the German party was allowed to continue its present development, it would soon become impossible to bring it back to the Russian fold —for it must be remembered that in this period even Stalin was limited in general to the forms of regular Comintern procedure.

Thus Stalin planned either to bring Maslow under his command or to destroy the German Left. The major point of attack was again its trade-union policy. The German Left agreed with the Russian Politburo that the base for any mass action in Germany had to be the trade-unions; their difference lay rather in their attitude toward those in the German party who disagreed, the various Ultra-Left groups. The Russian Politburo demanded that these be expelled, a proposal that Maslow rejected; he recognized that these militants, numbering some tens of thousands, were among the best elements the party had in the industrial centers.

For Stalin, the prime aim of Communist trade-union policy was their infiltration by means of cells, the prime instrument of union manipulation and, moreover, of valuable industrial espionage. The Ultra-Left, sensing that working through cells led up a blind alley, wanted to form independent unions that would fight it out with the German Federation of Labor in the open and break its monopoly of labor control.[1] This policy, Maslow realized, could not be realized in this period, but he also fought the fetishism of the Communist cell. The fate of German labor, in his view, would not be decided by the most adroitly managed cell system, but by creating a political climate in which united action would be manifestly in the interest of the German workers, and not merely of the Russian state. This scepticism of Maslow's concerning the worth of the union-boring campaign resulted in a long period of vilification in which he was condemned for his anti-union attitude.

Stalin Explains Bolshevism to Maslow

Stalin had opened his attack on the German Left at the beginning of February 1925, two months before the election, with an interview he gave to Wilhelm Herzog, a Communist free-lance journalist. In prepared questions, Herzog asked Stalin for his views on German Communist policy, and Stalin used the occasion to express his deep concern about the decrease in Communist electoral support and the difficulties in trade-unions. This patriarchal benevolence was given publicity in the world press; in the German party, it was understood

---

[1] Of the 21,033,000 persons listed in the 1925 census as gainfully employed, 53.3 per cent were industrial workers, but only 4,156,000 of these were organized in the German Federation of Labor, which had not recovered from the 1923 crisis. (Ludwig Heyde, ed., *Internationales Handwörterbuch des Gewerkschaftswesens,* Berlin, 1932, I, 27; II, 1553 ff.)

"A deep disappointment has seized large strata of the working class," declaimed the chairman of the Twelfth Trade-Union Congress, meeting in Breslau on August 29–30, 1925, "following the non-fulfillment of the grand aspirations of the year 1918. The hope for a socialist organization of labor, which the workers had been for heart and soul, has vanished into thin air. The wonderful November dreams have not come true."

This disillusionment among trade-unionists was particularly rife among militants, which fact made Communist activity in the unions difficult during these years. "In a whole series of party districts there is still a large number of Communists not organized in unions, in some districts over twenty per cent. In such an important city as Remscheid . . . only thirty per cent of our comrades are in the unions." (Report of Fritz Heckert on trade-union work, *Bericht über die Verhandlungen des XI. Parteitages der Kommunistischen Partei Deutschlands in Essen,* Berlin, 1927, p. 358.) Following various splits, a series of Communist-dominated, so-called independent unions had been organized, with a total membership of some 300,000 (*Protokoll des III. Weltkongresses der Kommunistischen Internationale,* Hamburg, 1921, p. 810; the change in membership between 1921 and 1925 was immaterial). Cf. Note 4, pp. 223–224, *infra.*

that it had no other purpose than to prepare for the intervention of the General Secretariat against both Zinoviev and Maslow. The German delegation to the Comintern, unschooled in the proper courtliness of later days, protested vigorously. Max Hesse, a Berlin machinist, raged against this Moscow intervention in coarse and cynical Berlin slang. He attacked Herzog for allowing himself to be the servile tool for this manipulation in terms that led to blows. The Herzog interview, Manuilsky reported, had only embittered the German party.

Maslow, from his cell in Moabit, wrote a sharp letter to Stalin. He agreed, he said, on the necessity of a change of policy, but he strongly objected to Stalin's personal interference in the internal affairs of the German party organization. Intervention by a "proletarian state party" in power into the life of the Communist party of another country, one group in a composite society, would destroy the basis for fraternal coöperation and lead to disastrous consequences.

In reply, Stalin wrote a long letter, couched in party language, in which he made Maslow a new and more precise offer to come over to his side. It was delivered to Moabit by Maslow's lawyer, Kurt Rosenfeld. It is a document worth repeating here in full, for it is an excellent example of the method in this period by which the Russian Party intruded in the internal life of other parties. One volume of Stalin's collected works, not yet published, would contain nothing but just such letters as this, written to leaders and hopeful leaders of every party throughout the world.[2]

February 28, 1925

Esteemed Comrade Maslow:

I received your letter of February 20–25. First of all, accept my greetings and my fervent wish that you will soon be liberated from prison.

And now to business.

First: you, and not only you, have inflated the incident with Herzog much too much. I could not brush him off, and I would not, not only because he is a party member but because he came to me with a letter from Comrade Geschke imploring me to grant

---

[2] The original letter, written in Russian, was lost when the Nazis sacked Maslow's apartment in 1933. This text is from Maslow's translation into German, which appeared in the German Left monthly, *Die Aktion*, vol. XVI, no. 9, September 1926.

him an interview. I am sending you a copy of this letter; the original has already been sent to the German Central Committee. To conclude merely from this interview, given only at the written request of Comrade Geschke, that the Russian Central Committee is making a turn to Brandler or intends to do so, is to make an elephant not out of a fly but out of a nothing and to grasp at the air.

If the Russian Central Committee, particularly Zinoviev and Bukharin, learn that you and other members of the German Central Committee suspect the Russian Central Committee of sympathizing with Brandler and Thalheimer and making a turn from the Left to the Right, they will choke with laughter. Once again, you are too distrustful and are for that reason wrong.

Second: you are completely right when you say that the German party has had enormous successes. Thalheimer and Brandler are without doubt of a type of old leader whose time has passed and who must yield to leaders of a new type. With us in Russia, "old leaders" from among the literati wither away continuously. This process increased during periods of revolutionary crisis and slowed down during periods of crystallization of forces, but it took place continuously. The Lunacharskys, the Pokrovskys, the Stroyevs, the Rozhkovs, the Goldenbergs, the Bogdanovs, and the Krassins—this is the best muster that happens to come to my mind now of former Bolshevik leaders who have gone over to playing second fiddle. That is a process necessary for the renovation of the leading cadres of a living and developing party. The difference between Brandler-Thalheimer and comrades of this type is, incidentally, that in addition they drag along a Social Democratic ballast of which those in this list are free. This difference is, as you see, not to the advantage of Brandler and Thalheimer, but on the contrary. The fact alone that the German party has succeeded in removing Brandler and Thalheimer and throwing them out indicates that the German party is growing, is moving forward, has one success after another. I do not speak about the success of the German Communist Party of which you write, perfectly correctly, in your letter. To believe now that there are people in the [Russian] Central Committee who might intend to turn back the wheel of development of the German Communist Party, that is to have too low an opinion of the Central Committee of the Russian Communist Party.

Be more prudent, Comrade Maslow.

Third: you speak about the line of the German Communist Party. There is no doubt that your line—I speak of your political line—is correct. That is really the explanation for the intimate relation—the better than comradely relation—between the Russian

Communist Party and the German Communist Party that you yourself mention in your letter. Does that mean that we have to gloss over the errors in the political work of either the Russian or the German party? Of course, it does not mean that. Can one say that either the German or the Russian party is free from some mistakes? Can one maintain that a partial criticism of the German Central Committee (l'affaire Barmat was not sufficiently taken advantage of, the well-known vote of the Communist deputies in the Prussian Diet in the election of its president, the question of taxation with regard to the Dawes Plan) is incompatible with complete solidarity with the general policy of the German Central Committee? Of course, one cannot do this.

What would become of our parties, we ask each other when we meet, for instance, in the Comintern Executive Committee, if we close our eyes to mistakes of our parties? If we allow ourselves to be carried away in a parade of complete understanding, of complete tolerance, if in everything we Yes each other? I believe that parties of this type could never become revolutionary parties. That would produce rubber and not a revolutionary party.

I have the impression that some German comrades are not against a demand that we say Yes to everything that the German Central Committee does. I am most energetically opposed to this mutual yessing. According to your letter, you are also against it. So much better for the German party.

Fourth: I am most decidedly against throwing out all comrades who think differently. I am against such a policy not because I pity those who think differently, but because such a policy would produce a regime of intimidation in the party, a regime of fear, a regime that would not foster a spirit of self-criticism and initiative. It is bad if the party leaders are feared but not respected. The leaders of the party can be real party leaders only if the party does not fear them but honors them and recognizes their authority. To create such leaders is difficult; it is a long and complicated process, but an absolutely necessary one. In such a case, the party cannot be called a real Bolshevik party, and the discipline of the party cannot be a real, conscious discipline. In my opinion, the German comrades mutilate these self-evident truths.

In disavowing Comrade Trotsky and his followers, we Russian Bolsheviks have instituted a most consequential principle-clarifying campaign for the foundations of Bolshevism against the foundations of Trotskyism, although on the basis of the strength and specific weight of the Russian Central Committee, we could have managed without this campaign. Did we need this campaign? It was absolutely necessary, for with it we educated hundreds of thousands of new party members (and also those outside the party) in the spirit of Bolshevism. It is regrettable that our German comrades do not feel the necessity of preparing and completing measures suppressing the opposition by a broad principle-clarifying campaign, thus making the task of educating the party members and cadres in the spirit of Bolshevism more difficult for themselves. To throw out Brandler and Thalheimer, that is easy; that is not a difficult task. But to overcome Brandlerism, that is a complex and serious affair. Here one can only do damage by punitive measures alone. Here one must plow the soil and seriously enlighten the membership.

The Russian Communist Party has always developed in antithesis to non-Communist tendencies, and only in this struggle did it become strong and weld its real cadres. The German Communist Party has before it a similar period of development by antithesis, a really serious and drawn-out fight with non-Communist tendencies, especially with Social Democratic traditions, with Brandlerism. But for such a task it is not sufficient to take mass punitive measures. For that reason I believe that the internal party policy of the German Central Committee must be made more elastic. I do not doubt that the German Communists will overcome their shortcomings in this respect.

You are completely right with regard to work in the trade-unions. The role of the unions in Germany is different from that in Russia. In Russia the trade-unions rose after the party, and they are really auxiliary branches of the party. That is completely different from Germany, and Europe in general. There the party developed from the trade-unions, which competed successfully with the party in influencing the masses and often clung like lumps of lead on the feet of the party. If one were to ask the broad masses of Germany, or of Europe in general, to which organization they have a more intimate relation, the union or the party, they would undoubtedly reply that they regard themselves as closer to the union than to the party. It may be good or bad, but it is a fact that the non-party workers in Europe regard the trade-unions as their main fortress in their fight against the capitalists (wages, working hours, security, etc.), while in their estimate the party is necessary but auxiliary and of second importance. That explains also why the broad mass of the workers regard the fight of the Ultra-Lefts against the trade-unions from the outside as one against their main fortress, which they have built up over decades and which "the Communists" now want to destroy. If this specific feature is not taken into account, the entire basis of the Western Communist movement will be annihilated. But from this two conclusions have to be drawn: First, in the West we cannot conquer the trade-unions without working inside the unions and increasing our influence in them. Therefore we must pay special attention to the work of our comrades in the trade-unions.

That is all for the moment.

Don't be angry with me because I have been straightforward and sharp. I shake your hand.

JOSEPH STALIN

This letter, a textbook model in Stalinist technique with potential confederates in the international hierarchy, was published only a year and a half later, after Maslow's expulsion. It was an offer and a threat. Zinoviev was not mentioned by name, but the reference to anachronistic old leaders was clear enough. It was one of the first occasions on which Stalin posed as the benevolent patriarch of all Communists; in response to such a personal gesture, Stalin expected an immediate pledge of loyalty to his person and to his policy.

Through the same Rosenfeld, Maslow sent me the original letter with his translation, adding a few sarcastic comments on this blunt bid. I was permitted to visit him twice a week in Moabit and could discuss current affairs rather freely so long as they did not touch on the German scene too closely. We interpreted Stalin's offer as a danger signal for Zinoviev and decided to support him, for we were agreed that if Zinoviev was removed from the Comintern he would be supplanted by the most arrogant and anti-foreign type of Russian. We were not at all satisfied with his Comintern policy, but he was the last thin barrier to the russification of the International.

The letter was discussed officially in the German Central Committee with Manuilsky present. It was impossible there to take too open cognizance of the meaning behind the polite party phrases, but the entire Central Committee could read between the lines and supported Maslow against Stalin unanimously.

At the Fourteenth Conference of the Russian Party, in April 1925, the conflict between Stalin and Zinoviev took uncompromisable form. Zinoviev was no longer master of his own Comintern apparatus, already infiltrated by the GPU, and he could send messages to his supporters abroad only with the greatest difficulty. Manuilsky got secret orders to intervene in Berlin and to remove the Left from leadership at any cost. This was veiled behind a justified criticism of Left errors, and Zinoviev, biding his time, was forced by Party discipline to support this intervention.

Manuilsky versus the German Left

Before the forthcoming convention of the German party met, Manuilsky gained one small victory for Stalin—the expulsion of the most ardent supporters of independent trade-unions. To his consternation, and with Maslow's full support, the party maintained excellent relations with those expelled and continued to collaborate with them on a local level. Moreover, the Ultra-Left faction in the party still maintained considerable support in Berlin, the Ruhr, and the Palatinate; the number of delegates they elected to go to the convention was large enough for them to be entitled to two representatives in the leading committees. They chose Werner Scholem for the Orgburo and Arthur Rosenberg for the Politburo.

Werner Scholem, a talented organizer, had been sent several times to Moscow, where he had met Stalin. The General Secretary disliked him heartily, for he turned aside any appeal couched in hyper-Bolshevist terms with the crude cynicism of the Berliner. He was proud of having been a member of the USPD, which he always regarded as a model workers' organization. Son of a wealthy family, he had left home because of his opposition to the Kaiser's war and had become a radical pacifist. He had been drafted into the army in 1914, when he was a member of the Social Democratic Youth; a short time later he was sentenced to a year's imprisonment, having been convicted of lese-majesty against Wilhelm II. After the war he became editor of the party newspaper in Halle and deputy to the Prussian Diet. Rapidly he became known throughout the Reich, for he was an excellent and pointed speaker.[3]

---

[3] Scholem was expelled from the party in 1926 for his opposition to Stalin; he continued his fight against him outside the party till the Nazis imprisoned him in 1933. Incarcerated in various concentration camps, he was killed in Buchenwald by SS-leader Blank in summer 1940, after having suffered the oppression of both the Nazis and the Communist inmates of the camp. (Cf. Benedikt Kautsky, *Teufel und Verdammte*, Zurich, 1946, p. 116.) Kautsky reports on the kangaroo court of the camp, which under the eyes of the SS sentenced political opponents to death and carried out the sentences. "Communist heretics were treated worse than Social Democrats, and there were quite a few of them, designated as Trotskyites, Brandlerites, trade-union oppositionists, etc." (Kautsky, p. 131).

Setting aside for the moment the consequential principle-clarifying campaign being led from Moscow, Manuilsky indiscriminately promised all three factions Comintern support for their conflicting policies. He listened with an especially sympathetic ear to the many complaints of the Ultra-Left groups against Maslow's parliamentarism and his bloc with the bourgeois Center Party. This opportunistic turn, he fulsomely admitted, constituted an enormous danger to the German revolution. He encouraged the Right wing, which had lost most of its electoral support in the party, to demand more salaried party functionaries, to be paid with Moscow's help. The deputies in the Reichstag and state diets found that Manuilsky understood their concern over the shrinking vote for the Communist Party, and he proposed that the reason was the narrow policy of the Left. To me, finally, he promised the unconditional support of Stalin in a principled fight against the Ultra-Lefts.

The party bureaucracy of whatever faction found in Manuilsky a sympathetic audience. The party had carried over from the 1923 uprising a swollen apparatus, which it could support only with substantial financial help from Moscow. As the Left rank and file was anxious to be rid of these salaried functionaries and supplant them with elected volunteers, and as they were adamant in their insistence that the party should look to its financial independence from Moscow, they continually demanded that Scholem cut down the party organization. Every one among those dismissed delivered a long plaint to Manuilsky and to Stalin, the substance of which was always that he had been fired on political grounds. Manuilsky was thus able to combine the defense of these ex-bureaucrats with that of the panacea of Communist policy, the infiltration of trade-unions.

The Brandler Central Committee had organized a special Trade-Union Division under Fritz Heckert and Jakob Walcher, which submitted periodic memoranda directly to A. Lozovsky, the chairman of the Profintern; and by this channel Stalin got many detailed reports, not only on the party but on German industry and all salient aspects of German economy. The several dozen employees of this division had a life independent from the German Central Committee, under whose formal jurisdiction the department had been set up and ostensibly remained; there were always three or four Russian experts from the

Profintern working in its office. Manuilsky insisted that this apparatus should not only not be cut but be continuously enlarged.

This dispute was less about trade-unions and how to work in them than about the delicate question of Moscow subsidies to the German party. Actually the party was large enough to finance itself. Membership dues, somewhat higher than the traditional fees of the Social Democratic Party, amounted to a fair sum. Moreover, the several hundred Communist deputies to the Reichstag and the various diets, though functionaries of the party, were paid by the state, and in addition each was required to donate a portion of his income to the party. Moscow's constant insistence that it was necessary to broaden propaganda beyond what the party could itself pay for perverted its activity toward sheer manipulatory methods. The party's annual budget was prepared in Berlin, but with an eye to pleasing the men in Moscow who would pass on it; the lists of musts among which funds were allocated always tended to be in accord with current Russian policy. During the years 1921–1930, it was Mirov-Abramov, the Comintern resident in Berlin, who was charged with transferring funds to the party.

The Tenth Congress of the German party convened in Berlin on July 12, 1925. There were 170 delegates, 142 of them workers from the bench, and representatives from various other parties, including one Hsia from China. Manuilsky, as Comintern delegate, was listed in the convention report under the name Samuely. The delegates had been elected after a full discussion of Maslow's program of defense of the Weimar Republic, and a substantial majority came with a mandate to support it.

In giving the various factions proportional representation in the Central Committee and the Politburo, the most difficult point was to find a suitable member of the Right, for Wilhelm Pieck was regarded as inadequate even by his own supporters. The solution was reached in the choice of Ernst Meyer, who had been the Politburo chairman before Brandler and before that a friend and disciple of Rosa Luxemburg. It was a symptom of reconciliation to have Meyer, who had fought at the Fourth World Congress for the expulsion of the Left, accepted into the direct leadership of the party. Though he maintained his fundamental position and remained loyal to his caucus, after the 1923 experience Meyer had revised his estimate of the Left wing and sympathized with their will to be more independent of Moscow.

From the beginning, the outcome of the convention was clear: it would be divided on political issues, but there would be a strong majority for Maslow's policy and the opposition, satisfied that it had been given full democratic representation, would be content to work amicably with this majority. This development alarmed Manuilsky, for there was general unanimity behind Maslow's criticism of Moscow. If the party could no longer be manipulated, then its integration into a stronger form could only be opposed by the manipulator. His job was clear: by some means to prevent the integration of the three principal factions of the German party into one working unit.

It was difficult for Manuilsky to find a formal starting point for disrupting the convention. He scrutinized its theses, but no single word gave him a pretext to intervene in defense of Marxist principles. Just before the election of the new Central Committee, he created the necessary dramatic tension. The convention chairman was Ottomar Geschke,[4] a railroad worker, who conducted the proceedings with his usual trade-union joviality. During the debate, Manuilsky asked for the floor after the chair had already granted it to another speaker. Geschke told Manuilsky to wait his turn, and this commonplace was dramatized by the Comintern delegate into a breach of the International's discipline. He had, he declared, the right to intervene at any moment of a party convention. He demanded that the proceedings be interrupted and convened the Central Committee, to which he stated that in his person the Comintern and the Russian Party had been offended by the convention chairman. He went on to criticize the spirit of rebellion and distrust of which this incident was symptomatic; another, and more important, indication of this anti-Bolshevist virus, he said, was the inclusion of the Ultra-Left in the party leadership, and he demanded that Rosenberg and Scholem be excluded from the list of nominees for the leading committees. In a closed session the convention unwaveringly rejected this intervention by the Comintern rep-

---

[4] This is the same Geschke who had requested an interview for Herzog from Stalin. After having spent twelve years in Buchenwald, in 1945 he was the chief of the Welfare Department in the Berlin City Council.

resentative and elected the proposed slate. The fight was on; it was clear that the party would now come into open conflict with Moscow. In the closed session, the delegates were as one in their determination to oppose the Russian Politburo. The rank and file suspected even the Left leaders, Thälmann and Fischer, of being too conciliatory. The membership wanted a rigid defense of the right of the German party to elect its own leaders and decide its own organizational principles, and demanded that interference from Russia be fought without stint.

An Open Letter to the German Party

After the convention, Manuilsky returned to Moscow and reported to a session of the Russian Politburo that there was a danger that the German party, the most important in the Communist International, would break away. He gave Stalin a weapon against Zinoviev by his statement that an alliance of the Communist parties of Western Europe, a "Fourth International" under German leadership, had been long prepared and was an imminent possibility. The German Left, according to his report, had been laying aside funds for this purpose since 1924. Thus accused by implication of conspiring with foreigners against the Politburo, Zinoviev had no choice but to demonstrate his loyalty by joining in the condemnation of the German Left and instituting corrective measures.

The convention had elected a Left treasurer, Arthur König, but Comintern funds remained in the hands of Wilhelm Pieck and Hugo Eberlein, who received the subsidy in foreign currency, mainly dollars, and paid current expenses monthly. It was impossible to deposit these sums in a bank, and until this period they had been secreted somewhere and drawn on as needed. With Eberlein's encouragement, König attempted to put these idle funds to work. It was his intention to invest them and get sizable returns for the party, but since the investments could be made only with sympathetic industrialists, the plan worked poorly and ended as a definite financial failure. Among these Communist business enterprises were a small textile plant in Chemnitz owned by one F. Aurich, the manufacturer of Red Front uniforms; a phonograph record factory; a publishing house on Lake Constance. The negotiations with various businessmen were to the accompaniment of much wining and dining, and waiters and busboys who recognized

Eberlein and König started a series of wild rumors going around Berlin.[5]

The Russian Politburo charged the International Control Commission with investigating this situation in the German party. In spite of his financial bungling, König was cleared, for the investigation was not able to unearth evidence sufficiently damaging to be used against the leaders of his caucus, Maslow and me. Maslow was in prison, and I had nothing to do with the party treasury. Zinoviev could point to the fact that only Wilhelm Pieck received funds from the Soviet Embassy and he and his friend Hugo Eberlein alone administered the party finances.

> After the failure of the 1923 uprising, Mirov-Abramov, the OMS agent in Germany, as well as Pyatnitsky in Moscow, spent many anxious hours wondering whom they could now trust with Comintern money. It was a relief to them when Wilhelm Pieck was retained in the new Central Committee, for both Pyatnitsky and Mirov-Abramov trusted this veteran labor leader.[6]

At the time of this incident, Heinz Neumann became one of Stalin's main supporters in Germany.

Born of wealthy parents, Neumann had left his bourgeois home and environment at the age of sixteen and joined the socialist youth. He wandered all over Europe, half tramp, half socialist missionary, and quickly picked up a facile French, Italian, Russian. During 1922–1924, he went to Moscow as an interpreter at Comintern conferences, and some of his Komsomol friends presented him to Stalin, who liked the bright ambitious youngster. In the German party, Neumann was becoming known outside Berlin as one of the young leaders of the Left caucus, a loyal and eager follower of Maslow. An incurable romantic, Neumann was inevitably drawn into the secret work of the party.[7] Stalin knew of these activities, and knew also that the young man admired him.

Immediately after the Berlin convention, Stalin called Neumann to Moscow, where he was assigned the task of writing a pamphlet against

---

[5] One of the principal agents of this Communist venture into free enterprise was Fritz Callam, then a party administrator in Essen, later, during World War II, a member of Paul Merker's Free Germany Committee in Mexico City.

[6] Walter Krivitsky, *In Stalin's Secret Service*, p. 54.

[7] Cf. Note 12, pp. 325–326, *supra.*

Maslow's Western Communism.[8] Up to this time he had done important work for the party but had not been elected to a leading post; Stalin promised him a promotion to the German Central Committee. This "confession," intended to help change the mood in the German party, created a sensation in the Comintern.[9]

With a background of the pending investigation, the Neumann

[8] Heinz Neumann, *Maslows Offensive gegen den Leninismus* (Hamburg, 1925).

[9] Heinz Neumann, for years Stalin's special confidant, was one of the few Germans who at that time could speak Russian. He was a guest at Stalin's intimate drinking parties, and with his lively intelligence and international background grasped more secrets than anyone should know of Stalin's rise to power. In December 1927 he and "Besso" Lominadze, a Communist Youth leader, were sent to China to organize the so-called Canton Commune. Back in Germany Neumann opposed the rising Nazis courageously and was often involved in street fights. In the summer of 1931, Neumann's sullen opposition to the Communist policy of toleration of the Nazis led to his elimination from his post as Thälmann's secretary. In February 1932, again by Moscow's orders, he was dropped from the German Politburo; and in May he was called back to Moscow. Here he discussed German policy at length with Stalin, and his later reports on these conversations are one of the most important evidences on the content of Stalin's German policy in this period. In August 1932, in order to eliminate him completely from German party affairs, Neumann was sent to Spain as a member of a Comintern delegation, which also included Medina, an Argentinean, and Salzmann, a Pole. At the end of the year, troubled by the news from Berlin, Neumann wrote to his friend in the German Politburo, Hermann Remmele, that vigorous opposition to the party line in Germany was necessary to save the party from its imminent destruction. The Nazis came to power the next month, and in March 1933, after Remmele's flight to Moscow, this letter was found by the GPU and forwarded to Comintern headquarters. Neumann was ordered to leave Spain and proceed to Zurich, where he lived in disgrace, with no contacts to the Comintern hierarchy; he earned a precarious living by petty assignments from the party publishing house. At the request of the Nazi government, which wanted him extradicted so that he could be tried for an assault on an SS-man just before he left Germany, the Swiss police arrested Neumann in December 1934 on a passport charge. After months of negotiations, he was finally permitted to go instead to Russia; he embarked at Le Havre in June 1935. Back in Moscow, Neumann and his wife were given small jobs as translators. Pyatnitsky wanted to save him by sending him to Brazil with the passport of a Canadian engineer, but at the last moment these arrangements were cancelled. After two years of intermittent hearings before the International Control Commission, Neumann was arrested in April 1937 for counter-revolutionary activity in the German party; specifically, he had given Fritz David (a defendant in the 1936 trial) a position as *Rote Fahne* editor in 1930 and thus facilitated the planned assassination of Stalin. Neumann is undoubtedly dead, but when and under what circumstances he died are not known. (Paul Merker refers to Neumann's opposition in an ambiguous passage; cf. *Deutschland, sein oder nicht sein?*, I, 256.)

In 1946, a small magazine (*Deutsche Blätter*, Santiago de Chile, September–October 1946, pp. 30–32) printed an anonymous report that in 1940 a group of German women, all of them relatives of political opponents of Stalin, had been handed over by the GPU to the Gestapo, which put them in the Ravensbrück con-

pamphlet, and more reports that the Germans were moving away from the Comintern, Stalin was able to extract a compromise from Zinoviev —an Open Letter to the German party criticizing the policy of its Left faction and recommending the elimination of Maslow and me from the leadership but the preservation of the Left Central Committee. With consummate skill, Stalin forged a double-edged instrument. On his initiative, the Russian Politburo ordered Zinoviev as Comintern chairman to send this Open Letter, thus at once showing that his authority in the Comintern was weakening and depriving him of his only substantial support among European Communists, the German Left. As Zinoviev had not yet decided when he could openly attack Stalin, he submitted to Party discipline, maintaining the vain illusion that he would be able to limit the damage by finesse.

As a preliminary, Zinoviev called a delegation of the German party to a plenum of the Executive Committee of the Comintern in Moscow to discuss a draft of the letter. The delegates were: Ernst Thälmann, Ruth Fischer, Philipp Dengel, Wilhelm Schwan, Ernst Schneller, Johnny Scher, Otto Kühne, Max Strötzel, and Heinz Neumann.[10]

In a document covering three pages in small print of the German Communist daily,[11] the Open Letter rehashed all the issues with which Manuilsky had attempted to disrupt the integration of the party. Its first point was to split Maslow and Fischer from the rest of the Left. All policy matters had been decided on by a majority—if not unanimous —vote of the Central Committee, but these two were made solely responsible for the errors of the party. The others had been "raped" into accepting an anti-Comintern policy.[12]

---

centration camp. The author of this article was Heinz Neumann's widow, Grete Buber-Neumann, who is now living in Stockholm. Mrs. Neumann has been kind enough to let me read her most interesting unpublished memoirs, which contain a detailed account of her life in the Karaganda camp after her arrest in 1938 and in the Ravensbrück camp after her transfer to the Gestapo.

[10] Kühne later entered the service of the GPU and was sent on various missions to European countries. In 1946 he emerged in Paris as the head of an association of German refugees in France. Scher was killed by the Nazis soon after they came to power. Imprisoned by the Nazis in 1933, Schneller died in a concentration camp in 1939 or 1940. Dengel signed Free Germany Committee proclamations from Moscow until 1944, when he suddenly disappeared; cf. note 7, p. 506, *infra*.

[11] Open Letter of the Executive Committee of the Comintern to the Communist Party of Germany, *Die Rote Fahne,* September 1, 1925.

[12] This convenient distinction between a few top leaders, who are to be disposed of, and their colleagues had an almost textual repetition in the United States in

After a long introduction, in which the Comintern Executive Committee reported that it had been difficult to convince the German comrades, that they had had to negotiate for weeks with several delegations, the Open Letter dealt with three important and complex problems: first, the Right deviation of Fischer and Maslow and their tendency to depend on parliamentary methods; second, the trade-union question, especially the necessity of rebuilding a large trade-union division in the German party; third, the internal party life and the attitude towards Brandler.

First the international setting was given; there was a "concentration of imperialist forces against the Soviet Union (the military-diplomatic ring around Moscow, the British policy, and the guarantee pact)." The Open Letter continued:

> A very important phase of this complex matter is the necessity of defining the new orientation of Germany towards the West. This change of orientation has created a different mood in the people, which is reflected in some parts of the proletariat, which lack class consciousness . . . In corrupted sections of the working class, an increase of so-called "anti-Muscovite" tendencies can be seen, the reflection of the new bearings of the bourgeoisie. In part, this mood exists also in the German Communist Party.

After the Frankfurt convention, the Executive Committee had sent the German Central Committee a telegram demanding the expulsion of the Ultra-Lefts, and this had been distributed by a circular letter to all the regional sections of the party. This had been done, the Open Letter complains, solely in order to arouse the party against the Executive Committee of the Comintern. A few months later, at the Fifth World Congress of the Comintern, Ruth Fischer had fought against a slogan of trade-union world unity, which she charged was solely a maneuver to prop Soviet policy in Britain.

> It was intimated that the fight for international trade-union unity was nothing more than "one move in the chess game of Russian foreign policy," an attempt to approach the MacDonald Social Democratic government.

1945, when Jacques Duclos intervened against Earl Browder. He also had the support of the majority of the Central Committee of the party, which in any case had only carried out a policy imposed by Moscow and accepted by the entire organization, but he was made solely responsible.

The anti-Bolshevist mentality of the Left was indicated also, the Open Letter continued, in its opposition to hiring a large group of salaried employees for trade-union work. (Once again, this point was made to attract the Right, who were hungry for these posts.) The Left is pessimistic, it was maintained; the Left does not believe in the imminence of the German revolution. Maslow in particular was singled out:

> Maslow's writings are a devious but extremely dangerous attack on Leninist fundamentals and on the entire policy in this period of the Communist International.

In his book, *The Two Revolutions of the Year 1917* (Berlin, 1925), Maslow had criticized the policy of the Third World Congress of the Comintern, which he considered jointly responsible for the errors of the German party. Some of these passages were quoted and answered with cries of indignation:

> This monstrous attack on Lenin and Leninism cannot be tolerated at any price . . . Under the cloak of fighting "West European" deviations, that is to say anti-Bolshevist deviations from Communism, Maslow propagates a West European Communism of the worst kind . . .
>
> Since the Third World Congress of the Comintern, the relation of Comrade Maslow's group to the Comintern has been incorrect and anti-Bolshevist . . .
>
> During the past years, Comrade Ruth Fischer has sent, over the protest of the ECCI, delegates to various sections of the Comintern, charged with changing the policy of the Executive Committee by factionalism.

Another symptom of the rebellious spirit of the Left Communists was an article of Maslow, "Some Remarks on the Tenth Congress of the German Communist Party," which had been published in the *Funke*. In it Maslow had related how, in August 1922, after the Jena convention, the Berlin organization had refused an invitation to send a delegation to Moscow because it disagreed with several Executive Committee criticisms of German Communist policy. Reporting this anecdote, in the words of the Open Letter, was "an unparalleled attempt to degrade the Communist International in the eyes of the German workers." The Comintern is without any doubt right, the Open Letter repeats several times; without any doubt Ruth Fischer and Maslow are wrong.

Maslow was attacked also because the party had advertised his book and pamphlets by "American" methods, incompatible with the tradition of the labor movement. Again he was attacked for his pessimism. He had said that it was ridiculous to suppose that it was possible at this moment to prepare to seize power, that the party needed a period of growth of at least ten years to become a real force in German political life.

The relation between the Left and the Ultra-Left was attacked several times. "At the end of the party convention, Scholem-Rosenberg's offer to unite against the ECCI was silently accepted, and that against all principles, for the convention's political direction had been toward a fight with the Ultra-Lefts." This link between Left and Ultra-Left was singled out as especially dangerous for Moscow.

Perhaps the most absurd section of this Stalinist intervention was its unctuous defense of party democracy. One of the reasons the Russian General Secretary cited for removing from office the German leaders just elected by a democratically run convention, was that they did not have a sufficient regard for political democracy. On the other hand, Ruth Fischer was accused of considering too much the political credo of the delegates elected to the Tenth Party Congress. "The party delegates have been mainly Ultra-Left in orientation." This quaint dismissal of elementary logic has also remained one of the main characteristics of Stalinist polemics.

The Open Letter ended by presenting another instrument to transform the party. The German Central Committee should be enlarged, as the Russian one had been after Lenin's death; in a larger body there would be more room for the Moscow Politburo to maneuver. With renewed demagogic denunciation of Maslow's parliamentarism, the Executive Committee demanded that the party concentrate its energies on "pure proletarian mass policy," that is, the formation of factory cells. This emphasis on pure proletarian policy was pure balderdash, intended to prevent any change of German Communist policy in a direction undesirable to Moscow.

> It must be understood [said the Letter] that one of the main errors of the German Communists in the last period lay precisely

in that they have given too much attention to "high," to "parliamentary" questions, and too little attention to work in the factories.

When I arrived in Moscow to attend the session of the Presidium called in August 1925, I saw the Open Letter for the first time. As there was a surface similarity between certain of my own criticisms of the sectarian character of the German party and several of the charges made in the Open Letter, I had planned to accept these points and to oppose mainly the organizational remedies suggested. By this stand, I intended both to win time, hoping that meanwhile Maslow might be liberated from prison, and in any case to shift the discussion from the faults of the German party to whether or not it should be independent of Moscow. The recurrent themes of Communist discussion—policy in the trade-unions, the Prussian Diet, and the others—had been talked threadbare, and bringing them up again could serve only to disintegrate the party further.

Stalin, however, had another plan. All members of the Presidium, myself included, were required under Comintern discipline to sign the Open Letter and then to defend it in our parties. Thus I was driven to sign my own political death warrant and to confess my sins in public.

The German Left still had too high a regard for the value of Communist discipline. That was our most vulnerable point, and Zinoviev, as head of the Russian "delegation" to the Comintern, made full use of it. My first decision was to refuse to play the game, and I announced that I would fight the Open Letter in public. Zinoviev, Bukharin, and Manuilsky iterated their argument: You can defend your point of view in a closed session of the Presidium and vote against the Open Letter, but if the highest world authority of Communism decides that all members of the Presidium must sign the letter, you cannot refuse without breaking Bolshevik discipline. No more can you refuse to defend the Open Letter in the German party. You are a member of the Presidium of the Communist International, elected by the Fifth World Congress, and this function has precedence over any that you have in the German party. Your first duty is towards the Presidium; Comintern discipline has priority over national party discipline.

Thus the principle of hierarchical discipline was applied against me. If there are differences in the Politburo, its decision by majority vote is binding on all members and they are not allowed by Bolshevik precepts to discuss their point of difference even in the Central Committee. Dissidents in the Central Committee must defend the committee's point of view even in the party; party decisions have to be defended outside the party even by members who disagree with them. Thus at every level disagreement is kept to the group of minimum size, and at each step down the hierarchical scale the next larger body is presented with a unanimous mandate. The secrecy of each body's deliberations is sacred; for a member of a committee to discuss them with someone in a lower hierarchical unit is the Communist equivalent of a serious misdemeanor.

The means of implementing this principle was in formation in August 1925, and this was the first important occasion on which it was carried out on a Comintern scale. Until this time, dissident groups in the Comintern had blared forth their views to all who would listen. The appeal to my Bolshevik loyalty was strong, but I would have resisted it had it not been supported by another, which Zinoviev made in another private conversation. His position, he told me frankly, was imperiled; the Comintern was under fire from all sides of the Russian Party. On the other hand, at the Fourteenth Congress of the Russian Party, to be convoked in a few months, he hoped to reverse this current. It had been the intention of Stalin, he informed me, to have Manuilsky remove Maslow and me from the German Politburo, and he had been able to prevent this. Your friends in the German party, he went on, will understand that when you now support with your signature a policy that you have vigorously fought for the past year, it will have been only because of formal Comintern discipline. It is the function of leaders to accept responsibility for the errors of the party, and by so doing you thwart an attack on your person. Your position in the German party is strong enough to withstand this ambiguous stand for a few months, after which we will be able to fight our opponents in the German and Russian parties openly.

Thus I signed the letter, after having voted against it in the Presidium. All our sophisticated calculations proved completely wrong; the Open Letter only facilitated Stalin's consolidation of power.

When I returned to Germany, his campaign was in full swing; Scholem and Rosenberg had already been eliminated from the Central

Committee. Stalin was able to split these two by promising Rosenberg a return, and for a time he collaborated with Thälmann and thus preserved his position in the Foreign Affairs Committee of the Reichstag. Under Manuilsky's auspices, the party was discussing "normalization" and "Bolshevization"; but the disintegration of the Russian Party then under way, to which this discussion would normally have led, was of course taboo. In spite of both Comintern discipline and the interfaction quarrels, the party as a whole was inclined to reject the Open Letter and the Russian domination it denoted. Perhaps the portion it liked least was that laying the responsibility for policy on Maslow, who had been in prison during the period, rather than on Manuilsky, who had been in Berlin coaching Brandler. I attacked the Open Letter in Berlin, Essen, and Stuttgart, and there was substantial and growing support for an anti-Moscow position. Never did I feel more genuine sympathy in the party than during these first weeks of Stalin's intervention.

In September 1925 Maslow had finally been brought to trial before the highest Reich court as a dangerous Communist leader. The evidence was based largely on *The Two Revolutions of the Year 1917,* the book he had written in prison. The day the trial opened, Maslow learned of the Open Letter, and he was even more anxious to get as short a sentence as possible so that he could fight for his policy in the party. Most of the Thälmann Politburo wanted Maslow's help in fighting Moscow interference more than they feared his opposition in the party, and they authorized him to make full use of the weak points of the indictment in his defense. There had been no 1923 uprising, and not only had Maslow been physically absent, being held in Moscow at the time, but he had not been a member of the German Central Committee. This defense, combined with the fact that the Open Letter made the court doubtful of Maslow's future status and policy, resulted in the relatively light sentence of four years. Since he had already served fifteen months, he could expect to get out in a year or two.

Maslow's defense of his person strengthened the anti-Moscow tendency among German Communists considerably. Stalin reacted with another Politburo decision against Maslow, accusing him of having behaved before a bourgeois court in an un-Bolshevik manner. He had publicly discussed internal party matters and had held the policy of

1923 up to public scrutiny, pointing out its weak spots. Not only all Communist papers but the world press were discussing the crisis of the German Communist Party and linking it correctly to that in the Russian Party. But Maslow had committed the greatest crime possible against the party by breaking conspiratorial secrecy, by lifting a corner of the rug that is supposed to veil Comintern matters from bourgeois eyes.

The day the trial ended, I was recalled to Moscow. I arrived there the end of September, only to learn that by a decision of the Presidium my return to Germany was prohibited. I had been promoted to higher duties in the Comintern office. Pyatnitsky took my passport, and I was consigned to the Hotel Lux, where for ten months I remained a virtual state prisoner. All my correspondence went through Comintern channels and therefore through GPU censorship, and I was thus cut off from all contact with the German party. The discussion in the German party was manipulated in our absence, while Maslow was in prison and I was held under surveillance.

In his Berlin prison, Maslow was much less restricted than I in my Moscow hotel. His correspondence was censored, but less strictly than mine, and he was allowed regularly to see his lawyer and a few friends, through whom he remained in contact with the party membership. I was surrounded by the growing hostility of the Russian Party hierarchy and systematically isolated, both morally and organizationally.

This first Stalinist intervention in German Communist affairs was a pattern for the many that were to follow, on all levels of all parties and of the International, and later in liberated countries. Stalin had based, and has continued to base his interventions on information from agents reporting directly to him. These reports are detailed on both the collective under observation and its individual leaders—enumerating their background, their past errors, their weaknesses, their vulnerabilities, their vanities. Each group is promised what it wants most and threatened with what it most fears, and thus the collective is disintegrated into conflicting subgroups, each angling for Stalin's favor. Certain individuals not yet tied to the Politburo are bid for and purchased.

What gives this process its peculiar Stalinist mark is the subsequent public confession of their past errors by former opponents, admitting that they had been at fault but that the General Secretary had not been.

This personification of party errors heightens the authority of the supreme leadership, whose ultimate wisdom is fallible only in the sense that it is thwarted by incompetent or unfaithful comrades. By its own inner logic, this system of intimidation cannot but end in permanent and ever-growing terror.

The years between the death of Lenin and the final victory of Stalin as his successor are marked by a curious paradox. On the one hand, it was recognized that a period of capitalist stabilization had set in and attempts were made to reëstablish Russia's relations with the bourgeois world; and, on the other, the Russian Party, disintegrating in this period, produced a series of provocations in various countries, from Britain to Estonia and Bulgaria.

Russia's efforts to reach a certain equilibrium in its foreign policy were from the beginning in conflict with the Comintern, the main target of all anti-Bolshevik propaganda abroad. A rearrangement with the capitalist world became essential from the point of view of internal Russian policy, which sought to quell all opposition by a maximum stability in foreign policy. Soviet Russia had been recognized by Germany in 1921, in the Rapallo Treaty, and with this opening wedge a number of other countries followed suit. During the next two years Soviet representatives abroad intensified their diplomatic efforts, and in the Party 1924 was called "the year of recognitions." The Soviet government was recognized by Great Britain, Italy, Norway, Austria, Greece, Danzig, Sweden, Denmark, Mexico, Hungary, the nascent Chinese Republic, France, and finally in January 1925 by Japan. This diplomatic rapprochement strengthened not only the international position of revolutionary Russia, but the hope that it might survive peaceably in a bourgeois world.

Speaking at the Thirteenth Party Congress in May 1924, Zinoviev pointed out that this policy, successful as it was, held a certain danger unless it was supplemented by continued support to all Communist parties. Fighting for power with Stalin, he emphasized the role of the Comintern in Russian policy; the class struggle had not ended by treaties between Soviet Russia and the capitalist countries. The capitalist offensive continued. On May 14, a week before the congress opened, a bomb plot had been discovered in Lisbon and Coimbra, Portugal. Felix Neumann and General Skoblevsky had been arrested in Berlin and would soon be the principal defendants in the Cheka Trial.

On the other hand, Zinoviev said, the Social Democrats are getting power in a series of countries. "The Second International is in the government in Britain, the greatest bourgeois country. Britain is not Poland, not Iceland, not even Germany. It is Britain." France, Belgium, Denmark, are following the trail of the British Labour Party. Berlin has half a million Communist voters, Paris more than 300,000. In the elections after the February revolution Petrograd and Moscow together had had no more than 800,000 Bolshevik votes. There are large Communist groups in Sofia and Prague, and the next task of the Comintern is "substantial Communist successes in London and New York."

Stalin had won his first important step in his struggle to control the Party, and through it the country, on April 2, 1922, when he had become General Secretary; but he was not able to infiltrate the Comintern apparatus substantially until after the Fifth World Congress, July–August 1924, the first at which he appeared as a Russian delegate. He took fullest advantage of Zinoviev's slogan of Bolshevization and made it one of his most effective instruments for the elimination of Zinoviev.

> The experience of unsuccessful class battles in various countries, particularly in Germany, where the leaders had committed a number of crass opportunist errors in the autumn of 1923, made it a matter of urgent necessity to tackle the tremendous task involved in the Bolshevization of the German and other Communist Parties . . . The Congress drew the attention of all Parties to the paramount importance of work in the trade-unions and

pointed out the need to organize shop nuclei as the basic units of
the Party organizations. Until then, some of the Communist Parties, retaining Social-Democratic traditions, had been organized
chiefly on a territorial principle, according to electoral divisions.[1]

The process of gaining control was a long one, and representatives
of Stalin's GPU were everywhere, taking advantage of every opportunity to disintegrate the Comintern.

The Zinoviev Letter

In Britain, the revolutionary policy of the Comintern was unpopular
and the British Communist Party had little influence among the
workers. The attitude toward Soviet Russia among British trade-
unionists, however, was friendly, and in this period it became much
more so.

During the summer of 1924, Russia tried to obtain a trade agreement with Britain. Negotiations broke down on August 5, principally
over the question of pre-war Russian debts, which Soviet representatives refused to recognize; but the desire for a trade agreement continued in Britain. If reasonable credit terms could be obtained, Russia
had offered to buy £15 million of machinery, and even after official
negotiations had broken off a purchasing commission of the Soviet
Textile Trust persisted in trying to arrange the purchase of £5 million
of textile machinery. Since unemployment figures were high, the
Trade-Union Congress was for accepting these trade offers on the terms
offered. Its chairman, A. B. Swales, pointed out that the shipbuilding
industry, which had been especially badly hit by the depression, could
be rehabilitated by building ships for Soviet Russia, and the TUC
passed the following resolution:

> In view of the abnormal and prolonged unemployment now
> existent in the United Kingdom, and the impossibility of restor-
> ing its pre-war foreign trade so long as Russia is not admitted to
> the Comity of Nations, this General Council calls upon the
> British government to reopen immediately negotiations with the
> U.S.S.R. with the following objectives: 1) Complete diplomatic
> recognition of the Soviet government of Russia. 2) Encourage-
> ment and support of trade relations with Russia by the application

---

[1] Popov, *Outline History of the CPSU*, II, 212–213.

of the Trade Facilities Acts and the Overseas Trade Acts to Russian trade.[2]

This desire of British trade-unionists for trade with Soviet Russia, based in the first place on nothing more than their wish to combat unemployment, developed into an increased Communist influence in the unions, which was to be reflected the next year in the general strike.

In this period, these negotiations with Britain were only one part of a general Soviet policy based on Stalin's hope that he could overcome economic difficulties at home by fostering trade abroad. The economists, diplomats, and administrators of the Party, busy seeking new trade relations, felt themselves frustrated by Zinoviev's Comintern, which blocked their efforts to improve political relations with the capitalist world. Attempting to continue a revolutionary policy was an outright damage to broader Russian interests.

On October 10, 1924, a few months after the first MacDonald cabinet had been installed, the British Foreign Office got possession of the text of a letter allegedly from Zinoviev to the Communist Party of Great Britain. In it, the party was instructed to go beyond the usual agitation for the ratification of the pending Anglo-Soviet treaty, and in particular to form cells in the British army:

> From your last report it is evident that agitation propaganda work in the Army is weak, in the Navy a very little better. Your explanation that the quality of the members attracted justifies the quantity is right in principle; nevertheless, it would be desirable to have cells in all the units of the troops, particularly among those quartered in the large centers of the country, and also among factories working on munitions and at military store depots . . . In the event of danger of war, with the aid of the latter and in contact with the transport workers, it is possible to paralyze all the military preparations of the bourgeoisie and make a start in turning an imperialist war into a class war. Now more than ever we should be on our guard . . .
>
> The Military Section of the British Communist Party, so far as we are aware, further suffers from a lack of specialists, the future directors of the British Red Army. It is time you thought of form-

---

[2] Statement of the General Council of the Trade-Union Congress, March 25, 1925; quoted in W. P. and Zelda K. Coates, *A History of Anglo-Soviet Relations* (London, 1943), pp. 199–200.

ing such a group, which, together with the leaders, might be, in the event of an outbreak of active strife, the brain of the military organization of the party . . . Do not put this off to a future moment, which may be pregnant with events and catch you unprepared.[3]

The letter was signed by Zinoviev and Kuusinen, as Chairman and Secretary of the Comintern Presidium. In one of the two forms in which the letter circulated in Great Britain, the British Communist Arthur McManus was also a signatory; in the other the letter was addressed to him.

As Prime Minister, MacDonald instructed the British Foreign Office to investigate the authenticity of the letter with the greatest care and meanwhile to draft a protest to the Russian government. On October 24, a week after these instructions, the Foreign Office sent a note to the Soviet Chargé d'Affaires to inform him that "His Majesty's government cannot allow this propaganda and must regard it as a direct interference from outside in British domestic affairs."[4] The Chargé d'Affaires replied that his government was willing to submit the authenticity of the document to an impartial arbitration by court.

Britain was in the middle of an election campaign, and the letter was used by the Tories, not only against the insignificant Communist Party but to damage the Labour Party. "It makes my blood boil,"

---

[3] *Anti-Soviet Forgeries,* foreword by George Lansbury, M.P. (London: Workers' Publications, Ltd., April 1927), p. 34. The same pamphlet was also issued in French and German: *Les Faussaires contre les Soviets* (Paris, 1926) and *Aus diplomatischen Fälscherwerkstätten* (Berlin, 1926).

According to this anonymous pamphlet, after the defeat of the capitalist military intervention, a new political war was opened against Russia by Lord Curzon's note of September 7, 1921, to the Soviet government, in which he complained about Comintern activities, particularly in the Near and Far East. The pamphlet exposed a series of anti-Soviet organizations and centers: several under White Russian emigrés; *Ost-Information,* "a secret journal of German spies," published by A. Winzer, Wilhelmstrasse 11, Berlin; Basil Thomson, chief of Scotland Yard, and Stieglitz, his German colleague. Some twenty false Comintern documents are enumerated, among them several Zinoviev letters; one, dealing with the situation in North Africa and addressed to Marcel Cachin, the French Communist, was published in the Paris newspaper, *Liberté.* Forgers of Comintern documents are listed: Druzhelovsky in Berlin; Yakubovich in Vienna; Kedolivansky in China; B. Weiss, the Social Democratic vice-president of the Berlin police; Singleton, an Englishman. Using photostats, the pamphlet contrasts real Comintern documents with these forgeries and points out the differences in the use of various emblems in letterheads.

[4] Coates, *A History of Anglo-Soviet Relations,* p. 186.

Stanley Baldwin said, "to read of the way in which M. Zinoviev is speaking of the Prime Minister of Great Britain." [5]

I was in England at the time as delegate of the German Central Committee to the British party convention, and I used my time to follow MacDonald's campaign. I heard him speak at mass meetings in Nottingham, Liverpool, Birmingham. The first Labour cabinet, an expression of the unrest created by unemployment, could not enact far-reaching social legislation, for it was weakly supported even by its own labor organizations. I was fascinated to observe how, in a country with only a sectarian Communist grouplet, Comintern politics could become so decisive an issue. When I was back in Germany, some British newspapers accused me of having smuggled the Zinoviev Letter into England.

The election was a serious defeat for the Labour Party, whose representation in Parliament fell from 191 to 151. The number of Liberal deputies was cut from 159 to 40, and the Conservatives regained a majority.

Austen Chamberlain, the new Foreign Secretary, sent the Soviet government a note to the effect that, in the opinion of the British government, the Zinoviev Letter was authentic. This was protested, and another offer to submit to arbitration was made, but in vain. On November 26, Zinoviev wrote a letter to the Trade-Union Congress protesting the document, and on the next day he granted an interview to foreign correspondents, a rare event for the Comintern Chairman. The trade-unions sent a delegation, Benjamin Tillett and George Young, to Russia; after examining all relevant ECCI minutes and proceedings, they concluded that the letter was a forgery.

In Britain the Labour Party set up a committee to investigate the authenticity of the Zinoviev Letter and the circumstances surrounding its publication. In a sworn deposition to this committee, a housemaid of a certain Mrs. Bradley Dyne testified that a Mr. J. D. Gregory, a Foreign Office chief, had received a White Russian there and discussed some money transaction. J. H. Thomas, the Labour leader, confronted Gregory with this statement and with the additional accusation that he had lost considerable money speculating on the French franc and

---

[5] Coates, p. 184.

had been paid well for his share in manipulating the Zinoviev Letter. Gregory denied the charges, and for the moment that was the end of the affair.[6]

In Britain, the Zinoviev Letter had been an important factor in returning the Tories to power, and its effect in Russia was hardly less. It divided not only Tories from Labour but in the Russian Party the conservative from the revolutionary wing. Zinoviev was defended in all official statements against the foreign attack, but inside the Party, and particularly in its higher brackets, the incident was used to intensify the campaign against the Comintern and its leaders.

The GPU manipulated a rather elegant diversion by getting a statement from Berlin police officials that the Zinoviev Letter and other Comintern documents had been forged in a White Russian office in Berlin.[7] On October 19, the same Berlin police administration had discovered a Berlin apartment completely equipped for manufacturing passports of all countries, and this news had been given world publicity.

In Britain, the incident closed with a clear-cut Russian defeat. Rakovsky, the Soviet Ambassador, did not get the apology he requested. On November 28, Rykov, the Russian premier, retorted in a speech to a congress of textile workers that the British Tories had returned to power on the crutch of the Zinoviev Letter, and that Britain had tried to unite Europe against Soviet Russia.

In my view, the Zinoviev Letter was indeed a forgery. It is neither the technical details—the fact, for example, that the various copies circulating in Britain were not identical—nor even the content, but the

---

[6] "On January 26, 1928, a trial was opened against the above-mentioned Mrs. Bradley Dyne . . . The plaintiffs were a City firm of bankers . . . who claimed £39,178, which they said was due them by the defendant in respect of foreign currency sold by her to the bank and resold by the bank to her . . . Mrs. Dyne had been introduced to the firm by Mr. J. D. Gregory. On February 1, 1928, the government appointed a special board of inquiry . . ." (Coates, p. 190.) The investigation was without results. On March 28, in the House of Commons MacDonald requested action against Gregory, but Prime Minister Stanley Baldwin replied that the government refused to lend itself to an inquiry that could serve no national end and was foredoomed by its very nature to futility. Gregory was dismissed from the Foreign Office none the less; he wrote of the affair in his memoirs: "It is no business of mine to say how I first got mixed up with this red object. Quite a number of people have written and said quite a lot of things on the subject, some true, some untrue: and I would prefer to leave it at that." (J. D. Gregory, *On the Edge of Diplomacy*, London, 1928, p. 217.)

[7] Cf. *New York Times*, November 21, 1924

political background in both Britain and Russia that makes it probable that it was not authentic. The whole of Zinoviev's political attitude toward Western Europe makes this letter a seeming anomaly, for the focus of Comintern activity in Britain was certainly not the relatively weak army but the massive labor organizations. On the other hand, the Tories, frightened by the first Labour victory, were looking for any material useful in their fight to regain control; a document against the Comintern would have been accepted with avidity and published immediately. At the same time, such a document would compromise Zinoviev as one disturbing the improving relations between Britain and Soviet Russia; Stalin, unscrupulous, eagerly sought any weapon that would serve in his fight to gain control of the Comintern. To say that it was clearly to the political advantage of the two groups involved —the Tories in Britain and the Stalinist faction in the Russian Party, both of them in the midst of a struggle for power—to have the Zinoviev Letter printed, is to say that in all probability both groups were involved in its fabrication. The expanding GPU had taken over the provocation tactics of the Tsarist Okhrana and applied them with a new skill in order to gain indirect access to the political police of other countries, by buying up anti-Bolshevist groups coöperating with those police and using them as a cover for infiltration and manipulation. Gregory, in financial difficulties and susceptible to bribes, was precisely the type of civil servant Russian agents sought. Zinoviev later told me that he had suspected that the letter was a GPU forgery but was unable to prove it. The housemaid and the White Russian produced in the Labour Party investigation have a definite odor of the GPU. The incident was finally settled only in 1928, when it had served its purpose; Zinoviev had been expelled, and the Tories were once again in power.

Adventure in Estonia

The incident in England increased Zinoviev's feeling of insecurity. He and Kamenev retreated to their urban bastions—Zinoviev to Leningrad and Kamenev to Moscow. In his Leningrad fortress Zinoviev conceived a plan to strengthen his Party bulwark by expanding into the Estonian glacis.

During the civil war, Estonia had been one of the bases from which the invasion started, particularly Yudenich's offensive against Petrograd. It had won its independence by joining no matter what current against the Great Russians. Its population of 1,125,000 was largely rural; in 1925, 70 per cent consisted of small peasants, tilling their shares of the former large estates that had been partitioned during 1919–1920. Industry was principally in small factories, employing 20 to 500 workers, and there was little pro-Communist sentiment among them. Estonia enjoyed her independence; her living standard was higher than that of her big revolutionary neighbor. There were three important political parties—Social Democratic, Labor, and Democratic; three deputies to the parliament were openly pro-German and only one pro-Russian. On February 2, 1920, Estonia and Russia signed the Treaty of Dorpat, in which each country recognized the newly won status of the other.[8]

The Communist Party of Estonia was small but very militant. At the end of November 1924, joining in the international campaign against the Comintern, the Estonian government raided the party headquarters and arrested several hundred Communists. Zinoviev's intimate friend and secretary, Mikhail Kobetsky, was Soviet Ambassador and Comintern agent in Reval,[9] and Zinoviev reacted to the November arrests with a decision to annex agrarian Estonia to industrial Leningrad. He came to an understanding with General Berzin, intelligence chief of the Red Army, thus to block the increasing power of the General Secretary. They agreed that in the case of a country like Estonia drawn-out preparations would be superfluous, that a coup d'état by a small group could settle its fate. A group of sixty Red Army officers was organized under the leadership of Zhibur, a civil war hero, and sent over the border.[10]

On December 1, this group of Russian officers, reinforced by a few hundred Estonian Communists whom they had armed, made a simultaneous attack on the government buildings, following the standard pattern for seizing power by taking the symbols of power. The Estonian army reacted with surprising energy, suppressed the "uprising," and declared martial law. The Russians withdrew back across the border, and 150 of the Estonian Communists were executed

---

[8] Henry de Chambon, *La république d'Estonie* (Paris, 1936).

[9] Alexander Barmine, *One Who Survived* (New York, 1945), reports extensively on Kobetsky and his end in the purges.

[10] Cf. W. G. Krivitsky, *In Stalin's Secret Service*, p. 48.

within twenty-four hours after their attempt. One of these was Victor E. Kingisepp, a close collaborator of Zinoviev, and in memory of the Estonian martyrs his name was given to the little town of Yamburg on the Russian-Estonian border.

Relations between the two countries remained estranged. Fifteen months later, N. V. Paderna, a former Tsarist officer, confessed in a trial at Leningrad that Estonian spies had sold Red Army secrets to a British officer, one Colonel Frank; and thirteen of the forty-eight Estonians on trial were executed.[11]

Stalin's supporters in the Russian Party welcomed the Estonian incident as a personal defeat for Zinoviev, as one more weapon in their struggle to depose him from the Comintern chairmanship. I was in Moscow several times during this period, and the overtone to discussions on the matter was always that Russia was struggling too hard to rearrange her economic and diplomatic relations with the world to be yet further burdened with this Comintern business.

Postlude in Bulgaria

The Comintern crisis culminated in Bulgaria.

Bulgaria had lived in a state of permanent civil strife since Tsankov's coup of June and the quelling of the Communist uprising of September 1923.[12] Tsankov had tried to merge all governmental parties in a Democratic Bloc (comparable to the Fatherland Front of today), but in an election five months after his coup, 35 per cent of the votes went to opponents of the government. The Communist Party continued to have its deputies in the Sobranye but was hampered in its organizational activities.

The country lived in a state of permanent alarm, of plots and counter plots, of terror and counter terror. Thousands were imprisoned for political activity; many were assassinated. The Stamboliyski oppositionists had retired to Yugoslavia, where they published their paper, the *Zemledelsko Zname* ("Peasant Banner"); they made constant armed incursions back across the border. The Macedonian nationalists, the IMRO, were no less active; they had organized a state within a state in the Petrich district. One year and eight days after the coup,

---

[11] Cf. *New York Times*, March 12, 1926.
[12] See above, p. 306 ff.

the Minister of the Interior declared in the Sobranye: "I walk in the streets of Sofia with the same feeling as when I was visiting the trenches during the war." [13]

The Comintern, through Zinoviev and Dimitrov, attempted to point a way out of this internecine Balkan strife. In the spring of 1924 a meeting of Communist deputies at Vienna drafted a program for a Balkan federation, of which Albania, Croatia, and Macedonia were to be autonomous members. The manifesto of the conference called on progressive European labor and revolutionary movements, and particularly the Russian Communists, to support these countries in resisting the imperialist aims of Yugoslavia, Greece, and Bulgaria. On May 5, 1924, the banner of the Balkan Federation was hoisted, and all Balkan revolutionaries were called to unite under it.

The sensational aspect of this manifesto was the united front it announced between the Communists and the IMRO. It was signed by several genuine IMRO leaders, among them Todor Alexandrov, who was assassinated two months later. In Bulgaria, no deals would be made with the Sofia government. The program of self-determination of oppressed nationalities would be carried out by simultaneous action in all the Balkan parliaments; but in the Sobranye the six Macedonian deputies would continue to be organized as a separate group.

This unification of Communists and Macedonian nationalists was followed with anxious eyes, in London as well as in all Balkan capitals.

---

[13] George C. Logio, *Bulgaria* (Manchester, 1936), p. 452.

The IMRO (Internal Macedonian Revolutionary Organization) had been founded in 1893 as a conspiratorial fraternity with the purpose of gaining Macedonian independence. Macedonia, situated around the Vardar valley and claiming Salonika as its capital, is a key strategic spot of the Balkans, important for Bulgaria, Greece, and Serbia (or Yugoslavia). The banner of the IMRO was a piece of black cloth, symbolizing oppression, with the words "Liberty or death" embroidered across it. The organization, financed by a general levy on all Macedonians, was based on local committees—*komitadji*—which elected delegates to a regular national convention. Terrorist acts were carried out by special detachments of two or three, called a *dvoika* or *troika*. The IMRO had representatives abroad who negotiated indiscriminately with any political figure or organization that could be interested in furthering Macedonian independence. Of the many attentats its members perpetrated, three important ones of this period may be mentioned. "Raykoff Daskaloff, Stamboliyski's minister of the interior, was shot in Prague in August, 1923. Peter Chauleff, the leader of the federalists, was murdered in Milan in December, 1924. In May, 1925, Todor Panitza, an old Macedonian voivode, was perforated with bullets in the Burg Theater in Vienna by a young woman." (Joseph S. Roucek, *The Politics of the Balkans*, New York, 1939, p. 146.)

The tension it created was heightened by a private little war organized by Pangalos, the Greek dictator. He invaded Bulgaria, but at the insistence of the League of Nations withdrew and paid an indemnity for the damage his troops had done.

Among the many political assassinations, one led to important results—the murder on April 14, 1925, by an unknown assassin of Konstantin Georgiyev, a Bulgarian general and president of the government party in Sofia. Two days later, at his funeral in the Svetya Nedelya Cathedral, a time bomb exploded and killed a group of important government officials—fourteen generals, three Sobranye deputies, the mayor of Sofia, and its chief of police—128 persons in all.

The Bulgarian cabinet reacted to the terror with counter terror. It declared martial law, proclaimed a curfew, arrested scores. The investigation was cloaked in secrecy, and it is impossible to follow the clues to the real facts of the conspiracy. Two officers of the Bulgarian army, Captains Minkov and Yankov, who had been killed by the police at the moment of their arrest, were accused of having placed the bomb. Various minor players were rounded up—the sacristan, Peter Zadgorski; and two men accused of having sheltered Minkov and Yankov, a Jewish lawyer, Marco Friedman, and reserve Colonel Koyev, both protesting their complete innocence. No clear report was given to the public. Ten were court-martialed; five were condemned to death, among them Georgi Dimitrov *in absentia*. One of his brothers, Todor, was arrested and killed in the Sofia prison; his mother and sister, Lena, fled to Russia. Three were burned before the trial. Zadgorski, Friedman, and Koyev were hanged in public, and this "unique entertainment drew 40,000 spectators."

> The former ministers Petar Yanev and Kyril Pavlov were burned alive with several of their friends in the great heating furnace at the Sofia police headquarters. The reserve General Topaldjikov and Yetchev (who served Stamboliyski) were carried off to Küstendil and never again heard of.[14]

Official figures report eighty-one trials involving 3557 persons, of whom 300 were condemned to death and 611 imprisoned. According to the opposition, at least 5000 were killed or disappeared. Tsankov

---

[14] Joseph Swire, *Bulgaria's Conspiracy* (London, 1939), p. 199.

admitted that, between June 1923 and April 1925, five Agrarian ministers, forty-seven Agrarian and Communist deputies, and hundreds of
teachers were killed. This period of extreme terror added a new term
to Comintern slang, and during and after World War II, opponents
of Russian expansion into Eastern Europe were often promised "the
Bulgarian treatment." But even this apex of terror did not result in
subduing the country; there was a series of peasant revolts leading to
many clashes with the army.

The time bomb in the Sofia Cathedral is one of the provocations
that mark the currents of terrorism between the two world wars.
Public opinion in Britain, France, and Germany immediately pointed
to the Comintern; Zinoviev was the plotter, the incendiary, the con-
spirator against world peace. He was the terrorist who, uniting with
other terrorists, sought to overthrow the bourgeois world by violence.

We in the German party were startled by the events in Bulgaria,
and we sought information from our representatives in Moscow on
what part, if any, the Comintern apparatus had played. We got an
official report from Mayer A. Trilisser, the GPU chief for the Balkans,
that neither he nor Zinoviev had had anything to do with the plot.
This official denial was countered even inside the Comintern by
constant rumors that Zinoviev had indeed maneuvered the conspiracy,
that both the idea and its execution were the result of the confusion
and despair that pervaded the Comintern in this period. Minkov and
Yankov, the two captains shot "while trying to escape," had both been
members of the underground Communist Party. Bulgarian Communists, by reason of their geographical propinquity and language affinity,
were much more intimately involved in the Russian Party crisis than
other "foreigners," and after the death of Lenin most of them believed
that a catastrophe could be averted only from outside Russia. The
struggle among the hierarchy—Trotsky, Stalin, Zinoviev—could not in
their view end otherwise than in the victory of anti-Bolshevik elements,
based on the NEP-men. GPU leaders, vitally interested in the maintenance of the Party dictatorship, were eager to take the initiative. It
will probably never be disclosed who in the Moscow GPU headquarters
told the Sofia agents to set the bomb.

Bulgaria was a fertile soil for GPU activities. In the underground
Balkan parties, patterned after the terrorist IMRO, in the maze of

conspiracies, it was a natural development to seek to solve the Balkan riddle by the organized destruction of leading groups. A Communist-controlled Balkan Federation would have been a much more effective way out of the Russian impasse than a sovietized Estonia. The Sofia affair was probably the meeting place of terrorists of all varieties, supplementing each other's activities in the Balkan atmosphere, where terrorism is endemic.

This interpretation is confirmed by Trotsky's veiled references. He blames the Russian bureaucracy for the "unreasonable acts" of "violence" in Estonia and Bulgaria.

> Nobody demands of the Soviet government international adventures, unreasonable acts, attempts to force by violence the course of world events. On the contrary, insofar as such attempts have been made by the bureaucracy in the past (Bulgaria, Estonia, Canton, etc.), they have only played into the hands of the reaction.[15]

The only direct allusion in the literature to the involvement of the GPU in the Sofia affair is in Bessedovsky's memoirs, where he relates how Yaroslavsky, a GPU agent, was killed.

> The OGPU decided that he must be done away with at all costs since he knew too much—including the true story of the Sofia Cathedral affair. One of the Cheka squads was ordered to carry out the sentence of death. This was made easier by the fact that Yaroslavsky, knowing that his silence brought him a certain degree of safety, did not take much trouble to hide himself. One of his former friends asked him to dinner and poisoned him. The body was photographed and a print was sent to Moscow as proof of his execution.[16]

Elensky, like Yaroslavsky a Red Army staff officer, was also involved. "It was he," Bessedovsky continues, "who supplied the dynamite and prepared the terrorist attacks. After the outrage on Sofia Cathedral he was recalled to Moscow."

According to official Comintern literature of the time, the Sofia plot was a provocation organized by the Tsankov government itself, to give it an excuse to exterminate the opposition. Some credence was given

---

[15] Trotsky, *The Revolution Betrayed* (New York, 1937), p. 232.
[16] Grigory Bessedovsky, *Revolutions of a Soviet Diplomat*, p. 35.

to this theory by the fact that neither Tsankov nor any of his closest followers was among those killed by the bomb; but no one in the Comintern actually believed this legend, concocted for bourgeois ears, and we were all certain that somehow the GPU had been involved, though how and through whom none outside the terror machine was able to find out.

Stalin took full advantage of this new loss to Zinoviev's prestige. Preparing for the Fourteenth Party Congress, he won one provincial branch after another, until only Leningrad, with Zinoviev at its head, remained as an important anti-Stalinist center.

The control that Stalin won over most branches during the period of preparation for the Fourteenth Congress did not make the Party accept him as the rightful successor to Lenin. He represented himself as the spokesman for a group that would give the Party a new leadership and a new policy. This group, comprising such prominent Old Bolsheviks as Rykov, Molotov, Kalinin, Voroshilov, Ordjonikidze, together with such representative younger men as Kirov, Lominadze, Zhdanov, had its most important figure other than Stalin in Nikolai Bukharin. If he had not taken Bukharin into his combination and reached a compromise with him concerning policy, Stalin would not have been able to rally the Right wing around himself. For the Right, Stalin was primarily the organizer, the man capable of implementing a new moderate policy.

Bukharin's Neo-NEP

The reason Bukharin found himself even for a time in alliance with Stalin was in part the same that had motivated Zinoviev and Kamenev earlier—fear that Trotsky might become Russia's Bonaparte. He was afraid, moreover, that the policy of Zinoviev and Kamenev, who spoke for the Russian proletariat, would make difficult a balance with the peasantry. Offering another version of Lenin's "democratic dictatorship of the workers and peasants," Bukharin counseled a mood of self-moderation, of abstention from state intervention in the peasant economy.

Like all Russian leaders in 1925, Bukharin believed that the route out of the Russian impasse by a European revolution had been blocked, and that therefore a new historic phase had set in. Russian policy had to be redefined in a new world setting, and the principal factor to be taken into account was the hostility of the Russian peasant. The New Economic Policy had broken the straitjacket of War Communism, but the market did not begin to function spontaneously. The revolution had broken the connections between industry and the village, and new ones were not easily built up. "In immense portions of Russia . . . not a single trader, whether coöperative or private, has yet penetrated. Until very recently there has been trade only along the railroads." [1]

Where relations between state trade bureaus and peasants had been established and were maintained into the NEP period, the growing discrepancy in prices between industrial and agricultural goods stiffened the sullen opposition of the countryside. The series of peasant revolts reached a peak in 1924 in the Georgian uprising, which was more nearly a civil war than the abortive Hamburg uprising a year earlier. Despite the better harvest of 1925, tension between Party and peasantry increased. There were riots in the villages, and many Party organizers and tax collectors were assassinated. The so-called village correspondents, whose function was to report to the party on the degree of hostility, often reported only indirectly—by their sudden death.[2]

Starting from Lenin's conviction that coöperation between Russian worker and Russian peasant was imperative, Bukharin developed it to an extreme, by which the peasant economy would be the real center of Russian economic progress. State economy would be limited by his proposal to heavy industry, which had to be rebuilt after the war and civil war; light industry and trade would be given a maximum freedom of movement under conditions of free enterprise. Thus the commodities so urgently needed in the village would be produced faster, and the tension between state industry and peasantry would decrease. The

---

[1] A. I. Rykov, quoted in Friedrich Pollock, *Die planwirtschaftlichen Versuche in der Sowjetunion, 1917–1927.* (Leipzig, 1929), p. 143.

[2] *The Oath,* a 1946 Soviet film glorifying Stalin as Lenin's successor, opens in 1924 with the murder by a kulak of a Stalingrad worker while he was on a Party mission in a village.

peasants, better provided with industrial goods, would offer their agricultural produce on the market without coercion. *"Enrichissez-vous!"*
Bukharin told the peasants.[3]

With her rich soil, Russia could provide generously for several times
her population, once modern agrarian methods were introduced.
Bukharin hoped to stimulate such a modernization through the individual initiative of the upper stratum of the peasant class. The poor
and middle peasantry would be helped through coöperatives, but,
Bukharin stressed, coöperation should not be allowed to hamper the
development and improvement of individual farms. The workers'
living standard would be raised principally through the organization
of consumers' coöperatives, which could trade directly with peasant
producers' coöperatives and thus circumvent the price-raising speculations of the Neo-NEP businessmen.

Bukharin's proposals were favorably received by many strata of Russian society. Those intelligentsia—engineers, economists, technicians—
the so-called *Spetsy* (specialists)—who had survived the civil war and
been integrated into the Soviet apparatus were outspokenly critical of
the state economy. At the Thirteenth Party Congress, in May, 1924, Zinoviev had complained of an "Indian summer" of Menshevism. Among
students and engineers, he said, there is a renaissance of bourgeois
mentality. In their demand for a rise in pay, engineers compared themselves with bison—even the Tsarist government had cared for the few
surviving specimens of that animal. If rare beasts, why not also rare
technicians? The term *Spetsy* they found offensive, and they demanded
equal status in Soviet society with the workers. One of the spokesmen
of this group, Professor Ustryalov, welcomed Bukharin's Neo-NEP as
a return to normal capitalist production, distinguished from production
abroad only by the fact that heavy industry was state-owned. His
article, entitled "Change of Signposts," created a sensation. Zinoviev
replied to this theory of capitalist restoration in "Philosophy of an
Epoch": "The working class fought and died in the October revolution for the idea of equality. It is time to transform this idea into
reality." Ustryalov's article made too explicit the implications of

---

[3] Guizot, who had given this advice to the French peasantry, was attacked by
Marx in the opening lines of the *Communist Manifesto* as one of the symbols of
European reaction. In 1885, just after a depression, Bismarck voiced an idea sim-
ilar to Guizot's: "How I would like to have several millionaires in Germany!"

Bukharin's position, and for that reason had to be formally rejected by Stalin and Bukharin.

Bukharin's Neo-NEP was the domestic section of a much broader reëvaluation after the defeat of the international revolution and the stabilization of the capitalist world. Capitalism had not only recovered from the post-war decline and reached its pre-war level, but it had also changed in quality. Rationalization of industry, new forms of division of labor and of management combined with a higher stage of monopolistic cartelization, had produced an "absolute" strengthening of capitalism, both economically and politically, and presaged a period of prosperity under capitalism. This transformation was a transition to a fundamentally different phase, in which the anarchy of production was yielding to higher forms of monopolistic organization. This new monopoly, breaking through national boundaries, forms world-wide organizations; on a national scale, Bukharin held, it will become so strong as to be almost fused with the state apparatus.

This does not mean, Bukharin noted, that Hilferding and other theorists are correct in their concept that capitalism will be able through monopoly to integrate competitive nations peacefully into a world economy. On the contrary, the fusion of state machinery with economic monopolies will ultimately aggravate the conflict between competing state economies. The antagonism between capitalist society and non-capitalist Russia, the unrest in the colonies, the class struggle in industrial countries—these continue, and these will make such a peaceful development ultimately impossible. But meanwhile a period of "relative stabilization," of temporary armistice between Russia and the capitalist world, should be the starting point from which to delineate Russian policy, both domestic and foreign.[4]

---

[4] Bukharin was one of the few great economists of the Old Bolshevik school. His work has been largely suppressed, and much of it is not available in an English translation. The thesis he presented in this period, to which we have no more than referred—that the World War had started a process of fusion of political with economic functions in capitalist society—is most interesting now, with the development since then of the Nazi and Stalinist states. Bukharin's principal economic work, *Oekonomik der Transformationsperiode* (Hamburg, 1922), is a provocative presentation of issues relevant to the present day.

After 1929, Bukharin was never in doubt about the real nature of the new Russian state. In 1938, in his trial, to the extent that he was able to break through the carefully formulated questions of State Prosecutor Vyshinsky, he presented a theory of compromise with Russia's antagonists, at that time principally Japan and

Bukharin's concept of the current relation between Russia and the capitalist world was shared by the group most fervently opposed to him in this period, the Workers' Opposition. Their agreement, however, started from different premises. The Workers' Opposition feared that the development of a rich peasantry would aggravate the class differentiation in the village and also in the city. The kulaks would prosper by Bukharin's policy at the cost of the poorer peasants, who would be driven to the city to become cheap labor. The villages were overpopulated, and the cities could not absorb the surplus; the only way out of the dilemma was aid from abroad.

> To conclude that we should be able to extract enough capital for the development of our extinct industry from taxation would be to console ourselves with hollow illusions. To flatter ourselves that we could raise this capital "out of pennies" would be to add to the old delusion another . . . The government should take energetic steps to raise the necessary means by foreign and internal state loans and by granting concessions with greater loss and greater sacrifice than the state is prepared to take on itself for granting credits. Great material sacrifices to international capital, which is prepared to build up our industry, would be a lesser evil than the condition into which we might drift in the next few years.[5]

Thus Medvedev wrote in 1924 to Baku, one of the centers of the Workers' Opposition. The next year the city sent a delegation to Berlin with a flag of the Baku soviet, of which I was made an honorary member. Like all contacts between Russian and German Left Communists, this openly rebellious ceremony increased the nervousness of the Politburo.

As this Baku Letter indicates, the cumulative dissatisfaction had led to increasing estrangement from the Party even of the factory workers,

---

Germany, in order to destroy the monopolistic power of the Stalinist state machine. He confessed that he wanted even to cede sections of the Soviet Union, specifically the Ukraine, the Maritime Province, and Byelo-Russia, to Germany, Japan, and indirectly to Britain, if that would have weakened the Stalinist dictatorship. "Psychologically, we, who at one time had advocated Socialist industrialism, began to regard with a shrug of the shoulders, with irony, and then with anger at bottom, our huge, gigantically growing factories as monstrous gluttons which consumed everything, deprived the broad masses of articles of consumption, and represented a certain danger . . ." (*Report of Court Proceedings in the Case of the Anti-Soviet "Bloc of Rights and Trotskyites,"* Moscow, 1938, p. 381.)

[5] Quoted in Maurice Dobb, *Russian Economic Development since the Revolution,* p. 298.

in theory the kernel and principal promoters of the new state. The working class, an isolated minority in a peasant country, was disillusioned with the result of the revolution, alienated from the state apparatus, indifferent to the State Party. As the dissatisfaction grew, the pressure of the Party in the factories was increased, which again aggravated the estrangement. The collection of frequent voluntary contributions for the Party or one of its many ramifications was regarded as an additional tax on workers' incomes and especially resented. Introduction of piece work, stricter definition of the "norms of production," increasing distinction between skilled and unskilled labor, marked the process that over the next ten years led to a wider wage differentiation than in any other industrial country. The occasional wildcat strikes with which these conditions were fought were suppressed ruthlessly.

The new state trusts, experimenting with new methods, sought a way out of every difficulty by tightening the control over labor. In this period factory directors formed a society, Club of the Red Directors, to agitate for greater authority. Industrial methods were in flux, and this ephemeral grouping was an attempt to guide the change in a favorable direction.

The pressure groups of the workers, the trade-unions, had already been broken as organizations independent of state management. Union leaders and assistant leaders were Party members almost to a man; at the Fourteenth Party Congress, Molotov reported that in 1924 and 1925 respectively 95 and 97 per cent of the regional trade-union committees were made up of Communist Party members. The factory councils, however, were more difficult to handle. They were more than half non-Communist; for the same years Molotov gives the figures respectively of 46 and 42 per cent of Party members.[6] The Party was doubly and triply isolated; it maneuvered, and the working class, indifferent to the state, watched in sullen and hostile silence.

The conflict between the workers and, on the one hand, the peasants

---

[6] *Inprekorr*, January 5, 1926. The same phenomenon was observable in Germany during the Nazi State Party regime. The 1936 election in the factory councils reflected a large resistance to Party control, and the councils were soon thereafter abandoned as a medium of manipulation. There was a similar development in Britain in 1946, where once again the unions were organized into the government and the shop stewards gained in importance. "It is painfully apparent that the workers will not follow their chair-borne leaders; they prefer to follow the shop steward in the street" (*Economist*, London, January 18, 1947).

and, on the other, the Neo-NEP advocates found expression in the Zinoviev-Bukharin polemics on the status of the peasantry. Bukharin's proposal, apart from its world-wide economic implications, was factional support to Stalin in his fight for control. In his support of Bukharin's peasant policy, Stalin expressed the will of the Party bureaucracy to defeat the aspirations of the working class to rule the new state; the Party itself, rather, would be raised to the key position of arbiter between the conflicting groups. Zinoviev recognized that the emphatic return to peasant economy that Bukharin advocated would leave no room for a Comintern of proletarian revolution, and in his desire to defend the disintegrating International he let himself be drawn into an interminable scholastic debate on "the peasant question." Increasing the economic weight given to the upper stratum of the peasantry and businessmen, Zinoviev pointed out, would certainly be reflected in corresponding political influence for these classes. The worker would be overwhelmed and lose all the advantages the revolution had brought him.

As before in the fight against Trotsky, Stalin sharpened the debate demagogically. He accused Zinoviev of proposing in effect a return to War Communism, that is, to the control of the peasantry by terror. Zinoviev and Kamenev protested in vain against this distortion of their views; the basis of their program was that the alliance between the poor peasants and the workers should be continued, that the dominant role of the working class was in the interest of both. For the past years Zinoviev had sought a political avenue to implement this policy—a peasants' international, the Krestintern, among others. He quoted from Lenin on the relation between the two classes:

> Ten to twenty years of correct relations with the peasantry and (even in the case of a delayed proletarian revolution) victory will be assured on an international level. In the other case, we face twenty to forty years of White terror.[7]

Having aggravated the dispute between Zinoviev and Bukharin, Stalin then came forward in the name of the Party bureaucracy as objective arbiter between the two factions. He had used Zinoviev and

---

[7] Quoted by Zinoviev at the Fourteenth Party Congress from Lenin's article "Taxation in Kind," *Bolshevik*, Moscow, No. 7, 1921.

Kamenev as his spearhead against Trotsky, and now he used the unpopularity they had thus earned to attack them. Stalin admitted his brutality, but pointed out that it was he who had protected Trotsky from Zinoviev's plot to expel him. Now he had to protect Bukharin from these same revolutionary desperados. "You cry for the blood of Bukharin. We won't give it to you, this blood, be sure of that." [8]

Stalin defended Bukharin with such fervor partly because in the first phase of the fight he was opposed by Lenin's widow, Nadyezhda Konstantinovna Krupskaya. Krupskaya, whom I knew well at this time, was a model of unobtrusive modesty. During Lenin's life, she had been his loyal assistant but had never interfered in Party affairs and had therefore no authority of her own. During the last years of his life, while the hierarchy was jockeying for the succession, Krupskaya was more completely in Lenin's confidence than ever before, and if anyone knew the order of his uncolored preference among the various leaders, it was she. The various factions, each anxious to present itself as *the* true successor to Lenin, watched her diffident lips to learn her secrets. In October 1925, Krupskaya had been one of four signatories of the oppositionist platform, together with Zinoviev, Kamenev, and Sokolnikov. At the convention two months later, however, her timid voice was drowned out in the chorus of Stalinist hoodlums. History shows, she said, that the ideas of great revolutionaries have often been distorted after their deaths, that while their names have been deified their revolutionary teachings have been cast aside. This cautious opposition to the general trend of the Party, coupled with discreet encouragement to Zinoviev off the floor of the convention, was as much as she was capable of.

Is State Industry Socialism?

The Fourteenth Party Congress convened in Moscow in December 1925, after having been postponed three times. It revolved around two major points: the coördination of state industry with agriculture and small business, and the reorganization of the Party hierarchy. "The Congress," Popov writes in his official history, "opened . . . in such a tense atmosphere as had not been witnessed at our Party Congresses

---

[8] Souvarine, *Staline,* p. 378. Souvarine's biography of Stalin is the only work that deals with the Fourteenth Party Congress more than summarily.

for many years." [9] Moscow lived in an extraordinary fever, reflecting the tension both of the country and of the convention. Delegates streamed in from the four corners of the vast land and corroborated each other's reports that the situation everywhere warranted pessimism.

Stalin, reporting for the Central Committee, was concerned with maintaining the Party monopoly in industrial management as the basis of its monopoly in power. Paraphrasing Lenin, he adjusted old Party terminology to the new situation; the state enterprises were represented to the congress as a fulfillment of socialism, as "enterprises of a consequential socialist type." The state enterprises were defined as the "socialist sector" of the economy. Any increase in their production figures, then, would be a victory for socialism: industrial statistics became a part of a totalitarian propaganda. This identification of state industry with socialism is the premise on which Stalin built his original and far-reaching theory of socialism in one country, the first fully developed statement of national socialism, the totalitarian state and its party monopoly.

Does not socialism mean, Zinoviev answered, more than the nationalization of industry? By all the standards of Marx and Lenin, by every criterion of international socialism since the founding of the First International, does not socialism mean a fundamental change in the relations between man and man? State industry is as exploitative as private industry, or even more so. Exploitation can be abolished only by a change in a multitude of factors governing the relation between the workers and the Party, the workers and the state. Nothing is further from possible realization in present-day Russia alone than socialism. If the transitional state of all Soviet institutions, if our poverty and misery, are designated as socialism, then socialism will lose its appeal and its theoretical basis.

A certain balance, Stalin rebutted, had now been reached between Soviet Russia and the capitalist countries. A period of peaceful cooperation between "the world of the bourgeoisie" and "the world of the proletariat" had set in, and peaceful contact between the two was now possible. Capitalism had overcome the chaos of production characteristic of its situation immediately after the war; the years of decay had come to an end, and "the political power of the bourgeoisie is

---

[9] N. Popov, *Outline History of the CPSU*, II, 249.

developing." The center of this political power, however, had shifted from Europe to the United States, and European capitalism had been stabilized only by paying the price of financial submission to America.

> Previously, Britain, France, Germany, and partially the United States were the most important centers of exploitation. Today, the United States and in part its helper, Britain, are the most important financial exploiters of the world.[10]

Stalin made the greatest possible appeal to the general sentiment that the policy of Comintern should be changed.

> The seizure of power is not on the order of the day, neither today nor tomorrow . . . We have to find new forms of the proletarian movement, new forms of the mass movement, forms of trade-union unity.

In eliminating revolutionary Comintern perspectives, Stalin did not, however, discard the perspective of a German "revolutionary" nationalistic war against the West.

> The Dawes Plan increased the exploitation and contains the kernel of an unavoidable revolution . . . Germany has to pay 130 billion gold marks, and she will never accept her present borders and the loss of her colonies. To believe that Germany, developing and becoming stronger, will accept this state of affairs, is to believe in a miracle.

Stalin devoted a large portion of his report to embellishing this thesis with a survey of various peace treaties deep in the past history of Russia and Germany, to prove that they all had been unworkable. Germany was given such prominence in his speech because of the Berlin treaty of 1926 between the two governments, negotiations for which were then in process.

There is danger, Stalin warned, of a new European war, a war which can be nothing but another intervention of "the Western powers" against Soviet Russia.

> Locarno is the nucleus of a new European war . . . Locarno is a plan for the arrangement of the forces for a new war and not for peace . . . The British Tories intend, on the one hand, to

---

[10] *Inprekorr*, No. 172, December 31, 1925. All the quotations are taken from this official and complete report.

retain their status quo policy toward Germany and, on the other hand, to utilize Germany against Soviet Russia. It is a bit too much to ask.

Concerning Soviet policy in Asia, however, Stalin drew a very cautious line. Right and justice were "two hundred per cent" on the side of the Chinese revolutionaries, but the Western notion that Russia would therefore adopt a more aggressive policy toward Japan was mistaken. On the contrary, "our interests demand a closer collaboration between us and Japan" against the United States.

> There are two conflicting centers of attraction in the world today. Anglo-America is the center of attraction for bourgeois governments, and Soviet Russia is the center of attraction for the proletarians of the West and the revolutionaries of the East.

Europe was not yet completely transformed into an Anglo-American colony; European countries continued to exploit their own colonies. The trend, however, was toward complete subservience to the United States, and therefore "we must now count on a trend to the Left in the European working class."

This trend to the Left in Europe should be met half way with a mixed economy in Russia. The Communist Party should direct its efforts toward the middle peasant, the peasant eager to improve himself and thereby the national agriculture; it should "liberate the poor peasants from the psychology of War Communism."

> The poor peasants . . . look to the OGPU, to the administration; they rely on everyone except their own forces. We have to teach them how to fight against the kulak, not by appeals to the OGPU but through a political struggle, an organized struggle.

The role in the village of the kulaks and other capitalist elements, the NEP businessmen, has been exaggerated by the Opposition, who have created a panicky attitude concerning these elements. Leningrad demands that the class struggle be unleashed in the village, that we return to War Communism, which "would be nothing but the announcement of civil war in our country."

Such a civil war, Stalin continued, would destroy all the constructive work thus far accomplished. It would run counter to Lenin's plan for coöperatives, and to the general Leninist concept that the peasant economy must be included in the system of socialist reconstruction. By this appeal to a moderate policy, coupled with energetic suppression of extremism, Stalin was able to rally around him all the elements in and out of the Party, in and out of Russia, who wanted peace abroad and a gradual change at home.

People were dreaming that Ustryalov and the bourgeois specialists for whom he spoke were delighted by the change in policy—and dreaming was not prohibited. He and all others like him, however, would get into serious trouble if they failed to "bring grist to our Bolshevik mill."

The Leningrad Opposition, Stalin continued, had taken over Trotsky's complaint, and before him that of the Workers' Opposition, that the Party was losing its revolutionary and proletarian character. These laments on the degeneration of the Party, he shouted, would frighten no one. "Our Party has not degenerated and will not degenerate. It is not made of a material that can degenerate." The Party had just published an edition of Lenin's *Collected Works,* and if the Party cadres would read these, that alone would make them invulnerable to degeneration. "The lament that the Party is degenerating will therefore frighten no one. You can lament on the degeneration of the Party as much as you like, but . . ."

The Opposition had proposed that the Party reverse its process of degeneration by fundamentally changing its class base, by organizing the Russian workers en masse. The Russian Party had never been a workers' mass party in the Western sense of the word, the Opposition had pointed out, and especially in the sense of the model party of the West, the German Social Democratic Party. The Opposition had proposed that 90 per cent of the Russian workers be organized into the Party in a short period, a plan that Stalin characterized as idiotic. Counting plants with twenty or more workers as industrial units, he cited the following figures:

	Total Number of Industrial Workers	*Industrial Workers in the Party*	
		Number	*Per cent*
July 1, 1924	5,500,000	390,000	7
July 1, 1925	6,500,000	534,000	8
October 1, 1925	7,000,000	570,000	8

Admitting 90 per cent of these seven million industrial workers would swamp the Party; the Bolshevik elite would lose its central position. (That was exactly the purpose of the Opposition, who hoped thus to check the *embourgeoisement,* the bureaucratization, the degeneration, of the Party.) Moreover, Stalin continued, of the 8 per cent of industrial workers in the Party, only 5 per cent were working in large plants, and even this figure had been artificially increased by transferring Communists into large factories.

Of the 1,025,000 Party members and candidates on November 1, 1925, a month before the congress, only 58.6 per cent were classified as workers, the rest of the Party membership being divided between 23.8 per cent of peasants and 17.6 per cent of employees. It is impossible, Stalin reiterated, to proletarianize the party without losing power.

He then gave comparable figures concerning the Russian peasantry:

	Total Number of Peasants (18 to 60)	*Peasants in the Party*	
		Number	*Per cent*
Thirteenth Party Congress	53,000,000	136,000	0.26
Fourteenth Party Congress	54,000,000	202,000	0.37

Stalin gave these impressive figures to emphasize the insignificant participation of the peasantry in the Party, the complete isolation of the State Party from the peasant base of the Russian population.[11]

In conclusion, Stalin remarked that Trotskyism was no longer a danger to the Party; it was completely liquidated. The Party would show the same masterful mature force in overcoming the Leningrad Opposition. This statement on Trotskyism is most interesting and curious, taken in relation with the secret manipulations behind the scenes.

Speaking in the name of the Leningrad Opposition, Zinoviev presented a minority report for himself and Kamenev; not since the Tenth Congress, when the trade-union question had divided the Party, had a minority report been given. The fight against Trotsky since 1923 had been possible only on the basis of a united Politburo, which had been molded by the common fear of Trotsky's strength and ambition

---

[11] In 1926, there were only two cities in Russia with a population of more than a million, only one more with more than half a million. The following table

but which was interpreted by the membership as a complete ideological unity. The Troika was presented as one, almost in the same mystical sense that the Trinity is One. For the revered leader of Russia was still Lenin, who could guide Russia safely through his pupils, but only if they acted together. The legend of a unified leadership, thus born out of fear, was fostered out of political expediency; the Politburo spoke as one man, and no hint of the deliberations by which it had arrived at its decisions was permitted to reach the membership. The mere fact, then, that Zinoviev presented a minority report, quite apart from its content, brought anxiety to the hearts of the delegates. The times were difficult, and it was hard to find the right answers even with a unified infallible leadership, but if that leadership was once divided, if the heirs of Lenin began to fight among themselves—

The differences in the Politburo, Zinoviev began, were a year and a half old; that is, they had started immediately after Lenin's death. He continued by clearing away the demagogic side issues that Stalin had emphasized. It is not, he said, the relation between the state and the peasantry that is the crux of the problem; it is not the problem of the kulaks nor that of the industrialization of Russia that divides the majority of the congress from the minority. On the proper attitude

---

gives the population of the largest proletarian centers and the membership figures for the corresponding largest Party branches.

	Population (1926)	Party membership (1927)
1. Moscow	2,025,947	91,647
2. Leningrad	1,614,008	82,245
3. Kiev	513,789	10,838
4. Baku	452,789	18,976
5. Odessa	420,888	9,250
6. Kharkov	417,186	16,179
7. Tashkent	323,613	7,865
8. Rostov	308,284	10,183
9. Tiflis	292,973	9,098
10. Dnyepropetrovsk	233,001	9,735
11. Nizhniy-Novgorod	230,428	9,796
12. Saratov	215,369	7,173
13. Tula	152,677	7,011
14. Stalingrad	148,370	5,648
15. Sverdlovsk	136,404	5,319
16. Ivanovo-Voznesensk	111,443	5,669
17. Perm	84,815	8,885

(*Bolshaya Sovetskaya Entsiklopediya,* XI, 534.)

toward the peasantry there are differences, but no fundamental difference, between the two wings. The Opposition emphasized more that
it was necessary to help the poor peasant get back on his feet, to give
him state help in buying agricultural implements, to back his attempts
to organize coöperatives; for without this help from the workers' Party
the poor peasant would get poorer. But, Zinoviev emphasized, the
minority did not propose a return to the methods of War Communism,
by which the civil war would be renewed in the villages, nor that the
backward peasant economy be socialized by force. He fought these
accusations with the utmost vigor, and pointed out that Stalin had
made them only in order to cloud the issue. Following Trotsky,
Zinoviev demanded that the Party expend more energy on the central
task of industrializing Russia. Trotsky's program had been designated as super-industrialization; Stalin feared that an emphasis on
industrialization would endanger the support he was seeking from
the upper stratum of the peasantry.

Then Zinoviev came to the vital issue, the one dividing the congress into two bitter irreconcilable groups. The central issue is the
relation between the Party and the workers, between state industry
and the working class. Nationalization alone is not enough to define
the character of the industry as socialist: it is one of several factors,
of which another, and a more decisive one, is a change in the relation
between workers and the industrial management. A nationalized industry, or partially nationalized industry, can be integrated into a
classic capitalist economy without breaking its contour. What decides
the character of a nationalized economy is the relation between man
and man, is whether the working class has the key role in its control.
Without a fundamental change in the class structure, nationalization
alone equals not socialism but state capitalism. Under state capitalism
the exploitation of the worker continues and can even be intensified.

For the first time in Bolshevik history, and with a burning fervor,
Zinoviev made of this question—this modern question, the nature of
state industry—the central issue of the congress. In defending this
concept, Zinoviev, Kamenev, and Sokolnikov had to fight both Stalin,
who made the thesis that socialism could be built in Russia alone
the premise of his bid for absolute power, and Stalin's unenthusiastic
(in this point) ally, Bukharin, who added that its development in Russia

would be "at a snail's pace." (Later, after socialism had been officially proclaimed, this phrase of Bukharin's was used to prove him a counter revolutionary.)

If the mode of production in Russia remained exploitative, said Zinoviev, then a whole series of fundamental issues were altered. Such questions as the nature of the Russian state, the role of the working class in the state, the role of a workers' party, hinged fundamentally on this problem of whether nationalization of industry equals socialism. In an economy that exploits the proletariat, one cannot speak of a proletarian dictatorship. If there is no proletarian dictatorship, the proletariat cannot mandate it to the Party. But there is a dictatorship in Russia, which Stalin is in the process of reinforcing, and if it is not a proletarian dictatorship, then it is a dictatorship of something else.

The Soviet economist, Larin, pungently countered this line of reasoning:

> The concept of the Opposition on state capitalism has many important practical implications. If, because of our technological backwardness—because, that is, of the petty bourgeois character of our country—Zinoviev and Kamenev stake everything on the international revolution, is that not much worse than the concept of the 1923 Opposition?

Larin also emphasized that the answer to this central question, whether Russia was state capitalist or not, determined every Party decision.

In his wish to appeal to the working class, Zinoviev linked the "New Opposition" to the trade-unionist opposition at the Tenth, the NEP, Congress. The differences then between Lenin and Bukharin, who always had contradictory opinions on state capitalism, were repeated in the fight on the NEP, which again centered around the relation between state and worker.

Zinoviev referred to the passage in which Lenin had defined five forms of Russian economy.

> No one, I think, in studying the question of the economics of Russia has denied their transitional character. Nor, I think, has any Communist denied that the term "Socialist Soviet Republic" implies the determination of the Soviet government to achieve the transition to Socialism, and not that the present economic order is a Socialist order.

But what does the word transition mean? Does it not mean, as applied to economics, that the present order contains elements, particles, pieces of both capitalism *and* Socialism? Everyone will admit that it does. But not all who admit this take the trouble to consider the precise nature of the elements that constitute the various social–economic forms which exist in Russia at the present time. And this is the crux of the question.

Let us enumerate these elements:

1) patriarchal, i.e., to a considerable extent natural, self-sufficing peasant economy;

2) small commodity production (this includes the majority of those peasants who sell their grain);

3) private capitalism;

4) state capitalism; and

5) Socialism.[12]

The concessions to foreign capitalism were one, but not the only, phase of state capitalism. State capitalism is not separated from socialism by the Great Wall of China; according to Lenin, state capitalism is three quarters socialism—given social and political changes of comparable profundity.

Zinoviev buttressed the meager support he was able to muster from this reference by a quotation from Lenin's article on the coöperatives.

You thought that we could not call this kind of system [Note: *system*, Zinoviev interpolated] in which the means of production belong to the working class and the state power belongs to the working class, a state capitalist system. You have not taken into account the fact that I have used the term "state capitalism" to link historically our present concept with that in my polemics against the so-called "Left Communists." Already at that time, I pointed out that "state capitalism" would be a higher form than our present economy. It was important for me to indicate the hereditary continuity between ordinary state capitalism and that extraordinary—yes, completely extraordinary—state capitalism of which I spoke when I introduced the reader to the New Economic Policy.

There is, therefore, Zinoviev emphasized, a "hereditary continuity" between the task of a workers' party in a capitalist economy and a workers' policy against state capitalist exploitation. New ways must

---

[12] Lenin, *Selected Works*, IX, 165–166. Cf. Lenin's report to the Fourth World Congress, *Selected Works*, X, 320 ff.

be found to defend Russian workers against the exploitation of the Russian state industry. The working class must be able to organize against the exploiter state. Its independence has been lost, and it must be regained.

Both factions defended their views by long quotations from Lenin. After 1921, when the NEP had been established, Lenin had spoken several times on the character of Soviet economy, but these remarks had never been developed into one coherent analysis of the new trends in Russia. The exegesis of these occasional and almost casual observations is of a scholastic nature, for since none of them was fully developed, they are all open to various interpretations.

If the Stalinist center had yielded to this theory of state capitalism that Zinoviev proposed, its claims that the monolithic Party was the only possible representative of the working class would have been invalidated. If state industry is socialism, the monopolistic State Party is a workers' party, and the dictatorial state is identical with a workers' state.

In his closing remarks, Zinoviev summed up the immediate demands of the Opposition:

> 1) Fight the revisionist theory of the "Red Professors."
> 2) Fight the revision of Leninism on the question of state capitalism . . .
> 5) Party democracy.
> 6) End the campaign against the Leningrad organization.
> 7) Offer Party and Comintern coöperation to all oppositionist tendencies and groups that had been expelled or estranged. [*There was a noisy interruption, with cries of* Repeat, repeat.]
> 8) Safeguard the principles by which Party functionaries are nominated and elected.
> 9) Reëvaluate the problem of the General Secretariat at the first session of the newly elected Central Committee.

With this program, the Opposition passed from scholastic comment and citations from Lenin to a direct attack on the plan to give Stalin unlimited power. Once the real issue was thus brought into the open, the bitterness and virulence of the debate reached new depths. Stalin had prepared for this fight by assuring himself the support of the two most important Soviet institutions outside the Party—the army and the trade-union staffs. In spite of all his careful manipulations, the degree to which his acquisition of power at the Fourteenth Congress was a touch-and-go matter is indicated by the division between the two top army representatives.

M. V. Frunze, the successor to Trotsky as head of the army, had died a month before the convention; he had supported Zinoviev and Kamenev against Stalin, and many of the delegates were convinced that he had been disposed of in a novel fashion. Frunze's health had been failing, and he was given a Party order to undergo an operation on his digestive system; his death on the operating table was a decisive blow to the Opposition.[13] After his death, Stalin had K. Y. Voroshilov appointed to his post, but was still not strong enough to keep Lashevich, a Zinoviev supporter, from the second post in the war commissariat. The split in the Party leadership was thus reflected in the army command, a fact that increased the general anxiety.

> The Opposition [Voroshilov said] wants to change the entire relationship between Politburo and Secretariat, but the Opposition does not understand what an important job is done by the Secretariat. The Secretariat does not make the policy of the Party . . . I don't understand all your palavers on the collective leadership of the Politburo. We don't want direction even by the Politburo. The entire Central Committee shall guide our Party.

The Opposition fought for its life.

> KAMENEV: . . . We are against creating a theory of "leader"; we are against raising up a "leader." We are against the fact that the Secretariat, by uniting his political and organizational functions, stands above the body politic. We are for a Party constitution which shall give the full powers of our highest bodies to the Politburo, in which all the political leaders of our Party meet, and which at the same time shall designate the Secretariat as the technical executor of the larger body's decision. [*Applause*] . . .

---

[13] Boris Pilnyak published a story in a Moscow literary magazine under the mysterious title "The Story of the Unextinguished Moon," with the subtitle "The Assassination of the Commandant." In the story, the country was ruled by three men, one military and two political leaders. One of the politicos forces the military leader to undergo an operation, against both the advice of the physicians and his own wishes, for he is beset with strange and horrible presentiments. The mood this story created reached a climax when Stalin had the issue of the magazine confiscated and took action against the editor. I was in Moscow at the time, in the months before the Fourteenth Congress, and heard the suspicions concerning Frunze's death from various comrades. Cf. Souvarine, *Staline*, p. 371; Trotsky, *Stalin*, p. 418.

We cannot consider as normal or as desirable for the Party the continuation of a situation in which the Secretariat unites political with organizational functions and, in fact, determines political decisions.

. . . I have come to the conviction that Comrade Stalin cannot fill the role of unifying the Bolshevik general staff. [*Cries:* That's a lie! Rubbish! Wouldn't you wish it? Now the cards are on the table! *The delegates arise and salute Comrade Stalin. Cries:* This is how to unite the Party. The Bolshevik general staff has to unite.]

YEVDOKIMOV, *from his seat:* Long live the Communist Party of Russia! Hurrah! Hurrah! [*The delegates rise again and cry* Hurrah! *Lively and prolonged applause.*] Long live the Central Committee of our Party! [*The delegates cry:* Hurrah!] The party before everything! [*Applause and cries of* Hurrah!]

VARIOUS VOICES: Long live Comrade Stalin! [*Lively and prolonged applause. Cries of* Hurrah!]

Tomsky, who had come to Stalin's side in support of Bukharin's policy, rose after Kamenev and in rebuttal gave an indirect but understandable warning to Stalin.

Equally ridiculous are Kamenev's attempts to depict the present situation as if Stalin is striving for autocratic domination, and as if the majority of the Politburo supports him in this attempt. There is a real collective direction in the Politburo, and the system of autocratic leadership will never be accepted. Such a system cannot and will not be.

Tomsky was given, according to the convention minutes, "stormy prolonged applause," which for Stalin was an indication that despite his majority the fight had not yet come to an end. He had planned this convention carefully. He had organized the discussion, the smear campaign; of the 150 who wanted to speak, most filed in a monotonous parade, repeating the same arguments against the Opposition, reassuring, reaffirming, reasserting. Stalin had achieved the silence of Trotsky, and he had won over Bukharin. He had arranged a show of force, including important representatives of all Soviet institutions, which impressed those who came to the convention with doubts. All this careful preparation bore fruit: he was confirmed as General Secretary of the Party. But the battle was not over; rumblings of dissent even among his own supporters warned him that he needed another preparatory period of maneuvering before he could go further. Now, in his closing speech, he donned a democratic toga and addressed the European working class as one true democrat talking to another. The unity of the whole working class, he said, is more precious than party regulations, the unity of the working class is the highest value in the battle for socialism.

> In increasing numbers foreign workers come to us, not only as friends or as brothers, but really as auditors for the European working class. They travel everywhere freely, and we show them our factories and our institutions, not as these things are shown to curious scholars whom we want to instruct, but as to persons to whom we report our achievements and our shortcomings. Soviet Russia is the property of the European working class, which has a right to intervene. We hope, then, and we expect that in case of capitalist intervention the working class of Europe will defend Soviet Russia. Some 1550 delegations have already been here, and sixteen others are expected.

The Party convention accepted the Stalin-Bukharin platform by 459 votes to 65, with 41 abstentions.

A Personal Note on the Fourteenth Congress

I was one of the auditors for the European working class, invited to Moscow, it will be remembered, to effect my physical withdrawal from the German scene. I was living in the Hotel Lux in a kind of honorary confinement. According to the Comintern constitution, as a member of the Presidium regularly elected at the Fifth World Congress, I had the right to attend and participate in the convention of any Communist party. European parties, particularly the German party, were often visited by members of the Presidium, who attended all party meetings and sessions of the political and organizational bureaus and of the secretariats. These informal delegates from the world organization did not have the right to vote, but their mere expression of opinion was in most cases enough to influence political and organizational decisions. In Germany, they delved into the smallest details of organizational and financial technicalities of the party and its affiliates.[14]

---

[14] Only the elected members of the Presidium, however, had these prerogatives. In this period, the German party had rejected a repeated proposal that Comintern

The Russian Party, however, never applied this constitutional rule to itself. Foreign Communists were admitted from time to time to special sessions of the Russian Politburo, when the agenda was limited to non-Russian matters. If Russian affairs were debated before foreign comrades, it was always a show discussion, prearranged with the didactic purpose of explaining and defending some particular points of view. Until this time, however, larger Party gatherings, and in particular Party congresses, had always been open to a large group of foreign Communists. That was a harmless courtesy, for the serious decisions on major issues were always made behind the closed doors of the Politburo sessions preceding the conventions. This time, however, the political leaders of Russia had not achieved a compromise in the Politburo and would fight for their positions on the open floor of the convention.

I requested a guest ticket to the convention and repeated this demand several times in writing to Stalin's Secretariat. There was no question of my right to attend the congress and participate in the debate. Not only was I a member of the Comintern Presidium with the special prerogatives I have described, but I had a special mandate from the Berlin organization of the German party to represent it at this convention. "The German question," which meant in this case a smear campaign against Maslow and me, was included as a part of the Comintern report. Ironically enough, I had been summoned to Moscow ostensibly because my presence was needed to clarify differences on German politics. It was symptomatic of Stalin's uncertainty that he did not risk letting me attend the convention; I would have had no vote, but my presence might have swerved a few votes to the Leningrad Opposition. Stalin's welcome to European working-class *contrôleurs* applied in the case of Germany, however, to Clara Zetkin, whose greeting to the congress was, "We salute you on the Leninist road as the iron phalanx that will lead the world proletariat to victory, marching forward in well-disciplined and unbreakable ranks."

Though I was not able to attend the congress, I got full reports

---

technicians be invited to the sessions of the German Politburo. Two of these, N. Grolmann and M. Idelsohn, both GPU staff members, lived for months in Berlin during 1924, trying vainly to intervene in the political life of the Central Committee.

from both sides. Characteristically, Stalin combined his smear campaign against me and his denying me the opportunity to answer it from the floor of the convention with an effort to win me over to his side. He sent me various private messengers with this task, among whom Béla Kun, the leader of the Hungarian party, was by his crude and direct manner an almost refreshing change. Kun had until recently sung the praises of Zinoviev, "the great organizer of the world revolution," and now that he had switched his loyalty to Stalin, dozens of anecdotes circulated in Moscow on his unscrupulous intrigues to organize Comintern cadres for his new master. He paid me several courtesy calls during the congress, to keep me up to date; and just before the decisive vote against Zinoviev, he made a very precise proposal. It centered around Maslow's behavior in his trial by the Leipzig court, which was condemned in a resolution not yet passed by the congress.

"It's very easy, Ruth; we can arrange everything. You can go back to Berlin and return to your position in the German party. We don't want any long political statements on Russia. What we want is two lines against Maslow. Don't yell! No one is asking you to repeat the accusations of the party against him. You can play your part very quietly and matter-of-factly. Concentrate on the fact that you don't agree with Maslow's behavior before the court, where he talked to a bourgeois audience on party matters. That doesn't bind you to any political commitments; it's really nothing. When you do that, Stalin and I will fix everything with the German Central Committee, and you'll see how wonderfully everything will work out."

This kind of bribe-threat was typical. On the one hand, I was offered a party sinecure; on the other, by a combination of ideological Party terror and state compulsory measures I was made to feel more and more insecure, so that such a sinecure would seem more and more desirable.

Shortly after my arrival in Moscow in September, the Comintern secretariat had as usual asked for my passport, and I was unable to get it back. I demanded repeatedly that I be allowed to return to Berlin. The repeated refusal was against Comintern rules, for I had not been removed from office. Such compulsory measures were still unusual. But while I was not wanted in Berlin, they did not want me to remain in Moscow either; a series of doctors investigated my health at short intervals and invariably prescribed a stay in a sanitarium at Kislovodsk, in the Caucasus. These diagnoses were discussed at length by the secretariat of the Presidium, which sent me its decision, complete with the ornate Comintern seal, that I be asked in the name of Comintern discipline to proceed immediately to the Caucasus to regain my health (I had this curious document in my possession until March 1933, when my Berlin apartment was raided by the Gestapo).

Besides Kun and others like him, I was attended by a delegate from the GPU, one Comrade Bogrebinsky, who under various pretexts visited me every day, morning and evening, to keep me informed of the progress of the convention—and to pump me on the plans and prospects of the Opposition and check my activity and visitors during the day with the GPU man at the entrance desk. Once again, this emphasized for me the insecurity of the majority: its consciousness of the deeply ingrained dissatisfaction of the Russian workers with the Party dictatorship; its panic. Bogrebinsky was particularly interested in Trotsky, who attended the convention as a member of the Central Committee but did not participate in the debates. Both groups feared him—they had united to oppose him—and now both hoped to win him over; Trotsky's attitude might have been decisive among the wavering delegates from the provinces. Trotsky, Bogrebinsky noted each day, had looked well or badly; he had spoken with this person or that. "I saw Trotsky today in the corridors. He spoke with some of the delegates, and I could hear a little of the conversation. He said nothing on the decisive questions. He did not support the Opposition, even by hints and allusions. That is wonderful. Those dogs from Leningrad will get a thorough beating."

Bogrebinsky, a man in his early thirties, was typical of the new bureaucracy. He wanted a strong Soviet state power and greater privileges for the state officials. For him, Stalin personified a sound Russian policy, based on stabilization inside Russia and abroad. His hatred of the old generation, who were impeding progress to the new course, was genuine and strong, for in addition to their incorrect policies they barred the rise of such late comers as himself to the highest Party and state ranks.

From the basis laid at the Fourteenth Congress, socialism in one country became a state religion, sacrosanct against all heretics. Stalin wrote after the congress:

> Lack of *faith* in the victory of socialist construction is the basic mistake of the New Opposition, because all the other mistakes of the New Opposition spring from it: . . . on the question of the New Economic Policy, state capitalism, the nature of our socialist industry, the role of coöperation under the dictatorship of the proletariat, the methods of the kulaks, the role and importance of the middle peasants—all these mistakes are the outcome of this basic mistake of the opposition, of their lack of *faith* in the possibility of constructing socialist society with the efforts of our own country . . .
>
> The historical significance of the Fourteenth Congress of the Communist Party of the Soviet Union lies in the fact that it was able to expose to the very roots the mistakes of the "New Opposition," that it threw aside its lack of *faith* and snivelling, clearly and distinctly indicated the path of the further struggle for socialism, gave the Party prospects of victory and thereby armed the proletariat with invincible *faith* in the victory of socialist construction.[15]

---

[15] Stalin, *Leninism*, emphasis added; quoted in Popov, *Outline History of the CPSU*, II, 258–259.

5

THE STATE PARTY IS
INSTALLED

After the Fourteenth Congress, Zinoviev maintained only formal authority over the Comintern apparatus. Of the innumerable problems
of the International, Stalin chose Germany as his special province.
Manuilsky had accumulated a wealth of detailed information on the
internal life of the Thälmann group and of the entire German party;
with a group of advisers, he again made his headquarters in Berlin
and continued to refine the crude German party methods with superior Russian techniques. As an impartial arbiter from the Comintern
Olympus, Manuilsky was able to manipulate the various Left and
Right factions and grouplets, promising support to all of them, playing
one against the other, offering political amnesty to all oppositionists who
were not "anti-Bolshevist" and who came over in time. The right of
party democracy was secure under him; the Comintern endorsed not
only criticism of German Communist policy but the sharpest attack
of the Thälmann leadership, provided only that two conditions were
fulfilled: first, that there be no reference to the Russian question, no
"intervention" by German comrades in the Russian Party crisis; second, that there be no criticism of Soviet foreign policy and especially
of contacts between the Red Army and the Reichswehr.

In the name of party democracy, Manuilsky sponsored a splitting
of the party into numerous groups; a disintegrating party was more
easily manipulated. Rank-and-file members were encouraged to study
ten assorted platforms with no practical differences on German ques-

tions; local units were forced to hear and discuss reports on these ten views. Blocs—that is to say, joint platforms of oppositionist groups that agreed on the major issue, resistance to Stalin's policy—were not permitted. By this strategy of attrition, by hampering any merger of forces among the resistance, Moscow intended first to crush the oppositionist tendencies and then to reconstruct the party in such a manner that it would have complete control. This aim was reached by changing the party structure, using the factory cells as instruments.

The Ulbricht-Pieck System

The pattern by which the German party was to be re-formed was decided on in two special organizational conferences in Moscow, held in March 1925 and February 1926.[1] Participants included Paul Merker, Maurice Thorez of France, Viola Briacco of Italy, and representatives of Moscow factories. The new form of Communist organization was described in great detail. Exactly what effect, for example, a cell of thirty-five Communists could have on a factory of two to three thousand workers was estimated. Sample factory reports were produced, which tried to imitate those from Russian factories. Correspondence was initiated between the Putilov factory in Leningrad and the Krupp cell.

The central German figure at these two conferences was Walther Ulbricht. Ulbricht, whose party name used to be Zelle, has made a career of cell organization. In 1923 he was a colorless party organizer from Thuringia, a member of the so-called Center group. He studied the organizational structure of the party from the point of view of how most effectively to disintegrate the Left organization and very early was singled out by Stalin as an adequate instrument for this work. He worked under the GPU men in the Comintern and gradually developed a technique of atomizing organizations into easily manipulated cells. By the time of the two Moscow conferences, he had become a specialist.[2] "As the industrial proletariat is the basis of the

---

[1] Reported in *Inprekorr*, 1926, pp. 655 ff.

[2] One of a large group of German Communists sent to Spain during the civil war, Ulbricht organized a German division of the GPU there. He established his headquarters at Albacete, where he personally led the investigation of German, Swiss, and Austrian "Trotskyists." He was responsible for the torture of many of these German dissidents, who suffered torments similar to those later imposed by

Communist movement," he wrote, "so the cell is the fundamental basis of our party organization."[3] "The System Pieck" is also the System Ulbricht. The two men, acting together under GPU orders, smashed the German party organization and regrouped it into Stalinist cadres. The German Communist Party could be Bolshevized only through this smashing and regrouping.

The Communist Party had grown organically out of the civil-war period. Almost 95 per cent of its members were workers. The German Left intelligentsia (especially the Jewish intelligentsia, who had been excluded from the civil service under the Kaiser) in general preferred the Democratic or Social Democratic Parties, which gave them greater access to government positions. The rank-and-file Communist had broken from the strong traditions and organization of Social Democracy by a violent process of clarification on matters of vital importance, a process that had left him with a bitter distrust of any party bureaucracy whatever. This contempt for bureaucracy, developed to an extreme among German Communists and to a less extent among German workers in general, was used by the Nazis during their rise in their campaigns against the *Bonzen*—the "bigshots."

Communists, then, were very jealous of their "democratic birthrights." One such right was the regional general assembly, at which all political and organizational issues were discussed and decided on the basis of equal weight to every voice, regardless of rank or position in the party. This regional organization had an intimate cohesion, based on the common background, the living in the same neighborhood, the every-day contacts outside of party work proper. The several hundred Communists it comprised had known one another for years, having shared the danger of the civil war and the same political experiences in the old Social Democratic and trade-union organizations.

---

the Gestapo. For days at a time they were imprisoned in windowless cells without food, interrogated all night, stood up for many hours in closet-like cells, beaten with lashes. Women were not exempt.

After the defeat of the Spanish Republicans, most of the German Communists went to France. After the collapse of France in 1940, during the Russian-German pact, Moscow ordered most of them to return to Germany; as a special privilege, Ulbricht was ordered back to Moscow. As a leading member of the Free Germany Committee in Moscow, Ulbricht was one of the first to be transferred to Berlin after the defeat of the Nazis. He is now second in command of the Socialist Unity Party.

[3] *Inprekorr*, 1926, p. 39.

The functionaries of these organizations, unpaid, had been chosen by a process of selection, the survival of those militants who had proved themselves the fittest; and not only the local leaders but the local rank and file were the fiber of a democratic organization. They were a body of men who had passed together through the fortunes and misfor-fortunes of the German labor movement of the past turbulent ten years. They had formed a close solidarity, based on free and volun-tary agreement, arrived at on the basis of this substantial equality of political experience and political knowledge. This body of men, whom no one who has ever lived among them can forget, developed in their struggle against adverse circumstances the finest qualities of human behavior—independence of character and the sacrifice of personal to group interest, solidarity with the group and personal integrity, the energy to face difficult tasks and accept responsibilities.

This group of individuals, who of their own free will had come together and stayed together in a strong group, struggled with a diffi-cult heritage of sectarian abstractions on German politics. Just in this period, these coalesced personalities, this differentiated collectivity, was beginning to overcome its handicaps and develop a more adequate German policy. They struggled for a democratic party structure, by which the Central Committee would be an executive of the various local bodies and no more. The local bodies, according to this emerg-ing concept, would make party policy, and the Central Committee would carry it out, and not vice versa. The members of the Russian Workers' Opposition who visited Germany were fascinated by the German party organization, for it exemplified the type of party they had hoped to organize in Russia. Stalin reacted no less strongly, for this type of organization, in which policy-making decisions are made on the base, was the antithesis of a Stalinist party. The increasing trend toward strengthened local home rule, expressed on a national scale through freely elected delegates to the party's conventions, was broken. By conspiratorial methods, Stalin's agents organized from the top down and reduced the local bodies to easily manipulated units.

In these local bodies, report and minority report on the pending problems would have given large majorities to the anti-Stalinist Left Opposition throughout the country. With the experiences of 1923 fresh in the memory of all the members, the distrust of the Russian state apparatus was immense. These revolutionary workers, who detested Prussian militarism, the Social Democratic leadership, and the Weimar police, included the Russian state bureaucrats as objects of an equally passionate antipathy. Stalin and Manuilsky were right in recognizing in the general Communist assemblies a fertile ground for prolonged resistance to the policy of the Kremlin.

Against these local party assemblies the Moscow apparatus declared open warfare. Under the slogan, "Concentrate party work in the factories," the old stratification of the party into regional assemblies, with town groups and factory cells within the framework of the regional groups, was liquidated. The System Pieck was introduced; party units larger than one single factory cell were formally prohibited, and even large factory cells were split into smaller units of no more than ten to fifteen members. The party was atomized; every coherent group of militants was disintegrated. Convention delegates were thrice screened: first small cell groups elected representatives; these representatives elected delegates to a regional party convention; and only this regional convention had the right finally to elect delegates to the Reich congress.

Another democratic birthright was the election of paid and unpaid party functionaries. By a sacred and eagerly guarded tradition of the German labor movement, no one could get a position in a labor organization without being nominated, discussed, and voted on by the rank and file. From now on, paid functionaries were nominated by the Central Committee, with prior approval by the Moscow control men. Candidates for state diets and the Reichstag, up to now also nominated by the membership, were also "proposed" by the Central Committee with the approval of the Moscow apparatus, and then endorsed by the delegates to a party convention.

There were hundreds of German party members who became paid employees of the various Soviet agencies in Germany. A job with one of these was a haven, eagerly sought by many German Communists. Salaries were considerably higher than in comparable German institutions, working hours were shorter, and there were other privileges. Employees of the Soviet Trade Legation in Berlin, for example, could buy motorcycles, fur jackets, and similar luxuries at a large discount, and with their families could enjoy cheap holidays in Russia or sojourns to Russian sanatoriums. Prestige and social status accompanied these material advantages. Many revolutionaries, with careers in the Weimar Republic closed to them by their Communist activity, considering such sacrifice futile now in a period of "relative stabilization," found compensation in the service of the Russian state. These careers changed completely the material and psychological conditions of their lives.

During these years the German party numbered between 125,000 and 135,000 members—by German standards it was a weak organization.[4] The apparatus of the party, however, was strong, comprising in its important elements the following:

The Central Commitee, its secretaries, editors, technical employees	850
Newspaper and printing plants, including advertising staffs	1800
Book shops, with associated agit-prop groups	200
Trade-union employees (principally in Stuttgart, Berlin, Halle, Thuringia, Chemnitz)	200
Sick-benefit societies	150
International Workers' Aid, with affiliated newspapers	50
Red Aid, including Children's Home in Thuringia	50
German employees of Soviet institutions (Soviet Embassy, trade legations in Berlin, Leipzig, and Hamburg, the Ostbank, various German-Russian corporations)	1000
Total	4300

All these employees became directly dependent on continued endorsement by the Moscow apparatus. One word against the party line, or even failure to defend it with sufficient vigor, was enough to cause them to be discharged on the spot, and they knew it. They were given liberal leaves of absence for "party work" and allocated as "responsible party militants" among the reorganized factory cells. This

---

[4] According to *The Communist International between the Fifth and Sixth World Congresses, 1924–28* (London, 1928, pp. 109–110), the German party had the following membership, based on dues paid:

1924	121,394
1925	122,755
1926	134,348
1927	124,729

The German party congress in 1927, on the other hand, was based on a party membership of 145,000. The circulation of the party press was estimated at about double the membership.

fool-proof manipulation was made palatable to the rank and file by the pompous and flattering argument that Soviet employees should be protected against bureaucratization and *embourgeoisement* by intimate and daily contact with workers at the bench.

In addition, the invisible undercover agents must be estimated at at least the same figure. Hence, almost one twelfth of the party membership was in direct Russian pay; and this was the most active element of the party, those who could be ordered to do any kind of party work, who could not refuse to participate in even the most insignificant factory cell meeting. Bureaucrats are everywhere the props of a political apparatus; the peculiar feature of these Russian cadres within German labor was their secret coördination, their military control by secret agents, their direct affiliation with the center in Moscow. This network of Stalinist agents became so dense that eventually it broke the German labor tradition in the German Communist Party and strangled all anti-Stalinist forces, eliminating every potential anti-Stalinist.

The system of factory cells did not bring about a better contact between the party and the broad mass of the proletariat, which was the principal reason given for foisting it on the party. In this period, large plants were almost completely emptied of Communist workers. Many had been blacklisted and, even during a time of relative economic improvement, could get jobs in large shops only with difficulty; some of those who had been able to keep their jobs were discovered to be Communists and discharged. More and more, the typical Communist worker was pushed into marginal industries, out of the main flow of German economy. Ulbricht's dictum that "ten workers in a big plant are more important than ten barbers" was a truism, but irrelevant to the situation. German plants had been purged of Communists six, seven, eight times. The party was strongest in the industrial regions, but even in these regions a large plant, employing hundreds of workers, might have only a handful of Communists.

The remnants met in their new factory cells in a depressed mood. In the big industrial centers, in Berlin and Hamburg and particularly in the Ruhr-Rhineland, residential quarters were far removed from the factory districts. The old intimacy of the regional organizations was destroyed, and nothing similar ever took its place. In their political combinations, the "responsible party militants" skillfully calculated the timetables of various suburban trains and bus lines, the hours at which the shift changed—the weariness caused by these circumstances. A contemporary Left Communist report of a cell meeting is an accurate description of this state of affairs:

> You must visualize an average factory cell meeting. There are perhaps seven or eight genuine workers present, and three or four attached party employees. A speaker delivers a violent tirade against the Opposition. There is usually no spokesman for the Opposition, for the cell committee has forgotten to invite him or has sabotaged the invitation . . . In the discussion period the employees of the party apparatus stigmatize as an anti-Bolshevist, as an enemy of Communism, everyone who does not vote for the Central Committee. Perhaps a worker remarks that he does not agree with all that; perhaps he proposes that the *Bonzen* should stop bickering and get together. The whole pack falls on the poor fellow to enlighten him, to demonstrate to him that he has not yet attained Bolshevik perfection.[5]

The fight against the imposition of this system was especially passionate in the Berlin organization. Several times a Berlin regional convention voted down every proposal of secretaries nominated by the Central Committee. When the Central Committee was able by artificially constructed delegate conferences to achieve, step by step, a majority vote for Moscow, immediately afterwards the Opposition again gained control in such important boroughs as Neuköln and Hallesches Tor, where the party meetings broke up in riots. "Without the reorganization, we could never have won the Berlin Communists."[6] In 1927, at the Eleventh Party Congress, Philipp Dengel,[7] the reporter for the Central Committee, declared:

---

[5] *Kommunistische Politik* (Berlin, End of May 1926), Vol. I, No. 5.

[6] Franz Dahlem, *Inprekorr*, No. 27, 1926, p. 270.

[7] Philipp Dengel, one-time secretary of the Cologne branch, had been won over to Stalin during the Open Letter affair in August 1925. He was active in the Thälmann group until 1933; after the victory of the Nazis he went to Russia. Here he survived the trials; he was mentioned several times during the war as a Communist exile living in Moscow. In 1943 or 1944, he disappeared from the dispatches and has never been mentioned since. He was not included among the German Communists sent back to Germany after the war.

For long months, we had to concentrate three-quarters or four-
fifths of our work on the isolation of such elements as Katz and
Korsch, Ruth Fischer and Scholem, in order to detach great numbers of workers in the party from them. It was a hellish job.[8]

During all these transitional years, the German Communist workers
revolted against the Stalinist course. It was not easy, even with the help
of the reorganized cell system and the secret agents integrated into the
party, to quell the Opposition. During 1926–1927 there was a state of
siege in the party. The steps by which the Opposition was gradually
stifled included the following:

1. Declarations of the Opposition were no longer published in the
Communist press, particularly at first if they referred to the Russian
crisis. For instance, the statement of Fritz Engel, the delegate of Berlin-
Wedding to the plenum of the Executive Committee in February 1926,
expressing the solidarity of the Berlin Left Communists with the Leningrad Opposition, was printed in neither *Pravda* nor the *Rote Fahne.*

2. After a short interval, minority reports were no longer permitted.
At the Eleventh Party Congress, those documents of the Opposition
that had been distributed were seized. "These scandalous, odious, per-
fidious documents of shame," Wilhelm Pieck declared, "can be inspected upon special request at the party center."

3. When even the cell meetings of the atomized party became in-
convenient, which was the case for a long period in some areas, the
cell members were deprived of their right to meet. In place of a cell
meeting, there was a conference of "responsible party functionaries";
that is, the party employees got together and voted support to their
employer.

4. Private letters were stolen from suspected comrades and used in
the German organization as political blackmail or sent to Moscow.

5. The secret apparatus intervened in party discussions. N-men
raided oppositionist meetings, surrounded meeting places with armed
groups, closed the doors and searched the participants for oppositionist
literature or revealing letters.

6. The same N-service made raids on private homes and undertook
regular police searches. Comrades were taken to headquarters and

---

[8] *Parteitagsbericht*, Essen convention, March 1927, p. 41.

interrogated there, not by the regular party organization but by secret-service men.

7. The secret service organized special campaigns of defamation against certain persons, who were represented as personifications of evil. Moscow-fabricated data were spread both through the party organizations and elsewhere.

8. There were various party punishments. Dissidents were prohibited from holding party posts for a year, participating in membership meetings—a peculiar Moscow invention in a German environment, speaking or writing on political subjects, whether in the general or the party press, writing on any topic. They were banished to Moscow, to the Russian hinterland, to Asiatic or Latin American countries, especially to China. During such an exile, they were forbidden, for example, to read any German material.

9. Selected oppositionists, groups of oppositionists, entire local units were expelled as "counter-revolutionary"; for instance, small industrial hamlets in the Ruhr, Ickern and Hückeswagen. München-Gladbach in the Rhineland, Triebes and Suhl in Thuringia, and many others were expelled as a unit after six town conferences had taken place without giving a majority to the Central Committee.

Party members were not permitted to have any relations with one who had been expelled; they were forbidden even to speak with him or to answer his greeting on the street. Thus thousands of rank-and-file members were expelled for no greater political crime than having continued personal contacts with comrades whom they saw in the factories or the unemployment offices. "Expulsion for contact" was applied first in the higher brackets of the party. Korsch was expelled for contact with Katz, Ruth Fischer for contact with Korsch; Zinoviev and Trotsky had to declare that they had no contact with Fischer. In some cases, particularly if he was a member of one of the secret services, a Communist was expelled for fraternizing with his counter-revolutionary spouse. In Halle a young comrade named Springstubbe was expelled because he was supposed to have written, under a pen name, in a Left Communist magazine. In Dresden a member of the Right faction, Erich Melcher, was expelled because he had been seen in the People's House in conversation with a Social Democrat. In München-Gladbach three members of the Red Front Fighters' League were expelled because they had ridden to a League meeting in a "non-party" automobile, the property of the expelled München-Gladbach party branch.[9]

The Party Hierarchy under GPU Control

In 1926 the first Lenin School was founded in Moscow. The direction of the school, ostensibly by the Comintern, was actually in the hands of the counter-espionage of the Red Army. There was a secret annex in the outskirts of the city where conspiratorial methods were taught. Here conspiracy was raised from "party dilettantism" to the level demanded in a state in which it was the general rule of behavior, the background of all interdepartmental relations. An assignment to this school was a special award, granted only after faithful years in the

---

[9] "The central question of the development of the party [Radek later wrote] is the question of the splitting of the party. Everybody who sees things politically and does not allow himself to be blinded by hatred, knows that Ruth Fischer, Maslow, Urbahns, Scholem represent a whole stratum of Communist workers. In the first post-war years this stratum represented revolutionary impatience. We had to combat it, in order to make clear to the Communist workers that a hopeless minority is in no position to capture power. But we did not want to separate ourselves from this mass, for it represented the hope of our class . . . That is why, on my own initiative, I insisted at the Leipzig convention of the party that Ruth Fischer should be put on the Central Committee; the latter rejected the proposal. I wanted the Left wing representatives in the Central Committee so that they might constitute a counterbalance against the pure-and-simple daily politicians, against the comrades who did not understand the difference between a USPD and a Communist party . . .

"Later that summer, when Brandler, Thalheimer, Pieck, Guralsky, and other members of the Central Committee wrote a letter to Zinoviev, Bukharin, and me to demand the removal of Ruth Fischer and Maslow, and Brandler declared in a private letter to me that the patching up will no longer work, I told him that I cannot go along with such insanity. He climbed down. But there was no collaboration with the Left wing . . . I sought to keep Brandler not out of friendship, although I value him highly and as a man he stands close to me, but because I was convinced that the Left-wing comrades alone are not in a position to lead the party and to maintain its contact with broad masses. A Communist party without the Left-wing workers is threatened with the danger of becoming a USPD. A Communist party without the collaboration of people like Brandler, Thalheimer, Walcher, and the thousands of old Spartakists courts the danger of becoming a KAPD . . .

"On the anniversary of the death of Karl and Rosa I spoke at a meeting of the Moscow Youth League, at which you too were scheduled to speak. I prepared for my speech, thumbed through old articles by Rosa, and it is my deep conviction that we Left radicals in Germany awakened not too early but too late, fought against the dangers not too sharply but too weakly."

This is a portion of a letter Radak wrote to Clara Zetkin after she had attacked him, as the representative of the Bloc in Germany, at the ECCI plenum in December 1926. It was published for the first time in December 1934, in the Trotskyist monthly, *The New International* (New York), vol. I, no. 5, pp. 155–156.

party and after thorough tests had been passed. Pupils took a two-year course, and graduates were the elite of the secret-service men, eligible for the most responsible tasks in the most important regions. They had a certain contempt for the *legalshchiki,* the functionaries in posts where strict observance of the law was prescribed.

Thus, under the title of democratization and normalization, the German Communist Party was russified in the simplest sense of the word: all of its units became completely subservient to Moscow, eager to carry out the Kremlin's orders. Every German Communist who entered the secret services was under Moscow discipline; when summoned, he had to go to Moscow headquarters and report to his superiors. These transfers were disliked and feared, for in Moscow the agent was isolated as he faced the Party and state judiciary. But to refuse a summons was "open lack of discipline," leading directly, for the small fry, to loss of salary and milieu. "Bigshots" were in greater personal danger. In several cases secret agents who refused to go to Moscow were taken there by force, and their friends' or families' queries were never answered.

Two years of this normalization sufficed to change the party cadres completely. In place of the internationalist militant Communist of the civil-war times, there arose a new type of National Communist—the Stalinist, the Moscow agent. The new cadres did not feel that they represented an international workers' party, but the Russian State Party; they were secret agents of a foreign state. The legal party apparatus, the legal party organizations, became empty shells, façades concealing ruins. The nucleus of the party was now the bulwark of secret agents, grouped so solidly that every attempt to resurrect independent tendencies would be crushed.

This network had been developed during the period of the 1923 crisis.[10] As a new uprising in Germany receded from the Kremlin calculations, the secret apparatuses were concentrated on espionage of all varieties. "Out of the ruins of the Communist revolution," Krivitsky writes, "we built in Germany for Soviet Russia a brilliant intelligence service, the envy of every other nation."

> At the head of the Party Intelligence Service we named Hans Kiepenberger, the son of a Hamburg publisher. He worked tire-

---

[10] See p. 172 ff., *supra.*

lessly, weaving an elaborate spy net in the ranks of the army and police, the governmental apparatus, and every political party and hostile fighting organization . . . Elected to the Reichstag in 1927, he became a member of the Committee on Military Affairs . . . [and] supplied the Soviet Military Intelligence with valuable information for many years . . . In the fall of 1933 he fled to Russia. In 1936 he was arrested as a Nazi spy . . .

"Didn't you know General Bredow, head of the Reichswehr Military Intelligence?" asked the OGPU examiner.

"Of course I knew him," replied Kiepenberger . . . (General Bredow had frequently appeared before the Reichstag Committee.) [11]

Kiepenberger had been in contact with Bredow on Russian orders; part of his job was to sound out German officers. After six months of questioning, however, he confessed that he had been in the service of the German Military Intelligence as well and was executed.

No one knows how much truth there was in Kiepenberger's confession, but undoubtedly many of the agents served both sides. It is difficult to distinguish between military espionage and the endless National Bolshevist discussions on the possible coöperation between the German and Russian armies against the West. It is no less difficult in such a milieu to know who was who, and to which side these double agents were finally loyal.

The *M–Apparat,* the military branch of the party, was no longer favored. Military instructors were recalled to Moscow; there was no more money allotted for the purchase of weapons. Many of the old militants were disturbed by this neglect and constantly lamented the decreasing support and funds granted the military organization. These malcontents were grouped by some of the Russian instructors and assigned to minor espionage tasks; their complaints were turned against the party and used to further its disintegration. A skeleton of the *M–Apparat* was maintained, consisting of experts in the new forms of warfare—artillery, radio, aviation, and chemical warfare. This "General Staff" continued to maintain a secret headquarters, where military maps, a library on military subjects, and other appropriate material were collected. Regular conferences were held on the progress of warfare. Under Russian and German direction, several smaller research

---

[11] W. G. Krivitsky, *In Stalin's Secret Service,* pp. 39–40.

outfits studied German military science and occasionally published instruction pamphlets and military propaganda literature. Small armed groups still organized military exercises, but larger maneuvers were discontinued.

In this period Soviet information services in Berlin were numerous and varied. The Comintern had its own information service, the embassy another, the trade legations still others. Berlin correspondents of *Pravda* and *Izvestia* could count on the continued benevolence of their Russian superiors only if they produced, in addition to their published stories, confidential reports on the situation in Germany. From every German circle—the liberal intellectual, the Social Democratic, the trade-unionist, the military—information, masked for example as research material for a Russian magazine, was bought by Soviet agents. Although often anti-Communist in their politics, these varied individuals thought it unobjectionable to sell information and analyses for Russian money. This large and multifarious group of informers surrounded the kernel of secret agents and facilitated their penetration into all levels of German society.

One particularly interesting aspect of this organization was the system of "Workers' Correspondents" built up in this period. In each factory where the party had any strength, it designated one of its members as a correspondent. Officially his task was to write letters to the Communist press; actually it was to submit confidential reports on the situation in the factory and the industry. These reports were filtered by experts, digested, and forwarded to Moscow.

During this transitional period, the secret service of the German party, controlled by GPU men, prepared a complete index of German Communist local leaders for the Stalin Secretariat—not only the social and political background of each man but a continuous detailed report on the position he took in party disputes and especially his attitude towards Stalin. This index, compiled in the Comintern headquarters in Moscow on the model of the secret Russian Party index, has been perfected during the last two decades. The decimation of German Communists by the Nazis has of course destroyed the value of large parts of it, but anyone who has survived and is now accepted into the apparatus was admitted because his record showed a long period of subservience to Stalin's Russia.

In the synchronization of the party, the intelligence and terror groups, the *N–* and *T–Apparate,* were decisive. It was they who weighed the character and behavior of oppositionists, decided which had to be eliminated, and regrouped the remnant into a malleable form. In the 1923 days, the T-groups had comprised energetic types directing their militancy against the counter-revolutionary organizations. These German partisans were transformed into subservient auxiliaries of the Russian terror apparatus; honest revolutionary workers, who had joined the groups in their passionate hatred of the Black Reichswehr, became filthy instruments, salaried assassins.[12]

The GPU got its agents into every important party branch; in the policy-making bodies of the party—the Central Committee and the Politburo—first of all; in city councils and Reichstag factions; among the teachers of the Marxist Workers' School; in the leading bodies of every wide ramification of Communist activity. Over the next years increasing numbers of the personnel of the International Workers' Aid, the party publishing houses, the party press, entered the service of the GPU and added a few marks to their regular salaries. At the time of the Left Central Committee, Pieck was assigned to report on its sessions to the GPU; later Ulbricht became the principal contact between the Russian secret service and the German party.

A minor but not uninteresting evidence of the corruption of the German party is the fact that Berlin became a second headquarters for the Russian agents penetrating the rest of Europe. The German party supplied the Soviet agents traveling through with safe apartments, bodyguards, stenographers, and other facilities. Often a GPU agent hired his assistants on the spot, selecting them from among those recommended by the Central Committee, and so it was that in the decade

---

[12] In the first period of the civil war, the three Golke brothers, all skilled workers in Berlin, had joined the secret organization of the party. After 1925, in order to escape the permanent unemployment that resulted from their Communist activity, they became members of a T-group. I met them again in Moscow during my exile there in 1925–1926, and they were still typical sober German skilled workers. They had to live in Moscow because of the part they had played in the assassination of a White Russian officer working for the Paris Deuzième Bureau. An old Russian acquaintance had invited him to dinner in Wiesbaden and served him with poisoned beer. The Golke brothers had done no more than watch on a street corner or listen through a door, but this incidental participation cut their links to Germany and tied them to the Russian apparatus.

before 1933 thousands of German Communists entered the service of a foreign state and were scattered, often under assumed names, to the four corners of the world. A novitiate was impressed with the importance of his new task, and the difference between crude party methods and the refined conspiracy of "the Comintern" was stressed. By a series of minor assignments the candidate was tested for his fitness and loyalty. Many got only temporary tasks, but an important group was signed up for life.

Side by side with the open party functionaries, who were in any case increasingly selected from the top rather than elected from below, there grew up a parallel invisible hierarchy, a secret elite whose every aspect was antithetical to the workers' representatives elected in the pre-Stalinist era. This body of GPU "officers" had a life of its own, a solidarity apart from the parties it manipulated. Rank and title, and corresponding salary and privileges, depended on the value of the services to the Russian state. Underlings and peripheral elements were divided into occasional and regular informants, between "friends" and sub-agents; and since these GPU men were decisive in deciding the fate of a man in the party, the rank of a comrade came to be measured by the sort of assignment he was trusted with. "He has *very* responsible work to do," was the standard introduction to a coming man, a comrade considered reliable by Moscow agents.

In New York in 1945 I listened to a discussion on the relative "importance" of this or that past GPU assignment. These remnants of the German GPU apparatus talked as would a group of veterans discussing the military prowess of the soldiers they had fought with. This peculiar mentality, this measure of every man by his "reliability," carried me back to Berlin in the middle twenties, where I had watched this movement of Russian instruments destroy the German Communist Party I had helped to build up.

The Dawes Plan, in effect for only one year, had set off an industrial recovery in Germany that was amazing in its speed and efficiency. The most significant political result of this recovery was the Locarno Pact, which was signed on October 16, 1925. By this pact, the British Conservative government intended, consciously and articulately, to end the identification of Germany as an aggressive militarist power. The pact stipulated that the forces occupying the Rhineland would be considerably reduced; that Germany, even before she regained full civil sovereignty there, would participate in the Allied control bodies; that Cologne would be evacuated immediately. These central political clauses, which were supplemented by an array of economic stipulations to help implement them, froze the Western frontiers of Germany. The Eastern frontier was still fluid, however, and it was a common remark that an Eastern Locarno might become necessary. (Exactly the reverse is true today: Potsdam and Yalta, supplemented by Soviet *faits accomplis* of transferred populations, have seemed to settle the issue of the Polish border in accordance with Russian plans, while the question of the Saar and the Ruhr remained in a state of dangerous flux.)

Stabilization of the German Economy

Lord D'Abernon, "the Ambassador of Peace," noted in his diary for October 16, 1925:

> Pact of mutual security initialed at Locarno. Formal signature is to take place in London on December 1. All is well. This

date marks the turning point in the postwar history of Europe, not only diplomatically speaking but psychologically. It was a decisive blow to the preponderance of the war spirit, which hitherto had maintained a stringent line of demarcation between the victorious and the vanquished nations. The Pact was a negotiated, not a dictated, Treaty. It also ended the system of one-sided alliances by the undertaking of Great Britain and Italy, in the event of any future Franco-German conflict, to throw all their weight, both moral and material, on whichever side was deemed to be the innocent one. In this way, the Pact was designed and destined to reassure France and Belgium against the peril of any renewed attack from Germany. Similarly, it reassured a disarmed Germany against any abuse of power by a fully armed France and her numerous allies. In a word, it restored the necessary balance of power.[1]

Locarno was the cement of the new Western bloc. It would temper the mutual fear and distrust between Germany and France; it would prevent Germany from falling into close collaboration with Russia. It would begin such a period of European stability as had followed the Congress of Vienna in 1815, when Napoleon's defeat had been consummated.

> At the signing of the Locarno Treaty in the reception room of the Foreign Office, Sir Austen Chamberlain hung one single picture, a portrait of Lord Castlereagh. He wished thereby to draw a parallel between that which had been accomplished at Vienna and that accomplished at Locarno.[2]

The same exaggerated hopes that war-torn Europe was settling down to a relatively permanent peaceful stability were voiced in the columns of every liberal newspaper throughout Europe.

> If Locarno is a fact, and an agreement on the European debts has been reached in America, these facts are symptomatic evidence that Europe is settling down to a new existence that will last for about a century.[3]

---

[1] Lord D'Abernon, *An Ambassador of Peace: Vol. III, The Years of Recovery* (London, 1930), p. 199.

[2] Otto Hoetzsch, *Germany's Domestic and Foreign Policies* (London, 1929), p. 74. For progressives, Castlereagh, the post-Napoleon stabilizer of Europe, was a symbol for reaction. In his poem, "The Mask of Anarchy" (written after the Peterloo massacre in Manchester on August 16, 1819), Shelley attacked him: "I met Murder on the way — he had a mask like Castlereagh."

[3] The Prague Social Democratic daily, quoted by Zinoviev, *Protokoll: Erweiterte*

As a culmination of the Locarno concept, Germany was admitted with full rights into the League of Nations, but only after months of maneuverings. In March 1926 the motion to admit Germany was defeated by Brazil's veto; the United States feared a too close British-German alliance, which would be detrimental to American interests in Germany. Moreover, France and Poland, who had a secret treaty guaranteeing the German-Polish border, would not lightly acquiesce in a step toward the revision of Versailles. Some six months later, however, Germany was admitted.

Germany's reintegration into European politics was balanced by a revival of her economic life. Based on American loans, German industry was rebuilt, strongly influenced by the American model. Industrialists everywhere were talking of Henry Ford. In Central Germany, in the Ruhr, in the large harbor cities of the Northern coast, large funds were invested in modernizing the production machine; in 1926, the process was worked out to convert coal into synthetic gasoline and the German chemical industry was rapidly expanded, to take its predominant place in the German economy. In 1927 the Rhenish industrialist Albert Vögler founded the Dinta Institute in Düsseldorf, to rationalize and streamline labor-management relations.

This new prosperity reduced unemployment substantially.

German Federation of Labor
Percentage of Membership Unemployed at End of Year

1922	2.8	1925	19.4
1923	28.2	1926	16.7
1924	8.1	1927	12.9

The unemployment in these years, moreover, was of a different kind, due not to depression but to technological change. Each year about a quarter of a million workers were thrown out of work by rationalization, when non-profitable factories or mines were shut down, either permanently or for renovation. The number of industrial workers increased to about 28 million, the peak figure for the entire period of the Weimar Republic.[4]

Exekutive der Kommunistischen Internationale, Moskau, Februar-März 1926 (Hamburg, 1926), p. 21.

[4] Wladimir Woytinsky, *Zehn Jahre neues Deutschland: Ein Gesamtüberblick in Zahlen* (Berlin, 1929), p. 133 ff.

Between 1925 and 1928 German unions broadened out into social and economic functions. The German Federation of Labor founded the Arbeiter-Bank (Workers' Bank), intended to finance trade-union expansion through union investments. Based on this, coöperatives of various kinds sprang up—the Gehag (a non-profit housing company), consumers' coöperatives, Bücher-Gilde (a combined publishing house and book club, founded by the printers' union). A Trade-Union University was founded at Bernau; scholarships were available for the study of labor law at regular universities.

The rise of unions was reflected in the strengthening of the Social Democratic Party on all levels. The party's influence was particularly great on the municipal level, where with the help of American loans it began to construct quasi-socialist communities; cities competed with one another in the number and beauty of their sport stadia, municipal crèches, libraries, hospitals, museums, city halls. The socialist constructive spirit of the German workers, which was thwarted on a national level, reached its full development in the cities, and combining the best of industrial genius with the honest and efficient management of the Social Democratic bureaucrats built up all the impediments of a raised standard of living.

These institutions, which by American standards were not overwhelming, were none the less the cause of amazed envy among Germany's poor neighbors, her victors in the war; and the Repco in Berlin looked on this spending as sheer waste of American money. Among Germans as well, these projects of municipal improvement were under constant and heavy attack; a few unwise speculations, such as the Sklarek scandal in Berlin, were inflated to enormous proportions.

On a Reich level, the strengthened influence of the trade-unions and the Social Democratic Party was reflected in a greatly increased welfare budget, in a mushrooming of welfare services, especially in child care, as well as much new social legislation, especially concerning public health. This era of social peace culminated in state unemployment insurance and compulsory arbitration of industrial conflicts. The new social legislation, which on the whole was far in advance of that of any country of comparable size, generally worked well in the industrial centers, but the rural areas were as yet little affected by it.

German labor was moving forward, and there seemed to be no

reason why the progress of the past years could not be continued indefinitely. Fritz Naphtali, member of the board of directors of the Arbeiter-Bank, was the leading spirit of a group including Clemens Nörpel, Richard Seidel, Adolph Braun, Robert Schmidt—trade-union theorists who emphasized the pre-war Social Democratic doctrine of gradual change from monopoly capitalism to socialism by citing the facts and figures of present improvement. According to these analysts, German economy was so greatly centralized that its monopolies were a preview of socialist economic organization. They could point to the German cartels in shipbuilding, in chemicals, in coal, in potash, in electrical equipment. Many of these, including first of all the Central European Steel Cartel, had wide international ramifications. By their trust agreements, cartels were destroying the free market of the classic capitalist society; on the other hand, unions, by organizing the bulk of society, were gradually eliminating the free market in labor. German society, thus organized from the top by cartels and from the bottom by trade-unions, could develop into the socialist society through the medium of the arbiter in the middle, the state, which would come increasingly under the democratic control of the broadest strata of the population. At the 1927 Social Democratic convention in Kiel, Rudolf Hilferding, who had developed this theory to the fullest and deepest degree, was the principal reporter; in the same year the trade-union congress at Hamburg took a stand for "organized capitalism," for transforming capitalism by "economic democracy."

At international trade-union congresses, German unionists were sometimes under severe attack. At the 1925 congress in Vienna, for example, Bramley, the British delegate, said that the German delegates, Sassenbach and Grassmann, represented not the German workers but the German capitalists. When Grassmann spoke against the German Communist Party, Bramley retorted, "What did you do with Rosa Luxemburg and Karl Liebknecht?" At the 1927 congress in Paris, Hicks, the British delegate; Jouhaux, the French; Fimmen, the Dutch; all joined in condemning the German unions for their lack of class consciousness. While these criticisms were usually made in socialist terms, a good part of the reason behind them was the envy of the better standard of German labor as compared particularly with Britain, where unemployment was rife. A stiffer attitude on the part of German

workers would hamper German industrialists, who would not be able
to dump their goods on the world market and take over former British customers.

Shall the Princes Be Expropriated?

During these years, the nationalist extremists were reduced to a
provincial grouplet centering around Munich. Hitler struggled to
hold his remaining followers together, and it seemed that the Nazi
movement was dying out. Stresemann's policy of playing the East off
against the West was winning much more for Germany than the
intransigent opposition of the *Völkische* extremists; the more successful he was, the more bitterly they attacked him.

The other end of the German political spectrum, the Communist
Party, also lost influence during this period of relative prosperity, of
normalcy, but it was never reduced to the insignificance of the Nazis.
In general, the German worker, particularly the skilled worker, in
spite of certain dissatisfactions with the harsh reparations burden and
the rationalization costs, more or less accepted the Social Democratic
interpretation of German and world affairs, more or less followed the
Social Democratic Party, which again became the leading force in
German labor. The Communists were reduced to the task of organizing the unemployed, many of whom lacked, because of the war and
postwar crisis, the education and experience that would fit them for
good jobs. The rupture between these two labor groups became of
decisive importance later, during the depression, when the Communists again organized at the kernel of German labor, and when their
disadvantage became an advantage.

Lenin's ideas had never really taken root in German soil, and the
various perverted forms of his thought that had developed all ended
up in blind alleys. Though in this period of economic stabilization the
Stalinist version of Bolshevism was pushed to the periphery of society,
it jibed better with the Germany that had been produced by the civil
war. As soon as American dominance was withdrawn, the Communist
Party moved in from the periphery to somewhere near a central
position. The Colossus of the East was not able to draw Germany into
the concentric rings of its power system, but its influence was none

the less decisive. Bolshevism, processed by the experience of 1918–1923, came to Germany after Stalin had coalesced the fascist tendencies floating around Europe into "Leninism," the state religion of socialism in one country. Once planted in German soil, Bolshevism fed on the many totalitarian elements there and grew into a specific German form, with German gods and slogans. Once the German Communist Party was completely Bolshevized—once, that is, it had been deprived of any independence from Moscow—its only remaining role was to act as the carrier of the totalitarian virus to the German body politic, which could resist only as long as it was getting transfusions from America. The Communist Party of this period is a peculiar bastard form—the body of a group of men who had shared the dangers and hopes of the civil war, with their appeal to dissatisfied youth and unemployed hardly lessened, with many of the slogans and banners intact—such a body, and the soul of Stalinist despotism. The transfer of totalitarian ideas was not merely by loose propaganda, but by direct and tight control of the core of a close-knit institution. Germany was the first big country in Europe to harbor a significant group of men who had given up their faith in international socialism for subservient deference to the policy of a foreign government. From Thälmann down to the Communist factory worker, party members lived in a kind of twilight, with lingering memories of the bright noon of 1918 hopes and illusions, but moving ever faster into the night of GPU-maneuvered squadrons.

German Communists, cut off from direct control of most of German labor, still maintained an important pressure on trade-unions and the Social Democratic Party; this was based on sympathy remaining from 1917, fostered by a growing propaganda machine advertising Russian culture, Russian society, socialist Russia. The principal difference between the Right and the Left wings of the Social Democratic Party concerned the proper attitude toward coöperation with Communists on domestic issues, on the proper limits of a labor united front; but by this route of Soviet culture, the Communists were able to pervade the Social Democratic Left and to influence the whole of the Social Democratic movement. Stalin's elimination of the Old Guard was the subject of much confused theorizing among Social Democrats, but in the end they reached a general accord that it indicated a return to a more reasonable, a saner world policy. That German Communists no longer interfered so violently with Social Democratic aspirations, a result of the entire change of German society in these years, was interpreted as in part due to a more friendly attitude in Moscow, and the resultant benevolence of the German liberal and Social Democrat did more than meet the Russian propaganda without obstruction. As the Communist Party lost its revolutionary potential, the sharply critical attitude of its opponents decreased; it gained important influence as an indirect pressure group, not merely among the Left but in every group in German society. In every party there was a faction that was yet willing to seek an improvement of Germany's status by an alliance with Russia, and that therefore took in the tales of Stalin's reconstruction there.

The influence of the Communist Party as a pressure group is illustrated in its role in the plebiscite to expropriate the Hohenzollerns, a campaign that combined in a peculiar way all the symbols and thoughts of the past ten years with the new trends—in particular, the new methods of mass manipulation.

The fortune of Wilhelm II had been sequestered by Prussia in 1918, but a complete confiscation had been postponed by a dispute, dragging through the courts and the Reichstag Judiciary Committee, on whether there should be partial compensation. For years, the Imperial family, as well as the former ruling houses of Bavaria, Saxony, Wurttemberg, and other states, were given large sums in partial payment for their estates; the Kaiser used a good portion of this money to finance political activities in Germany. When the Social Democratic Party proposed a compromise, to settle the matter by a Reichstag bill to pay the Hohenzollerns a portion of their claim, the Communists stepped in and demanded that the Imperial fortune be confiscated without any compensation whatsoever. Their stand won wide support among liberal groups and Social Democratic organizations, and various liberal-socialist committees were formed to organize a plebiscite on the issue; the Reich committee was headed by Robert Kuczynski, later an important fellow-traveling economic analyst. For the first time, liberal bourgeois democrats and Communists were organized together to fight for a common political cause.

The monarchists led a vigorous counter-campaign.

> What is happening today to the Hohenzollerns or the Braun-
> schweig-Lüneburgers can happen tomorrow to Herr Schultz or
> Frau Müller if "the commonwealth" should happen to need his
> savings or her wedding ring . . . This confiscation will bring a
> real palpable advantage to no one, for no one can get a little piece
> of a museum or a picture gallery or a royal park . . .[5]

President Hindenburg himself took up the fight; in an open letter
he pointed out that he had spent his life in the service of the Prussian
king and the German emperor; that this proposal to expropriate
the Hohenzollerns violated the concept of private property on which
the Weimar Republic was based. The proposed expropriation was a
great injustice, a regrettable lack of tradition, a crude ingratitude.

As the campaign between "monarchists" and "anti-monarchists" un-
folded, every scandal, every symbol, every event, during the years of
the civil war was revived—the Fehme affairs, the flag question. Whether
the Hohenzollerns got more or less or no compensation would not in
itself have greatly affected the course of the Republic, but the campaign in which this issue was decided did much to influence the formative process of the Nazi forces. This was the last occasion of any
scope in which conservatives and reactionaries of the old school tested
the efficacy of the monarchy as an instrument of mass manipulation.
It did not work. Many proponents of compensation, the Center Party
for example, were able to rally voters behind them only by very carefully delineating themselves from monarchists; the nationalist extremists became convinced that the Hohenzollern eagle was dead,
that it could no longer be used to regroup Germans behind their
Völkische programs. Ludendorff, sensitive to the mood of the nationalist masses, was reconciled with Hitler and, in December 1926,
again began to coöperate with the staff of the *Völkische Beobachter*.

A referendum was held on June 20, 1926; it was a preliminary vote
to determine whether there should be a plebiscite by which the actual
question of expropriation would be voted. Twenty million *Ayes* in
this primary were the precondition to the plebiscite; the nationalists
boycotted the vote. Of the almost 40 million eligible voters, only 15

---

[5] "A" [Adolf Stein], *Durch Volksentscheid zur neuen Revolution*, Politische
Schriften (Berlin, 1926), no. 9, p. 3.

million voted, 14.5 million *Yes* and 0.5 million *No*. This nationalist victory had its compensation for the Left. The 14.5 million votes the joint program of the two parties had won in the plebiscite were several millions more than their combined votes in the preceding Reichstag elections. In unity there is strength.

> SPD and KPD ziehen jetzt an einem Strick;
> Das bricht den Fürsten das Genick.

("The Social Democratic and Communist Parties, now marching down the same road, will together break the neck of the reactionaries.")

The German-Russian Treaty of 1926

The 1923 crisis in Germany had given Britain and America a deeper understanding of the decisive role that Germany plays in Europe. Seen by a participant, the Communist attempt in that year was perhaps the most lamentable of the series of Comintern fumbles, of the various portions of that grandiose plan struggling to be born. With their inadequate preparation, torn by internal strife, the revolutionary internationalists lost their last and greatest chance to end the anachronism of chopped-up Europe and to grow to maturity in a socialist federation. But seen from the outside, the Communist coup came too close to success: the Russian-German alliance was so threatening that a counter action by the West was imperative. One of the immediate results of the 1923 crisis was France's loss of status. Her attempt to incorporate the Ruhr and to separate the Rhineland from Germany, to support her alliances with the small successor states of the Balkans and Eastern Europe, had failed. Now Britain and America shouldered France out of the way and integrated Germany into the Anglo-American power system.

In her Foreign Minister, Gustav Stresemann, Germany had a man able to take full advantage of this East–West rivalry. He looked like a beer-bloated burgher—bald, clumsy—but he had a Machiavellian mind that cut through diplomatic verbiage to the central question, what could Germany gain by this? The situation of Germany was personified in him: a defeated nation, which could regain its status in Europe only by playing one neighbor off against the other and thus maintain an uncertain and improbable equilibrium. Stresemann's

every clever móve was in part to get something for Germany immediately, in greater part to give her an improved bargaining power
against the others: the treaty with Russia, in order to move lagging
American loans; rearrangement with France, in order to display to
Russia a strengthened Germany. (The famous *déjeuner* with Briand
at Thoiry was an empty gesture.) The steps back for Germany were
first, the evacuation of the Rhineland; second, the return of the Saar;
third, *de facto* if not *de jure* incorporation of Austria; fourth, on the
basis of the Reich thus strengthened, to realign the Polish frontier and
get Danzig and the Corridor back. Stresemann was willing to forego
other frontier problems—Alsace-Lorraine with France, Eupen-Malmédy
with Belgium—and concentrate on a demand for a relatively moderate
revision of the Versailles Treaty, enough only to reconstitute a Germany
able to play her full role in a reconstituted Europe. Above all, this
program was not a mere nationalists' dream; in 1925, it seemed not
only realizable but the natural course of events.

The entrance of Germany, the only uncertain friend Russia had
left, into the League of Nations brought the Politburo's apprehension
to a new pitch. Increasingly, Russia posed as the defender of Europe's
weak nations against the new imperialist plot from overseas, the
guardian of Europe from American hegemony. "Fight united against
the League of Nations," was the title of a manifesto.

> The pacifist aspect of Locarno is a mask behind which the crimi-
> nal gambling of imperialists with the lives of the working class is
> continued . . . The Second International has participated openly
> and directly in the activity of the League of Nations . . . The So-
> cial Democrats have refused all proposals for a united fight against
> the League of Nations, and have instead directly and actively par-
> ticipated in the League of Nations council and its subcommit-
> tees . . .
> As a French newspaper wrote, the miracle of peace has not
> been fulfilled. The "miracle" of a new war, however, is approach-
> ing with terrific power. American finance-capital . . . is prepar-
> ing new compulsory measures by which the fate of defeated and
> plundered Germany will become the fate of all European states,
> of the whole of Europe . . . By her financial pressure, America
> holds the whip of starvation over the working masses of Europe.
> The fate of Germany, the transformation of a great industrial
> country into a powerless destitute colony, threatens Poland, France,

> Italy, the Danube countries, the whole European continent . . .
>
> There is only one way out against the threat of war, against plundering, against submission to the dismemberment of Europe by American capital. Together with the Soviet Republic and with all the suppressed peoples of the world, fight for the Socialist United States of Europe! [6]

In this role of guardian of Europe against the super-imperialism of the United States, the Politburo developed Radek's National Bolshevism and adapted it to the new situation in Europe generally.

The Berlin Treaty between Russia and Germany, a major implementation of this policy, was accepted in Berlin because it increased Germany's leverage against Britain and America. From his Berlin embassy, Lord D'Abernon watched uneasily the coöperation with Soviet Russia.

> I still hold that prolonged coöperation between the German Right and the Russian Left is unthinkable, but I must admit that the other night at the Russian Embassy, I was somewhat shaken to see how many gentlemen there were with stiff military backs and breasts bedecked with iron crosses, all partaking freely of Soviet champagne. [7]

The Berlin Treaty, signed by Stresemann and Krestinsky on April 24, 1926, was presented to the Reichstag for acceptance on June 10. The first of four articles reads: "The German government and the government of Soviet Russia will remain in friendly contact in order to come to an understanding on all political and economic questions affecting these countries." For a period of five years, [8] the two nations pledged that each would remain neutral in a war against the other and that neither would participate in a boycott against the other. There had been a preparatory commercial treaty signed on October

---

[6] *Inprekorr*, 1926, p. 786. This relatively moderate version exploded into nationalist frenzy after the American depression of 1929, when the Young Plan was attacked, for example, as a vulture sucking blood out of a German baby's neck. The Young Plan, which was adopted in 1928, required payments from Germany until 1988 but released all the remaining controls on Germany's economy. The control of the Reich Bank and the railroads reverted to the German government, the Reparation Commission left Berlin, and, in 1930, the last Allied soldier left the Rhineland.

[7] Lord D'Abernon, *Ambassador of Peace,* III, 205.

[8] The treaty was renewed on June 24, 1932, for another two years. On May 5, 1933, after Hitler's accession to power, it was renewed again.

12, 1925, and there were complementary secret arrangements concerning collaboration on military matters. In one of a series of notes between the two signatory powers, Stresemann specifically declared that Germany's participation in the League of Nations was not to be interpreted as "an obstacle to friendly relations between the German and Russian governments."

According to the German Communist Party, the treaty "eliminated all possibility of war between Soviet Russia and Germany," [9] and this sentiment voiced the hope of substantially the whole country. In the Reichstag, from the extreme nationalist Right through the Social Democratic middle to the Communist Party, there were only three votes against the treaty—those of Karl Korsch, Ernst Schwarz, and Heinrich Schlagewerth, dissident communists who had been expelled from the party on May 1. Inspired by Korsch, these three attacked the treaty as contrary to the interests of both the Russian and the German workers; in his speech before the Reichstag on June 10, Korsch referred to Rosa Luxemburg's warning, given in her eleventh Spartakus Letter, September 1918, that there was a danger of an alliance between Bolshevism and German militarism. That was the first time that even dissident communists attacked Soviet foreign policy openly from the floor of the Reichstag.[10]

Germany Rearms with Russian Factories

One of the best guarded secrets of the Russian Politburo was the collusion between Red Army and Reichswehr. Apart from the usual diplomatic reasons, there were special factors that made it especially important to cloak this inter-army collaboration. Opposition to the Reichswehr and its illegal divisions was the solid base on which militant German labor policy was built, and if the contacts that have since come to light had been known at the time it would have been utterly impossible to build a German Communist Party.

---

[9] *Die Rote Fahne,* April 25, 1926.

[10] Paul Levi, for example, and the others who had left the Communist Party to enter the Social Democratic Party, continued to defend an alliance with Russia and, above all, refrained from attacking Russian foreign policy from the Reichstag rostrum. The support of the treaty among Social Democrats was particularly strong in the party's Left wing and among the Austro-Marxists (see, for example, the *Leipziger Volkszeitung,* January 1, 1927; the *Wiener Arbeiterzeitung,* December 24, 1926).

During the negotiations that led to the signing of the Versailles Treaty, German officers, looking around for a way out of the impasse, had begun to think of coöperating with the rising power to the East against the Entente. Some time around the date of the treaty, June 1919, the first tentative contacts between the two armies started; from 1921 on, they were solid and continuous. It was the political brains of the Reichswehr that paved the way to the momentous Rapallo Treaty, in April 1922. There were many voices in the General Staff calling for an alliance with Soviet Russia, among whom the most important were those of Generals von Schleicher and von Hammerstein, General von Seeckt, the creator of the new army, Colonel von Nikolai, a military espionage expert. These officers and others made frequent trips to Russia, official and unofficial, participated in Red Army maneuvers, built up close contacts with members of the Russian General Staff. The German officers were fascinated by the new Soviet army, envious of its rapid revival and growth.

In March 1921, after the suppression of the Kronstadt uprising, the Russian General Staff sent Karl Radek to Berlin with a secret proposal. This was in line with the general political line that Radek was to help propagate over the next years: that the European revolution had stagnated, and that Russia, the young workers' state, and Germany, the industrial colony of Anglo-America, could save themselves from destruction only by combining into a vast Eurasian power to crush the imperialistic West. This theory he discussed in ever less discreet terms, but the precise terms of the military plan by which it was to be implemented remained for the ears of the Reichswehr officers. The German army was offered Russian assistance in building up its armament, contrary to the provisions of Versailles, by establishing arsenals on Russian soil.

These proposals developed over the next three or four years into concrete collaboration.[11] The Junkers firm built factories at Fili, Samara,

---

[11] Among other sources for this information, the following should be mentioned: German pacifist groups, particularly the Deutsche Friedensgesellschaft, the Neues Vaterland league, and Carl von Ossietzky's *Die Weltbühne;* and the two Paris newspapers, *La Liberté* and *Echo de Paris.*

Part of the story came out in a rather curious way. The Junkers firm had contracted with the Reichswehr to build military installations in Russia, and a contingent of officers was assigned to the company to direct the work. Later the army refused to pay the costs, and since all arrangements had been made in secret the

and Saratov, and an airfield in the Tambov region. The Hugo Stolzenberg Company constructed a plant to produce Bersol, an explosive salt, and Phosgen and Lost, two types of poison gas. Reichswehr Major Lohmann tested submarines in the Baltic and the Black Sea. German officers were sent to Russia to conduct training courses for experts in chemical warfare and for pilots.

In 1921, the Reichswehr Ministry founded the Society for the Advancement of Industrial Enterprises, the so-called GEFU (*Gesellschaft zur Förderung Gewerblicher Unternehmungen*). Its credit was well supported, particularly by the Dresden and Darmstadt banks. Its chairman was General Karl von Borries, formerly commander of the army corps at Metz, later a member of the history commission of the Reich Archive. In the spring of 1925, responding to wide public clamor, the Reichswehr Ministry disbanded the GEFU but immediately set up in its place the WIKO (*Wirtschaftskontor*) to perform the same function. The bank account was transferred to a private name and administered by a Colonel Senftleben.

The desks of German trusts were overflowing with Russian projects in these years. The beet sugar industry of the Ukraine was to be enlarged with German capital. The Stinnes group had a plan to increase the production of the Don coal mines. Krupp got one concession to the oil of the Caucasus, but wanted more. There was a plan to settle, as a first installment, 25,000 Germans in the Ukraine. For a period these plans filled the air, and then they dissipated, leaving but few results behind.

Late in 1926, three German-owned ships—the *Gothenburg, Artushoff,* and *Kolberg*—arrived at Stettin from Russia with a cargo of

---

company could not present its contract to a court and sue. It issued a detailed memorandum on the matter to each of the Reichstag deputies; possibly it also sent a copy of this memorandum abroad, for in December 1926 the *Manchester Guardian* published a sensational series on German rearmament in Russia. (A. P. Rosengoltz confessed in the 1938 Moscow trial that in 1926 he had given "information concerning the foreign policy of the USSR" to Farbman, an English journalist. Cf. *Report of Court Proceedings in the Case of the Anti-Soviet "Bloc of Rights and Trotskyites,"* Moscow, 1938, p. 261.)

Ossietzky was imprisoned under the Weimar Republic, on November 23, 1931. By a secret oral decision of the Reich court, his publication of the details of collaboration between the German and Russian armies, even after these had been discussed in the Reichstag committees, was adjudged high treason. The Nazis found him in prison when they came to power and put him in a camp. There he received the Nobel Prize and later died.

grenades for the Reichswehr. The longshoremen who unloaded them were paid a special bonus for their silence, and during the period of their work were confined to the dock area. Some Social Democrats among them, however, contacted Franz Künstler, a Social Democratic Reichstag deputy and at that time chairman of the party's Berlin organization.[12] This news was a double-barreled weapon for the Social Democrats, to be turned against both the hated Reichswehr and the Communists; Künstler, a former Independent Socialist and a convinced pacifist, carefully recorded all the witnesses' reports. He was also able to gather evidence concerning the poison-gas factory in Troitsk, Samara; the permits of German workers who had been sent there were photographed.

In the Reichstag session of December 17, Scheidemann poured his contempt over the Communists. From now on, he said, when they were killed by the Reichswehr, they would have the pleasure of knowing that it was done with Soviet grenades. The Social Democratic *Vorwärts* and the Democratic *Berliner Tageblatt* gave wide publicity to the incidents. The demand of the Social Democratic Party for a parliamentary investigation, however, never came to fruition, for the Reichswehr was powerful enough to suppress it.

This publicity had less effect among German workers than might have been expected, for millions of them, even those not organized in the Communist Party, had been conditioned not to believe anything in the Social Democratic press against Soviet Russia. The *Rote Fahne* was able to becloud the issue by exposing again the collaboration of Ebert and Noske with the German General Staff, by tying the present issues to the long, bitter controversy between the parties in the civil-war period. It was for this reason, rather than because of any special intrinsic merit, that the publications of the dissident communist groups assumed such importance. These were three in particular: the *Kommunistische Arbeiter Zeitung* ("Communist Workers' Gazette"), organ of the 1920 split; the *Kommunistische Politik* ("Communist Policy"), organ of the 1925 split; and *Fahne des Kommunismus*

---

[12] Künstler was killed by the Gestapo in Berlin during 1943. See *Sowjetgranaten,* issued by the Executive of the Social Democratic Party (Berlin, 1927); the full text of the pamphlet is given as an appendix to Cecil F. Melville, *The Russian Face of Germany* (London, 1932), p. 177 ff.

("Banner of Communism"), organ of the 1926 split. It is amazing how much invective was applied against these oppositionist journals, none of which had a large circulation. The gamut of abuse ran from the standard "traitors to the socialist fatherland" to the favorite in this period, "agents of Chamberlain and Pilsudski." Ernst Schwarz, a man without stature and quite unimportant in himself, became the principal target of Moscow's counter propaganda.

Any discussion of the Reichswehr's attempts to circumvent the Versailles prohibitions was regarded as high treason. German pacifists or socialists who attacked this secret rearmament were labeled traitors to the fatherland and threatened with judicial proceedings. For the German Communist there was also high treason against the Workers' Fatherland, the home of socialism, to be considered. The Communist rank and file distrusted Radek; in spite of every precaution, some news of his secret missions to the German military leaked out. Many workers, Communist and non-Communist, demanded of the German Central Committee whether these rumors were true. I went to see Manuilsky and asked for information; he advised me to speak to Zinoviev and Pyatnitsky. In December 1926 I was called to Moscow to appear before an international control committee headed by Kuusinen, which was assigned to review my expulsion from the party.[13] There I got nothing but smooth denials; the mere mention of contacts between the two armies was met with irritability and hostility. Interference, or even curiosity, from European Communists concerning this secret sector of Soviet diplomacy was "anti-Bolshevist."

After my return to Berlin, I spoke at public meetings in opposition to the Russian-German military alliance, and the Russian Politburo answered with an article in *Pravda,* later reprinted in *Inprekorr,* entitled "From Ruth Fischer to Chamberlain." By forming an amalgam of Schwarz with Chamberlain, it sought to divert the issue from the military alliance to a fight against "world reaction."[14]

---

[13] For details, see pp. 571–572, *infra.*

[14] ". . . Schwarz's arguments are pitiful. They do not stand up under a critical analysis and correspond to the miserable and disgusting role that Schwarz has played. For Schwarz, among others, the fact that Soviet Russia could have supported the Germany of Cuno during the Ruhr occupation is evidence that Soviet Russia is an 'imperialist country' and that the general Comintern line is treachery to the proletariat. That is, however, a case in itself. In order to liberate the proletariat, a socialist republic must support even bourgeois countries if they

Thus the military alliance was under simultaneous attack from three sides—Left communist, Social Democratic, and pacifist-liberal. Large sections of German public opinion were subjected to an exposure of the details of this alliance between the socialist fatherland and Prussian militarism. For several weeks, the German Communist Party conducted meetings to fight the Soviet grenade "forgery," but without success. The facts could not be denied, and the knowledge of these facts penetrated deep into the hearts of German Communists, disintegrating still further the international solidarity of the early period. In Communist dogma, the whole affair was labeled anathema—in the words of Thälmann, "one of the dirtiest and most subtle methods of anti-Bolshevism" [15]—and thus disposed of, for the faithful.

The effects of these exposures were fought with expulsions, with shouting down the opposition, with demagogy. But resistance to this policy was so strong, even in the Thälmann Central Committee, that Stalin himself intervened at a meeting of the Comintern Executive Committee to defend "Left" Communism. Stalin's followers, who had defended the pact in veiled terms as "a necessary swing to the Right" had to be corrected; a Right policy, Stalin said in a closed session, is always to some degree a betrayal of the working class. This indirect reference to the pact was understood for what it was: a command to forget the matter and be silent. Thus, an official discussion in the Comintern was prohibited.

Stalin's attempt to counteract the effect of the German-Russian alliance among German workers by posing as more revolutionary than the revolutionaries is to be seen even more clearly in an attack at the same meeting on a German Left memorandum. This statement, edited by Maslow, demanded that each national proletariat follow "a consistent policy in fighting for the overthrow of its own bourgeoisie, even

---

have been crushed by the military force of imperialist robbers . . . Of course, Junkers has built factories here. Who does not know that Junkers is an aircraft factory?—of course it builds aircraft. But whoever pretends that this constitutes cooperation with the German army betrays the interests of Soviet Russia and, with it, of the proletariat . . . Schwarz forms a bloc with Chamberlain, with the intriguers of the British Foreign Office, with that senile chief among traitors, Kautsky, with the Russian White Guardists, with the followers of Pilsudski, with the Lithuanian gendarmes and secret police . . . Every simple worker must understand that Schwarz commits abject treason, that he is a monstrous traitor." (*Inprekorr*, 1927, p. 63.)

[15] *Parteitagsbericht*, Essen convention, 1927, p. 49.

if this bourgeoisie was friendly with Soviet Russia." To attack Maslow's memorandum as anti-Bolshevist was no longer enough; Heinz Neumann, the delegate of the German party, got a specific directive from Stalin to attack it from the Left and not from the Right. Neumann complied and characterized Maslow's memorandum as "social patriotic" and "counter-revolutionary." Ever since Lenin had invented the term, social patriotism meant national unity between bourgeoisie and working class, the precise opposite of "a consistent policy in fighting for the overthrow of its own bourgeoisie."

In a long speech before the committee concerned with German affairs, Stalin dealt extensively with the various German oppositionist groups. By his amazing display of details and his often accurate characterization of the leaders, he succeeded in aggravating the centrifugal tendency among them. Amadeo Bordiga, representative of the Italian party, an excellent militant but abstract in his criticism, was called a confused but honest man. The leaders of small splinter groups were flattered by the attention and by the fact that they were criticized as erring sons, who would soon be back in the fold of the family. The Ultra-Lefts—Korsch, Schwarz, and Maslow-Fischer—were designated as especially dangerous because of their anti-Bolshevism. Thus, after they had been expelled as well as while they were in the party, the various oppositionist groups were hindered from coming together on the basis of their common resistance to Stalinist policy. Within the party the dangerous subject of collusion between Russian Communists and German militarism was dropped, and no one risked raising it again.

In Berlin, one of the outspoken sponsors of German-Russian military collaboration at this time was Reichswehr Minister Otto Gessler. In public he of course denied every charge that there had indeed been such collaboration, but in the restricted circle of the Reichstag Foreign Affairs Committee, of which I was a member, he defended every measure as necessary for the defense of the fatherland. At the committee's meetings, Gessler lost his inhibitions and expanded freely, particularly on his favorite theme, the Polish danger. Against the Poles all nuances of German nationalism were united; even those nationalists who rejected any compromise with Bolshevism on domestic issues recognized the worth of Gessler's argument that against the new Polish state, against this French stronghold in Eastern Europe, German interest could be best served by a German-Russian alliance.

Communists had a special status in the Committee for Foreign Affairs. In the plenum and in almost every other Reichstag committee, Communists were treated as enemies of the state—the permanent irreconcilable opposition to domestic policy. In this committee, however, the same Communists were confidential agents of a friendly power, reliable enough to be informed of plans the details of which were withheld from other groups of the parliament. Much of the information on this ultra-secret matter was given the committee members informally, even casually. Gessler and the group of officers with whom he usually attended committee sessions would discuss, for example, the results of one of the trips that hundreds of German officers were making to Russia. Some went under false names; sometimes, in the case of more important missions, they were formally dismissed from the service and pensioned and then, after their assignments had been completed, reintegrated into the army.

Gessler, a jovial Southern German, often used the disparity between the German Communist Party and the Russian state to push his point home. All this quarreling between German Communists and other Reichstag groups, he would say, has become completely senseless. We officers have such good relations with Moscow that you Communists have become superfluous, the fossil remains of the civil-war period. We are impressed with the cleverness of these Russian politicians, and we will align ourselves with them to build up a powerful Russian-German military organization. This is the basis of real Soviet policy in Germany, and at the appropriate moment Moscow will shut up its Communist shop here.

At a session of the Foreign Affairs Committee on February 24, 1927, Gessler was tightly cornered, and in reply to the questions fired at him was compelled to give some important information. At that time the Communist representatives on the committee were Ernst Torgler (later a defendant in the Reichstag-fire trial) and August Creutzburg. (With my expulsion from the party, I had lost my place on the committee, though I remained a Reichstag deputy till May 1928.) The collaboration between the two armies, Gessler stated, had begun on the initiative of the Russians. After the Russian-Polish war of 1920, the Soviet government had approached Germany for assistance in reorganizing the Red Army, and this offer, since it gave Germany an opportunity to rearm secretly and coöperate in military research, had been accepted. According to Scheidemann's estimate, some 250 million marks, a third of the Reichswehr annual budget, had been spent in Russia in the last quarter of 1926 alone. In view, however, of the effect the disclosure of this secret armament would have on Germany's relation with the West, Gessler promised under strong pressure that this coöperation with Russia would come to an end.

Immediately after the committee meeting, I spoke to Torgler, who had not changed his friendly attitude toward the Left Opposition. He was tremendously impressed with Gessler's testimony. The Soviet government betrays us directly to the Reichswehr, he said; if our rank and file ever learned of these facts, there would be a mass exodus from the party. I proposed that he quit the party and support our effort to build an independent German communist organization by revealing the content of Gessler's testimony. Torgler agreed with me in principle, but tactically he thought it wiser to remain in the party.

Military coöperation between the two countries did not end after Gessler's statement; in 1927–1928 the number of officers sent to Russia was increased. In 1928, there were at least eight hundred men assigned by the Reichswehr Ministry to work with the Red Army. These permanent delegates of the German army were intimately involved in the training program, particularly the training of pilots and artillery and chemical-warfare officers. Eminent German physicists and chemists, Dr. Fritz Haber among them, went to Russia and coöperated in organizing, for example, the Moscow Institute for Chemical Warfare. In Leningrad, Perm, Sverdlovsk, and the Ukraine, munition plants were set up and run with expert German assistance.

In August 1928 General von Blomberg went to Moscow at the head of a group of high officers. A year later Freiherr von Hammerstein, a close intimate of General von Schleicher, went to Russia accompanied by Colonel Kühlenthal. Colonel Heim was there in 1929. General von Seeckt, one of the heads of this secret German-Russian military organization, was especially active in it after he left the Reichswehr Ministry in 1926. One of the important contacts with Seeckt was Valeriu Marcu, a German writer of Rumanian origin, who had quit the German party in 1921 with Paul Levi. He remained in contact with Moscow circles and later transmitted by word of mouth many messages too dangerous to put on paper.[16]

Over a long period, one of the contacts between the two armies was Ritter Dr. Oskar von Niedermayer, lieutenant colonel in the Reichswehr Ministry until 1936. He instructed hundreds of the German officers sent to Russia. He was very friendly with Tukhachevsky and until 1934 regularly spent his vacations in Russia; after the Röhm purge of the Nazi Party, he was afraid to continue these trips but continued to send his wife to Russia to maintain his contacts there. In 1916, Niedermayer had been the chief of a military mission to Afghanistan, exploring the possibilities of a land attack on India from German bases in Turkey and Mesopotamia.[17] He is the author of an excellent book on Afghanistan and of another on the Soviet Union; the latter, published in 1934 in collaboration with the Russian writer Semyonov, was intended to present the enormous geopolitical and economic potential of Russia to German readers.[18]

The continued collaboration between the two armies has remained one of the best kept secrets of contemporary history. In this relationship, however, we must seek the basic explanation of many factors of both Stalinism and Nazism. At various decisive points in the history of the two dictatorships, the armies strove to reach a common policy: The Politburo tried during the short chancellorship of Schleicher, December 1932–January 1933, to find a working arrangement between him and the Communist Party. After Hitler came to power, Stalin tried incessantly via army channels to get an alliance with Nazi Germany, a policy that reached its fruition finally in August 1939. When this alliance broke down in 1941 with the German invasion of Russia, it was revamped in 1943 with the creation of the Free Germany Committee and, despite the many complicating factors that disguise its essential character, in the Generals' Revolt of July 20, 1944.

---

[16] Marcu broke with the Russian Party completely after 1933; he died in New York, a convinced anti-Stalinist.

[17] Cf. [W. Griesinger], *German Intrigues in Persia: The Diary of a German Agent. The Niedermayer Expedition through Persia to Afghanistan and India* (London, 1918).

[18] Oskar von Niedermayer and Juri Semjonow, *Sowjet-Russland, eine geopolitische Problemstellung*, with an introduction by Karl Haushofer (Berlin, 1934).

Chapter 25 · Trotsky and Zinoviev Form a Bloc · · · · · · · ·

At the Fourteenth Party Congress, December 1925, Stalin had won a battle but not the war. Among the men elected there to the new Central Committee were Stalin and his supporters, but also the leaders of actual and potential oppositions. There were not only Bukharin, Rykov, and Tomsky, whom Stalin regarded—rightly as events later proved—as insecure and only temporary allies, but also Trotsky, Zinoviev, Kamenev and Sokolnikov, who were still formidable opponents. Trotsky was still the key figure for the outcome of the struggle, both at the convention and after. Both Stalin and Zinoviev-Kamenev watched his every move and tried to determine its direction.

Stalin maneuvered to increase the advantage the convention had given him by further weakening Zinoviev and his followers. In the election to the new Politburo on January 2, 1926, Sokolnikov was ousted and Kamenev was demoted to the position of candidate. Two weeks later, Sokolnikov lost his post as Commissar of Finance and Kamenev was relieved as vice-premier of the People's Council of Commissars. Zinoviev was replaced by Komarov as head of the Leningrad soviet, and Kamenev by Ukhanov as chairman of the soviet of Moscow. Both Komarov and Ukhanov were metal workers, and Stalin seized the opportunity to boast that the lord mayors of Russia's two metropolises were steel workers. Would that London and Paris, he said, would follow their example! [1]

This little speech is indicative of the role in the Party that Stalin

---

[1] *Inprekorr,* 1926, p. 2803.

played in this period—the leader of the proletariat against the intellectuals and bureaucrats. Not even the leader, for in those days he spoke of "the leaders" in the third person. He made a virtue of his shortcomings—his lack of intellectual or oratorical brilliancy. In this respect, he was the prototype of the mass leaders of the following totalitarian period, who boasted of their plebeian origin, their simple living habits, and often even their lack of intellectual sophistication. Stalin was one responsible Party worker among others—direct, uncomplicated, even crude and brutal if necessary; and this anti-intellectual appeal found a wide response among the middle strata of the Party. By vulgarizing the Marxist tenet that the proletariat could, by its class position in society, arrive at a correct political position almost intuitively, Stalin in fact nullified Lenin's refinement of just this aspect of Marx's doctrine. A party elite is necessary, Lenin had emphasized, in order by its scientific analysis to crystallize the spontaneous reactions of the workers into political theory and political action. Stalin's direct appeal to proletarian instincts, begun in the 1923 fight against Trotsky, was continued and amplified into a new manipulatory device which developed to its full flower during the dekulakization period of 1928–1929.[2]

To substantiate this proletarian pose, Stalin was particularly concerned with breaking the Opposition in Leningrad, the center of the proletarian elite of the Party. While the Fourteenth Congress was still in session, before the election of the new Central Committee, before it was formally assured that Stalin had a majority of the Party behind him, Stalin sent his agents to Leningrad. "Comrades Molotov, Kirov, Voroshilov, Kalinin, Andreyev, and others," Stalin writes, "were sent to Leningrad to explain to the members of the Leningrad Party organization the criminal, anti-Bolshevik nature of the stand taken up at the congress by the Leningrad delegation."[3] Accompanied by a strong

---

[2] The new leaders of the Comintern parties, such as William Z. Foster, Maurice Thorez, and Ernst Thälmann, were also simple sons of ordinary workers. Not only they but Stalin's competitors in Europe in transition as well, Mussolini and Hitler, were compelled to imitate this attitude of their model; this appeal to the vanity of the unprocessed raw material of society has been made in every modern dictatorship. The most clear-cut example is in Argentina, where Perón has built a power monopoly resting on his shrewd manipulation of *los descamisados,* the shirtless, against the middle layers of Argentine society.

[3] [Joseph Stalin], *History of the CPSU,* p. 278.

GPU contingent, these plenipotentiaries met an excited and aroused Party membership. The Leningrad branch, they explained, had unknowingly elected un-Soviet and un-Bolshevik delegates, elected them under the "false pretenses" that they were Bolsheviks. "You have been betrayed by your leaders," Stalin's messengers told the Leningrad Party. The acceptable reply was, "Yes, Comrade, I confess I was betrayed. I did not realize that in voting for Zinoviev I was voting for an anti-Bolshevik." This answer brought not only grace but an immediate place in the reorganized branch, a promise of a promotion.

The Opposition, however, continued the fight in Leningrad. According to Party ritual, all the decisions of the congress, including the condemnation of Zinoviev, had to be endorsed by the Leningrad branch, but the Stalinists could not be sure whether or not this endorsement was merely verbal, given for the sake of gaining time. It was a delicate operation, for each oppositionist won over, to some extent a doubtful acquisition in any case, had to be cut from the Leningrad organization carefully, so that those remaining would still be amenable to further wooing. After some weeks, Stalin's delegation returned to Moscow, leaving behind as his new whip Sergei Kirov, who became a most important figure in the development of Party terror.

Sergei M. Kirov, a member of the Party since 1904, had been elected to the Central Committee in 1922, the year that Stalin began to attract men in the middle stratum of the Party to him. He had gone as a delegate to the Fourteenth Congress without definite commitment to either faction; Stalin maneuvered behind the scenes and was able to win him over to the majority. He got his reward almost immediately; after the convention, he replaced Zinoviev as secretary of the Leningrad branch. Sent in from the outside, the representative of the Central Committee began his task of regrouping the branch surrounded by hatred and disgust.

The Opposition was especially strong among the youth.

> Immediately following the congress, Zinoviev called a meeting of the Leningrad Provincial Committee of the Young Communist League, the leading group of which had been reared by Zinoviev, Zalutsky, Bakayev, Yevdokimov, Kuklin, Safarov, and other double-dealers in a spirit of hatred of the Leninist Central Committee of the Party. At this meeting, the Leningrad Provin-

cial Committee passed a resolution unparalleled in the history of
the Young Communist League: it refused to abide by the decisions of the Fourteenth Party Congress.[4]

Moving cautiously at first, Kirov implanted Stalin's rule. The Leningrad workers, inhabitants of the most Western-minded of Russia's
cities, did not react well; each wave of terror succeeded only in driving
the Opposition underground and increasing its stubborn resistance.
When in December 1934 the GPU wanted a fuse to explode the mass
purge of the Party, it arranged to have Kirov killed, setting off the
show trials of the middle thirties and threatening, by this choice, the
people of Leningrad first of all. The choice of Leningrad as the site
of Stalin's Reichstag fire illustrates the connection between the semi-
legal opposition of the twenties and its conspiratorial continuation in
the thirties.[5]

In the period following the Fourteenth Congress, then, Stalin concentrated on removing the members of the Leningrad Opposition from
posts of power. Leaders of the other oppositionist groups were wooed.
Alexandra Kollontai, representative of the Workers' Opposition, for
example, had been sent to the Oslo embassy, thus at once separating
her from her friends and flattering her. In particular, Stalin made it
clear to Trotsky that the fight during the two years past had not
obviated the possibility of a new combination. Trotsky maintained his
position on the new Politburo, and he was later appointed chairman
of the Scientific and Technical Collegium. This was a gesture, but not

---

[4] [Joseph Stalin], *History of the CPSU*, p. 278.

[5] The GPU tool, the man who killed Kirov, was Nikolayev, who was designated a member of the Zinovievist Leningrad Opposition. The men arrested as
his co-plotters were Zinoviev, Kamenev, Zalutsky, Yevdokimov, Feodorov, Safarov,
Kuklin, Bakayev, Sharov, Faivilovich, Vardin, Gorchenin, Bulak, Gertik, and Kostina;
the reader should compare this list with the one from Stalin's history on page 539.
(Cf. Trotsky, *The Kirov Assassination*, Pioneer Publishers, New York, 1935.)

All these Zinovievists, whom Stalin denounced in 1926, were taken back into
the Party and formed a new nucleus of opposition. In 1935, they were tried in
connection with Kirov's murder and sentenced to various prison terms. In 1936,
the same group was taken from prison and tried a second time on the same charges;
this time they were executed.

That the GPU was implicated in the Kirov affair has now been established.
Twelve agents of Russia's secret police, headed by F. D. Medved, chief of the Leningrad unit, were charged with negligence in the case. One of the principal insiders
in the Kirov provocation was GPU chief H. G. Yagoda, who was himself sentenced
to death in the 1938 trial.

an empty one; it was intended to hamper the formation of a bloc between Trotsky and Zinoviev.

A few weeks later, Trotsky was given even more favorable treatment: he got permission to go to Germany to consult with Berlin specialists.

> Moscow physicians . . . had been urging me for some time to take a trip abroad . . . The matter . . . was taken up at the Politburo, which . . . left the final decision to me. The statement was accompanied by a note of reference from the GPU indicating the inadmissibility of my trip . . .
>
> Arrangements with the German embassy were completed without difficulty [the Berlin Treaty was being negotiated during these weeks] and about the middle of April [1926] my wife and I left with a diplomatic passport in the name of Kuzmyenko . . . We were accompanied by my secretary, Syermuks, by the former commander of my train, and by a representative of the GPU.[6]

Thus, as with Kollontai, Stalin removed Trotsky from contact with his supporters and at the same time made him a gesture of compromise. There was no substantial danger of Trotsky's influencing any group in the German party, for at this time he had no base there. The Thälmann leadership was thoroughly hostile. Brandler and his followers were too cautious to side with him; they hoped to be restored to the leadership of the party by Stalin. Maslow was in prison and I in Moscow, and in any case the German Left had been enveloped in the 1923 labyrinth of anti-Trotskyist scholasticism.

Stalin's cautious conciliatory approaches had some slight effect. There were "many" among his supporters, Trotsky says, who opposed a bloc with Zinoviev and Kamenev. "There were even some, though only a few, who thought it possible to form a bloc with Stalin against Zinoviev and Kamenev."[7]

Talks with Bukharin and Zinoviev

I was still in forced residence in Moscow during this period, but I could nevertheless participate in the last above-ground fight against the rising totalitarianism of Stalin's Secretariat. The Hotel Lux, on Tverskaya Street, the domicile of foreign Comintern representatives in

---

[6] Trotsky, *My Life*, pp. 522–523.
[7] *Ibid.*, p. 521.

Moscow, was a peculiar place. Formerly a merchants' hotel, decorated and furnished in the rococo style of the nineties, it was well kept but overrun with bad plumbing and undefeatable bedbugs and rats. Rat-hunting was a favorite pastime of the German Communists there, who had the German notion that, if attacked with perseverance, the rats could be exterminated.

The Lux was very unpopular among the workers of Moscow. Comintern delegates led a life apart from the Russian people. The foreigners had many privileges and prerogatives; their living standard was much higher than that of even the average Russian Party functionary. The hotel was under strict GPU control. Every employee from the door-man up, as well as some of the foreign guests, was on its staff, and through this GPU cordon no Russian could enter the building without a special permit. Some of these GPU agents were known—for example, Heimo, Kuusinen's secretary—but usually there was only a suspicion, which spread from one room to another and poisoned the atmosphere. I frequently visited the several German families living at the Lux—families of men who had been forced to leave Germany because of their Communist activity; and they all told me of the constant GPU sur-veillance. In the factories where their friends worked, in their party cells, in the hotel, among their comrades, there were GPU agents. Just because of my high rank in the Comintern, they warned me, I would not escape this GPU control; every step I took would be carefully ob-served and reported.

Stalin approached me constantly, always making new offers. I cite one of them here, as an example of the type of corruption to which Comintern leaders were subjected. I had reinforced my constantly iterated request for permission to leave Russia by the argument that my father was seriously ill and wanted to see me. Instead of being allowed to go, I was offered the opportunity to bring my whole family, including my young son, who needed my care, to Russia at state expense. My father, though he was not in any sense a Marxist, would be able to substitute for the modest circumstances in which he lived in Vienna a position in a Russian university.[8] Palmiro Ercoli-Togliatti,

---

[8] Rudolf Eisler died on December 13, 1926. He was the author of the *Wörter-buch der philosophischen Begriffe und Ausdrücke* and many other works on phi-losophy and sociology.

who wavered long between Stalin and the Opposition, got a similar offer, and accepted it. The whole of his numerous family was moved to Russia, where he arranged that they live in material comfort—and where they remain as hostages to guarantee his close adherence to the Stalinist line forever more.

Early in February 1926, just before the ECCI plenum, Stalin invited me to the building of the Central Committee for a personal interview. As a translator we had Petrovsky, with whom I had journeyed to London in 1924. This time Stalin did not beat about the bush; he did not repeat his ridiculous questions about women's organizations in Germany. In a cold and brutally frank discussion on the situation in Russia and the Comintern, Stalin revealed an iron will to "reorganize" the Russian Party and the international against any opposition whatever. In this two-hour personal conversation he did not make the kind of crude offer I have described; that sort of thing he left to his subordinates. He promised me his full support in Germany if I withdrew from Zinoviev. I would return to Germany with the approval of the Russian Politburo, carrying a letter to Thälmann instructing him to end the slander campaign against me; I would participate again in the direction of the German party. With the bloc in formation between Trotsky and Zinoviev, Stalin was willing to pay a good price to deprive it of a German following.

In spite of his adherence to Stalin's caucus, my relations with Bukharin were good. Of all the great Russian Communist figures after Lenin's death, he was one of the most human and lovable. He lived not in the Kremlin but in two rooms in a Moscow hotel, with his invalided agreeable companion, who never participated in Party disputes. He was everywhere in Moscow, in the universities, at youth meetings. When I talked with him he tried to win me over to his cause, which was already visibly different from Stalin's concept. He wanted a temperate policy; he did not want to go to extremes, either with the oppositionists or, more generally, with the peasantry. Our country is so terribly poor, he told me one evening; our peasants work inefficiently, with primitive tools. We have no rich peasants in the Western sense of the word; our kulaks cannot be compared with the rich peasant of Germany or France or the farmer of America. Everyone who owns two horses and some agricultural machinery has been dubbed a kulak. It will take years to transform this peasant economy into a modern agriculture. The Party monopoly is not threatened if a few of these kulaks get rich; we hold the key posts, and we can maintain control through them. An enforced collectivization would change the whole character of our regime; it would be disastrous in its consequences. The correct policy for the peasantry is to raise Russian agriculture to a higher level through a network of state-assisted coöperatives.

As a member of the Comintern Presidium whose return to favor was still possible, I was treated with a certain consideration. I was given a *propusk,* a permanent permit to enter the Kremlin, and I could circulate in Moscow pretty much as I pleased. After the Fourteenth Congress, however, my conversations with the various Russian leaders had to take on a certain conspiratorial color. When I went to the Kremlin to talk with Zinoviev, for example, I entered the gate on some pretext and then went to a side door of the Comintern Chairman's office, where I was admitted by Zinoviev himself. The advantage of this was not that I was not observed, for I was, but that the observation was unofficial; if I had entered through the front door and been registered by the guards, Zinoviev would have been required to report my visit.

In this manner, I saw Zinoviev a few days after the Fourteenth Congress adjourned, and we had a discussion, the first one uncomplicated by Bolshevik rhetoric, on the new situation created by the defeat of the Leningrad Opposition. While not discouraged, he was much concerned by the size of the majority, for he had hoped for stronger support among the provincial branches. In his estimation, there was real danger. Uninhibited by Comintern discipline, he spoke to me frankly and for the first time gave me his view of Stalin, whom he characterized as the spearhead of the Thermidor, the leader of a counter-revolutionary resurrection. Stalin, he said, is still far from having won a definitive victory. We have a good chance of beating him. If we do not recoup our forces, however, if we do not reverse the trend, then this will be the first link of a chain leading either back to capitalism or to Bonapartism. The final result will be White terror in Russia and in Europe.

This language shook me profoundly. During the past months, cut off from the German party and not daring to discuss matters too freely in Moscow, I had developed a similar feeling toward the new situation. I was particularly impressed by Zinoviev's sudden change of attitude; gone were all talk of Bolshevik discipline, all dialectic oratory. Despite my criticism of certain of its practical applications, I had lived in the past years with the myth of the infallibility of Bolshevik discipline, and in these months I found the myth disappearing. Faced by Stalin's realism, by his single-minded drive for monolithic power, Zinoviev and I with him were forced to shed the baggage of obsolete shibboleths and prepare ourselves for a new fight.

In our semi-clandestine meetings, Zinoviev not only communicated to me the secret Politburo reports, which were specially translated by one of his trusted secretaries, but enriched them in long conversations. I learned more about the complicated problems of the Russian situation than I had by reading the collected works of Lenin. Soon after Lenin's death, as early as the fall of 1924, Zinoviev and his friends had begun to ask themselves whether Stalin would ruthlessly attempt to change the Party into an instrument of power for his group. They did not interpret this transformation merely in terms of Stalin's ambition or his particularly sinister character. His drive for power was one aspect of the general backsliding of the proletarian revolution in Russia and in Europe, which would lead eventually to counter-revolutionary forms of government and state power throughout the Continent. Stalin's attempt to get all the key posts into the hands of his group was analyzed as a form of fascistoid reaction to the October revolution. The Party cadres were not hopelessly degenerated, Zinoviev emphasized; the main task was to encourage them to regroup themselves and to fight against the Stalin clique. This regrouping could gain sufficient momentum to cut the Bonapartist adventure at its root.

When we discussed an alliance with Trotsky, Zinoviev often repeated that he sincerely regretted his fight against Trotsky in 1923; this serious error had enabled Stalin to win the first round. However, he never blurred the political differences continuing between him and Trotsky. Zinoviev was in the process of revising his belief in "iron Bolshevik unanimity" as a guiding principle for a State Party. In discussing the question of party organization, he said, we must differentiate the task of the Communists before and after the seizure of power. Continuing the conspiratorial methods necessary in the fight for state power, maintaining iron unanimity in a million-man State Party, can result only in disastrous degeneration and a change of the social character of our movement. We must find a type of organization in which all tendencies of revolutionary socialism can find enough air to exist. Much larger political differences than those between Trotsky and our group, whether in the past or those that may develop in the future, must be able to exist side by side within the framework of Soviet and Party legality. If we are not able to unfold many facets of Communist thought and of Communist action, we are lost.

Zinoviev discussed which of the different types of Soviet democracy should be made legal: factions inside the Bolshevik Party, the later admission of the Mensheviks and a peasant party into the soviets. This subject of the relation of the State Party to other parties, however, was never thoroughly thrashed out among the oppositionist leaders themselves. It was assumed that once the Stalin group had been removed from the monopoly of power, the new regime in the Party would be able to maintain itself only by appealing to those elements who wanted wide extension of Soviet democracy. The oppositionists were afraid, on the other hand, to support the demand for other Soviet parties, for this was the Stalinist rallying point against them. Substantial groups in the Party who agreed with their general policy and their fight against Stalin's power would never accept such far-reaching changes in the organizational set-up. The Zinoviev group differed from the Workers' Opposition mainly in this point: whether to demand that several workers' parties be legalized immediately, or to fight first for power in the State Party and apply this principle later. Trotsky needed years of exile and Hitler's coming to power before he dissociated himself from the tenet of a State Party monopoly, and he was killed before he had clarified this point.

With these frank discussions in his office, I came to know Zinoviev very well during this stay in Moscow. The Stalinist campaign of vilification has so covered his name that little of the real man is known abroad. Born in a petty bourgeois Jewish family in the Southern Ukraine, Gregory Y. Zinoviev had been a member of the Bolshevik faction of the Russian Social Democratic Party from its formation in 1903. He was a product of the movement; his education was received, his personality was shaped, in his day-to-day underground struggle against Tsarism. During the years of reaction following the 1905 revolution, he shared Lenin's physical exile, devoting his entire energy abroad to working for the underground party in Russia. He was from the beginning Lenin's right-hand man; and from the beginning the vituperative polemics against Lenin's ideas were often directed at Zinoviev's person, as the weaker of the two. This role as the butt of all criticism was increasingly his after he became Chairman of the Comintern. Here he was made responsible for not only every weakness of every weak Communist party and for every defeat of each abortive revolution, but eventually for the failure of a secretary to get the job he wanted. The often-repeated allegation that Zinoviev had not sufficient stature to lead the Comintern is true, but true in the sense that, once the European revolution had subsided, the Moscow-dominated Comintern was an anachronism through which no man or group of men could "organize" world revolution. After 1923, Comintern headquarters should have been transferred to a European capital; Comintern life and Comintern policy should have been divorced from the Russian Party.

Under Zinoviev's cold demeanor, under the mask he had constructed through the years of personal attack, was hidden a very emotional personality. Like the socialist tribunes of the nineteenth century, Zinoviev had a messianic faith in the invisible force of the masses once set in motion. In this respect, he was one with Lenin and Trotsky and Bukharin, with the whole first generation of Russian Communists, who inculcated a new religion of internationalism. As a younger person, as a member of the next generation, I did not share the same indomitable faith in the invincibility of the masses; as I saw it, Zinoviev was feeding himself with illusions. This messianism was Zinoviev's weakness and his strength. When he was carried away by a sympathetic response, he was a brilliant revolutionary orator and had courage; when he met silence, he became "panicky." The crime for which he has been most reviled, that in 1917 he wanted a coalition with all the parties represented in the soviets, derived from the same character structure; he was afraid of cutting the Party from other workers' parties, of isolating it from the Russian masses.

In one of the meetings I have described, a few days after the Fourteenth Congress, Zinoviev reviewed with me the various possibilities of combating Stalin, and broached, almost timidly, an alliance with

Trotsky. This is, he said, a fight for state power. We need Trotsky, not only because without his brilliant brain and wide support we will not win state power, but because after we have won it we need a strong hand to guide Russia and the international back to a socialist road. Moreover, no one else can organize the army. Stalin has opposed us not with manifestos but with power, and he can be met only with greater power, not with manifestos. Lashevich is with us, and if Trotsky and we join together, we will win.

What we want, he continued, is not a coup but an awakening of the Party rank and file, and through them of the Russian and European working class, to the danger of the hour. (This is perhaps the surest measure of the historical worth of the Trotsky-Zinoviev bloc; other conspirators, those plotting against Hitler in 1944, for example, feared nothing more, not even the discovery of their plans by the dictator, than that the people as a whole would join them in overthrowing him.) The victim of the counter revolution would be the Russian working class. Behind the smoke screen of continued revolutionary phraseology, in the process of establishing socialism in one country, the rising Stalin hierarchy would eliminate the remnants of workers' power and open a campaign to exterminate the revolutionary generation. In this period, this threat cannot be overcome by Party methods alone. A majority in the Party has to be won over, but that majority has to be assured that the violent attempt to prevent it from taking power can be met, and overcome, by violence. Only an alliance of all the oppositionist forces can put through such a program.

Kamenev, he told me, had begun to negotiate with Trotsky and hoped soon to come to a definite arrangement. Zinoviev meanwhile had approached the leaders of the Democratic Centralism and other Workers' Opposition groups, and he was endeavoring to overcome their distrust, particularly of Trotsky. The anti-Stalin faction in Georgia had been contacted.

I went away from this conference and wrote a letter to Berlin to the effect that Zinoviev and Trotsky would form a bloc and that in my opinion the German Left should support it.

From more or less the same premises, Trotsky had reached the same conclusion: that Stalin had to be defeated, that only a bloc could defeat him. Trotsky, no less than Zinoviev, needed the help of the

other. During the 1923 fight, his supporters had been mainly in the
higher brackets of the state and army; inside the Party the Old Bolsheviks, even those who sided with him in one or another of the faction
fights, never regarded him as completely one of themselves. He was a
brilliant and effective statesman, a military leader of first quality, an
orator and writer unsurpassed in the Party, but not "a 100 per cent
Bolshivik." Trotsky had stepped from the outside into the Party and,
on the basis of his personal genius, into the top ranks of the Party.
He was a permanent member of the Politburo, but he was never the
head of a regional organization; he had enthusiastic admirers, but he
did not have enough organized support in the Party. Zinoviev, chairman of the Comintern, had also been head of the Leningrad organization; by a special car and the fastest train, he had commuted between
the two capitals, spending half the week in each. Kamenev, member
of the Politburo, had directed the Moscow branch. This kind of key
post within the Party delineated Party rank; Trotsky's silence during
1923–1925, in spite of the support a word from him would have received among broad circles of the army, the youth, the intellectuals,
in and out of the Party, was due in part to the fact that he lacked
comparable organized support in any of the provincial branches.

Trotsky's strong point was still the army. He had been removed as
People's Commissar for War in January 1925, but among the divisions
built up under his leadership during the civil war his enormous prestige was virtually intact. After Frunze died, or was killed, Stalin and
Zinoviev faced each other in the army in the persons of Voroshilov
and Lashevich, and this compromise between the two halves of the
Troika hampered both of them. The result was in part a maintenance
of the status quo, the dominance of Trotsky.[9]

Whatever his strength, however, at the beginning of 1926 Trotsky
was weaker than in 1923. The two-year campaign against Trotsky and
"Trotskyism" had not been without effect. His opponents had been
strengthened, the waverers had parted from him, and his supporters
were disgruntled and anxious because of his continued silence. An
offer of an alliance from Zinoviev-Kamenev, who though the weaker

---

[9] "In 1923–24, the Trotskyist opposition had a considerable number of supporters in the Party nuclei of the Red Army and of Soviet and higher educational
institutions." (N. Popov, *Outline History of the CPSU*, II, 273.)

half of the Troika and just roundly defeated at a Party convention were still Party leaders in full standing, was not to be put aside lightly. Together, a bloc formed of these with Trotsky could win a majority of the Party, or if not an arithmetic majority the support of the important industrial centers—Leningrad, Moscow, Baku, Kiev, Kharkov, Odessa. Even if Stalin maintained his majority in the provinces, he would be beaten by the urban weight of the bloc.

Several times in the months after the Fourteenth Congress, Trotsky, Zinoviev, and Kamenev met secretly to discuss the possibility of joining forces. The deep estrangement between Zinoviev and Trotsky had to be overcome; Zinoviev had been, after all, the chief propagandist against Trotsky. On a personal level, between the two men only, this could be done; the knowledge that each needed the other was daily reinforced by the mounting impetus of the Stalinist machine. During the time that Lenin had lain dying, Kamenev had reported his conversations with him to Trotsky, as well as to Zinoviev, and the friendship between Trotsky and Kamenev had to some extent survived the two years of backbiting. When Trotsky left for Germany, he remarks, "Zinoviev and Kamenev parted from me with a show of real feeling; they did not like the prospect of remaining eye to eye with Stalin." [10]

Among the rank and file of the two factions, however, it would be more difficult to overcome the hatred and distrust of "the permanent foe of Bolshevism," or of the man who had so labeled Trotsky. Rearrangement of principles, rewriting of theses, were easier for leaders than for followers. None the less they entered the fight in high spirits; Trotsky writes: "At our very first meeting, Kamenev declared: 'It is enough for you and Zinoviev to appear on the same platform, and the party will find its true Central Committee.'" [11]

Long before the Trotsky-Zinoviev bloc became a fact, Stalin was busy fighting it. With the sure instinct of the born power politician, he attacked it first at the crux, in the army. It was necessary to change the structure of the Red Army, which, created by Trotsky, still remained in its centralized form the fundament of his potential power and his prestige. As so often since then, Stalin masked his process of gathering monolithic power by calling it democratization.

[10] Trotsky, *My Life*, p. 523.
[11] *My Life*, p. 521.

> With 1925 a new era began. The advocates of the former proletarian military doctrine came to power . . . In the course of the next few years 74 per cent of the army was reorganized on a militia basis! [12]

This reorganization had nothing to do with military doctrine, least of all with the "proletarian military doctrine" on which it was ostensibly based. Each decentralized unit of the fragmented army was firmly tied to the local Party branch; increasingly, the local Party branch was tied to Stalin. Even if some of the army units could not be won over, some could; and those that could not were immeasurably less effective than they would have been under a united command relatively independent of the General Secretary. Even apart from the accidental factor that in general the army supported Trotsky, Stalin was right to fear it. During the civil war, he had organized the opposition to the military—to Trotsky, that is; and he learned in that fight that the political power monopoly of the Party can be seriously threatened by the army.

On a broader scale, Stalin answered the threatened bloc against him by hastening the reorganization of the parties of the Comintern. Zinoviev still represented enough power in the Russian Party to maintain his post as Chairman, and this in itself was an important hindrance; if Stalin had been able to replace him, as he had replaced Frunze with Voroshilov, even with another Lashevich as second in command, the reorganization of the Comintern would have proceeded faster. As a realist, Stalin did what could, for the moment, be done; the Comintern delegates were subjected to an increasing campaign of bribe-threats.

Roll Call of Stalin's Comintern Candidates

In February–March 1926 the enlarged plenum of the Executive Committee of the Communist International met in Moscow. There was a temporary armistice between Stalin and Zinoviev; following the suggestion of the Russian delegation, the plenum decided not to discuss the Fourteenth Congress of the Russian Party. This enabled Zinoviev to continue as Comintern Chairman, but in return he gave Stalin complete freedom in fighting all the groups in the Comintern opposed to him. The German Left in particular, the Maslow-Fischer group and its

---

[12] Trotsky, *The Revolution Betrayed*, p. 218.

immediate neighbors, was the target of Stalinist intervention. According to a prearranged ceremony, each delegate to the plenum expressed his hostility; the statements were stereotyped, accusing the German Left of lack of interest in the trade-unions, of neglect of the united front with the Social Democratic Party, of insufficient democracy in internal party matters. All of these criticisms, however, were only preliminary to the central one that the German Left was anti-Bolshevist and disloyal to the Russian state. Since the delegates were strictly bound not to mention the real content of the crisis—neither the conflict between Stalin and Zinoviev nor the Russian-German military alliance—the attack on this anti-Bolshevism had to be made by various nice subterfuges. Thus the delegates at once publicly avowed their loyalty to the new boss, Stalin, and their desertion of Zinoviev, and by these very statements helped indoctrinate themselves and their respective parties with the new Stalinist dogma of socialism in one country. Moving uneasily in this twilight, Zinoviev was sure that, if and when he regained control of the Russian Politburo, he would be able to win back the Comintern parties to his policy. As the delegates were not required to attack him personally, he felt that he would not lose face by waiting.

The most important problem for me during this period was how to protect my correspondence with Maslow and my other German friends from GPU tampering. I adopted a method I learned from some Russian comrades: I sewed the letters through with a large cross of cord and then sealed the cord in several places. I presumed that my letters would be read if it were possible to do it surreptitiously but that the GPU would not openly break the seal. These precautions, however, proved to have been childish. One day during the February plenum Ewert took the floor and began reading, one after the other, the letters I had written to Maslow in his prison cell. He not only read the political passages, but amused the audience by including large completely personal sections. I went to the platform and took the letters away from him by force, striking him as he tried to struggle with me. I left the hall immediately and returned to the Lux. Zinoviev telephoned to ask what had happened; Stalin sent Béla Kun around to learn the exact details of the incident. But in spite of Ewert's attempt to impose disciplinary action against me, no one attempted to get the letters back.

An important item on the agenda was the discussion of the new key role of the United States in European affairs. The Dawes stabilization and the industrial rationalization flowing from it were analyzed as the premises of a growing antagonism between the super-capitalistic and imperialistic United States and an impoverished and increasingly dependent Europe. This American domination of European economy would bring about "the unification of a Left Europe," led by the trade-unions and developing into the United Socialist State of Europe. Béla Kun proposed the slogan, "Pan-Europe against the hegemony of America."

Such a trade-unionist Europe, bound to Soviet Russia in a united front, was the basis of Stalin's socialism in one country. Repetitiously, the new line was hammered from the Comintern platform into the representatives of the Communist parties. This was another act in the Stalinist show, an indoctrination with another facet of the new Stalinist policy and political philosophy. Discreet Stalin supporters supervised the parade; each delegate was made to understand that he was expected to demonstrate his loyalty to the new leader. The speaker at this first international meeting after the Fourteenth Party Congress demonstrated that the European parties had already been rearranged in Stalin's support. Semard spoke for France, Ercoli-Togliatti for Italy, Dimitrov for Bulgaria, Geschke and Ewert for Germany,[13] Bogutski for Poland, Kilboom for Sweden, Ogjanovich for Yugoslavia, Darcy for the United States, Ferguson for Norway. Of the Russian delegation Stalin received the most eager support from Manuilsky, supported by Lominadze and the Finnish delegate, Kuusinen. There was also an opposition at this last Comintern plenum over which Zinoviev presided. The German Left was represented by Urbahns, Scholem, Engel, and Fischer. The Italian Left Communist Bordiga attacked the Russian Party openly, as did Arvid Hansen, minority representative from Norway. Bukharin, somewhat discomforted by the accusations, an-

---

[13] The permanent German delegate to the Comintern, Clara Zetkin, had been somewhat in the background during the period of the Left Central Committee in Germany. She made a passionate speech against the German Left, richly studded with personal remarks, particularly against me. Stalin, with a translator at his side, listened with attentive pleasure to her long tirades; later a friend reported to me that several times he had exclaimed, "What a witch! What a wonderful old witch!"

swered Bordiga by pointing out that the ECCI plenum itself, with minority representatives present, refuted the charge that the Comintern was undemocratic. "What terror is ruling in the German party and the Comintern if such a discussion is possible?" Bordiga's concept of party democracy, and Scholem's proposal to take back the Left factions that had been expelled, Bukharin rejected as "contradictory to the continuity of leadership."[14] Scholem interrupted him with, "Incomprehensible!" Bukharin polemized especially against Ruth Fischer's statement that the Comintern was on a slippery road and Korsch's reference to Red imperialism. Bordiga's proposal for a special Comintern congress to deal entirely with the relation between Soviet state policy and that of the revolutionary proletariat was indignantly denied.

Zinoviev's moderate and cautious summary against the Ultra-Left tendencies avoided definite commitments.

> We have been of the opinion that we have to count on two or three years of relative stabilization. Some representatives of the Ultra-Left have even said ten years. [*Interruption by Scholem:* Who?] Maslow! Maslow is of the opinion that we must wait at least another ten years [before German Communism would be strong enough to decide the fate of Germany].
>
> Decidedly we must reckon with the possibility of an improvement in capitalist prosperity. It is evident that America will not give up Germany. If there should be a sudden repetition of the October 1923 situation in Germany, America would not watch these events with folded arms, after having invested so much capital there. There is on the one hand, a "stabilization" of Europe through America; on the other hand, Europe is being revolutionized by this same America.[15]

The European labor movement, especially that of Germany, Zinoviev continued, was also being Americanized. He quoted from several leaders of the American Federation of Labor, who had said that the road of gradual change of society was by way of mutual understand-

---

[14] Thälmann, on the other hand, complained of the difficulties in breaking the continuity of the Left leadership. "In Berlin we had a staff, little changed for the past five years, which under the leadership of Ruth Fischer had a strong influence. In a slow process, step by step, we have conquered them." (*Protokoll: Erweiterte Exekutive der Kommunistischen Internationale, Februar-März, 1926*, Hamburg, 1926, p. 205.)

[15] *Protokoll . . . Februar-März 1926*, pp. 37–38.

ing between employers and employees, stressing the common interests
of all classes in the future development of American society. The AFL
was characterized as "an organization of a labor aristocracy within a
labor aristocracy."[16]

The Comintern economist, Professor Eugen Varga, enlarged on
this theme.

> Europe has lost its preponderance as the factory of the world;
> also, it can no longer compete with America in exporting capital
> to non-European markets . . . This disintegration of European
> capitalism and its structural change warn us against over-estimat-
> ing the duration and strength of the stabilization . . . Europe
> will suffer long crises, interrupted by short intervals of prosperity;
> in each crisis, the number of unemployed will be greater . . .
> The civil war [in Europe] will continue, undecided for a long
> time. It can end with annihilation of the "superfluous" by war,
> starvation, and epidemics; and on this foundation Europe can be
> resurrected as an annex to the United States.[17]

After the plenum, the Stalinization of all parties continued. The
March 16 issue of *Pravda,* reporting on the ECCI session, demanded
that the Bolshevization of the Comintern be intensified. At its July
convention in Lille, Maurice Thorez, one of the staunchest supporters
of Stalin at the February plenum, became the new leader of the French
party.[18] At the 1925 convention of the Workers Party (as the Communist party in the United States was then called), the Foster-Cannon
faction was deprived of its majority and, on the basis of a cable from
Moscow describing it as more loyal to the Comintern, the Ruthenberg-
Lovestone minority was installed. This was the first of a series of similar incidents; a wit described the American party as being suspended
from Moscow cables.

The Anglo-Russian Trade-Union Unity Committee

Over the next year the struggle between the factions developed in
the plenums of the Russian Central Committee, which met every three

---

[16] *Ibid.,* p. 34.

[17] *Ibid.,* p. 109 ff.

[18] Jacques Doriot, in these years one of Stalin's ardent admirers in the French
party, had been awarded the title of "the French Karl Liebknecht." In 1944, when
he was killed by an Allied plane, he was a Nazi supporter.

months. In these plenums Stalin was able to change the Central Committee man by man, a procedure contrary to the tradition still strong in the Party that the political composition of the Central Committee could be fundamentally changed only by a Party discussion leading up to a duly elected convention. These plenums were way-stations on the road to the next convention, at which the antagonists could win support and take new measure of each other; but in this period they were also one of the means by which Stalin fashioned the dictatorship of his group. It was possible to oppose Stalin by only two avenues: in the Party institutions, or illegally. Renouncing the legal fight would have meant giving up the hope for immediate victory, for it was possible to group oppositionist forces around a common program only by using the state institutions to broadcast that program. Once the Zinoviev-Trotsky bloc was formed, and only then, would it be relevant to raise the question of direct action.

At the plenum of the Central Committee in April 1926, just before Trotsky's departure for Germany, each oppositionist group presented a separate statement. The alliance among them had not yet been concluded. Zinoviev particularly wanted all the Workers' Opposition groups included in the bloc; he wanted to conduct the fight against Stalin under the slogan "Workers against the state apparatus!"

> At this very same April Plenum of the Central Committee, Zinoviev, shamelessly distorting the program of the Party, reproached the Central Committee for the fact that the Party had hitherto refrained from handing over the management of industry to the trade unions, i.e., directly defended the demands of the former "Workers' Opposition." [19]

Immediately after Trotsky's return from Germany, various factors pushed the coalition to completion. The situation in the country was bad: decreased production, reduced wages, few commodities. The increasing apathy of the workers had been indicated, for example, in the recent election to the soviets, in which by oppositionist estimates only 52 to 57 per cent of the proletariat participated. [20] Between April

---

[19] N. Popov, *Outline History of the CPSU*, II, 272.

[20] Only 36 per cent of the delegates were workers, a decrease of 10 per cent from 1925. In the city soviets there was a steady decrease of Party members; in part Stalin maneuvered against opposition in the Party by finding support outside it. In 1922, 70 per cent of the city soviets had been Communist; in 1923, 60 per cent;

and July 1926, the Bloc came to a formal agreement. It was composed of the following groups:

1. The Trotskyist Opposition.

2. The New Opposition, centered around Leningrad.

3. The Democratic Centralism group, represented by Sapronov.

4. The Workers' Opposition, represented by Shlyapnikov and Medvedev.

5. The anti-Stalinist faction in Georgia. The last three groups already had one foot outside the Party. Their support was among the Party rank and file and among non-Party workers.

The oppositionist Bloc thus mustered a substantial portion of the Bolshevik Old Guard. It represented the mood of the industrial centers against the new caste rising in the Party hierarchy and the resistance of the civil-war generation to the Stalinist course. The Stalinist faction had risen above the control of the Party membership by a series of maneuvers, and it "mercilessly" exploited the state power thus won to crush any opposition. These tactics had finally pushed together every group among the membership that, by increasingly totalitarian methods, had been eliminated from Party control.

The Bloc had good support abroad. Ever since the Fourteenth Congress, Stalin had been weakening oppositionist factions in Russia by sending their adherents abroad, and by this time most of the embassies and commercial legations were staffed with men sympathetic to either Zinoviev or Trotsky. These official state employees had to support the Stalin line, but they formed an excellent network of information from the Bloc to oppositionist factions in the parties abroad, and to the Bloc concerning developments in other countries. By their sabotage of Stalinist policy, they increased the pressure on the General Secretary. If the Bloc gained a victory, it could draw on this large reservoir of Old Bolsheviks and Trotskyists who had gained a wide experience and valuable contacts abroad.

Immediately after the April 1926 plenum, there were two events outside Russia that had an important influence on both factions—the Pilsudski coup in Poland and the British general strike.

On May 12, Pilsudski marched on Warsaw, and after three days of

---

in 1924, 57 per cent; in 1925, 46 per cent; in 1926, 36 per cent. (Molotov's report to the Moscow Party organization, *Inprekorr*, 1926, p. 1854.)

street fighting he overthrew the cabinet of Witosz, the peasant leader. A few days later his new government, based largely on "the colonels" who had participated in the coup, was approved by a majority vote of the Polish parliament. This event in Russia's front yard disturbed everyone, and over the next months the Party leaders analyzed it from all angles.

The Polish Communist Party, split into several wings, was inclined to give Pilsudski various degrees of critical support. He had not gone far enough, was the general tenor, but his revolution should be incorporated, as one step forward, into the general movement of the Polish working class. This policy was quickly corrected by the Russian Politburo, which interpreted Pilsudski's coup as an Anglo-American thrust at Russia's flank. An American expert, Dr. E. W. Kemmerer, had been conducting an investigation in Poland since the fall of 1925, to lay the ground for a loan on the Dawes model; and this attempt to spread American influence to the very border of Soviet Russia was noted in Moscow with inquietude.

On the other hand, Pilsudski's putsch was Poland's contribution to the general European trend toward totalitarian rule, which in this case never reached maturity. Pilsudski started with a program, never realized, of nationalizing industry and developing and stimulating agriculture by state aid. By the interpretation of the Politburo, Poland was another of the small countries of Europe following the Italian example toward fascism and militarism.

The coup also had its effect on the factional struggle; the Bloc gleaned another kind of insight from it. In three days, with a minimum of bloodshed and disorder, Pilsudski had taken over the government, but without changing the social structure of the country. Could not what had been done so easily in Poland be repeated in Russia? Could not the oppositionists also take over the government and still maintain the social base of nationalized economy? The oppositionists pondered thus, and Stalin, who also could read political portents, tightened his controls.

The British general strike, by the very fact of its occurrence, seemed to confirm Stalin's thesis that an alliance between Russia and British labor would soon be possible. Stalin had based his socialism in one country on his version of Lenin's "law of the uneven development of capitalism during the epoch of imperialism." [21] The American attempt to dominate Europe would force the development of a Trade-Union Europe against the hegemony of Capitalist United States, and Socialist Russia would be accepted in this conclave first as a collaborator and then as a leader.

From the 1917 revolution on, there had been a strong pro-Soviet sentiment among British workers. To a large extent this was reflected in British trade-union policy, but even when it was not directly reflected, often rank-and-file pressure modified what would otherwise have been an anti-Russian attitude. Sidney and Beatrice Webb, Fabian socialists, the chroniclers of the British trade-union movement, exemplify a general mood in their development into almost the official non-Communist apologists for Soviet Russia. In 1920 a British delegation, including among others Mrs. Philip Snowden, the wife of the well-known Labour leader, Albert A. Purcell, [22] and Robert Williams, visited Russia. During the incident of the Zinoviev letter, British unions had defended the Soviet Union against the attack of their own government. One of the most ardent defenders of the Soviet Union was A. G. Cook, chairman of the miners' union. He was supported in his drive for an alliance between the two countries by such labor leaders, among others, as his old friend, Arthur Horner, for long years a leading member of the Communist Party and chairman of the South Wales district of the miners' union; Ellen Wilkinson, who had left the party in 1924; Phillips Price; George Lansbury. England was the one country where dissenters from the local Communist Party, like Ellen Wilkinson,

---

[21] "In its first chapter the draft [of the program adopted at the Sixth World Congress, 1928] states that 'the unevenness of economic and political development is an unconditional law of capitalism. This unevenness becomes still more accentuated and aggravated in the epoch of imperialism.'

"This is correct. This formulation in part condemns Stalin's recent formulation of the question, according to which both Marx and Engels were ignorant of the law of uneven development, which was allegedly first discovered by Lenin . . .

"It would have been more correct to say that the entire history of mankind is governed by the law of uneven development . . . The extreme diversity in the levels attained, and the extraordinary unevenness in the rate of development of the different sections of mankind during the various epochs, serve as the *starting point* of capitalism." (Trotsky, *The Third International after Lenin*, New York, 1936, pp. 18–19.)

[22] In 1925, under the auspices of the British Trade-Union Congress, Purcell toured the United States in an effort to enlist trade-union support for American recognition of the Soviet Union.

could leave quietly and continue to display a demonstrative friendship for Moscow.

This sympathy with Soviet Russia, which during the whole period ran counter to official policy of the British Foreign Office, was concretized in 1925 with the formation of the Anglo-Russian Trade-Union Unity Committee. Supported by the International of Transport Workers, headed by the Hollander Edo Fimmen (who was among the most important of the fellow-travelers in European trade-union circles during the thirties), its Left wing was strong enough to swing the British union movement, the most conservative of Europe, to collaboration with Russia. At the sixth congress of Russian trade-unions, a resolution was adopted to form such a committee, and this proposal was accepted in Britain. Another British trade-union delegation, this one headed by Purcell, had toured Russia during the last months of 1924 and written an enthusiastic account of what they had seen.[23] Tomsky, as head of the Russian trade-unions, returned the visit; he was fraternal delegate to the Trade-Union Congress at Hull in May 1925. On May 14, an agreement was drawn up to form the Anglo-Russian Committee and signed by the union representatives of the two countries.

Stalin hoped that the British unions would break from the Amsterdam trade-union international, which was markedly anti-Russian, and form the nucleus of a new one. The Profintern, the Moscow-controlled trade-union international, would then be merged into this or allowed to die. Strong as were the antagonisms that had developed in the Russian Party, the faint hope that it would yet find a way out of its impasse by a fundamental change in Europe had not died out. Zinoviev and Bukharin alike watched this rapprochement with British unions with intense interest, and during the first months following the formation of the Anglo-Russian Committee both they and the Russian leadership generally interpreted it as the harbinger of a new day. These representatives of a weak and deteriorating labor movement, chained in the stone fortress of the economic facts of Russian society, met each move of labor outside with exaggerated hope. For Stalin, this was the

---

[23] *Russia.* The Official Report of the British Trades Union Delegation to Russia and Caucasia, November and December 1924 (London, 1925).

As a curiosity, it may be noted that the Austrian Left socialist Fritz Adler, who during World War II became sympathetic to Soviet Russia, polemized violently against this policy; he was supported by his compatriot, Otto Bauer.

fruition of his socialism in one country; the main task had now become the defense of Soviet Russia. Socialism was to be achieved not by a proletarian revolution, but by the *example* of Russia.

Trotsky was most critical of the prospects of British-Russian trade-union coöperation; the alliance, he warned, would break down at the first real test. The British unions, fundamentally loyal to their government, would support it in any serious conflict between Britain and Russia. The British Empire was still far too strong to be manipulated from the office of the General Secretary in Moscow, through the Anglo-Russian Trade-Union Unity Committee and Comrade Tomsky. The conflict of interest between Russia and Britain could not thus easily be overcome. In England the class struggle had not yet matured, and in Russia, having reached its peak in the revolution, it was receding. To attempt to tie the two groups together by linking the top layer of the working class of the two countries could not but fail. It was characteristic of Stalin that in his deep rooted miscomprehension of the British labor movement he thought that he could maneuver the unions into his power system.

The test of the new concept came with the British general strike in May 1926 and the nine-months miners' strike that followed it. The strike demonstrated the latent militancy of the British working class; it shook British society profoundly. During the year the membership of the Communist Party rapidly grew to 12,000, with a circulation of its paper to ten times that. Soviet unions supported the British strikers by allocating large sums for relief. The strike was broken; most of the British union leaders, especially Ernest Bevin, had taken a firm stand against it. Petrovsky, Tomsky, and Ewert, the men Stalin had sent to London, in fact endorsed the strike-breaking policy of the General Council of the TUC, in the hope of maintaining the Anglo-Russian Committee. They won nothing by this attitude, for they failed to win over the leaders, and the deep bitterness among British unionists against their leaders was directed also against the Communists, whose influence again decreased considerably.

The Meeting in the Woods

The defeat of the British general strike was deeply felt in Moscow. The presence of Tomsky and the other Russians in England had increased the tension between the two countries, which developed over the next months to the brink of war. The British unions offered no effective resistance to the policy of the Baldwin cabinet, and the "unity" between British and Russian unions was broken on the sharp rocks of international conflict, especially in China. On June 26, 1926, a stormy session of the House of Commons debated documents the Home Office had published the day before proving the connection of British Communists to Moscow. The next day, under the welcome necessity of protecting the country against the infiltration of British intelligence agents, a new law was passed in Russia intensifying GPU control.

Stalin used the strengthened authority principally against the Opposition, which had gained considerably from the defeat of his policy in Britain. In spite of this new law, Trotsky and Zinoviev felt encouraged, for throughout the country there was response to their attempts, now necessarily conspiratorial, to build up support of the Bloc. Contacts were established as far as Vladivostok. The scattered, illegal organizations were led by committees of three. Oppositionist couriers, sent out with a code for communications, distributed documents of the Politburo—which was itself a serious crime. They stayed secretly at the homes of oppositionist members, for official quarters were completely rigged with GPU spies. The couriers traveled with bodyguards, so as to avoid a stray bullet of a "White Guardist"; when they met, guards were posted to protect them against GPU raids.

Meanwhile the expulsions went on. As an indication of the caliber of the men who were being dumped from the Party, it is perhaps worth while citing the biographical notes given by the Central Control Commission of the group in Moscow that it expelled on July 26, 1926:

> 1. Mikhailov, director of a Moscow factory, supported Myasnikov, of the Workers' Opposition. Together with Chugayev, Ossip, Yatsek, he mimeographed and distributed clandestine documents; the group called itself "Workers' Truth."
>
> 2. G. Y. Byelensky, born 1884, socialist since 1901, Bolshevik since 1903, self-educated, soldier 1908, professional revolutionary since 1912, secretary of the Krasnaya Pryesnya district organization in Moscow. [I knew Byelensky. He was a simple type of worker-socialist, very popular among the Moscow rank and file, devoted to the cause of the revolution to the very marrow of his bones.]

3. Y. S. Chernyshov, born 1892, of peasant origin, in the party since 1918, in the Tsarist army and later the Red Army 1919–1921. Member of Byelensky's organization.

4. B. G. Shapiro, born 1898, blacksmith, in the Party and Red Army since 1918.

5. M. W. Vasilyev, born 1895, textile worker, in the Party since March 1917.

6. N. M. Vlassov, born 1884, blacksmith, in the Party since 1918.[24]

Under this increased pressure, the Bloc leaders began to plan the final steps. Even if they won a numerical majority, they were certain that Stalin would not cede the Party leadership to them, and they had to be prepared to back up the Party will by force. They expected to have to combat more and more terror, perhaps the accidental death of the oppositionist leaders. Trotsky and Zinoviev both took personal precautions, and went around even the restricted quarter of the Comintern buildings only in the company of one or two devoted friends.

> After Zinoviev and Kamenev broke with Stalin in 1925, both of them placed letters in a reliable place:
> "If we should perish suddenly, know that this is the work of Stalin's hands."
> They advised me to do the very same thing. "You imagine," Kamenev said to me, "that Stalin is preoccupied with how to reply to your arguments. Nothing of the kind. He is figuring how to liquidate you without being punished."
> . . . These were not guesses; during the honeymoon months of the triumvirate its members talked quite frankly with each other.[25]

The situation in the Party is best summed up in the often-quoted remark of Lenin's widow that if Lenin were still alive, he would be living in prison.

Thus, when the oppositionist leaders decided to discuss the military aspect of their program, they did not meet in any room. No place in all Moscow was considered entirely safe; any room might have GPU ears. They met in a wood near Moscow and discussed the role of those army units that had remained loyal to Trotsky if and when the "legal" opposition gained sufficient strength. This was an affair largely of

---

[24] *Inprecor,* 1926, p. 912.
[25] Trotsky, *Stalin,* p. 417.

technicalities, to be arranged between the two military leaders, Trotsky and Lashevich. Since as second in command of the Red Army Lashevich was still in a better legal position, he was charged with laying the groundwork for military action against Stalin, which would take place at a time to be set by the leading committee of the Bloc. Meanwhile he was to organize oppositionist nuclei among the officers and prepare them to take simultaneous action. It was anticipated that, with enough military influence built up by the combined prestige of Trotsky and Lashevich to support a potential majority in the Party, Stalin might not fight the inevitable but might resign.

While I was still in Moscow I heard of these preparations from my friend G. L. Shklovsky, and later again from friends in Berlin, and I know how complex the discussion was. The Bloc was divided on the issue of the extent to which military pressure should be combined with the fight, largely underground, for Party control. Nothing is more correct than Trotsky's repeated declaration that he never intended a coup, that he never hoped to overthrow Stalin without the support of the Party and the country. These men, all of them revolutionaries of the old school, hesitated long before a course that might lead to such a disturbance in the country as to result in the overthrow of both factions by a counter-revolutionary force. This fear of precipitating the first in a chain of disorders that might end with the dismemberment of Russia and the restoration of capitalism has been the most serious handicap to anti-Stalinists in and outside Russia. Over the past quarter of a century, it has been an important contributing factor to the disintegration of one anti-Stalinist group after another.

While the Opposition floundered in their fear of disturbing Soviet society, the foundations of this society were being reforged into a Stalinist power machine. Stalin learned of the meeting in the wood through his agents, and the mere knowledge that the oppositionist leaders had thus met, though he knew nothing of the content of their discussion, frightened him into arousing the Party against a threatened coup. At the meeting, Popov relates, Lashevich "related the plan of the united opposition 'to bring the Central Committee to its knees,' urging his hearers to pay special attention to the need of organizing activities in the Red Army." [26]

---

[26] N. Popov, *Outline History of the CPSU*, II, 274.

The next plenum of the Central Committee met in July, but before that time I managed to get back to Berlin. Maslow had been in prison for more than two years, and would be released by one of the amnesties common in Germany on July 10. At the beginning of June Zinoviev told me that Stalin was leaving Moscow for a short vacation in the Caucasus, and that I should take advantage of his absence to make my getaway. He asked me whether I would be able to produce a scene, and I answered that I would very much prefer a less bizarre procedure. Bukharin, he told me, will be in charge of the Politburo. He likes you personally and would like to help, but you must give him a pretext for acting against orders. Finally I agreed, and we cooked up an act.

The next day I pushed my way into a meeting of the Politburo. Zinoviev stood up and with well-feigned anger ordered me out; he reprimanded the guard for having allowed me to get past him. I began to pound the table, to cry that I must be allowed to go home. The long suppressed emotion, once released, burst; I fainted. When I came to, Bukharin was trying to feed me tea. Ruth, he told me, you will go home. We are not terrorists against our own comrades. I have just given Pyatnitsky the order to prepare your passport.

I was taken back to the Lux in a Comintern automobile. A few hours later, Pyatnitsky appeared with my passport, grim and most unfriendly. He refused to give me traveling expenses, and several of my friends (particularly the Pole, Henryk Domski, who was shot in Moscow in 1936) went about collecting money. I departed the same day, rather tense till I had passed the Russian border and could be sure that the GPU would not take me off the train there. I had gone through my baggage and papers several times to be sure that I was carrying no incriminating material; the rest of my things was brought to Berlin later by a diplomatic courier sympathetic to the Zinoviev group.[27]

This anecdote, a trifle in itself, is significant because it illustrates the

[27] On July 4, 1926, the Comintern delegations of the German and Russian parties unanimously adopted the following resolution. "The Presidium of the Executive Committee states that Comrade Ruth Fischer has returned to Germany, breaking the decision of the Comintern of March 31, 1926, protocol number 55, paragraph 11–A, and the decision of the Executive Committee Secretariat, dated June 5, 1926, protocol number 19, paragraph 19. This action represents a grave and conscious violation of international party discipline." (*Inprekorr*, July 1926.)

indirect ways resistance to a totalitarian regime uses. I have no doubt that Zinoviev arranged the details of the escape with Bukharin and Pyatnitsky, who though under Stalin's discipline were disposed to participate in this little action against him. But they needed protection against Stalin and had to be furnished with a pretext. Bukharin could well point out that in my excited state I might have attracted the attention of foreign correspondents, some of whom would have relished a story of a Comintern official being kept in Moscow against her will. Pyatnitsky could point out that he had followed orders and furnished a passport but had done no more; he had refused to give me traveling expenses.

At the July plenum of the Central Committee, the Bloc appeared before the entire Party membership for the first time as a united opposition. In a statement read by Trotsky in the name of the entire group, Trotsky and Zinoviev acknowledged their past errors in attacking each other. Trotsky, Zinoviev declared, had been correct in 1923 in his attack on the *organization* of the Party bureaucracy. On the other hand, Trotsky admitted that when he had charged Zinoviev and Kamenev in his *Lessons of October* with "opportunism," he had committed a gross error. This reciprocal amnesty was immediately attacked as a "supreme lack of principle," for the unification of all its opponents was a serious danger to the Stalin group. There were many differences remaining in the oppositionist Bloc, but it was united around two fundamental points: it is impossible to build socialism in Russia alone; in abjuring revolutionary internationalism the Bolshevik Party is degenerating. Paraphrasing Lenin, the platform spoke of "a workers' state with bureaucratic distortions." It charged the Stalin group with:

> 1. An immoderate growth of those forces which desire to turn the development of our country into capitalistic channels;
> 2. A weakening of the position of the working class and the poorest peasants against the growing strength of the kulak, the NEP-man, and the bureaucrat;
> 3. A weakening of the general position of the workers' state in the struggle with world capitalism, a lowering of the international position of the Soviet Union.[28]

---

[28] From the oppositionist platform, quoted in Trotsky, *The Real Situation in Russia*, p. 33. One member of the Opposition, J. A. Ossovsky, demanded the immediate legalization of a new proletarian party. He was expelled from the Party

The Bloc proposed a policy of industrialization based on a complete transformation of the State Party into a democratic workers' party. The official report of the plenum overflows with Stalin's denunciation of this "super-industrialization" program. The program of the Opposition was based on the premise of an indivisible link between industrialization and "workers' management," which was a battle-cry against monopolistic control of Soviet industry by the State Party. Stalin, on the other hand, began his all-out industrialization only after every remnant of independent workers' organization had been crushed. At this period, rather than risk the weakening of the State Party, he preferred the status quo of a peasant Russia.

Without an understanding of the process by which Stalin fought for the monopoly of power by the State Party, and within it for the monopoly of power by his group, Stalin's sharp rejection of Trotsky's "super-industrialization" plan is one of the riddles that so often puzzle liberal observers. The Opposition's industrialization plan and Stalin's Five-Year Plans are not the same; they start from different points and proceed to different patterns of society. As early as 1924, Zinoviev had considered admitting a poor peasants' party into the soviets. At the April 1926 plenum, this oppositionist slogan of workers' democracy had been pushed by the demand that management be given to the trade-unions. Industrialization in the terrorist style of the Five-Year Plans could be undertaken only after the "workers' groups" had been crushed.

A major point of the agenda of the July plenum was Comintern policy. The defeat of Stalin's policy in Great Britain, the open split of the German party, the effect of this on other European parties—all these were used to denounce the disintegrating influence of Stalinist intervention. Stalin replied by exploiting to the utmost Zinoviev's denunciation some months before of the Maslow-Fischer group, with which the Bloc now sided openly.

The July plenum ended with moral successes for the oppositionist

---

immediately after the July plenum. Born in 1893, Ossovsky, a blacksmith, joined the Party in 1918 and became a member of the Plan Commission. First expelled in March 1923, he was readmitted in January 1924 and expelled again on August 10, 1926. He had demanded that oppositionist parties, including Mensheviks and Social Revolutionaries, be given legal rights. While in Moscow the mere mention of admitting these reformist socialists was high treason, the drive continued for unity with reformist trade-unionists of Europe.

Bloc. Its ranks were unified, and there was a favorable echo from the Party. The Party now knew in every corner that a new fight was on, that there was a chance to overthrow the Stalin group. The economic situation was bad; the "grain-collections policy" had left the state without grain reserves and made it necessary to buy in the open market at high prices.[29] The Opposition, however, lost important organizational posts. Zinoviev was dropped from the Politburo and Lashevich from the Central Committee. Kamenev was removed even from his insignificant post as Commissar of Trade and replaced by A. I. Mikoyan.

Stalin Deprives the Opposition of Party Legality

The fight in the Comintern was intensified. Kollontai was transferred from Norway to Mexico, to remove her still farther from Moscow. Kamenev was offered the post of ambassador to Tokyo, but refused it. On August 20, Bukharin, as presumptive heir to Zinoviev, flew to Germany to clean up the German party.

On my return to Berlin two months before, I had found the various groups in the German party still in heated struggle. Maslow was released from prison on July 10, and together we supported the Zinoviev-Trotsky Bloc in Russia. When Bukharin arrived, he pretended terrible anger at having been fooled in Moscow; following out Stalin's orders, he arranged the immediate expulsion of not only Maslow and me but three other Left leaders, Hugo Urbahns, Werner Scholem, and Wilhelm Schwann. We, together with several other deputies who accepted our platform, formed a separate group in the Reichstag. We set up a headquarters in Berlin and propagandized extensively. In the middle of 1927, the Suhl district of the party in Thuringia came over to us, bringing with them a daily, *Die Volkstimme* ("People's Voice"), which began to promote the policy of the Russian Opposition.

After the July plenum, the Bloc became very active in Russia. Its members went to individual cell meetings and tried to create a demand for a new convention. This interference in cell discussions was to Stalin an unpardonable crime, for the undisturbed manipulation of cell mem-

---

[29] Dzerzhinsky, chairman of the Supreme Council of National Economy, defended the Central Committee against Pyatakov's various criticisms concerning the relation between the state economy and the Neo-NEP traders. Dzerzhinsky died a few hours after his speech and was replaced by V. V. Kuibyshev, who was succeeded in 1930 by Ordzhonikidze.

bership was the basic premise of monolithic control. Trotsky and Zinoviev, for example, attended a meeting of the Aviopribor airplane factory in Moscow; and this attempt to win over the airplane workers was regarded as especially dangerous.

> The apparatus counter-attacked with fury. The struggle of ideas gave place to administrative mechanics: telephone summons of the party bureaucrats to attend the meetings of the workers' locals, an accumulation of automobiles with hooting sirens in front of all the meetings, a well-organized whistling and booing at the appearance of oppositionists on the platform.[30]

The Central Committee ordered the formation of "special fighting detachments" against the Opposition. A multitude of informers was organized and sent to cell meetings to observe and report back. Just before the October plenum, Stalin ordered a displacement of oppositionists throughout the country. Some were arrested; many were transferred, on the pretext of Party assignments, to remote places in Far Eastern and Northern Asiatic Russia. Man and wife were ordinarily ordered to different posts.

This persecution was synchronized with a new offer from Stalin to the oppositionist leaders; if they repudiated the crime of all crimes—the splitting of the Party—Stalin would readmit most of the Trotskyists and Zinovievists to their Party and state positions. The oppositionist leaders, fearing the atomization of their supporters by the GPU, decided to accept the offer, in order to gain time for continued conspiratorial work against the Stalinist machine. On October 16, a week before the plenum,

> we made a declaration announcing that although we considered our views just, and reserved the right of fighting for them within the framework of the party, we renounced the use of activities that might engender the danger of a split. . . . It was an expression of our desire to remain in the party and serve it further. Although the Stalinists began to break the truce the day after it was concluded, still we gained time. The winter of 1926–27 gave us a certain breathing spell which allowed us to carry out a more thorough theoretical examination of many questions." [31]

---

[30] Trotsky, *My Life*, pp. 528–529.
[31] *Ibid.*, p. 529.

As part of this declaration, Trotsky and Zinoviev dissociated themselves from the Workers' Opposition in Russia and the Left Opposition in the Comintern.

On October 14, Arvid Hansen, the Norwegian Left Communist, had arrived in Berlin with a parcel of secret material from the Russian Opposition, which he had brought out with great personal danger. Devoted to Zinoviev, he had become his courier, aware that if he was searched at the border his Norwegian citizenship would not save him. We went through the documents, deciding which to translate and publish, which to use for the private information of our group. It was a large batch, and we worked continuously for three days. Then, on a Sunday evening, we took a stroll; we bought a newspaper and read in its headlines that Zinoviev and Trotsky had renounced their oppositionist activities and broken with the Maslow-Fischer group. Hansen was completely shattered. He had left Moscow a week before, and in a long and intimate talk Zinoviev had asked him for the utmost firmness. He could not understand this "treason"; he ended by breaking with the Opposition and going back to Stalin.

Hansen was not the only one who failed to understand the motivation of the declaration; it had disastrous consequences for the cohesion of the oppositionist Bloc, particularly outside Russia. Time and again, this has been cited as an example of "lack of character," "lack of principle," "capitulation." Such an estimate, however, misses the point. Neither this nor later withdrawals can be judged by liberal yardsticks; they did not take place in Hansen's Norway. In these transition years, resistance to the growing totalitarian character of the state and Party had to be adapted to the increasingly dictatorial forms of Party life. It was necessary when pressed too hard to withdraw and regroup, and then attack again. The Bloc did not sin by too little fight for "principles" in its struggle against the Stalinist monolithic Party, but withdrew often too late when the danger of annihilation became imminent and reëntered the fight not on its own terms, nor at its own time, but on Stalin's provocation.

By these methods, the Stalinist group was able to win an overwhelming majority in the joint plenum of the Central Committee and the Central Control Commission, which met October 22–26, 1926. It removed Trotsky from the Politburo, Kamenev as alternate to that body, and Zinoviev as Chairman of the Comintern.[32] Even this clean sweep, however, did not win the fight. Stalin had won his majority by a tremendously increased intimidation and terror in the Party, and he had paid a price for it. Party members had been pushed to his support, but they had also been antagonized. If the Bloc was able to get a new start in and outside Russia, Stalin's majority might dissipate.

After the October plenum, the Central Control Commission invited the leaders of the German Left to come to Moscow for a review of their expulsion. We discussed long in Berlin whether to accept this offer, and decided finally that Maslow, a Russian citizen, should not go, but that for the rest of us the possibility of exploiting the occasion to propagandize our views was worth the indubitable danger. In Moscow, Shklovsky met me with the words, "Are you mad?" Having won a move against Zinoviev and Trotsky, Stalin undoubtedly hoped to capitalize on their declaration against us and win us over to him.

The chairman of the commission was Ottomar V. Kuusinen. Most of the sessions were secret, but a stenographic report of one portion of the hearings was published [33] to defend the Russian Politburo against the accusation of destroying the German Communist Party. As a model of Stalinist intimidation, it is reproduced here in part from that official transcript.

> KUUSINEN: . . . We had to deal with the appeal of the five who were expelled from the German Party: Ruth Fischer, Maslow, Urbahns, Schwann, and Scholem, and to go through all the material which refers to their expulsion . . . We gave them a hearing in order to establish whether they are Communists, or anti-Communists, whether they deserved to be taken back into the Party and the Comintern, or whether their expulsion was to be finally ratified. The appellants were not satisfied with this procedure, and they complained, for instance, to Comrade Radek. [*Interjection:* Hear, hear!]
>
> FISCHER: We did not come here as accused, but as accusers [!] against a policy now being carried on in the Comintern and Communist Party of Germany, which will bring the Comintern and the Communist Party of Germany to their ruin.

---

[32] On November 22, Trotsky was also removed from his shadow presidency of the Scientific and Technical Collegium. A few days later, by a genuine Stalin maneuver, Zinoviev was appointed a member of the presidium of the State Planning Commission.

[33] *Inprecor,* 1927, pp. 180–183.

KUUSINEN: One of these "accusers" of ours was missing from the Commission. Of the five, only four arrived. The Kapellmeister did not show up. He preferred to continue his charges against the Comintern and the German Party under the protection of the German police, instead of defending his charges before the Commission of the Enlarged Executive. The four who did come said, as they had been instructed to say by the fifth:

"We did not bring Maslow along, in order not to deliver him into your hands."

His colleagues implied in the Commission that Maslow's freedom to return might have been endangered if he had come here. We said that the Party organs have only moral means at their disposal, that the decisions of the Party court are but morally binding. But these people replied: "We have no faith in the Soviet organs!"

All together we put sixteen questions to them. I will report very briefly on their replies to these questions . . .

"Do you recognize that there is no antagonism whatever between the policy of the USSR, the state of the proletarian dictatorship, and the interests of the international revolution?"

Ruth Fischer replied: "On this question we stand upon the viewpoint of the Russian Opposition and join fully with the formulations of Comrade Zinoviev."

To this we remarked: "But Comrade Zinoviev has publicly disavowed you." But Ruth Fischer only repeated the first part of her answer in the following form:

"On all these Russian questions we stand by the viewpoint of the Russian Opposition . . . Especially the honest supporters of the proletarian dictatorship must *most sharply combat* this policy," viz., "the policy of the Soviet state" and "this Stalin policy"—she used both of these expressions . . .

These people have no mistakes, no blame whatever. One could question them for weeks on end and they would still recognize no blame, no mistakes. Last Sunday, we questioned them for many hours with the greatest patience, and finally, we grew somewhat tired of all these questions and answers—because these people pulled themselves up as really without error or fault . . .

They talk about a "crisis," a "decay," a "disintegration" of the Comintern.

Stalin's majority at every Party plenum during this period was formally well established; the number of votes he got for every resolution was apparently impressive. But this majority was not a strongly welded whole. Three major groups in the Party seeking an equilibrium had come together under Stalin's leadership—the rising Party hierarchs, best personified by Molotov; the trade-union wing, represented by Tomsky; and the moderates, led by Bukharin and Rykov. The expected transmutation of "socialism in one country" into successes in foreign policy had not been achieved, and every failure abroad was reflected in the Party by a centrifugal tremor in Stalin's heterogeneous majority; after every setback he reëstablished his authority by increased violence against the Opposition. Stalin's experiment in Britain in 1926 had lowered his status in the Politburo, and his policy in China in 1927 brought him close to losing his majority altogether.

Stalin and Chiang Kai-shek

From the beginning the relation between Russian and Chinese revolutionists had been cordial. Immediately after the Bolshevik coup, Sun Yat-sen sent Lenin a congratulatory telegram. In July 1919, in a "manifesto to the Chinese people," the Soviet government renounced all Tsarist claims on Chinese territory and property. During these first years, however, contacts were rather tenuous, for during the Russian civil war the Kolchak armies blocked direct intercourse for eighteen months.

In 1921 Maring-Sneevliet, the Dutch Communist,[1] contacted Sun Yat-sen and reported favorably on the young Chinese nationalist organization, the Kuo Min Tang. In January 1923 Sun and Adolf Joffe, the Soviet diplomat, issued a joint declaration at Shanghai, and during that year the Kuomintang received a group of Soviet advisers, the most prominent of whom was Borodin.

Through this mission to China, Michael Borodin became one of the best known of Comintern figures. A Russian socialist of indefinite past and color, he had emigrated to the United States under the name of Grusenberg some time after the revolution of 1905. Here he made a precarious living at various jobs; for a while, under the name of Berg, he ran a business school in Chicago. He returned to Russia in 1918; having lived in America, he was regarded as an expert on foreign affairs and was sent on various missions abroad to Germany, to Turkey, possibly to Mexico. His big chance came when he was sent to China.

Borodin insisted that there be "a definite body of party principles, unity of party organization, strict party discipline." From the beginning, the party structure of the Moscow-counseled Kuomintang was an adaptation of the Russian model to the Chinese scene. Borodin helped establish the Whampoa Academy, where German and Russian officers trained Chinese cadets. In Moscow a Communist University for the Toilers of the Orient was founded and, in 1925, the Sun Yat-sen University, with Karl Radek at its head, where at its height nearly a thousand students were in attendance. Chiang Kai-shek, Sun's chief lieutenant, attended a Red Army school in Moscow and studied Russian Communism at its source.

In 1924, the Chinese Communists were instructed by Moscow to join the Kuomintang as individuals.[2] Later two Communists became

---

[1] Henryk Sneevliet left the party during the middle twenties and became the leader of an anti-Stalinist socialist group, which elected him to the Dutch parliament. During the Nazi occupation, he was arrested together with six comrades; killed by the Gestapo, he went to his death courageously. For his role in China, compare Harold R. Isaacs, *The Tragedy of the Chinese Revolution* (London, 1938), pp. 61–65.

[2] The First Congress of the Chinese Communist Party had been held in Shanghai in July 1921. Among the thirteen delegates was Mao Tse-tung, the present leader

ministers in the new Nationalist government.[3] Stalin and Bukharin, seeking to compensate for the loss of Russian prestige in Germany by manipulating a Communist success in the East, adapted every "principle" to the new effort. Theories were made to order, enunciated in long, involved, and dogmatic declarations. Bukharin's concept of the "bloc of four classes" in the national revolution of China was made the starting point of a new Soviet policy in all Asia. The united front of the national bourgeoisie, oppressed by foreign imperialists, with the peasants and workers, was to be the Asiatic version of Stalin's National Socialism.

As early as 1923, Trotsky had begun opposing the Stalinist policy in China. Through a maze of irrelevancies and scholastic refutations, he kept hitting at the vulnerable point—the illusion that the Comintern had found loyal allies in Chiang and his Kuomintang. Trotsky, later joined by Zinoviev, warned the party that the Chinese Communists would be the victims of this policy. But Stalin's dream of controlling all Eurasia from Moscow was not to be easily shattered.[4]

In July 1925 the Communist wing of the party, riding on the sweeping mass movement of the time, won control of the Kuomintang in Canton. Chiang, who had succeeded Sun Yat-sen as the movement's leader on his death in March 1925, suddenly swept down on the city in March 1926. He arrested several Communist leaders, whom he accused

---

of the party. In 1924, the year it was merged into the Kuomintang, the party's membership was still only about 1000.

[3] "You know there were two Communist ministers in the Government . . . Afterwards, they . . . stopped coming around to the ministries altogether, failed to appear themselves, and put in their places a hundred functionaries. During the activity of these ministers, not a single law was promulgated which would ease the position of the workers and peasants. This reprehensible activity was wound up with a still more reprehensible, shameful end. These ministers declared that one is ill and the other wishes to go abroad; . . . they did not resign with a political declaration." (F. Chitarov at the Fifteenth Party Congress; quoted in Trotsky, *Problems of the Chinese Revolution*, New York: Pioneer Publishers, 1932, p. 286.)

[4] "In Russia in 1905, if we had had a large revolutionary organization of the type of the present Left Kuomintang in China, it is possible that we would not have had soviets . . . What would have been the consequences of that? The consequences would be that the Left Kuomintang would play approximately the same role in the contemporary bourgeois democratic revolution in China that the soviets played in the Russian bourgeois democratic revolution in 1905." (Stalin at the plenum of the Executive Committee of the Comintern, June 15, 1927, quoted in *Die Fahne des Kommunismus*, June 24, 1927.)

of plotting against the Nationalist government, and shot some of their supporters. No hint of these events was allowed to appear in any of the Comintern papers, and there was no change in the policy of the Chinese Communists. On the contrary, two months after this episode in Canton, the party renewed its policy of taking over the Kuomintang from within.

> A special plenary session of the [Kuomintang] Central Executive was held in May 1926, which laid down the following rules concerning the Communist Party: 1. They were not to criticize the principles of Sun Yat-sen but were to abide by them implicitly. 2. The Communist Party must hand over its complete membership list to the Kuomintang . . . 3. Communists could not control more than one-third of the higher executive committees. 4. They could not serve as heads of departments in the central party headquarters. 5. Without authorization from the party, no member of the Kuomintang could call any meeting in its name to discuss party affairs. 6. Without authorization from the highest body in the party, no member of the Kuomintang was allowed to be a member of any other political organization or to engage in any other political activity. 7. If the Communist Party wanted to send instructions to its members in the Kuomintang, such instructions first had to be submitted to a joint committee of which the majority was non-Communist, for approval. 8. No member of the Kuomintang could join the Communist Party before tendering his resignation and, once a member had resigned, he could not rejoin the Kuomintang. 9. All those who violated the rules were to be punished.[5]

The Seventh Plenum of the Comintern Executive Committee, December 1926, seated delegates from the Kuomintang[6] and endorsed the expulsion of the German Left. Stalin himself reported on "the Russian question"—an indication that he was weak as well as his opponents; almost politely he repeated the previous designation of the Bloc as a

---

[5] Albert Weisbord, *The Conquest of Power* (New York, 1937), p. 1001.

[6] "After the Canton coup d'état, engineered by Chiang Kai-shek in March, 1926, and which our press passed over in silence, when the Communists were reduced to the role of miserable appendices of the Kuomintang and even signed an obligation not to criticize Sun-Yat-senism, Chiang Kai-shek—a remarkable detail indeed!— came forward to insist on the acceptance of the Kuomintang into the Comintern: in preparing himself for the role of executioner, he wanted to have the cover of world Communism and—he got it. The Kuomintang, led by Chiang Kai-shek and Hu Han-min, was accepted into the Comintern (as a 'sympathizing' party)." (Trotsky, *Problems of the Chinese Revolution*, pp. 270–271.)

"Social Democratic deviation in the Communist Party of the Soviet Union." By their compromise in October, the Bloc leaders were enabled to appear and defend themselves.

> Zinoviev, Kamenev, and Trotsky spoke in defense of their anti-Party views, protesting against the charge of a Social Democratic deviation made against them by the Fifteenth Conference. Kamenev even went so far as to accuse our Party, before the representatives of the international proletariat, of national reformism.[7]

The plenum intensified the fight against the Bloc's international support; in France, Boris Souvarine was expelled and Alfred Rosmer and Pierre Monatte were designated counter-revolutionaries; and the fight against the Italian Left Communist Amadeo Bordiga was continued.

At its Fifth Congress, in April 1927, the Chinese Communist Party numbered 60,000, compared with only 1,000 two years earlier.[8] In a speech on April 5, Stalin praised Chiang Kai-shek as a fine revolutionary fighter; the two men exchanged portraits. A week later, Chiang made his decisive about face and began to purge the Kuomintang of its Communist wing. Some tens of thousands of Shanghai workers were massacred. Even then, Communist policy remained the same—to work inside the Kuomintang; Stalin declared that to fight Chiang openly would mean to give him victory. On May 21–22, the massacre was repeated, this time in Wuhan.

> This march was set for May 21. The peasants started to draw up their detachments in increasing numbers toward Changsa. It was clear that they would seize the city without great effort. But at this point *a letter arrived from the Central Committee of the Chinese Communist Party in which Tchen Du-siu wrote that they should presumably avoid an open conflict and transfer the question to Wuhan.* On the basis of this letter, the District Committee dispatched to the peasant detachments an order to retreat, not to advance any further; but this order failed to reach two detachments. Two peasant detachments advanced on Wuhan and were annihilated by the soldiers.[9]

---

[7] N. Popov, *Outline History of the CPSU*, II, 308.

[8] The exact membership was 59,967, compared with 964 at the time of the Fourth Party Congress in January 1925. In 1927, 53.8 per cent of the membership were workers, most of the rest students. At the same time the Young Communist League had a membership of 35,000 and the Young Pioneers a membership of 120,000 children.

[9] Trotsky, *Problems of the Chinese Revolution*, p. 290.

The effect of these events in Moscow cannot be expressed by a few adjectives. Stalin and Bukharin were in the middle of self-congratulatory speeches on the success of their Chinese policy; Stalin's articles had to be hurriedly suppressed and a book by Bukharin made to vanish. The resolution adopted at the July 1927 plenum by the Stalinist Central Committee shows the uneasiness even through a heavy coat of whitewash.

> While the Chinese revolution, in spite of the correct tactics of the Comintern, has suffered a great defeat, this can be explained first and foremost by the correlation of the class forces within the country and also from the international standpoint . . . On the other hand, it is necessary to recognize that the leadership of the Chinese Communist Party, which systematically rejected the directives of the Communist International, bears its share of the responsibility . . .
>
> The present period of the Chinese revolution is characterized by its severe defeat and simultaneously by a *radical* re-grouping of forces, in which a bloc of workers, peasants and urban poor is being organized against all the ruling classes and against imperialism. In *this* sense the revolution is passing to a higher phase of its development, to the phase of the direct struggle *for the dictatorship of the working class and peasantry*. The experience of the preceding development has clearly shown that the bourgeoisie is incapable of carrying out the tasks of . . . the *bourgeois democratic revolution* . . .[10]

During the period of the Soviet-Kuomintang alliance, British-Russian relations had deteriorated. By the beginning of 1927, trade between the two countries had come almost to a standstill. There was a campaign in the British press to break off diplomatic relations with the Soviet Union, and meanwhile the British Foreign Office intensified its collaboration with Poland and Rumania. On February 23, Britain sent Russia a warning note; on May 12, the office of Arcos, Ltd., a Russian trading company in London, was broken into by two hundred policemen. Two weeks later Prime Minister Baldwin summed up the British grievances against Russia in five points, in substance as follows: (1) Soviet agents had tried to obtain British military secrets. (2) A top-secret document was missing and it was suspected that Soviet agents

---

[10] Quoted in Popov, II, 314–315.

had taken it. (3) Secret documents had been found in the Soviet Trade Legation, proving that the legation was acting as a go-between to the Communist parties of Great Britain and the colonies. (4) The Soviet chargé d'affaires had supported a political campaign in England against British policy in China. (5) In its propaganda against British interests in China, the Soviet government had violated the terms of the Anglo-Russian trade agreement of March 16, 1921.

At the end of May 1927 Great Britain broke off diplomatic relations with Soviet Russia. In general, the immediate reaction in labor circles was opposed to the rupture; but at the beginning of July, at the annual conference of the National Union of Railwaymen, J. H. Thomas denounced Tomsky for having interfered in the domestic affairs of the British trade-union movement.

A few days later, Peter Voikov, the Soviet ambassador to Warsaw, was assassinated. He had taken his post over serious objections by the Polish government, for he had allegedly been one of the group that had killed the Tsar and his family. Now, a Russian monarchist had killed him.

Throughout the world, the tension between Britain and Russia was felt. In France, for example, Jacques Doriot and nine others were imprisoned for their subversive propaganda in the French colonies. Two municipal councilors of St. Cyr, the site of the national military academy, were charged with selling military secrets to Russia. On June 12, Pierre Semard,[11] head of the railway union, was accused of inciting soldiers to mutiny and was imprisoned. Crémet, a member of the party secretariat, was charged with espionage for Russia. Paris issued a semi-official warning to Moscow that its agents must be withdrawn.

Thus with the sudden collapse of Stalin's policy in China, aggravated by the inflammatory tension between Britain and Russia, yet further aggravated by the renewed anti-Communist moves in all Europe, Russia was again dangerously isolated. Stalin's socialist fatherland, which only months before had hoped to lead trade-unionist Europe against American hegemony, which only days before had been in firm alliance with Chiang Kai-shek's China, was alone in a hostile world. In all Europe, she had only one weak and uncertain friend,

---

[11] Executed by the Gestapo in 1942.

Germany, which stood with one foot in the camp of the enemy. Germany substantially increased guaranteed credits to Soviet Russia; on the other hand, on July 27, the Berlin police arrested 700 Communists and charged them with property damage and attacks on police officials.

George V. Chicherin was hurried off to Berlin. He conferred with Reich Chancellor Marx and with Brockdorff-Rantzau; on June 7, on the eve of his departure for a League of Nations session, he spoke to Gustav Stresemann, Germany's Foreign Minister. Later, in Geneva, Stresemann reviewed the international situation with Chamberlain, and Germany's reluctance to join in was an important factor in preventing the outbreak of conflict between Britain and Russia.

To Strike or Not to Strike

In Russia, with Stalin's foreign policy toppling down about his head, the Opposition was in the ascendant. The higher ranks in the Party, who had seen in Stalin the man to lead the country into a period of peaceful coöperation with the capitalist world, found Russia and themselves before an abyss. Alexander Barmine, who describes himself in this period as "a typical Communist functionary," has described the reversal of feeling that took place in the country.

> No one at that time foresaw the rise of Stalin to personal dictatorship. Our general mood was one of healthy optimism. We were sure of ourselves and of the future. We believed that, provided no war came to interrupt the reconstruction of Russian industry, our socialist country would be able— . . . The permanent revolution seemed to us a dangerous theory . . . I was one of those who invariably backed up the findings of the Central Committee . . . Political passion reached its climax when the Chinese revolution, spurred by the Communist International and by Soviet advisers, began to stride from victory to victory . . . Stalin . . . remained deaf to warnings from all sides that Chiang Kai-shek was preparing a military coup . . . The disastrous effects of these tactics were soon dramatically revealed . . . Stalin's prestige was sharply compromised. The Opposition redoubled their efforts.[12]

Stalin's foreign policy was bankrupt. His machine tottered, and only increased GPU terror kept it from falling. Britain's rupture of diplo-

---

[12] Alexander Barmine, *One Who Survived*, pp. 161–166.

matic relations at the end of May, and the assassination of Voikov on June 7, were utilized to the utmost for persecuting the Opposition. On May 20 five "Polish spies and counter-revolutionaries" were executed. On June 6, five more were shot in Odessa, and on July 13 ten more. In Moscow, on June 20, twenty were shot for "counter-revolutionary activities and connection with the British government."

In Leningrad in particular, the critical international situation was used as a pretext to annihilate the oppositionists. On June 7, the GPU announced that an unnamed number of Leningrad workers, accused of having sent threatening letters to the administration, had been shot without trial. Wherever opposition was particularly strong, the GPU was adept at finding amalgams between Russian "counter-revolutionaries" and foreign "spies." In Kronstadt, for example, Klepikov, a former commander of the White Army, was condemned to death as an agent of Great Britain on June 17; a few weeks later his wife was named as his accomplice. In Moscow, on July 5, the GPU conveniently discovered a plot to blow up its headquarters; three of the conspirators, who tried to escape, were shot on the spot, and thus further investigation was made impossible.

The Politburo dramatized this attempt to blow up the headquarters of the state police and all other activities of "the captured spies of British imperialism," whether actual or "objective." In a hostile capitalist world, the salvation of the socialist fatherland lay in counter terror. Rumors began to circulate that Stalin intended to shoot the leaders of the Bloc; on August 17, at the express command of the Politburo, Trotsky denied the rumors. From one session of the Central Committee to the next, Stalin was looking for an opportunity to oust the oppositionist leaders; he was able to consummate his plans only after another year of bitter fighting, during which he suffered many reverses.

On September 7, the General Council of the TUC recommended that the British unions break their ties with Soviet labor; the following day, this recommendation was accepted and the Anglo-Russian Trade Union Unity Committee was dissolved. With scant ceremony, the representatives of the Russian unions were finally dropped—because they had interfered in the internal affairs of the British labor movement.

The increased popularity that the Bloc won by the crashing defeat of Stalin's policy in Britain and China posed the question of immediate action. There were those among the Opposition who, in view of the threatening war, counseled withdrawal—if need be, capitulation. Before the increased danger of another foreign intervention, the prime consideration was that the foreign armies should meet a united Russia.

Trotsky opposed this defeatist mood by his so-called Clemenceau thesis. In 1914, at a moment when the German armies were approaching Paris, Clemenceau had not hesitated to lead a most vicious campaign against the disastrous policy of the French cabinet. By these audacious tactics, he had overthrown it, rallied the wavering French people to the new government, turned the tide, and led France to victory. In the view of Trotsky, just the immediacy of the war danger made the success of the Bloc not only more possible but more urgent, for the country would not now follow Stalin into a war. The necessity of combating capitalist intervention would, it was hoped, revive the spirit of the October days.

In Russia the parallel between Trotsky and Clemenceau was accepted as the password to an anti-Stalinist uprising. Stalin sent Kamenev as ambassador to Rome; his departure from Moscow was marked by a protest demonstration at the station.

There was a plenary session of the Comintern Executive Committee in June, just after Britain had broken off diplomatic relations. Stalin posed as Russia's military leader; by his usual simple attire of tunic and Wellington boots, he emphasized to the Comintern delegates his combined role as Party and army commander-in-chief. The danger of war and the Chinese debacle were discussed; "the Russian question," again taboo, could only be whispered of in the corridors of St. Andrew's Hall.

At Stalin's instigation, the Russian delegation proposed that Trotsky and Vuyo Vuyovich be expelled from the Executive Committee. In the four-day debate, the Italian delegation (including Palmiro Ercoli-Togliatti), Albert Treint of France,[13] Victor Stern of Czechoslovakia, and Béla Kun, spoke against the motion. Stalin was most ardently supported by Ernst Thälmann, new leader of the German party. Zinoviev, who had been ousted from his post as Comintern chairman, was barred from the meeting hall by the armed guard posted at the door.

---

[13] Treint left the French party after the June plenum; he published a pamphlet in which he declared that Stalin's hands were red with the blood of Chinese Communists.

There was not enough room to seat him, Heimo told the delegates. But this cheap little maneuver was opposed even by Arthur Ewert, who was afraid of the bad impression it would make abroad. The defeat in China had been so decisive, and so clearly the result of their policy, that Stalin and Bukharin were afraid of having the delegates even hear the oppositionist attack. The petty vexation by which he tried to humiliate Zinoviev was a typical Stalinist gesture for by this attempt, which he was able to abandon without loss, he tested out how far he could go in more serious matters.

At the July 1927 plenum of the Central Committee, Trotsky and Zinoviev, apparently hopelessly beaten, showed that they had done better than merely survive the intervening months. With Stalin's defeat in China, the Bloc had won more authority. Stalin of course maintained his numerical majority—a reversal would have meant the consummation of a coup—but his faction was obviously wavering. The very resolution that Stalin's majority passed indicated that his power was shaky.

> Of late, in connection with the special difficulties in the international position of the USSR and the partial defeat of the Chinese Revolution, the opposition has concentrated its attack against the Party along the line of our international policy (in China and Great Britain) . . .
>
> The statements regarding the Thermidorian degeneration of the Central Committee, the policy of conservative nationalism, the kulak-Ustryalov line of the Party, the declaration that *"the greatest of all dangers is the Party regime"* and not the menace of war —all of these statements, tending as they did to weaken the will of the international proletariat for the defense of the USSR, were characterized by the Plenum of the ECCI as "a means, in the face of the war danger, . . . of camouflaging their desertion before the workers." [14]

Stalin extracted another pledge from Trotsky and Zinoviev to refrain from factional activity, but this declaration was rather vague, much weaker in its disintegrating effect than the one in October 1926. Against the background of the crisis, no one in either the Russian Party or the Comintern took it at its face value.

The crisis in the Russian Party was coming to a head; one or the other faction must soon win the decisive victory. Scarcely a month

---

[14] Quoted in Popov, II, 316; emphasis added.

after the July plenum, the leaders of the Bloc issued their platform preparatory to the Fifteenth Party Congress; in it they accused the Politburo, in Popov's words, "of the intention to dissolve the Comintern, to betray the Chinese revolution, to recognize the Tsarist debts, to abolish the foreign trade monopoly, to adopt a policy favoring the kulak in the countryside, and similar insolent nonsense."[15] In a decisive step forward, the Bloc sent out directives to organize non-Party workers as supporting groups around oppositionist party cells. Organizational links in the army were tightened, and special groups were assigned to liaison with the Komsomol.

One of Stalin's main instruments for counteracting the mounting danger was the Central Control Commission, which was headed in this period by G. K. ("Sergo") Ordzhonikidze, Stalin's close friend.[16] The procedure by which those who had been expelled or were threatened with expulsion were processed was much more subtle than simple physical torture. In "discussions" averaging three days in length, the Central Control Commission applied a peculiar combination of psychological with physical terror; offers of a promotion to a good assignment abroad were alternated with threats of banishment to Siberia or execution. In some cases, as for example with Vladimir Smirnov, the discussion was continued over eight days. The resistance of weaker minds broke down under this prolonged interrogation—the over-refined questions on Party dogma, the appeal to patriotism, the reminder that if they lost their Party status their children would be deprived of educational facilities, and above all, the constant pressure to divulge everything about other oppositionists.

This parade of penitents, this dress rehearsal for the show trials of the thirties, gave Stalin's Control Commission an opportunity of culling a sizable section of the Opposition. Many that had been expelled were readmitted.

---

[15] Popov, II, 317.

[16] Like so many who helped boost Stalin into power, Ordzhonikidze was not allowed to live to share it. In 1936, "to the complete surprise of his family and his attending physicians, Ordzhonikidze died. There are those who believe that in a moment of despair he took poison. There are others who believe that he was poisoned by Dr. Levin—the same doctor who later confessed to having poisoned Maxim Gorky. That he died by violence, that his end was not 'natural,' my sources have not the slightest doubt." (Victor Kravchenko, *I Chose Freedom,* New York, 1946, p. 240.)

In this way [Ordzhonikidze reported] we have readmitted almost 90 per cent of all those expelled from the Party. With one hand, we fight the oppositionists and expel them from the Party, and with the other hand, it has been said, the Central Control Commission readmits them all. This happened in several regions, such as Transcaucasia, where we have readmitted almost all the oppositionists.[17]

In the opinion of the oppositionists, this relative clemency was a good omen, for it reflected their influence within the Party. The readmissions also had another objective: by being allowed to circulate as seemingly free Party members for a time, the oppositionists and all their contacts were drawn into the GPU network.

While the supporters of the Bloc were thus being brought into line by the Central Control Commission, Stalin intensified his mass manipulation. The usual pre-revolutionary corner of the home reserved for an ikon and saints' pictures had changed its character; the pictures of the saints were replaced by those of Lenin and Stalin, but the mood of reverence was encouraged to continue. In this period the number of these so-called Red Corners in the factories was increased from 7,000 to 42,000. Various military auxiliary societies were founded—*Osoaviakhim* (a group to study chemical and air warfare), rifle clubs, and the like. Propaganda by movies and radio was increased.[18] The Communist Youth organized carnivals and parades in the streets of Moscow. Women's organizations and Pioneer groups received more attention; school children were indoctrinated with the latest Party line.

This last point can be illustrated by a personal anecdote. During my stay in Moscow in this period, I saw much of my good friend G. L. Shklovsky. He had been an intimate of Lenin in exile, the Russian consul in Hamburg in 1923, a devoted friend of Zinoviev and the German Left. An old man with a wide experience, he brushed aside involved dogmatic discussions with the simple statement that things were going from bad to worse. As a chemist in the office of the Central Control Commission, he had a good insight into the GPU-ization of the Party; for him all Party programs were sheer verbiage unless they

---

[17] Ordzhonikidze's report to the Fifteenth Party Congress, quoted in *Inprekorr*, 1927, p. 2881.

[18] Cf. Kossior's report on organizational activities, quoted in *Inprekorr*, 1927, p. 2809 ff.

began with breaking the GPU terror in the country. Shklovsky had spent years in Western Europe; he spoke German, French, and English. A man of deep integrity, he was of the best type of Bolshevik revolutionary. I visited him often at his modest three-room apartment, where he lived with his wife and their three teen-age daughters. One day the youngest, twelve years old, came home from school completely bewildered by the hour's instruction she had been given on the trade-union deviations of Ruth Fischer. She knew me as the woman who had often sat at her father's dinner table; she asked me some questions but was of course unable to grasp what was going on. During the last weeks of my stay in Moscow I discontinued these pleasant visits to Shklovsky's home, as well as the weekends at his *dacha* at Silverwood; we used to meet in the park.

New mass manipulatory elements were also developed in the international field. Workers' delegations to Soviet Russia in particular became more important as instruments of propagandizing. On November 9, 1927, there was a world congress in Moscow of the Friends of the Soviet Union. Of the 947 delegates from forty-three countries, there were 173 from Germany, 146 from France, 127 from Britain; about a third of them were Communists. On November 13, Stalin granted a six-hour interview to a workers' delegation of eighty workers from Germany, France, Austria, Czechoslovakia, Belgium, Finland, Denmark, Estonia, China, and Latin America.[19]

The Fourth International?

In the international field, the Bloc planned to hold an international conference of Left Communists in Berlin at the end of 1927. The Opposition's coup in Russia was thus to get international support; the new leadership would take power not as national but as international Communists. Zinoviev in particular was interested in the preparations for this conference; using the code and couriers of the embassy, he sent out his ideas concerning it through Safarov in Istanbul.[20]

---

[19] There were two well-prepared questions on the Maslow-Fischer opposition, which Stalin answered at length. To another question, "What are your plans for collectivization of the peasantry?" Stalin answered, "Step by step, through measures of an economic, financial, cultural, and political nature . . . In three ways: by private economy, by coöperatives, and by state economy."

[20] A Bolshevik and a member of the Leningrad organization since 1908, George

The prospects for an international bloc supporting Zinoviev and Trotsky looked very good in 1926–1927. The greatest difficulty was maintaining contact with the Russian oppositionists, and various Soviet functionaries risked their jobs and their freedom in bringing out material through the GPU control. Turov, who worked at the Berlin Trade Legation, was very helpful, as were Kaplinsky and Isayev. Pereverzev, who had been sent to a Geneva committee as a railroad technician, had a pass that was accepted at every station in Europe. We in Berlin were sent material from supporters of the Bloc everywhere—in Rome, in Paris, in the Balkan embassies, in England and America; we were particularly well connected with the Chinese Trotskyists.

Most of the oppositionists who were sent abroad by Stalin made their way through Berlin, and we saw them all and discussed the problems of the Bloc undisturbed. I saw Kollontai, for example, on her way to Norway. She impressed us as a weak and emotional character, tied to the Opposition only by vague sympathy with its aims; we were not surprised when she switched sides and supported Stalin. At the beginning of 1927, Solntsev, a close friend of Trotsky, was transferred to Berlin. A brilliant young man, he was a fanatical Trotskyist, and in the many heated discussions with him on, for example, the theory of the permanent revolution, we recognized the important differences between him and such Zinovievists as Kaplinsky and Pereverzev.[21]

In the late summer of 1927, when Kamenev passed through Berlin on his way to Rome, we worked out the plan for the Berlin conference in detail. During the next month or so, we contacted oppositionist groups in various countries—in France, Albert Treint; in Czechoslovakia, a group of Sudeten Germans around Alois Neurath and a group around the youth leader Karl Michaletz; in Austria, a group led by Joseph Frey. Our program at the conference would depend in part on what happened in Russia; if the Bloc regained power, then the Left Communists would return to a united Comintern. If not, even if a second party was not yet possible in Russia, we intended to form a

---

Ivanovich Safarov had been banished to Peking after the Fourteenth Party Congress. In the spring of 1927 he had been transferred to the Trade Legation in Istanbul.

[21] Solntsev was sent to the United States in 1928. In 1935, having returned to Russia, he was sent to Siberia; he died there while being transported from one prison to another.

Left communist international as the base for continued underground resistance in Russia.

Through these various contacts we learned of the opinion of the so-called Ultra-Left wing within the Bloc, among whom were, for instance, Safarov and Mrachkovsky [22] and various Trotskyist officers. Stalin was unpopular, they held, and could maintain his power against the Opposition only by terror, which he would not hesitate to use. As long as the Stalin group remained in power, most of the potential support of the Opposition would not dare to show itself. Therefore, they recommended no street demonstration, no illegal meetings, but the simultaneous arrest of the leading figures in Moscow and Leningrad and a few other key points, a few hundred persons in all, the proclamation of a provisional Politburo. Only then, after the Party was freed from the fear of GPU terror, would a regular Party convention have its full democratic content, and a convention held under such circumstances, this group was convinced, would return a large majority for the Opposition.

Maslow and I did not accept this view, for it meant risking the success of the Bloc on a single action; if it failed, Stalin would not hesitate to exterminate his adversaries. We thought rather, in this period of rising totalitarianism in Russia, the oppositionists should dig in, should follow a policy of silent resistance, until the approaching European crisis offered the most favorable moment for action. Our German comrades differed in many nuances, but the prevailing mood among them was "either–or—." Either build up in Germany an independent communist party, whose central function would be not merely to support the Russian Opposition but to play an important role in German labor. Or, in view of the repeated "capitulations" of the Russian oppositionist leaders and their effect in Germany, renounce the fight for factional differences and return to the official Communist Party, to help fight against the growing danger of Nazism. Some went by one road, to devote their lives to maintaining one of the dozen tiny grouplets that mushroomed in pre-Hitler Germany, and some by the

---

[22] Sergei V. Mrachkovsky, a Bolshevik since 1905, had commanded the partisan troops that defeated Kolchak. Then he became commander of the Ural Military District, a post he lost during the fight against Trotsky in 1923. Arrested in November 1927, he was in prison during the Fifteenth Party Congress. He was sentenced to death in the 1936 trial and killed.

other, to build up Stalin's Comintern. At this time no one in Germany, or in the West generally, appreciated sufficiently the difficulties that the Opposition faced in Russia; there was a general tendency to measure their actions, taken in the face of increasing GPU terror, by the standards of liberal democracy.

In Russia, the Opposition intensified its underground work. Under Mrachkovsky's direction, it set up a small clandestine printing plant; some of the leaflets were printed in the GPU plant itself. The Opposition, encouraged by its successes, tried to walk the wire between this dangerous alliance and provocation. The unfolding terror of Stalin's regime met resistance within the terror apparatus itself; the desertion in 1937 of two agents abroad, Ignatz Reiss and Walter Krivitsky, gave belated evidence of the continued tension in the Russian terror machine.[23]

A new "breakthrough to legality" was planned. A platform signed by eighty-three of the leading members of the Opposition, was circulated in the Party and through the Comintern and, in spite of the

---

[23] The Stalin eulogists, Sayers and Kahn, discuss this fear that the Soviet bureaucracy has of the terror apparatus it has built in a most revealing passage:

"When Zinoviev and Kamenev were arrested [after Kirov's assassination on December 1, 1934], four agents of the Soviet secret police had brought them to NKVD headquarters. The agents were Molchanov, Chief of the Secret Political Department of the NKVD; Pauker, Chief of the Operations Department; Volovich, Assistant Chief of the Operations Department; and Bulanov, Assistant to the Chairman of the NKVD [who with Bukharin and Yagoda was later one of the defendants of the 1938 trial].

"In arresting Zinoviev and Kamenev, the four NKVD agents acted in a most extraordinary fashion. They not only failed to search the apartments of the suspects for incriminating material; they actually permitted Zinoviev and Kamenev to destroy a number of incriminating documents.

"Still more remarkable were the records of these four NKVD agents. Molchanov and Bulanov were themselves secret members of the Trotskyite-Right conspiratorial apparatus. Pauker and Volovich were German agents.

"These men had been specially picked to make the arrests by Henry G. Yagoda, the Chairman of the NKVD." (Michael Sayers and Albert E. Kahn, *The Great Conspiracy: The Secret War Against Soviet Russia*, Boston, 1946, pp. 252–253.)

That a police state breeds conspiracy within the police itself was shown also in the last years of Hitler's Third Reich. Gisevius says that in the cellar of Strünck he used to meet Nebe, the chief of the *Kriminalpolizei*, and Count von Helldorf, chief of the Berlin police. As part of their job, both these men reported daily to the Gestapo, and hurried from their luncheon meetings at Gestapo headquarters, with many a backward glance, to the underground cellar meetings, which were preparing the July 20 coup against Hitler. (Cf. Hans Bernd Gisevius, *Bis zum bittern Ende*, Zurich, 1946, II, 285–358.)

GPU terror, it won considerable support; in Kharkov, for example, there were 180 Party members who dared sign it. "This was," Stalin writes, "perhaps the most mendacious and pharisaical of all opposition platforms."

> In their platform, they professed they had no objection to Party unity and were against splits, but in reality they grossly violated Party unity, worked for a split, and already had their own illegal, anti-Leninist party which had all the makings of an anti-Soviet, counter-revolutionary party.
>
> In their platform, they professed they were all in favor of the policy of industrialization, and even accused the Central Committee of not proceeding with industrialization fast enough, but in reality they did nothing but carp at the Party resolution on the victory of Socialism in the USSR . . .
>
> In their platform, they professed they were in favor of the collective-farm movement, and even accused the Central Committee of not proceeding with collectivization fast enough, but in reality they scoffed at the policy of enlisting the peasants in the work of Socialist construction . . .[24]

This Platform of the Eighty-Three was signed by Trotskyists and Zinovievists only; the Workers' Opposition, though maintaining contact with the Bloc, had built up its own organization, so that they could continue their independent opposition to the Stalinist Politburo if Trotsky and Zinoviev withdrew from the struggle. Some months before, the Democratic Centralism group had issued a Platform of the Fifteen, which centered around three main points: (1) The State Party is hopelessly degenerated and cannot be reformed. The fight for another Party majority, the struggle to break through to Party legality, is futile, a senseless form of resistance that forces the anti-Stalinist cadres into GPU traps and alienates the workers from the oppositionist Bloc. (2) The degeneration of the State Party expresses the end of the October revolution, which has been betrayed by a hierarchy rising on its shoulders. (3) The workers have never in fact been in power in Russia, but the October revolution gave them the base on which a workers' society could have been built. That base has been destroyed by the Stalinist counter revolution, and the workers have been thrown back into the position of a class in opposition to the monolithic state.

---

[24] [Joseph Stalin], *History of the CPSU*, p. 284.

They must organize resistance against the hostile state power; they must form a genuine workers' party, not in order to struggle for state power—which in this period is to be regarded as of no more than abstract and theoretical interest—but to defend labor's rights against the further encroachments of the Stalinist state.

In preparation for the Fifteenth Party Congress, which was to be held in December, oppositionists attempted to speak at Party meetings in defense of the Platform of the Eighty-Three.

> The Party convention was planned for December, and its preparation was undertaken with feverish zeal. It began with meetings at which reports on the Central Committee plenum were given. Admission to these meetings was by personal invitation only; comrades known to be oppositionists obviously did not have access to them. If in spite of these precautions some did get in, there were storm troops, composed of declassed elements of the apparatus, assigned to sabotage oppositionist speeches with noise and turbulent interruptions.[25]

Under GPU command, these shock brigades rang bells, shouted, started fights. There were emotional outbursts from outraged comrades, who could no longer bear to listen to the counter-revolutionary arguments of the Opposition; they stood up and with Bolshevik zeal tore the oppositionist literature to bits. At some meetings it was ceremoniously burnt. Sometimes when an oppositionist speaker took the floor the lights were turned off. As Stalin puts it in his history, "the Party members gave the oppositionists a severe rebuff, and in some places simply ejected them from the meetings."[26]

Meanwhile, despite the readmission of the "90 per cent" that Ordzhonikidze was to report, the expulsions and banishments continued. "During the night of September 12–13, the GPU made a series of raids, searching the houses of oppositionist Communists and non-Party workers."[27] In particular, the homes of the oppositionist secretaries were searched; the GPU invariably confiscated their typewriters, which were at that time very rare in Russia.[28]

---

[25] Letter from Russia, *Die Fahne des Kommunismus,* September 30, 1927.

[26] [Joseph Stalin], *History of the CPSU,* p. 283.

[27] Letter from Russia, *Die Fahne des Kommunismus,* October 14, 1927.

[28] The lack of all types of technical equipment in this period can perhaps be best pictured by a curious anecdote. Nadezhda Krupskaya, Lenin's widow, sent

The principal tactical device of Stalin was to form an enormous amalgam, by which the members of the Bloc were somehow entangled with British spies, underground White Guardists, the assassins of Voikov in Warsaw. For example, it was alleged that Trotsky had been in contact with one Shcherbakov, not a Party member, the son of a former factory owner. Shcherbakov had approached a former Wrangel officer to ask him for a mimeograph, and a certain Tverskoi spoke to the same officer, telling him that a military coup was imminent. From such slight beginnings, by adding new characters and enriching the plot with more picturesque details, every move of the Opposition was poisoned by intrigue. Their very existence came to be interpreted as a danger to the socialist state: if they met with anyone at all, it was to conspire; if they did anything at all, it was intended to overthrow the socialist state; if they did nothing, it was only because they were awaiting a more opportune moment. It was in this period that the situation began which in its full development would make the mere mention of the name of Trotsky or Zinoviev an oppositionist act.

Cut out in practice from discussion within the Party branches, the Opposition organized its own secret pre-convention meetings. Leaders

---

out an appeal for help in furnishing the Russian countryside with spinning wheels. In an article published in the official Comintern weekly (*Inprekorr*, 1927, p. 1863) in several languages and distributed throughout the world, she described "the terrible scarcity of spinning wheels in the villages of the Soviet Union" and appealed for help. The peasant woman, who slaved in the field all summer, had no respite during the winter. In her dark, windowless hut, she sat and spun flax and hemp with a manual spinning wheel. In the Bryansk district, the girls never went to school because they had no time.

The peasant women of Smolensk and Konotop, hearing of the existence of machines that facilitated the spinning and weaving of cloth, appealed for state help in getting them. They were of course very poor; in many villages they lacked even the kopeks it cost to subscribe to *The Peasant Woman*. The Textile Syndicate in Moscow answered, "We have investigated this problem and discovered that there is no such spinning wheel in existence, one designed to facilitate home industry."

Krupskaya appealed, therefore, to all inventors, Russian or foreign, to help the Russian peasant women. Writing on the tenth anniversary of the Russian revolution, she declared, "Give us a spinning wheel, an October spinning wheel, that will raise the cultural level of the peasant women!"

The *Inprekorr* editors added a comment to German inventors. Proposals could be sent to the committee formed to judge the competition that had been organized, but the inventors should take into account the fact that "even the spinning wheel of our forefathers (operated with a pedal) is very rare in the peasant regions of Russia. The yarn of the Russian peasant is spun with a *hand* spinning wheel."

of the October revolution spoke in two-room apartments of workers, who risked everything by this hospitality; from twenty to two hundred stood or sat on the floor to listen. When the GPU came to break up an illegal meeting, they were invited to join in and listen to the discussion. In all, according to Trotsky's estimate, some twenty thousand persons attended meetings of this kind in Moscow and Leningrad.[29] As a test of its strength, the Opposition seized the Moscow Technical School, and for two hours Trotsky and Kamenev spoke to an audience of two thousand without interruption. Though Stalin had enough police to break up the meeting, he did not dare force the issue. Outside Moscow, however, the Bloc had to discontinue larger illegal meetings.

Stalin's uncertainty is illustrated, too, in a speech before the October plenum of the Central Committee.

> STALIN: Have we ever accused the Opposition, or do we now accuse them, of organizing a military conspiracy? Of course not. Have we ever accused the Opposition, or do we now accuse them, of participating in such a conspiracy? Of course not.
>
> MURALOV: In the last session you did make just such an accusation.
>
> STALIN: You are wrong, Comrade Muralov. We have two communications about an illegal printing plant and about non-Party intellectuals connected with this printing plant. You will not find one sentence, one word, in these documents by which we accuse the Opposition of participating in a military conspiracy. In these documents the Central Committee and the Central Control Commission assert only that the Opposition, in organizing this illegal printing plant, has allied itself with non-Party bourgeois intellectuals, and that moreover some of these intellectuals have been proved to be in alliance with White Guardists, who are considering a military conspiracy.[30]

This same October plenum, however, expelled Trotsky and Zinoviev from the Central Committee.

It was the eve of the tenth anniversary of the Bolshevik revolution, and throughout the country mass demonstrations were being organized. All the Party leaders were in Leningrad, attending the Central Com-

---

[29] Cf. Trotsky, *My Life,* pp. 531–532.

[30] *Die Fahne des Kommunismus,* November 18, 1927. N. E. Muralov was sentenced to death in the 1937 trial, together with Pyatakov and eleven others. Radek and Sokolnikov, defendants in the same trial, were sentenced to ten years.

mittee plenum there, and there was an official celebration before the Tauride Palace. Zinoviev and Trotsky deliberately chose the last motor truck lined up for the occasion and thus disconnected themselves from the Central Committee group reviewing the demonstration at the head of the line. Their supporters massed around the last truck and gave the two leaders of the Bloc a stormy ovation; they left the demonstration in high spirits.

Stalin marked the anniversary, November 7, with a maneuver designed to soothe the unrest in the country. In a manifesto of the Central Committee, a series of measures favoring the working class, headed by the seven-hour day, was solemnly ordained as law in socialist Russia. The poor peasants were promised exemption from taxation and proffered state assistance in improving their situation. On October 1, as part of the same maneuver, an amnesty had been granted minor offenders. This political turn, "a turn to the Left, to Marxism and Leninism," which apparently had adopted its program, was of decisive influence in quelling the Opposition.

The response which the oppositionist supporters had given the October 27 rally in Leningrad pushed the leaders of the Bloc to the culmination of their plans. In accordance with Communist tactics usual outside Russia, Trotsky and Zinoviev were to organize street demonstrations in Moscow and Leningrad against the Central Committee. Dissatisfaction with Stalin's policy was so widespread that, it was hoped, these two meetings would spread to other industrial centers and the Party hierarchy would be forced to yield. "Out of secret small gatherings into open street demonstrations!" Posters were prepared, groups organized, speakers assigned.

In Berlin, when Maslow and I heard of the plan from Herzberg,[31] who was in a mood of exalted optimism, we sent word to Zinoviev that in our opinion the plan would not work and that, in case of failure, Stalin's revenge would not permit a second attempt. Though we then considered the plan immature and dangerous, I recognize today that Herzberg and the other Russians who shared his enthusiasm knew much better than we how little relation there was between Stalin's

---

[31] Herzberg was a Party organizer from Leningrad. He had a minor post at the Soviet Trade Legation but spent almost all his time working for the Opposition. He was shot during the trial period, 1935–1937.

numerical majority and his actual support in the country. The isolation of the State Party had reached a point where the rupture between it and the bulk of the people was visible. Even if it did not reach its immediate objective, the demonstration would intimidate Stalin and weaken and postpone his plans.

In the week before the anniversary, the cadres of the Opposition were further decimated by arrests. Naked terror reigned. Turov, who had been suddenly recalled from the Berlin Trade Legation, was found dead near Moscow. A few days before the planned demonstration, the Central Control Commission extracted declarations of capitulation from several important members of the Opposition, including Krupskaya, Sokolnikov, Zalutsky.

When Trotsky appeared in the Moscow streets, he was pelted with rotten apples. Wherever he went, fights broke out and the demonstration was transformed into a riot. Surrounded by this "belt of incidents," he was never able to address the crowd. "A policeman, pretending to be giving a warning, shot openly at my automobile."[32] In Leningrad, the GPU was even more effective. The riot was organized so well that the police found it necessary to put Zinoviev and Radek under protective arrest before they reached the streets. They were locked up for the duration of the demonstration, and a large detachment of armed guards was posted before the building.

Thus the "break-through to legality" ended in disaster. As Popov wrote, "By coming out in the streets on November 7, the Opposition passed an even more annihilating verdict upon itself. It signed its own death warrant."[33]

Four days later, another ultimatum was issued to the Opposition: The Party line must be defended by every Party member; there must be no discussion outside the Party. Nor inside: illegal oppositionist meetings were prohibited again. While the GPU was thus building an iron wall between the oppositionist leaders and all who might otherwise hear them, Kollontai paid for her job in the diplomatic service with an article in *Pravda,* entitled "The Masses Do Not Believe in the Opposition."

On November 14, one week exactly after the planned demonstration,

---

[32] Trotsky, *My Life,* p. 534.
[33] Popov, II, 319.

a joint session of the Central Committee and the Central Control Commission expelled Trotsky and Zinoviev from the Party.

Two days later, Joffe, Trotsky's close friend, committed suicide. Once the top leaders were expelled, the followers throughout the country were subjected to extreme terror. Not a defendant's crime, but his behavior, was decisive—his importance to the Bloc's organization, his popularity among his fellow workers, his intellectual and moral qualities. Strong characters had to be broken, those of high intellectual caliber isolated from all sources of information, popular figures removed from their environment. Thus, by measures varying in degree from simple demotion to a death sentence, the GPU realistically went about disintegrating the remnants of the Opposition. For those leaders who capitulated "totally," there was always the possibility of starting life anew—for a short while.

Trotsky Is Banished to Central Asia

The Opposition was shattered, its leaders expelled from the Party, many of its middle-rank leaders in prison or killed, its rank and file frightened into silence. Moreover, the delegates to the Fifteenth Party Congress were even more carefully selected than those to the Fourteenth; those who indicated a lingering sympathy for oppositionist views on even minor points were discarded. Mere verbal endorsement of Stalin's policy was not enough; the delegates were chosen, as were the men who were imprisoned, on the basis of their behavior. The convention was completely rigged, and there was no doubt that it would give Stalin an overwhelming majority. Nevertheless, Stalin felt the pressure of the silent resistance throughout the country, and he felt that the congress would need a shot in the arm. This stimulus was furnished by what has since been called in official Party histories the "Canton Commune."

Immediately after Chiang's about face in April and May, Stalin had sent a group of his followers to China to see what could be salvaged out of the mess. Among these was the German, Heinz Neumann, who was at that time fanatically devoted to Russia's new leader. He was able to set off a series of special fireworks in Canton, to take the mind of the delegates to the Fifteenth Congress off the Stalin-led Chinese debacle.

During the period of the rising revolution, the Communist Party of China, following Stalin's orders to the letter, had tied themselves like a second tail to the Kuomintang, and when the time came Chiang had cut off this unwanted appendage. Now that the revolution was crushed, now that tens of thousands of Chinese Communists had been killed, Stalin turned to the Left. At a party çonference in August, the old leadership was denounced (for having followed all too faithfully the instructions it got from Moscow), and the new leaders ordered preparation for an immediate insurrection.

During the height of the Chinese revolution, Stalin had declared that with such an organization as the Kuomintang soviets could be dispensed with. Now, in December 1927, he ordered soviets. The "Canton Commune," made to order, lasted exactly three days before Chiang crushed it in an ocean of blood. Neumann and his Russian friends escaped, but the Canton Communists paid with their lives to decorate the walls of the Fifteenth Congress with revolutionary slogans. As late as February 7, 1928, *Pravda* wrote, "The Chinese Communist Party is heading towards an armed insurrection. The whole situation in China speaks for the fact that this is the correct course." [34]

The Fifteenth Party Congress convened on December 2, 1927, and met for more than two weeks. It was attended by 898 delegates and 771 candidates, representing about 890,000 Party members and 350,000 candidates. Half of the delegates (449 out of 898) were attending their first Party convention; they would have no measure by which to gauge the Bolshevik realism of the convention proceedings. As the official report points out, there was a "complete renewal of cadres." [35] The number of Party officials among the delegates decreased from the 70 per cent at the Fourteenth Congress to 45 per cent; the number of workers increased from 5 to 18 per cent. Thirty-eight per cent of the delegates, as compared with 59 per cent at the Fourteenth Congress, had been in the Party since before 1917.

By the official figures, 724,000 Party members had voted for Stalin, and 4,000, or less than 1 per cent, for the Opposition. [36] The GPU had

---

[34] Quoted in Trotsky, *Problems of the Chinese Revolution*, p. 294.

[35] *Inprekorr*, December 1927.

[36] The figures are from Stalin's *History of the CPSU*, p. 285. Popov (II, 323) gives the figures as 725,000 votes to 6,000; even from one official history of the Party to the next, the oppositionist vote is reduced by one-third.

done its work well. But, as before, numerical majorities made up of
delegates coerced into their position need not have been decisive. During the first days of the convention neither Trotsky nor Zinoviev recognized the depth of their defeat; they both retained illusions of influencing some of the delegates and salvaging a working minority out
of their apparent rout. This could be done, it was felt, only if once
again the Opposition pledged itself to follow Party discipline. The
convention therefore opened with a formal declaration of loyalty from
the Bloc, which Stalin immediately characterized as a "complete disarmament."

Stalin reported for the Central Committee. He was furnished with
an appropriate background: a document by Krichevsky, "former member of the Ukraine Opposition," was circulated; Krupskaya spoke
against the Bloc; Bukharin quoted a letter from Lenin. Stalin centered his attack on the oppositionist demand for "Party unity"—that
is, for Party legality. He pointed out the splits in the Bloc itself—with
the various Workers' Opposition groups, with the Maslow-Fischer
group. To the nth degree he emphasized every difference between
Trotsky and Zinoviev, old or new, real or fancied, personal or political. In spite of the heaviest possible attack on the Opposition as a
whole, there were yet undertones indicating that Trotsky, as contrasted
with the Old Bolsheviks, was the most criminal.

When Rakovsky, one of Trotsky's most intimate friends, appeared
on the platform, he was met by an uproar. Constant shouts interrupted him—"Shame! Splitter! Counter-revolutionary!" Rakovsky's
statement went unheard in the noise, and he was not granted an extension of time. His speech ended in a renewed burst of heckling—
"Resign from the Party! Drag them off the platform; the platform is
not for Mensheviks. Drag him off! Drag him off!" [37]

Yevdokimov spoke against the expulsion of leaders like Zinoviev.
Shouts—"Plekhanov was also a leader and went astray." Kirov, a
delegate from Leningrad, scoffed at Lashevich and his "Sermon on

---

[37] Christian Rakovsky, a native of Bulgaria, had a revolutionary past beginning
long before the First World War. After 1917, he became first president of the
Ukrainian Soviet Republic. He was a Soviet diplomat often seen abroad, as delegate to the Genoa conference in 1922, as ambassador to both Paris and London.
He was sentenced to death in the 1938 trial, together with Bukharin and others,
and killed.

the Mount," as he called the meeting in the wood. He pointed at Safarov, saying that he had conducted an illegal meeting in the Narva district of Leningrad.

Then Kamenev came to the platform and tried for the last time to save the legality of the Bloc. He spoke on the issue, did the Bloc intend to form a second party? Only the Old Guard, the Zinoviev-Kamenev group in the Opposition, was held capable of realizing such a plan, and it was therefore given better treatment than the Trotskyists. Kamenev was heckled less than the other speakers; to some extent he was even listened to. We do not want the organization of a second party, he said. We are for reconciliation, because of the danger to the Soviet Union. The Opposition forms a minority within the Party, and when we ask for reconciliation we are proposing the appropriate measure to save the Party—and with the Party, the country. We have fought a bitter fight, but now we are willing to subordinate ourselves to the will of the majority.

Kamenev strongly protested the arrest of the oppositionists.

> A situation facing you with men like Mrachkovsky in jail while we are free—that cannot continue. We fought together with those comrades; we bear the responsibility for all their actions . . . It is not possible to separate us from them. Such is the situation. When you try to separate us, you lose respect for us. [*Voice:* We have had no respect for you since October 16.] [38]

Kamenev's attitude was dignified; he did not disavow the political platform of the Opposition, but fought hard to preserve its legal status. His implied suggestion that the delegates compromise again with the Bloc was not accepted, but he impressed them and saved at least some of the oppositionists from immediate exile to Siberia.

It was a dangerous moment for Stalin when for the last time the Old Guard spoke from a legal platform. As Stalin well knew, Kamenev had been until the end Lenin's closest personal friend. As he died, Lenin had personally charged him with editing his writings and with various missions, of which the liaison with Trotsky was only one. Thus, to eliminate Kamenev from the Party symbolized a break not

---

[38] *XV. Sezd Vsesoiuznoi Kommunisticheskoi Partii* (B), second edition (Moscow, 1928), p. 256. Only one of the many interruptions noted in the minutes is quoted here.

only with the revolutionary past but with the person of Lenin; it made even the Stalinist hooligans pause for a moment in their rough ride to unbridled power.

Rykov rose immediately after Kamenev to destroy the impression he had made.

> The substance of Comrade Kamenev's speech is the outcome of the decision of the illegal Central Committee of the Trotskyist party. From that speech it is obvious that the Central Committee of the Opposition decided not to capitulate and to try to preserve its future legality within our Party (also preserving unchanged its Menshevik ideology) and to screen its illegal activity. [Hear, hear!] This is the only logical explanation of Comrade Kamenev's speech.

In the last part of his speech, Rykov attacked especially Trotsky's Clemenceau thesis and tried to separate him from Kamenev. He said that the oppositionists were consulting in three separate chambers, each group by itself, and then together. They held their group discipline higher than Party discipline, he said.

> Do they not understand that they have attempted to prepare or organize to overthrow the government by these street demonstrations against the Party, against the government? . . . They were, in fact, organizing what is usually called civil war.[39]

Every speech by a Stalinist speaker emphasized that another statement accepting Party discipline would not be accepted. The time for maneuvering was past; what was required was complete capitulation. This message was directed less against the Opposition than against those in Stalin's own group who were hesitating.

Illusions of retaining Party legality disappeared quickly and completely. The question now was how to avoid deportation to Siberia, for there the Bloc leaders would lose every contact with their supporters both in Russia and abroad. At this point in the process of milling the Opposition, we come to a chapter peculiarly Stalinist. The Bloc, in complete verbal defeat, which by resolutions of the congress had been routed, was approached by the leader himself to negotiate the terms of their surrender. Under the guise of Party discipline, the individu-

---

[39] *Minutes*, p. 264.

als of the disintegrated Bloc were now invited to strengthen the victory against those still wavering. These negotiations, whose bait was always the promise of a possible comeback, were repeated ten years later, when most of these same men were taken from their prison cells to the Kremlin to work out the details of their confessions.

Before the Fifteenth Congress ended, Stalin made an explicit offer: if the capitulation was complete enough, expulsions from the Party would be limited in time—readmissions would be considered later—and the Bloc leaders would be allowed to remain in Moscow. On this offer, the Opposition split in two. Trotsky refused it; such a statement, he said, would only complete the demoralization of the oppositionist forces and would not affect the GPU terror. The Zinoviev group again decided to win another respite. In the second half of the convention there were two oppositionist platforms presented. On political issues their wording was almost identical; Zinoviev and Kamenev added a declaration of submission to the Party. Stalin had reached his goal: the Bloc had been split.

The Fifteenth Congress expelled the Opposition *en bloc*. It resolved—

> To instruct the Central Committee and the Central Control Commission not to accept applications from leading members of the former opposition who have been expelled from the Party unless submitted individually and not to make decisions on such applications until at least six months after their submission, provided that: 1) the conduct of those submitting the statements has conformed to the pledges made by the authors of these statements; 2) the statements themselves of the former oppositionists are fully in accord with the demands of the Fifteenth Congress . . . and hence are based on a repudiation of the platform of the eighty-three, of the platform submitted on September 3, and of the platform of the fifteen.[40]

---

[40] *Minutes,* p. 1319. Note that the defeated Opposition was required not only to give up their fight, dissolve the faction, and accept the discipline of the Party, but to give up the ideas they held. Kamenev had pleaded with the convention not to make such a demand: "But if to this unconditional and complete submission to all congress decisions, the complete cessation, complete liquidation of every form of factional struggle and dissolution of the factional organizations, we should add a renunciation of our views—that, in our opinion, would not be acting like Bolsheviks . . . This demand that views be renounced has never been put forward in our Party. If we should renounce views which we advocated a week or two ago, it would be hypocrisy on our part, and you would not believe us."

According to official figures, over 2500 submitted declarations repudiating the Opposition.

Trotsky had to pay the price for the attempt of Zinoviev and Kamenev to win another breathing spell. Stalin took immediate advantage of the split in the Bloc and singled Trotsky out for particularly harsh treatment. Thus the shrewd calculations of Zinoviev failed of their purpose; Stalin alone won by the split, for he was enabled to eliminate his most dangerous competitor for state power.

Trotsky was notified by the GPU that he was to be deported to Alma Ata, on the border of China, 2500 miles from Moscow, 150 miles from the nearest railroad station. There was a sympathy demonstration at the station on January 16, the day he was scheduled to leave, and his departure was postponed. This incident, which the GPU had not been able to suppress, caused almost a panic in the Politburo; if Trotsky continued in Moscow, they feared that the GPU-built unanimity of the convention would melt before their eyes. According to Trotsky's report, Stalin diabolically charged Bukharin with organizing his final send-off. GPU men carried him forcibly out of his apartment, in which he had been completely isolated; the only protest was from Sedov, his son, who shouted, "They are carrying Comrade Trotsky away!" He left from a suburban station, and no one knew whom the departing train carried.

The International Left Meets in Berlin

Parallel with this struggle in the Russian Party, the one between Manuilsky and the German Left was approaching its climax. On German issues alone, the differences between the Stalinist party and the various Left communist groups were not sufficient in 1927 to form the basis of a second party. On the contrary, concerning the relations with the trade-unions and the Social Democrats, concerning the plebiscite, the fight against the monarchists, the Stahlhelm and the other nationalist organizations, there was basic agreement. The fight between the two groups was none the less sharp; by Stalin's orders the purge he was carrying out in Russia was repeated in Germany, and throughout all the Comintern. At the beginning of 1927, some 1300 party functionaries were expelled. Important local units were forced out of the party as a whole—in Hanover, Hamburg-Schiffbek, Frankfurt an der Oder, Rathenow, Schneidemühl; elsewhere branches were decimated by expulsions, especially in the Rhine-Ruhr—in Dortmund, Essen, Hamm, Cologne, and Düsseldorf—as well as in Mannheim, the Palatinate, East Prussia.

These expulsions shook the party and disintegrated it into many factions and splinter groups. At the time of the Essen convention, in February 1927, there were ten Communist groups in and out of the party, reading from Right to Left: (1) The Brandler faction, in which were Paul Böttcher, Jakob Walcher, Rosi Wolfstein, Arthur Rosenberg.[41] (2) The Ernst Meyer faction, a more conciliatory edition of the Brandler tendency. (3) The group of party bureaucrats—Wilhelm Pieck, Walther Ulbricht, Arthur Ewert, Hans Pfeiffer.[42] (4) The Thälmann faction, including Philipp Dengel, Heinz Neumann, Ernst Schneller, Theo Neubauer, Heinrich Süsskind,[43] Karl Volk. (5) The Chemnitz Left faction, led by Paul Bertz, which had groups also in Berlin and Cologne. (6) The Left opposition, led by Arkadi Maslow, Hugo Urbahns, Ruth Fischer. (7) The Palatinate Ultra-Left group, led by Hans Weber. (8) An Ultra-Left group led by Paul Kötter, with its principal strength in the Wedding, the proletarian suburb of Berlin. (9) The Ultra-Left group of Karl Korsch. (10) The Ultra-Left group of Ernst Schwarz, principally in Berlin. These factions and grouplets were in part artificial creations; the Weber and Kötter groups in particular had been handwrought by Manuilsky. There were only three principled differences: the Right, which wanted a close collaboration with the Social Democrats; the Center, which wanted close collaboration with Moscow; and the Left, which wanted a German Communist policy independent of both Stresemann and Stalin.

Manuilsky had in fact accomplished the disintegration before the Essen convention, which endorsed what had been done and completed the job. In spite of the eighteen months of bitter fighting and the thou-

[41] Rosenberg had been with the Thälmann group; he left the party six months later and published an open letter to Stalin urging him to abandon the Third International.

[42] Pfeiffer, who was secretary of the Berlin organization in this period, was sent to Norway and Sweden after 1933. He was shot in 1936 in Russia, one of the victims of the Moscow trials.

[43] Neubauer was in a concentration camp from 1933 to 1939, when he died. Süsskind, editor of the Chemnitz Communist daily, was shot in Moscow in 1936.

sands of expulsions, there were 10 Left delegates of a total of 133. At the convention, the last representative of the Left opposition was expelled; Manuilsky finished his work in Berlin ten months before his boss in Moscow was able to complete the defeat of the Bloc.

That the oppositionists had been expelled over a period of eighteen months, in various little grouplets each of which thought its particular wordy manifesto the answer to every problem, hampered the unity among them that the situation demanded. Sometimes their delegates to the Reichstag worked together as a bloc, but there was little common action beyond that. This splintering of the opposition, a product in part of Moscow's manipulation, was repeated in every party of the Comintern; two years later, the international Right opposition, led by Bukharin, was disintegrated by the same methods. Still half bound to the mysticism of the Stalinist Party, oppositionists maneuvered clumsily; they had to learn the hard way that it is not thus that one fights a totalitarian power.

All during the summer and fall of 1927, we tried to integrate the European Left and prepared for an international conference to be held in Berlin at the same time as the Fifteenth Party Congress in Moscow. In the middle of November the Zinovievist, Safarov, arrived from Istanbul and criticized the Trotskyist, Solntsev, for the slow pace at which the European Left was being organized. From now on, things had to move faster. We met at the beginning of December; there were about twenty Russian comrades present from the various embassies and legations and representatives from the Left factions of almost every European country.

As chairman of the conference, Safarov made a report on its background; it was, he said five minutes to twelve, and the organization of a new international should begin forthwith. In the middle of Sarafov's report, he was handed a telegram from Moscow. Sarafov became pale; controlling himself with visible effort, he continued with his report but changed its content completely. He now stressed the necessity of party discipline, and covered the break so well that some of the delegates did not understand what was happening. Maslow interrupted to ask whether there was another capitulation in the offing; Safarov denied it. The manifesto, however, that he and Maslow had written, which was to be issued by the conference as the rallying point for a new international, was never signed. The end of the Bloc in Russia was in fact the end of the Communist Left in Europe as well.[44]

---

[44] The defeat of the Left was a pattern for the later general defeat of European labor; their experience in the Comintern taught them the nature of a terrorist one-party state, how such a regime is set up, the implications it has for socialist organization—lessons that socialists generally were to learn only later from Hitler.

For a year or two the Left Communists continued as an independent group, and then they split up into grouplets. Contact with Zinoviev, more and more hazardous and infrequent, continued until 1933; several times Shklovsky brought the message to Berlin that the only way out was by a second party in Germany. But it was too late. After 1929, when Bukharin was demoted by Stalin, he also sent calls for help to Germany, but after the Nazis began their rise to power there was even less chance than before of building a second communist party.

A group of the Left rejoined the Communist Party; others joined the Social Democrats or became active in the trade-unions. Within the general resistance to the rising Nazis, Left communists formed a particular subcurrent, enabled by their experience to warn against the developing Nazi regime. In concentration camps after 1933, many of them met a new generation of Trotskyists, workers and students attracted by Trotsky's criticism of Thälmann's policy.

Werner Scholem, one of the outstanding Left leaders, spent years in a concentration camp and was finally killed, but he was only the most prominent among many others. Heinz Langerhans was captured in Berlin in the act of mimeographing anti-Nazi leaflets and incarcerated for six years in Brandenburg and the camp at Sachsenhausen. In 1936 Karl Schröder, a former leader of the KAPD then in the Social Democratic Party, was taken as the leader of an underground group called the *Rote Kämpfer* (Red Fighters). In 1937, in Berlin-Charlottenburg, a group of workers led by Karl Hippel was sentenced to long terms.

This far from complete list had its Soviet counterpart. In 1937, Heinz Neumann and Hermann Remmele, members of the last legal German Central Committee, were killed in Russia. Not only was there parallel terror against German dissident communists in Nazi Germany and Stalinist Russia, but coöperation between the two police bodies. A characteristic story is that of Emil Klubsch, a toolmaker who had emigrated to Gorky in 1928. In 1937, having been branded a Hoelzite, he was handed over by the NKVD to the Gestapo, which placed him in the Sachsenhausen camp.

The transformation of the German Communist Party into one division of the Russian Politburo was strikingly illustrated by the new propaganda forms that were imported and fostered during the middle twenties. Russian propaganda methods, first adapted to the West in Germany, were developed there in one field after another, and with the emigration of thousands of Germans after 1933 spread through the world in their German version. Communist organization of non-Communists in the United States in particular shows an amazing resemblance to earlier German varieties.

The Red Front Fighters' League

The Red Front Fighters' League, an imitation of the Stahlhelm and a precursor of the Nazi storm troopers, had developed surprisingly since its foundation in 1924. Uniformed Communists, young men with a good bearing, marching in military formation under disciplined command, became a frequent and popular sight in Germany; and when their bands played workers' songs and military marches in the market squares, they attracted big crowds. League members marched in formation to all Communist meetings and, standing at attention at the side of the platform, greeted each speaker with a raised-fist salute and *"Rot Front! Heil Moskau!"* They guarded the entrance to the hall and protected party members distributing literature; at street meetings they surrounded the speakers' platform. When

Clara Zetkin or Ernst Thälmann spoke, they formed an honor guard, standing at attention while the Communist dignitary made a ceremonious inspection. They accompanied party members in their rounds seeking donations from small businessmen. The Red Front Fighters' League attracted many socialist and Catholic workers to its ranks. Its regional conventions became local events, in which the population of the small towns joined; as they marched through the streets, League members were cheered by men and girls from the sidewalks and windows; after the march they were treated to free beer. Once a year, traditionally each Whitsunday in Berlin, there was a national jamboree.

In 1926, a quarter of a million League members, most of them young men, came to the jamboree and marched about Berlin's streets. The nationalist newspapers were startled by the fine demeanor of these young fellows. The *Deutsche Tageszeitung* noted their "incomparable discipline and the considerable progress of the organization." The *Börsenzeitung,* organ of the Berlin stock market, wrote: "These demonstrators were not gangsters, not racketeers. They were our German boys, dressed as we have seen them in times past in smart uniforms, who are now, to our great regret, under the spell of Communist fanatics."

With the change in Russia, there was a change in the League's mentality. Founded as a party division assigned to defend the Communist organization, it was soon transformed into a propaganda medium for "the defense of the socialist Fatherland." League delegations were frequently seen in Moscow; on December 7, 1925, for instance, before a crowd of several hundred thousand in the Red Square, a League delegation ceremoniously bestowed a flag on Mikhailov, the Moscow Party secretary. In Germany, the League paraded with pictures of Stalin, Molotov, Voroshilov, and other Russian leaders. A frequently repeated ceremony was a parade to Berlin's Lustgarten, where, to their commander-in-chief, Ernst Thälmann, the members would swear a solemn oath to defend the Soviet fatherland.

In 1925 the women members were organized separately into one of the first uniformed women's groups in Germany. There were many women's organizations in this period: the newly founded International League against Compulsory Motherhood, which demanded that birth control be made legal; the League of Large Families, to help in the welfare of infants and mothers; the Luisenbund, a patriotic women's group, named after Luise, the Prussian queen. At the end of 1925 the Red Women's and Girls' League was founded, with Clara Zetkin as its president. An international women's conference in Moscow was attended by a large German delegation.

In the campaign to expropriate the Hohenzollerns, the women organized their own demonstrations. "The castles of the princes for our children's playgrounds." Women carried six-yard garlands made of billion-mark inflation notes inscribed, "This is Wilhelm's compensation."

In 1924, at a Reich children's conference in Weissenfels, a youth magazine, *Der Junge Genosse* (The Young Comrade), was founded. The Young Pioneers, a Communist children's group organized in 1920, began to flourish in these years. Squadrons of Communist children were pushed to the front on every occasion.

Communist demonstrations changed from the rather dull Social Democratic pattern to a cross between new-style Russian propaganda and American advertising. Party affairs were enlivened by organized mass choruses, and figures of the party's enemies, who were burned in effigy. The rifle clubs of this period used the faces of Chamberlain and other enemies of Soviet Russia as targets.

In 1925, at its Tenth Party Congress, the party tried drama for the first time as a propaganda technique. The Berlin Grosse Schauspielhaus, which was rented for the purpose, had been designated by Max Reinhardt, its first producer, as "The Theater of the Masses." The play was directed by Erwin Piscator, the party's theatrical expert, in collaboration with Ernst Torgler, the educational director of the Berlin branch; the sets were by John Hartfield.[1] In twenty-three scenes, the pageant developed an anti-war theme: the first showed Berlin in 1914 waiting for the declaration of war; others were Liebknecht in the Potsdam Square inciting the soldiers to mutiny, the Social Democratic Reichstag group on July 25, 1914, the assassination of Liebknecht and Luxemburg, a finale of a group of Young Spartakus chil-

---

[1] Piscator is now director of the Dramatic Work Shop, a subsidiary of the New School for Social Research in New York. Hartfield was in London during the war; his brother, Wieland Herzfelde, is with the publishing house, Aurora Company, a German Communist front in New York.

dren marching on the stage followed by a squadron of the Red Front
Fighters' League in uniform.

Soon there was a book, *Rote Tribüne,* an anthology of similar plays.
One was a chorus of the working class, by Ernst Wangenheim, now
director of a Berlin theater. Another was Emil Halupp's *Die Internationale,* in which the struggle against the Social Democratic betray-
ers is developed in a soldiers' barracks during the war. Every branch
of the party, in village and city alike, every party affiliate (the Red
Aid, for instance), turned to this dramatic propaganda, which ran the
gamut from pathos to satire. Blue Shirts, an organization in Russia
to stimulate artistic propaganda, was transferred to Germany as the
Rote Rummel (Red Shindigs). Revues became very popular, combinations of variety and comic acts with tableaus of current events.

This kind of dramatic appeal, which was developed during the
middle twenties to a considerable success in Germany, was later imitated by other Communist parties, particularly in the Far East. There
were Chinese, Japanese, and Indian Communists in Berlin in this period, sent there to study these propaganda methods. Kunio Ito, for
example, a highly gifted painter-actor from Tokyo, worked for several years in the Agit-Prop department of the German party, as well as
for the *Arbeiter Theater-Bund* (Workers' Theater League). He ex-
celled in stage designs and masks for demonstrations, exhibition layouts,
transparencies, posters. When I now read [2] of the propaganda methods
in Communist China, which during the war were largely sponsored
by the People's Anti-Japanese Dramatic Society, every detail carries me
back to the Berlin Communist theater of 1925–1928.

This striving for theatrical effects, in which all the seven arts were
combined into one enormous effort to attract the masses, developed
steadily during these years. But there was a sharp break in content.
The anti-war themes, the internationalism, the German scenes even,
of the early plays and pageants gradually disappeared, and in their
place were introduced increasingly obsequious tributes to the Russian
state and its leaders.

[2] In, for example, Edgar Snow, *Red Star over China* (New York, 1939); Har-
rison Forman, *Report from Red China* (New York, 1945).

Willi Münzenberg

These new propaganda methods reached their apotheosis in the person of Willi Münzenberg, one of the founders of the German party, a veritable genius in this art.

Willi Münzenberg was born in 1889 in Thuringia.[3] He joined a socialist youth group called, significantly, Propaganda. After six years as an unskilled worker in a shoe factory, Münzenberg left his native Erfurt and traveled to Switzerland. Here he worked in a Zurich pharmacy during the day, and in the evenings sat at the table of Fritz Brupbacher, an anarchist intellectual of broad culture and singular charm. He discussed life and politics with the anarchist and syndicalist circle there, and absorbed basic attitudes that he never lost till the end of his life.

In Zurich, Münzerberg came in contact with many of the leading Russian Bolsheviks, with Lenin and Krupskaya, Trotsky, Zinoviev, Radek, Manuilsky, Chicherin. He was influenced in particular by Lenin, who channeled his vague radicalism into practical activities. From 1916 on, Münzenberg had an inner loyalty to the Lenin group. In November 1917, when the Bolsheviks took power in Russia, he participated in a demonstration in their support; a year later the police expelled him from Switzerland.

As soon as he returned to Germany, Münzenberg became a member of the Spartakusbund and joined in the fight against its Right wing. Just after the outbreak of the war he had taken over a defunct magazine, *Jugend-Internationale* (Youth International) and, beginning with an international youth rally in Stuttgart on Whitsunday 1914, had organized a youth secretariat. In 1920, when the Communist Youth International held its First World Congress in Moscow, Willi Münzenberg, thirty-one years old, "a professional youth," became its first president.

Some of the extraordinary ability in mass propaganda that he later developed was to be seen in this early period. Even before the war, he began to use theatrical techniques, crudely; "the proletarian theater," though it supplanted dreary speeches by drama, was still rather

---

[3] Cf. Willi Münzenberg, *Die Dritte Front* (Berlin, 1930), a history of the socialist youth movement with much autobiographical material.

heavily class-conscious. In an attempt to draw young girls into the movement, he organized a meeting on the subject, "Whom Should the Working Girl Marry?" Many came to listen, but when he talked of nothing but socialist principles, half of them fled. Nevertheless, at a time when their presence in political organizations was still unusual, Münzenberg got more girls into the youth movement than any other organizer.

In 1921, after the Kapp putsch in Germany and the Kronstadt rebellion in Russia, Münzenberg retired from party activity and began his real life's work. Russia was in the throes of a severe famine; millions of people were starving. At the Third World Congress, it was decided to appeal for help from sympathetic individuals outside Russia. A month later, on September 12, 1921, in Berlin, Münzenberg founded the International Workers' Aid, the first Communist organization that penetrated deep into non-Communist circles of workers and intellectuals—the pattern for a thousand other such organizations that were to follow.

Under Münzenberg's guidance, the IWA was an enormous success. The workers of a Berlin automobile plant sent a truck; a Chemnitz factory sent fourteen knitting machines; a Stuttgart factory sent five milk separators; the workers of a Leipzig factory sent pharmaceutical goods; other groups donated refrigerators for hospitals, tools, supplies. In 1921, twenty-one shiploads of material left for Russia; in 1922, seventy-eight shiploads. In 1926, according to Münzenberg's figures, the IWA collected material worth twenty-five million gold marks. All together some two million dollars' worth of commodities was collected. Much of it was second-hand and perhaps of dubious value, and in any case its effect on the economic crisis of a country the size of Russia could have been only very slight. But as propaganda the value of these collections was inestimable: everyone who donated his little bit felt tied to the workers' fatherland.

Money was also collected, by a whole series of measures: workers contributed a day's wage to the Russian people; there were collections on all occasions and special benefit concerts and art exhibits; all sorts of things were offered for sale: picture postcards of Russian scenes, busts of Marx and Lenin, special IWA stamps, flowers, medals, special emblems, special pamphlets, newspapers, books. A one-billion-dollar loan was floated, with interest at 5 per cent, guaranteed by a special decree of the Council of People's Commissars and signed by Rykov, Smolianov, Glazer, and Kamenev on September 13, 1922, to be redeemed on July 1, 1933. Of the many writings designed to stimulate this bond issue, a poem by Max Barthel, a close friend of Münzenberg's (and later a member of the Nazi Party), was typical:

> To immense Russia, to Europe,
> The slogan in the rhythm of the humming cylinders,
> Machines, machines, motors, tractors, turbines, harrows,
> And just machines.
> Workers, brothers, world-changers,
> Give, give and help to reconstruct
> The great classless proletarian community,
> Workers, proletarians around the earth.

The whole scheme was exploded by the inflation.

The Münzenberg Trust began in Germany, but it soon spread over the world. First Europe, then the Americas and the Far East, contributed to Russian relief. In the United States, Sidney Hillman donated $450,000. In Japan, the IWA had nineteen sympathizing newspapers and magazines. The soup kitchens and child welfare that the IWA had organized in Germany during the 1923–1924 economic crisis were transferred to Japan during the 1925 strikes and the next year to Britain during the miners' strike. In Russia itself, Münzenberg founded a series of children's homes; he organized shops for the repair of machinery, drew up contracts with Soviet factories.

To support his relief campaign, Münzenberg began to supplement the official Communist press with lively and well-written magazines. *Die Rote Fahne* and the other party papers were written in a jargon non-Communists found repulsive and hard to understand, and their pages were weighed down with long resolutions and manifestoes. Münzenberg founded a magazine, *Sowjet-Russland in Bildern* (Soviet Russia in Pictures), whose name he changed finally to *Arbeiter Illustrierte* (Workers' Illustrated Review), in imitation of the German counterpart of *Life,* the *Berliner Illustrierte.* The first issue of the *Arbeiter Illustrierte,* in August 1921, was 5000 copies; five years later it had a circulation of almost a million. Among the many other magazines he founded was *Der Rote Aufbau* (Red Construction), which later was one of the best propagandizers for Stalin's Five-Year Plan. He published two daily newspapers, *Berlin am Morgen* (Berlin in the Morning) and *Die Welt am Abend* (The World in the Evening). He published a magazine for amateur photographers, another to exploit the wide interest in radio. He organized his own publishing house and, to facilitate the sales of its books, he founded a book club.

When Sergei Eisenstein's *Potemkin* was shown in Germany, it was acclaimed by all the critics, and the German public looked forward to seeing more Russian movies. Very soon, Münzenberg had organized a company with exclusive rights to distribute Soviet films; it soon had agents in London, Paris, Rome, Amsterdam, New York. Beginning simply as a distributor, the company later produced films of its own.

Münzenberg did not participate in the faction fight raging in the party during these years. He was sympathetic to the Left (Zinoviev's expulsion from the Russian Party shattered his faith in it), but he preferred to remain with one foot out of the party, busy following his oft-repeated precept, "We have to organize the intellectuals." During this transitional period, when the political life of the party was postponed until it was brought under Stalin's control, activists flocked to his numerous organizations, finding in this work a compensation for their frustration in other fields. They worked together with a new species, one that Münzenberg had discovered, "the fellow-traveler." They worked together in the type of organization he had invented, "the front."

During the depression years, 1929–1933, the Münzenberg Trust burgeoned with every variety of anti-fascist propaganda, with ballyhoo for Russian culture, films, literature, science, scenery. Progressives and liberals the world over, who wanted to join in the fight against fascism but were reluctant to join a political party, found a haven in one of the numerous organizations Münzenberg founded. Of these the most important was the League against War and Fascism,[4] which had the enthusiastic support of such prominent figures as Edo Fimmen, the secretary of the International Transport Union, and Ellen Wilkinson, a leader of the British Labour Party.

---

[4] In the United States, it changed its name successively to the American League for Peace and Freedom; in September 1939, to American Peace Mobilization; in June 1941, to American People's Mobilization; in April 1946, to National Committee to Win the Peace.

In 1935, when the Popular Front was organized in France, and throughout the world, Münzenberg was in Paris, and with him thousands of German émigrés. The success with which the Communist line was propagated among Social Democrats and liberals during these years, the publication of *Ce Soir* in Paris and *PM* in New York, the thousands of painters and writers and doctors and lawyers and debutantes chanting a diluted version of the Stalinist line—all this had its root in Willi Münzenberg's International Workers' Aid.[5]

Though Münzenberg was overwhelmingly the dominating figure in the Communist Party's expansion among sympathetic elements, his were not the only party wares offered up for wider sale in this period. At the "Masch" (*Marxistische Arbeiter Schule*—Marxist Workers' School), many young sympathizers studied a wide variety of subjects. Thus, the more sterile the German Communists became in the political field, the more active they became in the invention of organizational devices. With a new fervor, they began to study "the market"—German society, and with sociological methods to plan their campaigns accordingly. In a delusion of organizational grandeur, Ernst Schneller, a member of the party's Orgburo, reported to the 1927 convention on the organizations that must be brought under party control. They were, he said: 30,000 sport clubs, 9,000 gymnastic clubs, 8,000 rifle clubs, 5,000 football clubs, 30,000 cycle clubs, 12,000 hiking clubs,

---

[5] From 1928 till the Nazis took power, together with Heinz Neumann and Kurt Sauerland (both of whom were killed in Moscow), Münzenberg was testing out the possibilities of building up another communist party in Germany. During the period in Paris, his organizations were infiltrated by NKVD agents, among whom André Simon-Katz, a Czech from Pilsen, played an especially sinister role in spying on him.

After the Moscow trials, Münzenberg was summoned several times to Moscow. He procrastinated as long as he could, and ended by refusing to go. From 1938 on, he was among the outcasts; he joined no group but on the contrary avoided NKVD attention by having no contact with "Trotskyites."

In May 1940, Münzenberg was interned, together with all other German nationals in France. A month later he fled with the other German inmates before the Nazi invasion. A few miles from the camp he was found hanged; the Stalinists spread the story that he had killed himself.

I do not believe that Münzenberg committed suicide. The two men with whom he had fled from the camp disappeared without a trace; they may very well have been NKVD agents. Within reach of the place of his death, on the French Riviera, lived his good friend, Valeriu Marcu, where Münzenberg would have found a haven, money, influential friends. He did not believe in the Nazi victory; he was not depressed. Fifty years old, he had still an immense vitality, a hundred new plans to be fulfilled.

2,000 rabbit- and chicken-raising clubs, 1,000 bowling clubs, 10,000 choral societies, 20,000 branches of the Young Men's and Women's Christian Society. The total membership of this array was almost six million. Schneller's ambitious project was fulfilled only after 1933, by the Nazis.

At the Sixth World Congress, in 1928, Kuusinen described the task of the Communist parties as building up a solar system in which every planet, from large to tiny, revolves around the Communist sun.

Bert Brecht, the Minstrel of the GPU

The changed character of the party can be illustrated well in the works of the one gifted poet the German Communists ever had, Bertolt Brecht. Brecht joined the party only in 1930, and his poetry glorifying it was written during the years of the depression; he had never known, he had never participated in, he had not been drawn to Communism in its original form. On the contrary, the young Brecht, the son of an Augsburg paper-mill owner, was indifferent, if not hostile, to German Communism as long as it was a fighting and democratically organized body; during the civil war he was a disinterested outsider. He joined the party without previous links to it, with little knowledge of it. His works are the reflection of the transitional period and its finished product, the Stalinist party.[6]

---

[6] Brecht left Germany in 1933. After traveling about Europe, he settled down during the Hitler era in Svendborg, Denmark. When the Nazis invaded the country in 1940, he left, going finally to Santa Monica, California, where with his old friend, Hanns Eisler, he formed the nucleus of a Communist literary and artistic group. Another member of this group was Lion Feuchtwanger, who learned the reason for the Moscow trials in a personal interview with Stalin. During the anti-Nazi decade in the United States, this group—Brecht, Eisler, Feuchtwanger, Heinrich Mann, among others—all of them linked to German Communism, represented for many Americans the anti-fascist German. Brecht presented himself to the American public by his dramatization of Gorky's *The Mother,* which is unadorned Communist propaganda; with music by Hanns Eisler, it was played in 1932 in Berlin and in 1935 in New York. Brecht has never broken his allegiance to Moscow, but since his poetry is not unconditionally endorsed by Russian Party critics, he prefers to remain in America as long as possible. The two other German party poets, Erich Weinert and Johannes R. Becher, both far inferior to Brecht as artists, went to Moscow in 1933 and got important Party assignments, Weinert, for example, in the leadership of the Free Germany Committee with Paulus and Seydlitz. Becher was among the first to return, and has become a leading figure in Germany's re-education.

Since the end of the war, Brecht has been played widely in Germany, Czechoslovakia, Hungary—wherever Communist control is dominant. The most original of

Brecht was among the young poets who, profoundly shaken by the war and its results in Germany, reacted with negativism; he was one of the poets of Germany's social disintegration. Discarding realism for *avant-garde* forms, he attempted to express in his early works the horror and destruction of the time of troubles. His first play, *Drums in the Night,* is a bitter satire on the Weimar Republic. A soldier, long believed dead, comes home unexpected, unwanted, to find his sweetheart in the arms of a black-marketeer. The Spartakus revolt and Rosa Luxemburg are mentioned, but only as backdrops, to give color. The soldier, undecided between *Bett und Barrikade,* chooses the bed with the blue canopy and ignores politics.

In a series of works following this, Brecht expressed his nihilism in various and bizarre forms. For him, there are no forms of society, past or present or future, no values, no goods; his message is: There is nothing. In another play, Brecht takes us to Mahogany, one of his imaginary towns, this one situated somewhere in the Western Hemisphere—a center of a brutal, noisy pleasure business, of drinking and gambling and love-making. Johnny, the Alaskan woodcutter, comes here and spends his hard-earned money. In the final scene he discovers not only that pleasures are empty but that there is nothing to which a man can hold—*da ist nichts, woran man sich halten kann.* The climax of this period came with Brecht's best known work, *Die Dreigroschenoper* (Beggar's Opera), which shows thieves and prostitutes as the only people of worth. To the accompaniment of Kurt Weill's music, this became Germany's first depression hit. Its climactic line, *Erst kommt das Fressen und dann die Moral* (First we stuff ourselves and then we think of morals), became a folk saying.

From this over-all negation, from this cynical withdrawal from all values, from this bitter empty nihilism, Brecht collapsed into the polar opposite, the adoration of the discipline and the hierarchical order of the German Communist Party. Hypnotized by its totalitarian and terrorist features, he became the most original poet the party ever possessed. The *avant-garde* critic of society became the minstrel of indoctrination, the medium for transferring party philosophy to the crowd. In this period he calls his works didactic plays or school operas.

the German Communist poets, he may have a measurable influence on the postwar youth, who prefer his *avant-garde* forms to banal eulogies made in Moscow.

The German edition includes portions of a discussion on the school opera, *Der Neinsager* (The No-Sayer), by students of the Karl Marx School of Berlin-Neukölln, a progressive high school so named by its Social Democratic directors.[7]

Brecht's plays were produced with a minimum of props, as abstractly as possible. On a bare stage, with no naturalistic scenery to distract the audience, one symbolic object is pushed into the foreground, almost a member of the cast. They were written to be put on in the open air, in a meeting hall, in a barracks. Frequently the small cast is supplemented by a Greek chorus, symbolizing the masses, who comment on the deeds and misdeeds of the actors. The themes are parables, often adaptations of ancient or medieval plots to modern environment. They are repeated like drum beats—the sacrifice of the individual to the collective, the substitutability of any individual for another, the non-validity of individual morality with respect to the collective, the necessity and the inflexibility of the hierarchical order, the inevitability and the strange beauty of terror. Brecht teaches that the individual has not only to sacrifice himself for the cause but also to sacrifice the cause to the higher insight of the hierarchy. Brecht developed a technique of his own, based on the epic drama: events are not reproduced at the time of their happening but are reported on later, often by flashbacks in the form of plays within the play. In his forms and sometimes in his themes, he shows the conscious influence of Shakespeare; the typical Shakespearian soliloquy summing up the moral of the play is often transferred in Brecht to the chorus. Brecht is fascinated by Chinese philosophy and presents Marx and Lenin as the Classical Teachers, the Wise Old Men.

One of the first didactic plays of Brecht was *Man Is Man,* the theme of which is that the individual is futile and replaceable. In a prologue, a single actor appears and announces that Bert Brecht is of the opinion that things happen thus. The scene opens on a group of soldiers in Calcutta; by some misadventure, one of them disappears, but is replaced immediately; there is no change in the collective. *Es ist ganz egal auf wen die Sonne schien* (It doesn't matter at all on whom the sun shone). An incident in 1947 Germany reads like the synopsis of this early Brecht play. In Potsdam twelve German prisoners of war

---

[7] Bertolt Brecht, *Versuche 11–12* (Berlin, 1931), IV, 308 ff.

are escorted by a Russian soldier, to be shipped to an unknown destination. At the Stadtbahn station the detachment passes a crowd of
men and women hurrying home from work. One middle-aged, ill-clad
woman suddenly throws herself on one of the German prisoners; it is
her husband, returned from the dead. The Russian guard allows the
reunited pair to depart together, followed by the amazed stare of the
eleven and the civilians. A young civilian in the crowd, with a brief
case under his arm, is singled out of the crowd. "You come with us,"
the guard says. Again the little detachment numbers twelve, and it
marches off as though nothing had happened.[8] Those who had been
in concentration camps remembered the technique. As Brecht writes
in his epilogue, "This was to be demonstrated: Q.E.D."

Die Massnahme

The one didactic play of this series by Brecht that best digests all
the terroristic features into a mirror of the totalitarian party and its
elite guard, the NKVD, is *The Punitive Measure,* written under the
impact of the defeat of Chinese Communism.[9] The accompanying
music was written by Hanns Eisler, whose brother, Gerhart, had been
sent to China at the end of 1929 to liquidate the opposition to the
Russian Politburo. The play, a parable on the annihilation of the
party opposition, is a preview of the Moscow trials. With a sensitivity
to Stalinist methods that denotes his genius, Brecht was able to write
in 1931 a play about the show trials his master would produce five
years later.

Four Agitators report to a Controlchorus concerning their mission
to Mukden. We see the Controlchorus in the background, and in the
foreground the Agitators act out the incidents of their mission. Many
passages are set to music, and the others are recitative interludes. The
play begins:

> CONTROLCHORUS: Step forward. Your work has been blest.
> In this land also the Revolution is on the march, and the ranks of
> the fighters have been formed here too. We are in agreement
> with you.
> THE FOUR AGITATORS: Stop. We have to say something. We
> announce the death of one comrade.

---

[8] Reported by John Scott, *Time,* New York, April 21, 1947, p. 32.

[9] *Die Massnahme,* in *Bertolt Brecht, Gesammelte Werke,* II, 329–359. Copyright
1938 by Malik-Verlag Publishing Company, London W.C. 1.

CONTROLCHORUS: Who killed him?

THE FOUR AGITATORS: We killed him. We shot him and threw him in a lime pit.

CONTROLCHORUS: What had he done, that you shot him?

THE FOUR AGITATORS: Often he did the right thing, but sometimes the wrong, but in the end he endangered the movement. He wanted to do the Right but he did the Wrong. We seek your judgment.

CONTROLCHORUS: Show how it happened, and why, and you will hear our judgment.

THE FOUR AGITATORS: We will accept your judgment.

In the first of a series of flashbacks, this one called *The Principles of the Classics* (Marx and Lenin), the Four Agitators report how they stopped at the last party house at the border to get a guide into China, and there meet the Young Comrade.

THREE AGITATORS: We come from Moscow.

THE YOUNG COMRADE: We have waited for you.

THREE AGITATORS: Why?

THE YOUNG COMRADE: We are stalled. There are disorder and want here, little bread and much fighting. Many have courage but few can read.

The Young Comrade asks whether they have brought with them locomotives and tractors and machine guns and ammunition. On the contrary, they failed to bring even a letter from the Central Committee to tell them what to do.

THREE AGITATORS: It is thus. We bring nothing for you. But over the border to Mukden we bring to the Chinese workers the Principles of the Classics and of the Propagandists: the ABCs of Communism; to the ignorant, knowledge of their situation; to the oppressed, class consciousness; and to the class conscious, the experience of the Revolution. From you, however, we have to get an automobile and someone to guide us.

After this first scene the Controlchorus sings a song, "In Praise of the USSR."

In the second scene, called *The Extinguishing,* the Four Agitators are ready to enter China, but they must first extinguish their faces.

DIRECTOR OF THE PARTY HOUSE: You shall go over the border as Chinese. You must not be seen.

TWO AGITATORS: We are not seen.

DIRECTOR OF THE PARTY HOUSE: If one of you is wounded, he must not be found.

TWO AGITATORS: He is not found.

DIRECTOR OF THE PARTY HOUSE: You are ready to die and to hide the dead?

TWO AGITATORS: Yes.

DIRECTOR OF THE PARTY HOUSE: Then you no longer are yourselves. No longer are you Karl Schmitt of Berlin. You are no longer Anna Kyersk of Kazan, and you no longer Peter Savich of Moscow. You are all without name or mother, blank leaflets on which the Revolution writes its orders.

The Director gives them masks, which they put on their faces.

CONTROLCHORUS: Who fights for Communism must be able to fight and not to fight, to say the truth and not to say the truth, to render and to deny service, to keep a promise and to break a promise, to go into danger and to avoid danger, to be known and to be unknown. Who fights for Communism has of all the virtues only one: that he fights for Communism.

The first episode in China is entitled *The Stone*. The Agitators first go downtown, to stir up the coolies. The Young Comrade is admonished not "to fall in the trap of pity." The coolies are pulling a boat up the river, and they slip and fall in the mud. The Young Comrade, becoming one of them, helps by placing a heavy stone in the mire so that they do not slip. Three times The Young Comrade places the stone, and then cries out for something more than this primitive improvement, for better shoes for the coolies. Having thus exposed himself, he is seized by the overseer, and the Agitators have to depart.

The next episode is called *The Small and the Great Injustice*.

THE FOUR AGITATORS: We founded the first cells in the factories, educated the first militants, established a Party school, and taught them to put out illegal literature.

The Young Comrade is assigned to distribute leaflets before the factory gates, but without exposing himself. He is instructed to avoid conflict with the authorities under all circumstances. When a policeman beats a worker, however, The Young Comrade interferes and even cries for help. Again he and the Agitators have to flee.

His supreme test, in the episode entitled *What Is a Man After All?* concerns his attitude toward the business world.

THE FOUR AGITATORS: We fought daily with the old unions, with hopelessness, and with submission. We taught the workers to transform the fight for better wages into a fight for power. Taught them the use of weapons and the art of demonstration. Then we heard that the businessmen were wrangling over custom duties with the British who rule the town. To utilize this conflict among the rulers for the sake of the ruled, we sent The Young Comrade to the wealthiest of the businessmen with a letter. In it was written, Arm the coolies. We instructed The Young Comrade, Act so that you get the weapons. We will show how it happened.

ONE AGITATOR: I am The Business Man. I wait for a letter from the coolie union about common action against the British.

THE YOUNG COMRADE: Here is the letter of the coolie union.

THE BUSINESS MAN: I invite you to eat with me.

THE YOUNG COMRADE: It is an honor for me to be permitted to eat with you.

The Business Man points to the common interest of the coolie union and himself; both are clever; both live off the coolies. The Young Comrade remembers his instructions and agrees. Until the dinner arrives, The Business Man sings his favorite tune, "The Song of the Commodity":

> There is rice down the river,
> Up the river people need rice.
> If we store the rice
> They will pay more for it.
> Those who tow the rice-boats
> Will get even less of it.
> Then for me the rice will be even cheaper.
> Do I know what a rice is?
> Do I know who knows that!
> I know not what a rice is!
> I know only its price . . .
>
> Do I know what a man is?
> Do I know who knows that!
> I know not what a man is!
> I know only his price.

Outraged, The Young Comrade refuses to continue eating with The Business Man.

THE YOUNG COMRADE, *getting up:* I cannot eat with you.

THE FOUR AGITATORS: He said that. And not ironic laughter

nor any pressure could induce him to eat with the one he despised. And The Business Man threw him out. And the coolies got no arms.

Here the play is interrupted by a discussion of Communist tactics.

> CONTROLCHORUS: But is it not right to cherish honor above all else?
>
> THE FOUR AGITATORS: No.
>
> CONTROLCHORUS: Long since we ceased listening to you as judges and began to learn.

Then the Controlchorus sings the song, "Change the World, It Needs It":

> What vileness would you not commit to
>   exterminate vileness?
> Could you change the world, for what
>   would you be too good?
> Who are you?
> Sink into the mud,
>   embrace the butcher, but
>   change the world: it needs it.

The last scene is called *The Betrayal*.

> THE FOUR AGITATORS: In these weeks the persecutions increased beyond measure. We had only a hidden room for the typesetter and the pamphlets. One morning large hunger revolts broke out in the town and there was news of unrest in the countryside.

The Young Comrade discusses with the Agitators whether the time is ripe for an uprising. He revolts against the party, which wants to postpone the action till a better moment.

> THREE AGITATORS: You go to the unemployed and convince them that they must not go ahead alone. We demand that of you in the name of the Party.
>
> THE YOUNG COMRADE: But who is the Party? Is it sitting in a house with the telephone? Are its ideas secret, its decisions unknown? Who is it?

The Controlchorus sings "In Praise of the Party":

> One man has two eyes
> The Party has a thousand eyes.
> The Party overlooks seven states

> One man sees one city.
> One man has his hour
> But the Party has many hours.
> One man can die
> But the Party cannot be killed.
> For it is the *avant-garde* of the masses
> And leads their fight.
> With the methods of the Classics
> Ladled out of
> The knowledge of reality.

The Young Comrade, who has already torn up the Scriptures of the Classics, cries:

> That no longer has any bearing. At the moment of the fight, I reject all that was yesterday valid and do only what is human. My heart beats for the Revolution.

He takes off the mask, and cries:

> We have come to help you. We come from Moscow.

He tears the mask in pieces.

> THE FOUR AGITATORS: We saw him. In the dusk, we saw his naked face, human, open, guileless. He had torn up the mask. He kept on crying out in the open street. We knocked him down, picked up his unconscious body, and hurried out of the town.

The climax is called *The Punitive Measure.*

> THREE AGITATORS:
> We decided:
> he had to disappear, and totally.
> For we had to return to our work
> and we could not take him with us nor leave him there
> so we had to shoot him and throw him in the lime pit
> for the lime will burn him up.
> CONTROLCHORUS: There was no other way?
> THE FOUR AGITATORS:
> With time getting short we found no other way.
> For five minutes, with pursuers at our heels,
> we deliberated over
> a better possibility.
>
> Terrible it is, to kill.
> But not only others but ourselves we kill when it

becomes necessary.
But we cannot, we said,
permit ourselves not to kill. Only on our
unbending will to change the world can we base
the measure.

FIRST AGITATOR: We will ask him if he agrees, for he was a brave fighter.

SECOND AGITATOR: But even if he does not agree with us, he must disappear, disappear totally.

THREE AGITATORS: So we ask you, do you agree?

THE YOUNG COMRADE: Yes. I see that I have always acted incorrectly. Now it would be better if I were not.

THREE AGITATORS: Yes. Do you want to do it alone?

THE YOUNG COMRADE: Help me.

THREE AGITATORS: Lean your head against our arm, close your eyes.

THE YOUNG COMRADE: For Communism . . .

THREE AGITATORS: Then we shot him and threw him into the lime pit, and when the lime had absorbed him we returned to our work.

CONTROLCHORUS:
Your work has been blest.
You have propagated
the Principles of the Classics
the ABCs of Communism.
And the Revolution is on the march here too
and here too the ranks of the fighters have been formed.
We are in agreement.

In its language, in the symbols it uses, this didactic play, *Die Massnahme,* is characteristic of the transformation of the Comintern. The defeat in China and the subsequent purge are used in Germany to indoctrinate the party in docility to Moscow and in passivity to the Nazis. In *avant-garde* abstractions, Brecht achieves the transfiguration and beatification of the Stalinist Party. The audacious use of the Controlchorus symbolizes the intervention of the GPU in Party life and the voluntary acceptance of its hierarchical discipline. Stalin's reorganized Comintern is presented in the figure of the naïve Communist, who submits himself to final judgment by the representatives from Moscow. On every Russian border, there are Party houses, with Moscow missionaries en route to every country, under a mask, to lift which is the supreme crime. Under the mask they manipulate the native movements, which may be sacrificed to a union with The Business Man when the fight against the British, against the West, makes this advisable. In a simple and very German way, Brecht is able to present the German Communist Party, stripped of every revolutionary impetus of its early years, with no trace of a life of its own, a docile instrument in the hands of the Russian hierarchs.

6.

SUMMARY AND CONCLUSION

The regime that issued from the October revolution has passed through a series of transformations, each distinguishable by specific features. The Soviet state was born during World War I, and the new forms of Soviet society developed in the five years immediately following, against a background of civil war not only in Russia but in Europe. With Germany's defeat, Europe had lost its precarious balance of power, established in the second half of the nineteenth century, and was not able to find another. Among the successor states to the Hapsburg monarchy, in a chain of friction points along the Danube and in Central Europe, unrest persisted, culminating in the short-lived Hungarian Soviet Republic. The formation of the new Soviet state, however, was more influenced by the civil war raging in Germany and the in-between lands. During these years revolutionary internationalism was the motive force of Lenin's party, which had taken power with the concept that the overthrow of Tsarist autocracy would be the beginning of a socialist revolution whose central figure would be the German worker.

The Leninist party was far from being the iron-disciplined monolithic group that it has been pictured, both by Stalinists, who seek to buttress their absolute continuity with the October revolutionists, and by most anti-Stalinists, who are convinced that nothing fundamental has changed in Moscow since November 1917. On the eve of the 1917 uprising, the Leninist party had split. Two of Lenin's most intimate collaborators, Zinoviev and Kamenev, "deserted" him to defend a government of soviet parties against the tendency to establish a one-party dictatorship. An outsider, a man who for decades had fought him with all the virulence associated with Russian socialist polemics—Leon Trotsky—became his alter ego. In 1918, when the very life of the young Soviet state depended on reaching a solution to the problem posed by the still powerful German army, the conflict between revolutionary objectives and the will to resist the German invasion split the Bolshevik Party again, only a few weeks after it had taken power.

Though the general criticisms of Luxemburg and Bukharin were far from identical (they differed sharply, for example, on the national question), they did agree in pointing out that a separate treaty between Soviet Russia and the German General Staff could not but retard the German revolutionaries. Undoubtedly the efficient quelling of the revolution in November 1918 by the German military was possible partly because of the breathing spell they had been given by the peace on the Eastern front; but would the downfall of Soviet power in Russia—the possible alternative to the Brest-Litovsk Treaty—have helped the revolutionaries in Germany? Would it have inspired them to fight the German General Staff harder? The relations between Russia and the border countries, as between Russia and Germany, were resolved by neither the Brest Treaty nor its aftermath. The manifold national aspirations, arising out of the Russian revolution and the defeat of the Central Powers and increasing in complexity with the years, were ever before the Europe that saw the rise of the Hitler and Stalin empires. The present Stalinist solution, to incorporate not only the border countries but a large portion of Germany into a Greater Russia, has only aggravated the problem.

Lenin's companions were fanatically devoted to a cause, but they were free from any hint of a Führer fixation; Lenin was able to enforce his authority only by dint of rigorous logic, pounded indefatigably into the resistant heads of men who shared his all-consuming faith in socialism and respected him as one leader among others. Not only was there not automatic unanimity; it was not automatic that Lenin held the majority. He had to struggle with men of almost equal caliber to win his point, and that he did usually win had nothing to do with the threat of a GPU standing behind his chair.

The deep affection, the love, that Nikolai Bukharin, Lenin's principal opponent in the Brest-Litovsk crisis, felt for Vladimir Ilyich can be compared only to the feeling that sometimes develops between two soldiers who have seen danger together, immensely reinforced by a deep intellectual affinity; but these early Bolsheviks were first of all men of principle. For Bukharin, the vision of international socialism was disappearing behind the parchment of the Brest Treaty, and he fought desperately to save it. Leader of the majority of the party, he considered putting the rebellious Lenin under house arrest for long enough to carry out his policy. This audacious plan never materialized, and eventually Lenin won over the majority to his program. But the crux of this story is not the conflict but the total reconciliation between the two men afterward. Lenin, who fought for thirty years for the dots on his *i*'s, was able to reintegrate his dispersive associates with the most amazing flexibility. Not only did he win the party to his policy, but he managed to reëstablish an atmosphere of friendly solidarity among the men who had fought each other so hard, a unity in which the past was forgotten and all eyes were on the difficult task of the present and the prospect of the future. It was not a crime once to have opposed Lenin's view; there remained no subterranean current of dark suspicion. Without inhibition, with rare objectivity, this first generation of Bolsheviks was able to discuss the struggle and learn from it what they could.

When I was in Moscow in the early twenties, one of a group of young Communists from Western Europe, Bukharin, spoke to us without reserve concerning his Left Communist faction and the struggle he had waged against Lenin. There was much in post-Kronstadt Russia to disquiet us young idealists from the West, but there was certainly no skeleton in Bukharin's closet. Only one who lived through the early years of the revolution and could observe Lenin and Bukharin together can grasp the full monstrosity of Vyshinsky's charge twenty years later that Bukharin had planned to assassinate Lenin.

On the basis merely of his role during the Brest crisis, Stalin would not appear. He supported the view that a treaty with Germany was necessary and out-Lenined Lenin in pointing out that there was no prospect of a German revolution and that policy in Russia should be made without regard to Liebknecht.

"There is no revolutionary movement in the West; there are
no facts; there are only potentialities, and we cannot take into
account potentialities." "Cannot take into account?" Lenin at once
repudiated Stalin's support; it is true that the revolution in the
West has not yet begun; "however, if we should change our tactics
because of that, we would be traitors to international socialism."[1]

With the defeat of the German uprising of 1923, this concept of
internationalism finally broke down; these hopes, these aspirations,
were once and for all destroyed. The disaster of German Communism
in 1923 was due partially to the internal structure of German Social
Democracy and Communism, their congenital weakness, the immaturity of the Communist Party and the comfortable middle age of the
Social Democratic Party, and partially to the fact that the transfer of
Leninist concepts to a highly industrial Western country proved to
involve more than translating a set of dogmatic formulas from Russian
into German. Despite defeat in the war, German society retained a
high degree of organization, with a closely knit institutional network,
by which the ruling classes were able to defend their status much
more effectively than could their counterparts in the disintegrating
Russia of 1917. To defeat the forces of restoration demanded more
than a carefully prepared coup d'état; it required an art of revolutionary politics, which that high-strung ideologue, Rosa Luxemburg, had
never acquired. The antithesis of the power politician, she groped for
a German alternative to the Russian experience, but her ideas were
never developed to full vigor. German Communism, however, could
have matured, could have exploded the fetters of inhibiting dogma,
trade-union narrowness, and lack of realistic audacity, if the revolution
in retreat in Russia had not added a new bridle.

The isolation of the October revolution did not lead to the direct
dispossession of the Russian Communist Party that, in this case, had
been expected, but to the withering away of all the original trends of
the revolution without the return to power of the dispossessed classes,
the landowners and the big capitalists. In a disintegrating but none
the less still strongly capitalist Europe, the Bolsheviks found their
original aspirations unrealizable. Determined to hold a power that
had been acquired under different prospects, they reached the point

---

[1] Trotsky, *Stalin*, p. 250.

where they could maintain it only by adjusting the Soviet regime to the paradox that a party of revolutionary internationalism ruled over a country unfit for the realization by itself of a socialist society. The disintegration of the October trend, setting in in 1920–1921, had already corroded the timid beginnings of the Communist International as an international socialist fraternity. By this corrosion, proceeding in perceptible gradations, the German revolt of 1923, which from the outside appeared to be undertaken under the most favorable conditions, was by inner necessity transformed into an impossible adventure. The details of this abortive coup reflect the process of disintegration of Russian Communism. The defeat of the German Communists marks the close of *the period of revolutionary internationalism, 1917–1923*.

The 1923 revolt had as its international background social convulsions in Italy, in the Balkans, and, on another Soviet frontier, in Turkey. The year 1923 saw the rise of the three European dictators who were to share the destiny of the continent for two decades or more—Mussolini, Hitler, and Stalin. Stalin, elected General Secretary for the first time on April 2, 1922, thus gained the premise for his struggle for complete power, which he began to wage by eliminating Trotsky from the leadership and introducing GPU methods within the party. In a short flash on the historical screen, Hitler appeared in his Munich putsch, a provincial crackpot who for a number of years would not be able to overcome the still unbroken force of German labor. In October 1922, Mussolini took power under a program of democracy and partial nationalization, and spent the next years in reinforcing his dictatorship, the completion of which process was marked by the assassination of Matteotti in 1924. Meanwhile, in the neighboring Balkans the insecure new states, politically squeezed between Russia and Germany, struggled to find an equilibrium between the peasants and the rising urban classes. The Stamboliyski-Tsankov episode, with all its terrorist features, is a history of the peninsula in miniature. In defeated and weakened Turkey, by a successful coup Mustapha Kemal Pasha adapted a semi-modern dictatorship to an anachronistic despotism, for which his People's Party substituted a program of nationalism and modernization. In China, Chiang Kai-shek, protégé and disciple of the Bolsheviks, revolted against his teachers after a short alliance and established on the basis of Chinese nationalism his own dictatorship, which adapted all the devices of their power control to the different social content of the Chinese scene.

In our times, the model of totalitarian power is a party state, governed by the disciplined hierarchy of a State Party and its secret police. The party fuses economic with political power into a complete unity; the nationalization of the means of production, complete or in part— which with this background of combined controls is first of all a means of infiltrating political power through economic life—has been effected in various countries by a State Party that has eradicated from itself and from the society it controls all vestiges of a democratic or socialist past. The State Party of our times is a new phenomenon, which can be identified with neither the Jacobins of the great French Revolution, nor the terrorist conspirators against Tsarism, nor the revolutionary fraternity of Lenin. The State Party is, however, the heir to these predecessors; its language, symbols, ideas, flow directly from the experiences of this earlier tradition. Without either Jacobinism or Leninism, the State Party would have a different pattern of thought and organization, and detailed studies of these earlier social phenomena reveal many similarities between them and the State Party as it exists today. But here, in my opinion, the historical parallel ends, or becomes so inadequate as not to give a suitable basis for fruitful analysis.

Lenin, whose life was a fight against Tsarist autocracy, wanted to supplant it through industrialization and democratization. The Leninist party had been formed as an instrument in the fight against Tsarism; its conspiratorial methods, the product of this despotism, were mirrored in every anti-Tsarist revolutionary group—in both wings of the Social Revolutionary Party, in the Menshevik Party, among the anarchists and the various national-minority groups. The centralism of the Leninist party was the result of an attempt to maintain the militancy of its predecessors but throw off the futile posturing of terrorist attacks upon individuals and substitute for it an attack on the system. The small, weak, ineffectual Bolshevik bands were held together by the bold revolutionary vision of the party's leaders, especially that of Lenin; its members obeyed the general staff in exile because of their common fanatical belief in the common cause, because each was willing to sacrifice himself for the common goal. To create an *esprit de corps* and to enforce party discipline, Lenin had nothing more than his spiritual superiority; he had no salaried trade-union posts to offer, no publicity, no political careers, not even the pleasure of personal recognition; for the work had to be done anonymously, in the dark, under cover, in spiritual isolation even from the brother parties of the International.

Such an organization bred another type of man than the agent of the party in power—a statement that remains valid irrespective of whether such a party was adequate to fulfill the tasks it set itself, or of whether such an organization could be successfully transplanted from its native Tsarist Russia to the West, where labor had developed democratic institutions formed on the pattern of its environment, the bourgeois democratic state. The great lacuna in Leninist theory was precisely its failure to anticipate that such a party, when it reached the pivotal position of unlimited state power, would develop unexpected forms, make unforeseen jumps, encounter new and complex problems of social organization. When it became clear that the dictatorship of the proletariat was not a short span to proletarian democracy, the Russian rulers were faced with the vista of a new historical era and with problems on a comparable scale.

Lenin's sickness had reached such a state in 1923 that he never consciously lived through the final crushing of German Communism. During the years of the civil war in Russia, he had watched with sorrow the beginning rupture and fossilization of the Soviet structure. In his every defense of the party against alternative tendencies—the Workers' Opposition groups, the Kronstadt rebels, the Trade-Union Opposition, the various factions in the party or the Comintern—he was fully aware of the implied danger and tried to succeed each use of the surgical knife with a suitable ointment. The last years of his life were filled with tragically ineffective attempts to hamper the crystallization of totalitarian power, of which he foresaw the catastrophic consequences. Lenin's struggle from his deathbed to prevent Stalin's succession is one of the great dramas of human history, here drily told; and when a new generation of Russians is able to explore it thoroughly, the story will afford much help in facing new problems.

Lenin's attitude toward German Communism is characteristic of his political physiognomy. He tried to integrate the conflicting forces within the German party, to limit the dogmatic and often infantile discussions, to reconcile the personal competitors fighting each other with unnecessary bitterness. Lenin's concept of Germany and of German socialism in particular is an important chapter in the history of the Russian revolution which has never been adequately dealt with and is here also treated only as a background to the main story, with nothing like the completeness it warrants. I hope to be able to expand this theme in ensuing volumes, contrasting Stalin's and Lenin's diametrically opposed attitudes toward Germany.

Trotsky, the other founder of the Soviet Republic, from different personal and theoretical premises, opposed the installation of the State Party regime. Just because, by his post as military commander during the civil war, he had participated more in laying the foundations for this totalitarian regime, Trotsky saw its dangers more sharply than others.

> The demobilization of the Red Army of five million played no small role in the formation of the bureaucracy. The victorious commanders assumed leading posts in the local soviets, in economy, in education, and they persistently introduced everywhere that regime which had ensured success in the civil war. Thus on all sides the masses were pushed away gradually from actual participation in the leadership of the country.[2]

Just because Trotsky was an outsider to the internal dictatorship of the Old Guard within the Bolshevik Party, just this handicap in the struggle to succeed Lenin limned for him the symptoms of degeneration more clearly and earlier. Trotsky's fight in 1923 to set "a new course" in the Party is one of the landmarks dividing two historical periods. With an enormous energy, he stressed the fallacy of identifying the fourteen-year period of the Bolshevik Party before it seized power with the present period, he combated the myth of organic unity between the pre-revolutionary and the post-revolutionary party, he fought the myth of infallibility. He tried to stem the new class clambering to top personal power with a set of dogmatic and schematic formulas, designed to pass from one generation to the next as an ideological barrier to any change.

Stalin, pushed forward by the Party hierarchy in their need for a

---

[2] Trotsky, *The Revolution Betrayed*, pp. 89–90.

man to secure the party's power against all resistance, showed his manipulatory genius by uniting, against the warnings of the dying Lenin, the Old Guard against the principal danger of the moment, Trotsky. He carried out this brilliant maneuver without a blueprint, hesitatingly, pragmatically, feeling his way through the pattern of party tradition and the meshes of personal ambition, cautiously removing, one after the other, each obstacle to his undisputed power. Utilizing the despair that followed the German defeat, Stalin transformed the internationalism of 1917 into "socialism in one country," into Russian national socialism, which, though it was born through a labor of dogmatic and sterile discussion, was a bold and far-reaching reassertion of Russian nationalism, the extension of every aspiration of Imperial Russia.

> Of course the question under dispute [writes his temporary chronicler, Popov] was not whether socialism could be built up in any country, irrespective of its size and level of economic development. It was precisely a question of our country, with its territory, natural resources, and the stage of economic development already attained by it, which was typical also of other countries with an average level of capitalist development.[3]

In this Stalinist concept, the word *socialism* has lost all the meaning it had during the nineteenth century; it has nothing left in common with any of the schools, factions, deviationists, exegetes of Marxism; it stabilized a set of concepts in direct conflict with those encompassed in Lenin's socialist philosophy. In the early years of Stalinist power, socialism meant only this: We, the Stalinist Party, can conserve power as a minority group, can strengthen it, need not share it with any other group in the country, can defend it against any pressure from abroad, successfully and alone. "Socialism in one country," or the defense of the power monopoly, became in the course of events always more narrowly defined. The power to be defended is neither soviet nor Party power; it is the power of a group that identifies its interest so completely with that of the Party, and the interest of the Party so completely with that of the country, that elementary national self-interest justifies using the most dictatorial methods to maintain this monopoly.

---

[3] N. Popov, *Outline History of the CPSU*, II, 276, note.

The transitional period of the middle twenties is characterized by the fight to maintain this monopoly of power, and marks the beginning of Europe's Totalitarian Era. Such a power monopoly cannot be maintained by a fraternal group, even with a hierarchical order; it demands the person of a dictator. Stalin had to eliminate the representatives of the Old Guard, Zinoviev, Kamenev, and later Bukharin, from control in the Politburo, because they were obstacles to his personal dictatorship. The adoration of The Leader, with its beginning in this period, was an essential lubricant to the system. It was the peculiarity of post-revolutionary Russia that leadership was institutionalized by concentrating power in the hands of the Party's General Secretary. The totalitarian regime in Russia, the result of the recession of the revolution, nevertheless took over the forms and institutions the revolution had created: Stalin had to present himself to the Russian masses according to the images set during its progress, as the first son and closest disciple of Lenin, the founder of the regime. Though the manipulations and manipulators that helped Hitler into power were the by-products of the revolutionary upsurge in Germany, and not its creators, Hitler achieved power as the plebeian son of the masses, marching at their head to solve the deep social crisis. In 1923–1924, Stalin appeared as dictator in Russia from the other end of the road, not at the head of the masses in rising discontent but as the representative of a new ruling class delegated by it to quell preventatively every oppositionist trend and ensure its new status eternal life.

Thus, as Stalin grasped for personal dictatorship, the new State Party began to unfold. To establish his personal power, he had to remove all opponents within the power system and therefore to change the internal structure of the Party. Despite the retrogressive features of these years, the carry-over of revolutionary tradition bulked so large, the spirit of October so deeply impregnated every corner of Party life, that he could perform his cold, but by no means unbloody, coup only in installments. He had to seize power within the power machine, first one part and then the next, group by group, organization by organization, man by man. He had to isolate, vilify, demoralize, bribe, threaten, and, if all else failed, eliminate all competitors and aspirants to competition, who in an hour of crisis might be acceptable to a dissatisfied Party. This array of power-political vices, or virtues, reflects not only Stalin's single-minded determination to take personal power against all odds, but also the unusual length of those odds, the persistent force with which he was opposed, despite the apparent apathy of the Russian people, by the spirit of 1917. The heritage, the customs, the traditions, the patterns, of the revolution had so enormous a weight within the Party that, Stalin discovered, even within the deteriorating framework of soviet and Party democracy, he could not achieve his goal. Even the most extreme limitation of Party life, even the strictest hierarchical discipline, did not give him adequate security. He needed not a revised instrument, but a new one. To control the Party, he had to build a new vehicle of power control.

In 1923, when Stalin began to make substantial use of the Cheka, he changed its function. Created in the civil war as a weapon against the enemy, the hostile classes, the landowners and the bourgeoisie, it became also the Stalin group's instrument within the Party to achieve and maintain its power monopoly. Every Party function was now guaranteed doubly, the second time by an elite within the elite, rising like a dark shadow behind the open Party. Without the terrorist elite within the Party, Stalin would not have been able to utilize the combination of economic with political power against his opponents and to centralize the state functions completely in the hands of a chosen few ten thousands, erasing in the process the last traces of democratic control by the Party rank and file or even by one portion of the Party hierarchy against another. As the Cheka became master within the Party, it moved nearer the center of Russian society generally and became more firmly entrenched there.

This *period of transformation, 1923–1929,* described in this study in detail, has been elucidated in one feature that until now has not been sufficiently analyzed or even clearly seen, namely, the parallel coördination of the Comintern with the new regime. Confused by the national socialist dogma of Stalin, most analysts have presented him as a realistic dictator, who, having renounced the early concept of world revolution, rules wisely behind the high borders of his vast empire, with no ambition to control other areas of the world. The development after World War II has exploded this myth of Stalinist moderation. In the detailed presentation given here of the origin of the State Party regime, the implications of socialism in one country become obvious. With their roots in the social conflicts of their native countries, the Communist parties outside Russia, bound to the remnants of the revolutionary period, to the Leninist phraseology still extant, were living bodies not easily destroyed. In the Comintern policy of this period, the rhetorics of readjustment of Communism to a trade-unionist Europe were in contrast to the dynamism of a State Party, which can tolerate independence of its international affiliates no more than of its national branches. The Comintern, with the empty symbols and furled banners of an irrevocably dead past, was molded into the form of its new master, and became an image of its model, the terrorist State Party of Russia; it received in miniature all the accoutrements of such a State Party excepting only that the state from which it derived its power and which it served was no longer its own national state but "socialist Russia," the center of the globe, the pivot of a power system conceived by geopolitical rather than internationalist concepts.

With the transformation in Russia in 1926, the Comintern parties were purged. Not only programs were changed, not only leaders expelled or dispensed with—that would have been a surface overhauling; the very party structure was melted down. The European parties, the product of the European civil war, were atomized into helpless cells, in most cases by craftsmen from Moscow and with violence. Contemporaries described this smashing-up process as the end of the Comintern, the final victory of democracy over Communism, the beginning of a lasting stabilization of Europe; but in this euphoria of illusions they failed to note that the broken parts had been welded together into a new whole, that the scattered groups had been realigned, that a new type of organization, which was to get its name of "quisling group" or "fifth column" only later, had been formed in the middle twenties. This process of regrouping the Comintern cadres by direct Moscow manipulation has been described in detail in the one example of Germany. As I was deeply involved in the process, many nuances derived from a full and painful personal experience have been reproduced here. It seemed desirable to give the contemporary reader an opportunity to wander through the labyrinth of Comintern crises, with some of the blind alleys noted only in passing, for the Comintern of 1925–1927 is the greenhouse of totalitarianism, in which the full plants of later years can be observed as seedlings.

There have been many post facto attempts to explain the origins of the Nazi regime. German political and economic history have been pored over in an endeavor to find in German experience or the character of the German people a clue to Nazi barbarity. One analyst has gone so far as to present the German problem as one of psychotherapy.[4] Antagonism between the rising Nazi power and the West has virtually blacked out the contribution of Stalin's totalitarianism to the making of totalitarian Germany.

It would of course be an error to overlook the specific German features that gave Nazism its particular forms. Nazi philosophy and policy were derivative from German nationalism as transmuted by the defeat in the First World War. Germany's belated but intense industrialization, which made it difficult to adapt her growing plant to the home market, was grafted on a semi-feudal society. Not only a monarch but a score of princelings cluttered up Germany's unaired corners, and this stratum of feudal left-overs and their retainers continued to form a substantial bloc in German life even after the Kaiser's abdication. The German army, bound by such strong social relations as, for example, intermarriage to the heavy industry of the country, which from its side had expanded largely along lines set by armament needs, was composed in its upper layer principally of members of the landed aristocracy; hence the army expressed the interests of both the landed and the industrial gentry. It reflected the paradoxical dichotomy of German society proper, for it was in technique among the most modern armies in the world. Under a pretense of aloof impartiality, it maintained its tradition as a political army, the result in part of Germany's situation in Europe and in part of the fact that, with Wilhelm's abdication, the defense of Wilhelmian society passed to it. Germany's borders were wide open to a series of countries in tumultuous political and social change. After her defeat, this peripheral pressure increased the separatist tendencies of the states, whose local patriotism was still a live force, and aggravated the difficulties of the Reich. At the same time, the defeat increased the social struggle within the Reich, the struggle between vested interests and restive labor. Under the illusion that it was possible to restore Wilhelmian society, which for it was the precondition to reconstituting Germany's status in Europe, the army made

---

[4] Richard M. Brickner, M.D., *Is Germany Incurable?* (New York, 1943).

itself the defender of the Reich's unity and traditions. Labor, which had grown up in its fight against the Bismarckian Reich, wanted to fulfill the promise of a fifty-year struggle by using Germany's defeat to eradicate completely every remnant of monarchism and feudalism. The revolutionary internationalist ideas sweeping in from the East met the native idealist pacifism, deep-rooted among German workers, and combining with it became a fundamental opposition to the German army and its aspirations. In the ensuing civil war, the army was able to get an alliance with the Right wing of the Social Democratic Party, which for a time had lost its influence over the masses: the economic results of Germany's defeat, however mild they may seem by comparison with conditions in Europe since World War II, were yet sufficiently harsh to deprive a gradualist program of any attraction.

Protracted over three years, the German civil war is full of revealing incidents; the defeated revolutionaries left a deep imprint on the young Republic. The abortive military coup d'état labeled the Kapp Putsch, a culmination of the clashes between army and workers, indicates the narrow margin by which the ante-bellum classes, represented now by the army, maintained their vestigial power, the danger they suffered of complete annihilation. The wavering of the unions best illustrates how precarious was the equilibrium reached; after having for the first time tasted their full power in the general strike of 1920, they considered a dictatorial labor government against the military and the conservative classes they represented.

The Imperial Army had been destroyed by the defeat and the Versailles Treaty. The reconstitution of the Reichswehr was by the regrouping of the 100,000 men permitted by the treaty, and the supplemental Freikorps and Black Reichswehr. The war had left a remnant of jobless junior officers, who having planned a career in the Imperial Army were not willing to renounce this military life for a bare civilian existence in precarious post-war Germany. With this group of ex-officers as their nucleus, the Freikorps attracted to their ranks the embittered, the cynical, the hopeless, the adventurous sons of all classes, among whom the futureless middle class formed the bulk. This type, called in German by the untranslatable term *Landsknecht,* were indoctrinated with a Bismarckian heritage of hatred for the workers, detestation of the internationalist socialists, who formed the principal obstacle to the rebirth of the German Reich. Marching through Germany, terrorizing, slaughtering, burning, the Freikorps were the direct forefathers of the SS hordes who in the Hitler era became the horror of Europe and the disgrace of Germany. With the end of the civil war the Freikorps petered out, and during the short period of stabilization every attempt to reconstitute a monarchist movement in the old style failed. Neither the Freikorps nor the monarchists had been able to achieve their common goal: to eliminate labor from post-war German administration by smashing its institutional strength. Monarchy was dead and could not be revived; a revival of German imperialism needed a new symbol around which to crystallize.

After 1917, the long affinity between Germany and Russia had been intensified. The osmosis of Russian influence through the thin wall of the unstable border is not to be measured by the electoral successes of the German Communist Party. In his National Bolshevik mission to Germany, Karl Radek met half way the nationalist aspirations of the Schlageters, of the German military and middle-class dispossessed, who were increasingly willing to be counseled on how to adapt successful Bolshevik power politics to the resurrection of a mighty Reich. With German internationalism broken by the resurgence of nationalism in Russia, German nationalism blossomed anew, not only unfettered by any significant resistance but abetted by many of the forces that had once bitterly fought it. The resurgence of Russian nationalism was the key by which the Nazis were able to unlock doors to wide areas of industrial Germany, until then firmly closed to any but socialist visitors. The relations between Reichswehr and Red Army, which under other circumstances might have been no more than routine military liaison, became against this background of rising Russian and German nationalism a factor of significance.

After Manuilsky finished the reorganization of the German Communist Party, it was able to serve doubly in the disintegration of the country's society. No longer was the party the representative of one class of Germans, but of the ruling body of a foreign state, superior to Germany in territory and manpower. The numerous fellow-travelers, tied by threads of varying thickness to Russia, scattered widely through the many social milieus into which they penetrated in this period, were increasingly agents of a foreign country. Of these agents, perhaps the most clumsy and the least effective were the actual members of the German party, who had a far less important influence than those in high business circles, among the upper civil servants and diplomats, and, in particular—the most important promoters of a Russian-German continental bloc—in the army. In this complicated game of power politics, the Communist Party attracted to itself none the less the virulent hatred of every nationalist grouping, which although often willing to deal with Russia directly and on its own terms, was afraid that a Communist victory in Germany would mean the incorporation of the Reich into the Russian empire. Thus the very existence of this sizable fifth column stimulated the aggressiveness of the nationalists, tended to cancel out their mutual jealousies and help produce an increasingly united front against this Russian enclave in German society. The fury of the Nazis following 1929, when the American depression gave them a new start, reflects this real and not at all imaginary danger of Germany's russification.

It is necessary, also, to stress the *direct* influence of the Stalinist Party on the structure of the National Socialist Party. The struggle in the Russian Party over the succession to Lenin, and the new type of Party regime and Party state that ensued from it, were closely observed and critically analyzed, with a passionate interest not easily to be found outside Germany. The fight of the Left Communists against this trend, stretching over several years, was unable to restore the revolutionary international socialism of the early period, but it had enough weight —once again, much more than in any other country—to bring Manuilsky's maneuverings into the open, to make the rise of a new type of society apparent to a broad public. With its direct link to the Opposition in the Russian Politburo and the resulting informed comment on Russian affairs in its press, the Left played a more important role in the large discussion on which way Germany was going than would be supposed from its always insignificant membership. Every German of policy-making stature watched through as many eyes as he could muster the envelopment of Russian society, by sometimes almost imperceptible gradations, in the maw of Stalin's personal dictatorship. Stalin's success was admired. His methods, the ruthless extermination of every opposition, became the studied model of every pimpled Nazling, who after 1933 and even more in the face of the Nazi Party's decay, at the time of the Himmler terror, imitated his preceptor. Hitler's reëmergence in 1928–1929 was into a country remarkably different from 1923 Germany: the Freikorps had been pushed into the background, and the neo-Nazis had taken over whole the methods, the style, the songs, the uniforms, the slogans, of the Communists—of the Red Front Fighters' League, of Münzenberg's various propagandist fronts. The West was impressed by the similarity of flags—the large red expanse with a small black and white swastika pinned to it; but behind this flag marched Stalin's slogan: socialism in one country, socialism for one chosen nation, consecrated to the task of grasping all power to the fulfillment of its historical destiny—National Socialism.

In Russia, the Trotsky-Zinoviev Bloc fought the new phenomenon in full awareness of its character. Their resistance to it was in the face of a number of harrowing difficulties, of which the persecution of them and their followers by the Stalin machine was only one, and not the most important. The strongest force opposing them was the recession of the revolutionary wave that had brought them to power, the weakness of revolutionary socialist internationalism in a Europe settling down to Dawes-based capitalist prosperity. After Lenin's vision of a revolutionary Germany rising beside and above revolutionary Russia had vanished into nothingness, the fight of the internationalist center of Leningrad and its inevitable defeat by Stalin's nationalism are a pathetic spectacle. Stifled already in the contracting discipline of the Party, already gasping in the ever-constricting regulations of Stalin's State bureaus, the oppositionists were not free even to fight a losing fight openly. Because they remained loyal, they were stigmatized as traitors. They fought a good and bitter fight, displaying sometimes audacity, sometimes cunning withdrawal, but over all an obdurate courageous endurance that is hard to match in the annals of a totalitarian country. Trotsky, Zinoviev, Kamenev, Bukharin—names besmirched by the most tremendous campaign of calumniation ever organized—are the names of men, of living beings, who like other men were both strong and weak, with moments of confusion and despair, of fear and even of panic. They did not always behave as we, with our comfortable armchair post facto analysis, would advise; they were not models of Marxist righteousness, of proletarian strength. Since they were every one of them deeply involved in the making of the new Russian state, they shared the responsibility for the product of their creation. Ten years later, when they were defendants in the Moscow monster trials, those of them present revealed, through the cipher of the confessions that was their only possible language, a fundamental criticism of Soviet society. But with all their faults and all their weaknesses, one merit remains with them, a *plus* that will increase with the years: Russia's dictator rose to power only against the conscious, articulate, selfless resistance of tens of thousands of the October generation, whose bodies form the foundation for his throne. The fight of these men has left its mark on Stalinist society, and another generation of young Russians may be able to extricate itself from the contradictions, may be able to break out of the recurring series of disaster and purge, because of the mistakes made by the Bloc.

The account of the formation and defeat of the Trotsky-Zinoviev Bloc is based principally on my own experiences, carefully checked against and supplemented by other presentations, particularly those of the official Party histories and of Trotsky. Twenty years afterward, I am not able to identify myself with any one of the groups involved. In particular, I have subjected Trotsky's stand to a searching criticism, which is not meant to detract a whit from the lasting admiration I feel for this great revolutionary figure. But the story of the Opposition, the story of these years of my life, is given not in full but only to the extent that it is relevant to the main theme—the development of the State Party in Russia and in Germany. The struggle of the Bloc is so rich in ideas, so interesting in revealing episodes, so fascinating in the many unusual personalities involved, that it deserves for itself, in a different work, a fuller and richer development. This study only marks a trail through the maze of Russian Party history, which will become of increasing interest in the years to come. When the GPU dragged Trotsky, the co-founder of the Soviet state, to a suburban railroad station and shipped him off to Alma Ata, contemporary observers said that with the enormously dramatic incident the fight of the Opposition was closed and Stalin would rule over his empire in undisturbed harmony. But the roots of resistance went deeper than the personality of any one man: very soon Stalin's allies of yesterday—Bukharin, Tomsky, Rykov—became the center of a new fight against his totalitarian dictatorship. The story of their struggle belongs to a new period, which will be treated in another volume, that of *the rise of State Party regimes in Europe, 1929–1939.*

In 1929, even Trotsky's presence in a remote spot in Central Asia, where he was separated from the country and his supporters by miles of Russian wilderness and by the strict surveillance of the GPU, still threatened the power of the Stalin dictatorship; he was banished to Turkey. Some months before, Bukharin had been removed from the Comintern Presidium and, in effect, from all policy-making bodies; until the middle thirties, he lived on borrowed time in a recess of the Party. In 1929, the ousting of Mikhail Tomsky from his post marked the extinction of the last trace of trade-union independence. During the transitional period, the peasants had been granted a respite, while Stalin concentrated on overcoming the opposition of the October generation. Now, in 1928–1929, the whole of the increased power of the state machine was turned once more against the peasant. Stalin's concept of a State Party was unfulfilled so long as the major portion of Russian society remained essentially outside state control; in his policy of collectivization, Stalin developed his socialism in one country to its logical end. This, Russia's "second," or better, counter, revolution, changed Russian economy and society completely.

Lenin's concept that socialism in Russia was possible only in alliance with one or more technologically advanced countries, in particular with Germany, meant specifically that the Russian peasant would be induced by the incentives that industry offered to change his centuries-old way of life, to become first a farmer and then a coöperative farmer. Lenin had defended his belief in the alliance between workers and peasants on many occasions, under many circumstances, in many forms. The peasant had a right, he reiterated time and again, to adjust only gradually to the new life that industrialization could bring him, but had a right also to that new life. Lenin never forgot that Russia was a peasant country, that the typical Russian was a peasant, that a workers' party could rule with the peasants but could rule against them only by a mountainous and ever-growing terror. His genius as a leader in a peasant country, in contrast to, for example, Béla Kun in peasant Hungary, or to the general trend of West European socialism, was evidenced in his coördination of a Marxist party with the main flow of the peasant revolution. In 1904, during the formative years of the

Bolshevik Party, Lenin had coined the term "the democratic dictator-ship of workers and peasants," by which he meant dictatorship against bourgeoisie and landowners, and democracy among workers and peasants.

Lenin defended this concept against attack from all sides, against Mensheviks on the Right, and on the Left against Trotsky's theory of permanent revolution, which meant in substance that a workers' vic-tory in Tsarist Russia could be sustained only by reinforcing it through far-reaching socialist economic measures.[5] The content of the struggle between Bolsheviks and Mensheviks embraced every aspect of the change that a revolution would bring about. The Mensheviks insisted that social conditions in Russia were not ripe for socialism and that their task was to lead a democratic bourgeois revolution against Tsarist autocracy; and Lenin, contrary to Leninism as later fabricated, agreed fully with his Menshevik adversaries that it would be folly to hope that from the starting point of overthrowing feudal Tsarism a socialist society could be realized in Russia. His fundamental difference with them lay rather in judging which class should be the motive force of the revolution, the liberal bourgeoisie or the peasants. The victory of the liberal bourgeoisie, Lenin declared, would neither give the peasants full freedom nor move the workers to a pivotal position; it would not change fundamentally the imperialist character of the Russian state. The workers' party, therefore, should seek an alliance not with the liberal bourgeoisie but with the peasantry, and by this alliance achieve victory. The victorious workers and peasants would not go on to socialism in one country; rather Russian society would be thoroughly revolutionized and democratized, would be cleansed of its feudal vestiges. The unfavorable objective conditions of Russian technical equipment would impose on a victorious proletariat the necessity of self-moderation in carrying out socialist measures. Had we believed in 1905, Lenin says, that we could have achieved socialism, we would have marched toward political catastrophe.

---

[5] Cf. Trotsky, *Die russische Revolution, 1905* (Berlin, 1923), particularly the chapter entitled "Our Differences of Opinion," pp. 222–231. There has been waged over a period of decades a scholastic battle between proponents of Lenin's democratic dictatorship of workers and peasants and those of Trotsky's permanent revolution. Stalin's realization of "socialism" has made the historic forms of this dispute mean-ingless, but has given its content a new importance.

The Bolsheviks were able to take power in 1917 in spite of their numerical insignificance not because they had fashioned a fool-proof coup d'état but because they advanced on the crest of a revolutionary peasant wave, which in the hinterland had carried out revolutionary slogans months before they were taken over by the Bolsheviks. At the head of this vast peasant mass, the Bolsheviks were enabled, in the first phase, to overcome the resistance of large urban groups and, later, when foreign intervention and the regrouping of the White forces had reduced Soviet Russia to the Grand Principality of Moscow, to overcome all counter-revolutionary attempts and throw the invaders back to the borders of the country. Lenin advocated the peasants' seizure of the land and defended it against the attacks of many West European Marxists, in particular Karl Kautsky and Rosa Luxemburg, who proved in the abstract that larger areas under cultivation are more productive than small parcels. This agronomic argument is valid and may one day be relevant, but in Russia this abstractly desirable program could have been introduced only by the retention of feudal holdings or by state compulsion in creating state collective farms.

After the abortive attempts at workers' management and local power had petered out, the positive residuum of the October revolution was the peasants' expropriation of the big estates. This did not in itself solve the agricultural problem of Russia; the disparity between agriculture and the weakened and disorganized industry continued and became worse. During the transitional period, Stalin's policy in both areas, agriculture and industry, was vacillating and indecisive; he neither completely accepted Bukharin's program of encouraging the peasantry to transform itself into a class of self-sufficient farmers, which in form he agreed to, nor entirely dispensed with the program of the Opposition for more highly centralized industry, which in form he rejected. All his force and energy in this period were concentrated on the one central task of building the State Party around him and interlinking it with every administrative branch of the state. Through the increased use of his terrorist apparatus he was able to do this, but in the process the Party was cut off from every live force in the country; though he alienated the workers, he did not thereby attract the peasants. After Trotsky's exile to Alma Ata, Stalin was more alone than in 1922, when he began his struggle for power. Having already cut himself off from first the Trotskyists and then the Zinovievists, he was now opposed in the Politburo by Bukharin, Tomsky, and Rykov, who almost gained a majority against him. The Party, unable to attract any class to its support, was transformed into a terror machine for the mobilization of forced-labor armies. Concepts and methods that had had a timid beginning during the travail of the civil war period were revived and, under completely changed circumstances, developed to a new fulsomeness. This uprooting and transfer of millions over Russia's vast expanses, the enormous labor projects carried out by primitive methods, are comparable only to the great achievements of Asiatic despots. The Russian peasant lost everything he had gained through the October revolution—his land, his personal dignity, his enfranchisement, his freedom of movement; once again, he became bound to the land, changing the old landowner for the state-manager of the *kolkhoz* or the GPU supervisor of the forced-labor camp.

During the civil war, terror in the Russian village had been as cruel, as brutal, as abhorrent, as is war per se. Beginning with the spontaneous acts of the peasants themselves against their oppressors, the landowners and their agents, it was continued by guerrilla groups of all factions, White and Red, anarchist and restorationist. The terror of the Communist guerrilla bands, made up of both workers and poor peasants, was the terror of rising classes against old despotic classes. The new terror of Stalin, on the other hand, was the terror of a monolithic state power against all classes, including oppositionist factions within the ruling Party. Civil war had raged in the villages; houses had been burnt, peasants had been killed. Each successive army as it took and retook the village hanged some leaders of the opposing side, requisitioned food where it could find it. But the main body of the peasantry remained; millions of persons were not uprooted and shipped thousands of versts across a barren tundra. As so often with Stalin, he took the revolutionary experiences of the past and applied them to a different present; his war on the peasant was termed a fight against the kulak. His policy of collectivization added a new word to the language of totalitarianism—dekulakization.

On February 15, 1928, three weeks after Trotsky was banished to Alma Ata, an anonymous article in *Pravda,* obviously written by Stalin, pointed out that the methods of the New Economic Policy were not giving satisfactory results in feeding the army and the cities. By a series of rapid steps, this alarm was converted into a full program of collectivization of agriculture. The first decree prescribing "a greater use of penal labor" appeared on March 26.[6]

The principal new feature of the first Five-Year Plan, conceived in this period, was not the planning of industry or even the extension of planning over the whole of the national plant, but this enforced collectivization of the land. Between 1929 and 1934, several millions of peasants, men, women, and children, were forcibly transferred from the villages of their forefathers to a far-off corner of Russia. This punitive measure, which must be pictured against the primitive transportation facilities of Russia, against the extreme heat and the biting cold of the Russian climate, was the first since 1918 of the enormous forced mass migrations characteristic of our time, engineered just as the Nazis were entering the European scene. In the forced-labor camps, an integral and important part of the Five-Year Plans, the uprooted peasant met the banished worker. When the Russian famine reached its peak in 1932–1933, most of the peasantry had been collectivized, either in the forced-labor camps or on the collective farms. On the *kolkhoz,* the peasant had, exactly as before the revolution, a small plot of his own, not quite sufficient to feed himself and his family adequately; but the major portion of his labor power was forcibly directed into cultivating the land of his masters. Terror, from a weapon in the class war, had become the motive power of a new type of economy.

The status of national minorities in the Soviet Union can be appreciated only against this background of enforced collectivization. Here again the original trend of the October revolution was turned into its opposite. One of the most important sections of Lenin's revolutionary policy had been his support of national independence, which he defended to the point of accepting secession from the Tsarist conglomerate. In 1923, Stalin's terrorist subduing of the revolting Georgians contributed substantially to Lenin's break with him. Ukrainian na-

---

[6] Cf. David J. Dallin and Boris I. Nicolaevsky, *Forced Labor in Soviet Russia* (New Haven, 1947), p. 206. Dallin continues: "The intention was 'to bring about the realization of a series of economic projects with great savings in expenditures . . . by means of widespread use of labor of individuals sentenced to measures of social protection.' In July of the same year the Commissariat of Justice ordered the introduction of compulsory prison work for *all* able-bodied prisoners."

tionalism was strongly reflected in the Ukrainian Communist Party, which was tamed by, among others, the same Manuilsky who did the job in Germany. With the dekulakization, it was enormously easier to solve "the national question," for those national minorities aspiring to be free of Great Russian domination could all be dubbed kulaks and counter revolutionaries. The enforced collectivization deprived them of the very core of national independence, the right to remain together, in a bloc, among compatriots; the score of diasporas to which the peoples of Russia have been subjected has reduced the right to sing Stalin's praise in twenty languages, to the accompaniment of twenty native folk dances, to less than a gesture.

As a logical and necessary outgrowth of this beginning in the dekulakization period, the mass deportation of millions has become a permanent and important feature of Soviet life, a central clause of its unwritten constitution. By the order of the Supreme Soviet of August 28, 1941, the German Autonomous Soviet Socialist Republic ceased to exist, and approximately two-thirds of its population of 600,000 was transported to Siberia. In 1943, the Kalmyk Autonomous Soviet Socialist Republic, with a population of some 200,000, was deported in toto from its territory between the lower Volga and the Don. More than half of the 280,000 citizens of the Khara-Chay Autonomous Region were deported. The Chechen-Ingush Soviet Socialist Republic of more than 700,000 souls has been moved from the Northern Caucasus. These three peoples were moved in 1943, during the war; in 1945, after the victory, large areas of the Crimea were depopulated by the deportation of a million Tatars. Those brought from afar to settle in the homes thus vacated also proved to be unreliable, and the deportations continued; as in Georgia in 1923–1924, the land had to be "plowed anew."

This feature of domestic policy became one of the most effective auxiliaries to foreign policy. After the Russian-German pact of 1939 divided Poland, almost one million Poles were deported by the NKVD to Siberia, and another million by the Gestapo to forced labor in Poland and Germany. About one tenth of those in Russia have since been released, and it is to this group that we owe the most complete and best documented account of this phase of Soviet economy.[7] Mass

---

[7] A study of permanent value on the fate of the Poles deported to Russia is the anonymous *The Dark Side of the Moon,* with a preface by T. S. Eliot (New York,

deportation was an important accompaniment to the russification of East Prussia, the Baltic states, the Balkans. The same methods of forced migration were applied to Germany, into which some millions of Germans were driven from the Sudetenland and the East. On their way, some hundreds of thousands perished.

The new science of social engineering had its genesis in the transitional period, when the Opposition inside the Party was eliminated by terror; once developed there, the system was refined and broadened to include in its vast scope one sixth of the world's surface, 175 millions of human beings. The fight against Trotsky and Zinoviev had been a pilot plant where new types of trip hammers and giant pincers were tested. Though the Opposition was shattered, annihilated, opposition continued, grew; in the army, in the administration, in the Party, in the cities and in the countryside, each wave of terror brought its echo of resistance. One thing was changed: no one thought any longer in terms of a break-through to legality; resistance from this time on was only in the forms and by the methods possible in a completely totalitarian state. Thus the terror sent out from the Party center made a tour of the country and its institutions, ending up finally back in the Party. The second Five-Year Plan, 1933–1937, coincided with the ruthless extermination of anti-Stalin groups in the Party—from the Kirov assassination in 1934 to the Bukharin trial in March 1938. In these trials Trotsky and Zinoviev were joined not only by Bukharin and his associates but by the chief of the GPU, H. G. Yagoda, as well as a Red Army marshal, Mikhail N. Tukhachevsky. In these trials the principle not of thought control but of the prevention of thought reached its climax. These "trials" have been probed thus far only by novelists and journalists; their thorough analysis would reveal the permanent

---

1947). The story of the Poles rounds out the story of the German concentration camps, details about which were not known till after the end of the war. Two of the most interesting of several hundred titles on the German camps are Benedikt Kautsky (son of Karl Kautsky), *Teufel und Verdammte* (Zurich, 1946), and Eugen Kogon, *Der SS-Staat: Das System der deutschen Konzentrationslager* (Frankfurt am Main, 1946). Kogon's study is particularly interesting because of his analysis of the concentration camp as one increasingly important branch of the Hitler economy. The Polish and German books are complemented by the sharp psychological studies of the French, particularly David Rousset's two works, *L'Univers Concentrationnaire* and *Les Jours de Notre Mort* (Paris, 1946). A comparison of the large number of books on German camps with such works as Dallin's on the Russian camps brings out strikingly the structural congruence between the two.

division that exists, hidden behind terrorist discipline, among the various elements of the top stratum.[8]

---

[8] The charge against Yagoda, who was head of the state's secret police for sixteen years, is the pivotal point of the trials. If a man in such a position could be accused of having used his post to plan and carry out the poisonings of various top officials, then the Stalin court was indeed a reincarnation of its Byzantine predecessor. In this new type of world, all sorts of rumors were bruited about; in this atmosphere, one particular rumor, that Stalin had poisoned Lenin (cf. Trotsky, *Stalin,* pp. 377–379), gained a certain currency. These dangerous rumors had to be pulled down out of the air in which they were floating and crystallized around some object, some person other than Stalin. The object had to be Bukharin, the principal opponent of Stalin's program of dekulakization. The secret popularity won by those who had fought the terror regime had to be uprooted; it had to be proved that, like Trotsky and Zinoviev, Bukharin also had been the enemy of the workers' state from 1917 on, that already in 1918 his collaboration with Lenin had been only apparent; it had to be proved that the same group of men now accused of planning to assassinate Stalin had begun their dastardly careers by planning to assassinate Lenin. For this purpose, the Brest-Litovsk crisis had to be resurrected in the show trial of 1938, and it is worth noting that episode for the light it focuses both on the terror system of Stalinist society and on the methods of increasing that terror.

In this pageant of Stalinist history marched a parade of former Left Communists (V. N. Yakovleva, V. V. Ossinsky, V. N. Mantsev) and former Left Social Revolutionaries (B. D. Kamkov, V. A. Karelin), who dug up details to prove the guilt of the accused. But with all these props Vyshinsky was unable to wrest a confession from Bukharin that he had planned Lenin's assassination. Throughout the entire investigation, Bukharin maintained that his opposition to Lenin's policy during the Brest-Litovsk negotiations could not be defined in terms of conspiracy, plotting, and terrorism, but had to be understood as a struggle for an alternative program. With the majority of the Party and of the government behind him, Bukharin was trying to put his policy into effect.

"VYSHINSKY [*to Bukharin*]: Did you at this period conduct illegal work, fighting the Soviet power?

"BUKHARIN: Here one must deal with various periods. If it is a question of the period prior to the Brest-Litovsk Peace, there was nothing illegal in the strict meaning of the term, for the simple reason that everybody knew about the struggle, there was an open organ of this struggle, conversations took place openly . . .

"VYSHINSKY: Did you speak openly of the arrest of Lenin, Stalin, and Sverdlov?

"BUKHARIN: There was talk of arrest, but not of physical extermination. This was not in the period prior to the Brest-Litovsk Peace, but after. Before the Brest-Litovsk peace, the principal orientation of the 'Left Communists' was to gain a majority in the Party by legal means.

"VYSHINSKY: What legal means?

"BUKHARIN: Discussions, voting at meetings, and so on.

"VYSHINSKY: And when did the hope of this disappear?

"BUKHARIN: That was after the Brest-Litovsk Peace. I want to clarify this question in order to refute V. N. Yakovleva's evidence. She speaks of a period prior to the Brest-Litovsk Peace, which is patent nonsense, because at that time we and the Trotskyites had the majority in the Central Committee and we hoped to win the majority in the Party, so that to speak of conspiratorial activities at that time is nonsense. . . .

"VYSHINSKY: Were your feelings profoundly rancorous?

"BUKHARIN: It was not a question of personal rancor against persons and against leaders.

The dekulakization and the purges made an enormous impression on the outside world. Only now, after the defeat of Germany and Japan, will it be possible to evaluate the stimulus that this social engineering gave to latent totalitarian forces in Europe and Asia.

Lenin's grand strategy had had as its cornerstone the German revolution; Stalin's German policy found its basis in the fear of the German revolution. In the years of Nazi ascendancy, 1929–1933, his manipulations in Germany were motivated by a determination that a joint Communist-Social Democratic action against the increasing danger of National Socialism should not be permitted to interfere with his larger schemes in Europe. The Communist Party of Germany grew in this period to a substantial size, not only in indirect influence as before but in membership figures and electoral support. Manipulated from Moscow, it was directed into a policy of silent agreement, not disturbed by name-calling, with the Nazis, and virulent opposition to the Democrats and Social Democrats. This policy was carried out through the new theorem of "social fascism," which Stalin enunciated in person. The trade-unions, the Social Democratic Party—in this period, that is, the least totalitarian stratum of German society, and one fighting for its very life—were denounced as worse than just plain fascists, were stigmatized as the most dangerous enemy, the first target. The hatreds of

---

"VYSHINSKY: I ask, was the atmosphere heated enough?

"BUKHARIN: Yes, heat along the line of the factional struggle was very great.

"VYSHINSKY: The atmosphere was intensely heated?

"BUKHARIN: Yes, intensely.

"VYSHINSKY: And in such an atmosphere, the idea of arrest and in the case of some, perhaps, of assassination was not precluded?

"BUKHARIN: As regards arrest, I admit it; as regards assassination, I know nothing whatever.

"VYSHINSKY: But the atmosphere was—

"BUKHARIN: The atmosphere was the atmosphere.

"VYSHINSKY: The atmosphere was appropriate for such ideas and plans to arise in certain heated minds?

"BUKHARIN: Perhaps, they did arise in somebody's mind, but I personally saw no symptoms of it.

"VYSHINSKY: And nobody urged you in this direction?

"BUKHARIN: No, nobody.

"VYSHINSKY: Nobody suggested that Lenin, Stalin, and Sverdlov must be removed?

"BUKHARIN: No, Citizen Procurator, nobody."

(*Report of Court Proceedings in the Case of the Anti-Soviet "Bloc of Rights and Trotskyites,"* Moscow, 1938, pp. 447 and 508.)

the German civil war were rekindled and fanned to new heights with the bellows of mass propaganda spreading this Stalinist message, exactly when the rise of the Nazi Party made the old enmities obsolete, when in the imperative need of a common fight they had begun to be overgrown. During the depression the disappointment in the Weimar Republic general among the workers had turned to bitterness, and the trade-unions were in the early stages of transformation, in the process of discarding the heritage of Ebert and Noske. With the growing threat of Nazism before his eyes, the German trade-unionist of 1930 was much more disposed to throw off his passivist tradition for any realistic alternative, but he was paralyzed by the Communists in his midst. Moreover, the integration of military and conservative forces around the reactionary extreme, the Nazis, tended to polarize all liberal and Republican groups as well. The Germany of 1930 was split into two almost equal parts: the Nazi-military camp, filled with an audacious courage by its increasing cohesion, and the anti-Nazi camp, which foreseeing the possible victory of the Nazis, the preparation for a new war, the possible destruction of the German people in that war, was none the less unable to achieve the cohesion it knew was essential. The anti-Nazi camp also was split down the middle, split by an ax wielded by Stalin—an ax called social fascism—by which the Communist half of the anti-Nazi camp was made into the silent ally of Hitler.

In 1933 the second fully developed State Party regime in one of the main areas of Europe came to power. Hidden behind ideological veils of Hitler's anti-Bolshevism facing Stalin's anti-fascism, the two totalitarian societies approached each other asymptotically in their principal structural features, driven by the power-political antagonisms that have disfigured Europe since 1917. The features of Hitler terror, developed out of the struggle to eliminate German labor, stimulated and reinforced the Stalin terror; and Hitler's St. Bartholemew's night against Röhm and the Left wing of the Nazi Party, July 30, 1934, marks the beginning also of the great purges in Russia. In the other direction, the mass expulsion of millions in Stalin's Russia was used as a primer in Hitler's Germany, which imported some twelve million slaves during the war.

The insecurity of Germany's position in Europe continued, and with it her attempts to get advantages from both the West and the East, to

Rosa Luxemburg at an August Bebel memorial, about 1912

Karl Liebknecht in a punishment company

Bolshevik leaders, 1919

Zinoviev, 1918

Trotsky, Commissar for War, crossing the Red Square, 1921

Freikorps troops in Berlin, 1919

Freikorps marching in Munich, 1919

The Red Army in the Rhine-Ruhr, 1920

Albert Leo Schlageter

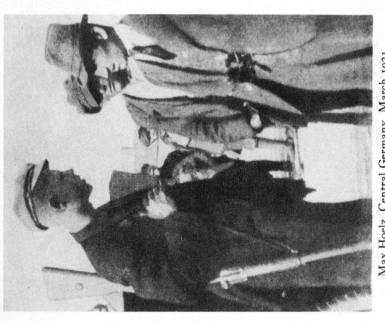

Max Hoelz, Central Germany, March 1921

Radek setting fire to Germany

Bukharin

The Lion Trotsky crushing the counter revolution

Early Bolshevik cartoons

Die Kommunistin

Organ der Kommunistischen Partei Deutschlands (Sektion der Kommunistischen Internationale)
Herausgegeben vom Frauen-Reichssekretariat. Gegründet und unter ständiger Mitarbeit von Clara Zetkin

| Nr. 18 | Die Kommunistin erscheint am 1. und 15. jeden Monats. Infolge der immer weiteren Geldentwertung mußte der Preis wieder erhöht werden. Einzelnummer 500000 Mark | Berlin, 15. September 1923 | Verlag: Friedrichstadt-Druckerei GmbH. (Abteilung Zeitschriften). Berlin SW 48, Friedrichstr. 226. — Verantwortlich für die Redaktion: Martha Arendsee, Berlin. | Jahrg. 5 |

Die Aktion des gesamten Proletariats bringt das Ende der Wucherherrschaft

Clara Zetkin's women's magazine attacks the inflation

Red Front Fighters

Thälmann marching at the head of the Red Front Fighters

A GPU school

General Secretary Stalin voting for his reëlection, Fifteenth Party Congress, Moscow, 1927

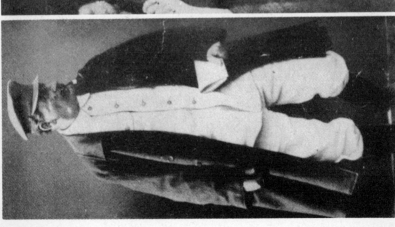

Stalin, about 1927

play one off against the other. The Schlageters who had listened sympathetically to Radek's National Bolshevik message, who had dreamed of the grandiose phantasmagoria of a united Eurasia against the West, were now in the Nazi Party, and in the Party they held to the concept that one day collaboration with Soviet Russia might materialize. In the Kremlin, Stalin maintained his hope that Russia might break out of her isolation by way of an alliance with Germany. For a time, outwardly at least, there seemed little hope for such a policy. In 1935, Russia officially opened the Anti-Fascist Decade at the Seventh World Congress of the Comintern; and in 1936, Germany organized the Anti-Comintern Pact. But neither of these moves was definitive; they were both in part a direct reflection of policy, in part an indirect threat and an offer. Krivitsky relates that, on the special order of Stalin, he tried during this period to maintain his contacts in Germany, but in vain. That collaboration was continued on a reduced scale comes out, with the distortion with which every fact appears in this mirror, in the Moscow trials of 1936–1938. In the testimony of Radek, of Rosengoltz, and especially of Krestinsky, a portion of the story is divulged; one of the purposes of this manipulated testimony was to warn Germany that the political contacts still continuing between the two countries could also be broken off. But Hitler was unenthusiastic; as Niedermayer remarked to a friend, "the highest person" did not understand that a German-Russian alliance was imperative. The break, however, was in the relation between the two armies; the secret political contacts were never completely cut and in 1938, after Munich, they were once again strengthened. Under the noses of the British and French missions in Moscow, the Nazis laid the basis for the pact of August 1939, which marked the beginning of a new war and, for those who had swallowed whole the anti-fascist fulminations of the Comintern, of a new era.

The German army, which had never regained the aplomb of the Wilhelmian days, which was reduced during the Weimar Republic in part to a 100,000-man morsel and in greater part to illegal maneuverings, was shaken to its bowels by the rise of National Socialism. But in spite of all reverses, by conserving its upper layers, the German army had maintained its continuity. During the civil war it had made use of its illegitimate children, the Freikorps, but after order was restored, during the period of transition, it relegated these unsavory condottieri again to the background. These toughs of the Freikorps became the storm troopers of a later day; from the beginning the Nazi Party had been nursed by the army, at first rather indifferently, but later with increasing attention. But also, from the onset, there had been strong currents in the army against this policy of fostering revolutionaries, and as the Nazis grew the recognition of the dangerous competition offered by this plebeian bastard also grew. This division among the top generals and marshals resulted in a series of army conspiracies against the Third Reich, which, beginning in 1933, developed through one abortive plan after another to the crescendo of July 20, 1944. Both wings of the General Staff maintained almost to the end the illusion that power remained fundamentally in its control of the armed forces, that the Nazi rabble could be dispensed with whenever it became convenient.

German generals were accustomed to handling large bodies of men; in 1914 they had already deployed eleven million soldiers. Hitler's decree of March 16, 1935, reinstituting compulsory military training, immediately increased the number of men under army control from the poor 100,000 permitted by the Versailles Treaty to six times that number. Precisely at this time, the conspirators around the General Staff considered undergoing the slight surgical operation, the removal of Hitler. With his amazing instinct for power control, Hitler always intervened at the right moment, and by demoting some of the conspiring generals and promoting others defeated their plots.[9]

From the beginning of the Russian-German war, Stalin undoubtedly followed the reports he received of this division in the German General Staff with consuming interest. With an eye to the future, the old National Bolshevik slogans were revived, in order to prepare for the absorption of a portion of the German army if that ever became possible. On October 8, 1941, in Moscow, that "well-known anti-fascist" as the record designated him, Walther Ulbricht, presided over the first conference of German prisoners of war captured on the East-

---

[9] Cf. Hans Bernd Gisevius, *Bis zum bittern Ende*, 2 vols. (Zurich, 1946); a one-volume abridged translation was published in 1947 by Houghton Mifflin Co., Boston, under the title *To the Bitter End*; Fabian von Schlabrendorff, *Offiziere gegen Hitler* (Zurich, 1946); Ulrich von Hassell, *The Von Hassell Diaries, 1938–1944* (New York, 1947); Count Folke Bernadotte, *The Curtain Falls: Last Days of the Third Reich* (New York, 1945).

ern front.[10] Following this beginning, there was a tremendous propaganda along the Eastern front, a repetition in Stalin's own fashion of the 1918 appeal to the German soldier. The loudspeakers set up on the battlefield reached many ears receptive to their National Bolshevik message—the younger officers with the hope still that by a German-Russian alliance they could rule the world, the older ones with the more sober intention of ridding Germany of Hitler by such a change of policy.

In July 1943, after the defeat of the Sixth German Army before Stalingrad, the Free Germany Committee was founded in Moscow, with Communist Erich Weinert as its chairman and Count von Einsiedel, a direct descendant of Bismarck, as its vice-chairman. On October 11, 1943, the Committee created a branch, the League of German Officers, under the intelligence chief of the Sixth Army, Colonel Hans Günther von Hooven.[11] As the German armies surrendered on the Eastern front, one important group of generals after another joined this movement. Of these, Field Marshal Friedrich von Paulus, who joined later than others and with more trepidation, was pushed to the fore as an impressive figurehead; General Walther von Seydlitz became chief of the group. They were given special privileges and full facilities to carry on propaganda among prisoners: a budget to cover military as well as agitational activities, broadcasts, a weekly magazine, *Freies Deutschland,* etc.

The Free Germany Committee was officially disbanded in August 1945, but the secret German army on Russian soil has continued till today. For a time it was garrisoned in Eastern Germany and Poland and given cleaning-up assignments there. Neither Paulus nor Seydlitz —nor such other German generals as Edmund Hofmeister—was either returned after Hitler's defeat to Germany or tried as a war criminal in Russia. Paulus appeared for a short while at Nuremberg but soon returned to his Moscow headquarters.

Around this Free Germany Committee there was a world-wide

---

[10] Cf. *First Conference of German Prisoners of War Privates and Non-commissioned Officers in the Soviet Union* (Foreign Languages Publishing House, Moscow, 1941).

[11] *Deutsche, Wohin?* Protokoll der Gründungs-Versammlung des National-Komitees Freies Deutschland und des Bundes Deutscher Offiziere, with a foreword by Paul Merker and Arnold Vieth von Golssenau (Mexico City, 1944).

campaign to involve German refugees and anti-fascists of all varieties in a Moscow-controlled group. In the Western Hemisphere its head-quarters was in Mexico City, where about eighty German Stalinists set up their own publishing house.[12] There were branches in the United States and virtually every Latin American country; in Europe the prin-cipal branches were in Britain, France, and Sweden. The Free Germany Committee had deeper repercussions in Hitler Germany than have yet been revealed. Moscow was not able to establish contact with army groups behind the lines, but an organization of German officers, led by scions of the best feudal families, planned to assassinate Hitler and turn German policy Eastward.

The contrast between these purposive officers inspired by the Seyd-litz committee and the wavering and indecisive Western-oriented civilians and officers who opposed Hitler comes out strongly in Gisevius' memoirs. An anti-Nazi conservative, Gisevius participated, both before and during the war, in one plot after another, all of them long and carefully planned but all leading to a coup that never materialized. The conspirators centered around Dr. Karl Goerdeler, mayor of Leipzig, who was in touch with British and American in-telligence through Stockholm and Switzerland. Three noblemen—Schulenburg, Stauffenberg, and Helldorff—entered the group and cut through the endless discussions with a new incisive activism. The three National Socialist counts were for close relations with Soviet Russia; Schulenburg had been German ambassador to Moscow.

In the last days before July 20, 1944, the small group of plotters was shaken by their discussion of the vital question—East or West? In a Berlin cellar, Goerdeler and Stauffenberg led opposite sides of an ex-amination, constantly interrupted by air-raid alarms, of the two possible roads out of Hitler Germany. "East" meant that Hitler would be killed and the German armies on the Russian front would relax their pressure and permit the Red Army to enter Berlin without opposition. Against this, Gisevius and Goerdeler pushed for the *Westlösung*.

> I suggested once more [Gisevius writes] the 'Western' solution, which we had repeatedly discussed in Switzerland. By that I meant that we would abandon the attempt at assassination and a

---

[12] Cf. *Unser Kampf gegen Hitler*. Proceedings of the First National Convention of the Free Germany Movement in Mexico (Mexico City, 1943).

Putsch in Berlin in favor of a unilateral action in the West. If
Kluge and Rommel had crossed their psychological Rubicon, then
let them refuse to obey Hitler and make an offer for a separate
armistice to Eisenhower. Practically this would mean that the
front in the west would be broken and the Anglo-American troops
would pour across the Siegfried Line into Germany, meeting very
little or no resistance. At the very least they would reach Berlin
before the Russians.[13]

This plan was opposed by Colonel Klaus Schenk Graf von Stauffenberg; the young officers for whom he spoke did not want a civilian
government headed by bourgeois and reactionary has-beens. What
they wanted was

> the salvation of Germany by military men who could break with
> corruption and maladministration, who would provide an orderly
> military government and would inspire the people to make one
> last great effort. Reduced to a formula, he wanted the nation to
> remain soldierly and become socialistic. . . .

> Stauffenberg wanted a military dictatorship of 'true National
> Socialists.' Now that the Nazi leadership had failed and Hitler
> had been exposed as the bungling strategist he was, the soldiers
> were to spring into the breach and save the lost cause. Stauffen-
> berg wanted to retain all the totalitarian, militaristic, and socialistic
> elements of National Socialism.

> Stauffenberg had been playing hide-and-seek with me. A few
> weeks before he had counted upon playing off the West against
> the East; now he was imagining a joint victorious march of the
> German and Red armies against the plutocracies. It was an open
> question whether the recent military disaster had not accelerated
> this radical reorientation.[14] [Moreover, it is difficult to deny one
> point. Why do the Russians have their Seydlitz committee? And
> why do the Western powers give us no hope?][15]

On July 20, 1944, Hitler narrowly escaped being killed. Field Marshal Erwin von Witzleben and General Ludwig Beck tried to organize

---

[13] Gisevius, *To the Bitter End* (Houghton Mifflin Company, 1947; copyright 1947
by Fretz & Wasmuth Verlag, A–G.), p. 526. Quoted by permission of the American
publishers.

[14] *Ibid.,* pp. 503, 504, 516.

[15] Sentences in square brackets do not appear in the American edition, and are
here translated from the German text, II, 319.

an army uprising against him; when it failed, Beck committed suicide, and Witzleben and three generals and four staff officers were sentenced to death by a Nazi court and publicly hanged.

The German army controlled enough power in Hitler Germany, had the General Staff used it, to give the genuine German anti-Nazis an opportunity to lead Germany out of the impasse into which Hitler had taken her. A certain number of officers, typified by Stauffenberg, displayed in the best tradition of the Prussian Junker a personal courage and willingness to sacrifice self to the fatherland, but to no avail. Split between Nazi and anti-Nazi wings, with the latter split again between Western- and Eastern-oriented, with these political differences complicated and reinforced by personal antagonisms, the General Staff failed to save Germany from destruction and dismemberment.

Stalin's myriad organizations, which had been grouping refugees all over the world into Communist parties and fellow-traveler leagues, stood ready to take over.[16] The main contingent came from Moscow, led by Wilhelm Pieck, accompanied by his son Arthur in a Russian major's uniform. Together with Ulbricht, he organized a bitter fight

---

[16] A few weeks after the Führer's suicide among the ruins of Berlin, a German Communist poet fresh from Moscow, Johannes R. Becher, presented the Führer anew to the German people:

> "When in the reconstructed plant
> Machines again begin their roar,
> They sing a song, and we understand it all,
> A hymn of praise rung out—Stalin, we thank thee.

> "When again the peasant walks his fields,
> Freed from the foe, and sows again,
> Often he stands and looks afar
> And offers a thanksgiving prayer: Stalin . . .

> "Whenever a man begins his work,
> At dawn, before he leaves the chamber
> He will gaze on thy picture;
> So early art thou awake in his heart.

> "So if again we see the realm of peace,
> We thank for it thy holy effort.
> With its blossoming the earth thanks thee.
> Thee the world thanks for Liberty's resurrection.

(*Internationale Literatur, Deutsche Blätter*, Verlag für Schöne Literatur, Moscow, vol. XV, June–July 1945. These verses comprise the opening editorial of the first post-war issue of this official periodical.)

with the only serious competition, the Social Democratic Party; after a year Stalin's agents succeeded in splitting the Social Democrats in the Soviet zone and absorbing the pro-Soviet wing into the Socialist Unity Party, which unites the features of its two totalitarian predecessors, the Communists and the Nazis.

Index ·